An Important Message to Our Readers

Take Charge of Your Workers' Compensation Claim

An A to Z Guide for Injured Employees

by Attorney Christopher A. Ball
edited by Beth Laurence

...tions periodically. ...New editions contain ...ons. To find out if a later ...Nolo at 510-549-1976 or check our ...site at http://www.nolo.com.

To stay current, follow the "Update" service at our website at http://www.nolo.com/lawstore/update/list.cfm. In another effort to help you use Nolo's latest materials, we offer a 35% discount off the purchase of the new edition of your Nolo book when you turn in the cover of an earlier edition. (See the "Special Upgrade Offer" in the back of the book.)

This book was last revised in: **March 2002.**

Third Edition	MARCH 2002
Editor	BETH LAURENCE
Illustrations	MARI STEIN
Production	SARAH HINMAN
Book Design	TERRI HEARSH
Cover Design	TONI IHARA
Index	JANET PERLMAN
Proofreading	SUSAN CARLSON GREENE
Printing	BERTELSMANN SERVICES, INC.

Ball, Christopher A.
    Take charge of your workers' compensation claim : an A to Z guide for injured employees / by Christopher A. Ball. 3rd California ed.
        p. cm.
    Includes index.
    ISBN 0-87337-803-2
    1. Workers' compensation--Law and legislation--California--Popular works. I. Ball, Christopher A. How to handle your workers' compensation claim. II. Title.

KFC592.Z9B35   2002
344.794'021--dc21

97-20972

CIP

For information on bulk purchases or corporate premium sales, please contact the Special Sales Department. For academic sales or textbook adoptions, ask for Academic Sales. Call 800-955-4775 or write to Nolo, 950 Parker Street, Berkeley, CA 94710.

Acknowledgments

The Law Offices of Rose, Klein & Marias, my employer, without whose encouragement this book would never have been written. I am proud to be associated with a firm that has always fought for and put the needs of injured workers first and foremost.

Robert I. Vines, my mentor and dear friend, for his unselfish willingness to share his vast knowledge and experience in workers' compensation with anyone who asks (and I asked plenty!). If it were not for his faith and support, I would not have been in a position to write this book.

Linda Foley and Kathryn Phillips, two extremely competent paralegals, whose expertise in the area of vocational rehabilitation was greatly utilized by this author, and whose review of the vocational rehabilitation chapter is gratefully acknowledged and appreciated.

Ralph "Jake" Warner, founder and owner of Nolo, who took an unwieldy and seemingly unmanageable subject matter and somehow managed to put it in a format that makes sense.

Lisa Goldoftas, editor extrordinaire at Nolo, who in my humble opinion deserves all the credit for making this book readable. Her expert guidance and suggestions were always right on target and appreciated.

Judge Kenneth Peterson and Judge David Hettick (Oakland Workers' Compensation Appeals Board), for their exemplary reading of the manuscript and excellent suggestions for improvement.

Applicants' attorney Jeffrey E. Friedman (Jones, Clifford, McDevitt, Naekel & Johnson law firm, San Francisco), whose expertise greatly enhanced the book.

Attorney Moiece Palladino (State Compensation Insurance Fund), for her careful reading of the manuscript and outstanding suggestions.

John Hopper, Information & Assistance Officer (Van Nuys), for his review and excellent comments.

Robert S. Lichtenstein, M.D. (Mountain View, California), Board Certified Neurosurgeon, for his fine and compassionate reading of the medical chapters; Mike Mansel (insurance broker), for his excellent critique of the book; and Bill Nickoloff, for his helpful suggestions.

Stephanie Harolde, for her careful and patient treatment of so many drafts of the manuscript; and Terri Hearsh, for her beautiful design and artful handling of a complicated manuscript.

Dedications

To Mom—You gave me what money can't buy, and I'm forever indebted.

To my children, Jennifer and Christopher—I'm certain I neglected you while writing this book, but you understood and accepted my commitment. You are both responsible and caring young adults and I'm very proud of you. Thank you both for your help.

To my loving wife, Marian—Without your support and understanding, this book would never have been completed. Thanks for putting up with me when the long hours made me irritable, and for the encouragement you gave when it seemed as though this book would never be finished. You are truly my inspiration.

Table of Contents

Part I: All About Workers' Compensation

3 Is Your Injury Covered By Workers' Compensation?

4 Cumulative Trauma Disorders

Part II: Protecting Your Rights

5 What to Do If You're Injured

6 Keep Good Records to Protect Your Claim

7 The Insurance Company's Role

8 Dealing With Your Employer

9 Taking Charge of Your Medical Case

10 Medical-Legal Evaluations

Part III: Workers' Compensation Benefits

11 Payment of Medical Benefits

12 Temporary Disability Benefits

13 Permanent Disability (and Life Pension)

14 Vocational Rehabilitational Benefits

15 Death Benefits

16 Extraordinary Workers' Compensation Benefits and Remedies

17 Benefits and Remedies Outside the Workers's Compensation System

Part IV: Settling Your Case

18 Rating Your Permanent Disability

19 Figure Out a Starting Settlement Amount

20 Negotiating a Settlement

Part V: The Workers' Compensation Appeals Board

21 Preparing Your Case

22 Arranging for a Hearing or Trial

23 How to File and Serve Documents

24 Going to a Hearing or Trial

25 Appealing a Workers' Compensation Decision

Part VI: Beyond the Book

26 Lawyers and Other Sources of Assistance

27 Legal Research

28 Case Law Review

Appendices

A1 Summary of Important Workers' Compensation Laws for Injuries Between 1/1/90 and 12/31/93

A2 Temporary Disability Benefits Compensation Chart

A3 Permanent Disability Indemnity Chart

A4 Workers' Compensation Forms

A5 Workers' Compensation—District Offices

1

Introduction to Workers' Compensation

As a workers' compensation attorney, I advise injured workers about how the law applies to their particular workers' compensation claim. I have yet to talk to an injured worker who felt that the workers' compensation laws were fair or adequate. There is good reason for this. Legal limitations and restrictions as to how much an injured worker may recover result in many workers receiving inadequate benefits. Unfortunately, the workers' compensation system was not designed primarily to benefit the injured worker. Instead, it was created to protect employers and workers' compensation insurance companies by limiting their legal liability and obligations.

Despite these negatives, workers' compensation has evolved over the years to include some fairly decent worker protections. Although many of these are buried in hard-to-understand rules and procedures, informed workers who understand how the system works and are willing to assert their rights have a good chance of being treated fairly. Sadly, most workers have little, if any, knowledge about their workers' compensation rights. This book aims to change that.

This book can help you if you're handling your own workers' compensation case or filing a claim on someone else's behalf, such as a minor. (In legal terms, this is referred to as acting in the capacity of a Guardian ad Litem, where you file a workers' compensation claim on behalf of a minor or someone who is incompetent.) If you're represented by an attorney, she will be better able to guide you through the process if you're well-informed about workers' compensation procedures and understand the important decisions you'll need to make.

If you were injured on or after January 1, 1994, this book will provide up-to-date information on California workers' compensation laws. Due to changes in the law, this book cannot be relied on for injuries occurring prior to 1994, although it should still be very helpful.

INJURIES BETWEEN 1/1/90 AND 12/31/93

If you were injured before 1994 and your case hasn't settled yet, you will need to go beyond this book to find information that applies to your date of injury. Appendix 1 provides a summary of the important laws for injuries that occurred between 1/1/90 and 12/31/93. In addition, the Workers' Compensation Information and Assistance Unit provides free help, as discussed in Section C1, below.

LEGAL CITATIONS

Throughout this book, you'll see references to laws that govern the California workers' compensation system. If you want more information, you can look up these legal citations, as discussed in Chapter 27.

Labor Code (LC). The vast majority of workers' compensation laws are contained in the California Labor Code, the basic state laws that regulate employment matters.

California Code of Regulations (CCR). These rules and regulations expand upon, interpret and explain procedures for implementing and enforcing the California Labor Code.

United States Code (USC). Many laws that apply to people not covered by California workers' compensation laws can be found in the United States Code.

A. What Is Workers' Compensation?

Workers' compensation is a system of benefits set up to help employees who are injured on the job. If a worker dies as a result of work injuries, the employee's dependents are entitled to receive workers' compensation death benefits.

Work-related injuries (which broadly include injuries, occupational illnesses and diseases) are also referred to as "industrial injuries." For workers' compensation purposes, an industrial injury is any injury—in any occupation—that occurs as a result of your employment. Put another way, "industrial" is synonymous with "work." You may also hear the term "compensable injury," another term that refers to an injury that's covered by workers' compensation.

The workers' compensation system is sometimes described as a "no fault" system of give and take. The injured employee gives up the right to sue an employer in court. In return, the employee receives compensation without having to prove that the employer caused the injury. In exchange for providing compensation regardless of fault, the employer's liability is limited to benefits specified in the California Labor Code. Not surprisingly, these amounts are almost always significantly less than what might be available if employees could sue in court. For the vast majority of cases, the rule that all work-related injuries must go through the workers' compensation system is a fact of life. (There are a few situations where an injured employee is not covered by workers' compensation and may sue an employer in the regular (municipal or superior) court system; see Chapter 17 for a discussion.)

At first glance, a no fault system sounds like a fair deal—workers who are hurt are taken care of without having to go through a costly process of assigning blame. Unfortunately, the existing system is complicated and hard to understand. It has evolved into what too often becomes a bureaucratic nightmare that commonly intimidates and hinders people with valid claims. But perhaps the worst aspect of the California workers' compensation system is that it doesn't deliver on its fundamental promise to cover all injured workers on a no fault basis. The employer and its workers' compensation insurance company will often fight an employee's perfectly legitimate claim every step of the way.

B. What an Injured Worker Is Entitled to

Enough about the problems with workers' compensation laws. If you've been injured on the job, you probably want to know how you'll be compensated. California workers' compensation laws provide a *limited* number of benefits (mostly money payments). Workers' compensation benefits are tax exempt; in other words, they are not considered income for income tax purposes.

1. Take an Active Role in Obtaining Benefits

It's a fact of life that you're the one who must see to it that the insurance company provides you with benefits. If you (or your attorney, if you have one) don't go after all the benefits to which you are entitled, you will likely be shortchanged. In the workers' compensation system of limited benefits, you cannot afford to be complacent.

Lest you let your pride get in the way, clearly understand that workers' compensation benefits should not be considered charity. Whether you like it or not, the existence of the workers' compensation system means that you have given up valuable legal rights. For example, you cannot sue your employer, you are not entitled to payments to cover lost wages (past, present or future) and you cannot receive compensation for your pain and suffering.

Accept workers' compensation benefits for what they are: part of a system set up to get you medical treatment for your injury, provide minimum income while you are off work, and help you get back to work in some capacity as soon as possible.

WORKERS' COMPENSATION FRAUD

Over the last several years, alleged workers' compensation fraud (the filing of false claims) has been a major concern of employers and workers' compensation insurance companies alike. In response to these concerns, California passed major revisions to its workers' compensation laws, which are incorporated in this book. *It is now a felony for anyone to knowingly file a false or fraudulent workers' compensation claim.* The laws that make it harder to commit fraud unfortunately also make it much more complicated for injured workers to file and receive compensation for legitimate claims.

WORKERS' COMPENSATION JARGON

In few places on earth will you find a system that uses more confusing, contradictory and just plain batty terminology. Unfortunately, you will simply have to master a number of confusing terms and acronyms used in the workers' compensation system or you won't understand how to handle your claim. Whenever you hit a mind-boggling term, take a moment to learn what it means. In no time at all, you'll be talking with ease about your TTD, VRMA, QME, P&S and QRR.

2. Workers' Compensation Benefits

The following summary discusses what is available and refers you to the chapters that explain how to obtain and make the best use of available benefits:

- **Medical Treatment and Related Costs.** You are entitled to medical treatment, at no cost to you, to cure and relieve the effects of your industrial injury. You are also entitled to be reimbursed for costs of mileage going to and from your medical appointments. You are not, however, entitled to mileage reimbursement for attending court hearings or traveling to the insurance company's office. (Chapters 9, 10 and 11 cover all aspects of medical benefits.)
- **Temporary Disability.** You are entitled to receive monetary payments while you are off work and temporarily disabled due to your injury. The amount of temporary disability is based upon two-thirds of your average weekly wage, with established maximums, depending upon the date of your injury. In short, don't expect to receive as much money as when you were on the job. (See Chapter 12.)
- **Permanent Disability.** If your injury affects your ability to participate in the open job market in the future, you may receive a set dollar amount as compensation. How much you'll receive is determined by the part of your body that is injured, your age, your occupation and any work restrictions as determined by various doctors. These factors are plugged into a standard rating schedule to determine how much you can recover. If you're 70% to 99.75% disabled, you may additionally receive a small pension for the rest of your life. If you're 100% (totally) disabled, the amount you are entitled to receive increases substantially. (See Chapter 13.)
- **Vocational Rehabilitation Benefits.** If you cannot return to your former job because of limitations caused by your industrial injury, you are entitled to assistance in finding other employment. Vocational rehabilitation is a program designed to assist you in returning to the labor market. To this end, vocational rehabilitation employs a number of means, including possibly a retraining program designed to help you acquire the skills necessary to return to suitable gainful employment. (See Chapter 14.)
- **Death Benefits.** If you were a total or partial dependent (one who relied upon another for support) of an employee who died as a result of an industrial injury, you may have the right to recover certain benefits, including burial expenses and a sum of money. (See Chapter 15.)

OTHER WORKERS' COMPENSATION BENEFITS

In unusual circumstances, you may be entitled to benefits that are not available in a typical workers' compensation claim. Turn to Chapter 16 if any of the following remedies may apply to your situation:

- **Subsequent Injuries Fund Benefits.** You may be eligible if you had a prior injury or illness before your present workers' compensation injury, regardless of whether or not the prior injury happened at work.
- **Uninsured Employer's Fund.** This fund is available if your employer does not have workers' compensation insurance and is not self-insured.
- **Discrimination Benefits Under LC § 132(a).** You may be eligible to file a separate claim if your employer discriminated against you because you asserted your right to file a workers' compensation claim.
- **Employer's Serious and Willful Misconduct.** You may qualify for increased benefits if your employer's seriously improper action or inaction—such as the failure to remedy an obvious safety violation—contributed to or caused your work injury.

---

3. Other Benefits and Remedies

You may qualify for benefits and remedies outside the workers' compensation system, including:

- **State Disability ("SDI").** Most workers have a small amount deducted from each check for "SDI." In the event of disability for any reason (work or otherwise), you may be entitled to disability payments. SDI is usually paid where workers' compensation temporary disability is not being paid. (See Chapter 17, Section A.)
- **Social Security Benefits.** If your injury is severe enough, you may qualify for social security disability, which is paid by the federal government. (See Chapter 17, Section B.)
- **Claims or Lawsuits for Personal Injuries.** If your work injury was caused, entirely or in part, by an outside third party (someone not working for your employer), you may be able to sue that person or entity in civil court for damages. (See Chapter 17, Section C.)
- **Claims or Lawsuits Based on Discrimination.** In some instances where you have been discriminated against, you may be able to file a claim under the Americans with

Disabilities Act, the California Fair Employment Housing Act or other legal avenues. (See Chapter 17, Section D.)

C. Where to Get Additional Information and Help

While this book may answer most of your questions, it's quite possible that you'll need further assistance. You may contact any of the agencies listed below for help. In addition, Chapter 27 provides information on how to utilize the law library and the Internet to do legal research. If you decide that you want to be represented by an attorney, you may also find Chapter 26 on lawyers helpful. Be aware, however, that it may be difficult to find a workers' compensation attorney willing to take your case, as lawyer fees are relatively low and most workers' compensation attorneys have many more possible cases than they can handle.

1. Information and Assistance Officers

The Workers' Compensation Appeals Board is the place where your matter is heard by a workers' compensation judge, and where documents in your case are filed. Despite its name, all workers' compensation matters (not just appeals) are handled by the Workers' Compensation Appeals Board, also known as the "Appeals Board" or the "WCAB." There are approximately 18 Appeals Boards in the State of California.

Each Workers' Compensation Appeals Board has at least one Information and Assistance officer (also called an I&A officer). The Information and Assistance officer's role is to assist injured workers in navigating their way through the workers' compensation system. Some Information and Assistance officers can be your best source of information and help in resolving problems you encounter.

Information and Assistance officers are there to give you free help in pursuing your workers' compensation claim. See Appendix 5 for the number of your local workers' compensation office. You may get helpful general information from the automated Workers' Compensation Information and Assistance Unit line at 800-736-7401, which provides prerecorded information about workers' compensation.

In addition, "Injured Worker Workshops" are held the first Tuesday of every month at every district office. These free one-hour workshops consist of a presentation by an Informa-

tion and Assistance officer followed by a question and answer session. Call your district office for more information. (See Appendix 5 for the phone number.)

2. Workers' Compensation Insurance Rating Bureau (WCIRB)

The Workers' Compensation Insurance Rating Bureau (WCIRB) is helpful in finding out who your employer's workers' compensation company was at the time of your injury. Here's where to reach the WCIRB:

Workers' Compensation Insurance Rating Bureau
525 Market Street
Suite 800
San Francisco, CA 95105
Telephone 415-777-0777

3. Division of Workers' Compensation Website

The Workers' Compensation Division has developed a helpful website at http://www.dir.ca.gov/DWC/dwc_home_page. htm. Here you can find an overview of workers' comp laws and rules, an FAQ (frequently asked questions) area and guides for injured workers on topics such as how to object to a summary rating, how to file an appeal and how to fire your attorney. This site also provides workers' compensation forms and the manual for rating permanent disabilities in PDF format (readable by Adobe Acrobat Reader).

D. How to Use This Book

No two injuries are alike, and no two injuries are ever handled the same way by the same insurance company, let alone by different companies. How much of this book you'll choose to read will depend on your individual circumstances.

I suggest that you read Chapter 2 (Overview of a Workers' Compensation Claim) to get a good understanding of the workers' compensation system, and to determine where your claim is in the system. Read Chapter 21 (Preparing Your Case) in conjunction with Chapter 2, as trial preparation should begin on day one of your claim and continue until the day of trial.

If you have a cumulative trauma, or repetitive stress injury, read Chapter 4 (Cumulative Trauma Disorders).

A thorough reading of Chapter 6 (Keep Good Records to Protect Your Claim) will assure that you properly prepare and maintain the information you will need for trial.

At least glance through Chapter 5 (What to Do If You're Injured) to make certain that you have done everything you should following your injury. Feel free to turn to relevant chapters as the need arises and skip any chapters that do not apply to your situation. For example, if the employer's workers' compensation insurance company has already accepted your case and begun providing benefits, you may want to skip Chapter 3 (Is Your Injury Covered By Workers' Compensation?). Likewise, if the insurance company has proposed a settlement, you'll want to turn to Chapter 19 (Figure Out a Starting Settlement Amount).

While great care has been taken to provide you with a comprehensive and informative book on your workers' compensation benefits, this book cannot cover each and every aspect of workers' compensation law in detail. Particularly if your claim has been denied or delayed, you'll need to go beyond this book. (See Chapters 26 and 27 on hiring a lawyer and doing your own legal research.)

Finally, to avoid using the cumbersome "he or she," I have randomly alternately used masculine and feminine pronouns throughout the book.

E. What This Book Does Not Cover

Workers' compensation laws have changed tremendously over the last few years. This has inevitably resulted in uncertainty, as three different sets of laws are on the books—laws that apply to years prior to 1994, to 1994–1997 and after 1997. Many of the new or revised laws are subject to various interpretations, and will continue to be interpreted for many years to come as workers' compensation cases are brought to trial and legal decisions are appealed. I have given my best effort to provide you with accurate explanations of the law for injuries on or after 1/1/94. However, this book is not a legal opinion on any issue or law and should not be relied on as such. If you have questions or concerns regarding a workers' compensation issue or law, you should attempt to consult with a workers'

compensation attorney, get help from an Information and Assistance officer or do your own research. If you face any of the following issues, you should seek help beyond the book:

- **You were injured before January 1, 1994.** Appendix 1 gives an overview of workers' compensation laws between 1/1/90 and 12/31/93 and gives some suggestions for where to find additional information.

- **Your employer was not insured.** By law, your employer must carry workers' compensation insurance or be permissibly self-insured. If, however, your employer does not have workers' compensation insurance, you'll probably need to seek compensation from the Uninsured Employers Fund, discussed in Chapter 16, Section B.

- **An injured worker died.** If an employee's death was due to a work injury, at least in part, the worker's dependents may file a claim for death benefits. The worker's estate may be entitled to any accrued workers' compensation benefits as of the date of death. (See Chapter 15 for more information.) If you feel the death was due to the work injury and the insurance company denies coverage, seek help from an Information and Assistance officer or see a lawyer.

- **You have a stress-related (psychological) injury.** Insurance companies almost always deny these claims and will fight you every step of the way. If at all possible, find a workers' compensation attorney to represent you or seek help from an Information and Assistance officer. (See Chapter 3, Section B4, for more information.)

- **If the statute of limitations has run.** If the insurance company has denied your claim because it asserts that you failed to file your claim in a timely manner, you'll need help beyond the book. Contact an Information and Assistance officer or see a lawyer. (See Chapter 5, Section C1, for more information.)

- **Apportionment.** Insurance companies sometimes claim that all or part of a permanent disability is due to preexisting or subsequent factors, such as a non-work-related auto accident. If so, seek help from an Information and Assistance officer or see a lawyer. (See Chapter 3, Section B7, for more information.)

- **Post-termination claim.** Sometimes an insurance company will deny a claim if you were terminated or laid off. If this happens, seek help from an Information and Assistance officer or see a lawyer.

ICONS USED IN THIS BOOK

Look for these icons to alert you to certain kinds of information.

 Caution: Alerts you to potential problems you may encounter in your workers' compensation case.

 Tip: Gives practical suggestions for handling a legal or procedural issue that may come up.

 Fast Track: Lets you know when you may skip reading some material that is not relevant to your situation.

 Resources: Refers you to additional books or resources.

 See a Lawyer: Advises you to see a workers' compensation attorney or other source of assistance.

 Case Law: Lets you know there is an important court decision or case on this legal area, discussed in Chapter 28, Case Law Review.

■

2

Overview of a Workers' Compensation Claim

If you've been injured on the job, your workers' compensation claim will stumble and saunter its way through the workers' compensation system. It will seem that all you do is wait for something to happen. When you request medical treatment, you may wait weeks for a response. You may wait for a doctor's appointment, then wait for the medical report. And if you file for a hearing before the Workers' Compensation Appeals Board, you may wait months for your hearing date.

And so it will go. At every turn, it is likely to take months before anything is accomplished. Unfortunately, it probably won't make you feel much better to realize you are not alone. An average workers' compensation case takes two to three years to be resolved. And many cases take much, much longer.

It probably won't come as a surprise that the workers' compensation system is also bureaucratic: lots of forms, reports and other documents are shuffled through what sometimes seems like an endless maze. Above all, the workers' compensation system is confusing. It's fraught with rules and regulations—and it sorely lacks understandable information for the injured worker.

This chapter helps take the mystery out of the workers' compensation system by clearly outlining the steps involved in a "typical" workers' compensation case. Inevitably, there will be some variations depending on your particular situation and whether or not you're represented by an attorney. But the basic steps are usually similar in workers' compensation cases.

DEATH CLAIMS

If you were totally or partially dependent upon someone who died due to an industrial injury, you may have a workers' compensation claim for death benefits. Skip ahead to Chapter 15.

Step 1. Notify Your Employer of the Injury

If you sustain a work injury, immediately notify your supervisor or boss of the injury at your first opportunity. If your injury developed over a period of time, as with a repetitive stress, or cumulative trauma, injury, notify your employer as soon as you have symptoms and realize you've been injured as a result of your job.

Although you may initially verbally tell your supervisor of the injury, it is important that you also give your employer written notice of the injury within 30 days of the injury. This will prevent any misunderstanding about whether or not you reported the injury, and will protect your right to workers' compensation benefits. If you have a union representative, contact that person right away; you may need help obtaining additional benefits that are secured by a union contract. (Your union representative may be instrumental in protecting your legal rights should your employer attempt to terminate you because you can't return to work for a while. Also, some employers may have salary continuation agreements for those injured at work.)

Make certain that you complete any required in-house accident reports. Also, review any accident reports prepared by your supervisor or employer for accuracy and obtain a copy for your records. If you disagree with the report, write your employer a letter explaining your position. (Chapter 5 takes you through all the rules and procedures involved with reporting your injury and filing a claim.)

Step 2. Get Medical Treatment If Needed

It is important to promptly seek medical treatment if needed. Not only will prompt medical treatment protect your health, but it will establish a medical record of your work injury. If you gave your employer the name of your own doctor or health plan *before* your injury ("designated your treating physician," in workers' compensation jargon), you may go to that doctor. If not, the employer usually has the right to send you to a doctor it chooses, which often turns out to be the "company doctor"—a doctor or medical clinic that the employer sends its injured workers to on a regular basis.

If you have a medical emergency that requires immediate medical attention, you may go to the nearest emergency room for emergency treatment. But after your emergency medical condition has been stabilized, you must continue follow-up medical treatment with the physician selected by your employer, unless you designated a doctor in advance. (See Chapter 9 for a detailed discussion of medical care.)

Step 3. Paying for Medical Treatment If Employer Refuses Authorization

If you report what you believe to be a work-related injury to your supervisor, your employer will most likely agree to accept responsibility. Authorization may be given verbally or in writing to the doctor by your employer or its workers' compensation insurance company.

Sometimes employers will refuse to authorize medical treatment, claiming that the injury is not work-related, or that it is not serious enough to warrant medical care. Should your employer refuse to authorize your medical treatment, it may work to your advantage. By doing so, your employer gives up its right to control your medical treatment for the first 30 to 365 days depending on the circumstances. Instead, you may choose any doctor you want to treat with and are not bound to go to the company doctor for treatment. (Another advantage, discussed in Chapter 10, Section C, is that you are not limited to selecting your Qualified Medical Evaluator (QME) from a three-member panel, and may select one from all qualified QMEs, LC § 4060.)

If the insurance company has refused to authorize medical treatment, and your injury requires emergency medical treatment, you may go to the nearest emergency room for treatment, and your employer must pay, even if the insurance company will not authorize it.

For non-emergencies, seek prompt treatment by relying on private health insurance, if you have it. If you do not have medical insurance and your employer refuses to pay, you have three choices. You may pay for treatment yourself and seek reimbursement later. You may find a doctor to treat you on a "lien basis," where the doctor waits for payment until your workers' compensation case is settled. (See Chapter 9, Section B2b, for more on liens.) Or you may get a judge to order your employer's insurance company to pay for treatment. The Information and Assistance officer can help with this procedure. (See Step 10, below.)

⚠ **ALWAYS APPLY FOR STATE DISABILITY (SDI)**
Whenever you have an injury that results in your inability to work, *always—and immediately—*apply for SDI from the Employment Development Department (EDD). That way, you'll receive income from this source in case of a delay or denial of your claim. When your workers' compensation benefits begin, it's important that you promptly inform the EDD, and it will discontinue payments. (You may also be entitled to retroactive temporary disability if you receive less in SDI payments than you would have from the workers' compensation insurance company. We cover SDI in Chapter 17, Section A.)

Step 4. What to Tell the Doctor

The doctor's first report will often be relied upon by the insurance company to determine the extent of your injuries and whether they resulted from your employment. Tell the doctor that you injured yourself at work (if that's true) and how the injury occurred (if you know). In addition to giving the doctor a complete history of your medical problems (if asked), be sure to cover all your symptoms and sources of pain. For instance, even if most of your pain is in your back, if your arm hurts even a little, *tell the doctor!* You'll find detailed information on dealing with doctors in Chapter 9.

Step 5. The Doctor Decides If You Need Time Off

The first doctor you see will determine whether or not you need some time off from work to recover from the effects of your injury. Depending on the doctor's findings, you will receive one of the following:

- off work order
- limited duties work order (also called a light duty work order or modified work order), or
- return to work order—that is, you can return to work with no restrictions.

Especially if you are given an off work order, it's essential that you keep your employer advised of your medical status. If you neglect to do so, you may be fired for failing to report to work without a valid excuse. If, however, you keep your employer informed, you cannot legally be fired for injuring yourself, filing a workers' compensation claim and obeying doctor's orders.

INJURED WORKERS WHO ARE FIRED

Employees often ask if they can be fired while off work because of an industrial injury. The answer is "not usually," unless the employer can prove that the termination is due to "business necessity," such as where the company went out of business or closed a factory store. Otherwise, an employer cannot terminate a worker until his condition stabilizes (called a "permanent and stationary" designation in workers' compensation jargon) and doctors determine that permanent disabilities prevent the worker from returning to his usual job. Even then, an employer may be prohibited from discriminating against an injured worker. Under the Americans with Disabilities Act, a new or former employer must make a reasonable effort to accommodate your disability.

If you have an employment contract with your employer, or a union bargaining agreement, review the contract or check with your union representative to determine if your employer may terminate you after a specified time off work. For example, members of the Retail Clerks Union (grocery clerks and checkers) arguably have one year from the last date worked to return to work before an employer may terminate them—and even then, they may be able to get their job back.

Step 6. Complete Workers' Compensation Claim Form and Application for Adjudication of Claim Form

Your next step is to protect your rights as an injured worker under the workers' compensation system by promptly completing two forms:

- **Workers' Compensation Claim Form (DWC-1).** Your employer is required by law to give you this form within 24 hours of learning of the injury. (LC § 5401.) You must fill in the DWC-1 form and give it to your employer. A copy of form DWC-1 is provided in Appendix 4.
- **Application for Adjudication of Claim.** You must also complete an Application for Adjudication of Claim form and file it with the Workers' Compensation Appeals Board. An Application for Adjudication of Claim form is included in Appendix 4.

⚠ TIME LIMITS TO FILE A CLAIM

Your workers' compensation claim form (DWC-1) and the Application for Adjudication of Claim must by law be filed within one year from the date of injury. But as a matter of common sense, you should complete and file these within 30 days of your injury, or at your first opportunity. (We provide forms and detailed instructions in Chapter 5, Section C2.)

Step 7. Secure Control of Your Medical Care

As emphasized throughout this book, your treating doctor makes many important decisions that affect your workers' compensation case. Among other things, this doctor decides when and if you can return to work, what type of treatment you need and whether you are seriously injured. Most importantly, the treating doctor's report is given a presumption under the law as being correct if you have to go to court. Therefore you need a doctor who is sympathetic to your interests.

Obviously, it is important that you take maximum advantage of your legal rights and select a treating doctor of your choice. If you gave your employer a written designation of your treating physician prior to the injury, you may receive medical care from that doctor. Otherwise, you cannot pick your own doctor until a certain period of time has passed after your injury. Pay attention to this time period and choose your own doctor as soon as you legally can. (See Chapter 9, Section B, for details on how and when to do this.)

Step 8. Receive Temporary Disability Benefits If You're Eligible

When an injury limits you from returning to your job, you are entitled to receive temporary disability benefits. These payments are designed to help support you while you are not receiving full pay and are recovering from the effects of the injury or illness.

If the treating doctor determines that you are temporarily disabled, and the insurance company has not begun payments, you'll need to take charge. Contact your employer's workers' compensation insurance company and request payment of temporary disability indemnity (also referred to as TD). It's okay to make your request by telephone, but it is always wise to follow up with a confirming letter, such as the one in Chapter 12, Section C3.

Within 14 days of your request, the workers' compensation insurance company should begin making temporary disability payments or advise you by mail why payments cannot be made within the 14-day period (known as a "delay letter"). If you have an off work order and your claim is accepted, the insurance carrier should promptly begin making temporary disability payments for all but the first three days you were off work, unless you are temporarily disabled for more than 14 days or your injury requires an overnight stay in the hospital, in which case you will be paid for these three days. (LC § 4652.) See Chapter 12, Section B, to determine the amount you are entitled to receive.

If you receive a delay letter, you may be asked to provide additional information to the insurance company so that it can decide whether temporary disability payments are owed. The delay letter will also state when the insurance company expects to have the information required to make the decision. (LC § 4650, CCR § 9812.) The insurance company has 90 days from knowledge of your claim in which to make a decision as to whether you are eligible for temporary disability.

If you do not receive either a check or a delay letter within 14 days of your request for benefits, the insurance company is liable for a 10% penalty on any temporary disability payments that you should have received by the 14th day. But don't sit around waiting for your check to appear. This is just one more instance where the old adage "the squeaky wheel gets the grease" holds true.

Step 9. Handling a Denial of Your Claim or Benefits

If you're unable to work because of your injury, the last thing you want to face is a battle with the insurance company. Unfortunately, this isn't in your control. Some insurance companies deny many claims as a matter of course, or routinely reject requests for temporary disability payments, medical treatment or other benefits.

If your workers' compensation claim or any request for benefits is denied, the insurer should notify you of the reason in writing, namely that:

- the insurer does not believe you sustained an industrial injury
- the insurer does not believe that you are temporarily totally disabled

- the insurer does not believe you need medical treatment, or
- your case involves two or more employers or insurance companies who refuse to pay benefits, each claiming that the payment of benefits is the other's responsibility.

In any of these situations, you may need to take immediate steps to secure benefits. If a letter or phone call proves fruitless, you'll probably need to request a hearing before the Workers' Compensation Appeals Board, as discussed in Step 10, below. Consider seeing a lawyer, if you haven't already. (See Chapter 26 for information on hiring a lawyer.)

Step 10. Taking Problems to the Appeals Board

The Workers' Compensation Appeals Board oversees the California workers' compensation system. You may request a hearing (either expedited or regular) before the Appeals Board to resolve virtually any disputed issue. Examples of problems that may necessitate a hearing include:

- **refusal to authorize for medical treatment.** Your employer or its insurance company refuses to pay for your medical treatment.
- **refusal to authorize for surgery or tests.** Your treating doctor requests authorization to do surgery or perform tests, such as an MRI, and the insurance company refuses to authorize it.
- **refusal to provide benefits.** The treating doctor says that you are entitled to benefits, such as vocational rehabilitation services, and the insurance company refuses to provide them.
- **insufficient benefits.** The insurance company pays temporary disability at a lower rate than your earnings justify.

• **inadequate medical care.** You believe the quality of medical treatment you are receiving is inadequate, and the insurance company refuses to send you to another doctor.

Information on requesting a hearing before a workers' compensation judge is contained in Chapters 22 and 24.

Step 11. After You Are Determined to Be Permanent and Stationary (P&S)

You may continue to receive temporary disability payments until your doctor says that your medical condition is "permanent and stationary" or that you can return to work. Permanent and stationary (also referred to as "P&S") is workers' compensation jargon meaning that your doctor believes your medical condition has plateaued and medical treatment at this time won't improve your condition.

Exactly when this determination is made depends upon the severity of the injury, the length of your treatment and your prospects for your further recovery. It could be weeks, months or even several years before your doctor concludes that your condition has reached a plateau. Once you are determined to be permanent and stationary, you are no longer entitled to temporary disability payments, even if you cannot return to work or have not been released to return to work. You may, however, still be entitled to further medical treatment on an as-needed basis.

After your doctor's permanent and stationary diagnosis, you can expect to receive a letter from the insurance company advising you of the company's position on several critical issues in your workers' compensation case, including:

• whether you have a permanent disability (if so, the insurance company will begin making payments)
• whether you qualify for vocational rehabilitation, and
• whether you are entitled to future medical care.

If you, or the insurance company, disagree with the treating doctor's opinion on any issues, the disputing party has 30 days to request that the issue be determined by going to a Qualified Medical Evaluator (QME). (See Chapter 10 for a detailed explanation of medical-legal evaluations.)

Step 12. If You Recover Completely and Return to Work

Many work injuries result in a minimum amount of time off from work—perhaps a few days or weeks. After recovering, the injured worker returns to the job without any work restrictions or long-term disability. In such situations, your main concern is to make certain that you were fairly paid by the insurance company for the days you were off, and that all medical treatment was paid by the insurance company, or you were reimbursed if you paid your own medical bills. Be aware that even if you go back to work, you may still be entitled to a monetary permanent disability award. (See Step 14.)

Step 13. If You Are Entitled to Vocational Rehabilitation Benefits

If your ability to do your customary work is permanently impaired, you may be entitled to vocational rehabilitation benefits (job training and placement) under either of the following conditions:

• the treating doctor has indicated that you can return to your former employment with certain restrictions, and the employer won't or can't accommodate you, or
• the treating doctor has indicated that you should not return to your former employment under any circumstances.

If both you and the insurance company agree with the treating doctor's determination and/or the actions of the employer, you can mutually agree to begin the vocational rehabilitation process. Otherwise, either party may voice its objections and get another doctor's opinion. (See Chapter 14 for more on vocational rehabilitation. Chapter 10 discusses how to get a medical-legal evaluation to obtain another doctor's opinion.)

Step 14. If You Are Permanently Disabled— Negotiate a Final Settlement

If you can't go back to your former job, or you can, but only with work restrictions or limited duties, you may be entitled to permanent disability payments. After your condition becomes permanent and stationary, you should try to negotiate a settlement with the insurance company. By negotiating your settlement, you eliminate the hazards of litigation. For example, if the case goes to trial, you're likely to wait many months or more to finally get to trial. You may even end up with less than you'd have received if you had settled the case.

The factors you should consider when negotiating a settlement are covered in detail in Chapters 19 and 20, and should include the value of your permanent disability, any past due benefits (such as retroactive temporary disability) and either the right to future medical treatment or its dollar value.

Step 15. Go to Trial If There Is No Settlement

If the case doesn't settle, either side may file appropriate documents with the Workers' Compensation Appeals Board to set the case for trial. First, you'll attend a preliminary hearing, called a pre-trial conference or mandatory settlement conference. There, you will have a final opportunity to settle the case. If you and the insurance company still cannot reach a settlement, you will be assigned a trial date to have your case heard before an Appeals Board judge. The trial date will probably be set anywhere from two to eight months later, depending upon how crowded the trial calendar is.

Step 16. Judgment Is Paid or the Matter Is Appealed

If the judge rules in your favor, the insurance company must either pay the judgment to you within 25 days or file a Petition for Reconsideration, which is the first of three steps in the appeal process. If you don't agree with the judge's ruling, you may also file a Petition for Reconsideration. If a petition is denied, the appealing party may file a Writ of Review with the Court of Appeals, and finally with the California Supreme Court. (Appeals are covered in Chapter 25.) ■

3

Is Your Injury Covered by Workers' Compensation?

→ IF YOUR CLAIM WAS ACCEPTED

If you filed a claim that has already been accepted by the workers' compensation insurance company, you can safely skip this chapter. Your claim is "accepted" if the insurer considers yours a work-related injury and agrees to cover it. Acceptance by the insurance company may come in the form of a letter or may be inferred if the insurer provides benefits, such as temporary disability and medical treatment. However, if at a later date the insurance company denies your claim because of a claimed coverage problem, you may need to review this chapter.

If you are in doubt as to whether your *job* or injury is covered by workers' compensation, this chapter will help you decide. You need only read the sections of this chapter that address your situation, so please follow these instructions:

- If you don't know whether your *job* is covered by workers' compensation, read Section A.
- If you aren't sure if your *injury* is work-related (compensable), turn to Section B.
- If you significantly contributed to the injury, see Section D.
- If your injury didn't occur while you were working on the job, see Section D8.
- If you didn't file a workers' compensation claim within one year of the injury, see Section D9.

A. Is Your Job Covered by Workers' Compensation?

If you work for almost any employer, whether it's a large multinational corporation, a small business or a mom and pop store, you are almost surely covered by workers' compensation. As long as you were hired in California or are regularly employed in California and you suffer a work-related injury (either inside or outside of the state), that injury is covered under California workers' compensation laws. The fact is, most injured workers are covered by workers' compensation and must exclusively seek benefits through that system. But a few categories of workers—notably some federal workers and independent contractors—must pursue other avenues for compensation.

1. Most Employees Are Covered by Workers' Compensation

To be eligible for benefits, you must be an employee—not an independent contractor (see Section 2a, below). If you receive a salary or hourly wage, you are probably an employee, even if that term is not used. In fact, even a salary or hourly wage is not a requirement, as long as you aren't volunteering. There is no need for you to have a written employment contract.

Employees include legal and illegal aliens, minors (even if they are too young to be legally employed) and prisoners. You may even be covered by workers' compensation through a homeowners' policy if you were hired by a homeowner to perform gardening, maintenance, housecleaning, child care or the like. (LC § 3351.)

To qualify as an employee, you do not have to be employed full-time, or employed by only one employer or employed for any particular number of days or months. An exception to this rule applies to industrial injuries involving emotional stress or injury to the psyche. For emotional injuries, you probably must be employed for at least six months prior to the date of injury to qualify for workers' compensation. (See Section B4b.)

⚠ SPECIAL PROCEDURES FOR MINORS

Although minors (people under age 18) who are injured are entitled to workers' compensation benefits, they cannot legally file a claim for benefits because they are not of legal age to do so. Therefore, a minor must have an adult "Guardian ad Litem" (someone who is legally responsible for pursuing a claim) appointed to file a claim on his behalf. (We discuss this requirement in Chapter 5, Section C4b.)

You are covered by workers' compensation from the moment you start work, and sometimes even before you're hired. For example, if you are "trying out" for employment and are injured in some required activity—say an agility test—you are eligible for workers' compensation benefits.

In short, never assume that because yours is an unusual employment situation, you are not covered by workers' compensation. For workers' compensation law purposes, the definition of an employee is extremely broad. With few exceptions described, if your injury had any connection with any sort of employment, you are presumed to be an employee covered by workers' compensation. (LC § 3357.)

2. Workers Not Covered by Workers' Compensation

Certain categories of workers are not covered by workers' compensation. If injured on the job, these workers may not use the workers' compensation system—although other ways of seeking compensation may be available.

 IF YOU ARE EXCLUDED FROM FILING A CLAIM

If you're not entitled to file a workers' compensation claim, you may have the right to file a claim in a federal or California civil court. To do this, you'll probably need the help of a lawyer. Don't delay in finding a lawyer, since you must file your claim within a specified period of time or you will be barred from doing so.

a. Independent Contractors Excluded

Independent contractors are not employees—and therefore aren't covered under the workers' compensation system. People who often work as independent contractors include freelancers, plumbers, electricians, building contractors, auctioneers and doctors.

If the person who hired you has no right to control how you get the job done, you may be an independent contractor. Here are some other indicators that you may be an independent contractor rather than an employee:

- Independent contractors do not get vacation, holidays, medical insurance or other benefits. They pay their own social security and self-employment taxes.
- Independent contractors generally offer services to the public at large, and do not work for just one person or business.
- Independent contractors generally provide their own equipment and supplies and have a definite business location.

EMPLOYEES MISCLASSIFIED AS INDEPENDENT CONTRACTORS

Some employers or insurance companies may try to claim that you are an independent contractor when you are really an employee. Even if you have a contract stating that you are an independent contractor, it doesn't necessarily mean you are. You'll probably need the help of a workers' compensation lawyer if the insurer denies your claim on the premise that you're not an employee.

b. Certain Business Owners Excluded

If you work for yourself or own a business, you may not be covered by workers' compensation. Sole proprietors, partners, LLC members and officers of closely held corporations are generally not considered employees unless specifically listed under the business's workers' compensation insurance policy.

Of course, if a small business hires employees, they are covered under workers' compensation, even if the owner is not.

c. Certain Part-Time Workers Excluded

Certain part-time workers are excluded from workers' compensation coverage. The most common of these are household employees, such as gardeners or housekeepers, who were employed fewer than 52 hours during the 90 calendar days immediately preceding the date of the injury or who earned less than $100 in wages from the employer during the 90 days preceding the date of injury. (LC §§ 3352(h).)

d. Most Federal Employees and Transportation Workers Excluded

Most federal employees and certain types of workers in the transportation industries who are injured on the job must file a lawsuit in federal court to receive compensation, rather than using the workers' compensation system. Employees excluded from workers' compensation include:

- **Seamen.** Under the Jones Act, a seaman (someone who works in or around the oceans or seas) who is injured because of an employer's failure to provide a seaworthy vessel may recover damages only in federal court. (46 USC § 688 et seq.)
- **Railroad employees.** Under the Federal Employer's Liability Act (FELA), all railroad employees have to file in federal or state court for injuries sustained at work. FELA applies to any injury sustained due to an accident, but does not apply to injuries due to continuous traumas or occupational diseases. (45 USC § 51-60.)
- **Other federal employees.** Under the Federal Employers Compensation Act (FECA), injured federal employees must file in federal or state court (5 USC § 8101-8193), but they cannot use the workers' compensation system.

e. Longshoremen, Harbor Workers and Defense Workers Excluded

People whose injuries occur at a few specified locations—most commonly on the ocean or other navigable waters or on defense bases—are excluded from filing under California workers' compensation. Here are the rules:

- The Longshore and Harbor Workers' Compensation Act covers injuries occurring upon the navigable waters of the U.S., including any adjoining pier, wharf, dry dock, terminal or other adjoining area customarily used by an employee in loading, unloading, repairing or building a vessel. The majority of these types of injuries involve longshoremen, whose job involves loading and unloading seagoing vessels. Anyone so injured has to file a lawsuit in state or federal court. (Someone who actually works full time upon a vessel would probably be considered a seaman, and thus be subject to the Jones Act. See Section 2d, just above.)

- The Outer Continental Shelf Lands Act covers all persons injured on the ocean beyond three miles from shore. (43 USC § 1331-1356.) Anyone so injured may have a choice between being compensated under the California workers' compensation laws and the Longshore and Harbor Workers' Compensation Act. (If in doubt, see an attorney.)

- All deaths at sea beyond the three-mile limit are covered by the Death on the High Seas Act. (46 USC § 761 et seq.)

- Employees doing work on defense bases or public works outside the continental United States are covered by the Defense Base Act.

f. Employees Hired Outside of California Excluded

If you were hired in another state and are only temporarily working in California, you are not covered under California law. Fortunately, you are probably covered under the workers' compensation laws of your home state or where you were hired. (LC § 3600.5(b).)

IF YOU LIVE AND WORK IN DIFFERENT STATES
If you live in another state, but work permanently in California, you are probably covered under both states' workers' compensation laws. File your claim in the state with the best benefits (probably not California).

g. Volunteers Often Excluded

Persons who volunteer for a public agency or private nonprofit organization and receive no payment other than meals, transportation, lodging or incidental expenses generally are not covered by workers' compensation. (Volunteers who work for a for-profit business may be considered employees, especially if they receive something of value, such as food or lodging.)

Usually excluded from workers' compensation coverage are:

- unpaid volunteers who provide services to charitable institutions
- volunteer ski patrol workers, and
- volunteer disaster service workers.

VOLUNTEERS ARE SOMETIMES COVERED

Under workers' compensation laws, the following are considered to be employees, rather than volunteers:

- sheriff's reserve deputies while on duty
- any volunteer who assists a police officer at the officer's request
- volunteer police or fire fighters while on active duty
- state fish and game reserve officers while on active duty, and
- anyone who performs hazardous work at the request of a fire or law enforcement officer.

In addition, it is possible for organizations to elect to cover volunteers under workers' compensation. For example, a church may specifically cover a person who does repairs for the church on a volunteer basis.

---

h. Nonworking Students Not Covered

A student injured at school while participating in normal school activities is not covered by workers' compensation. Even student athletes who participate in amateur sporting events sponsored by the school are excluded from coverage.

There is one exception to the rule that students aren't covered by workers' compensation. A student injured while participating in a school work-experience or community occupational training program is covered. And of course, a student employed at a regular job, such as a hamburger joint or a campus store, is an employee and is fully covered under workers' compensation.

B. Do You Have a Compensable Injury?

To qualify as a compensable injury (one covered under workers' compensation), you need to have suffered some form of work-related physical or emotional harm. Because some industrial injuries are not easy to spot, many people are working today with industrial injuries and don't even know it. Let's look at some of the major categories of compensable injuries.

1. Specific or Traumatic Injuries

The most straightforward injury can be traced back to a single incident that happened to you while working, even if you didn't realize you sustained an injury until later. Following are a few examples of specific or traumatic injuries:

- You are hit by a falling object at work.
- You slip on something while at work and fall, dislocating your knee.
- You cut your hand with a knife or tool.
- You are involved in a car accident while delivering packages at work. You think you're fine, but several days later you trace the pain in your neck to a whiplash sustained in the car accident.

2. Cumulative Trauma or Continuous Trauma Injuries

An injury caused by work activities that extend over a period of time may not be easily identified. In the workers' compensation world, this is called a continuous trauma or cumulative trauma injury. This type of injury may also be referred to as a repetitive motion or repetitive strain injury. The common denominator in these types of injuries is the repetitive nature of the activities that caused the injury.

EXAMPLE 1: A computer user does eight hours of programming and design work every day. She gets tingling and numbness in her fingers after one year of work.

EXAMPLE 2: A laborer who does heavy lifting often has a sore lower back after work. Over a period of time, the symptoms get worse. Eventually, his back hurts so much he can't go to work.

EXAMPLE 3: A grocery store checker pulls thousands of groceries across her check stand every day. One day, she realizes that her hands are going numb. Her doctor tells her she has carpal tunnel syndrome, brought on by the repetitive motions used in scanning groceries.

EXAMPLE 4: A factory worker is constantly exposed to toxic chemical fumes on the job. Over a period of several years, she develops respiratory problems due to this exposure.

There is no required time period for an injury to qualify as a cumulative trauma injury. Some injuries occur over years, while others can develop over a relatively short time. The final determination of whether you have a cumulative trauma injury will be made by your doctors.

A continuous trauma does not have to occur all at one job. You may have done similarly repetitive work for several different employers over many years. If so, the employers (and their respective insurance companies) for which you worked during the last year of the continuous trauma are responsible for paying workers' compensation benefits. See Section B7, below. (Also, in Chapter 5, Section C, we discuss how to file a claim form that lists all employers who may be responsible for your workers' compensation coverage.)

3. Sickness Due to Harmful Exposure

An illness or disease may qualify as an industrial injury if it was caused or made worse by conditions at work. You probably would have a claim for workers' compensation in situations such as these:

- A construction worker is exposed to asbestos while working and many years later develops a condition called asbestosis.
- A maid is required to use a cleaning solution at work and breaks out in a rash, develops a migraine headache and suffers severe stomach problems.
- A doctor is pricked by a needle at work and later tests HIV-positive.

If you are thinking that some of these injuries are also cumulative injuries, you are correct. For example, sickness that results from long-term exposure to a toxic substance is also a cumulative injury.

⚠ IF YOU HAVE ASBESTOSIS

Do not attempt to represent yourself in this very specialized field, as you'll probably miss out on important rights. Find a workers' compensation attorney who deals with asbestos claims.

4. Stress-Related Injuries

To qualify for workers' compensation benefits for a stress-related injury, you must be able to show by competent medical evidence that you have a psychiatric and/or perhaps a physical injury as a result of stress on the job.

⚠ BEWARE OF STRESS CLAIM SCAMS

Be leery of television or radio commercials that ask you to call an 800-number if you were subjected to stress on the job. For the most part, doctors who solicit business from workers with stress-related injuries are interested in fattening their own wallets, not in workers' health or legal rights. You may get medical or psychiatric treatment (whether you need it or not), but you probably won't get any monetary benefits from the workers' compensation insurance company.

a. Psychiatric Injuries

 See *California Youth Authority v. WCAB (Walker)*, *Rodriguez v. WCAB* and *Cristobal v. WCAB* in Chapter 28.

A stress claim generally involves injury to the psyche (one's emotional well-being) due to stressful conditions at work. In other words, this is an emotional injury that limits one's ability to perform certain job functions, such as following instructions or communicating with others.

Although workers' compensation is supposed to be a "no fault" system that covers employees pretty much across the board, this is no longer true for psychiatric injuries. For starters, you must have been employed by your employer for at least six months (not necessarily continuous employment) prior to the date of injury. You may lose your eligibility for

workers' compensation if you were terminated or laid-off prior to filing a stress claim. See the sidebar below, "Special Rules If Job was Terminated."

In addition, you must demonstrate by a preponderance (51%) of the evidence that the actual events of your employment predominantly caused the psychiatric injury. In other words, if you are disabled due to a variety of factors—such as stress at work, personal financial problems and a recent divorce—you may qualify for workers' compensation benefits only if the work stress contributed at least 51% to your overall psychiatric disability.

EXAMPLE: Manuel works on a production line in a factory. His supervisor constantly pressures Manuel to work faster, and frequently threatens to terminate him. His supervisor humiliates Manuel in front of his co-employees on a daily basis, calling him a "stupid wetback" who can't follow instructions or saying he's too fat to do factory work. As a result of the constant harassment, Manuel becomes too nervous to continue working and files a workers' compensation claim. Manuel has no stresses other than his work life, so he is sure he can prove that at least 51% of his disability was caused by his work environment.

There is an important exception to the 51% requirement. If you were the victim of a work-related violent act or were directly exposed to a significant violent act, you qualify for workers' compensation benefits if your employment caused at least 35% of your overall psychiatric disability.

You may need medical treatment and temporary disability payments as a result of your psychiatric injuries. But bear in mind that if you qualify for permanent disability, you will have proven to the world that you have a *permanent* psychiatric disability. Be sure that this is something you are willing to live with. Although future employers may not legally discriminate against you because you have a psychiatric disability, realistically you may face that possibility.

▣ SEXUAL HARASSMENT ON THE JOB

Sexual harassment by co-employees or superiors at work may also result in physical or emotional injury. In addition to workers' compensation benefits, you may be entitled to pursue other remedies in civil court. To do this, you must take action within one year from the date of the alleged harassment, or your case may be forever barred. If you are interested in learning more about your rights in this area, refer to *Sexual Harassment on the Job*, by Barbara Kate Repa and William Petrocelli (Nolo).

PROBLEMS FINDING ATTORNEYS TO HANDLE PSYCHIATRIC STRESS CLAIMS

Most psychiatric stress case cases result in little or no permanent disability, because once the employee leaves the stressful environment (the job), he will generally have a full recovery. This means you will probably have difficulty finding a lawyer to represent you, because attorney fees are based on a percentage of permanent disability recovery. In short, you may have no choice but to represent yourself if you have a psychiatric stress claim. But because this type of claim is often contested and can be particularly complicated, I recommend you make a concerted effort to find competent counsel to represent you.

b. Physical Stress-Related Injuries

Sometimes stress at work causes not only emotional injury, but manifests itself in physical injury to the body. Depending on the circumstances, emotional injury may or may not be present as well.

EXAMPLE 1: Ted works for a convenience store. While at work one evening, he is held up at gunpoint. After the incident, Ted finds that he is fearful of every customer that comes into the store. He has difficulty sleeping, and has frequent nightmares about the incident. Before long, Ted develops an ulcer and suffers a nervous breakdown.

EXAMPLE 2: Larry is a sales representative for a large pharmaceutical company. He has been under a great deal of pressure from his supervisor to meet monthly sales quotas and has been told that he will be terminated if he fails to do so. Larry's wife is expecting their third child, and he can't afford to lose his job. Larry begins working 18-hour shifts, constantly worrying about failing to meet quotas and being fired. Larry suffers a heart attack, which he alleges is due to the stress at work.

It's even possible to have a legitimate stress claim for an injury that results from the stress experienced because of a workers' compensation injury and claim.

EXAMPLE: Denny slips a disk in his back at work. The insurance company denies him benefits, causing him severe financial hardship. This results in further physical and emotional injury from the stress placed upon Denny due to the lack of money.

SPECIAL RULES IF JOB WAS TERMINATED

Additional rules apply for stress injuries if you were fired, laid off or voluntarily quit prior to filing a claim for workers' compensation benefits. In addition to other requirements, you must show that at least one of following applies:

- **Sudden and extraordinary events of your employment caused the injury.** This means that your psychiatric injury was due to something one would normally not experience in the workplace; for example, witnessing a violent act.
- **Your employer had notice of the psychiatric injury prior to the notice of termination or layoff.** Sufficient notice might be a memo to your supervisor saying that you were planning to file a stress claim. Certainly, an actual filing of a claim would qualify.
- **Medical records prior to the notice of termination or layoff contain evidence of treatment of the psychiatric injury.** For example, you may have seen a doctor or therapist about your problems before receiving notice of a layoff.
- **Your date of injury is after the date of notice of the termination or layoff, but prior to its effective date.** If you receive notice of termination that is to take place in a week or a month, you could file a stress claim without being subject to the termination rules above.
- **You were sexually or racially harassed at work.**

---

leukemia), hernias or similar stress-induced diseases. (If you are employed in any occupation that involves protecting the public, please refer to Labor Code Sections 3212-3213 for a complete list of the types of injuries that are presumed to be work-related.)

- **Injuries where there was no other reasonable explanation for the injury.** In certain situations, no one knows how the injury occurred and there's no evidence to contradict that it was work-related. For example, an employee was welding a pipe at work one day. The next thing she remembers is waking up in the hospital with a gash to her head. Unless there is evidence to the contrary, it will be presumed that the injury occurred as a result of her employment.
- **Injuries that resulted in the employee's dying or becoming incompetent or otherwise mentally incapacitated.** Since, for obvious reasons, the injured employee cannot explain how the injury occurred, it is presumed that the injury occurred as a result of her employment.

6. Injuries Resulting From a Prior Condition

If you're injured at work as a result of a pre-existing or underlying condition, you may still have a workers' compensation claim. (LC § 4663.) But to be covered, there must be something new about the injury. It can't just be a recurrence or one-time flare-up of the old injury. To qualify for workers' compensation, the injury must be either:

- an aggravation (worsening) of an underlying condition, whether work-related or not, or
- a new injury that developed as a result of a prior industrial injury.

5. Injuries That Are Automatically Work-Related

Certain injuries are assumed to be work-related unless the employer or its insurance company successfully offers sufficient evidence to dispute it. If an employer disputes whether one of the following kinds of injuries is job-related, the employee still has an excellent chance of winning, because all laws and facts must be liberally construed in the employee's favor. (LC § 3202.)

- **Injuries in high-risk law enforcement professions.** This applies to police officers, fire fighters and other law enforcement personnel who develop heart trouble, cancer (including

EXAMPLE 1: Marci suffered a mild carpal tunnel injury in her right wrist as a result of repetitive data entry work. She filed a workers' compensation claim and eventually settled her case. Marci returned to work, and after several months, began feeling pain in her right wrist again. Her doctor determined that Marci had exacerbated (suffered a recurrence) of her original injury, but that she did not have a new or additional injury, and therefore did not have a new workers' compensation claim.

EXAMPLE 2: Farhad breaks his leg at work and files a workers' compensation claim. The bone heals, but because of the break, Farhad develops an altered gait (he begins to walk differently). Over time, this eventually causes pain and disability to his back. Farhad has a subsequent injury to his back as a result of the original industrial injury to his leg.

An important concept to remember is that an employer "takes each employee as is." This means the employer cannot deny workers' compensation coverage simply because a person in perfect health would not have been injured. Nor does it matter that the employer did not know about the employee's previous underlying condition, even if the employee withheld information about the condition prior to employment.

EXAMPLE: Dan injured his back playing football in college and had back surgery. Twenty years later, Dan lifts a 15-pound weight on the job and ruptures a disk in his back. Dan is entitled to workers' compensation coverage, despite the fact that someone without Dan's back condition probably would not have been hurt lifting 15 pounds. (But it is possible that if Dan has a permanent disability, his employer will not be responsible for the full amount. See the discussion on apportionment that follows.)

7. Apportionment

 See *County of Los Angeles v. WCAB (McLaughlin)* in Chapter 28.

Even if you are legitimately injured on the job and suffer a permanent disability, the insurance company may claim that it is responsible for a portion—but not all—of your perma-

nent disability. This issue is likely to arise if you had a pre-existing injury to the same body part as your workers' compensation injury. It is often medically difficult to determine how much disability is due to the injury on the job, and how much is due to a pre-existing condition or other factors.

If a portion of your present permanent disability is not due to your current job, it may be legally be allocated (apportioned) to outside factors. This allows the insurance company to reduce its payments to you and escape liability, to some extent.

EXAMPLE: Cathy was involved a car accident, which resulted in an injury to her back. She received medical treatment and then recovered. Two years later, she moves a heavy filing cabinet and injures her back at work. The workers' compensation insurance company claims that part of Cathy's present permanent disability is due to the earlier automobile accident. As a result, the insurance company asserts that it is not responsible for paying Cathy the total amount of permanent disability that she otherwise would be entitled to receive. Cathy must get evidence to support her contention that she completely recovered from the automobile accident and had no problems working until she was injured on the job.

Apportionment based on a claim of a pre-existing injury or for another reason can be a difficult and confusing issue for many people, including insurance adjusters. You will likely need to get medical reports to back your claim. Look into getting an attorney if apportionment is raised as an issue in your case, or seek help from an Information and Assistance officer.

Apportionment is discussed in greater detail in Chapter 18, Section D1.

C. Injuries Not Covered by Workers' Compensation

When an employer carries workers' compensation insurance, the usual rule is that any work injury falls under that coverage. For example, an injured employee is not excluded from coverage just because he was careless, negligent or even just plain dumb. However, as you'll see, a few types of injuries can legally be excluded from workers' compensation coverage.

1. Injuries Caused by Intoxication or Drugs Excluded

If you were intoxicated at the time of the industrial injury, you may not be entitled to workers' compensation benefits. (LC § 3600.) But be careful not to jump to conclusions. Mere intoxication or illegal drug use or misuse of legal drugs is not an absolute bar to recovery. It must be proven that your intoxication basically caused the injury.

2. Self-Inflicted Injuries Excluded

An injury that is intentionally self-inflicted is not covered by workers' compensation. (LC § 3600.)

EXAMPLE: Jorge gets angry at Cathy, his supervisor. Because Jorge knows that Cathy is criticized by her superiors whenever an employee files a workers' compensation claim, he intentionally slams his fist into a wall, injuring his hand. He is not entitled to benefits under workers' compensation.

However, self-inflicted injuries can be covered where the employee's action is deemed to be an "irresistible impulse," meaning that the action could not be helped.

EXAMPLE: Jorge slams his fist into the wall in an immediate and direct reaction to learning that he has been denied a promotion. Court cases seem to indicate that Jorge will be allowed recovery under the theory that his was an irresistible impulse. But in this situation, Jorge must prove that his actions were really the result of an irresistible impulse—in other words, he slammed his fist into the wall in a fit of rage, without thinking.

Claims filed by dependents of employees who died as a result of a work injury will be denied if it is proven that the employee intentionally committed suicide. However, it's up to the employer to prove that such a death was suicide, not an accident.

An exception to this rule involves a situation where an employee commits suicide because of an industrial injury. (This area usually requires the help of an attorney.)

EXAMPLE: Martin is paralyzed in an accident at work. He experiences continuous pain. In addition, Martin becomes deeply depressed by the injury and the resulting financial hardships, and commits suicide. Even assuming the employer can prove that Martin's death was a suicide, his surviving dependents can still recover if they can show that the suicide was directly caused by the industrial injury.

3. Injuries From Fight Started by Employee Excluded

If employees begin an argument at work and a fight ensues, the initial physical aggressor will be barred from workers' compensation benefits. (LC § 3600.) It's possible that the argument need not even be related to the workplace; courts have held that an argument about anything will do, as long as it started at work.

Who the initial physical aggressor is may be difficult to prove. It is not necessarily the person who threw the first punch. The initial physical aggressor is the one who first engaged in physical conduct that a reasonable person would believe presented a real threat of bodily harm.

EXAMPLE: Joe stands 6'3" tall and weighs 250 pounds. Tom, a co-employee, stands 5'2" and weighs 105 pounds. Joe and Tom begin arguing about the quality of work each is doing. Joe calls Tom's mother a name Tom doesn't care for, and Tom pushes Joe. Joe breaks Tom's hand, then grabs his throat and starts choking him, yelling all the while that he's going to kill Tom for touching him. Fearing for his life, Tom grabs a pipe and strikes Joe over the head, sending him to the hospital. Since Joe could not have reasonably believed that Tom's push presented a threat of bodily harm, Joe will probably be considered the initial aggressor. Joe will not be allowed to collect workers' compensation benefits, but Tom will.

In certain situations, the initial aggression may be forgiven as reasonably necessary. This might occur, for example, where an employee initiates force to protect herself from a sexual advance, or to retrieve stolen property from another employee.

4. Horseplay-Related Injuries or Injuries in Violation of Company Policy Excluded

Simply put, horseplay is equivalent to "goofing off" or acting in a careless and immature manner. If an injury is caused by horseplay that is clearly discouraged by the employer, it probably will not be covered by workers' compensation. (LC § 3600.) On the other hand, if the employer condoned the horseplay, the injury should be covered.

EXAMPLE 1: Gina's boss, Tony, installs a basketball hoop in the back of the shop. During breaks, he shoots baskets with his employees. One day, while shooting baskets, Gina sprains her ankle. Because this activity was condoned by the employer, Gina should receive workers' compensation coverage.

EXAMPLE 2: During work, Sam sneaks outside and shows off his "double loop flip" on his skateboard. In the process, Sam breaks his leg. Sam's employer had reprimanded him several times for skateboarding on company premises. Sam's injury is not covered under workers' compensation laws.

IF HORSEPLAY WAS A FACTOR
The issue of "horseplay" is often a gray area. If this concerns you, it would be wise to do some legal research or see a lawyer.

5. Felony-Related Injuries Excluded

An employee who is injured as the result of committing a felony (a serious crime, such as murder or burglary), or a crime that could have been prosecuted as a felony, even if it was prosecuted as a less serious misdemeanor, is not covered by workers' compensation if the employee is convicted. (LC § 3600.)

EXAMPLE: Audrey works as a nurse at a hospital where several patients die under suspicious circumstances. Audrey is investigated by her employer because she's suspected of murder. As a result of the investigation, she suffers a mental breakdown. If Audrey is later convicted for murder, she would not be entitled to workers' compensation benefits for the breakdown.

6. Off-Duty Recreational Activity Injuries Excluded

An injury that arises out of voluntary participation in any off-duty recreational, social, or athletic activity generally is not covered by workers' compensation. (LC § 3600.) If, however, the activities are a requirement of the employment, or are perceived as such by the employee, the injury is covered. It doesn't matter if the employee was mistaken, as long as the belief is reasonable.

EXAMPLE 1: Lanny is invited by his boss to dinner. His host accidentally drops a heavy platter on Lanny's foot, breaking several bones. Lanny would be entitled to workers' compensation benefits if he thought it would be "suicidal to one's career" to refuse an invitation by the boss.

EXAMPLE 2: Jerry and a few of his co-workers get together after work to play racquetball at the request of their supervisor. Jerry fractures his ankle during the game. Whether or not Jerry is entitled to workers' compensation benefits depends upon whether Jerry felt he was obligated to play because his supervisor made the request.

Other common non-workplace situations where workers' compensation coverage may be granted might include playing on a company-sponsored softball team or attending a company picnic.

7. Injuries Claimed After Employee Was Terminated or Laid Off Excluded

You generally must have filed a claim for workers' compensation benefits before you were fired, laid off or voluntarily quit. You may, however, be entitled to workers' compensation benefits if you can show at least one of the following:

- **Your employer had notice of the injury prior to the notice of termination or layoff.** For example, if you told your supervisor that you were planning to file a workers' compensation claim and received a layoff notice the following week, you would qualify under this exception.
- **The date of injury is after the date of notice of termination or layoff, but prior to its effective date.** If, for example, you receive notice that you'll be laid off at the end of the month, you could file a workers' compensation claim before then.

• **You received medical treatment for the injury.** This applies if you receive treatment before receiving notice of the termination or layoff and your medical records contain evidence of the injury prior to the notice of termination or layoff.

8. Injuries Outside Work or Job-Related Activities Excluded (AOE/COE)

Most industrial injuries happen at the job site, during regular work assignments. But to qualify, an industrial injury need not be so cut and dried. To be covered by workers' compensation, your injury or illness must meet two important criteria:

1. The injury must have happened as a result of your work activities or environment. In legal jargon, this is known as "arising out of the employment" or "AOE."

2. The injury must have occurred while you were performing activities required by your job. In legal jargon, this is known as "in the course of employment" or "COE."

IF POSSIBLE, SEE A LAWYER FOR AOE/COE ISSUES
If your employer or the insurance company raises these issues, it is highly recommended that you consult with a workers' compensation attorney or discuss your case with an Information and Assistance officer. These issues are critical to your entitlement to workers' compensation benefits and involve complex legal arguments.

THE DIFFERENCE BETWEEN AOE AND COE

To the uninitiated, AOE and COE can seem like pretty much the same thing. Here's how they differ.

AOE (arising out of the employment) refers to the requirement that the injury must have happened as a result of your work activities or environment. AOE addresses whether or not the type of injury you have is consistent with the type of work you did. For instance, did the exposure to heavy smoke while burning trash at work *cause* the lung cancer?

COE (in the course of employment), on the other hand, refers to the criterion that the injury must have been caused while you were performing job-related activities. It addresses whether or not the *activity* that caused the injury was a work-related activity—for example, was burning trash part of the employee's job? Taking an on-premises break, using the restroom and even changing a tire in the company parking lot are all covered in the course of employment.

---

9. Injuries Where Claim Not Filed on Time

You must make your claim for workers' compensation benefits within certain time limits—usually within one year from the date of injury. See the discussion in Chapter 5, Section C1.
■

Cumulative Trauma Disorders

A cumulative trauma disorder (CTD) is an injury that occurs over a period of months or years. Cumulative trauma disorders are commonly known by many other names, such as repetitive stress injuries, continuous trauma injuries, repetitive trauma injuries, repetitive microtrauma injuries, repetitive strain injuries, repetitive motion injuries, repetitive motion syndrome, occupational overuse injuries or overuse syndrome.

Cumulative trauma disorders now account for about 60 percent of all job-related injuries, and one in eight American workers has been diagnosed with a CTD. Is it any wonder that employers and workers' compensation insurance companies look at these claims with increasing scrutiny?

Although many insurance companies now realize that these injuries are legitimate, if you have suffered a cumulative trauma injury, it is not unlikely that your claim will be initially denied by the insurance company. It is therefore very important that you know as much as possible about the nature of your injury so that you can effectively prove the injury is work-related.

In Section A of this chapter, we review the different kinds of cumulative trauma disorders, as well as their respective treatments. We also explore the various factors, including improper ergonomics, that lead to the development of a CTD. In Sections B through F, we introduce you to the practical aspects of properly handling a CTD claim: reporting your injury, getting a diagnosis and getting medical treatment, which might include taking time off, returning to work and being compensated for a permanent disability. These issues are then discussed in more detail in the remaining chapters of this book.

A. What Is a CTD?

There is no one accepted definition of cumulative trauma disorder, but here is a general definition that combines the more common theories:

A cumulative trauma disorder is defined as a disorder of the muscles, ligaments, bones, nerves, tendons, and/or vascular system, alone or in combination with each other, that is caused by repeated exertions or movements. A cumulative trauma disorder develops over a prolonged period, usually requiring months or years.

Other CTD definitions concentrate on soft tissue as the focal cause of the injury: CTDs are painful and limiting soft tissue disorders that result from repeated or continual application of physical stress to a particular body part over extended periods of time. This physical stress causes microtrauma and overwhelms the tissue's normal adaptive ability to repair itself, and the result is often damage to muscles, tendons, tendon sheaths, bursas, cartilage, bone, joint surfaces, nerves or other soft tissues.

1. Common CTDs

Some of the more common upper extremity CTDs include nerve entrapment syndromes (for example, carpal tunnel syndrome and ulnar nerve compression), bursitis, tendinitis, de Quervain's tenosynovitis, epicondylitis and others. To better understand these various injuries let's consider the various body parts that can be affected by cumulative trauma.

a. Muscles

Muscle problems can include muscle strain or muscle spasm. This may start with injury to a few muscle fibers, which can lead to spasm and eventual pain in the whole muscle. The cause of this type of injury includes awkward positions or sustained static positions. The most commonly affected muscles include those along the neck and lower spine, the shoulders and arms.

b. Tendons

The most common injury to the tendons is tendinitis, or inflammation of the tendon. Tendons attach the muscle to the bones, and repetitive movements that decrease the lubrication of tendons located in hands and other areas can lead to inflammation, swelling and scarring. Tendinitis can cause great discomfort that can either be a dull ache or a sharp pain. The most common locations for tendinitis are the front and back of the wrists, the elbows and the shoulders.

Epicondylitis is a form of tendinitis involving the tendons attaching to the elbow (outside elbow for "tennis elbow," and inside elbow for "golfer's elbow"). This injury is not just limited to tennis players and golfers, however. Overuse of computer mice and keyboards as well as playing musical instruments can lead to this form of tendinitis. Another form of tendinitis common today is de Quervain's tenosynovitis, a painful inflammation of the thumb side of the wrist, which can be caused by repetitive activities requiring sideways motion of the wrist while gripping the thumb, as in hammering, filing and joystick or mouse use.

c. Nerves

An increasingly common CTD is nerve entrapment syndrome. Repetitive motion can sometimes squash or pinch the nerves that run through the shoulders, inside the arm muscles, along the bones, through the wrist to the hands.

Carpal tunnel syndrome, which results from repetitive or awkward positioning of the wrist, can increase pressure and/or cause tendons in the wrist to swell up and compress the median nerve in the carpal tunnel at the wrist. Symptoms include numbness in the hand; tingling in the thumb, the index, third and fourth fingers; pain; weakness and clumsiness. The causes of carpal tunnel syndrome include working with the wrist bent in any non-neutral (flexed) direction, forceful pinching or gripping and exposure to constant vibration.

Ulnar nerve compression involves your "funny bone" nerve, which runs down the upper arm alongside the triceps, through the bones of the elbow (called the "cubital tunnel") and down the outside of the wrist. The ulnar nerve feeds the fourth and fifth finger, and symptoms can include numbness and tingling in those fingers plus elbow and wrist pain. It is not yet known exactly what causes ulnar nerve compression, although it can occur as a result of repetitive or awkward positioning of the wrists and hands and frequent bending of the elbows at angles of more than 90 degrees.

Both of these nerve entrapment syndromes can be exacerbated by poor posture—allowing the shoulders to slump and roll forward can trap the nerves and vessels as they travel to and from the arm, worsening the pain and numbness.

Yet another nerve entrapment syndrome is thoracic outlet syndrome. This problem occurs when the blood vessels or nerves that pass into the arms from the neck are squashed, and can be due to weak shoulder muscles and/or enlarged chest muscles. Thoracic outlet syndrome can also be caused by repetitive activities that require the arms to be held overhead or extended forward or by poor posture, especially when the shoulders are dropped and slouched forward. Symptoms include pain in the shoulder, arm and/or fourth and fifth fingers.

d. Bones, Joints and Discs

Repetitive bending, reaching or twisting is a primary cause of injuries such as degenerative arthritis and degenerative disc disease. The most common locations for this type of problem are the lower back (lumbosacral spine), neck (cervical), shoulder and elbow.

e. Bursas

Bursas are fluid-filled sacs located near the body's joints that reduce friction between the body's bones and muscles. Bursitis occurs when bursas become inflamed from injury or overuse. The most common areas affected are the shoulders, elbows, hips and knees.

f. Associated Problems

Depression and reflex sympathetic dystrophy syndrome (a constant, burning pain at the site of an injury) can develop following any of the above CTDs.

2. Activities That Cause CTDs

There are probably as many factors that cause cumulative trauma injuries as there are types of jobs. Virtually any repetitive, sustained or forceful exertion over a long enough period of time can lead to a cumulative trauma injury. Other causes include vibration, repetitive impact and working in a fixed position for a long period of time.

The most common CTDs today involve injury to the upper extremities (wrists, elbows) due to repetitive keyboard activities. Employees often spend hours at a time inputting or manipulating computer data, and if this is done without regard to proper ergonomics, a nerve entrapment syndrome such as carpal tunnel syndrome may develop.

Another occupation that has a higher than normal incidence of CTDs is that of the grocery checker. With the advent of scanners that read bar codes on grocery products, grocery checkers are required to pull or slide the product across the scanner. This repetitive activity often leads to the development of cumulative trauma injury to the upper extremities. The repetitive turning of the neck from side to side may also cause a CTD to the neck or shoulders. In addition, constant lifting activities may cause injury to the back.

Occupations that require working in a fixed position for a prolonged period of time, called static posturing, can also lead to CTDs. Some examples of static posturing include prolonged sitting or standing, prolonged gripping or grasping, or holding a particular position for long periods. For example, an operator or front desk clerk who holds a telephone receiver between the head and shoulder, or an airline mechanic who has to crawl and work in a twisted position, may both develop cumulative trauma disorders.

Other work-related activities that lend themselves to repetitive stress injuries include:

playing musical instruments	working in an assembly line
polishing, grinding, sanding, painting	pipesetting and other overhead work
jackhammering	sawing, cutting
butchering/meat packing	driving
writing	massaging
stocking shelves and packing	operating a cash register
working as a mechanic	

Improper ergonomics, such as poor workstation setup or posture, is a primary cause of today's CTDs, regardless of the type of activity someone performs. Ergonomics is the study of how people interact with their physical environment and how that interaction might be modified to prevent or reduce musculoskeletal disorders.

Ergonomics is starting to play an important role in the cause and prevention of work-related cumulative trauma injuries. Ergonomic experts work with some employers to improve their employees' ergonomics. For example, the proper ergonomic model for the prevention of carpal tunnel syndrome (a CTD injury to the wrist) would include keeping the wrists in a neutral position (straight), the elbows down by the sides and the shoulders back, and would aim for reducing the frequency of repetitive activity.

Remember, however, that workers' compensation is a no-fault system. Even if you wouldn't have been injured at work if you hadn't typed while slumped in your chair or with your feet on your desk, your injury still falls under the workers' comp system because it happened at work.

B. Becoming Aware of Your Injury

Because it can be months after a CTD starts to develop before you realize that your work is causing you pain, identifying a CTD is more complicated than discovering you've sprained an ankle.

1. Warning Signs

There are no clear early warning signs to alert you that you are headed for a cumulative trauma injury. Often by the time you realize that something is wrong, damage has already been done. As a result, don't ignore the following signs; report them to a physician knowledgeable in cumulative trauma injuries as soon as possible:

- **Pain.** You may feel sharp or dull, aching pain in your limbs that increases in intensity over time. Some feel this pain after working on the computer or cash register for a few hours, while others start to notice pain only when they make certain movements outside of work, such as twisting a doorknob to open a door or washing their hair.
- **Tingling or numbness.** Sometimes your hand or arm may have a tingling sensation or you may experience numbness or tingling in certain fingers. This is a sign that damage to your nerves may have already occurred and should be taken seriously.
- **Fatigue.** You may notice that you tire easily and can no longer do the same amount of work you used to be able to do.
- **Weakness or clumsiness.** You may notice a loss of strength or find that you are dropping items or have difficulty in picking things up.

In their early stages, prior to the development of real impairment, CTDs often go unreported because the involved individual considers the signs and symptoms of the disorder as necessary characteristics of aging or as normal "aches and pains" that do not represent a potentially disabling process.

If you have a physical problem (for example, pain or limitation of movement) but you don't know its cause, you should make an appointment with your family doctor or primary care physician. Discuss with the doctor your symptoms and all of your activities during the past six months, both on and off the job. The doctor will probably be able to identify the cause of your problem, and chances are it will be your job activities. If your family doctor does tell you that your injury is work-related, you must immediately report the injury to your employer (discussed just below).

2. Reporting Your Injury

Reporting your injury to your employer is discussed in detail in Chapter 6. However, since it can be difficult to identify a work-related cumulative trauma injury, reporting a CTD is more complicated than reporting specific injuries. Recall that a continuous trauma injury is one that occurs over a period of time, as opposed to a specific injury that occurs on a specific date and time. Because of this, there are a few things you can do to protect your rights if you suspect that you may be suffering from a CTD.

First, if you suspect that you have any injury (for example, you have pain in your wrist that's getting worse with time), before reporting the injury to your employer, advise your employer that you wish to designate a physician to treat you in the event you have an injury at work. A sample of such a letter can be found in Chapter 9, Section B1.

Designating your doctor in advance will allow you to be treated by this doctor right after you report the injury, rather than having to see the company doctor for the first thirty days or longer. This prevents the possibility that the company doctor will send you back to your job before you are medically able to work, or worse yet, write a report after only one or two visits saying that you have fully recovered and have no disability whatsoever.

Second, once you have designated a physician, don't delay in reporting the injury to your employer. The labor code requires you to report a work injury to your employer within 30 days from the date of the injury. If you fail to timely report the injury, your employer might try to argue that your workers' compensation claim is barred by the statute of limitations.

How do you determine the date of your injury when the damage may have occurred over a long period of time? Good question. The law says that the date of a continuous trauma disorder is the date that the employee first suffered disability and knew or "should have known" that the disability was caused by work. Let's break this down one part at a time. You first suffer disability when you take time off of work because of the problem (even one sick day) or go to a doctor for the problem. When you knew or should have known that the disability was caused by your job is when you have reason to

believe your pain or other symptoms are caused by activities you do at work. This can be when:

- you go to a doctor and tell the doctor you believe you injured yourself doing your job, or
- you go to a doctor and the doctor tells you your injury is probably work-related.

What this means for practical purposes is that once you have taken time off work or seen a doctor for the problem, you should report the injury to your employer within 30 days. If you haven't seen a doctor or taken time off work for the problem, you should report your injury when it becomes clear to you that your symptoms are being caused by your job.

There is one exception to the rule that you must report your injury to your employer within 30 days of the date of injury: If you failed to officially report the injury to your employer within 30 days, you may still file a workers' compensation claim if your employer had knowledge of the injury from some other source. Perhaps you told a supervisor that you were having pains during work or a co-employee told a manager that you were complaining of pain.

Follow the instructions in Chapter 5 to report your injury and file a workers' compensation claim.

⚠ BE CAREFUL WHAT YOU SAY!

Once you file a CTD claim, you may be interviewed by an investigator or the insurance company adjuster. You will be asked when you first believed your symptoms were caused by your work. Make sure your answer is within the 30 days prior to the date you reported the injury to your employer. If you say that you knew six months before you finally reported the injury that your disability was caused by your work, you may have a problem.

3. The Insurance Company's Response

Within 14 days of filing a claim, your employer's insurance company will send you written notice that it has received the claim. This initial letter will advise you if the insurance company accepts your claim, denies your claim or needs more time to investigate your claim before accepting or denying it. In that case, the insurance company then has 90 days to accept or deny your claim.

When you file a cumulative trauma injury claim, you can be fairly certain that the insurance company won't accept your claim right off. At the very least, the insurance company will probably send you a letter stating that it is investigating your claim and that you will be advised within 90 days as to its decision on whether or not it is accepting or denying your claim.

If the insurance company notifies you that it is investigating your claim (or even that it accepts your claim), it will probably ask you for a statement about how your injury occurred. You're best off sending in a written statement rather than giving your statement over the phone. An example of a written statement is shown below; see Chapter 7, Section E for further guidance.

SAMPLE STATEMENT

1. Date of Injury 6/26/XX

2. How injury happened: Repetitive keyboard activities on the computer.

3. Parts of body injured: Bilateral upper extremities.

4. Reporting the injury: I told my supervisor Mary Akins I was having pain in both wrists when I worked on my computer. She had me fill out a company injury report.

5. Medical Treatment: Mary Akins sent me to the Industrial Medical Clinic at 1444 W. Main St. in Los Angeles. I was examined and told take off work for two weeks. I was also given a prescription for Ibuprofen, 800 mg.

If the insurance company denies your claim, it won't pay for medical treatment or temporary disability benefits so that you can take time off work to recover from your injury. You'll need to get what's called a "medical-legal evaluation" to establish that your injury should be covered by workers' compensation.

Medical-legal evaluations are medical assessments to prove your case, not to provide medical treatment, and are performed by doctors approved by the workers' compensation system, called qualified medical examiners (QMEs). See Chapter 10, Section C for more information on medical-legal evaluations.

If your QME files a medical-legal report that says the insurance company should compensate you for your injury, the insurance company should begin providing you benefits. If not, you have one year from the date of injury to file an "Application for Adjudication of Claim" with the Workers' Compensation Appeal Board. See Chapter 5, Section C for instructions on how to file this application.

If your claim is denied, you should give serious consideration to obtaining an attorney who specializes in workers' compensation law. A claim that has been denied by the insurance company, whether it is a specific injury or a CTD, is usually one that requires legal assistance.

C. Diagnosis and Treatment

When you have a CTD, you may be treated by a doctor for six months to a year or longer. As with any work-related injury, the fate of your case will be in the hands of your treating doctor, so it important to find one who understands your problem and has experience in dealing with your specific CTD.

1. Diagnosis of Your Injury

The diagnosis of cumulative trauma injuries can be difficult because by definition the injury usually involves soft-tissue, not broken bones that can easily be x-rayed, and because most doctors have become familiar with these injuries only in recent years, if at all.

The types of injuries caused by cumulative trauma usually can't be validated by objective testing such as x-rays. This can make it both harder for the doctor to diagnose your injury and easier for a company doctor to report that you did not sustain a true injury.

Sometimes the primary—and often times only—evidence of injury is the pain and other symptoms that you feel. This is particularly true with injuries such as back strain from prolonged sitting or standing, a stiff or painful neck from staring at a computer monitor, or pain in one or both wrists from using a computer keyboard for extended periods of time. This lack of objective evidence can make it difficult to convince some doctors and insurance companies that you really are injured.

2. Documenting Your Injury

There are a few ways a doctor can try to objectively document an injury, but they are far from perfect. Currently the best source of objective testing for soft tissue injuries are magnetic resonance imaging (MRI) and nerve conduction studies (NCS), but these tests often come out negative even in patients with valid injuries. Again, many cases involve pain that can't be verified by any type of objective test, but the pain is no less debilitating.

As a result, it is extremely important that you tell each and every doctor exactly what it is that you are experiencing. Here is a short list of the things you should discuss with any doctor you see for your injury:

- For each part of your body that hurts, tell the doctor exactly where the pain is.
- Tell the doctor about the type of pain you have. Is it a dull or sharp pain? Is it a shooting type of pain or is it an aching type of pain?
- Tell the doctor the frequency of the pain. Is it constant, frequent, intermittent or just occasional?
- Tell the doctor about the severity of the pain. On a scale of 1 to 10, with 1 being minimal and 10 being unbearable, give the doctor your best estimate of each type of pain you are experiencing. Most doctors are familiar with this pain scale.
- Maintain a pain diary. A few sample diary entries are shown below; see Chapter 6, Section C10 for information on how to keep a pain diary.

SAMPLE PAIN DIARY

Saturday, 6/26/xx. Doctor Jones took me off work yesterday for two weeks. He prescribed Ibuprofen, 800 mg, twice a day. Pain seems a little less today with medication. My left wrist is a 4 on a scale of 10, but is a constant dull ache. Right wrist is little worse—maybe 6 on scale of 10. Pain in right wrist seems to shoot up into elbow area.

Tuesday 7/1/xx. Doctor returned me to work today on a trial basis with a limitation of no repetitive keyboard activity. My employer had me on the computer for an hour straight today. My wrists started hurting again after typing. Tonight I notice a definite increase in pain. Before work today, my pain was probably 3 on scale of 10. Tonight it's a 6 on scale of 10. I am calling the doctor tomorrow a.m. to advise and will also tell my supervisor.

Again, since CTDs often can't be documented by objective tests, the doctor must rely heavily on your subjective complaints to make his diagnosis and treatment recommendations. This can affect whether your claim is accepted by the insurance company and whether you are provided with temporary disability payments for time off work. And later on, the amount of your permanent disability will be rated according to how the doctor records your symptoms, which will dictate the amount of monetary benefits you'll receive. Therefore, whether or not the doctor believes what you tell him is critical to your case.

You should never exaggerate your symptoms, and at all times, you should be truthful and cooperative with the doctor. Doctors have furtive methods of determining whether you are actually experiencing pain or loss of mobility. For instance, a doctor may do several tests that test the same thing. If you have different results in two tests that should have the same result, the doctor may decide that you are not being truthful. Company doctors and qualified medical examiners in particular are constantly observing your movements and actions, looking for inconsistencies in your story. But as long as you are truthful and do not exaggerate, you shouldn't have any problems.

3. Seeking Medical Treatment If Your Claim Is Denied

Early and aggressive treatment of cumulative trauma injuries is critical to stopping the injury from getting worse. Unfortunately, treatment can be delayed if a CTD claim is denied or delayed by the insurance company.

If the insurance company denies your claims or puts off a decision on your claim for 90 days (discussed in Section B3, above), you won't be allowed to see a doctor through workers' compensation. You should immediately seek treatment through your group medical insurance carrier if you have one.

Sometimes the insurance company will still agree to pay for you to see a doctor while it is taking 90 days to decide whether to accept or deny your claim. In that case you should accept the offer and go to a doctor through workers' compensation, not to your personal physician (unless you have predesignated your personal physician as your treating doctor for work-related injuries, as discussed in Section B2, above).

4. Treatment of Your Injury

Early treatment of CTDs focuses on diminishing your pain, controlling any inflammation and reducing activity levels. Treatment may include taking time off work, taking prescribed anti-inflammatory medications and participating in physical therapy, which can include applying superficial heat or cold, ultrasound, splinting, bracing and massage.

As a last resort, surgery may be indicated for certain CTDs such as carpal tunnel syndrome. For other CTDs, such as ulnar nerve compression, surgery is rarely helpful or recommended.

Obtaining a good treating physician is important in all cases of CTDs because early, aggressive treatment can often times prevent further injury. Treatment of CTDs requires specialized knowledge and understanding of the underlying causes of the problem. Almost all doctors will say that they can treat the problem, but only a few really have the specific training and patience to treat these injuries (CTDs often take longer to treat than specific injuries).

You should seek out a doctor who specializes in the diagnosis and treatment of continuous trauma disorders, and in your type of injury in particular. For example, a particular doctor may have developed a reputation for successfully treating pianists with repetitive strain injuries.

In my opinion, you don't want to start off with a surgeon—surgery should be a last resort. A surgeon may often offer you a surgical alternative right off the bat, and if you decline, many surgeons won't be able (or willing) to offer much in the way of alternative treatment.

I would recommend finding a doctor that specializes in physical medicine and rehabilitation, otherwise known as a physiatrist. Physiatrists are often sports medicine doctors, but increasingly they are being called upon to treat work-related repetitive stress injuries. These doctors treat acute and chronic pain and musculoskeletal disorders, and they focus on restoring as much function to the patient as possible, similar to what occupational and physical therapists do.

Physiatrists are accustomed to injuries that can take a long time to heal, and are not averse to referring patients out for non-traditional treatments such as acupuncture. If your physiatrist can't "cure" you, he or she can always recommend you for a surgical consultation, but will do so only after all possible conservative avenues have been explored.

The American Academy of Physical Medicine and Rehabilitation is the best place to start in finding a good doctor (go to http://www.aapmr.org/find.html). You might also consider contacting other people who have gone through what you are going through now. There are many groups of people that get together either in person or on the Internet to discuss their injuries and treatment. To find a website or online group that focuses on your type of injury, use a search engine such as Google or try Yahoo Groups at http://groups.yahoo.com.

5. Temporary Disability

When or for how long a doctor takes you off work (puts you on temporary total disability) for a CTD is not as clear cut as for a specific injury like a fractured ankle or a hernia. Most doctors will rely heavily on what you tell them in deciding on whether or not you need some time off work.

If your doctor has not taken you off work and you believe that your symptoms are not getting any better or are getting worse, tell your doctor. Do not be afraid to ask her if some time off work might help you recover faster. Your doctor may take you off work for a week or two initially and extend that to a month or more depending on your progress. In Chapter 12, we discuss temporary disability in detail.

6. Permanent and Stationary Status

Once your treating doctor has determined that your medical condition will not substantially improve with further medical treatment, she will declare you to be permanent and stationary (P&S) and release you from further treatment. At this point, your temporary disability payments will stop, even if you have not yet returned to work.

The doctor will write a final report (called the permanent and stationary report, or P&S report). In that report she will list what restrictions you should follow to avoid worsening your condition, the type of future medical treatment you might need for flare-ups or if your condition disintegrates, and your factors of permanent disability, if any.

If you have suffered permanent disability as a result of your injury, the doctor's P&S report will then be used to determine the percentage of disability you have suffered (called "rating" your disability, which is discussed in Section F, below).

Often times, a treating doctor may release you from medical treatment (declare you to be P&S) before you think you are ready. This is because continuous trauma injuries take longer to treat than most other type of injuries. Especially if you have been recovering for a long period of time, the doctor may feel pressured by the insurance company to declare you to be P&S even if she thinks you may get better with more therapy and even more time off work. If this happens to you, and you don't think you can handle returning to work, don't be afraid to tell the doctor that you don't think you are ready to go back to work. Be prepared to be specific as to why you don't think you can resume working (for example, you still can't do any lifting or you still have significant pain on typing) and why you think further medical treatment could help.

Do not be discouraged if you disagree with the doctor and he releases you from treatment anyway. Remember that a declaration that you are P&S does not mean that you have no permanent disabilities or that you should necessarily go back to work. It just means that the doctor does not think you will get any better with further medical treatment. For a complete discussion of permanent and stationary status, please refer to Chapter 9, Section E.

If your condition gets worse after the doctor has declared you P&S, you can always return to your doctor for a re-evaluation. However, if you follow your doctor's orders, it is likely that your condition may continue to get better over time, even after you are released from treatment.

If the doctor doesn't think you can go back to doing your former work activities, she may return you to work with restrictions such as no heavy lifting or no working on the computer for more than three hours per day. Alternatively, if the doctor decides you can't return to your former job at all, you may be entitled to vocational rehabilitation benefits, which will help you retrain for other employment. See Section D, below, for a discussion of returning to the workforce.

7. Permanent Disability

Unless you have recovered 100%, your treating doctor's final (P&S) report will probably indicate that you may have some permanent disability from your injury. In that case, the insurance company may ask the workers' compensation Disability Evaluation Unit to rate your disability. This means that it will review the doctor's report and assign a percentage, such as 25%, to your permanent disability. The insurance company will send you a letter stating the amount of permanent disability benefits it believes is payable, and it may even propose a settlement at that time.

If you disagree with your disability rating, you may request an "advisory rating" from the administrative director of the workers' compensation system. See Chapter 18, Section A2, for how to do this. In this case, it helps to understand how the rating system works.

Ratings for CTDs are largely based on the work restrictions the doctor sets out in the P&S report, as well as your subjective complaints, rather than on objective tests. However, rating a continuous trauma disability follows the same rules as a specific injury, such as a ruptured spinal disk from falling off a ladder. This is because, for CTDs, the rating manual uses the same rating percentages for work restrictions and subjective complaints as it does for specific injuries.

Common work restrictions for an upper extremity disability such as carpal tunnel syndrome might include no repetitive gripping and grasping, no heavy lifting and no forceful pushing and pulling—very similar to restrictions for a rotator cuff injury or ruptured disk, for example. As a result, you can use the general information in Chapter 18 to rate your cumulative trauma permanent disability and the information in Chapters 19 and 20 to negotiate a settlement in your case.

D. Returning to the Workforce

After you have finished with your medical treatment (your doctor has said you are permanent and stationary), you should receive a letter from the insurance company telling you:

- whether you should go back to work
- whether you may have a permanent disability, and
- whether you qualify for vocational rehabilitation.

If the doctor's report states that you are well enough to return to your old job, the insurance company may direct you to go back to work. In this case, the doctor's report may contain restrictions on the type of work you can do—permanent limitations that you should observe as a result of your cumulative trauma disorder.

Of course, your doctor may not want you to return to your previous job once your condition becomes permanent and stationary. Because CTDs result from doing a particular job activity over and over, it is common sense that returning to a job doing the exact same thing is likely to result in further injury. In that case, the insurance company will work with your employer to determine if modified or alternative work is available. Considering whether to take a modified or alternative job is your first step in a vocational rehabilitation program.

1. Vocational Rehabilitation

Vocational rehabilitation is a re-training and job placement program in which you work one on one with a vocational rehabilitation representative (a counselor trained in job training and placement) to develop a vocational rehabilitation plan to get you back to work.

A vocational rehabilitation plan consists of first trying to get you modified or alternative work with your current employer. If that won't work, your rehab representative will help you to find another job using skills you already have. Or, if you don't have any skills that transfer to a job you can do within your physical limitations, the vocational rehabilitation program can provide on-the-job or educational training to put you to work in a new trade.

In Chapter 14 we explain how to hire a vocational rehabilitation representative and create a vocational rehabilitation plan, both of which are paid for by the insurance company. Here, we'll discuss a few points that are important for workers with CTDs.

If you are first offered modified or alternative work by your employer, make sure that the proposal and job description are written up as part of a formal vocational rehabilitation plan. That way, if you lose your modified or alternative job for any reason in the first year, you are entitled to another vocational rehabilitation plan. Also, before you accept an offer of modified or alternative work, make sure that your doctor reviews a job analysis (J.A.) or job description of the new position and approves it. A job analysis or job description can be prepared by a vocational rehabilitation representative.

Modified or alternative work may not available in your situation; it is often more difficult for an employer to find modified work for someone who has a continuous trauma injury. Modifying your job to take out the activity that caused the injury often times changes the job duties so significantly that the employer has no need for someone to do the remaining duties.

If modified or alternative work is not available, you can seek job training and placement through vocational rehabilitation. Try not to worry about whether or not you will be able to find another job you can do. Even though you may no longer be able to do computer work, for example, vocational rehabilitation representatives are trained in helping you to find a job you *can* do despite your work restrictions and limitations. If, however, your vocational rehabilitation representative can't find any work you can do that's within your restrictions (this is rare), you may be entitled to total permanent disability (discussed in Chapter 13).

2. Preventing Reinjury

Again, when you return to work, it should be to a job that fits within your new physical limitations. Your doctor's P&S report should list all of the preventative restrictions (probably called "prophylactic" restrictions in the report) that the doctor recommends. For example, restrictions for bilateral (both arms) carpal tunnel syndrome might prohibit you from doing work that requires repetitive gripping and grasping. In other words, the doctor is saying that if you return to any type of work that requires repetitive gripping and grasping activities you are likely to cause further injury to your wrists.

Other work restrictions for someone who suffers a computer-related injury might include:
- no prolonged sitting
- no prolonged fixed positioning of the neck
- a time limitation on computer use
- a weight limitation on lifting and carrying, and
- a weight limitation on overhead reaching.

If you return to your previous job, make certain that your employer receives a copy of the doctor's restrictions before you go back to work, and make sure the employer abides by them. Don't feel bad about declining to do certain work that your doctor has recommended against. If your employer has provided you with modified or alternative work, you can't legally be fired for refusing to do work that your doctor says you can't do.

In addition, you should provide your treating physician with a detailed and accurate description of your job duties so that she can make appropriate recommendations or changes that should be made to your work environment to prevent further injury.

If your injury is caused by repetitive use or overuse of a computer, an ergonomic evaluation of your workstation is critical in preventing its reoccurrence upon your return to work. Necessary and appropriate modifications to your workstation, taking into consideration your height, weight and body build, are mandatory if you are to return to the same type of work.

If you go to work for a new employer, make sure that your employer is aware of your work restrictions. Employers are required to make a reasonable accommodation for your disability under the federal Americans with Disabilities Act (ADA) and California's Fair Employment Housing Act (FEHA). Generally speaking, if you have a disability, a new or former employer must make a reasonable effort to change the duties of your job so that you can do the "essential functions of the job."

EXAMPLE: Your doctor has given you a permanent work restriction of "no lifting objects over 50 lbs." You find a new job as a receptionist at a doctor's office. The "essential functions" of the job are greeting patients, answering the telephone and scheduling appointments with the doctor. However, every Friday the doctor's office gets a delivery of supplies, which you would normally be required to unload from the truck and carry into the office. Some of the boxes of supplies weigh over 50 lbs. If it's reasonable for the employer to accommodate you so that you can avoid having to lift the supplies (for example, by having someone else help you or providing for a dolly to roll the supplies), then you can't be refused employment or terminated because of your work restriction.

Disability discrimination is a very complicated area. If you suspect that an employer is not being fair with you, failed to hire you or terminated you because of your disability, you should contact an attorney who specializes in this area.

3. Reinjuring Yourself

If you do return to work, whether with the same employer or a new one, and you reinjure yourself, your options depend on whether you have suffered a new injury or simply an exacerbation of your original injury. This determination is up to your doctor.

a. New Injury

If your doctor concludes your new pain is a new injury, you should file a new workers' compensation claim against your current employer so that you will receive medical treatment and time off work if you need it.

EXAMPLE: In the year 2000, Mary Sater is diagnosed and treated for bilateral carpal tunnel syndrome due to computer activities that required her to enter data by way of a keyboard. After Mary is released by her treating doctor, she returns to work in 2001 in an alternative job as a receptionist. Her new job duties require her to answer the telephone and take messages. Her employer does not provide a headset and she must cradle the phone between her neck and ear as she writes messages. After six months, Mary again begins to experience pain in her wrists. She thinks that she has exacerbated her original carpal tunnel syndrome from writing, so she returns to her doctor. After doing an MRI of her neck, the doctor determines that Mary is experiencing pain in her wrists due to an injury to her neck resulting from constantly holding her neck in a crooked position while taking messages on the phone. This is a new injury, and she should file a new claim against her current employer.

b. Exacerbation of a Previous Injury

If your doctor concludes your new pain is a worsening of your original injury, and you have not yet settled your case, you're in luck. You can simply continue to be treated by your doctor until you are once again declared to be permanent and stationary and the doctor writes a final report setting forth your increased factors of disability.

If your doctor concludes your pain is a worsening of your original injury and you have settled your case by Stipulations With Request for Award (see Chapter 19, Section B1), the insurance company will pay for the medical treatment you need. In addition, you may be entitled to receive more permanent disability payments. If your case is not more than five years old from the date of injury, you may file a petition to reopen your case for new and further disability (see Chapter 19, Section B1c) so that your disability may be re-rated. However, if it has been more than five years from the date of your injury, you can't reopen your case for new and further disability. (Again, however, you can go to a doctor for treatment of the original injury, and the insurance company will pay for it.)

If your doctor concludes your pain is a worsening of your original injury but you already settled your claim by Compromise and Release (see Chapter 19, Section B), you may be out of luck. The only way you can get workers' compensation benefits in this case is to file a new workers' compensation claim, and you can do this only if you can show that at least 1% of your current disability is due to your current employment (see the discussion of apportionment in Section 4, below), and not to your prior injury.

If you try this route and your employer denies your claim because a doctor says your problems are due 100% to a prior injury that was settled by Compromise and Release, you should get an attorney. You will have to treat this like any other denied claim and proceed to develop medical evidence that your injury is at least partly due to your current employment. (See Chapter 10 on medical-legal evaluations.)

4. Apportionment

Apportionment—when an employer says another company is wholly or partly responsible for paying for your disability—is often an issue in continuous trauma disabilities. That is because if you have a subsequent reinjury at a new job, it is very likely that at least part of your current medical disability is due to your prior injury.

> EXAMPLE: While working for a software company as a computer programmer, Sherri experiences pain in her elbows, wrists and trapezius muscles. Her doctor diagnoses her with ulnar nerve neuropathy and takes her off work for several months. A year later, Sherri is hired by a different employer. While the employer is aware of her past disability, Sherri and the employer do not anticipate a problem because Sherri will be doing light computer and office work rather than computer programming. Unfortunately, Sherri does develop repetitive strain problems; this time her injury presents itself as carpal tunnel syndrome in her wrists. Her doctor concludes that 20% of her disability is due to her new employment, and 80% is due to her previous injury.

If you have a subsequent injury that is apportioned, you may receive fewer permanent disability benefits from your current employer since you were presumably compensated for your previous injury by your previous employer. To avoid having a new injury apportioned, you must have rehabilitated yourself completely so that you have no remaining disability

at the time of the reinjury. Please refer to Chapter 18, Section D1 for a complete discussion of apportionment.

E. Further Medical Treatment

After your doctor has released you from medical treatment and you have settled your claim and returned to work, you may need to seek medical treatment from time to time to treat flare-ups of your cumulative trauma disorder. Whether you treat with a doctor authorized by the workers' compensation insurance company or go to your own group medical insurance for treatment depends on several factors.

If you settled your case by Stipulations With a Request for Award or were awarded future medical treatment in a findings and award (see Chapter 19), you have the right to be treated by a doctor of your choice and have the workers' compensation insurance company pay for it.

If you settled your case by Compromise and Release (see Chapter 19), you gave up your right to have your future medical treatment paid for by the workers' compensation insurance company. You will therefore have no choice but to go to your group insurance carrier for treatment. Whether or not your group insurance carrier will agree to pay for this treatment depends upon their policy regarding pre-existing medical conditions. Many group insurance carriers will treat pre-existing conditions; some will cover treatment only if you have gone treatment-free for a period of time (usually 6 months).

Often times what you tell (or don't tell) your group insurance carrier will determine whether or not it will authorize treatment for your cumulative trauma injury. If you point out to the doctor that you are seeking treatment for a prior work injury, you will cause "red flags" to appear and may have problems getting authorization for treatment. If you simply go in for treatment "because my wrists have been hurting lately," you'll be less likely to experience problems in getting treatment.

Of course, if you are specifically asked whether you injured your wrists at work, you must be truthful and say so. But if there is some activity that you recently did that you believe "lit up" your work injury (such as gardening), be sure to tell the doctor. That may be reason enough to allow the doctor to treat you through your group insurance. ■

What to Do If You're Injured

This chapter explains the four most important things you need to do if you are injured on the job:

- Request medical treatment. (See Section A.)
- Promptly report your injury. (See Section B.)
- File a workers' compensation claim, which consists of filling in and filing two documents: a DWC-1 form and an Application for Adjudication Claim. (See Section C.)
- Take appropriate steps to protect your workers' compensation rights. (See Section E.)

A. Request Medical Treatment

If you're injured in the course of your employment, it's important to seek prompt and appropriate medical treatment. Whether you get first aid on the job, are rushed to the emergency room, see your family doctor after work or report to a company doctor, you should always see that you get the treatment you need. You won't gain a thing by being stoic and delaying treatment.

1. Which Doctor Will Treat You

A fundamental principle of this book is that it is always best to get treatment by a doctor of your own choice. For starters, you are likely to get better medical care from someone you know and trust. In addition, the doctor who provides your medical treatment will be extremely influential in determining whether you're entitled to workers' compensation benefits and how much you'll receive. It's even fair to say that whoever has control of your medical treatment (called the "treating doctor") has control of your case. One big reason for this is that the treating doctor's report is given a presumption of being correct should your case go to trial.

An obvious question is: Who has the right to pick your doctor if you are injured on the job? If you read Chapter 2, you know that you have that right only if you notify your employer of the doctor you wish to see in advance of your injury. If you fail to do this, with the exception of emergency treatment, your employer has the legal right to decide what doctor you see for the first 30, 90, 180 or 365 days after you are injured. (The number of days depends upon the facts of your case; refer to Chapter 9, Section C.) Although not all employers will insist on exercising this right, if yours does, you must see your employer's chosen doctor.

Because being treated by a doctor who is picked by your employer may mean you receive an unsympathetic diagnosis, I recommend that you designate your doctor or health organization *now*, whether you have already been injured or not. Once your written notification is on file, it will protect you should you ever suffer any work injury in the future. (See Chapter 9, Section B1, for a step-by-step explanation of how to do this.)

2. How to Get Medical Care

Now let's review the steps to take if you are injured on the job:

- **Emergencies.** If your injury is life-threatening or requires immediate emergency attention, call an ambulance or get to the nearest emergency room. Under these circumstances, your employer has no immediate control over what doctor you see for treatment, even if you have not filed a written request asking for a specific doctor in advance. Your employer (or its workers' compensation insurance company) is required to pay for emergency medical treatment.
- **Non-emergency injuries.** If your injury does not require immediate medical attention, notify your supervisor or employer and request medical treatment. It's a good idea to ask someone to accompany you when you make this request. It may be necessary later to have a witness who can verify that you notified your employer of your injury and requested medical attention.

If you previously designated your treating doctor, simply tell your employer that you will see this doctor. Otherwise, your employer may choose which doctor you'll see for treatment. If your employer does not specify a doctor or is unavailable to authorize medical treatment, you may arrange for it yourself.

MEDICAL CARE IS COVERED IN CHAPTER 9

This chapter gives only a brief overview of how to handle your medical care. Please refer to Chapter 9 for an in-depth discussion of your medical treatment, including:
- the role of the treating doctor
- when and how you may change treating doctors
- the importance of medical control and how to get it
- what to do if your employer or its insurance company won't authorize medical treatment, and
- what to say to the doctor to best preserve your legal rights.

B. Report the Injury Within 30 Days

An employer is not responsible for providing any workers' compensation benefits until it has notice of your job-related injury. It's up to you to provide this notice in writing within 30 days from the date of the injury. (LC § 5400.)

1. When to Report Slow-Developing Injuries

It may be months or even years after an injury first starts developing—or after you first feel mild discomfort—before you realize the link between your pain and your job. Injuries that occur over a period of weeks, months or even years, are usually known as continuous trauma or cumulative trauma injuries. These injuries are usually the result of:
- continuously doing an activity that causes wear and tear on your body over a period of time—such as constant bending and stooping activities or repetitive hand movements, or
- being subjected to working conditions that cause you to gradually become ill—for example, an allergic reaction to workplace toxins.

Many of these types of injuries occur in occupations requiring continuous heavy lifting activities, data entry, computer use or being present in an atmosphere containing dust, smoke, chemical fumes or other air- or waterborne hazards.

As a practical matter, you should report the injury as soon as you feel your symptoms are job-related or are told the injury is job-related. By law, you must report the injury within 30 days from the date you knew about the injury. This is the date that you first suffered disability (lost time from work or

got medical treatment) and knew, or reasonably should have known, that the disability was caused by your job. (LC § 5412.) See Chapter 4, Section B2, for more information.

2. How to Report Your Injury

At your first opportunity, report your injury to someone in a position of authority. This may be your foreman, supervisor or perhaps the owner of your company. If you have a union, you should also report the injury to your union steward or business agent. If yours is a medical emergency, get treatment first and report the injury promptly when things calm down.

If your company has a standard form for reporting injuries, make certain that you either personally fill out the form or at least check it very carefully for accuracy. You may also use the workers' compensation DWC-1 form as your formal written notice of injury. (Instructions for completing this form are in Section C2, below.)

If you'll be out of work for a while, call your boss or send a note and keep a copy. As a practical matter, you should give written notice, even if your employer was told about the injury. Should your employer later deny that it received notice, it is much easier to produce a written notice than to call witnesses to testify that the employer received notice. You may give a note to your employer or send it by certified mail, return receipt requested. The note should be dated and specify:
- the date of injury
- the parts of body injured
- where the injury occurred, and
- how the injury occurred.

SAMPLE

To: G & H Technologies

I, Jamie Gordon, wish to inform you that I injured my right leg on 3/3/XX at 9:30 a.m. I was hit from behind by a forklift driven by David Letz. The injury occurred in the main warehouse at G & H Technologies.

_____   _____
Date   Signature of employee

I, (supervisor's name) acknowledge report of such injury.

_____   _____
Date   Signature of supervisor

Once your injury has been reported, your employer will likely want to document and review what happened. It's your responsibility to see that the appropriate forms are filled out and that you get copies.

3. If You Don't Report the Injury on Time

 See *Reynolds v. WCAB* in Chapter 28.

If you fail to give your employer written notice within 30 days of an injury, you may be barred from receiving workers' compensation benefits unless either of the following applies:

- You can show that your failure to give notice didn't mislead or otherwise prejudice your employer. Stated differently, the employer must not be able to show that your delay harmed your employer's ability to dispute your claim of injury (LC § 5403), or
- The employer knew about the injury. If the employer found out about the injury from any source, it is equivalent to written notice by the employee. (LC § 5402.) For instance, if you strain your back working for a small retail store and another employee tells the owner, that's adequate notice. Similarly, if you are a secretary for a law firm and complain to your supervisor that your wrists and lower arms hurt all the time, that's notice.

EXAMPLE 1: Mary is working alone and slips on some oil, causing her to twist her knee. Mary doesn't mention the injury to her employer. After more than 30 days, Mary's knee is still bothering her, and she tells her employer of the injury. Because the employer had no other way of knowing about the injury, and since more than 30 days have elapsed since the date of injury, Mary may be barred from receiving workers' compensation benefits.

EXAMPLE 2: While working on a forklift in the yard of his employer, Mark falls off and is knocked unconscious. Several employees witness the accident. One co-employee tells Mark's supervisor what happened and the supervisor calls an ambulance. Mark is not required to give written notice because the employer has already been put on notice of the injury.

C. File Your Workers' Compensation Claim

Reporting an injury to your supervisor or boss simply informs your employer that you have been injured; it is not the same thing as filing a workers' compensation claim. You must still take care of the paperwork necessary to initiate a claim. For injuries occurring on or after 1/1/94, you must file two forms:

- a DWC-1 claim form, which you give to your employer, and
- an Application for Adjudication of Claim, which you file with the Workers' Compensation Appeals Board.

We cover how to complete these important forms later in this section. For now, let's look at the rules governing when you need to file them.

1. When to File Your Claim

By law, you must file your workers' compensation claim within certain time limits or you won't be entitled to any benefits. The time limit within which to file a claim is known in legal language as the "statute of limitations." You must file a workers' compensation claim:

- **within one year from the date of injury** if the insurance company denied responsibility for your injury (for instance, sent you a letter denying your claim) or did not acknowledge your injury (neither responded nor provided any benefits)

- **within five years from the date of injury** if the insurance company provided benefits—for example, paid temporary disability or medical treatment, or
- **for death benefit claims, within one year from the date of death.** In addition, the death must have occurred as a result of the industrial injury and within 240 weeks of the date of the injury.

To protect your rights, you should always file a claim for any injury requiring anything beyond minor first aid, even if you do not think the injury is serious. If there is any possibility that future complications could develop, file your claim! You'd be wise to file your workers' compensation claim within 30 days of your injury, if possible. If you neglect this important task, you may lose your right to compensation.

EXAMPLE: Julie slips at work and injures her back. She reports the injury to her supervisor, who gives Julie a DWC-1 form. Julie takes the day off, puts the form in the glove compartment of her car and returns to work the next day. Although Julie gets a letter from her employer stating that she may have a workers' compensation claim, she continues to work with the pain in her back, thinking that it will eventually go away. Over a year later, Julie sees her family doctor for a checkup. The doctor discovers that she has two slipped disks in her back, which were likely caused by her injury at work the previous year. Julie digs out the DWC-1 claim form from her car and files it. She gets a letter from the workers' compensation insurance company denying her claim. Because Julie failed to file a claim within one year from the date of her injury, her claim is barred forever by the statute of limitations.

IF YOU DIDN'T FILE A CLAIM ON TIME

If the insurance carrier denies your claim on the basis that the statute of limitations has run, get help from an Information and Assistance officer or an attorney. You may have another chance. For example, if your employer didn't give you written information that you may have a workers' compensation claim (a blank DWC-1 form would be sufficient), the statute of limitations does not begin to run until you learn of that right.

a. Specific or Traumatic Injuries Statute of Limitations

If you were involved in an accident at work, the statute of limitations begins to run from the date of the injury or accident.

EXAMPLE: Fred falls at work on 12/11/01 and breaks a leg. He has until 12/11/02 to file his claim.

b. Continuous Trauma Injuries Statute of Limitations

For continuous trauma injuries, including occupational diseases, the date of the injury is calculated from the date on which two conditions are met. First, the employee takes time off from work due to the injury. Second, the employee knows (or should have known, as a reasonable person) that the disability was caused by his work.

EXAMPLE 1: Stan misses work on and off for several months because of ill health. After a series of tests and doctor's visits, Stan's doctor tells him that he has toxins in his system due to exposure to cleaning chemicals at work. Stan's date of injury is the date the doctor told him that his injuries were work related. Stan has one year from that date within which to file a claim.

EXAMPLE 2: Laura does data entry at a computer terminal all day long. She notices pain in her right wrist and sees her family doctor, who does some testing. Laura's doctor tells her that she has carpal tunnel syndrome, an injury involving the nerves in her wrist, which is caused by her constant typing at the computer terminal at work. Laura continues to work for another five months before finally telling her supervisor that she can't work anymore because of carpal tunnel syndrome and goes home. Laura's date of injury is the date that Laura first took off work. She has one year from that date within which to file a claim.

2. Complete and File a DWC-1 Form

The DWC-1 form (Employee's Claim for Workers' Compensation Benefits) documents the date you were injured and provides details about the injury. Your best bet is to file the DWC-1 form as soon as possible so that you can qualify for all benefits that you may be entitled to.

By law, your employer must give you the form and written information within one working day of finding out about an injury (from any source), if the injury results in:

- lost work time beyond the date of injury, or

• medical treatment beyond first aid—one-time treatment of minor injuries such as scratches, cuts, burns or splinters. (CCR § 10119, LC § 5401.)

If your supervisor does not give you the form within 24 hours of your request, make a written request to higher management. If you still cannot get the form, use the blank DWC-1 form provided in Appendix 4.

a.   How to Fill in a DWC-1 Form

You must complete and file a separate DWC-1 form for each incident resulting in injury. If yours is a continuous trauma injury involving more than one employer, you'll have to prepare one form for each employer.

EXAMPLE 1: Tom slips and falls on a greasy spot in the warehouse and injures his wrist and knee. He need only file one DWC-1 form listing both injuries, since they both arose from the same incident.

EXAMPLE 2: Martha injures her right shoulder lifting a heavy box off an overhead shelf at her work on 7/4. She goes to a doctor who says that while she did injure her shoulder lifting the box on 7/4, her shoulder also has a cumulative trauma injury stemming from the warehouse work she is currently doing for two different employers. Martha files three DWC-1 forms: one for the specific injury of 7/4 at Job A, one for a continuous trauma injury (for the previous one-year period) at Job A, and one for a continuous trauma injury (for the previous one-year period) at Job B.

The DWC-1 claim form has two parts to it: an upper part, which you complete as the employee, and a lower part, which your employer fills in. If you get the DWC-1 form from your employer, it will probably be a carbon form in quadruplicate; however, you may use a single form and make copies. Either fill in the form using a typewriter or neatly handwrite the information using a pen. Here's how to fill it in.

1. Name and Today's Date. Provide your full name. If you go by a nickname or use another name at work (some women use a pre-marriage name, for example), provide that as well—for example, "Richard (Skip) Whitmore" or "Susan Davis, AKA Susan Smith." ("AKA" stands for "also known as.") Also fill in today's date.

2-3. Home Address. Fill in your home address, including the city, state and zip code.

4. Date and Time of Injury. The date you were injured controls important rules about your case, such as how long you have to file a workers' compensation claim and what benefits you may receive.

If your injury resulted from a specific incident, such as an accident at work, simply fill in the date and time it happened, and proceed to the instructions for item 5 on the form.

If yours is a cumulative injury the date of injury can be a little less obvious, and you'll need to carefully read the rest of this discussion. The date of injury for these types of injuries should be set out as a period of time, rather than one specific date—for example, 9/20/01 to 9/20/02. To determine the continuous trauma period, you first need to determine the ending date of the continuous trauma and then go back up to a *maximum of one year*. The ending date is the date you first suffered disability as a result of your injury—meaning you took off work due to your injury—*and* knew, or should have known, that your disability was caused by your present or prior employment. (LC § 5412.)

The one-year limit for a continuous trauma period is purely a legal technicality to determine which insurance companies are responsible for your claim. Only the companies that insured your employer during the last year of your cumulative injury are responsible for paying benefits. Of course, the actual injury may have occurred over many years. When discussing your injury with doctors, the insurance company, or the workers' compensation judge, you should point out all periods that you believe contributed to your injury, not just the last year.

EXAMPLE 1: Shawn works as a carpenter, building cabinets for new homes. He works with wood and spends a great deal of time sanding. He has worked in this capacity for the same employer for the past five years. On 12/3/01, Shawn leaves work because he has difficulty breathing. After about 10 days he returns to work, but is scheduled for some tests the following month. On 1/6/02, Shawn's doctor tells him that his lungs have been damaged from breathing sawdust particles at work. The ending date for the continuous trauma would be 1/6/02, the date Shawn lost time off from work *and* knew that his illness was due to his work. While it's likely that Shawn's exposure to dust over the five years of employment caused the injury, the continuous trauma period he lists in the DWC-1 form is for only one year: 1/6/01 to 1/6/02. Only insurance companies that insured Shawn's employer from 1/6/01 to 1/6/02 would be responsible for his claim.

State of California
Department of Industrial Relations
DIVISION OF WORKERS' COMPENSATION

Estado de California
Departamento de Relaciones Industriales
DIVISION DE COMPENSACIÓN AL TRABAJADOR

EMPLOYEE'S CLAIM FOR WORKERS' COMPENSATION BENEFITS

If you are injured or become ill because of your job, you may be entitled to workers' compensation benefits.

Complete the "**Employee**" section and give the form to your employer. Keep the copy marked "**Employee's Temporary Receipt**" until you receive the dated copy from your employer. You may call the Division of Workers' Compensation at **1-800-736-7401** if you need help in filling out this form or in obtaining your benefits. An explanation of workers' compensation benefits is included on the back of this form.

You should also have received a pamphlet from your employer describing workers' compensation benefits and the procedures to obtain them.

Any person who makes or causes to be made any knowingly false or fraudulent material statement or material representation for the purpose of obtaining or denying workers' compensation benefits or payments is guilty of a felony.

PETICION DEL EMPLEADO PARA BENEFICIOS DE COMPENSACIÓN DEL TRABAJADOR

Si Ud. se ha lesionado o se ha enfermado a causa de su trabajo, Ud. tiene derecho a recibir beneficios de compensación al trabajador.
Complete la sección "Empleado" y entregue la forma a su empleador. Quédese con la copia designada "Recibo Temporal del Empleado" hasta que Ud. reciba la copia fechada de su empleador. Si Ud. necesita ayuda para completar esta forma o para obtener sus beneficios, Ud. puede hablar con la Division de Compensación al Trabajador llamando al 1-800-736-7401. En la parte de atrás de esta forma se encuentra una explicación de los beneficios de compensación al trabajador.

Ud. también debería haber recibido de su empleador un folleto describiendo los beneficios de compensación al trabajador lesionado y los procedimientos para obtenerlos.

Toda aquella persona que a propósito haga o cause que se produzca cualquier declaración o representación material falsa o fraudulenta con el fin de obtener o negar beneficios o pagos de compensación a trabajadores lesionados es culpable de un crimen mayor "felonía".

Employee: *Empleado:*

1. Name. *Nombre.* Penelope Watson   Today's Date. *Fecha de Hoy.* 4/4/year

2. Home Address. *Dirección Residencial.* 720 Ninth Street

3. City. *Ciudad.* Sacramento   State. *Estado.* CA   Zip. *Código Postal.* 95814

4. Date of Injury. *Fecha de la lesión(accidente).* 3/2/year   Time of Injury. *Hora en que ocurrió.* 9:30 a.m. ____ p.m.

5. Address and description of where injury happened. *Dirección/lugar dónde occurió el accidente.* Andrews Construction, 8978 Elk Grove Road, Elk Grove, CA

6. Describe injury and part of body affected. *Describa la lesión y parte del cuerpo afectada.* Fell from elevated platform and injured my back, neck and right leg.

7. Social Security Number. *Número de Seguro Social del Empleado.* 000-00-0000

8. Signature of employee. *Firma del empleado.* *Penelope Watson*

Employer—complete this section and give the employee a copy immediately as a receipt.
Empleador—complete esta sección y déle inmediatamente una copia al empleado como recibo.

9. Name of employer. *Nombre del empleador.*

10. Address. *Dirección.*

11. Date employer first knew of injury. *Fecha en que el empleador supo por primera vez de la lesión o accidente.*

12. Date claim form was provided to employee. *Fecha en que se le entregó al empleado la petición.*

13. Date employer received claim form. *Fecha en que el empleado devolvió la petición al empleador.*

14. Name and address of insurance carrier or adjusting agency. *Nombre y dirección de la compañía de seguros o agencia administradora de seguros.*

15. Insurance Policy Number. *El número de la póliza del Seguro.*

16. Signature of employer representative. *Firma del representante del empleador.*

17. Title. *Título.*   18. Telephone. *Teléfono.*

Employer: You are required to date this form and provide copies to your insurer or claims administrator and to the employee, dependent or representative who filed the claim within **one working day** of receipt of the form from the employee.

SIGNING THIS FORM IS NOT AN ADMISSION OF LIABILITY

Empleador: Se requiere que Ud. feche esta forma y que provéa copias a su compañía de seguros, administrador de reclamos, o dependiente/representante de reclamos y al empleado que hayan presentado esta petición dentro del plazo de un día hábil desde el momento de haber sido recibida la forma del empleado.

EL FIRMAR ESTA FORMA NO SIGNIFICA ADMISION DE RESPONSABILIDAD

Original (Employer's Copy)
DWC Form 1 (REV. 1/94)

ORIGINAL (Copia del Empleador)
DWC Forma 1 (REV. 1/94)

EXAMPLE 2: Let's use the same fact situation as in Example 1, but let's assume that Shawn began working for his current employer on 7/1/01, and prior to that worked for three years for another employer doing the same type of work. Shawn would have to file separate claims against each employer. The insurance carriers that insured Shawn's present employer from 7/1/01 to 1/6/02 would be responsible, as would be the insurance carrier or carriers that insured Shawn's prior employer from 1/6/01 to 7/1/01.

5. Address/place where injury happened. If the injury happened at work, list the work address. Otherwise fill in the address or location of the injury. For example, if you were involved in an accident while driving a truck on company business, the location of the injury would be where the accident occurred, not your employer's address.

6. Describe the injury and part of body affected. Give a brief and clear statement about how the injury occurred. For example: "fell from platform," "repetitive lifting of heavy objects," or "repetitive keyboard and mouse use."

Make sure you list *all* of the body parts injured. Be as thorough as possible, even listing body parts that may not be seriously injured. If you even suspect you might have injured a certain part of your body, list it. If you fail to list a certain part of your body, the employer or its workers' compensation insurance company may later deny that an injury occurred to that body part.

For example, if you injured your right hand, wrist, elbow and shoulder, list all of them: "entire right arm and shoulder, including hand, wrist and elbow." It doesn't matter if you use technical medical terms or not; "collar bone" is just as acceptable as "clavicle," for example. It is, however, better to use general terms rather than specific terms. For instance, if you injured your lower back, use the term "back" or "spine" instead of "lumbar region of back." If you limit yourself to "lumbar region of back" now, and later find out you really injured other parts of your back, the insurance company may try to deny your claim.

7. Social security number. Insert your social security number here.

8. Signature of employee. Sign the form, using the name you listed in item 1, above. Leave the rest of the form blank; your employer will complete it.

b. How to File a DWC-1 Form

To file a DWC-1 form, promptly give it to the employer you worked for when the injury happened. You may file the DWC-1 form by personally handing it to your employer, having someone else deliver it or mailing it by certified mail with a return receipt requested. Although you can send the form by regular mail, you could run into problems if the employer claims it didn't receive it or got it after the one-year filing deadline. (See the sidebar, "Two Employers and Other Confusing Situations: Who to File Against," if you had two or more employers at the time of injury.)

Within one working day of receipt of the claim form, your employer must complete the lower part of the DWC-1 form and send or give a dated copy both to you and its workers' compensation insurance company. (CCR § 10121.) The completed bottom part will contain the name and address of your employer's workers' compensation insurance carrier.

IF YOU'RE RUNNING OUT OF TIME TO FILE

If the one-year (or five-year) statute is about to run, you'll need to act quickly. Fill out and sign your half of the DWC-1 and keep a copy for your records. Give the original to your employer, or mail it certified mail, return-receipt requested. If your employer doesn't return a completed copy of the form prior to the statute running, the fact that you filed your part will protect your claim. As long as you file the form within one year of the date of injury, your claim will not be barred by the statute of limitations.

Two Employers and Other Confusing Situations: Who to File Against

Most people who are injured at work are employed by one employer with workers' compensation insurance coverage. In unusual cases, however, it can be confusing as to which employer you should file your claim against. Here are two of the more common situations:

Employee who worked for more than one employer. If you had separate specific injuries at each job, you should file against each employer for the injuries sustained. Likewise, if you suffered a continuous trauma that you think was caused by working for two or more employers in the last year, each is liable under workers' compensation for your injuries, and you should file a separate DWC-1 form against each of them. Do not confuse this with the situation where you hold two or more jobs and are injured solely as a result of working at one of them. In that case, only the employer where you were injured (and its insurance company) would be responsible.

Employee of an uninsured subcontractor. If you were employed by a subcontractor (usually in the construction business) who does not have workers' compensation insurance, and there was a general contractor on the job, you automatically become its employee for workers' compensation purposes. There is no point in filing a claim against a subcontractor who doesn't have workers' compensation coverage. Instead, file the claim with the general contractor and consider it your employer. If you aren't sure if the subcontractor is covered, file against both.

and Assistance officer. Or contact the Workers' Compensation Insurance Rating Bureau (WCIRB), which keeps current records of all employers' workers' compensation insurance companies. (The telephone number and address for the WCIRB is provided in Chapter 1, Section C2.) You need to send a written request, including the name of your employer, your date(s) of injury and your return address. Include a check for $5 for each year you want to know about.

Once you have the name and address of your employer's workers' compensation insurance company, send the original signed DWC-1 form to the insurance company. Remember to keep a copy for your records and send the form certified mail, return receipt requested.

SAMPLE

May 24, 20XX

Workers' Compensation Insurance Rating Bureau
525 Market Street
Suite 800
San Francisco, CA 94105

To Whom it May Concern:

Please provide me with the name and address of the workers' compensation insurance company for ACME Tools, 3333 West 4th St., Anytown, CA 99999. The date of coverage needed is April 5, 20XX. Enclosed please find my check for $5.

Thank you.

Darlene Chan

Darlene Chan
555 N. 7th St.
Anytown, CA 99999

c. If Your Employer Won't Complete DWC-1 Form

Sometimes employers refuse to complete a DWC-1 form because they don't want to tell their insurance company that a workers' compensation claim was filed. If this happens, you'll need to contact your employer's workers' compensation insurance company directly.

Employers are required to post the name of their insurance carrier or claims administrator on the premises. But if you can't readily find this information, check with an Information

d. Amending a DWC-1 Form

If, after filing your DWC-1 form, you learn of new body parts you injured that you did not know of when you completed the form, you should change (amend) the DWC-1 form. Photocopy your original and mark the changes directly on the copy. (This way, you will have the original without the amendments, should you ever need it.)

Draw a line through any parts you want to change and write in the changes above the lined-through parts. Because you want to be able to see what changes you made on the form, do not "white out" anything. On the top of the form, in front of the word DWC-1 write "amended" (or, if you go through this process more than once, "2nd or 3rd amended," such as the case may be). Finally, deliver the amended DWC-1 to your employer as if it were the original.

If you amend the DWC-1 form, make sure you also amend your Application for Adjudication of Claim, if it also needs to be modified. We cover this in Section 4e, below.

3. Complete an Application for Adjudication of Claim

You must also complete and file an Application for Adjudication of Claim form with the Workers' Compensation Appeals Board within the one-year or five-year deadline discussed in Section C1, above.

Let's take a step-by-step look at how to fill in the application, which is provided in Appendix 4.

Initial information. The application consists of a single page with numbered paragraphs from 1 to 9. The top six lines of the form are not numbered. There, you enter the basic information about your case.

Case No. Enter your workers' compensation case number if you have one. This would apply only if you previously filed documents with the Appeals Board, which is unlikely. If a case number has not yet been assigned, leave it blank.

M_____. Enter Mr., Mrs. or Ms. and the injured worker's full first and last names. If you go by a nickname or use another name at work (some women use a pre-marriage name, for example), provide that as well—for example, "Richard (Skip) Whitmore" or "Susan Davis, AKA Susan Smith." ("AKA" stands for "also known as.")

Injured Employee's Address and Zip Code. Enter the injured worker's home address, city, state and zip code.

Social Security Number. Fill in the injured worker's Social Security number.

Applicant If Other Than Injured Employee. If you are the injured worker, just enter "Same." If you are the applicant, but not the injured worker, enter your name here. For example, if you are filing an application on behalf of a minor (someone under age 18) who had a job-related injury, you would be the applicant.

Applicant's Address and Zip Code. Enter the address of the applicant if different from the injured worker. Otherwise, enter "Same."

Employer—State If Self-Insured. Enter the employer's full name. If the employer is self-insured, state that.

Employer's Address and ZIP Code. Fill in the employer's address and zip code. If it has a corporate headquarters, it is best to use that address.

Employer's Insurance Carrier, or If Self-Insured, Adjusting Agency. Enter the name of your employer's workers' compensation insurance company or, if self-insured, its adjusting agency. By now you should have this information from the DWC-1 form that was completed by your employer. (See Section C2c, above, if you don't know the name of your employer's insurance company.)

Insurance Carrier or Adjusting Agency's Address. Enter the address of the workers' compensation insurance company or adjusting agency. Again, you should have this information from the DWC-1 form that was completed by your employer.

Paragraph 1. Enter your birthdate in the space provided. Next, enter your occupational title. If you have more than one title or do more than one job, it's very important that you list them *all*.

On the next blank line, enter the date of your injury. Then enter the name, address and zip code of your employer.

On the last blank line in this paragraph, enter the parts of your body that have been injured. Be sure to list *all* the parts of body you are alleging as injured. This information should be the same as listed on the DWC-1 form that you filled out in Section C2a, above.

Paragraph 2. On the blank line, enter a short description of how the injury occurred. Simply describe as best as you can how the injury occurred, such as "lifting cartons of milk," "struck by falling boxes," "tripped and fell" or "computer programming."

Paragraph 3. Enter how much you were earning at the time of your injury. (If you have questions about how to compute your earnings, see Chapter 12, Section B1.)

STATE OF CALIFORNIA
DEPARTMENT OF INDUSTRIAL RELATIONS

WORKERS' COMPENSATION APPEALS BOARD

SEE REVERSE SIDE
FOR INSTRUCTIONS

APPLICATION FOR ADJUDICATION OF CLAIM
(PRINT OR TYPE NAMES AND ADDRESSES)

CASE No. __BV7777__

Mr. John Wu

(INJURED EMPLOYEE'S ADDRESS AND ZIP CODE): 111 North Hill Street

Social Security No.: __555-55-5555__

Los Angeles, CA 90012

__Same__
(APPLICANT, IF OTHER THAN INJURED EMPLOYEE)
vs.

__Same__
(APPLICANT'S ADDRESS AND ZIP CODE)

__TBA Industries__
(EMPLOYER — STATE IF SELF-INSURED)

__415 W. Ocean Blvd.__
(EMPLOYER'S ADDRESS AND ZIP CODE)

__SCIF__
(EMPLOYER'S INSURANCE CARRIER OR, IF SELF-INSURED, ADJUSTING AGENCY)

__Long Beach, CA 90802__
(INSURANCE CARRIER OR ADJUSTING AGENCY'S ADDRESS)

IT IS CLAIMED THAT:

1. The injured employee, born __10/06/50__ , while employed as a __Warehouseman__
(DATE OF BIRTH)   (OCCUPATION AT TIME OF INJURY)
on __9/9/XX__ at __415 W. Ocean Blvd., Long Beach, CA 90802__
(DATE OF INJURY)   (ADDRESS)   (CITY)   (STATE)   (ZIP CODE)
By the employer sustained injury arising out of and in the course of employment to
__Back and both legs__
(STATE WHAT PARTS OF BODY WERE INJURED)

2. The injury occurred as follows: __slipped on grease while walking on warehouse floor__
(EXPLAIN WHAT EMPLOYEE WAS DOING AT TIME OF INJURY AND HOW INJURY WAS RECEIVED)

3. Actual earnings at time of injury were: __$650 per week__
(GIVE WEEKLY OR MONTHLY SALARY OF HOURLY RATE AND NUMBER OF HOURS WORKED PER WEEK)

(SEPARATELY STATE VALUE PER WEEK OR MONTH OF TIPS, MEALS, LODGING OR OTHER ADVANTAGES REGULARLY RECEIVED)

4. The injury caused disability as follows: __9/9/XX to 1/6/XX__
(SPECIFY LAST DAY OFF WORK DUE TO THIS INJURY AND BEGINNING AND ENDING DATES OF ALL PERIODS OFF DUE TO THIS INJURY)

5. Compensation was paid __X__ $__Unknown__ $ __490__ __Unknown__
(YES) (NO) (TOTAL PAID) (WEEKLY RATE) (DATE OF LAST PAYMENT)

6. Unemployment insurance or unemployment compensation disability benefits have been received since the date of injury
__X__
(YES) (NO)

7. Medical treatment was received __X__ __3/2/XX__ All treatment was furnished by
(YES) (NO) (DATE OF LAST TREATMENT)
the Employer or Insurance Company __X__ Other treatment was provided or paid for by __N/A__
(YES) (NO)
Did Medi-Cal pay for any health care
(NAME OF PERSON OR AGENCY PROVIDING OR PAYING FOR MEDICAL CARE)
related to this claim __X__ doctors not provided or paid for by employer or insurance company who treated or examined
(YES) (NO)
for this injury are __None__
(STATE NAMES AND ADDRESSES OF SUCH DOCTORS AND NAMES OF HOSPITALS TO WHICH SUCH DOCTORS ADMITTED INJURED)

8. Other cases have been filed for industrial injuries by this employee as follows: __1989 injury to right__
__shoulder, case #BV 1234__
(SPECIFY CASE NUMBER AND CITY WHERE FILED)

9. This application is filed because of a disagreement regarding liability for. Temporary disability indemnity __X__
Permanent disability indemnity __X__ Reimbursement for medical expense __X__ Medical treatment __X__
Compensation at proper rate __X__ Rehabilitation __X__ Other (Specify) __Penalties and interest__
(AND APPLICANT REQUESTS A HEARING AND AWARD OF)
__Mileage (transportation)__
THE SAME, AND FOR ALL OTHER APPROPRIATE BENEFITS PROVIDED BY LAW.

Dated at __Los Angeles__ California, __5/24/XX__
(CITY) (DATE)

_____
(APPLICANT'S ATTORNEY)

_____
(APPLICANT'S SIGNATURE)

_____
(ADDRESS AND TELEPHONE NUMBER OF ATTORNEY)

132

DIA WCAB FORM 1 (REV. 7/81)

84 32595

Paragraph 4. Fill in all the dates that you have been off work as a result of your injury.

Paragraph 5. Check "yes" if the insurance company has been or is paying you any temporary disability benefits; otherwise check "no." On the next blank line, enter the total amount you have been paid to date if you know, otherwise enter "unknown." Next, enter the weekly amount you were paid by the insurance company. Finally, enter the date that you last received a check. (If you need more detailed information on temporary disability, see Chapter 12.)

Paragraph 6. On the appropriate line, indicate whether or not you have received any checks for unemployment insurance or state disability. (See Chapter 17 for more about these benefits.)

Paragraph 7. On the first line, place an "X" or check mark indicating whether or not you received medical treatment for your injury from any source. On the next line, enter the date that you last received medical treatment from any source, or the words "not applicable."

Place an "X" or check mark to indicate whether or not your employer or its workers' compensation insurance company paid for all of your medical treatment. If they paid for part, but not all, of your medical costs, indicate "no." If you don't know this information, enter "unknown."

Next, fill in the name of any person or agency, other than your employer, that provided or paid for any medical care. For example, you'd fill in the name of your group health insurance if it provided treatment. Enter "none," if appropriate, as would be the case if your employer paid for the whole thing. Place an "X" or a check mark indicating whether Medi-Cal paid for any health care related to your claim. Finally, enter the name and address of any doctors or facilities that treated or examined you for your injury, but were not paid by your employer or its insurance company. Enter "none" if appropriate.

Paragraph 8. On the blank line, enter "none" if you've never filed a workers' compensation claim. Otherwise, enter the case number of any other workers' compensation claims you have ever filed, whether in California or elsewhere. If you don't know the case number (or weren't assigned one), enter any information you have, such as "3/2/92 injury to right hand filed in Los Angeles, CA."

It's possible that you're not sure whether you filed previous claims—perhaps because you started the claims process and your injury then resolved itself. List all claims you might have made. The insurance company will prob-

ably track them down later and you could end up looking like you were trying to hide something.

Paragraph 9. Here you place an "X" or check mark for each issue on which you and the insurance company may disagree. Because a disagreement is always possible, and not in your control, check each and every line. On the blank line entitled "Other (Specify)," enter the words "penalties and interest" and "mileage (transportation)."

Date and Signature. Date and sign the bottom of the Application. Leave the lines for Applicant attorney blank.

4. How to File an Application

Follow the instructions below to file your application. You may also need to complete one or two short documents that must be filed along with the application.

a. Prepare Declaration in Compliance With Labor Code Section 4906(g)

This form states, under penalty of perjury, that you have not bribed or otherwise induced any doctor or medical facility to write a fraudulent report on your behalf. A blank copy of this declaration is provided in Appendix 4. All you need to do is date and sign the form and circle the word "Application" in the last paragraph.

b. Prepare Guardian ad Litem Papers If Applicant Is a Minor or Is Incompetent

 Skip this section unless the Applicant is a minor (under age 18) or an incompetent adult.

If the Applicant is a minor or is mentally unable to make legal decisions, you must prepare an additional form—a Petition for Appointment of a Guardian ad Litem and Trustee. This document requests that you, as the petitioner, be appointed to act on behalf of the injured worker in the workers' compensation matter.

A Petition for Appointment of a Guardian ad Litem and Trustee can be filed by a parent or court-appointed guardian or conservator. You can get copies of these forms from the Appeals Board. If you need help completing them, contact an Information and Assistance officer.

DECLARATION IN COMPLIANCE WITH LABOR CODE SECTION 4906(G)

The undersigned swear under penalty of perjury that they have to the best of their information and belief not violated California Labor Code Section 139.3 and they have not offered, delivered, received or accepted any rebate, refund, commission, preference, patronage, dividend, discount or other consideration, whether in the form of money or otherwise, as compensation or inducement for any referred examination or evaluation.

4/4/XX
_____   _Penelope Watson_
Date   Employee

_____   _____
Date   Employee's Attorney

_____   _____
Date   Employer

_____   _____
Date   Insurer

_____   _____
Date   Employer's/Insurer's Attorney

The document filed is an Application, Answer, Case Opening Compromise and Release or Case Opening Stipulations with Request for Award. **(Circle the document(s) filed.)**

c. Determine Where to File

You'll need to file the Application for Adjudication of Claim with a local Workers' Compensation Appeals Board. The Appeals Board will probably be located in the county where you currently live or where the injury occurred. If these are different, the choice is up to you.

In some larger counties, there are a number of Appeals Board offices. You can find out the correct office by calling the Workers' Compensation Appeals Board listed in the government section of your local telephone directory, under State of California, Industrial Relations Department. If you have questions about where to file, call the Information and Assistance Unit at 800-736-7401.

d. File Application and Other Documents With Appeals Board

There is no fee for filing your documents. You may file the application and accompanying documents in one of two ways:
- Photocopy the documents and mail the originals to the Workers' Compensation Appeals Board, following the instructions in Chapter 23, Section D.
- Take the documents down to the Appeals Board, following the instructions in Chapter 23, Section D. If you're under time constraints to file (say you're nearing the filing deadline), you should file the application in person.

YOU MAY NEED TO FILE MORE THAN ONE FORM
If you prepared separate applications for different injuries or different employers, remember to file all of these documents with the Appeals Board.

e. Amending an Application

If you need to make changes to the application form after you file it, you can follow the same general procedures covered in Section C2d, above, for amending a DWC-1 form. Finally, serve copies on all interested parties and file the amended application with the Appeals Board as if it were the original. If you amend the application, also amend the DWC-1 form if it's also incorrect.

D. The Insurance Company's Answer

After you file your application, the Workers' Compensation Appeals Board will do one of two things:
- **If you don't have a lawyer.** The Appeals Board will serve (properly send) a copy of your date-stamped application to your employer's insurance company and all other interested parties. You will also receive a copy.
- **If you have a lawyer.** The Appeals Board will send your lawyer a copy of your Application for Adjudication of Claim, which shows the date of filing. Your attorney must then properly send copies of the file-stamped application to your employer, insurance company and all other interested parties.

Within 15 days after service of the application (10 days if service was in person), the insurance company must file an answer with the Appeals Board. The answer should list any inaccuracies in the application and set forth any defenses. (LC § 5505, CCR § 10480.) You must be served with the answer.

Should the insurance company fail to answer in the required time, it may have waived its right to object. Check with an Information and Assistance officer for more information.

E. Take Steps to Protect Your Rights

As an injured worker, you should take steps to insure that your rights under the workers' compensation system are protected. Although it shouldn't be true—and wouldn't be in a fairer system—your case may be jeopardized if you say or do the wrong thing. In short, while hoping for fair treatment (which you may receive) it is best to prepare yourself from the very start for a long and hard battle (which you may have to fight).

Once you've filed your claim, you'll find the following particularly helpful:
- **Keep good records.** How you keep track of your claim can make or break your case. (See Chapter 6.)
- **Be careful when dealing with the insurance company.** Look at everything the insurance company does from all possible angles. Keep in mind that the insurance company represents your employer, not you. (See Chapter 7.)
- **Know how to deal with your employer.** Regardless of whether or not you're hoping to return to your job, your employer can help or hurt your case. (See Chapter 8.)
- **Take charge of your medical care.** Which doctors you see and how actively you take charge of your medical care will affect both your health and your overall case. (See Chapter 9.) ■

Keep Good Records to Protect Your Claim

Keeping good records is one of the best ways you can protect your rights. By organizing the papers you accumulate in your workers' compensation case and keeping track of benefits you receive, you'll improve your chances of:

- receiving all benefits you're entitled to, especially if the insurance company disputes what you're owed or what you've been paid
- receiving a fair settlement, and
- being able to prove your case at trial, if your case doesn't settle beforehand.

A. Set Up a Good Recordkeeping System

You will accumulate many papers in the process of handling your workers' compensation claim. Now is a good time to set up a system so that you can readily lay your hands on any document you need.

You may find it helpful to go to an office supply store or large stationery store to see what's available to organize your paperwork. File folders or large manila envelopes are a good start; even better is a cardboard accordion file with a top flap that can be tied securely. You might want an expandable file that holds separate file folders that are designated by category—such as medical reports, insurance company correspondence, medical benefits, vocational rehabilitation and so on.

I suggest that you place your documents in each category in chronological order, with the oldest documents on the bottom. Then add current documents to the top of the stack, so your file will automatically be in chronological order.

B. Read and Understand What You Receive in the Mail

You may feel overwhelmed at the volume of the documents you receive and be tempted to file them away without careful study. No—don't do it. It is imperative that you carefully read each and every letter, document, notice and medical report you receive and understand what it says. If you put aside even one document, you run the risk of failing to meet a required deadline or losing track of an important aspect of your case.

If you do not understand the meaning of any letter, notice or medical report you receive, immediately call the doctor, the insurance company's adjuster or an Information and Assistance officer for clarification.

C. Gather Important Records Pertaining to Your Claim

It is crucial that you keep an accurate record of everything that happens from the moment your injury occurs until your case is finished, a period likely to span several years. So take some time now to gather the records listed below.

1. Papers Documenting Your Injury

Gather together any work accident reports, completed DWC-1 forms and other records of your injury. For example, if you were a truck driver, you might have kept a log listing all your activities for each hour of the day. This might prove the date and time of injury.

2. Medical Reports and Records

Keep a chronological record of all medical reports and records you acquire directly from a medical facility, as well as those sent to you by the insurance company. If you request it, your employer and the insurance company must provide you with copies of all medical records and reports that come into their possession. We show you how to make a request in Section D, below.

3. Copies of Documents Filed With the Appeals Board

Include papers you or the insurance company filed in your case, including any Application for Adjudication of Claim, Declaration of Readiness to Proceed and Notice of Change of Address.

4. All Correspondence

Keep a chronological record of all your correspondence to and from your employer, the insurance company, doctors and anyone else involved in your case, such as a lawyer.

If you sent documents by certified mail, keep copies of all return receipts. Also keep copies of any proofs of service showing that documents were served (properly sent).

5. Earnings Record

You'll need a record of your earnings if the insurance company disputes the amount you claim you earned (which in turn may affect the amount of your benefits). If available, gather together copies of your pay stubs for all jobs you held during the year prior to being injured. Also keep copies of your W-2 and 1040 tax forms for the last two years.

6. Record of All Income and Benefits Received

Keep track of all money you receive from the date of your injury until your case ends. Include any money received from the State of California Employment Development Department, the workers' compensation insurance company, Social Security, SSI, AFDC, private disability policies and any other source of income not mentioned here. Use the form entitled Record of Income and Benefits Received, which you will find in Appendix 4. In addition, keep check stubs and any letters regarding payments made.

7. Record of All Time You Are Off Work

Keep a chronological log of those periods for which you have a doctor's report or off work order indicating that you are temporarily disabled. In Appendix 4, you will find a Record of Time Off Work form you can use for this purpose.

8. Record of Any Out-of-Pocket Medical Expenses

Keep track of any expenses you directly incurred due to your injury. For example, you may have paid for (or made co-payments on) doctors' and chiropractors' bills, emergency room bills, medical tests or prescriptions. Include all non-prescription medications you use. You may use the Record of Medical Expenses and Request for Reimbursement, which is covered in Chapter 11, Section A2, and provided in Appendix 4.)

9. Record of Your Medical-Related Mileage

You are entitled to be reimbursed at the rate of 31 cents per mile for the mileage involved in attending medical appointments and picking up medications. If you incurred parking or bridge tolls, list these as well. Use the Record of Mileage & Transportation and Request for Reimbursement form in Appendix 4 to keep track of the mileage. (See Chapter 11, Section A1, for a sample form.)

10. A Diary of Your Pain and Day-to-Day Activities

Your employer or its insurance company may contend that you were not disabled or were not injured as seriously as you claim. Because it may be several years before your workers' compensation case is settled or goes to trial, it is helpful to have a written diary of the pain you experienced and the problems you encountered as a result of your injury. If necessary, the diary itself may be used later as evidence before a judge. (See sidebar, "How to Keep a Pain Diary.")

RECORD OF INCOME AND BENEFITS RECEIVED

Name: _____Denise Wilson_____

Employer: _____World Designs_____

Insurance Carrier: _____Acme Insurance_____

Claim Number: _____99999_____

Date check received	Check number	Period (starting date through ending date)	Amount of check	Reason for check (temporary disability, permanent disability advance, vocational rehabilitation, unemployment, Social Security, etc.)
4/19/XX	1234	4/1/XX—4/15/XX	$298	TD
5/2/XX	1421	4/16/XX—4/31/XX	298	TD
5/17/XX	1500	5/1/XX—5/15/XX	298	TD
5/21/XX	1528	N/A	20	Travel to QME appointment
6/3/XX	1599	5/16/XX—5/30/XX	298	TD
8/20/XX	1904	8/7/XX—8/15/XX	150	TD

RECORD OF TIME OFF WORK

Name: _____Denise Wilson_____   Employer: _____World Designs_____

Insurance Carrier: ___Acme Insurance_____   Claim Number: ___99999_____

Starting Date	Ending date	Doctor's report or off work order?	Reason for time off work
4/19/XX	5/30/XX	off work order	recovering from hip injury
8/7/XX	8/20/XX	off work order	relapse of hip injury

How to Keep a Pain Diary

Keep your diary in a bound book (not a three-ring binder) and always use ink (not pencil), so the insurance company cannot claim you later inserted or changed pages. Keep your diary on at least a weekly basis, unless something unusual should occur (such as a fall brought on by severe pain), in which case you will want to make an additional entry for that day.

The diary should contain a detailed record of your day-to-day symptoms and pain. Do your best to rate your pain for the various parts of your body that were injured. A common scale is 1 to 10, 1 being only slight pain, and 10 being excruciating pain. In addition, include a record of particular problems or improvements you are having performing day-to-day activities. If you are claiming emotional or physical injury due to stress, include a record of how your relationships and financial affairs are affected by the injury.

While it is important to be honest (don't exaggerate), it is also necessary to adequately document your pain or inability to do certain things. So don't minimize your problems.

Sample

Tuesday, 1/6/XX: Went to emergency room. Pain was a 7 plus.

Friday, 1/9/XX: Ankle is in a cast. I believe the fall has further injured my knee; the knee pain is an 8 and is constant and throbbing. The knee is red and swollen. I made a doctor's appointment to have it looked at next Wednesday. When I tried to watch TV tonight, I had to take four pain killers. The pain makes me edgy and nervous, and I'm afraid I've been taking it out on my kids, who continue to be upset.

Friday 1/16/XX: Knee feels better this week. Pain is on the average around a 5 or 6. Saw Dr. Jones yesterday, and he gave pain medication.

11. Photographs, Videotapes and Other Evidence

If the insurance company is claiming that you did not injure yourself at work, try to put together some physical evidence that will substantiate your position. This may include photographs of the job site where you were injured and photographs or videos of the part of your body you injured (as close to the date of injury as possible). If you sprained your ankle, for example, videos of you moving around with crutches might be helpful.

If you find something that can help prove your injury—such as a piece of equipment that contributed to your fall—by all means keep it (or a photograph) as evidence.

12. A Witness List

You may need to have witnesses testify on your behalf to help prove your case. For example, if the insurance company claims that you must have injured your back outside of work, you'd want to find a witness to testify that he saw you fall from a forklift at work. It is never too early to get the names and addresses of people who could serve as witnesses. This would include people who have firsthand knowledge of such things as:

- how the injury occurred
- the safety records of any equipment involved
- the fact that you reported the injury
- anything the employer may have done that contributed to the cause of your injury
- what your work duties consisted of (this may be relevant if issues of occupation and eligibility for vocational rehabilitation arise), and
- the amount of pain you have, as well as the activities you can no longer do (usually a family member can be helpful here).

KEEP IN TOUCH WITH YOUR WITNESSES
If you don't see your witnesses regularly, ask them to contact you in the event they move. While you don't want to pester your witnesses, it's also important not to lose track of them. For instance, make a point of calling your witnesses every few months just to stay in touch. It's common sense that it's much easier to locate someone who has recently moved than someone who moved several years earlier.

13. Notes of Conversations Regarding Your Claim

It is especially important to keep written notes of conversations you have with the insurance company, the defense attorney and your employer.

14. Vocational Rehabilitation Documents

As you will learn, your workers' compensation claim and your vocational rehabilitation claim may be settled or resolved at separate times. Keep copies of all papers concerning vocational rehabilitation. Vocational rehabilitation is discussed in Chapter 14.

D. Request Copies of Documents and Evidence

It's to your advantage to have copies of important documents and evidence your employer and its insurance company have on your case. Fortunately, you have the right to this information. If you make a written request, your employer and its insurance company must send you copies of all documents and evidence it has or acquires in your case. Mail a request to your employer (certified, return receipt requested), with a copy to the insurance company. A form letter for this purposes is provided in Appendix 4.

SAMPLE LETTER

Date

[Employer's name and address]

RE: Workers' Compensation Claim
Injury Date: [Date]
Injured Worker: [Your name]
Certified Mail Return Receipt Requested

Dear [Employer's name]:

I request that you, your insurance carrier or administrator send me copies of the following:

1. All of my medical reports.
2. My wage statement.
3. Any statements taken from me pertaining to my injury.
4. Investigation reports regarding my injury.
5. Copies of any videotapes, film and/or photographs that have been taken of me.
6. Any statements made by me with reference to my right or desire to participate in vocational rehabilitation.
7. A history of all benefits paid, the dates and amounts.
8. Any statements prepared by a Qualified Rehabilitation Representative in my case.
9. Any reports or statements prepared by a case management worker in my case.

Please consider this a *continuing demand*, and serve me with the above if you should receive them in the future.

Thank you for your anticipated cooperation.

Sincerely,

_____

[Your name]
cc: [insurance company]

E. Keep Your Address Current

You are required to keep the Appeals Board and all opposing parties informed of any change in your address. If you move, send a Notice of Change of Address to the Appeals Board with a copy to all parties. See Appendix 4 for a self-explanatory form you can use. How to serve (send) copies to opposing parties is covered in Chapter 23. ■

CHAPTER

7

The Insurance Company's Role

Most employers pay premiums to a workers' compensation insurance company, which, in turn, pays any benefits due an employee who is injured at work. Your employer's workers' compensation insurance company, sometimes called the insurance carrier, will be responsible for managing and settling your workers' compensation claim, unless your employer is self-insured, as discussed in Section A of this chapter. In general, the insurance company makes most decisions on how the claim should be handled and ultimately resolved.

Although every workers' compensation case is unique, this chapter will give you some general guidelines about the most effective way to deal with the insurance company. By knowing what the insurance company expects and how it operates, you'll have a better chance of protecting your rights and being treated fairly.

Always keep in mind that your employer's insurance company is not in business to help you, but to represent your employer. This advice also applies to the State Compensation Insurance Fund (also called State Fund or SCIF). SCIF is a private insurance company set up by the state to make sure that workers' compensation insurance is available to all employers—including those unable to get coverage from a private company because of a bad safety history and very small businesses that can't find coverage elsewhere.

Insurance companies remain in business by paying out less in claims than they receive in premiums. Or to put it more bluntly, the less the insurance company pays you, the more it gets to keep. Thus, the insurance company has no incentive to see that your rights are protected; if anything, the opposite is true.

Unfortunately, workers' compensation has evolved into an adversarial system. Insurance companies often rely upon, and take advantage of, the fact that most injured workers have no idea of the how the system works. Many injured workers believe everything that an insurance adjuster tells them, thinking that the insurance company has their best interests at heart.

RECORD EVERY CONTACT WITH THE INSURANCE COMPANY

Keep accurate records of your dealings with the insurance company. This is important for a number of reasons, including the fact that the insurance company may switch the person in charge of handling your claim (the adjuster) many times throughout your case. If you don't have a written record of prior agreements, the new adjuster may not honor them.

Section E, below, gives advice on how to keep a paper trail of your contacts with the insurance company.

THE MANY NAMES FOR INSURANCE COMPANIES

In your dealings with the workers' compensation system, you will hear the terms "insurance company," "insurer," "insurance carrier" and "carrier." They all mean the same thing. The odd word "carrier" derives from insurance industry jargon, which refers to providing a person or business with insurance as "carrying" their insurance policy. Thus the ABC Insurance Company is said to be the insurance carrier (provider) for the Racafrax Company.

A. Self-Insured Employers

IF YOUR EMPLOYER IS NOT SELF-INSURED
Skip to Section B, below, if an insurance company is handling your workers' compensation claim.

Some employers choose to self-insure, rather than use an insurance company. This means that the employer handles its own workers' compensation claims and directly pays all benefits. Most self-insured employers hire an adjusting company that oversees and handles the day-to-day activities of workers' compensation claims. The adjusting agency may be an in-house agency (part of the company) or one that is hired by the employer.

Although you may believe that dealing directly with your employer instead of with an insurance company is an advantage, in my experience, this is often not true. Your employer may bring to the negotiating table its opinions and biases regarding your claim and how it may affect your ability to remain a viable employee. Also remember that a company that tries to save money by self-insuring is likely to be very concerned with the bottom line.

If you must deal directly with your company to settle your workers' compensation case, the general principles discussed in this chapter shall still guide you. Where this book refers to the "insurance company," simply substitute "adjusting agency" or "employer" for a permissibly self-insured employer.

B. The Insurance Company's Responsibilities

The insurance company has three primary (and interrelated) responsibilities:

- to promptly handle all claims
- to provide benefits, and
- to deal with you in good faith.

All too often, however, an insurance adjuster will delay or deny benefits, without any concrete evidence or proof that the claim is not valid. Typically, the insurance adjuster does so on information supplied by the employer that the injured worker "did not really injure herself at work" or "is really not as hurt as the doctor says she is." If you're subjected to such unfair behavior, you do have some recourse. There are financial penalties for not promptly paying a workers' compensation benefit. (See Chapter 19, Section C9.) In addition, if the insurance company takes action or uses tactics that are frivolous or solely intended to cause unnecessary delay in paying your benefits, the workers' compensation judge may order the insurance company to pay any expenses, including attorney's fees and costs, that you incurred as a result of the delay. (Although rarely done, under LC § 5813, the judge may also order the insurance company to pay a penalty of up to $2,500 to the General Fund, the bank account for the state of California.)

C. Your Responsibilities as an Injured Worker

As a person making a workers' compensation claim, you have certain legal responsibilities, namely, to cooperate with *reasonable* requests made by the insurance company in its investigation of your claim. Reasonable requests would entail such things as providing the insurance company with your medical history and a written authorization for release of your medical records.

DO NOT COMPLY WITH UNREASONABLE REQUESTS
Unless you filed a claim for psychiatric injury, your medical history and release of medical records pertaining to prior psychiatric treatment or counseling is irrelevant and unreasonable.

You must attend all reasonable medical appointments scheduled by the insurance company. I would say that an examination every three months or so by the insurance company's doctor is reasonable. Certainly, requiring you to be examined every week by the same doctor is not reasonable.

The insurance company must make reasonable accommodations for you to attend the medical examinations. If you do not have a car or can't drive, for example, the insurance company must pay your reasonable transportation costs. Medical appointments should also be set within your general geographic area. Requiring you to attend a medical appointment 100 miles away is not reasonable.

As a matter of practicality, remember that the insurance company is not going to tell you your rights or explain what is to your advantage. It is your responsibility to be aware of your rights and to assert them. With the help of this book, you should be in a good position to do so.

D. Who's Who in the Insurance Company

Let's back up a little and take a look at how workers' compensation insurance companies are set up. As your claim progresses, you'll deal with various people who work for the insurance company, including the following:

- insurance adjuster
- adjuster's supervisor
- attorney, house counsel or hearing representative
- case management worker, and
- qualified rehabilitation representative, also known as a "QRR."

By knowing who the various players are and what their respective roles are in the workers' compensation arena, you will have the best chance of resolving your claim fairly. Determine as soon as possible who is involved in your workers' compensation case. Keep a written list of their names, titles, addresses and telephone numbers, as well as a written record of all contact you have with them.

1. The Insurance Adjuster

Assuming you do not have an attorney, your primary contact will be an insurance adjuster (claims adjuster), whose job is to settle your claim. It is important to do your best to establish a good working relationship with the adjuster. You'll likely have to do this with more than one person, as it is common for adjusters to leave or cases to be rotated among adjusters.

Whatever the attitude of the adjuster (some can be uncooperative), remember that this person will decide when, and if, you get the various benefits you may be entitled to. A good approach is to treat the adjuster as you would want to be treated in business dealings. Start by making polite requests of the adjuster, but be willing to be more assertive (but not obnoxious) if need be, and confirm all agreements in writing.

If you get an adjuster who seems to be cooperative and kind, that's fine—it's always nice to deal with a pleasant person. But do remember that the adjuster was hired to bring your claim to a close as quickly and as cheaply as possible. Rule one: never confide in the adjuster. For example, if yours is a back injury, don't tell the friendly adjuster about the mild strain you suffered a few weeks ago helping your brother lay a new roof. This information may be taken out of context, exaggerated and used against you.

2. The Adjuster's Supervisor

No matter how good your working relationship is with the insurance adjuster, there likely will be times when you cannot get her to see things your way. If so, you may want to ask to speak to the adjuster's supervisor. The supervisor has authority to overrule any decisions made by the adjuster. Generally speaking, the supervisor has many more years of experience than does the adjuster. If your reasoning is sound, it is very possible that she will decide to grant your request and override the decision of the insurance adjuster on the case.

Going over the adjuster's head will probably negatively affect your future relationship, so only do this for important matters. In other words, don't complain to the supervisor if your $32 mileage check is late.

Before you call the adjuster's supervisor, think through your circumstances, what you want and why it's reasonable. Then calmly and clearly explain your position, setting forth the medical and legal reasoning behind your request.

> ### How to Negotiate With the Insurance Company
>
> Successful negotiation is based upon requests, and even demands, that are logical and reasonable and, if necessary, persistent. If you are requesting medical treatment authorization, point out the medical reports that support your request. If you are trying to negotiate a settlement, present sound medical evidence to back up a reasonable demand, not a request for an outrageous sum. If the insurance company realizes that you are well-prepared and know what you are entitled to, your reasonable demands should get serious consideration.

3. The Attorney, House Counsel or Hearing Representative

If you cannot settle your workers' compensation claim with the insurance adjuster or supervisor, you will eventually need to have your matter heard before the Workers' Compensation Appeals Board. If your case takes this twist, the adjuster will usually turn your file over to someone else, who will represent the insurance company at the Appeals Board hearing.

The person representing the insurance company may be an attorney, either house counsel (a lawyer who works only for the insurance company) or outside counsel (a lawyer hired by the insurance company to handle your particular case). Workers' compensation laws also allow non-attorneys to represent insurance companies at Appeals Board hearings. If the insurance representative is not an attorney, he will be referred to as a hearing representative, or hearing rep, for short. The hearing rep acts like an attorney on behalf of the insurance company, but is not licensed to practice law.

Who the insurance company uses is usually dictated by cost. Some companies find it cheaper to have an attorney working for them, while others find it less expensive to hire outside attorneys or non-lawyer hearing reps as needed. Regardless of who the insurance company decides to use, your case is going to be handled in much the same way.

4. The Case Management Worker

Some insurance companies hire outside case management workers to assist in the management of their workers' compensation claims. The case manager's job is to help you promptly get the medical care you need while reporting to the insurance company on how your medical treatment is progressing. Insurance companies hire case management workers for many reasons, such as efficiency, cost control and good will. If you're offered this service, you have the option to accept or reject it. If you have an attorney, discuss the pros and cons of a case management worker if one is offered.

A case management worker can be a big help with things like scheduling medical appointments and even arranging to get to the doctor. But be sure you request copies of all of reports the case management worker provides to the insurance company (discussed in Chapter 6, Section D). If you feel that she is not impartially stating everything that occurs, immediately terminate her services. Sometimes a case manager turns out to be little more than a "spy" for the insurance company, reporting to the insurance company anything that might be used against you. You do not need permission to terminate the services of a case manager; simply tell the case manager or the insurance company of your wishes.

5. The Qualified Rehabilitation Representative (QRR)

The qualified rehabilitation representative (QRR) is an independent company (rarely just an individual) in the business of providing vocational rehabilitation counseling to injured workers. Some QRRs are insurance company employees. QRRs who do not work for the workers' compensation insurance company are paid by the insurance company.

If you're eligible for vocational rehabilitation, you'll work with a QRR to develop a plan so that you'll be able to find a job that is within your physical capabilities. (For more on choosing a QRR and participating in vocational rehabilitation, see Chapter 14.)

E. How to Deal With the Insurance Company

If you are not represented by an attorney, you will eventually have to talk to someone from the insurance company about your claim. You may be contacted by an insurance adjuster, an attorney or even a private investigator. This sets up a dilemma—if you don't cooperate with the insurance company, it has the legal right to immediately deny your claim and deny you benefits. However, if you say the "wrong" thing, you could jeopardize your case or delay the receipt of your benefits.

Your best approach is to keep your responses to the insurance company's questions as short as possible. Try to limit yourself to the basic information about your claim.

Whenever you call the insurance company, be as prepared as possible. If the insurance company has assigned a claim number to your case, have it handy. Know exactly what you want to ask, and ask for your insurance adjuster by name if you know it. Otherwise, give your full name or claim number and ask to speak to whoever is handling your claim. Have a pen and paper handy so you can take notes of your conversation.

QUESTIONS TO WATCH OUT FOR

The following types of questions should be red flags, and require well-thought-out and careful answers:
- questions that imply your injury was not caused by your employment or was caused by activities that were outside of your job duties
- questions that imply your injury was due to your being intoxicated or because you started a fight, and
- questions about prior injuries or accidents that imply you may be lying about the cause or extent of your present injury.

If you encounter any trick questions, answer them truthfully, and in such a way as to leave no doubt that your injury occurred at work and was caused by your employment.

---

1. Initial Contact With the Insurance Company

The first contact you have with the insurance company probably will be by letter. By law, you must be sent notice within 14 days after the insurance company receives your claim. This initial letter will advise you whether the insurance company is accepting or rejecting your claim, or whether it needs additional time (up to 90 days) to investigate before deciding. This letter will have the name and telephone number of the insurance adjuster who will be handling your case.

If the insurance company fails to advise you in writing within 14 days of receiving your claim that it is delaying its decision pending further investigation, your claim is presumed to be accepted. There is no penalty for the first 14 days of delay. However, there is a 10% penalty for any benefits due and not paid after the 14th day. (See Chapter 19, Section C9.)

If you do not receive any correspondence from the insurance company within 14 days of filing your workers' compensation claim, you should call the insurance company. Your first telephone contact with the insurance company is very important. In many instances, it will set the tone of your entire case. In other words, it's to your advantage to establish a cordial but firm working relationship with the insurance adjuster.

Ask if the insurance company intends to accept or reject your claim, and request that you be paid any benefits that are due. If the insurance company claims that it was not notified of the claim, send the insurance company a copy of the DWC-1 form you gave your employer.

2.   Your Statement About the Injury

Even when an insurance company accepts a claim, it usually contacts the injured worker and asks for a statement about what happened (usually within the first 90 days). If the insurance company advises you by letter within 14 days that it is going to investigate your claim further before deciding whether or not to accept it, you can pretty much count on being asked to give a statement.

Before you are contacted, give some thought about what you want to say to the insurance company. Many people become nervous when interviewed, and as a result do a very poor job of stating their case. Even if you feel confident about talking to the insurance company, you're best off writing out your statement ahead of time. That way, you can think through your case and avoid making statements that are inaccurate or misleading.

If you simply don't feel comfortable giving an oral (spoken) statement, or feel too scared or shaky to do so, you may give a written statement instead. We give some guidelines below.

Whenever you give the insurance company any kind of statement, the most important thing is to *tell the truth*. As long as you follow this rule, you won't have problems with one statement contradicting another (unless you allow yourself to get confused or intimidated). Remember, you are the most important witness in your workers' compensation case.

a.   Prepare Your Statement in Advance

As noted above, never give a statement on the spur of the moment. If you are contacted by phone and asked to give a

statement before you have had a chance to prepare, tell the insurance company you don't have time just now, and make an appointment time for the insurance company to call you back for your statement. Or simply explain that you will send a written statement to the insurance company.

Whether you're planning to give your statement orally or in writing, take the time to write down all the important dates and times, as well as the name and addresses of the doctors you have seen. Include all important facts.

SAMPLE STATEMENT

1. Date of Injury: 1/3/XX
2. How injury happened: I was carrying a box of supplies down some stairs when I tripped and fell, injuring myself. I think I fell down about five stairs onto the landing.
3. Parts of body injured: My back and left leg. *[Include all body parts that could possibly be injured, even if only slightly.]*
4. Witnesses: Co-workers Jim Walters and Sally O'Leary witnessed the accident.
5. Reporting the injury: I immediately told my supervisor, Ted Felding, of the injury. He had me fill out and sign a company injury report.
6. Medical Treatment: Ted Felding told me to go to the Jason Medical Clinic at 3434 Smith St. in Los Angeles. I went there the same day of my injury at about 4:00 PM and they examined me and prescribed *[indicate medication]*, which I paid for and have been taking three times a day. No X-rays were taken.

Also see Chapter 4, Section B3 for a sample statement regarding a cumulative trauma injury.

b.   Giving an Oral Statement

If you give the insurance company an oral statement, it will take one of three forms:

- an interview by phone, which will probably be recorded after you're informed of that fact and agree to it
- an in-person interview, which will probably be recorded, or
- a deposition, where you are asked questions under oath. A court reporter (a specially trained transcriber) records everything and later transcribes your testimony into a booklet, which can be used in any legal proceeding involving your case. Depositions are usually taken only if you have an attorney. (If your deposition will be taken, please refer to Chapter 21, Section C, which tells you how to prepare for a deposition.)

If you don't have an attorney, you may wisely decide to have a friend, family member or other non-lawyer present at your interviews. Also, remember to have a written statement handy, as it will help prevent you from becoming confused or intimidated.

There is no reason to be afraid to have your statement recorded, so long as you get a written transcript of the recording. Begin your oral statement by specifically stating that the insurance company has agreed to provide you with a copy of the statement (the insurance company must give you a written copy of your statement upon request).

c.   Changing Your Statement

For obvious reasons, you should try your best to give an accurate statement in the first place. Your statement is always suspect if you have to change your story. However, if you made a mistake in your statement or left out something important, make arrangements to change your statement at the earliest opportunity. You can change your statement by writing the insurance company a letter setting forth your changes. Remember to sign and date your letter.

SAMPLE LETTER

12/8/XX

Mr. Tom Smith
ABC Insurance Co.
33 W. Pine Ave.
Smithville, CA 99999

Re: Clyde Johnson vs. Design Central

Claim No. 98765
Appeals Board No: BV 12345
Date of Injury: 9/9/XX

Dear Mr. Smith:

On 11/21/XX, I gave an oral statement to Jane Felsworth. I told her that the witness's name was Jose Flores. I have now learned that his name is Jose Torres.

Sincerely,

Clyde Johnson
Clyde Johnson
555 N. 12th St.
Smithville, CA 99999

3.   Make Notes of Your Conversations

Make a written note of every conversation you have regarding your claim. Include the date, time, who you talked with and what the conversation was about. This will help to avoid any misunderstandings on your part. Also, a dated record, made at the time of the event, is excellent proof to substantiate what was said.

EXAMPLE: 12/7/XX, 10:15 a.m. Spoke with Tom Smith, insurance adjuster. He agreed to begin payments of temporary disability payments in the amount of $336 per week. He said the first check will be mailed this week.

4.   Send Confirming Letters

If you reach any type of agreement with someone from the insurance company about your claim, it is best to follow up with a confirming letter. This may serve as a needed reminder to an over-busy adjuster. It also will avoid any misunderstanding about what you agreed upon, or claims that the conversation never took place.

Send a written or typed letter to the person you spoke with and keep a copy for your records. As the sample below shows, the letter can be very short.

SAMPLE LETTER

12/8/XX

Mr. Tom Smith

ABC Insurance Co.

33 W. Pine Ave.

Smithville, CA 99999

Re: Clyde Johnson vs. Design Central

Claim No. 98765

Appeals Board No: BV 12345

Date of Injury: 9/9/XX

Dear Mr. Smith:

This will confirm our conversation of 12/7/XX, where you agreed to begin making temporary disability payments of $336 per week. You indicated that you will mail the first check within the week. Thank you for your help and cooperation.

Sincerely,

Clyde Johnson

Clyde Johnson

555 N. 12th St.

Smithville, CA 99999

F. Tactics Insurance Companies Use to Deny or Minimize Claims

There are a number of techniques the workers' compensation insurance company may use to deny or delay your claim. By knowing what these may be, you'll be better prepared to explore your options and protect yourself.

1. Private Investigators

The insurance company will not only monitor your medical progress, it may also assign an investigator to your case. An investigator is likely to search public records and other sources, collecting information on your prior workers' compensation claims, automobile accidents and medical history. The investigator may interview your co-workers, witnesses, friends, relatives, neighbors and past or present doctors, as well as you. (Before you consent to an interview, read Section E, above.)

Many insurance companies hire private investigators to follow and videotape injured workers. The goal is to catch you engaging in an activity that is inconsistent with your claimed disability, such as strenuous sports, household repair tasks or other activities that contradict your doctor's orders. This type of surveillance (called a sub-rosa investigation) is so common that some workers' compensation insurance companies have their own team of in-house investigators.

Typically, the investigator will hide in a van with one-way glass, parked quite a distance (up to about 150 yards) from where the scene is being filmed. The investigator will usually be equipped with at least one video camera with a telephoto lens. Filming may take place at a number of locations, and it may occur over a long period of time.

It's not uncommon for investigators to film injured workers attending medical appointments, shopping, going to family gatherings or doing work around the house. Video clips may show you taking out the trash, picking up the mail (beware of large packages that you didn't order), changing a flat tire, lifting heavy items at a garage sale or doing yard work.

Investigators are also fond of using the phone to get information or to find out if you're home. They may pretend to conduct a survey or inform you that you're a prize winner. Instead of worrying about whether or not an investigator is calling, many injured workers use an answering machine to screen all calls. Be aware that if you're using a cordless phone (maybe you "won" one in a contest you didn't enter), your calls can be monitored with a radio scanner.

Be prudent about your physical activities and always follow your doctor's advice. If you claim you can't mow your lawn because of your injured back, don't allow yourself to be video-taped doing so—even if you're only giving the lawn a light trim because your mother-in-law is coming for dinner and you're in pain the whole time. Or, if you contend that you can't lift anything heavy, simply do not attempt to do so, no matter what the necessity. If you do, you're likely to find that it's all on videotape.

It's important to understand an investigation can happen for any case, and at any time in your workers' compensation case. You'd be foolish to think that an investigation won't happen to you because your injury is relatively minor, or you've moved or your claim is proceeding smoothly. I once had a client who moved from California to a small midwestern town (population of about 120), and was dumbfounded to discover that an investigator had filmed him doing farm work he said he could not do!

2. Delay Tactics

As mentioned, a favorite tactic used by workers' compensation insurance companies is to delay, and then delay some more. Even though you may be in pain and living from check to check, the insurance company is primarily interested in holding on to your money as long as possible. After all, the longer it delays paying you, the more interest it can earn on your money.

Some of the most common delay tactics include instances where the insurance company:

- delays in paying your temporary disability indemnity when due
- delays in accepting or rejecting your claim
- delays in authorizing medical treatment recommended by the treating doctor
- delays in setting up medical appointments for treatment or evaluation
- delays in authorizing vocational rehabilitation benefits after a doctor determines that you are entitled to it
- delays in the payment of valid medical or pharmaceutical bills, and
- delays in just about anything you ask the insurance company to do.

Your best approach is to always be diligent in making your demands. Don't let a deadline pass without making a phone call and sending a follow-up letter demanding that the insurance company promptly take appropriate action. If the insurance company fails to respond immediately, seek help from an Information and Assistance officer. You may even choose to have an Appeals Board judge hear the matter. (If your benefits or medical treatment are delayed, you may be entitled to an automatic 10% penalty under Labor Code §4650 and if the delay is unreasonable you may be entitled to a 10% penalty on the entire species of benefits under Labor Code §5814. In addition, an insurance company whose actions constitute "bad faith" may be responsible for expense incurred as a result of that delay and penalties under Labor Code §5813. See Chapter 19, Section C, for a more detailed discussion of penalties.)

3. Intimidation

Let's say your adjuster tells you that you have no case, and if you don't accept what's being offered, you'll get nothing. The best defense to this tactic is to know your case. Assuming you have a legitimate claim, you should never allow yourself to be bullied into settling your claim prematurely.

Make a note of anything said to you that you consider unfair or outrageous. Then write a letter to your adjuster's supervisor protesting this treatment. Save a copy of the letter; you'll need it if your case later goes before the Appeals Board.

SAMPLE LETTER

[Date]

Dear [Name of Supervisor]:

I believe that I have been unfairly treated by ___*[Name of adjuster]*___ . On 9/3/XX, I spoke with ___*[Name of adjuster]*___ and was told that, in her opinion, I have no case and that I could be prosecuted for filing a fraudulent claim if I do not drop my case.

I feel these threats are a direct attempt to intimidate and constitute a failure to deal in good faith. I request that your company immediately discontinue such activities.

Sincerely,

[Your name]

G. Settling Your Case

The insurance company will do its best to settle with you for the least amount of money possible. Your goal is to receive the amount you are rightly entitled to.

Some insurance companies may try to wear you out by delaying settlement. Others may try for a quick settlement in the hope that you lack knowledge and will settle your claim for less than you are entitled to. Above all, don't let yourself be pressured into settling before you're medically and vocationally ready.

Unless you're one of the lucky few for whom money is not a pressing concern, if you're on temporary disability, cut out all discretionary spending and put yourself on a tight budget. This will better prepare you to resist when the insurance company tries to tempt you to settle your case for less than it's worth.

Before you accept any settlement, take the time to carefully read Chapters 19 and 20 for details on how to figure out and negotiate a fair settlement. ∎

Dealing With Your Employer

Regardless of how well you and your employer get along, things can change—and often do—after a work injury. Especially if your injury is fairly serious, your employer can't count on your being able to resume your duties on a given date or at your old pace. It's very likely that your employer will fear that your injury will cause its workers' compensation insurance premiums to increase.

In the best of circumstances, your employer may support your efforts to get workers' compensation benefits so that you can recover and return to work. Unfortunately, it's probably more common for an employer to become unsympathetic, uncooperative and even hostile. If this is your situation, you may feel very vulnerable and helpless. You may feel that your boss is unfairly turning against you.

Understand that regardless of your employer's attitude about your injury, your employer has certain legal obligations. This chapter provides information about what your employer can and can't do, as well as some possible explanations as to why it may try to limit your benefits. Hopefully, by reading this chapter, you will be in a better position to protect your legal rights and deal with your employer in the best way possible.

WORKPLACE SAFETY: THE BEST WAY TO AVOID WORKERS' COMPENSATION CLAIMS

The easiest and best way for employers to prevent employees from filing workers' compensation claims is to prevent workplace injuries in the first place. Oftentimes, a workplace injury could have been prevented by the employer, had it implemented safety procedures or complied with regulations promulgated by Cal-OSHA (California Occupational, Safety and Health Administration).

Under LC § 6401.7, employers must establish an injury prevention program. Savvy employers will carefully study and track employee injuries, hold safety meetings and trainings and involve employees in identifying safety hazards. Employers that adopt a pro-active approach to making the workplace safer will find a marked decrease in employee work injuries and a corresponding decrease in their workers' compensation premiums. (For more on workplace safety, see *Your Rights in the Workplace,* by Barbara Kate Repa (Nolo) or *The Employer's Legal Handbook,* by Fred Steingold (Nolo).)

A. Self-Insured Employers

If an employer is large enough and meets certain requirements, it can legally be self-insured. This means that instead of paying premiums to an insurance company, the employer sets aside funds to pay workers' compensation claims directly to the insured worker. In other words, the employer becomes its own insurance company and is responsible for paying all workers' compensation claims. If your employer is permissibly self-insured, your employer has total control over every aspect of your claim.

In most cases, self-insured employers hire a claims adjusting service to manage and adjust (make recommendations regarding settlement) its workers' compensation claims. If so, you'll deal primarily with this entity. However, if the employer does not have a service, you will need to deal directly with the employer regarding all aspects of your claim, including settlement.

When we refer to the insurance company in this book, this also refers to self-insured employers who are acting as their own insurers.

B. The Employer/Insurance Company Relationship

It's important to realize from the onset that your employer is a separate business entity from its insurance company unless the employer is self-insured. Workers' compensation insurance works just like most insurance policies. Your employer pays the insurance company premiums determined by the number of workers, the amount of payroll paid, the type of work and the number of workers' compensation claims. In return, the insurance company provides your employer with a workers' compensation insurance policy. If the employer's workers suffer industrial injuries, the insurance company pays benefits.

The insurance company continually reviews how many claims have been filed and adjusts the employer's insurance premiums accordingly. Not surprisingly, adjustments are usually upward, especially if there have been any workers' compensation claims.

1. How Your Employer Can Help

It is unfair to suggest that all employers turn against injured workers. Some employers may express a sincere concern for the welfare of their injured employees and will go out of their way to help. This positive attitude is probably more prevalent with smaller employers who have close working relationships with their employees. Unfortunately, many employers, especially large corporate employers, are so concerned with the bottom line that an injured worker is looked upon as a disposable commodity.

If you are fortunate enough to have an employer who wants you to be treated fairly by its workers' compensation insurance company, request that your employer contact the insurance company and speak up on your behalf. Although the employer technically has little say about the outcome of your claim (unless it is self-insured), your employer can use its economic clout on your behalf. After all, it's the employer who decides which workers' compensation company to deal with and can always switch to another if its loyal employees are being treated unfairly.

2. How Your Employer Can Hurt Your Case

How the insurance company decides to handle claims can affect the amount of money your employer has to pay for workers' compensation insurance. Because workers' compensation insurance is mandatory in the state of California, your employer has no choice but to pay it or self-insure.

If a number of injured workers file claims for workers' compensation, the employers' workers compensation premiums will increase if the injury is very severe. Sometimes even one additional filing can trigger an increase. In addition, a workers' compensation claim may result in your employer's facing investigations or fines by state regulatory agencies, such as Cal-OSHA, for allowing unsafe work conditions.

While many employers will keep their noses out of their employee's workers' compensation claims, others will interfere.

a. Employer May Discourage Claims

Many employers realize that the only "real" control they have over costly insurance premiums is to try to limit the number of workers' compensation claims filed by injured workers. So a considerable number of employers, although they will not admit it, have unwritten (and illegal) policies designed to discourage their employees from filing claims. For example, some employers provide "bonuses" to all workers as a group if there are no workers' compensation claims filed during a quarter. If one employee files a claim, no one gets a bonus. This subjects employees to great peer pressure not to file a claim. When an employee files a workers' compensation claim, this type of employer may look upon the employee as a traitor, troublemaker or not a "team player."

A hostile employer may even attempt to harass or intimidate any employee who files a claim. The employer may attempt to make an example out of the injured employee to accomplish two things. First, the employer hopes to discourage other employees from filing a workers' compensation claim, even if they have serious injuries. Second, the employer wants to dissuade other employees from testifying on behalf of an injured employee at any workers' compensation hearing.

Illegal tactics employers sometimes implement include:
- reducing the number of the employee's work hours or overtime
- penalizing an employee, such as by writing the employee up (or putting a bad performance report in his file) for things he did not do
- verbally harassing the employee, such as by chastising the employee in front of other employees
- firing or laying off the employee, or
- if the employee is working, assigning him to the most difficult or boring duties.

If you are injured, never let your employer dissuade you from filing a claim and seeking medical attention. These unfair tactics, and any similar ones that have the effect of punishing an employee, constitute illegal discrimination. Under LC § 132(a), you or another employee who may be a witness on your behalf, may file a claim against your employer for discrimination. (See Chapter 16, Section C, for a complete discussion.)

b. Employer May Treat Claim as Fraudulent

Although most employers are responsible and treat their workers fairly, some employers take the position that employees' workers' compensation claims are almost always fraudulent and without merit. In rare instances, an employer may deliberately destroy an accident report and claim that the accident never occurred. I have even seen cases where the employer illegally threatened other employees by saying that they would be fired unless they testified against the injured worker.

Unfortunately, if your employer falsely advises its workers' compensation insurance company that your case is fraudulent, the insurance company is likely to investigate and possibly deny your claim. Although this will certainly be an inconvenience, it rarely will prevent you from ultimately getting benefits.

c. Employer May Prevent Settlement

Your employer has the right to veto or disapprove any settlement reached by you and the insurance company.

If your employer advises the insurance company that it disputes the validity of your workers' compensation claim, the employer must be notified of any workers' compensation hearings in your case. If your employer asks a workers' compensation judge in writing not to approve a proposed settlement agreement between you and the insurance company, the insurance company will probably not go forward with the settlement and your case will go to trial. If the insurance company proceeds with the settlement agreement over the employer's objection, it will not affect your settlement, but it could expose the insurance company to further proceedings by the employer.

For legitimate workers' compensation claims, employers will rarely try to prevent settlement. If your employer objects to a settlement without good reason, the court may impose a penalty upon the employer for acting in bad faith to cause unnecessary delay of the settlement of your claim. The employer may be required to pay you any expenses, including attorney fees and costs, that you incurred as a result of the delay. Although rare under LC § 5813, the judge also has the power to order the insurance company to pay a penalty of up to $2,500 to the General Fund (the checking account for the State of California). As you would also be entitled to payment of your expenses, including attorney fees, if it is found that your employer acted in bad faith, you should give serious consideration to getting an attorney at this time.

If you have a legitimate claim, you should never be afraid to go to trial, as you will generally gain more by going to trial because you did not give up anything to arrive at a compromised settlement figure.

C. The Employer's Responsibilities

An employer has a number of obligations under the workers' compensation system. If your employer does not fulfill these requirements, you may have legal recourse, ranging from being permitted to file a lawsuit to gaining control of your own medical treatment.

1. Employer Must Carry Workers' Compensation Insurance

If your employer lacks the workers' compensation coverage required by law you may do either or both of the following:

- **file a lawsuit against your employer in civil court.** You aren't limited to the benefits provided by workers' compensation in this case. For example, you may sue for lost wages as well as pain and suffering as a result of your industrial injury. Although this remedy may at first seem advantageous, its success depends on whether your employer is financially solvent enough to pay an eventual court judgment. Unfortunately, businesses that violate laws requiring them to maintain workers' compensation insurance are often close to insolvency.

  Winning a civil case against your uninsured employer should be merely a formality, as you don't need to prove that your employer was at fault for your injury. Uninsured employers are presumed responsible under the Labor Code. (LC § 3708.)

- **file a workers' compensation claim against the State of California Uninsured Employers Fund (UEF).** If you choose to file a workers' compensation claim, you'll need to follow the same paperwork procedures as with any other workers' compensation claim. However, also list the Uninsured Employer's Fund as a defendant. This fund is funded and run by the State of California to pay the claims of injured employees whose employers do not have workers' compensation coverage. (See Chapter 16, Section B.)

2. Employer Must Post Notices and Advise You of Your Legal Rights

Every employer must post certain notices in a convenient location frequented by employees during working hours. The notices contain important information about employees' rights and:

- provide the name of the company's workers' compensation carrier or the fact that the employer is self-insured, as well as who is responsible for claims adjustment
- state that injured workers have the right to receive medical treatment and to select or change treating doctors, and
- give details about available workers' compensation benefits. (LC § 3550; CCR § 9881.)

Employers must also notify new hires of the above information no later than the end of the first pay period. (LC § 3551; CCR § 9880.) If an employee requests it, the employer must provide a form to designate the personal physician by whom the employee wishes to be treated if injured at work. Some employers have contracted with at least two health care organizations to provide treatment for employees injured at work. At the time of hire, and at least once a year after, these employers must give employees an opportunity to designate a personal physician. (LC § 3552.)

Many employers fail to comply with all of the requirements listed just above. In that case, an injured worker is automatically allowed to choose which doctor will provide treatment for an industrial injury. (LC § 3550(a).) If your employer violated *any* posting or notice requirements, write a letter to the insurance company. Point out the violation and request that you immediately be allowed to treat with your doctor of choice. Remember to send the letter certified mail, return receipt requested.

3. Employer Must Provide Claim Forms and Pamphlet

If you were injured at work, your employer must provide you with a workers' compensation claim form DWC-1 within 24 hours of notification of the injury. (CCR § 10119.)

In addition, an employer has five days after it learns of a work-related injury to supply you with written information (usually a pamphlet) about your rights under the workers' compensation system. The written material explains your legal rights, and provides details about available benefits, procedures for filing a claim, when and how to contact an Information and Assistance officer and the fact that you're protected from discrimination. (CCR § 9882.)

If your employer fails to provide a DWC-1 form or give you written information on time, you may choose your personal doctor. Point out this fact in a letter to the insurance company and request that you immediately be allowed to treat with your doctor of choice. Remember to send the letter certified mail, return receipt requested.

D. If You're Out of Work Due to the Injury

This section applies only to employees who are off work because of their injuries. If you haven't lost work time, skip to Section E, below.

Being off work because of an injury can be a frightening and frustrating experience. Many injured workers cannot afford to lose much work time because temporary disability benefits paid under the workers' compensation system are not sufficient to live on. And of course, most employees have the reasonable fear of losing their jobs. While there are no hard and fast answers, the following suggestions should help you through this inevitably rough period.

SICK LEAVE AND VACATION

If you've accumulated vacation and sick leave at your job, it's yours to take whenever you wish. You are not required to take or use your vacation and sick time before drawing temporary disability payments under workers' compensation.

If you want to receive sick leave or vacation pay, see the discussion in Chapter 12, Section C5.

1. Communicate With Your Employer

If you're disabled and out of work, you need to ask yourself two questions: Do you want to return to work for this employer? Are you able—or will you be able—to go back to your old job?

If your answer is "yes" to both questions, it's an excellent idea to open up a line of communication with your employer. If your employer does not hear from you, it may assume the worst, especially if you were upset when you left or your accident or injury was your fault. Lack of communication may enforce an attitude that you are not a "team player" and that you only want to cost the company money. The employer may feel you are goofing off or trying to get a free ride.

If, on the other hand, you regularly check in with your boss, your employer is likely to see that you're still a loyal employee and you're doing your best to get better and get back to work. If possible, call your employer at least once a week and give an update about your condition and when you expect to return. If you feel it is appropriate, you may even want to tell your employer one or more of the following:

- You didn't want to file a workers' compensation claim, but since you were legitimately injured, you filled out the paperwork as required by law.
- You are looking forward to returning to your old job.
- Your main concern is to get better and get back to work as soon as possible.
- Your treating doctor has found that you did indeed suffer an injury at work.

2. Will Your Employer Keep Your Job for You?

Unfortunately, there is no law or legal policy that requires your employer to hold your job for you if you are injured or ill. Absent an employment contract to the contrary, your employer can terminate you at any time. Your employer cannot, however, retaliate against you—including terminating you—for filing a workers' compensation claim. If your employer has notice of or knows about your injury and does terminate you, your right to receive workers' compensation for any injury that has already occurred will not be affected.

Common sense dictates that your employer would prefer to have you return to work, rather than incur the time and expense involved in finding and training a replacement. But whether or not your employer is willing—or can afford—to hold your job for you will depend upon a variety of factors, including:

- how irreplaceable your employer perceives you to be
- how long you've been out and when you expect to be able to return
- how critical your position is to the overall operation of the business—in other words, how long your employer can comfortably operate without filling your position
- your employer's financial well-being
- the requirements of your employment contract, if you have one; many employment contracts require that the employer hold a job for a set amount of days, weeks or months, and
- your employer's willingness to put up with the inconvenience. How well you get along with your employer will likely contribute to its willingness to keep your job available. (See Section D1, above, on the importance of communicating with your employer.)

If you belong to a union, your union representative may be very helpful in negotiating on your behalf if your employer violated any provisions of your employment contract. Keep in touch with your union representative as your workers' compensation situation develops. That way, she can properly advise you of your rights under your employment contract, and assist you in enforcing them.

3. If Your Employer Offers an Alternate Job

If you can't ever return to the same type of work because of your injury, you may be entitled to a workers' compensation benefit known as vocational rehabilitation. This is a program designed to get you back to a job within your work restrictions.

If at all possible, you don't want to do anything that may jeopardize your future right to vocational rehabilitation if you need it. This is an area where you need to be very careful. Here's why. If you cannot return to your old job because of your disability, your employer may offer you an alternative position once you can do some work, sometimes at less pay. At the very least, your employer must inform you that alternative work is not available. If the job offers wages and compensation that are within 15% of those paid to you at the time of your injury, you must accept the job, or you will forfeit any future rights you have to vocational rehabilitation benefits. (For more on vocational rehabilitation, see Chapter 14.)

4. If You Go Back to Work

It's likely that you will return to work with your original employer long before your workers' compensation case settles. If that happens, you'll naturally be in close contact with your employer.

In most cases, going back to work is uneventful. You return, do your job and everything is the same as before the injury. It's a good idea, however, to be careful about what you say to your employer regarding your injury. Until your case settles, you should do your best not discuss your claim with your employer.

IF YOUR EMPLOYER HARASSES YOU

Sometimes an employer harasses a returning employee and starts laying a foundation for eventual termination. For example, the employer may single you out and write you up for things that other employees aren't being written up for. If you face problems with your employer, immediately see an Information and Assistance officer or consult a workers' compensation attorney.

E. Bankruptcy or Other Employer Financial Problems

As long as your employer had insurance coverage at the time of your injury, financial problems or bankruptcy by your employer will have no effect upon your workers' compensation case or your financial recovery. The insurance company makes decisions regarding settlement of your case and pays for the benefits you receive.

If, however, a bankrupt employer did not have workers' compensation insurance, or the employer is permissibly self-insured, you must file a claim with the bankruptcy court. You'll need to petition the bankruptcy court for what's called "relief from the automatic stay." Let's back up just a bit. When a bankruptcy petition is filed, an "automatic stay" goes into effect, which precludes any potential creditor (the telephone company, landlord or you) from proceeding with any actions, legal or otherwise, that would affect the bankruptcy. As an injured worker, you may ask the bankruptcy court to lift the automatic stay as far as you are concerned so that you can collect your workers' compensation benefits. (In situations such as these, it is best to get help from an Information and Assistance officer or contact a workers' compensation attorney.) ■

CHAPTER

9

Taking Charge of Your Medical Case

As an injured worker, you are entitled to receive medical care needed to cure or relieve your injury or illness at no cost to you. (LC § 4600.) That's great, you say. But wait; it's important to fully understand that the doctors who treat your medical problem will also make important decisions about the fate of your workers' compensation case. To best protect your legal rights, you'll need to address two important aspects of your medical treatment:

• the medical care you receive—you obviously want the right kind of high quality treatment, and

• how your medical treatment affects the legal status of your workers' compensation claim—you want to be sure your medical treatment supports and doesn't undermine your legal case.

In this chapter, you will learn about the importance of taking charge of your medical care, and how to do it. You may have seen some doctors already. That's fine. Reading this chapter should help you decide if it is in your best interest to keep seeing those doctors, and what to do if you decide it's not.

⚠ INJURIES BEFORE 1/1/94

The information contained in this chapter assumes your injury date is on or after 1/1/94. Significantly different laws apply to injuries before 1/1/94, as outlined in Appendix 1.

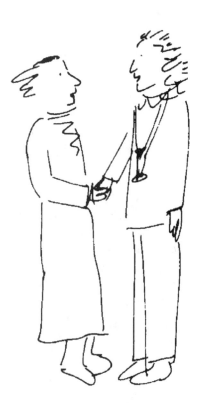

REIMBURSEMENT FOR TRAVEL AND MEDICAL EXPENSES

You are entitled to be reimbursed for costs of prescriptions, medical bills you paid and other costs associated with your medical care. You are also entitled to be paid for your round trip mileage to and from doctors' examinations, physical therapy sessions and trips to the pharmacy to pick up medications.

Keep copies of all medically related receipts and careful records of how much you travel. You'll need to submit these records to the insurance company when you request reimbursement. Chapter 11, Section A, gives step-by-step instructions.

A. Important Role of the Treating Doctor

The future of your workers' compensation case rests largely with the doctor who treats you or oversees treatment until you completely recover or your condition reaches a plateau. In workers' compensation jargon, this person is usually called the "treating doctor" or "primary treating doctor." Your treating doctor is so important to your workers' compensation case because she will report to the insurance company about the extent of your injury, your treatment and your prognosis for recovery. In addition, the treating doctor's opinion is generally presumed to be correct. (LC § 4062.9.)

If your primary treating doctor thinks it's necessary, she may refer you to treating doctors in other specialties (a heart specialist or orthopedist, for example) for treatment and consultation, but you will also continue to see and treat with your primary treating doctor.

1. How the Treating Doctor May Affect Your Case

Here are the main issues your primary treating doctor will address and convey to the insurance company:

• **Were you injured on the job?** If the treating doctor decides your injury or symptoms are consistent with your story of how the injury occurred, the insurance company will be more likely to accept your claim and agree to provide benefits.

- **What will be the type and extent of your treatment?** The treating doctor has the power to say you don't need any treatment. If you do need treatment, she may prescribe the type of treatment and medication you need. It's also up to the treating doctor to decide if you need physical therapy, chiropractic care and other types of help.
- **Do you need to see specialists?** It is up to the treating doctor to recognize when additional tests are necessary, or when you need to see a specialist in another medical field. If the treating doctor fails to live up to these responsibilities, you quite possibly won't receive the excellent medical treatment that you deserve.
- **Are you temporarily disabled?** The treating doctor determines whether you should return to work immediately or take some time off. If you need time off from work as a result of your injury, you are entitled to temporary disability payments. The treating doctor also decides when you are well enough to go back to work. Some doctors are very reasonable when it comes to making this determination; others are not.

  EXAMPLE: Joanne, who was working for a major grocery chain, injured her back when a heavy metal shelf gave way and fell on her. Although tests showed that Joanne had herniated (ruptured) two disks in her back, and she was in great pain, the treating doctor told her she could immediately go back to work. Eventually, Joanne required back surgery because of her injury.

  If you feel you need time off work to recover, don't hesitate to mention this to your doctor.
- **When is your condition "permanent and stationary?"** This bit of legal jargon means that your medical condition has reached a plateau, and additional treatment at this time is not expected to further improve your condition. Your doctor makes this determination, which can have a big effect on your monetary benefits.
- **Can you ever return to your former job?** The treating doctor is normally a crucial decision-maker in determining whether or not you can return to your former job. If you can go back, she may determine whether you can work full- or part-time, and whether your job will need to be modified to accommodate your disability. The treating doctor's findings will also affect your qualification for additional workers' compensation benefits, such as vocational rehabilitation.
- **Do you have a permanent disability or need future medical care?** The treating doctor's opinions on issues of whether you are permanently disabled and whether you need future medical treatment are presumed correct. This determination will greatly affect any financial settlement.

YOU ARE ENTITLED TO A SECOND OPINION

As we will discuss in detail in Chapter 10, if you or the insurance company objects to any of the treating doctor's findings, the objecting party may obtain another medical opinion. This is called a medical-legal evaluation. We mention this now to reassure you that all is not bleak if you end up with a treating doctor you don't trust.

There can be only one *primary* treating doctor at a time. If you are seeing or have seen more than one doctor for treatment, you'll need to establish which one is your primary treating doctor. The primary treating doctor must be identified in your permanent and stationary medical report. She must have examined you at least once for the purpose of rendering or prescribing treatment and must have monitored the effect of the treatment afterwards.

2. Treating Doctor Decides Whether You Should Return to Work

Following your injury, the treating doctor will determine whether your medical condition is such that you need time off or if you may return to your job.

a. Off Work Order

If the doctor determines that you need time off to recuperate, she will give you an off work order, either in the form of a note or written prescription. The off work order will specify a set period of time, usually a week or two for fairly minor injuries, that you should not work. The order will also specify a return appointment date (before the expiration of the order), at which time the doctor will decide if the off work order needs to be extended.

You must give the off work order to your employer or see that it's mailed or faxed. The off work order specifies that you are out due to an industrial injury and therefore not absent without reason.

b.   Limited Duties Work Order (Restrictions)

The doctor may determine that you need to take it easy, but that it's okay to return to work with limited duties (restricting certain activities that you can do at work). If so, the doctor will give you a note—called a limited duties, light or modified work order—indicating what those work restrictions are. A typical limited duties work order might be "no lifting at or above shoulder level," "no prolonged sitting," "no repetitive gripping or grasping" or "no climbing ladders." Make sure your employer gets this order promptly on the day you return to work; otherwise, you will be expected to do your normal duties.

c.   Return to Work Order

Another possibility is that the doctor may issue a written note indicating that you may return to your work without any restrictions (or with restrictions that aren't meaningful, given your injury). In essence, this means that your injury doesn't affect your ability to perform your duties.

If, in fact, you have fully recovered, that's great! Your goal should be to return to work as soon as possible. Unfortunately, some doctors try to get employees back to work as quickly as possible to save the employer and its insurance company some money. Even if a doctor acting in the best of faith returns you to work without restrictions (or with restrictions that don't adequately protect you), always remember that this determination is only an opinion. *The doctor can be wrong!*

The safest way to cope with what you believe is an erroneous return to work order is to call the insurance company and explain the problem. Then report to work. If you don't do so, your employer may legally fire you because you failed to report to work without a good excuse. If this occurs, you'll face an uphill battle trying to convince your employer that your opinion is more reliable than the doctor's.

If, after returning to work, you believe you cannot do your job—even if you have only tried for a few minutes—inform your supervisor and ask that you be authorized to return to the doctor for further treatment and evaluation. By law, your employer must honor your request. When you see the doctor, clearly explain that you returned to your job but could not continue working because of pain or an inability to perform the work. The doctor must reevaluate her position and will, in all probability, give you an off work order.

d.   If You Disagree With the Doctor's Order

If the doctor refuses to take you off work, or insists on restrictions that are completely unrealistic (you can't lift your right arm without pain and the doctor says not to lift more than 50 pounds), immediately call the workers' compensation insurance company (ask for the adjuster handling your case) or your employer. Explain what happened, why you are dissatisfied, and demand another treating doctor. By law, you are entitled to a one-time change of doctors *within five working days* of your request. If the insurance company does not provide you with the name of another doctor in that time, you may choose your own doctor, as discussed in Section C1, below.

e.   If You Are Reinjured or Your Condition Worsens

If you go back to work and reinjure yourself, in workers' compensation terms, the reinjury will be considered either:

- **an aggravation**—a new injury. In this case, you should fill out the paperwork required to file a new workers' compensation claim.
- **an exacerbation**—a worsening or flare-up of the same injury.

If your doctor concludes your new pain is an exacerbation of your original injury, your medical options depend on the status of your case:

If you have not yet settled your case, you're in luck. You can simply continue to be treated by your doctor until you are once again declared to be permanent and stationary and the doctor writes a final report setting forth your increased factors of disability.

If you have settled your case by Stipulations With Request for Award (see Chapter 19, Section A), the insurance company will pay for the medical treatment you need. You may need to get prior approval from the insurance company.

However, if you have already settled your claim by Compromise and Release (see Chapter 19, Section B), you may be out of luck. The only way you can get workers' compensation benefits in this case is to file a new workers' compensation claim, and you can do this only if you can show that at least 1% of your current disability is due to your current employment, not your prior injury. If your doctor says your problems are due 100% to your prior injury, you may have to get a medical-legal evaluation to decide the issue (see Chapter 10).

Either way, you should immediately report any additional problems to your supervisor and request a medical appointment with your doctor.

3. The Treating Doctor's Reports

While you are being treated for your injuries, the treating doctor is required to send written reports to the insurance company to keep it apprised of your condition and prognosis. If you have more than one treating doctor, it's likely that each specialist will write a report and the primary treating doctor will write a comprehensive summary report.

GET COPIES OF TREATING DOCTOR'S REPORTS
If you send a request to your employer and the insurance company, they must send you copies of medical reports. See Chapter 6, Section D, for instructions.

a. Doctor's First Report of Industrial Injury

Within five days of the initial examination, any doctor who treats an injured employee for an industrial injury must prepare a standard report that sets forth each treated occupational injury and illness. This is true for one-time treatments as well as emergency room treatments.

The first report of industrial injury is important because it is close to the date of injury. As such, the insurance company will often rely on it when initially determining whether to accept or deny your claim. The doctor will mail the first report of industrial injury to the insurance company, or, if the employer is self-insured, to the employer. (LC § 6409.)

b. Periodic Medical Reports

Assuming your claim is accepted, the treating doctor must file reports with the insurance company at least once every 30 days. The insurance company will carefully review these interim reports, which give an update of your condition. If you're receiving temporary disability, the insurance company will stop paying if the reports indicate you have recovered or can return to work.

Sometimes insurance companies cut off temporary disability payments if the treating doctor fails to keep the insurance company informed as required. If this occurs, you may need to act as a go-between with your treating doctor and the insurance carrier. Do this by immediately calling and writing your doctor and urging her to file the necessary reports.

c. Permanent and Stationary Report

When your treating doctor concludes that your condition is stable and additional medical treatment at this time will not help you improve, she will write a "permanent and stationary report." From the date of this report, you are no longer judged to be temporarily disabled under the terms of the workers' compensation law, and any temporary disability payments you have been receiving will stop.

The permanent and stationary report will incorporate the opinions of any specialists and will discuss such critical issues as the nature and extent of your permanent disability, your need for future medical treatment and your qualification for vocational rehabilitation benefits.

d. What to Do If You Object to a Medical Report

Carefully review the first report and each and every interim medical report, as well as the permanent and stationary report. If you object to anything significant in any treating doctor's report, you must make a written objection.

You must make your objection within 30 days of receipt of the medical report (20 days if you have a lawyer) if you object to your treating doctor's opinion regarding:

- issues of permanent and stationary status
- need for or reasonableness of your current medical treatment
- determination of whether you are a qualified injured worker (QIW) and thus eligible for vocational rehabilitation, or
- determination of most other medical issues, except compensability (whether your injury is covered under workers' compensation).

SAMPLE OBJECTION TO MEDICAL REPORT

Date

[Name of insurance company]
[Address]

Injured worker: [Your name]
Employer: [Employer's name]
Date of Injury: [Date]
Claim Number: [Number]

To Whom It May Concern:

Please be advised that I object to the findings of [doctor's name], my treating doctor, as set forth in her report of [date].

Specifically, I dispute the doctor's opinion regarding the following issues: [list those that apply]

1. My permanent and stationary status [or permanent and stationary date]
2. A finding that I no longer require medical treatment
3. My QIW status
4. The nature and extent of my permanent disability
5. My need for future medical treatment
6. Compensability of my injury
7. Apportionment
8. New and further disability
9. Other: _____

Please provide me with a form to request a QME panel.

Sincerely,

[Your name]

There are no time limits as to when you must object to the treating doctor's opinion regarding compensability, the nature and extent of your permanent disability or the need for future medical treatment. (But, of course, you must object before settlement or trial.)

 TREATING DOCTOR'S REPORT IS PRESUMED CORRECT
The findings of the treating physician are presumed to be correct under LC § 4062.8. Therefore, if you are satisfied with that report, you need do nothing. If your case goes to trial, the judge must rely upon the treating doctor's findings unless he believes that other medical reports are more believable.

 See *Minniear v. Mt. San Antonio Community College* in Chapter 28.

B. Choose Your Treating Doctor (Get Medical Control in Your Case)

Whoever selects your treating doctor obviously has great input and control over how your case will be handled. Unfortunately, as pointed out earlier, many employers and insurance companies pick doctors who will make decisions that will save them money, even if these decisions are not in your best interests. Doctors who are financially dependent on insurance company referrals quickly understand that if they want referrals to continue, they had better make workers' compensation-related decisions cost effective from the insurer's point of view.

And what makes employers and insurance companies appreciate a doctor so much that they make referrals? For one thing, getting you back to work as soon as conceivably possible. The sooner you're back to work, the less medical treatment and temporary disability indemnity they have to pay. Another thing that makes insurance companies happy is a diagnosis that you are 100% healed, or have very minimal disability as a result of your work injury. Finally, insurance companies are always pleased with a finding that you don't need any ongoing medical attention.

1. Designate Your Treating Doctor in Advance

The only sure way you can get immediate control in case of a work injury is by giving your employer *advance written notice* of your treating doctor. This must be your personal physician (or medical group) or chiropractor. Your personal physician is the doctor you regularly see, who has previously directed your medical treatment, and who retains your medical records. (LC § 4600.)

If you already reported an injury to your boss and did not previously designate a treating doctor, you are too late to do so for your present injury. It's still worthwhile to designate your doctor, however, in case you're ever injured again.

 DESIGNATE A DOCTOR BEFORE YOU REPORT A GRADUALLY OCCURRING INJURY

If you believe you have an injury that developed over time, such as a cumulative trauma injury, it's wise to designate your treating doctor before advising your employer of your injury.

To designate a treating doctor, simply notify your employer in writing. No special form is required, but you may wish to use the Employee's Designation of Personal Physician form provided in Appendix 4. Keep a copy for your records.

Note that you are entitled to designate only *one* primary treating doctor. That doctor will have authority to refer you to other medical specialists if he feels that's appropriate. Your safest bet is to designate a medical group, if you normally go there for treatment. That way, even if your injury is somewhat unusual, you can see the appropriate doctor within the medical group.

If your employer doesn't allow you to, or you don't wish to designate a group, choose a doctor who you feel comfortable with and who will refer you to appropriate specialists if needed. This could be your family physician or another personal physician. If you want to receive chiropractic care if it's warranted, make sure your medical doctor is willing to make referrals to chiropractors.

2. When You May See Your Doctor of Choice After an Injury

If you didn't designate your doctor in advance, you still may have the opportunity to immediately select your treating doctor rather than going to someone hand-picked by your employer. You may choose your treating doctor from the start in any of these situations:

- Your employer leaves the decision up to you.
- Your employer refuses to authorize (agree to pay for) treatment.
- Your employer has contracted with at least two health care organizations to provide medical treatment for employees injured due to work and you were not advised of your

---

EMPLOYEE'S DESIGNATION OF PERSONAL PHYSICIAN
(California Labor Code Section 4600)

To _____ :
    Name of Employer

In the event I am injured at work and require medical treatment, I designate the following as my personal physician:

_____
Name of Physician, Chiropractor or Medical Facility

_____
Address of Physician, Chiropractor or Medical Facility

_____
Telephone Number

_____   _____
Date   Signature of Employee

Given to: _____
      Name of Employer Representative

right to pre-designate your treating physician in writing when you were hired, by the end of the first pay period, and at least once a year after. (LC § 3551.)

- Your employer failed to properly post notices of your workers' compensation rights or advise you of your right to pre-designate your doctor when you were hired or by the end of your first pay period.
- After being informed of your injury, your employer did not provide you with claim forms and information about workers' compensation benefits, as discussed in Chapter 8, Section C3.
- You can go to the emergency room of your choice if you require emergency medical care.

a. If Your Employer Leaves the Decision Up to You

If you gave your employer an opportunity to tell you what doctor to go to for medical treatment and your employer declined, you are free to treat with whomever you want. However, if your employer did not have a chance to name the doctor you should see (as might be the case where you first go to the emergency room), you haven't been given the go-ahead to choose doctors. Your employer can select a doctor at its first opportunity.

b. If Your Employer Won't Authorize Medical Treatment

What happens if your employer or the insurance company says you are not eligible for medical treatment and refuses to authorize it? Your first step, of course, is to get needed treatment yourself. After all, your health is most important.

It's quite common for workers' compensation insurance companies to refuse treatment, claiming that your injury did not happen as a result of your work, or that you are not injured and do not need treatment. Do not panic if this occurs. You still have an excellent chance of getting workers' compensation coverage. Indeed, close to 90% of all claims or requests for medical treatment that are denied by employers or insurance companies are ultimately accepted or found to be valid by the Workers' Compensation Appeals Board.

It can even be to your advantage if you're denied medical treatment. By refusing to authorize treatment, the insurance company waives the right to designate your doctor. You are therefore free to go to any doctor you choose who is willing to treat you. (LC § 4600.)

The next question is, how do you get medical treatment when the insurance company won't pay? You may choose to seek treatment at a free medical clinic or county hospital. Barring that, there are generally four ways to obtain medical treatment:

- **Pay for treatment yourself.** If your workers' compensation case is accepted, you are entitled to be reimbursed by the insurance company for all treatment that was reasonably necessary. If you self-procure, be sure you get reimbursed from the insurance company if your case settles. If the insurance company won't reimburse you, you'll have to make this an issue at your trial.
- **Use your group health insurance coverage.** If you have group health insurance coverage provided directly by a health maintenance organization, such as Kaiser, or under a plan by which an insurance company reimburses doctors, use it. Your prepaid health insurance plan will provide or pay for treatment and file a green lien (discussed just below). The group company will be repaid by the workers' compensation insurance company at the end of the case. Be sure to tell your group insurance company that you injured yourself at work.
- **Find a doctor who is willing to file a "green lien."** You may ask the doctor you want to treat with if she is willing to treat you without payment and instead file a lien form in your workers' compensation case. This procedure is called a "green lien" in the jargon of the workers' compensation trade because the form is green. By filing a green lien, the doctor is entitled to be paid if you are found to have a valid workers' compensation claim. In short, the doctor agrees to wait for payment until your workers' compensation case settles. The green lien can be filed by the doctor any time prior to settlement or a trial on the merits of your claim.

Unless the doctor is familiar with the workers' compensation system and has treated injured workers in the past, it is unlikely that she will agree to file a green lien. In short, you may have to call around to find a doctor who devotes at least part of her practice to workers' compensation cases. In the event you don't qualify for workers' compensation, it is possible that you may be personally responsible for payment of your medical treatment.

- **File for an Appeals Board hearing.** You may ask a workers' compensation judge to decide whether you are entitled to receive medical care. (See Chapter 22, Section B.)

c. If Your Employer Failed to Post Proper Notices

Your employer is required by law to post a notice advising its employees about their rights under the California workers' compensation laws. If your employer failed to post such a notice prior to your injury, it forfeits its right to control your medical treatment and you are free to choose your own doctor. You should therefore check your workplace (or ask a co-worker or friend to do it) after your injury to see if the proper notice is posted. Doing this is not a waste of time, as many small employers, particularly, don't bother to post notices, or post them in a place where employees never go. (See Chapter 8, Section C2, for a detailed explanation of the notice posting requirements.)

d. If Your Employer Failed to Advise You of Your Right to Pre-Designate Your Treating Doctor in Writing

In addition to posting notices, your employer is required to give you written notice of your right to pre-designate your treating doctor in the event of an injury. This must be done at the time you are hired or by the end of the first pay period. (LC § 3551, CCR § 9880.)

Also, where your employer has contracted with at least two health care organizations to treat employees who suffer work injuries, your employer is required to place in your employment file either your choice of treating doctor or a signed statement that you declined to pre-designate a treating doctor in the event of an injury. This must be done at the time you are hired, and at least once a year after that.

If your employer failed to advise you of your right to pre-designate your treating doctor, you are free to choose your own doctor for treatment. (LC § 4600.3.) Because many employers fail to do this, it can be a valuable way to be sure you are treated by a doctor of your choice.

EXAMPLE: Jacob is injured at work. He informs his employer and requests to see a doctor. His employer tells him to go see the industrial medical clinic doctor. Jacob tells his employer he wants to treat with his own doctor because he feels he'll get better treatment. He tells his employer (or its insurance company) that he has the right to choose his own doctor because the employer failed to advise him of his workers' compensation rights in writing as required by LC § 3551. Jacob goes to his own doctor.

C. Changing Treating Doctors

As you now know, if you're injured and you haven't previously designated your treating doctor in writing, your employer or its insurance company has the right to choose the treating doctor (subject to the exceptions discussed in Section B2, above). But after you see this doctor, you have the right to change treating doctors, subject to certain rules.

YOUR RIGHT TO A SECOND OPINION

In addition to the other rights discussed in this section, if yours is a "serious" injury, you have the right to the services of a consulting doctor or chiropractor. In other words, you can check the first doctor's diagnosis with a second opinion. (LC § 601.) You do this by making a spoken or written demand on the insurance company.

What is considered a "serious" injury is anybody's guess, and may be the subject of contention with the insurance company. But if you feel your injury is serious enough to require a second opinion, by all means, demand it.

---

1. Automatic One-Time Change at Any Time

The good news is that you may request a *one-time* change of doctors from the insurance company at any time. (LC § 4601.) Unfortunately, there is also bad news. The doctor you change to will also be selected by the insurance company if it acts within five working days of your request. If you make your initial request by mail, you must allow an additional five days from the date of mailing, for a total of ten days.

The insurance company must provide you with the name and address of an alternative doctor as well as an appointment date. The information may be given to you by telephone, in writing or by any other means.

Pay careful attention to the five-day deadline. Often you can use your right to an automatic one-time change of doctors to get a doctor of your own choosing. Here's why. The insurance company's paperwork often will not allow it to respond to your request with five working days. If you aren't given the alternative doctor information within the five-day deadline, you are free to choose your own treating doctor. Do not count the day of the request in the five days. (See Section C5, below, for instructions on how to change doctors.)

EXAMPLE: Chris reports injuring his knee at work on Wednesday, July 18. The following day, the insurance company tells him to see Dr. Adelberg for treatment, which he does. Chris calls the insurance company on Monday, July 23rd, explains that he is not happy with Dr. Adelberg, and requests a different treating doctor. The company does not give Chris the name of an alternative doctor within five working days, so on Tuesday, July 31st, Chris sets up an appointment with Dr. Shell. Chris writes the insurance carrier a note explaining that he has decided to treat with Dr. Shell because he wasn't given the name of an alternative doctor within the allotted time.

2. Changing a Pre-Designated Treating Doctor

If you pre-designated your treating doctor in the event of industrial injury, you are free to change doctors at any time. Simply notify the insurance company of the change.

3. If Your Employer Did Not Offer Choice of Health Care Organizations (30-Day Wait)

 If your employer has contracted with at least two health care organizations to provide medical treatment for injured employees, skip to Section C4, below, to locate the rules that apply to you.

If your employer refers you to a doctor or medical group after you report an injury (but did not previously give you the choice of two health care organizations), you may usually change doctors after 30 days from the date of injury. You simply advise the insurance company that you are exercising your right to "free choice" and designate the doctor you want to treat with. From that point on, the company must honor your choice and pay your own doctor to treat you. (LC § 4600.3.) See the instructions in Section C5, below.

If, however, your doctor has reported that you won't need further medical treatment in the future and that your condition is "permanent and stationary" (further medical treatment at this time will not improve your condition), you do not have the

automatic right to change treating doctors. Instead, if you disagree, you must select a qualified medical evaluator (QME) to reevaluate your medical condition. (Chapter 10 discusses QMEs.)

4. If Your Employer Offered Choice of Health Care Organizations (90-, 180- or 365-Day Wait)

If your employer did not offer at least two health care organizations to treat with, skip this section.

Things are about to get a little confusing, so pay close attention. Your right to get rid of a doctor you don't like depends on what kind of health care coverage your employer offers. Obviously, this may require some checking on your part.

If your employer has contracted with at least two health care organizations to provide medical treatment to injured employees, and you chose one of the two, this organization now becomes your treating medical facility, and the doctor you see there will be your treating doctor. However, if you were given a choice and never exercised it, your employer or its insurance company has the right to choose which organization you must go to if you are injured.

Assuming you go to one of the health care organizations your employer has contracted with, you usually will be assigned to one "primary care" doctor, who will be considered your "treating doctor" for workers' compensation purposes. If you want to see another doctor or a specialist, you must first get permission from this primary care doctor.

You do have the right to change doctors on request within the health care organization. Within five days of a written or oral request, the health care organization must provide you with a list of participating doctors. (Although not specifically set forth in the law, I would argue that you have the right to go to a doctor of your own choice if you are not given the list of participating doctors within five working days of your request.) You also have the right to a second opinion from a participating doctor regarding a diagnosis from another participating doctor.

Even if your employer contracts with two health maintenance organizations and you were sent to one, you eventually have the right to stop going to the health care organization and instead to see a doctor of your choosing. But when you may choose to switch doctors depends on the kind of non-industrial medical coverage your employer offers, if any.

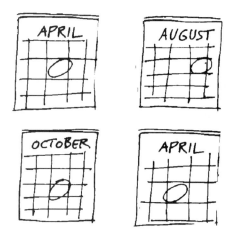

a. No Ordinary Health Care Coverage Offered by Employer (90-Day Wait)

If your employer doesn't offer health care coverage for non-industrial needs (this is entirely separate from any workers' compensation coverage related to your injury), you may change to a doctor of your choice after 90 days from the date you reported the injury to your employer.

> **EXAMPLE:** Jay is injured while working for Central Engineering. Central has contracted with two health care organizations to provide medical treatment to its employees only if they are injured on the job. Central provides no other health coverage for its employees. Jay must go to Central's health care organization for treatment for 90 days from the date he notified the employer of his injury. After that, he can freely choose another doctor.

b. Ordinary Health Care Coverage Offered by Employer (180- or 365-Day Wait)

Your employer is deemed to have offered ordinary health care coverage if it offers to pay more than half the costs of the coverage, or if the plan is established under a union collective bargaining agreement. In this situation, your right to change doctors depends on whether or not your primary care physician (your family doctor) participates in the health care organization.

- **If your doctor is not participating in the health care organization.** If you have been treated by a health care organization for your industrial injury, you may exercise your right of free choice of treating doctor after 180 days from the date

you reported your injury, or upon the date of contract renewal or open enrollment of the health care organization, whichever occurs first.

> **EXAMPLE:** Lori works for Beta Tools. Beta contracts with two health care organizations to provide health care coverage for its employees who are injured on the job. The contract also provides employees with the option of regular health care coverage, with Beta picking up 50% of the monthly cost. Lori decides not to participate in the ordinary health care plan, because she's covered under her husband's health insurance. Lori suffers an industrial injury on 3/3/01. The open enrollment for the health care plan is 12/1/02. This means she doesn't have the right to choose her own doctor from outside the health care organization until 180 days from the date she notified her employer of the injury. However, if the health care organization's net open enrollment date was 5/1/01, Lori could have chosen her own doctor after only 58 days.

- **If your doctor is participating in at least one of the two health care organizations offered.** If you are treating with one of the health care facilities, you may choose a treating doctor of your choice after 365 days from the date your injury was reported, or upon the date of contract renewal or open enrollment, whichever occurs first.

> **EXAMPLE:** Let's take the same example given above with Lori. This time, however, Lori's doctor participates in one of the two health care organizations. Lori cannot choose another doctor until 365 days from the date she reported the injury to her employer.

 IF YOU DON'T GET TO SEE YOUR PERSONAL DOCTOR, DON'T MENTION HER NAME

The only way the insurance company can determine if your personal doctor is participating in one of the plans offered to you is to review your medical records and check the names of all the doctors you have seen against the names of the doctors who participate in the offered plans. If, for some reason, you are forced to see a specialist you don't know or like, and you don't volunteer the information that your personal doctor also works with the plan, it is unlikely the insurance company will have the time or the inclination to check up on this. In all likelihood, you'd be able to choose a doctor after 180 days, instead of 365 days.

5. How to Request Change of Treating Doctors

 IF THE TREATING DOCTOR WROTE A PERMANENT AND STATIONARY REPORT

If your permanent and stationary report (discussed in A3, above) states that you don't need any more medical care, you no longer have the right to choose a different treating doctor. Instead, if you disagree, you must choose what workers' compensation jargon refers to as a qualified medical evaluator (QME) to determine if you need further treatment. Chapter 10 covers QMEs and how to pick one.

If, after reading Sections C1-4 just above, you've concluded that you have the right to change treating doctors, you must notify the insurance company. It's wise to call the insurance company, and then promptly send a confirming letter by certified mail, return receipt requested. Legally, your request need not be in writing. (CCR § 9781.)

SAMPLE LETTER REQUESTING OR NOTIFYING OF CHANGE OF TREATING DOCTORS

February 4, 2002

Acme Insurance
1200 Pepper Road
Anytown, CA 99999

Certified Mail, Return Receipt Requested

Injured Employee: Perry Downing
Employer: Jeffrey Sporting Goods
Date of Injury: 1/2/01
Claim No.: JT 372-B

To whom it may concern:

As discussed in our telephone conversation today, I have requested a one-time change of treating doctors pursuant to Labor Code Section 4601. Please provide the name and address of another doctor as required.

or

As discussed in our telephone conversation today, I am exercising my right of free choice of doctors. Accordingly, I select Dr. Joan Jenson, 3333 West 6th St., Anytown, CA 99999 as my treating doctor. Effective immediately, I will no longer be treating with Dr. Bruce Fellows.

Sincerely,

Perry Downing

Perry Downing

After the required waiting time has passed (30, 90, 180 or 365 days), you may change treating doctors as many times as is reasonably necessary unless your doctor has already designated your condition as permanent and stationary and stated that you don't need any more medical care. The insurance company may tell you that you only have the right to one "free choice" doctor. This is not true, as long as the change is reasonably necessary. (The insurance company will strenuously object if you change doctors for no reason.) Reasonably necessary, in my opinion, would include such reasons as:

- the treating doctor is not readily available (you can't get appointments within a reasonable time)
- the treating doctor is not providing adequate treatment (you are in real distress, but the doctor doesn't seem to take your symptoms seriously)
- the treating doctor is prejudiced against you for some reason
- you and the treating doctor simply don't get along, or
- the treating doctor is insisting on unreasonable and unwarranted tests.

6. If the Insurance Company Refuses Your Request to Change Treating Doctors

If you have followed the rules set forth in this chapter and the insurance company will not recognize your right to change your treating doctor, immediately write a letter. Explain that under the law as set forth in the court case *Emporium-Capwell Co. v. WCAB (Tidwell)*, 48 CCC 801 (1983), you have the right to change treating doctors at any time after waiting the appropriate time from the date of injury. If the insurance company still refuses authorization, you have several ways to get medical treatment, as discussed in Section B2b, above.

 See *Ralph's Grocery Store v. WCAB (Lara)* in Chapter 28.

D. Be Sure You Receive Excellent Medical Care

You should be an active participant in your medical treatment and healing. After all, you are the only one with a 100% interest and commitment to your own health. The more you know about your condition and treatment, the better able you will be to get the best possible medical care.

1. Knowing What to Say to the Doctor

For most people, seeing a doctor can be an intimidating experience. This is especially true if the doctor was selected by your employer and you're worried that you may receive an inadequate diagnosis or treatment. Even if you selected your own medical clinic or doctor, you still may be a little concerned. This is not only understandable, it's sensible. No matter how pleasant or impersonal the doctor appears, you should always protect your legal rights.

a. Come to the Exam Prepared

If possible, bring a friend or family member to the examination. It's always nice to have the support of a loved one. In addition, that person may be called on later to verify what happened in the examination.

Be prepared to keep a record of what is said. Take a pad and pencil with you to your examination. If the doctor appears to be hostile or to ask intensive questions about your personal activities, jot down these questions along with your responses. If the doctor sees that you are making a record, he may be less likely to make an "erroneous" report.

b. Give a Complete Medical History

The medical history you provide should include the following:
- **How you were injured**. Give a complete and detailed description of the workplace-related events that led up to your injury. If you were outside the workplace itself (driving on an office-related errand or attending a seminar required by your job), make sure you emphasize the fact that you were doing your job.
- **All specific body parts you may have injured**. Make sure the doctor records information about all of the parts of your body you think you may have injured. Be as thorough as possible, even if you think you only injured a certain body part or you think it's a minor problem. The workers' compensation insurance company is likely to deny coverage for any injured body part not reported promptly.

EXAMPLE: Sally slips and falls at work, hitting both her head and right knee. The knee causes such extreme pain that Sally forgets to tell the doctor about her mild headache. A month and a half later, Sally realizes she's had constant and worsening headaches since the accident and she requests medical treatment. The insurance company claims that any head problems are not covered by workers' compensation, since Sally did not tell the doctor about them at the time of the accident.

REPORT EVEN EMBARRASSING INJURIES

Never neglect to report an injury, even if you're embarrassed about the part of the body injured (you have a pain in your butt or genitals) or how the injury occurred.

- **An accurate history of any prior injuries**. Be sure to give a complete history about any prior related medical problems the doctor asks about. Do this even if you suspect that the information may be used to show that your present medical problems are due to prior medical problems. If you fail to mention possible related problems when asked (say the fact that your back was injured before), you may end up in a bad situation. For example, the insurance company may get copies of prior medical reports and deny your claim altogether by attributing it to injuries you hid. But don't get carried away. While you always want to be honest about your prior medical history, you also want to insist that your injury was caused by your current on-the-job injury, not by a flare-up of an old problem (if that's the truth). The best way to do this is usually to explain how the injury occurred in direct, and if necessary, graphic, terms.

EXAMPLE: Tommy sees Dr. Wu after injuring his ankle while working in a cafeteria. Tommy had broken his ankle five years earlier, playing basketball. He was treated at the emergency room at that time, and had follow-up care with his family doctor. Dr. Wu asks Tommy if he ever injured his ankle before. Tommy should tell the doctor about his prior injury and explain that he made a complete recovery. Tommy has absolutely no incentive to cover up the earlier injury, because the insurance company will surely obtain Tommy's past medical records and learn about it anyway. What Tommy should do is to emphasize how the current injury occurred: "I slipped on a greasy spot in the cafeteria and had a hard fall. As I went down, I felt my ankle twist slowly and then felt an extremely painful moment when my whole ankle seemed to fly apart."

c.   What Not to Tell a Doctor

To protect yourself from having your workers' compensation claim denied, there are certain things you should never say:

Rule 1.   Never speculate that it's possible that your injury may have occurred outside of work. To be eligible for workers' compensation benefits, your injury must have occurred as a result of your employment.

Rule 2.   Never say that you are 100%, or completely, recovered from your injury, unless that's absolutely true. If you do, you will not receive a permanent disability award that you might otherwise be entitled to.

Rule 3.   Never exaggerate your injury. Doctors are very good at spotting individuals who exaggerate their problems. If a doctor notes that you were exaggerating your pain or other symptoms, the insurance company may believe that you are faking your injury and deny a claim that otherwise might be allowed. (Don't understate your condition either. As long as you are truthful, you will avoid most problems.)

Rule 4.   Never say or do anything to antagonize the doctor. If you don't like the doctor's manner, either politely tell the doctor what's bothering you or don't say anything at all and exercise your right to change doctors (or if the injury is serious, get a second opinion).

d.   Watch Out for Inappropriate Questions by the Doctor

Some doctors, especially those selected by insurance companies or employers, may ask questions that seem to blame you for the injury. Although your actions rarely have anything to do with your entitlement to coverage (it's a no-fault system, remember), a doctor may establish the basis to deny you coverage. For example, a doctor may try to show that your injury was not work-related, was caused by something fairly outrageous you did, such as horseplay or starting a fight, or was the result of your intoxication or misuse of drugs. (It will help to read Chapter 3, Section D, which discusses when injuries may not be covered.)

A question like, "Isn't it possible your back hurts because of your gardening activities at home?" or "Do you ride horses or play an active sport like softball or soccer?" should be a red flag. Remember, the information you provide will be put in the doctor's report to the insurance company with an opinion on how you were injured. This report can make or break your claim.

If you face any hostile or trick questions by the doctor, slow down. Answer each question very carefully—and truthfully—so there can be no misunderstanding. For example, if you are asked, "Did you notice any increase in pain after gardening?" you should respond with something like, "Since the injury at work, my back has really been killing me. There are many activities I can no longer do since my injury at work, and gardening is now one of them." If you are convinced that a doctor is not treating you with your best interests in mind, request another treating doctor. (See Section C on changing doctors.)

2.   Stay Involved in Your Medical Treatment

For some injured workers, the treatment phase of the workers' compensation case seems to drag on forever. Especially if you are off work and in pain, you may feel very vulnerable at this time. It is not unusual to feel as though your world is falling apart and you can't do anything about it.

You must firmly believe that things will improve. Countless thousands before you have been through industrial injuries and have coped with the recovery and rehabilitation process. You can too. With this in mind, you may want to consider the following suggestions:

• **Keep informed about your medical condition.** You have the right to know exactly what the doctor believes is wrong with you, what treatment she recommends and why. It's your right and responsibility to ask questions about your treatment, recovery and ultimate prognosis. For example, ask the doctor's best estimate of the time frame for your treatment and recovery. This will help you plan your

affairs better. Also, make it your goal to be sure you understand exactly what the doctor is saying. If you don't understand medical jargon, ask the doctor for a plain-English translation. If this doesn't clear it up, write down the confusing terms and take time to go to the library to do some research. Many libraries have access to computerized databases of medical articles and other information (check with the reference librarian). Always remember that the better informed you are, the easier it will be to discuss your treatment with your doctors.

- Obtain copies of medical reports. If you request it, the insurance company is required to give you copies of all medical reports it receives from the doctor. If you don't receive copies from the insurance company within a reasonable time after your appointment (say within 60 days), call or write and request copies. You can also obtain copies of your medical files from the doctor's office, although some doctors charge for this service. (A fill-in-the-blanks letter you may use to request your medical records is provided in Chapter 6, Section D.)

- Keep a "pain diary" of your condition. It is always a good idea to keep a diary of the pain you suffer and of how your condition is progressing. Because some workers' compensation cases can go on for years, it's very important that you start this record and faithfully continue it. Otherwise, you may not be able to accurately recall what your condition was like at a particular time. (See Chapter 6, Section C10, for details.)

- Keep your medical appointments. It is your responsibility to keep your medical appointments. If you must cancel an appointment, do so well in advance. Many doctors require 48 hours or more advance notice to avoid charges. The doctor's office may charge you directly for missed appointments. If the insurance company pays for any appointments you miss without advance notice, the cost of the missed appointment may be deducted from your final settlement. In short, missing appointments may be equivalent to finding several $100 bills and deliberately tearing them up.

- Get a second opinion in important medical matters. This is particularly necessary where a doctor is recommending surgery. Under workers' compensation laws, you are entitled to a second opinion if your injury is serious.

- Seek alternative medical treatment if you want it. Alternative medical treatment is available for workers' compensation injuries under certain conditions, such as where tradi-

tional treatment is not working. Examples of alterna.. medical treatments might include acupuncture, massage therapy or bio-feedback. You and the workers' compensation insurance company may agree on alternative healing practices in writing, with each party reserving the right to terminate the agreement upon seven day's written notice to the other party. (LC §§ 4600.3, 3209.7.) If you want alternative treatment and the insurance company won't authorize it, you may have to file for a hearing and request that a judge order the treatment. (See Chapter 22.)

E. When Your Condition Becomes Permanent and Stationary (P&S)

The single most important turning point in your workers' compensation case occurs when you are declared to be permanent and stationary. "Permanent and stationary" (P&S) describes a doctor's opinion that your condition has reached a plateau. It means that further medical treatment at this time will not help to improve your overall condition. It does not, however, mean that your medical condition will never improve.

Although a P&S determination must be made by a doctor in the form of a medical report, the vast majority of injured workers are informed of their P&S status from the insurance company. Some receive a letter of explanation along with a final payment of temporary disability. Unfortunately, many injured workers find out they've been declared P&S only after calling the insurance company to find out why they didn't receive a temporary disability check.

1. What Happens Once You Are Permanent and Stationary?

As soon as a doctor declares you P&S, a number of different things may happen. Depending on your health and, to some extent, on the attitude of your treating doctor and the insurance company, the most important changes may include:

- Your temporary disability payments will stop.
- Current medical treatment may stop, depending on the doctor's opinion on your need for future medical treatment.
- You may be told to go back to work.

• You may be informed that your medical condition prevents you from returning to your former line of work, and therefore you may qualify for vocational rehabilitation. If so, you may begin to receive a maintenance allowance and instructions on how to begin participating in vocational rehabilitation. (Vocational rehabilitation is discussed in Chapter 14.)

• You may begin to receive permanent disability payments if the doctor considers you permanently disabled.

2.   Who Determines When You Are Permanent and Stationary?

Normally, the treating doctor determines when you are P&S. This is only logical, because it is the treating doctor's job to help you get better; at some point she will decide that further treatment at this time won't accomplish anything.

If you (or the insurance company) disagree with the treating doctor's opinion regarding your P&S status, such as whether you really are P&S or what date you became P&S, the objecting party may obtain something called a medical-legal report from another doctor. (How and when to obtain a medical-legal report, as well as its effect, is discussed in Chapter 10.)

3.   Review the Permanent and Stationary Report

If the insurance company doesn't send you a copy of the P&S report within two weeks after you know the report was written, you should request a copy. Or you may request a copy directly from the treating doctor.

The treating doctor's P&S report contains critical information and opinions about your workers' compensation claim. It is important to review the report because the treating doctor will render opinions on all medical issues necessary to determine your eligibility for various workers' compensation benefits. The P&S report may be relied upon by you, the insurance company, or both of you, in negotiating a settlement.

a.   Review the P&S Report for Accuracy

Carefully review your P&S report for accuracy, and write down any inaccuracies you may spot. As you go through the report, pay particular attention to the parts of the report that cover:

• your employment history
• description of your job duties
• how the injury occurred, and whether your medical problems were caused by factors other than the work injury
• history of prior injuries
• diagnosis
• basis for the doctor's finding that you are P&S (remember, this means that the doctor has concluded that further medical treatment at this time won't help your condition improve)
• subjective factors of disability (what type of pain you have as well as the frequency and intensity of the pain)
• objective findings of disability (what the tests results show—for example, test results for a shoulder injury would include the range of motion of the shoulder)
• any work restrictions the doctor recommends, and
• the doctor's opinion as to whether you can return to the type of work you were doing when injured or whether you are a Qualified Injured Worker (QIW)—someone who is eligible for vocational rehabilitation.

TREATING DOCTOR'S REPORT IS PRESUMED CORRECT

If you have chosen a top quality doctor to be your treating doctor and receive a report that satisfies you, you are in good shape. Even if the insurance company asks for another report from a qualified medicial evaluator (QME)—and this turns out to be less favorable—the law still says the treating doctor's report is presumed to be the correct one. Of course, if it turns out that the QME report is better for you than the treating doctor's report, you can always request that the QME report be relied on at trial. (Chapter 10 provides information about using a QME.)

b. Review the Treating Doctor's Opinion on "Critical" Issues

In the P&S report, your treating doctor will render an opinion on certain issues that I term "critical." A critical issue is one that, in and of itself, may determine whether or not you're entitled to a major benefit in your workers' compensation case. If the treating doctor's opinion on a critical issue is not in your favor, you may lose any right to that benefit unless you get a report from a qualified medical examiner (QME) that is more favorable to you.

Take plenty of time to study your P&S report. On a separate piece of paper, note any areas of the report that you believe to be wrong. As part of reviewing the report, pay very close attention to the doctor's opinion on the following critical issues. Answer the following questions very carefully:

1. Do you agree with the treating doctor's opinion that you are permanent and stationary? In other words, do you agree that additional medical treatment at this time will not help you?

2. Do you agree with the treating doctor's opinion about your need—or lack of need—for medical care in the future?

3. Do you agree with the treating doctor's assessment of whether or not you can return to the type of work you did before the injury? This may determine if you are entitled to vocational rehabilitation benefits.

4. Do you agree with the treating doctor's opinion as to the nature and extent of your permanent disability? Note that you will need to get the report rated to make this determination; that is discussed in Section c, below.

5. Do you agree with the treating doctor's opinion on apportionment, if any? Apportionment addresses whether or not your permanent disability is due in whole or in part to factors other than your current job-related injury. (For more on apportionment, see Chapter 3, Section C6.)

If you agree with the treating doctor on all critical issues, you can feel comfortable about contacting the insurance company to request benefits or to discuss settlement of your case.

If you disagree with the treating doctor's opinion, you have the right to object to the treating doctor's report within 30 days of receipt. You have the right to see additional doctors for evaluation of your condition if you disagree with the report. (The insurance company has the same right.) These other doctors, called qualified medical examiners (or QMEs), will review the P&S report and rely upon it to some extent in arriving at their opinion regarding your condition. Therefore, you will want to make them aware of any inaccuracies you found in the treating doctor's report.

 REVIEW ALL TREATING DOCTOR'S REPORTS CAREFULLY
Review all treating doctor's reports, not just the P&S report. If any interim treating doctor's report contains a medical opinion that you disagree with, you must object within 30 days of receipt of the report. (See Section A3d, above, for more details.)

c. Get the P&S Report Rated

After receiving and reviewing the treating doctor's permanent and stationary report, you need to arrange to have it rated. Rating is the process by which your permanent disability percentage is calculated. The insurance company will usually contact you about getting the report rated and will send you a form to do so. If you do not hear from the insurance company within 14 days after receipt of the P&S report, contact the company and request the form. (See Chapter 18 for details on rating reports.)

4. If the Permanent and Stationary Report Indicates a Permanent Disability

If in the treating doctor's opinion you have a permanent disability, the insurance company has three options.

Option 1: The insurance company may begin paying permanent disability benefits.

Option 2: The insurance company may dispute the conclusions of the P&S report and request a medical-legal evaluation, as discussed in Chapter 10. In the meantime, the insurance company must begin paying permanent disability benefits.

Option 3: The insurance company may object and promptly set the matter for trial before the Workers' Compensation Appeals Board to resolve the dispute. (LC § 4061(l).) In the meantime, the insurance company must begin paying permanent disability benefits.

HOW TO GET AN ATTORNEY FOR FREE

If the insurance company decides to request a hearing with the Appeals Board, the insurance company must pay for your attorney's fees if you retain one. In this event, I strongly recommend that you seek a workers' compensation lawyer. There is no reason not to be represented, since your attorney will be paid by the insurance company. If you see an attorney, be sure to tell her that you believe that the attorney's fee should be paid by the insurance company under LC § 4064 and explain why. Make sure the attorney gives you an opinion regarding this fee issue before you retain her. ■

Medical-Legal Evaluations

A medical-legal evaluation is used to resolve a legal dispute between an injured worker and the insurance company. The evaluation, done not to provide treatment, but to provide evidence for your case, is performed by a doctor other than your treating doctor (see Section A1, below). The workers' compensation judge will review the doctor's medical-legal report and may rely upon it in making a decision regarding disputed issues.

The most important disputes that may require a medical-legal evaluation include:

- whether or not the injury is covered under workers' compensation (also known as compensability of the injury), covered in Section C, below
- the treating doctor's opinion on the nature and extent of your disability, the need for future medical treatment and the nature of that treatment (see Section D, below), or
- opinions of the treating doctor regarding your permanent and stationary status, your eligibility for vocational rehabilitation, the extent and scope of your medical treatment, the existence of new and further disability or any other medical issue (covered in Section E, below).

A. Rules for Medical-Legal Evaluations

Your decision to obtain a medical-legal evaluation will depend upon several factors, including whether the insurance company has accepted your case and what issues are in dispute.

- **If the insurance company denied your claim:** You may get a medical-legal evaluation to help establish that your injury is a result of your work and should be covered by workers' compensation.
- **If your claim was accepted by the insurance company:** If there is a dispute over a treating doctor's report, you or the insurance company may get a medical-legal report to prove your position.

Depending on your situation, you may need to obtain a medical-legal report at various times in your workers' compensation case.

1. Who Will Perform the Medical-Legal Evaluation

A medical evaluator is a doctor who examines you and writes a comprehensive report (called a medical-legal report) commenting on various issues in your workers' compensation case.

A medical evaluator does not generally treat you; if she feels you need additional treatment, she will usually refer you back to your treating doctor. A medical evaluator need not be a medical doctor; she could be a chiropractor or other specialist.

a. Qualified Medical Examiner (QME)

If you are not represented by a lawyer, you will select a qualified medical examiner (QME), normally from a panel of three doctors. (This rule applies when there is a dispute pursuant to LC § 4061 (see Section D, below) or LC § 4062 (see Section E, below).) Selection of the doctor is discussed in Section B, below.

If you have an attorney, the procedure is different. If a treating doctor has already written a report, your attorney and the insurance company will normally try to settle your case based on it. If this can't be done, they will attempt to jointly choose one agreed medical examiner (covered in Section b, just below). Failing this, your attorney and the insurance company will each designate a QME and two reports will be issued.

b. Agreed Medical Examiner (AME)

An agreed medical examiner (AME) is only available if you're represented by a lawyer. For an accepted claim, your attorney and the insurance company must mutually agree on which AME will make a medical evaluation. Because the AME must be agreed upon, and people without lawyers aren't eligible in the first place, many injured workers will never see one. Generally speaking, the Workers' Compensation Appeals Board will follow recommendations of an AME, since the parties all found him acceptable.

2. Who Pays for the Medical-Legal Evaluation

For an accepted claim, the insurance company is responsible for paying for the first reasonable and necessary medical-legal evaluation you obtain. (LC §§ 4060, 4061, 4062.) If you have already obtained one medical evaluation, you cannot get another at the insurance company's expense for the same disputed medical issue. (LC § 4064(a).) If, however, a different medical-legal issue develops, the insurance company must pay for you to obtain an additional evaluation for the new disputed issue. If possible, you must use the same doctor you used for the first medical-legal evaluation.

If the insurance company has denied your claim, it must pay for a medical-legal evaluation on whether your injury should be covered, as long as you follow certain rules (see Section C, below).

3. Requirements of Medical-Legal Evaluations and Reports

For a medical-legal report to be valid, the doctor conducting the medical-legal evaluation must adhere to certain rules under the Labor Code. The report must satisfy all of the following criteria to be admissible evidence at any hearing on your case. (As a practical matter, however, if you don't object to a report that doesn't satisfy these requirements, it will be admitted as evidence.)

For starters, only the doctor who signs the report may take a complete medical history, review and summarize prior medical records and compose and draft the conclusions of the medical report. (LC § 4628.) If the evaluator delegates these tasks to anyone else, the report may be disregarded.

Assuming you are already permanent and stationary, the medical-legal report must contain the following information:
- your complaints
- all information received from the parties that the doctor reviewed in preparation of the report or relied upon to formulate an opinion
- the history of the injury, as well as your medical history (including any non-work-related medical problems and whether you are still experiencing any problems from them)
- what the doctor found upon examining you (also known as objective findings), as well as a diagnosis
- the cause of any disability and an opinion as to the extent of any disability and work limitations
- recommended medical treatment
- opinion as to whether or not permanent disability has resulted from the injury and whether or not it is permanent and stationary. If permanent and stationary, a description of the disability with a complete evaluation
- apportionment of disability, if any
- if the injury is alleged to be a psychiatric injury, a determination of the percent of the total cause resulting from the actual events of employment

- the reasons for the opinion, and
- the date of the examination and the signature of the physician. (CCR § 10978.)

Once you receive a report, check it for any defects; reports often lack one or more of the above items. Obviously, you will want to raise a fuss only if you want to discredit a medical-legal report you are not happy with, or where there is more than one report and you want to exclude a less favorable one from evidence. Later, at trial, you can tell the judge why you believe the report you don't like is defective under California Labor Code § 4628 and CCR § 10978. If the judge agrees, he can order a new medical-legal evaluation.

B. Picking a Qualified Medical Evaluator (QME)

In many cases, the QME's report will make or break your case. For obvious reasons, it's in your best interests to carefully select the doctor who will have this authority.

1. Assignment of the Panel

If you request a QME panel, it must be assigned within 15 working days or you have the right to obtain a medical-legal evaluation from *any* QME of your choice. (LC § 139.2(h).) This can be very important, because it is better to be able to choose your doctor from all QMEs in the state of California rather than having your choice limited to one of three.

The insurance company is generally required to send you a form with which to request the assignment of a panel of three QME doctors. The QME panel form must advise you that you should consult with your treating doctor prior to deciding which type of specialist to request. (CCR § 101.)

You will then receive a letter that contains the names of three QMEs, as well as this information about each one:
- the doctor's name
- the doctor's address and telephone number
- the doctor's specialty and number of years in practice, and
- a brief description of the doctor's education and training, as provided by the Industrial Medical Council. (CCR § 103.)

The three doctors for the panel are randomly selected from all QMEs who do not have a conflict of interest in the case (such as having a prior relationship with the employer or insurance company), who have the appropriate specialty selected by you, and who are within the general geographic area of your residence.

IF YOU'RE SATISFIED WITH THE TREATING DOCTOR'S REPORT

If the insurance company wants you to see a QME, it is very important that you inform the insurance company that you are only selecting a QME because of its request. Explain that you wish to rely upon the treating doctor's report, and will be raising the presumption of correctness of that report. To do this, send the insurance company a letter similar to the following.

9/19/XX

Dear Sir/Madam:

This letter will confirm that you have requested that I select a qualified medical evaluator pursuant to Labor Code Section 4061(d) because you disagree with the findings of the treating doctor, Dr. Hernandez, in his report of 3/3/XX.

Although I am doing so, please be advised that I do not dispute the findings of Dr. Hernandez in his report of 3/3/XX, and that I will, in fact, be relying upon the findings contained in that report should this matter proceed to trial. Furthermore, pursuant to Labor Code Section 4062.9, the findings contained in Dr. Hernandez's report shall be presumed correct.

Sincerely,

Terry Rose

Terry Rose

---

2. How to Pick a QME

Whether you are picking a QME from a panel of three doctors or from the entire QME list, it is obviously key that you pick someone who's competent and fair. This means you do not want to see a doctor who gets all or most of his workers' compensation business from insurance company referrals.

Instead, you want a doctor who gets at least half of his referrals from injured workers' attorneys.

The doctors you have to choose from are picked at random, and are supposed to be neutral. But don't be complacent about which doctor to select. I have seen panels consisting of three doctors known to work primarily for insurance companies. But in fairness, I have also seen well-balanced panels made up of doctors I consider to be caring and unbiased.

To know which doctor to pick, you have to take the time to investigate. Start by asking your treating doctor what she knows about the doctors and whether they have the expertise to evaluate your injury. The Information and Assistance officer may have heard of the doctors in question and have some recommendations. You may even want to call each of the doctor's offices and try to determine what percentage of their workers' compensation examinations are done at the request of insurance companies. Often if you tell a receptionist or other assistant why you are concerned, you will get a straight answer.

If you do not feel there is an acceptable doctor on the panel, write and request another panel; see the sample letter below.

SAMPLE

July 2, 20XX

Medical Director
Industrial Medical Council
P.O. Box 603
San Francisco, CA 94101-0603

Re: Janice Clemens v. Johnson Masonry
Case No. BV 7777
Objection to QME panel

Dear Medical Director:

Please be advised that I object to the doctors provided on the QME panel I received on June 28, 20XX. The doctors provided are all known by reputation in the community to be defense medical evaluators. I do not feel I can get an impartial evaluation with any of these doctors.

Please provide me with a new panel from which I can select a doctor for my QME evaluation.

Sincerely,

Janice Clemens

Janice Clemens

3. Setting an Appointment With a QME

You are responsible for making an appointment with the selected QME within 30 days of the assignment date on the selection form. (CCR § 103.) If you call the selected QME and he is not available within 60 days, the evaluator is deemed unavailable and you may request a new panel. (CCR § 110.)

When you make an appointment with the selected evaluator, you must indicate on the QME selection form which doctor was selected and return a copy to the Executive Medical Director (the address will be on the form) and to the insurance company. (CCR § 105.)

4. Exchange of Information

Within five working days of receiving the completed QME selection form you sent in, on which you selected a QME, the insurance carrier must supply you with some extremely important information:

- copies of all medical and non-medical information to be provided to the QME
- information about your right to object to any non-medical information being submitted to the QME (you'll have 10 days to do so; 15 days if the information was mailed to you), and
- notification that, 20 days prior to the evaluation, you must furnish your employer with all information you propose to provide the QME. Your employer has the right to object to non-medical evidence within 10 days of receipt. (CCR § 102.)

C. Compensability of Injury (Labor Code § 4060)

Skip this section if the insurance company accepts any part of your claim. For example, this might happen if the insurance company agrees that you injured your neck, but does not agree that you injured your arm (assuming you claimed both were injured). Go directly to Section D if the issue in your case is the nature and extent of your permanent disability or the need for future medical treatment. Skip to Section E if the dispute involves any other medical issue.

This section covers what happens if the insurance company denies your claim—in other words, says that your claim is not compensable. "Compensability" is the jargon the workers' compensation system uses to mean coverage. Compensability is denied if the insurance company claims that your injury is not covered by workers' compensation *for any reason*. (LC § 4060(a).) If compensability (coverage) is an issue, any medical-legal reports you obtain to support your position must be done following the guidelines of LC § 4060. Here are the rules.

1. When to Get a Medical-Legal Report

If the insurance company denies your claim, it won't pay for medical treatment or temporary disability you might otherwise be entitled to receive. Whether you obtain a medical-legal evaluation immediately or wait a while will depend upon the circumstances in your case and your personal needs. Especially if you are out of work and lack other sources of income, you may need to quickly establish that your injury is covered by workers' compensation.

If the medical-legal report says your injury is compensable, the insurance company should begin providing benefits. If not, you can request a hearing before a Workers' Compensation Appeals Board judge.

LOOK INTO ALTERNATIVES

Getting a QME report and going to a hearing is not a quick process. If you are getting state disability payments or have other sources of income, you may decide to wait until you are finished with your treatment before getting a medical-legal evaluation and report. Likewise, you may be able to get treatment under a lien (see Chapter 9, Section B2b) or use a private health insurance policy instead of getting a medical-legal report right away.

2.   How to Qualify for a Medical-Legal Report

Before obtaining a medical-legal evaluation to address issues of compensability, you must file your DWC-1 claim form to notify your employer that you have been injured. Then, your employer must either:

- reject your claim—in which case you are eligible to get a medical-legal report immediately, or
- delay your claim by sending you a "delay letter" within 14 days of the date you filed your DWC-1 claim (19 days if you mailed it). The insurance company then has 90 days from the time you filed your DWC-1 form to investigate your claim. If the insurance company rejects it within that time, or doesn't do anything and the 90 days runs out, you are eligible to get a medical-legal report.

The point of paying attention to all these fussy rules is that if you get a medical-legal report before the proper deadline expires, you—not the insurance company—will have to pay for it.

3.   How to Get a Medical-Legal Evaluation

If the deadlines necessary to qualify for a medical-legal evaluation have been met and you do not have an attorney, you and the insurance company may each obtain a medical-legal evaluation to address the issue of compensability.

The insurance company will pick a QME and schedule an examination. You will receive a letter advising you of the date and time of the appointment. You must also receive a check to cover your expenses prior to attending the examination; otherwise, you are not required to attend.

In addition, you have the right to an evaluation with a QME of your choice. You must first select a doctor from the approved QME list maintained by the medical director of the Workers' Compensation Appeals Board. (LC § 4060(d), LC § 139.2.) You can get help from the Industrial Medical Council, which is a division of the Workers' Compensation Appeals Board set up to oversee the QME process. Contact an Information and Assistance officer, or

Industrial Medical Council

P.O. Box 603

San Francisco, CA 94101-0603

Neither you nor the insurance company may obtain more than one comprehensive medical-legal report on the same issues at the insurance company's expense. However, any party may obtain additional reports at its own expense. (LC § 4060(d).) This may be a viable option if your QME report also supports denial of your claim. The cost of the additional report may be reimbursed to you when your case settles or goes to trial, but be aware that you may have to pay for it yourself.

INSURANCE EXAMS AFTER THE QME EXAM

If the insurance carrier tries to set you up to see another doctor after the insurance company has already sent you to a QME, because it doesn't like what the QME said, YOU DON'T HAVE TO GO. Please refer to Chapter 28 to read the discussion of the case *Regents of University of California, Lawrence Berkeley Laboratories v. WCAB (Ford)*.

IF YOU HAVE A LAWYER

If a medical-legal evaluation is required to determine whether your injury is covered by workers' compensation, your attorney may contact the insurance company and discuss the possibility of having you examined by a "neutral" agreed medical examiner (AME). Your attorney and the insurance company can agree to send you to an AME at any time, even after you have seen a QME. Depending on your situation, each side may decide to first send you to a QME that it chooses, and agree to send you to an AME only if issues cannot be resolved based upon the two QME reports.

4.   Issues Covered by the Medical-Legal Report

Obviously, if coverage (compensability) is being denied, the main reason you want a medical-legal evaluation is to determine that you are covered. But it's important to understand that the medical evaluation will not be limited to the issue of compensability, but will also address other medical issues in dispute at the time of the examination. (LC § 4060(e).)

What issues will be addressed depends on your permanent and stationary status:

- **permanent and stationary finding.** If at the time of the medical examination, the doctor determines that you are permanent and stationary, he will also render an opinion on such issues as the extent of any permanent disability, and whether or not you require future medical care.

• **no permanent and stationary finding.** If you are not permanent and stationary when the medical evaluation occurs, the only other issues the QME will address are whether you are temporarily totally disabled and whether you are in need of current medical treatment.

Fortunately, the doctor who conducts your medical-legal evaluation is allowed to consult with any doctors who have already treated you for injuries outside her field of expertise. When compensability is an issue, you usually will already have seen one or more doctors.

SEE SPECIALISTS BEFORE THE EVALUATION

Because the doctor performing the medical-legal evaluation may consult with other treating doctors who have already seen you, it is very important that you get treatment from doctors in each medical specialty for which you have alleged an injury *before* you obtain a medical-legal evaluation. Ask your treating doctor to refer you to the necessary specialists.

D. Nature and Extent of Permanent Disability or Need for Future Medical Treatment (Labor Code § 4061)

If your claim was accepted by the insurance company, but there is a dispute regarding the nature and extent of your permanent disability or your need for future medical treatment, read this section. Otherwise, skip ahead to Section E, below.

Your case may have reached this stage because the insurance company accepted your claim in its entirety or has agreed that at least one part of your body is injured but denies that another is. It's also possible that the insurance company may have initially denied coverage (compensability) completely, but after getting medical evaluations and possibly going before the Appeals Board, you won and compensability is no longer an issue. Regardless of how you get here, any additional medical-legal report you obtain to resolve the issues of permanent disability or need for future medical treatment must follow the rules under LC § 4061.

1. When to Get a Medical-Legal Report

Your need for a medical-legal evaluation under LC § 4061 will probably be triggered by an event such as the following:

• You receive a notice from the insurance company indicating that it disputes the opinion of the treating doctor on the nature and extent of your permanent disability or your need for future medical treatment.

• You review the treating doctor's medical-legal report and you disagree with his opinion on the issues of permanent disability or need for future medical treatment.

• You receive your last payment of temporary disability indemnity from the insurance company along with a notice stating that you have no permanent disability—and you disagree.

• You receive your last payment of temporary disability from the insurance company along with a notice stating how much permanent disability it believes you are owed—and you disagree.

2. How to Get a Medical-Legal Report

If you do not have an attorney, the insurance company must immediately provide you with a form to request the assignment of a panel of three qualified medical evaluators (QMEs). You then select a doctor from the panel to perform a medical evaluation and prepare a medical-legal report on your permanent disability and any need for future medical treatment. (LC § 4061(d).) As discussed in Section B3, it is your responsibility to make the appointment with the QME you select.

RELYING ON THE REPORT OF THE TREATING DOCTOR

The insurance company may force you to go to a QME if it disagrees with your treating doctor's report. If you agree with the opinion of your treating doctor regarding the nature and extent of your permanent disability and your need for future medical treatment, notify the insurance company of that fact in writing. We provide a sample letter in Section B1, above. That way, you'll be able to invoke the provisions of LC § 4062.9 that give the treating doctor's report a presumption of being correct.

The QME's report and the reports of the treating doctors are the only reports that can be obtained by either side for consideration by a judge on the issues. (LC § 4061(d).) In other words, neither side may get additional QME reports, even if they pay for them!

At the appointment, the QME must give you a brief opportunity to ask questions concerning the evaluation process and the evaluator's background. You must then participate in the evaluation unless you have good cause to discontinue the evaluation. "Good cause" includes evidence that the evaluator is biased against you because of your race, sex, national origin, religion or sexual preference, or that the evaluator requested that you submit to an unnecessary medical examination or procedure.

You definitely want to take advantage of your right to discuss the examination procedure with the QME before starting the examination. Don't be afraid to ask questions regarding the QME's background, including where the QME gets a majority of her business. If it comes from insurance company referrals, proceed with caution.

Try to get a feel as to whether the QME will give you a fair and impartial evaluation. If you don't think so, consider terminating the examination and requesting a new panel. Although, in theory, the cost of the exam may be deducted from any court award you get, this is usually a non-issue, since 90% of workers' compensation cases settle outside of court by agreement with the insurance company.

If you decide not to proceed with the evaluation, you have the right to choose another QME from a new panel of three. However, if the Appeals Board later determines that you did not have good cause to terminate the original evaluation, the cost of the second evaluation will be deducted from any award you obtain. (LC § 4061(f).)

IF YOU HAVE A LAWYER

Neither party may obtain more than one QME report at the expense of the insurance company. However, unlike a situation where you're not represented, the parties may obtain additional QME reports at their own expense. Your attorney and the insurance company must first try to agree upon a "neutral" agreed medical examiner (AME). They must agree on an AME within ten days (or if a delay is agreed to, 20 days) of either party's request to go to an AME. If the parties cannot agree on an AME within the time limit, the parties may not later select an AME. Instead, each side may rely on the treating doctor's report or send you to an additional QME. (LC § 4061(c).)

3. Issues Covered by the Medical-Legal Report

The medical-legal evaluation is not limited to issues regarding the nature and extent of your permanent disability or need for future medical treatment. It must address *all* other medical issues in dispute at the time of the examination, such as whether you should return to your former employment.

The fact that there can be only one QME if you do not have a lawyer means that this doctor may end up reporting in fields outside of her expertise if you have two or more very different injuries. For example, you may have a situation where the QME is an orthopedist and he has to also report on a psychiatric condition that developed as a result of your injury. If you obtained treatment for your psychiatric condition, the QME can at least consult with your treating doctor and rely upon that expertise when drafting a QME report concerning your psychiatric injury.

However, if you have not already been treated for your psychiatric injury, the QME is going to have to give an opinion regarding your psychiatric injury without the benefit of any medical expertise in that field of medicine! This is why it is critical that you obtain treatment in every medical specialty in which you are claiming an injury *before* your QME evaluation. Ask your treating doctor to refer you to the necessary specialists.

4. What Happens After You Attend the Medical-Legal Evaluation?

If you aren't represented by a lawyer, the QME will prepare a medical-legal report that addresses all issues in dispute at the time of your examination. The QME must mail the report and a one-page form that summarizes the medical findings to you, the insurance company and the administrative director of the Workers' Compensation Appeals Board.

Within 20 days of receipt of the medical evaluation, the Administrative Director is supposed to calculate the permanent disability rating, which is used to determine the dollar value of your disability, and mail the rating to you and the insurance company. (LC § 4061(i).)

Within 30 days after you receive the advisory rating, either you or the insurance company may request the Administrative Director to reconsider the recommended rating. Or you may obtain additional information from the treating doctor or the QME to address issues not addressed or properly addressed in the original QME evaluation. (LC § 4061(k).) For more on rating injuries, see Chapter 18.

If, after a medical-legal report is prepared, you (or the insurance company) object to any *new* medical issue, you must utilize the same medical evaluator who prepared the previous evaluation to resolve the medical dispute, if possible. Subsequent QME reports on different issues than those covered in the first QME report are done at the expense of the insurance company and are not considered to be a "second" QME report for which you have to pay.

IF YOU HAVE AN ATTORNEY

When the medical-legal report is issued, your attorney will evaluate and rate it. If you got a report from an agreed medical examiner (but not a QME), your attorney may agree with the insurance company to send the report to the rating bureau at the local Appeals Board for an opinion by a professional rater. This is similar to the summary rating procedure available for unrepresented workers. Again, see Chapter 18 for more on rating injuries.

5. If the Medical-Legal Report States You Are Entitled to Benefits

If an evaluation resolves any issue so as to require the insurance company to provide compensation, the insurance company must begin payment of compensation or promptly commence proceedings before the Appeals Board. (LC § 4061(l).)

HOW TO GET AN ATTORNEY FOR FREE

If the QME's medical-legal report requires the insurance company to pay permanent disability benefits or commence proceedings before the Appeals Board, and the insurance company decides to commence proceedings (request your matter be set for trial) instead of paying you permanent disability benefits, under LC § 4064 you are entitled to have your attorney's fees paid. If this happens, I strongly recommend that you seek a workers' compensation lawyer. There is no reason not to be represented, since your attorney will be paid by the insurance company. If you decide to see an attorney, be sure to tell her why you believe that the attorney's fee should be paid by the insurance company. Make sure the attorney gives you an opinion regarding this fee issue before you decide to retain her.

What happens if the insurance company refuses to take action? For example, let's say the insurance company refuses to begin payment of your permanent disability benefits and

also won't set a hearing with the Appeals Board to decide the issue. If that happens, write the insurance company a letter similar to the example below.

If the insurance company does not comply within 14 days, you should file a Declaration of Readiness to Proceed; see Chapter 22, Section D, for instructions. The insurance company will now be responsible for paying your attorney fees, so I strongly suggest that you contact a workers' compensation attorney for an appointment.

SAMPLE

9/21/XX

Naomi Hopkins
Greater West Insurance Company
P.O. Box 141
Anytown, CA 99999

Re: Sandy Yi
Claim No XYX114

Dear Ms. Hopkins:

You have been served by the Administrative Director with a copy of the QME report of Dr. McDermott dated 5/5/XX, as well as with a copy of the rating of my permanent disability. As you know, the QME found that I have a permanent partial disability that entitles me to 30.25 weeks of payments at the rate of $158 per week.

Under the terms of the Labor Code Section 4061(l), you are required to immediately begin payment of benefits or file a Declaration of Readiness to Proceed to have the issue resolved by the Appeals Board. You have refused and continue to refuse to do either of the above.

This letter will serve as formal notice that unless you either begin payments (which must include a 10% late penalty on all payments that are past due) or file with the Appeals Board within 14 days from the date of this letter, I will file a Declaration of Readiness to Proceed with the Appeals Board.

If I am forced to do this, it will be my position that I am filing the Declaration of Readiness to Proceed on your behalf. As such, if I should decide to obtain legal representation, you will be responsible for paying my attorney fees pursuant to Labor Code Section 4064.

Sincerely,

Sandy Yi

Sandy Yi

E. Other Issues to Be Resolved by Medical-Legal Evaluations (Labor Code § 4062)

If your claim has been accepted and there are any disputed issues other than the nature and extent of your permanent disability or your need for future medical treatment, read this section. Otherwise, skip ahead to Chapter 11.

1. When to Get a Medical-Legal Report

The need to obtain a medical-legal evaluation may arise because you (or the insurance company) have objected to a determination made by the treating doctor concerning medical issues such as the following:

- whether or not you are permanent and stationary
- whether or not you are a qualified injured worker (QIW), a worker entitled to vocational rehabilitation benefits
- whether the medical treatment you are receiving is appropriate or necessary, or
- the existence of any new and further disability.

2. How to Get a Medical-Legal Report

The objecting party must notify the other side of its objection to the treating doctor's report in writing within 30 days of receipt of the treating doctor's report. The 30-day time period may be extended for good cause by mutual agreement. If any party fails to object within the 30 days, that party may have waived its right to obtain a medical-legal report on the issue. (LC § 4062(a).) But as a practical matter, even if you miss the deadline, you should object; a judge may find that there was a good reason for the delay.

As soon as either party makes a timely objection, the insurance company must immediately provide you with a form with which to request assignment of a panel of three qualified medical evaluators (QMEs). You then select a doctor from the panel to perform a medical evaluation and prepare a medical-legal report on your permanent disability and any need for future medical treatment. (LC § 4061(d).) As discussed in Section B3, it is your responsibility to make the appointment with the QME you select.

Other than the treating doctor's reports, the QME evaluation will be the only medical report allowed to resolve the issues in dispute. (LC § 4062(b).) Neither you or the insurance company is allowed to get additional QME reports, even if the party is willing to pay for it.

IF YOU HAVE A LAWYER

Neither party may obtain more than one QME report at the expense of the insurance company. However, unlike a situation where you're not represented, the parties may obtain additional QME reports at their own expense. Your attorney and the insurance company must first try to agree upon a "neutral" agreed medical examiner (AME). They must agree on an AME within ten days (or, if a delay is agreed to, 20 days) of either party's request to go to an AME. If the parties cannot agree on an AME within the time limit, the parties may not later select an AME. Instead, each side may rely on the treating doctor's report or send you to an additional QME. (LC § 4061(c).)

3. Issues Covered by the Medical-Legal Report

After you attend the medical-legal evaluation, the doctor must mail a copy of the medical-legal report and a form that summarizes the doctor's medical findings to you, the insurance company and the Administrative Director.

The medical evaluation must address *all* contested medical issues arising from all injuries reported prior to the date of your initial appointment with the evaluator. (LC § 4062(c).) This means that no matter how many injury claim forms you have filed, you get only one medical-legal report.

4. Disputed Issues Arising After Report

If, after a medical-legal report is prepared, you or the insurance company objects to any new medical issue, you must utilize the medical evaluator who prepared the previous evaluation, if possible. (LC § 4061(g).) For example, if you get a QME to issue a medical-legal report on the issue of whether you are receiving proper medical treatment, and later a dispute arises as to whether your condition has become permanent and stationary, you would be entitled to an additional evaluation to resolve this issue, but you must try to use the same QME.

Subsequent QME reports on new issues are done at the expense of the insurance company. You are, however, limited to one QME report for each new issue, unless you are represented by a lawyer. ■

11

Payment of Medical Benefits

I f you're an employee with a work-related injury, you are entitled to receive all the medical care necessary to cure or relieve your injury or illness. The costs must be paid for by your employer's workers' compensation company or by your employer, if self-insured. (LC §§ 4600 to 4603.) You don't pay any deductibles. You must, however, give notice to your employer that you were injured. (See Chapter 5, Section B, for information about informing your employer of your injury.)

Expenses that are covered include, but are not limited to, medical, dental, surgical, psychiatric, chiropractic and hospital treatment. Nursing care, physical therapy, therapeutic massage, surgical supplies, crutches, apparatus (including artificial limbs), acupuncture and the like may all be covered if they're necessary to cure or relieve the effects of the injury. In addition, you are entitled to costs associated with your medical treatment, including medications and round-trip mileage to medical appointments. (For a thorough discussion of medical care, see Chapter 9.)

⚠ PAYMENT FOR DENIED CLAIMS

If your workers' compensation claim is denied by your employer's insurance company, payment will not be authorized for your medical treatment. You need to pay for medical treatment yourself or make other arrangements for payment until your claim is settled. Your options are covered in Chapter 9, Section B2b.

A. Payment for Accepted Claims

If your claim is accepted by your employer's insurance company, your medical bills should be sent by the doctor or hospital to the insurance company and paid promptly. If the insurance company doesn't pay the bills promptly or disputes any charges, the doctors must look to the insurance company, not you, for payment. (LC §§ 4622, 4625, 4621.)

WHY INSURANCE COMPANIES SOMETIMES WON'T PAY MEDICAL BENEFITS

Medical benefits are not always voluntarily paid for by the insurance company. This may occur because the claims adjuster assigned to your case:

- does not know the law
- misplaces your file
- has not had time to work on your case
- does not believe your injury is work-related, or
- does not believe that you need medical treatment (yes, some claims adjusters really try to make medical decisions).

To avoid disputes about payment, it's always best to contact the insurance company to request authorization for any additional tests or medical referrals made by your doctor. You can do this by telephone, but follow up any authorizations in writing.

1. How to Request Payment of Round Trip Mileage

You are entitled to be reimbursed by the insurance company for the cost of your round trip mileage to and from all doctors' appointments, physical therapy appointments, trips to a pharmacy to obtain medications and special medical examina-

RECORD OF MILEAGE & TRANSPORTATION AND REQUEST FOR REIMBURSEMENT

Name: _____William Johnson_____

Address: _____19 Spring Lane, Anytown, CA 99999_____

Employer: ____Mel's Motor Co._____

Claim Number: _00123_____   Today's Date: _____8/8/XX_____

To (Insurance Carrier): _Allied Insurance Company_____

I have incurred the expenses listed below in connection with trips for medical examinations, treatment and/or vocational rehabilitation. Receipts, if available, are attached. Pursuant to the California Labor Code, I request immediate reimbursement. Please send the payment to me at the address listed above.

Date	Medical or vocational rehabilitation appointment with (specify)	Parking fees/actual transportation fees	Mileage (round trip)
6/6/XX	Dr. Henry		20
6/10/XX	Dr. Henry		20
6/17/XX	Downtown Medical Center		10
6/18/XX	Dr. Henry		20
6/20/XX	Dr. Henry		20
6/27/XX	Dr. Henry		20
7/15/XX	Dr. Henry		20
8/1/XX	Dr. Henry		20

Total parking fees/actual transportation costs _____

Total mileage _____150_____

Total cost of mileage (Total mileage X .31) _____$46.50_____

Total fees to be reimbursed
(Total cost of mileage + Total parking fees/actual transportation costs) _____$46.50_____

tions. You are not, however, entitled to mileage reimbursement for attending court hearings or traveling to the insurance company's office. The current rate is 31 cents ($0.31) per mile. It doesn't matter if you drive, take public transportation or walk.

If the insurance company doesn't provide a form, keep track of the mileage using the Record of Mileage and Request for Reimbursement form provided in Appendix 4; a sample is below. About once every three months (or more often, if your expenses are significant), submit your mileage totals to the insurance company for payment. Remember to keep a copy of the completed form for your records.

SPECIAL EXAM TRANSPORTATION COSTS MUST BE PAID IN ADVANCE

If you are requested to attend a medical exam set up by the employer or its insurance carrier, you are entitled to be advanced transportation costs, which could include airfare and taxi fare. (LC § 4600.) See Section A3, below.

2. How to Request Reimbursement for Medical Treatment and Supplies

You are entitled to be reimbursed by the company for any out-of-pocket expenses you incur for such things as:

- doctors' bills
- medications, both prescription and over-the-counter
- medical supplies, such as crutches and braces
- medical tests, ordered by your doctors, and
- hospital bills.

To obtain reimbursement, you must submit copies of your receipts along with a request for reimbursement form. You can use the self-explanatory form in Appendix 4, entitled Record of Medical Expenses and Request for Reimbursement, or a form provided by the insurance carrier. Periodically, submit the request for reimbursement to the insurance company, remembering to keep a completed copy for your records.

3. Payment of Costs Associated With Special Exams

From time to time, you may be asked to submit to a medical examination by a doctor chosen by your employer, its insurance company or the workers' compensation judge. In addi-

tion to advance round trip mileage for these appointments, you are also entitled to:

- all reasonable expenses of meals and lodging incidental to reporting for the examination, and
- one day of temporary disability indemnity for each day of wages lost in submitting to the examination. If you only lose a half day, you are only entitled to a half day of temporary disability.

These expenses must be paid to you in advance of the medical appointment, or you are not required to attend. Before attending the exam, you should contact the insurance company, give a reasonable estimate of the costs you will incur and request payment.

B. Future Medical Care Costs

Future medical treatment, to be paid for by the insurance company, may be agreed upon in a settlement or awarded by the Workers' Compensation Appeals Board for an indefinite period, even for life, depending upon the facts of the case. You may, however, choose to waive your right to future medical care in exchange for a sum of money. (See the discussion of settlement options in Chapter 19, Section B.)

 See *Gardner v. WCAB*, *Stott v. WCAB* and *Jensen v. WCAB* in Chapter 28.

RECORD OF MEDICAL EXPENSES AND REQUEST FOR REIMBURSEMENT

Name: _William Johnson_

Address: _19 Spring Lane, Anytown, CA 99999_

Employer: _Mel's Motor Co._

Claim Number: _00123_   Today's Date: _8/8/XX_

To (Insurance Carrier): _Allied Insurance Company_

I have incurred the medical expenses listed below for prescriptions, medical treatment and other medical costs. Receipts for these expenses are attached. Pursuant to the California Labor Code, I request immediate reimbursement. Please send the payment to me at the address listed above.

Date expense incurred	Specify expense	Reason for expense	Amount spent
6/6/XX	Durant Pharmacy	Painkillers	$8.29
6/17/XX	Durant Pharmacy	Painkillers	8.29
6/18/XX	Downtown Medical	X-Rays	180.00
6/27/XX	Ace Medical	Knee brace	42.94

Total expenses to be reimbursed $239.52

Temporary Disability Benefits

If your industrial injury temporarily limits you from working at your previous job and hours, you are entitled to receive money to help replace your lost income. The payments you receive are called temporary disability indemnity (compensation) or temporary disability benefits, or even "TD."

A. Types of Temporary Disability

Depending on your injury and how it impairs your ability to work, your condition may fall into one of two temporary disability conditions:

- temporary total disability (TTD), or
- temporary partial disability (TPD).

LOOK FOR THE INITIALS "TTD" AND "TPD" ON YOUR CHECKS

Many insurance companies use the abbreviations "TTD" and "TPD" on checks to describe which benefit they are paying. When looking to see that you've been paid the correct amount, you'll need to know what payments you're receiving.

1. Temporary Total Disability (TTD)

You will qualify for temporary total disability if you temporarily cannot do *any* work as a result of your industrial injury. In this case, you are entitled to the full amount of any temporary disability benefits.

The determination of TTD status is usually made by your treating doctor. If, however, you or the insurance company dispute the treating doctor's opinion, a qualified medical evaluator (QME) may evaluate you and render an opinion about whether you are temporarily totally disabled. (If you have an attorney, an agreed medical examiner (AME) will perform the evaluation.) If the insurance company still won't pay temporary disability payments following a QME's affirmative report, you will have to request a hearing before the Workers' Compensation Appeals Board. Please see Chapter 10 for a detailed explanation of how to use a QME.

There is no time limit on how long you may collect temporary total disability benefits; you are entitled to payments for as long as your treating doctor indicates that you are still treating for your industrial injuries. Your right to temporary total disability benefits ends as soon as you reach one of these workers' compensation milestones:

- you return to regular work

- you are medically able to return to regular work (the doctor gives you a return to work order), or
- you are determined to be permanent and stationary—a determination by your doctor that you have reached a plateau and further medical treatment at this time would not improve your condition (see Chapter 9, Section E, for more about your permanent and stationary status).

2. Temporary Partial Disability (TPD)

See *Hupp v. WCAB* in Chapter 28.

You may be entitled to temporary partial disability (TPD) if a doctor determines that you temporarily cannot carry out your full duties at work, but can work a limited number of hours. TPD is also payable if a doctor says you can return to work full-time, but are restricted as to the type of work you can do, and your employer says it does not have full-time work for you with your limitations, but can provide restricted work on a part-time basis. TPD cannot extend for more than 240 weeks within a period of five years from the date of injury. (LC § 4656.)

As if this weren't already confusing enough, it is also possible to go from temporary total disability to temporary partial disability. For example, if your medical condition improves to the point where you can return to work on a limited basis, you might not earn as much as you would on total temporary disability, and thus be entitled to some temporary partial disability benefits. Of course it is also possible to go from TDP to TTD if your condition were to deteriorate so that you could not work part-time.

B. Amount of Temporary Disability Payments

See *Placer County Office of Education v. WCAB (Halkyard)* in Chapter 28.

The temporary disability indemnity amount is computed at the rate of two-thirds (2/3) of your average weekly earnings, with set maximum amounts. As you can see from the accompanying chart, if you are reasonably well paid, you'll receive a lot less from workers' compensation than you did on the job.

TEMPORARY DISABILITY AND MINIMUM/MAXIMUM RATES FOR THE FIRST TWO YEARS FROM YOUR DATE OF INJURY		
Date of Injury	**Minimum Weekly Payment**	**Maximum Weekly Payment**
7/1/94 - 6/30/95	$126 or 100% of your average weekly wages, whichever is less	$406 (based on weekly wages of $609 or more)
7/1/95 - 6/30/96	$126 or 100% of your average weekly wages, whichever is less	$448 (based on weekly wages of $672 or more)
On or after 7/1/96	$126 or 100% of your average weekly wages, whichever is less	$490 (based on weekly wages of $735 or more)

Note: The amounts in parentheses ( ) are the equivalent gross weekly wage amounts to qualify for the benefit listed.

Refer to Appendix 2 for a table of temporary disability benefits. Remember that you cannot exceed the maximum weekly payment listed above.

EXAMPLE: Santiago earns $900 per week as a supervisor for a construction company. He is injured at work on 6/22/95 and his doctor issues a report that says Santiago is temporarily totally disabled. His temporary disability amount is computed at two-thirds of his average weekly earnings. Two-thirds of $900 is $600. However, because the maximum temporary disability rate for his date of injury is $490, that is all he is entitled to.

You are locked into the temporary disability rate that applies to your date of injury for two years from your date of injury. If you are entitled to receive any temporary disability indemnity after two years from the date of injury (even if your disability has not been continuous), you are entitled to any higher rate in effect.

EXAMPLE: Darlene was seriously injured on the job on 5/5/96, and her doctor declared her temporarily totally disabled. When the injury occurred, her average weekly wage was $720. Two-thirds of $720 is $480, so Darlene is entitled to the maximum rate of $448 per week. If Darlene's temporary disability continues past 5/5/98, she will be entitled to the entire $480 per week, since the maximum disability rate in effect at that time is $490.

1. How to Calculate Weekly Earnings

 See *Hofmeister v. WCAB* in Chapter 28.

MAXIMUM DISABILITY RATE

If your temporary disability rate is the maximum rate set forth in the chart, you do not need to read the rest of this section on how to compute your weekly wages. That's the amount you'll receive, period. Skip to Section 2, below.

It's important to know how your temporary disability rate is established so that you can make sure you're receiving the correct disability amount. Because it's fairly common for the insurance company to pay too little, it's important that you check this.

When you receive your first temporary disability check, the insurance company will advise you in writing how the amount you are getting was calculated. You will be told the average weekly wage used in calculating your weekly benefit.

Your weekly wage is figured at the gross amount (before taxes and other deductions are made) that you were earning at the time of your injury. This amount should include income from all jobs you held that were affected by your inability to work, such as any independent contract work you were doing, a second job or a business you might own. You may also include overtime and the market value of board, lodging, fuel and other perks you receive as part of your pay. (LC § 4454.) You should not include income such as alimony, dividends or rental income, since these sources of income are not affected by your inability to work.

If you disagree with the insurance company's figure as to how much you earn per week, you will have to obtain evidence (actual documents) to prove to the insurance company your correct weekly wage.

The easiest method is to ask your employer for a wage statement, setting forth how much you earned over the past 12 months (or for however long you worked there if less than 12 months). Divide the grand total by the number of weeks of pay to get your average weekly wage. If you can't get this information from your employer, you can get a good idea of your earnings from your pay stubs or W-2 tax form provided by your employer.

If you need to compute your average weekly earnings, follow these guidelines:

- **If you work for two or more employers at the time of the injury:** The average weekly wage is the total of these earnings from all jobs. If you're paid at different rates, you must calculate your pay at the lower rate if the injury occurred at that job. If, however, the injury occurred on the job that pays the higher rate, calculate your pay at the higher rate for that job only.

  EXAMPLE: Tim works for employers A and B. He works 20 hours per week for employer A at $8 per hour, and works 20 hours per week for employer B at $10 per hour. Tim is injured while working for employer A. Tim's average weekly wage is taken by multiplying 40 hours (the total from both jobs) by $8 (the wage paid at the job he was injured at). If Tim had been injured at the higher paying job, he'd be able to use the higher wages for that job alone (20 hours at $10 plus 20 hours at $8).

- **If earnings are at an irregular rate (such as piecework), on a commission basis, or are specified by week, month or other period (not necessarily irregular):** The average weekly wage is figured by averaging the actual weekly earnings for the previous year or shorter period of time (if convenient to determine an average weekly rate of pay).

  EXAMPLE: Bert works as a commissioned sales rep for XYZ Co. He has worked there since February of 2001. On 8/6/01, he is injured on the job. Bert's wages depend upon his sales and are different every week. Bert's average weekly wage is computed by taking his total earnings for the period 2/1/01 to 8/6/01 and dividing by the total number of weeks he worked.

- **If you work for fewer than 30 hours per week, or for any reason the previous methods of arriving at the average weekly wage cannot reasonably and fairly be applied:** The average weekly earnings are taken at 100% of the sum which reasonably represents the average weekly earning capacity at the time of your injury. Consideration must be given to your actual earnings from all sources and jobs. (LC § 4453.) For example, if you just got a big raise, your average weekly

wage would be your current weekly wage, not your average over the last 52 weeks.

HOW TO QUALIFY FOR A HIGHER RATE
It's possible that a recent raise or change in the number of hours you're working could help you qualify for a higher temporary disability rate. In that event, use the higher wage (rather than prior earnings) to compute your temporary disability rate.

2. Calculating Partial Disability Benefit

If you go back to work for a limited number of hours, assuming your part-time work results in less pay than you'd receive if you didn't work and received temporary *total* disability benefits (TTD), you are entitled to receive two-thirds of your weekly loss in wages. (LC §4654.) Your "weekly loss in wages" is determined to be the difference between your average weekly wage (see Section B, below, for the definition of average weekly wage) and the weekly amount you are able to earn part-time. (LC §4657.)

EXAMPLE: Bonnie's earnings at work qualify her for the maximum TTD rate of $490 per week (for average weekly wages of $735 per week or more), as shown in the chart above. After an on-the-job injury, Bonnie returns to work on a part-time basis and only earns $300 per week. Her wage loss then is $435 per week (the maximum weekly wage of $735 minus the $300 she earns). The insurance company will pay Bonnie two-thirds of this $435 wage loss, or $290.

3. If You're Reinjured

If you return to work and are reinjured on the job, you need to know whether or not you have a new injury. If the injury is not new, but an exacerbation (flare up) of your prior injury, the original injury date controls for purposes of figuring additional temporary disability (subject to any increase you are entitled to after two years).

If, however, the injury is new, you are entitled to the temporary disability minimums and maximums in effect at the time of the new injury. You must also follow procedures to formally file a claim for the new injury. (See Chapter 5, Sections B and C.)

C. How Payments Are Made

Temporary disability is calculated weekly and payable every two weeks. The workers' compensation insurance company should begin sending temporary disability checks to you as soon as it determines that you both:

• have a valid claim, and
• are temporarily disabled.

PROBLEMS GETTING PAID

Unfortunately, not all injured workers get the temporary disability payments they're entitled to receive. The most common problems you are likely to encounter are:

• Your employer denies you have a workers' compensation claim and refuses to pay benefits.
• The insurance company claims your average weekly wage is less than it really is, so it pays you less than the amount you believe you are entitled to.
• The workers' compensation insurance company does not process your paperwork in a timely manner.

Most of these problems can be resolved by calling the insurance company or writing a letter (remember to keep copies). If you still cannot get results, you may have to file documents and set a hearing with the Appeals Board to have a judge determine if you are entitled to benefits.

---

1. Off Work Order or Medical Report Required

To qualify for temporary disability payments, you must have an off work order or a medical report from a doctor specifying that you are temporarily totally or partially disabled. As soon as you get the off work order, mail it to the insurance company with a written request for temporary disability payments.

It's possible that your treating doctor will authorize you to return to work on a modified basis or with certain restrictions, such as no lifting over 15 pounds, or no repetitive bending and stooping. If you can't return to work because your employer has no job within these restrictions, you are entitled to be paid temporary disability benefits.

If you are capable of doing the essential functions of your job with some reasonable accommodations from your employer on how you get it done, and you feel your employer has not attempted to make those changes, you may be entitled to file a claim for discrimination. (See Chapter 16, Section C, and Chapter 17, Section D.)

2. Special Rules for First Three Days Off Work

No temporary disability compensation benefits are paid for the first three days off work unless the injury requires hospitalization or the disability lasts more than 14 days.

EXAMPLE: Jerry is injured at work and takes 11 days off to recover. Because Jerry was neither hospitalized nor off work for more than 14 days, he is entitled to only eight days of temporary disability; he does not get paid for the first three days off work.

3. Payments Must Begin Within 14 Days

The first payment of temporary disability benefits must be made not later than 14 days after the employer learns of the industrial injury and temporary disability status. On that date, all benefits then due must be paid unless the employer denies liability for the injury.

If you do not receive your first temporary disability payment within two weeks after you forwarded the off work order to the insurance company, you need to follow up promptly. Call and request that payments begin immediately, retroactive to the date you were first taken off work. Always make a note of any telephone call and follow up with a written letter confirming what transpired in the phone call.

SAMPLE LETTER

April 22, 20XX

Katherine Bradford
ABC Insurance
333 West Third Street
Anytown, CA 99999

Re: Temporary disability payments for Henry Wilson
Employer: Brand X Corporation
Claim No: 11403-00-ABC

Dear Ms. Bradford:

On 4/5/XX, I notified you by telephone, and then by letter, that Dr. Smith, my treating doctor, gave me an off work order. The off work order is dated 4/2/XX and indicates that I will be temporarily totally disabled until at least 9/5/XX.

It has been more than 14 days since you were advised of my disability status. Please begin temporary disability payments immediately and include all payments due since 3/29/XX.

Sincerely,

Henry Wilson

Henry Wilson

4. Penalties for Late Payments

Temporary disability payments must be made every two weeks, beginning with the date designated on the first payment. If any payment is not made according to this time frame, you're entitled to an automatic 10% late fee in addition to the payment. (LC § 4650.) The insurance company probably won't pay the penalty unless you request it, although technically you're entitled to it automatically.

A 10% late penalty is not assessed if the insurance company cannot determine whether temporary disability payments are owed. To avoid liability for the penalty, the insurance company must advise you in writing within 14 days after you submit your DWC-1 form to your employer:

- why payments cannot be made within the 14-day period
- what additional information it requires to determine whether temporary disability payments are owed, and
- when it expects to have the information required to make the decision.

Most insurance companies pay temporary disability on time. If you are entitled to a 10% penalty, and do not receive it with your next disability check, you may wait until your case settles to request the penalty. This is particularly advisable if it's not much money and you don't need it right away. After all, you don't want to alienate the claims adjuster with unnecessary demands. If, however, you want to receive the 10% penalty soon, call the insurance company and request payment. If you need to, follow up with a letter.

5. Sick Leave, Vacation and Salary

If your employer pays you full wages in the form of sick leave or vacation pay during the time you are disabled, no temporary disability indemnity is payable to you. Even if you are paid less than your full salary, as long as it exceeds your temporary disability indemnity weekly rate, you are not entitled to temporary disability.

Some employers want injured employees to receive sick leave or vacation pay instead of temporary disability. If you have notified your employer that you have an industrial injury, the employer cannot do this without your permission. (LC § 4652.) If your employer allows it, however, you might wish to receive sick leave or vacation pay if it gives you more money than temporary disability. ■

Permanent Disability (and Life Pension)

When a doctor determines that further medical treatment at this time will not help you improve, your medical condition is referred to as "permanent and stationary." This might mean you have fully recovered or simply that your condition has stabilized. After you're found to be permanent and stationary, it's time to determine if you have a permanent disability as a result of your work injury. For workers' compensation purposes, a permanent disability is any disability or impairment that is expected to remain after you reach the maximum recovery or healing.

If you completely recover without any ill effects, you will not have a permanent disability. If, however, your maximum recovery from your injury is less than full and complete, you will have a permanent disability. A permanent disability is defined as how your injury has affected your ability to participate in the open job market.

PERMANENT DISABILITY AND TEMPORARY DISABILITY COMPARED

Do not confuse permanent disability with temporary disability (discussed in Chapter 12). A temporary disability exists if you temporarily can't perform your regular job. In that case, you'll receive temporary disability payments while you are off work receiving medical treatment and recovering from the effects of your injury. Once you are finished with treatment, or can return to work, temporary disability payments end. The amount you received in temporary disability payments is not deducted from your settlement.

If you don't recover 100%, you are entitled to a specified amount as a permanent disability award. Permanent disability awards are over and above any temporary disability payments and medical care costs. If permanent disability payments are advanced to you before your case settles, that amount will be deducted from your permanent disability award when you settle your case. You may receive permanent disability even if you are working again.

A. How Permanent Disability Award Compensates Worker

If you have a permanent disability, you are entitled to a limited sum of money, referred to as a permanent disability award. The money is intended to compensate you for your future loss of ability to participate fully in the open job market. In other words, if your permanent disability limits which jobs you can do, you should at least get some money as compensation.

If you qualify for permanent disability, payments are due even if you:
- return to work
- can do the exact work for which you had previously been employed, or
- didn't suffer any wage loss.

In fact, the vast majority of injured workers who recover a permanent disability award return to their former jobs.

EXAMPLE: Wesley falls and injures his right knee while working as a bank teller. After his condition stabilizes, his doctor gives a work restriction of "no very heavy lifting." Wesley is entitled to a permanent disability award because his inability to lift heavy objects would make it harder for him to find employment on the open job market. The fact that Wesley's current job as a bank teller (to which he returned) does not require very heavy lifting is irrelevant for permanent disability purposes. After all, Wesley may not work for the bank forever. Wesley will receive a small permanent disability award.

In case you're thinking that a permanent disability award is a pretty good deal, it's actually very limited. For example, a permanent disability award does *not* compensate you for pain and suffering stemming from your injury, nor does it account for past, present or future wages lost because of your injury or financial damage as a result of your injury, including loss of credit worthiness (if, for example, you don't have enough money to pay bills).

Finally, there is no right of survivorship to permanent disability awards. In other words, if you die before you receive the amount due, your survivors will not get your permanent disability payments.

B. Kinds of Permanent Disability Awards

If you have a permanent disability, you should be entitled to at least one of the following types of disability monetary awards:

- **permanent partial disability award.** The vast majority of injured workers with permanent disabilities have permanent *partial* disabilities. Any permanent disability that is ultimately determined to be less than 100% disabled is considered to be a partial disability. (Permanent disability is calculated in .25% increments.)
- **life pension award.** Permanent partial disabilities of 70% to 99.75% pay, in addition to permanent partial disability payments, a nominal lifelong pension. (LC § 4659.) This weekly amount is paid to you after your normal weekly permanent disability indemnity ends. The life pension is paid until you die, even if your condition improves.
- **permanent total disability award.** If it is ultimately determined that you have a total permanent disability (100%), you are entitled to lifetime payments at your temporary disability rate. This is similar to a life pension, but it is paid at a much higher rate. A total disability means you aren't expected to be able hold down any type of gainful employment whatsoever.

C. Establishing Your Permanent Disability Status

It typically takes quite a while to reach a final determination of a permanent disability, although the exceptional case is handled faster. Your doctors (treating doctors and perhaps medical evaluators) will write medical reports in which they set forth various limitations that result from your industrial injury. These opinions are usually contained in a permanent and stationary medical report, which is "rated" to convert the doctors' opinions on your limitations into a percentage of disability.

Unless you have an attorney, the rating process will be done for you automatically (called an advisory rating or summary rating) by the Administrative Director of the Workers' Compensation Appeals Board. Fortunately, advisory ratings are usually reliable and rarely contain errors. The percentage of permanent disability will be rated anywhere from .25% to 100% (in increments of .25). The advisory rating will also convert the percentage of disability into the amount of money you are entitled to based upon the percentage of disability. (See Chapter 18 for more on rating your permanent disability.)

1. Notification of Your Permanent Disability Status

If you were never temporarily disabled—for example, you continued to work while you were getting medical treatment—you will receive notice from the insurance company regarding permanent disability when your medical condition is determined to have stabilized (is permanent and stationary).

If you were receiving temporary disability, the insurance company will give you notice of your permanent disability status when it stops making temporary disability payments to you. Temporary disability payments stop either when your medical condition is determined to be permanent and stationary or when you return to work full time. At this point, the insurance company must send your last payment of temporary disability along with a notice stating one of the following:

- **No permanent disability will be paid because the insurance company believes that you don't have a permanent disability from the injury.** The notice must include information on how you can get a formal medical evaluation if you disagree with the insurance company's opinion. (LC § 4061(a)(1).)
- **The insurance company believes you have a permanent disability.** The insurance company must state the amount of permanent disability benefits that are payable, the basis on which the determination was made (usually your treating doctor's permanent and stationary report) and whether you'll need future medical care. (LC § 4061(a)(1).) The notice must include information on how you can get a formal medical evaluation if you disagree with the insurance company's opinion.
- **Permanent disability may be or is payable, but the amount cannot be determined yet because your medical condition is not permanent and stationary.** This usually occurs when you returned to work, but are still receiving treatment for your injury or illness. The insurance company will monitor your treatment until the treating doctor says that you are permanent and stationary. Within 14 days of that time, the insurance company will send you notice of its position regarding your permanent disability, as discussed just above. (LC § 4061(a)(2).)

2. Check the Basis for Your Permanent Disability Status

Insurance companies almost always base their decisions about whether you are entitled to permanent disability on the treating doctor's permanent and stationary report or the advisory rating of that report if it has been rated, although sometimes an insurance company makes its own estimate of the amount of permanent disability you are entitled to after reviewing a medical report.

If you agree with the insurance company's opinion regarding the nature and extent of your permanent disability (how much disability you have), you may begin settlement negotiations (see Chapter 19). To help you decide, carefully review the treating doctor's permanent and stationary report and any advisory rating to see what the treating doctor says about the nature and extent of your permanent disability. The doctor's opinion about permanent disability is generally set forth as a "work restriction" or as "subjective complaints." (See Chapter 9, Section A3, for a detailed explanation on how to read a doctor's report.)

If the treating doctor's permanent and stationary report hasn't been rated yet, immediately submit it to the Disability Evaluation Unit for calculation of a permanent disability rating. (See Chapter 18, Section A2, on how to do this.) If the insurance company wants to discuss settlement based only upon the opinion of the treating doctor's report, insist that the report be rated first. (If the insurance company reviews the treating doctor's report and thinks it has a low rating, it will request an advisory rating to help convince you to settle, knowing that the rating will be low. But if the insurance company thinks the report will rate fairly high, it might not request an advisory rating.)

3. Medical Evaluation Required When Permanent Disability Disputed

If, after reading Chapter 18, you disagree with the doctor's permanent and stationary report or any advisory rating, immediately call or write the insurance company within 30 days of receipt. If you call, always follow up with a written confirmation of your telephone conversation.

Explain that you dispute the determination of your permanent disability rating. Give your reason as to why you disagree. If your explanation makes sense to the insurance company, it may agree and improve its offer. If it doesn't, and you dispute the treating doctor's report, the insurance company will then send you the necessary paperwork to select a qualified medical evaluator (QME) to resolve the dispute.

The insurance company also has the right to object to the treating doctor's opinion or the advisory rating, and must

notify you of its objection. The insurance company will then provide you with a form to request a QME panel. (This process is covered in detail in Chapter 10, Section B1.)

PERMANENT DISABILITY IS SOMETIMES ARBITRARILY DENIED

If the insurance company has a valid medical basis for denying permanent disability, it should willingly tell you. If it refuses to tell you, you should wisely suspect that your benefits are being arbitrarily denied.

Workers' compensation insurance companies cannot legally deny permanent disability benefits without a legitimate reason. If the insurance company won't explain why it refuses to pay you permanent disability benefits, you may request that a workers' compensation judge resolve the matter. Under LC § 5814, the judge may find that the insurance company owes you a 10% penalty payment on the entire permanent disability award.

---

4. Using Non-Feasibility for Vocational Rehabilitation to Prove Total Disability

 See *LeBoeuf v. WCAB* and *Sandlin v. WCAB* in Chapter 28.

If you have been found "non-feasible" for participation in vocational rehabilitation because your injury prevents you from participating due to pain or physical limitations, you can use this fact to prove that you have a total, or 100%, disability. Please refer to Chapter 14 for a detailed explanation of vocational rehabilitation.

D. How Permanent Disability Is Paid

Unless you request that payments be postponed, the insurance company must begin paying permanent disability within 14 days after the date your temporary disability payments cease. (LC § 4650(b).)

Even if the extent of your permanent disability cannot be determined, the insurance company still must start paying permanent disability indemnity within the 14-day period if it has any reason to believe that you will be entitled to a permanent disability indemnity. Payments must continue until they total a reasonable estimate of permanent disability. (LC § 4650(b).)

Incidentally, don't worry about getting more money in advances than you are entitled to. The insurance company is very good at underestimating how much your permanent disability award will be. In addition, it will probably withhold 12-15% to cover possible attorney fees, even if you don't have a lawyer. In the unlikely event that you're overpaid, the insurance company could ask you to repay the overpayment, but I have yet to see this happen.

1. Bi-Weekly Permanent Disability Payments

The insurance company must make payments to you at least twice in each calendar month; typically, they're made every two weeks. (LC § 4650(c).) For permanent total disability, you will be entitled to receive permanent disability payments for the rest of your life. For permanent partial disabilities, payments end after a set amount of time based on a system that rates the dollar value of your injury.

These bi-weekly payments are also referred to as permanent disability advances, and will be deducted from any final settlement check you receive, even though they are really payments of your permanent disability, and not really "advances."

2. Lump Sum Permanent Disability Advances

In addition to receiving your bi-weekly payments, if you need money due to financial hardship, you can ask the insurance company for a lump sum advance such as $500 or $1,000. Most insurance companies are willing to advance some permanent disability money against your final settlement check if you have a good reason for requesting the advance. The request may be made by phone or by letter. It generally takes the insurance company several weeks to act upon the request.

Whether you eventually settle out of court or go to trial and receive an award from a workers' compensation judge, the insurance company is entitled to subtract any money it has paid you for lump sum permanent disability advances (for instance, $500 or $1,000) as well as any bi-weekly payments it has made.

EXAMPLE: Barbara received $1,000 in lump sum permanent disability advances and $7,000 in bi-weekly permanent disability advances. Her total permanent disability settlement is $10,000. At the time of final settlement, she will be entitled to receive an additional $2,000 for her permanent disability. Any amounts that she was paid for temporary disability are not credited against the final settlement.

The following questions should help you decide whether or not to request a lump sum permanent disability advance or accept the bi-weekly permanent disability advances:

- Do you need the money now?
- Will you need the majority of your money later?
- Do you have the discipline to save or invest it without touching it? If so, you may be better off having the money working for you now, rather than letting the insurance company use the money.

 PERMANENT DISABILITY ADVANCES MAY AFFECT OTHER DISABILITY POLICIES

Most long-term disability policies, as well as Social Security disability, take a credit or offset for any workers' compensation benefits you receive. You are required by law to advise these agencies of any money you get in your workers' compensation case. If you receive disability other than workers' compensation, it is better not to accept any permanent disability advances (either weekly or lump sum). In all probability, your other benefits will be reduced by a like amount. If your case later settles, you may be able to insert special language in your settlement agreement to minimize the amount of credit taken against your workers' compensation settlement by these agencies. (See Chapter 20, Section D2e.)

3. Penalties for Late Payments

If any bi-weekly permanent payment is not made on time, the amount of the late payment automatically must be increased by 10%. (LC §§ 4650(c) and (d).) The insurance company is supposed to include the penalty with the payment of any benefit which is late. If the insurance company does not, you may send a letter demanding the penalty or wait until your case settles.

If the insurance company doesn't have a reasonable basis for delaying payments, a judge may additionally award a 10% penalty on the entire permanent disability award. (LC § 5814.)

As a practical matter, you may need assistance from the Workers' Compensation Appeals Board to force payment of the late penalty if the insurance company is noncooperative. You can do this in a separate proceeding or, as is usually more convenient, wait until you are ready to settle or go to trial on your main case (called your case-in-chief), where all remaining issues are resolved.

4. Resolving Problems With the Insurance Company

If the insurance company refuses to provide you with bi-weekly permanent disability payments, and it has not denied that the money is owed to you, you may need to appear before the Workers' Compensation Appeals Board for a hearing to obtain an order that the insurance company must pay you these benefits.

Before taking this action however, try calling or writing the insurance company and demanding the benefits to which you are entitled. (If you need to set a hearing before the Appeals Board, see Chapter 22.)

E. Amount of Permanent Partial Disability Benefits

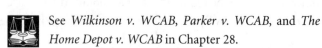

See *Wilkinson v. WCAB*, *Parker v. WCAB*, and *The Home Depot v. WCAB* in Chapter 28.

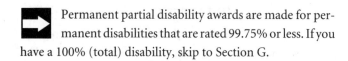
Permanent partial disability awards are made for permanent disabilities that are rated 99.75% or less. If you have a 100% (total) disability, skip to Section G.

A permanent partial disability benefit amount is determined by:
- your permanent disability rating, which converts from a percentage into the number of weekly payments you are entitled to, *multiplied by*
- your permanent disability indemnity rate, which is based upon your average weekly wage at the time you were injured.

It is always wise to double check the insurance company to make certain that it is paying you at the correct rate and for the proper amount of time. Here's how.

The first factor in determining the amount of money you are entitled to receive is your permanent disability rating—that is, the percentage of disability. This is expressed as a percentage in increments of .25, such as 26.75%.

This figure will be based on some or all of the following:
- the percentage of disability determined by the treating doctor
- the percentage of disability determined by the qualified medical examiner, and
- an advisory rating, discussed in Section C2.

The percentage of disability is subject to negotiation. If you and the insurance company cannot agree upon a permanent disability rate, the judge will make that determination at your trial. Disability rates are discussed in Chapter 18.

1. How Many Weeks of Benefits Will Be Paid?

Once you have your disability rate (percentage of disability), it must be converted into the number of weeks of payments. It's easy to do this. Refer to the Permanent Disability Indemnity Chart in Appendix 3. Find your percentage of disability in the first column and then find the corresponding number of weeks of indemnity payments in the column to its immediate right. The number of weeks to which you are entitled changes with the date of injury, so make sure you find the correct "Total Weeks" column (there are two) that corresponds to your date of injury. For example, 26.75% for an injury date of 7/30/01 would entitle you to 106.25 weeks of payments.

2. What Is the Weekly Rate of Payment?

You are entitled to up to two-thirds of your average weekly wage, according to your date of injury, within the minimum and maximum amounts allowed by law. (LC § 4658.) Refer to the chart below to determine the rate you're entitled to. (See Chapter 12, Section B1, if you're not sure how to compute your average weekly wage.)

EXAMPLE: Brad is injured at work on August 3, 2002, and has a 50% disability rating. Two-thirds of his $600 weekly earnings is $400 per week. The maximum weekly amount allowed for an injury occuring after 7/1/96 is $170 for a permanent disability rating of 25% or more. Brad is entitled to the maximum weekly amount, or $170.

PERMANENT PARTIAL DISABILITY RATES

Date of injury	Minimum weekly payment	Maximum weekly payment
7/1/94 to 6/30/95	$70 [$105 wages]	$140 for PD under 15% [$210 wages] $148 for PD 15% to 24.75% [$222 wages] $158 for PD 25% to 69.75% [$237 wages] $168 for PD 70% and over [$252 wages]
7/1/95 to 6/30/96	$70 [$105 wages]	$140 for PD under 15% [$210 wages] $154 for PD 15% to 24.75% [$231 wages] $164 for PD 25% to 69.75% [$246 wages] $198 for PD 70% and over [$297 wages]
On or after 7/1/96	$70 [$105 wages]	$140 for PD under 15% [$210 wages] $160 for PD 15% to 24.75% [$260 wages] $170 for PD 25% to 69.75% [$255 wages] $230 for PD 70% and over [$345 wages]

Note: The amounts in brackets [ ] are the equivalent weekly wage amounts to qualify for the benefit listed.

3. Determining the Amount You Are Entitled To

If you are entitled to the maximum weekly permanent disability amount, such as $170 for a rating of 25% or more, you can simply look up your disability rating in the Permanent Disability Indemnity Chart in Appendix 3 and follow the figures across to the column that corresponds to your date of injury. There, you will find the total dollar amount you are entitled to for the maximum weekly disability rate.

You'll need to do this calculation without the chart if your weekly permanent disability rate is below the maximum. To determine the amount of money you are entitled to, multiply the total number of weeks to which you are entitled by your permanent disability rate. For example, 33.25 weeks multiplied by $140 = $4,655.

4. Combining Injuries for Disability Rating Purposes

In Chapter 18, Step 7, we discuss combining multiple injuries to come up with a higher permanent disability rating. Here we'll explain how it works so that you can plan ahead if you have multiple injuries.

For rating purposes, it is often (but not always) to your advantage to combine successive injuries. This tactic can increase your overall monetary award because one higher percentage of permanent disability often pays more benefits than two or three smaller ones.

EXAMPLE: While working for Ajax Cleaning, Joe injures his lower back on 3/23/99. He files a workers' compensation claim and is treated by Dr. Smith, who treats Joe and send him back to work with certain modifications to his activities. Joe returns to work with the same employer, and while still being treated for his back injury of 3/23/99, Joe has another back injury. Joe files a second workers' compensation claim and is treated for that injury. Eventually the doctor releases Joe back to work and writes a report stating that Joe's back became permanent and stationary on 1/2/01 and that Joe has some permanent disability, caused 50% by the first injury and 50% by the second injury. The doctor gives Joe a work restriction of "no heavy work," which works out to an approximate rating of 30% permanent disability (we discuss how to rate injuries in Chapter 18).

Joe's insurance company tries to say that Joe has two separate injuries, each rated at 15% disability. This would result in two separate settlements for permanent disability of $8,040 each, for a total of $16,080. However, Joe demands that his injuries be combined for rating purposes, resulting in one permanent disability of 30%. This would result in one settlement for permanent disability of $21,420 instead of two settlements for $16,080, an increase of $5,340.

The legal justification for combining injuries can be found in the case of *Wilkinson v. WCAB* (see Chapter 28). The court in this case said that if an employee has two successive injuries to the same part of the body that occur with the same employer, and those injuries become permanent and stationary at the same time, the injuries can be combined. And in a subsequent case (*Rumbaugh v. WCAB*; see Chapter 28), the court threw out the requirement that the injuries need to occur with the same employer. It remains in controversy whether the injuries must actually involve the same part of body and must become permanent and stationary at the same time to be combined.

F. Life Pension Benefits

 Skip this section if you are not eligible for a life pension (available only for injuries rated between 70% and 99.75%). For injuries that result in 100% total disability, there is no life pension, but you are entitled to permanent total disability benefits; skip to Section G, below.

If you have a permanent partial disability of 70% to 99.75%, you are entitled to a relatively small life pension in addition to any money you receive for permanent partial disability. Life pension payments usually are paid bi-weekly and begin after all permanent partial disability payments have been made.

Don't get overly excited if you qualify for a life pension. It is a small amount of money, and certainly not enough to support you. For example, if you were injured between 7/1/94 and 6/30/95, the most you could possibly be entitled to would be a weekly payment of $94.02—and that would be for an injury of 99.75%!

1. How to Compute a Life Pension

You may want to seek help from an Information and Assistance officer. If you want to compute your life pension yourself, here are the steps; an example follows.

Step 1: Multiply your average weekly earnings on your date of injury by 1.5%, up to the maximum allowed in the "Maximum average weekly wage" in the chart below. If your average weekly wage is less than the maximum shown in the chart, use your average weekly wage.

Step 2: Subtract 60% from your percentage of disability to get a multiplier. For example, a disability of 70%

would have a multiplier of 10%, computed: 70% – 60% = 10%.

Step 3: Multiply the weekly wage you calculated in Step 1 by the multiplier in Step 2.

MAXIMUM WAGES FOR CALCULATING LIFE PENSION RATES	
Date of injury	**Maximum average weekly wage**
7/1/94 to 6/30/95	$157.69
7/1/95 to 6/30/96	$207.69
On or after 7/1/96	$257.69

EXAMPLE: Jim's industrial injury occurred on 6/2/95. His permanent partial disability was 72.25%, entitling Jim to a life pension in addition to his permanent partial disability award. At the time of his injury, Jim's average weekly wage was $480. Because his average weekly wage exceeds the maximum allowed for his date of injury, Jim must use the maximum allowable average weekly wage of $107.69. 1.5% of $107.69 is $1.61535. Multiplying $1.61535 by 12.25 (the difference between Jim's disability of 82.25% and 60%), Jim comes up with $19.79 (rounded to the nearest penny) per week. In addition to all other benefits, Jim is entitled to $19.79 per week for life after his permanent disability award has been paid in full.

G. Permanent Total Disability Benefits

 Skip this section if your injury does not result in a 100% total disability rating.

If you are 100% disabled, you are considered to be "totally" disabled for workers' compensation purposes. You may be 100% disabled even if you are perfectly able to hold down a job in the labor market.

Any one of these work injuries will automatically entitle you to a total permanent disability award:
- loss of, or loss of sight in, both eyes
- loss of, or loss of use of, both hands
- an injury resulting in a practically total paralysis, or
- an injury to the brain resulting in incurable imbecility or insanity. (LC § 4662.)

Other injuries, or combinations of injuries, may result in total permanent disability. This determination must, however, be made by doctors; it is not an automatic legal presumption. If agreed between the parties or determined by a judge after a trial that you cannot do any work at all, you are considered totally disabled.

1. Permanent Total Disability Rate

Permanent total disability payments are paid at your *temporary disability rate* (see Chapter 12). This rate is significantly higher than the rate paid for permanent partial disabilities, so don't confuse the two.

Unlike temporary disability benefits, however, you are not entitled to whatever maximum temporary disability rate is in effect two years from the date of your injury. Your total permanent disability rate is based upon your temporary disability rate in effect on the date of your injury.

See the total temporary disability chart in Chapter 12, Section B, to determine the maximum permanent total disability rate (based upon 2/3 of your average weekly wage).

2. How Long Payments Last

If you have an injury serious enough to result in a permanent total disability, you are generally entitled to disability payments for the rest of your life. You will note that permanent total disability is the only award other than life pension that is not capped at a set amount. How much you will receive depends upon how long you live. Your survivors will not be entitled to receive any of your permanent total disability payments after you die. ■

Vocational Rehabilitation Benefits

If your doctor determines that you should not return to your former type of work because of your work injury, you may qualify for vocational rehabilitation benefits. Read this chapter carefully for an overview of your rights to receive vocational rehabilitation.

If you returned to your former job, you may choose to skip this chapter. But be careful. Offers of modified or alternate work with the same employer may result in termination of your rights to vocational rehabilitation benefits. If you change your mind after working a few months, you may not be able to get vocational rehabilitation benefits at that point. At the very least, carefully read the sidebar, "No Vocational Rehabilitation Benefits If Employer Offers You a Job."

No Vocational Rehabilitation Benefits If Employer Offers You a Job

Your employer or its insurance company does not have to provide vocational rehabilitation benefits if the employer offers you at least 12 months of:

- **modified work.** This is a return to your former job with modifications made so that you can work with your disability. If you voluntarily quit prior to the end of the 12 months, you won't be entitled to vocational rehabilitation benefits.
- **alternative work.** The work must meet several requirements. Given your disability, you must have the physical ability to perform the job. The job must offer wages and compensation that are not more than 15% below those paid to you at the time of your injury. In addition, the job must be located at your present work site or within reasonable commuting distance of your residence at the time of the injury, generally no more than 25 to 50 miles, one way.
- **any work at all, if you fail to reject the offer of work in the proper manner.** If you are not offered acceptable, modified or alternative work, your rejection of your employer's unsatisfactory offer must meet certain requirements for you to be eligible for further vocational rehabilitation services. (We cover how to reject such an offer in Section B, below.)

MORE INFORMATION ON VOCATIONAL REHABILITATION
This chapter provides a basic overview of vocational rehabilitation. But you'll probably need help beyond the book if you plan to handle your own rehabilitation plan. Check the *Workers' Compensation Rehabilitation Manual* (Work-Comp Communications); see Chapter 27, Section B1, for ordering information.

A. What Is Vocational Rehabilitation?

Vocational rehabilitation (also called "voc rehab") is an individualized placement and training program. You may be eligible if you cannot return to your old job or your former kind of employment because of your physical or emotional condition. Vocational rehabilitation is designed to help you find "suitable gainful employment"—legal jargon for a job that can be gotten quickly and that pays enough to support you.

Vocational rehabilitation may be available if your doctor determines that you can't go back to your previous job or type of employment because you will further injure yourself or you are physically or emotionally incapable of doing the work. The role of vocational rehabilitation is to help you find work you *can* do. You generally work with a counselor to come up with a suitable individualized plan, taking into account a variety of factors including your disability, education, experience background and motivation.

In general, rehabilitation plans that utilize a worker's existing skills and experience are favored. For example, if you have secretarial experience, a rehabilitation plan to find you a computer job (assuming your disability allows it) is preferred over sending you to a vocational school to learn to be a dental assistant (assuming you had no prior experience in this field).

 VOCATIONAL REHABILITATION CANNOT BE EXCHANGED FOR CASH—OR CAN IT?
Although by law, you theoretically can't trade your vocational rehabilitation rights for a sum of money, there are, in fact, methods to do so if both you and the insurance company are so inclined. Please refer to Chapter 19, Section C10, for a detailed explanation.

1. The Rehabilitation Unit

Vocational rehabilitation is overseen by the Vocational Rehabilitation Unit, also referred to as the Rehabilitation Unit. The Rehabilitation Unit is an entity that approves rehabilitation plans and decides disputes involving vocational rehabilitation issues in much the same way the Appeals Board resolves other workers' compensation issues. The Rehabilitation Unit is usually, but not always, located in the same building as the Workers' Compensation Appeals Board. (See Section H1 for more on locating and using the Rehabilitation Unit.)

2. Benefits Provided by Vocational Rehabilitation

While you are participating in vocational rehabilitation, in addition to job placement and training, you may be entitled to certain monetary benefits, including:

- temporary disability payments
- vocational rehabilitation maintenance allowance (VRMA), and
- costs.

Let's briefly look at each of these benefits.

a. Temporary Disability

If you are participating in vocational rehabilitation while still temporarily disabled, you will continue to get your temporary disability payments. (See Chapter 12 for more on temporary disability.)

b. Vocational Rehabilitation Maintenance Allowance (VRMA)

If you are not receiving temporary disability payments, you are entitled to a vocational rehabilitation maintenance allowance, also called VRMA, for as long as you are participating in vocational rehabilitation.

VRMA payments must be made every 14 days figured from the day designated for the first payment. The maintenance allowance is based upon two-thirds (2/3) of your average weekly wage up to a maximum of $246 per week. Maintenance allowance payments cannot exceed 52 weeks total, unless your vocational rehabilitation plan is delayed as a result of the insurance company's refusal to provide benefits.

If your maintenance allowance is less than the temporary disability you received before engaging in vocational rehabilitation, you may elect to supplement your maintenance allowance with advance payments of permanent disability benefits, up to the amount of what your temporary disability payments were. (LC § 139.5(d)(2).) However, any money advanced from the amount of your permanent disability will be deducted from your final settlement amount by the insurance company. (If you are considering doing this, please read Chapter 13, Section D2.)

VRMA may be withheld if an employee does not reasonably participate in the vocational rehabilitation process, such as by failing to attend scheduled meetings or by refusing to follow up on tasks assigned in the vocational rehabilitation plan. However, if the claims adjuster (also referred to as the claims administrator in vocational rehabilitation jargon) intends to withhold payment, it must give the employee a written notice stating the reasons and the employee's right to object within ten days. The employee may object by filing for dispute resolution, discussed in Section F7, below.

DELAYS IN VRMA

If the insurance company delays any VRMA payment, you may be entitled to receive a higher amount. See the discussion about penalties for late VRMA payments in Chapter 19, Section C4.

c. Costs

In addition to your maintenance allowance, you may be entitled to reimbursement for certain expenses that you incur in your vocational rehabilitation program, such as costs of school tuition, student fees, books, tools and equipment, required supplies and uniforms. You also may be entitled to reimbursement for living expenses if your retraining takes place away from home. The costs of a rehabilitation counselor will be paid directly by the insurance company, so you won't need to be reimbursed.

3. Plan Restrictions

Vocational rehabilitation plans have several restrictions:

- **total cost.** Benefits under the vocational rehabilitation plan are limited to $16,000. Included in this $16,000 cap is any vocational rehabilitation maintenance allowance you receive and up to $4,500 in fees for the counselor who assists you in preparing the plan.

- **vocational rehabilitation maintenance allowance (VRMA) is limited to a total of 52 weeks.** You may receive VRMA for a shorter time if the VRMA and other costs exceed the $16,000 cap within the 52-week period.
- **length of time.** In general, a plan must be completed within 18 consecutive months after its approval, including a 60-day period of job placement. Most plans take under a year to complete, with nine months being average. Although you have 18 months to complete your plan, you can only get VRMA for a maximum of 52 weeks (12 months). For example, you would have to finish the last six months of an 18-month Vocational Rehabilitation plan without being able to get VRMA. If you can't financially afford to do this, make sure your plan can be completed in 12 months!
- **location of rehabilitation plan.** The plan must take place inside California unless the insurance company agrees otherwise, or a request for dispute resolution has been filed and the Rehabilitation Unit finds that out-of-state services are more cost effective than similar services provided in California.
- **number of plans.** You generally are limited to one vocational rehabilitation plan unless the original plan becomes inappropriate. This might apply if your disability deteriorates to the point where you cannot meet the physical demands of the plan, the plan is disrupted due to circumstances beyond your control (such as a school's closing down), or your plan becomes unsuitable because the insurance company failed to provide benefits to you in a timely manner.

B. Six Steps in a Vocational Rehabilitation Plan

With vocational rehabilitation, there are six possible methods of returning you to work. Technically, these methods must be addressed in the order that they appear below. In other words, you cannot skip over one to get to another option. If the first option does not result in getting you back to work, you move on to the next. However, depending on your qualified rehabilitation representative (QRR), you may be able to use more than one method at the same time, such as on-the-job training and educational training.

Step 1: Job Modification

Job modification is the first and primary method of getting you back to work. Under this arrangement, you return to your old job, but your duties are modified according to your work restrictions so that you are not required to do anything that may harm you.

EXAMPLE: Jane seriously injures her right elbow while employed as a sales clerk. Her doctor gives a work restriction of "no lifting over 25 lbs. with her right arm." Jane's job required her to regularly lift boxes weighing up to 40 lbs. Jane's vocational rehabilitation plan calls for a modification of Jane's sales clerk job so that she is no longer required to lift anything over 25 lbs.

A modified job must pay within 15% of your previous salary and must last at least 12 months.

If a modified job fits all of the above requirements, you must accept it, or lose any future vocational rehabilitation benefits.

Step 2: Alternative Work

The alternative work option involves working with your present employer to transfer you to another position. If the salary for the alternate position is lower, it must be within 15% of your previous salary. The job must last at least 12 months and be within your capabilities.

EXAMPLE: George works in a warehouse, which requires heavy lifting. After he ruptures a disk in his back and qualifies for vocational rehabilitation, his employer retrains him and places him as a telephone operator at a salary that is 10% lower than his previous salary. George's new job requires no heavy lifting at all. George must take the job.

HOW TO REJECT AN OFFER OF MODIFIED OR ALTERNATIVE WORK

Sometimes employers offer work that does not meet the requirements of modified or alternative work. If this happens, make sure you reject the offer in writing. Send a letter to your employer by certified mail, return receipt requested. If you fail to do so, you may not be eligible for vocational rehabilitation benefits. Here's a sample:

Date

Employer's name
Employer's address

Dear [name of employer or supervisor]:

Please be advised that I am rejecting your offer of ["modified" or "alternative"] work pursuant to Labor Code Section 4644(a)(5). This job offer ["does not satisfy the work restrictions set forth in my doctor's report dated (date)" and/or "does not offer me a salary within 15% of my previous salary" and/or "is not expected to last at least 12 months."]

Sincerely,
[Injured worker's name]

Step 4: On-the-Job Training

On-the-job training is basically a paid apprenticeship program. You learn a new job or trade by working for a new employer. The insurance company generally pays the new employer a portion of your wage or salary while you are training.

EXAMPLE: Daryl is a truck driver who has undergone back surgery. Because of his injuries, he can only sit for short periods of time and cannot lift anything heavy. He is placed with a locksmith to learn that trade. During the apprenticeship period, Daryl's insurance company pays part of his salary.

Alternatively, you can do an unpaid internship at a new company while you collect your maintenance allowance.

Step 5: Educational Training

This method consists of attending college or some sort of trade school to acquire new skills so that you may get back to work. What we are talking about here is a short-term trade school or possibly a college course that can be completed in the 18-month time frame. You won't, however, be entitled to attend college for four years or go to law school.

Step 3: Direct Job Placement

This method involves finding other employment using transferable skills that you already have. For example, if you were employed as a nurse practitioner, but you have bookkeeping skills, you may be placed in a job that takes advantage of those skills. It is the job of the vocational rehabilitation counselor to determine what transferable skills you possess.

In practice, direct job placement involves looking for almost any kind of employment you can do. You may be required to search the want ads in various papers and answer any ad for which you are qualified. However, the Labor Code requires that suitable gainful employment be employment that returns you, as close as possible, to your pre-injury salary.

Step 6: Self-Employment

Self-employment is the last resort method available through vocational rehabilitation. Self-employment also allows you to get the entire amount of vocational rehabilitation money ($16,000). This method involves helping you go into business for yourself. In addition to helping you develop a business plan, some start-up expenses—salaries, rent, utilities and the like— may be paid for a short period of time. You will, however, have to pay for capital items such as equipment or vehicles.

If you don't have an attorney, self-employment plans must be approved by the Rehabilitation Unit. It's difficult to get such a plan approved because the Rehabilitation Unit does not favor self-employment plans and will not approve such a plan unless convinced it will succeed. If you are entitled to vocational rehabilitation benefits and would like to explore the possibility of getting the maximum amount of money, you should see a workers' compensation attorney. Self-employment type plans do not require approval of the Rehabilitation Unit if you have an attorney. (See Section H3 for a discussion about hiring a lawyer.)

C. Eligibility for Vocational Rehabilitation (QIW Status)

To qualify for vocational rehabilitation—or to determine that you are a qualified injured worker (QIW, in workers' compensation jargon)—you must meet both of these requirements:

- **You must be medically eligible.** A doctor must determine that you cannot return to your usual job due to the permanent disability caused by the effects of your injury. It doesn't matter whether your condition is fully a result of your most recent injury or is partially a result of a prior injury or disability. (Medical eligibility is discussed in more detail in Section 1, below.)
- **You must be physically and emotionally able to participate.** It must be expected that vocational rehabilitation services will help you return to suitable, gainful employment. This means that you cannot be so physically or emotionally disabled that you are unable to work at all. In workers' compensation jargon, this is also known as a finding that you are "feasible" to participate in vocational rehabilitation. ("Feasibility" is discussed in more detail in Section 2, below.)

If you have been temporarily totally disabled for a total of at least 365 days (they need not be consecutive), there is a "rebuttable presumption" that you are a QIW, thus eligible for vocational rehabilitation services. (LC § 4636(c).) This means that unless the insurance company can convince the Rehabilitation Unit that you are not entitled to vocational rehabilitation services, you are entitled.

QRR MAY ASSIST IN DETERMINING YOUR ELIGIBILITY

A qualified rehabilitation representative, or QRR, is someone with job experience in evaluating, counseling or placing industrially injured workers. Almost all injured workers are required to use the services of a QRR when setting up a vocational rehabilitation plan. (See Section F1a for the one exception to the rule requiring a QRR.) Most injured workers also use the services of a QRR in determining their status as a QIW, although this is not required. (See Section F1 for information on choosing a QRR.)

1. Determination of Medical Eligibility

You are medically eligible for vocational rehabilitation if you're permanently disabled and can't return to your former job. Some injuries are so serious that it is obvious that returning to your former employment is out of the question, and the treating doctor will make the determination in a report while you are still temporarily disabled.

For most people, medical eligibility is not quite as cut-and-dried, because it takes time to see what your eventual condition will be. The treating doctor usually makes the initial determination of your eligibility for vocational rehabilitation benefits in the permanent and stationary report, although there is no legal reason why you must wait until then.

a. How the Doctor Determines Your QIW Status: The Job Analysis

The treating doctor or qualified medical evaluator probably will not be familiar with your duties at your pre-injury job. However, the doctor must know what activities you are required to do if you return to your former job before she can decide if your permanent disabilities will prevent you from doing that work.

To assist the doctor in making this determination, a job analysis (known as a JA in workers' compensation jargon) may be prepared and provided to the doctor. When you have been totally disabled for 90 days or more and you have not yet been determined to be a qualified injured worker (QIW), the insurance company is responsible for preparing and providing the doctor with a job analysis. The claims administrator must assist you in the joint development of a job description. (CCR § 10124(b)(1).)

You are entitled to participate in developing the job analysis, and when complete, you must sign it or it won't be valid. In this way, you can make certain that the job analysis fairly and accurately represents your duties. The job analysis sets forth in detail the physical requirements of your job at the time of your injury. These activities might include walking, running, standing, sitting, lifting, pushing and pulling, computer work and other tasks relevant to your field of work.

The job analysis can be a very powerful tool in obtaining vocational rehabilitation benefits (or in getting a medical opinion that you can return to your job, if that's what you want). Make sure that you're consulted regarding every aspect of your job analysis.

Oftentimes, the QRR or the insurance company will go to your place of employment and interview your boss and co-employees regarding your job duties. You are entitled to be there when this is done, and, if at all possible, you should take advantage of this right. This will allow you to immediately dispute any incorrect information. Pictures or videotapes may be taken of your work environment to be included in the job analysis.

If the QRR or insurance company will not agree on your estimates of your job activities in the job analysis, you can write down your position in the comments section of the job analysis for consideration by the doctor (before you sign it).

b.   Other Factors Considered by the Doctor

In determining your medical eligibility for vocational rehabilitation benefits, the treating doctor takes into account:

- your current and probable future medical condition
- an estimate of your current and potential work restrictions
- your ability to accept and participate in vocational rehabilitation services
- recommendations for subsequent evaluations or services, if any

- your ability to engage in light work in a modified or alternative capacity if available, and
- any other information the doctor feels is relevant. (LC § 4636(a).)

c.   If You Disagree With Treating Doctor's Opinion

You will be mailed a copy of the treating doctor's medical report containing the doctor's opinion of your eligibility for vocational rehabilitation. If you don't agree with this opinion, object in writing within 30 days of the date you receive the treating doctor's report. If you don't object within the 30 days, you may have forever given up your right to do so. (But you should object, anyhow, and seek assistance from a lawyer or Information and Assistance officer.)

If you object to the treating doctor's determination of your QIW status, you are entitled to be examined by a qualified medical evaluator who will make a determination of whether or not you are a QIW. (See Chapter 10 for more on qualified medical evaluations.)

SAMPLE OBJECTION LETTER

3/20/year

XYZ Insurance Company
333 N. West Ave.
Bartville, CA 99999

Applicant: David Wong
Employer: Urban Manufacturing
Date of injury: 3/2/year
Claim No: 8841
Case No: IF0123
Subject: Objection to ineligibility for vocational rehabilitation benefits

To whom it may concern:

As required by Labor Code Section 4062, I object to the determination of Dr. Wilson, as set forth in her report of 2/28/year, that I am not entitled to vocational rehabilitation benefits.

Please forward to me the form to request assignment of a panel of three Qualified Medical Examiners to decide this issue.

Sincerely,

David Wong

David Wong

d.   If the Treating Doctor Cannot Decide Your QIW Status

If your treating doctor cannot make a determination of your QIW status at the time he is first asked to do so, the insurance company must monitor your recovery and request a report from the treating doctor as soon as he is able. The treating doctor is required to send a report to both you and the insurance company no less than every 60 days, until the doctor either determines that you can or cannot return to your former employment, and are therefore entitled or not entitled to vocational rehabilitation services. (LC § 4636(b).) The insurance company or your qualified rehabilitation representative should keep in close contact with the treating doctor to assure that he does not delay in deciding this issue.

2.   Determination of Physical and Emotional Ability to Participate ("Feasibility")

The next step is to determine whether you are physically and mentally capable of participating in a vocational rehabilitation program, referred to in workers' compensation jargon as "feasibility."

As a practical matter, most workers who are medically eligible are also "feasible" to participate in vocational rehabilitation. If, however, an injury is very severe, the injured worker may not be physically or emotionally able to complete a vocational rehabilitation program. For example, if you are in such excruciating pain that you can't get out of bed for more than five minutes at a time, you quite possibly won't be considered feasible to complete a vocational rehabilitation plan.

If you are not presently feasible, but become so at a later date (your medical condition has improved), you can request vocational rehabilitation at that time. Note, however, you must make your request within five years from the date of injury, or one year from the date of your settlement (whichever is later).

The determination of feasibility is usually made by your QRR after the insurance company sends you written notice of your medical eligibility. (LC § 4637(a)(5).) As part of doing this, the QRR will ask you questions about your ability to do certain things, such as sit, stand and study.

Whether you are determined to be feasible is normally in your hands. Don't say you can't do a certain activity unless you are 100% certain you can't do it. However, if you are positive about participating in vocational rehabilitation, you will nor-

mally pass the feasibility test, unless you are obviously physically unable to participate.

While usually not necessary, a QRR may request a feasibility evaluation to help determine whether you are feasible for vocational rehabilitation. This is a comprehensive ten-day evaluation that measures your pain tolerance and ability to walk, stand, sit, lift and perform other actions. Because a feasibility evaluation is very expensive, the QRR will generally not request it unless she feels it is necessary to determine your ability to participate. If you are asked to participate in a feasibility evaluation, the cost of the study will be included in the $16,000 cap on your plan, meaning you can't use that money for other parts of your plan. For this reason, if a feasibility evaluation is requested, you should normally contact the QRR and seek other alternatives to the feasibility evaluation.

If the QRR determines that you are not feasible to participate, she must write you a letter and explain the basis for the decision as well as the procedure for contesting it. (CCR §§ 10009(c)(2), 10006(b), LC § 4637(b).)

If the QRR determines that you are feasible to participate in vocational rehabilitation, and you are medically eligible, she will contact you regarding the preparation of a vocational rehabilitation plan.

D.   How to Start Vocational Rehabilitation

See *Visalia School District, Petitioner v. WCAB and Lube Hernandez, Respondents* in Chapter 28.

The insurance company is obliged to inform you of your rights to vocational rehabilitation. You, however, must accept primary responsibility for requesting vocational rehabilitation benefits.

1.   Receive Notice of Your Rights

See *Double D Transport Company v. WCAB (Copeland)* in Chapter 28.

If you've been totally disabled for a total of 90 days (the days you have been disabled need not be consecutive), the workers' compensation insurance company must give you written information about your right to vocational rehabilitation. The written materials must inform you about a number of issues, including the maintenance allowance, the scope of services available to you and your rights under the Americans With Disabilities Act. (LC § 4636, CCR § 10008.)

Also after 90 days of total disability, the insurance company has ten days to provide you with a pamphlet entitled "Help in Returning to Work," along with information on how to contact an Information and Assistance Officer.

2. Insurance Company Informs You of Medical Eligibility

Within ten days of learning that you are medically eligible for voc rehab, the insurance company must notify you in writing of your entitlement to vocational rehabilitation services. The notice must advise you of certain rights and responsibilities. You'll then have 90 days to apply for vocational rehabilitation services.

A copy of the written notice also must be mailed to the Rehabilitation Unit (the entity that resolves disputes between you and the insurance company regarding your entitlement to vocational rehabilitation benefits).

3. Recommendation of a QRR

A Qualified Rehabilitation Representative (QRR) has experience involving the evaluation, counseling or placement of industrially injured workers. A QRR may be in-house (an employee of the insurance company) or an outside contractor. The insurance company must, with your input, recommend a QRR unless:

- your medical condition precludes your participation in vocational rehabilitation
- you decline to accept vocational rehabilitation services, or
- you qualify for the one exception to the rule requiring a QRR and notify the insurance carrier that you don't want a QRR. (For more on this, see Section F1a, below.)

Section F1, below, covers QRRs in detail and gives suggestions on how to choose one.

4. Request Vocational Rehabilitation

If your employer or its insurance company has notified you that you may be eligible for vocational rehabilitation benefits, you have 90 days to request (accept) them, or you may lose your right to benefits.

If you don't request vocational rehabilitation benefits within 45 days after being notified that you may be entitled to do so, the insurance company must remind you in writing of your right to these services. If the insurance company does not do so, you may still be entitled to benefits after the expiration of the 90 days.

⚠ REQUEST BENEFITS

You should *always* request vocational rehabilitation benefits within 90 days of receiving notice from the insurance company, even if you do not plan to participate or you want to wait and participate later. You may apply for benefits and not use them, but if you don't apply and later change your mind, it will probably be too late.

If you haven't been notified of your eligibility for vocational rehabilitation, but you have been made permanent and stationary, you'll have to be proactive.

Immediately review all of the medical reports to determine if the doctor has given an opinion on your qualified injured worker status. The treating doctor's opinion can usually be found in a sub-heading entitled "Vocational Rehabilitation." It is typically a one-paragraph opinion, which may read something like this:

> "*Vocational Rehabilitation.* Based upon the work restrictions as set forth in this report, it is my opinion that the injured worker is not capable of returning to his employment and is therefore a qualified injured worker."

If the treating doctor states that you are eligible for vocational rehabilitation benefits, and if you agree with that opinion, you should immediately send a written request to the insurance company to provide vocational rehabilitation benefits. A simple handwritten or typed letter or note will suffice.

If you have not been notified that you may be eligible for vocational rehabilitation benefits, you must usually make your request within five years from the date of injury, or you will no longer be able to do so. If, however, you have neither received nor formally requested benefits (filed an RU-104 form) during the five years, you may still request rehabilitation benefits within one year from the date your case settles. If, for example, your case settles six years from the date of injury, and you didn't request or receive vocational rehabilitation benefits, you have one year from the date of settlement to request benefits. (LC §§ 5405.5, 5410.)

Some injured workers may wish to return to their former job, and may believe that they are capable of doing so. In those cases, it is possible that the doctor could say the injured worker is entitled to vocational rehabilitation and yet the worker would not agree with that opinion. If you disagree with the treating doctor's opinion for any reason, immediately make your written objection to the insurance company. (See Section C1c, above.) If it is later determined that you are a QIW, you can still participate in vocational rehabilitation. In other words, the fact that you initially objected to vocational rehabilitation does not waive your right to it later.

E. Delays and Failure to Provide Rehabilitation Services

 See *Industrial Indemnity v. WCAB (Elizondo)* in Chapter 28.

Most insurance companies comply with legal requirements to provide vocational rehabilitation when it's warranted. But if the insurance company doesn't follow the correct procedure, you do have some recourse. Start by calling or writing the insurance company to determine why you were not provided with benefits. This may be all you need do to resolve the problem. Should the insurance company continue to fail to notify you of your possible entitlement to vocational rehabilitation services, fail to recommend a QRR, or fail to provide vocational rehabilitation services when required, you may request the administrative director of the Workers' Compensation Rehabilitation Unit to authorize vocational rehabilitation services at your employer's expense. (LC § 4639.) Section H1 discusses how to request the assistance of the administrative director.

If the insurance company causes any delay in providing you with required vocational rehabilitation services, you are entitled to payment of a maintenance allowance for the period of the delay at your temporary disability rate. The temporary disability rate may be higher than your VRMA rate. In addition, the maintenance allowance and any costs attributable to the delay will not be counted toward the overall $16,000 cap on vocational rehabilitation services. (LC § 4642(a).)

 PENALTIES FOR UNNECESSARY DELAY IN PROVIDING BENEFITS

If the insurance carrier unreasonably delays in providing you vocational rehabilitation benefits, a judge may require the insurance company to pay a 10% penalty on all vocational rehabilitation costs. (LC § 5814.)

F. Preparing a Vocational Rehabilitation Plan

A vocational rehabilitation plan is a written proposal of how to get a qualified injured worker back to suitable gainful employment—following the six steps discussed in Section B, above:

- job modification
- alternative work

- direct job placement
- on-the-job training
- educational training, and
- self-employment. (CCR § 10002(g), LC § 4635(e).)

In creating a vocational rehabilitation plan, the Qualified Rehabilitation Representative (QRR) must consider the injured employee's qualifications, extent of disability, pre-injury earnings, future earning capacity, vocational interests and aptitudes, as well as the present labor market.

1. Selecting a Qualified Rehabilitation Representative (QRR)

A QRR evaluates, counsels and places industrially injured workers. QRRs are often counselors or occupational therapists or hold some other title; however, that is not required.

a. Decide Whether to Waive Services of a QRR

The only way you can seek a waiver of a QRR's services is if you are well on your way toward completing a certificate or degree program from a community college, a California State University or the University of California prior to the date you requested benefits. (CCR § 10126(5).)

Here's why it may be to your advantage to not use a QRR. There is a $16,000 cap on the amount of money that can be spent on a vocational rehabilitation plan. By eliminating the QRR fee (up to $4,500), you may use the money to pay for other aspects of your plan, such as your maintenance allowance, tuition or textbooks.

Substantial progress toward completing a certificate or degree program includes, but is not limited to, situations where you can demonstrate all of the following:

- You were, are, or will be enrolled as a full-time student taking 12 units or more.
- You have completed 35% or more of the units necessary to complete your degree or certificate program and you have at least a "C" grade in those courses.
- You can produce a letter of recommendation from the school in which you are enrolled endorsing your course of study. This letter must be from the Dean of Admissions, the school department head or the school counselor. The letter must be accompanied by an outline of the courses to be taken and the estimated time for completion of each course.
- If your vocational rehabilitation plan requires additional expenses (money) over and above the $16,000 cap or will take longer than 18 months, you must show that you have the financial ability and time to complete the plan.

However, don't jump to conclusions when deciding whether you need a QRR. In fact, it may be to your advantage to have the assistance of a qualified QRR, because he can handle all the procedural aspects of your vocational rehabilitation case as well as assist you in formulating a plan and finding employment.

b. Picking a QRR

There are hundreds of QRRs in California, ranging from self-employed individuals to relatively large companies. It is important that you and the insurance company agree upon an experienced and knowledgeable QRR to put together your vocational rehabilitation plan. Don't agree to the first QRR recommended by the insurance company without investigating the person's credentials, experience and attitude. Because you must agree to the choice of the QRR, the insurance company has no rights to impose someone on you.

⚠ THE INSURANCE COMPANY MAY WANT AN IN-HOUSE QRR
The insurance company may recommend an in-house QRR—who is employed by the insurance company. Frankly, I would just say "no." I can't think of any reason why a person who works for the opposing side of your case will have your best interests at heart when preparing a vocational rehabilitation plan.

Because it is so important to get a qualified QRR, spend a little time checking out the QRR's qualifications and philosophy. Call the QRR and ask questions such as these: How long has he been in business? How many people has he placed in jobs in the last year? Ask specific questions regarding your type of injury and whether he feels he could write a vocational rehabilitation plan that would allow for the kind of work you would like to do. Make sure you feel comfortable with him.

You might also try calling a few workers' compensation law firms that represent injured workers (applicants) and ask to speak to whoever handles vocational rehabilitation plans. Ask that person what she thinks of the QRR recommended by the insurance company.

c.   Problems With the QRR

If you don't want the QRR the insurance company proposed, one good approach is to propose a different one. If you and the insurance company cannot agree on a QRR within 15 days, either party may file a Request for Dispute Resolution (Form RU-103) with the Rehabilitation Unit, requesting appointment of an Independent Vocational Evaluator (IVE).

If for any reason you are not satisfied with your QRR, you have the right to request one change. You can do this by calling or writing the insurance carrier and requesting a new QRR. If the insurance carrier refuses to authorize a new QRR, you will have to file a Request for Dispute Resolution (Form RU-103).

d.   Using an Independent Vocational Evaluator (IVE)

An Independent Vocational Evaluator (IVE) is an experienced QRR. Within 15 days of a request by one of the parties (or the Rehabilitation Unit's determination that an IVE is required), the unit appoints an IVE.

The Rehabilitation Unit may order that services be provided by an IVE at the insurance company's expense in any of these circumstances:

- The employer failed to provide vocational rehabilitation services in a timely manner (when required by law).
- An independent evaluation is necessary for the Rehabilitation Unit to determine if an employee is vocationally feasible.
- An IVE is necessary to determine if a vocational rehabilitation plan meets legal requirements.
- The employee and QRR cannot agree on a vocational goal. (CCR § 10127.2(f).)

2.   QRR Prepares a Vocational Rehabilitation Plan

The insurance company forwards all medical and vocational rehabilitation reports in your case to the QRR you've agreed upon. Within 15 days of receipt of the referral, the QRR contacts you, usually by letter, to arrange for a meeting and an initial evaluation to determine whether you are feasible for vocational rehabilitation services.

Within 90 days of the QRR's initial evaluation, the insurance company must:

- submit a vocational rehabilitation plan to you
- notify you that you are not a qualified injured worker (QIW) and the reason for the determination, or
- request the Rehabilitation Unit to resolve a dispute concerning your QIW status or the provisions of the vocational rehabilitation services. (CCR § 10009(c), LC § 4638.)

Assuming the QRR decides to go ahead and develop a plan, in a subsequent meeting, your QRR will begin the process of determining the best way to get you back to work. He will want to know about your education background, your work experiences and the type of work you may be interested in pursuing. The QRR probably will want to give you an aptitude test to determine what types of jobs you are best suited for.

Take an active role in the development of your plan. Try to get the QRR on your side by explaining your vocational goals and desires. If you communicate and work well with the QRR, there is a much better chance that you'll be pleased with your new job. Above all, make sure that the plan provides for employment in a field that you will be happy working in. Nothing could be worse than ending up in a job you don't like. Don't allow yourself to be "railroaded" into a line of work you know you will hate. After all, you may be doing this work for the rest of your life.

The QRR's aim is to come up with a plan that will provide a job with similar wages, hours and working conditions to the one you had when you had your industrial injury; however, this is not always possible. If you are not satisfied with the QRR's proposals, you need to sit down and carefully consider whether it is you or your QRR who is being unreasonable. If your QRR has offered reasonable explanations as to why the plan is appropriate, you should probably follow his advice. However, if you feel the QRR has not provided adequate reasoning, you might consider contacting the insurance company to request a new QRR.

After the QRR has determined your qualifications, he will look at the available job market. With the help of your aptitude test, and taking into consideration your physical restrictions, the QRR will put together a vocational rehabilitation plan to get you back to work. The written plan defines the responsibilities of the insurance company, the injured worker, the QRR and any other parties involved in implementing the plan. It also contains detailed information about your disability, the plan objectives and how these goals will be reached. In addition to training, the plan should include a period of job placement. For example, if you are retraining to be a plumber, your plan should include a period of assistance by the QRR in finding you a job with a plumbing outfit.

Use all available outside resources in developing a plan. Ask your QRR about available resources that may help you keep from using up the $16,000 cap for training expenses (thus allowing more maintenance allowance for you). This might include:

- **grants or loans for educational or vocational training.** Go to the library and research any grants available to you based on factors such as your sex or nationality.
- **special funds if your job was lost due to foreign competition under the Trade Relocation Act (T.R.A.).** If you lost your job due to foreign competition, you may be entitled to two years of school and a year of unemployment benefits.
- **the state vocational rehabilitation program.** This program is similar to workers' compensation vocational rehabilitation, but it is funded and run by the state. Anyone with a disability (caused by work or otherwise) may be entitled to participate.

The plan will discuss the expenses that will be paid by the insurance company. It will indicate the rate at which you will be paid temporary disability or a maintenance allowance. The plan must also contain a description of the level of participation in the plan expected of you in order for you to receive your maintenance allowance. If you fail to adhere to the agreement, the claims adjuster may petition to withhold your maintenance allowance.

LIST ANTICIPATED EXPENSES IN YOUR PLAN

To be reimbursable by the insurance company, all expenses you may personally incur while participating in vocational rehabilitation must be listed in the plan. Don't overlook these items:

- QRR fees
- transportation expenses to and from any vocational rehabilitation training facility (currently paid at the rate of 0.31¢ per mile)
- costs of retraining, including required supplies, tools and equipment, student fees, tuition, books, uniforms and other incidental costs
- additional living expenses if you must be away from home on a temporary basis or are too far to commute. For example, if your plan requires you to attend a two-week vocational training at a school located 300 miles from your home, you should be reimbursed for costs of your food and lodging, and possibly child care expenses
- clothing allowance, if you do not have suitable attire necessary to participate in training, placement or work activities, and
- relocation expenses, if you are required to permanently relocate. This includes costs of moving household goods and other personal items, transportation allowance to the new residence and reimbursement of non-refundable deposits and charges incurred by a permanent change of residence.

---

3. If the QRR Fails to Develop a Plan Within 90 Days

If the QRR cannot develop a vocational rehabilitation plan for the insurance company to submit to the Rehabilitation Unit within 90 days of the initial evaluation, the QRR must notify both you and the insurance company why a plan could not be developed and how much additional time it will take to do so. If there is any dispute regarding how the plan is progressing, you may request the assistance of the Rehabilitation Unit. For example, if you disagree with the type of work the QRR is trying to get you into, you can ask for help from the Rehabilitation Unit.

Within 90 days after determination of the your vocational feasibility, the QRR, in conjunction with the insurance company, must either:

- submit a vocational rehabilitation plan agreed to by you, to the Rehabilitation Unit for review and approval, or
- meet with the insurance company and request a formal resolution.

4. QRR Must File Periodic Reports

At periodic intervals, generally every 30 days, the QRR must file reports with the Rehabilitation Unit and give copies to you and the insurance company. These reports must set forth what has transpired in the previous 30 days (or since the last report) regarding vocational rehabilitation services (or lack of services).

5. Plan Approval

Once the QRR has developed a vocational rehabilitation plan, it must be submitted to you and the insurance company for approval. You and the insurance company must agree or object to the proposed plan in writing within 15 days of receipt. If you disagree with the plan, the insurance company must submit the proposed plan and a statement summarizing the dispute to the Rehabilitation Unit.

Assuming you agree with the plan, the next step is to submit the plan to the Rehabilitation Unit, unless your plan provides for modified or alternative work with the same employer, in which case this isn't necessary.

⚠ IF YOU DO NOT APPROVE OF A PLAN

If you object to a plan that the insurance company submits to the Rehabilitation Unit for approval, you have 15 days to file a written objection. Simply write the Rehabilitation Unit a letter stating that you object to the plan as submitted and specifying why you disapprove of the plan. (CCR § 10012(c).)

If you don't use the services of a QRR, your plan must be submitted by the insurance company to the Rehabilitation Unit within 15 days of your agreement to the provisions of the plan. (CCR § 10126(b)(2).)

The Rehabilitation Unit must approve or disapprove a submitted plan within 30 days and advise you, the insurance company and the QRR of its decision. If the Rehabilitation Unit does not take action within those 30 days, the plan is deemed approved unless you or the insurance company object to the plan in writing within that same 30-day time frame.

Any changes to a rehabilitation plan must be approved by the Rehabilitation Unit. You or the claims administrator may request that the Rehabilitation Unit approve a modification of a previously approved plan because of an unforeseen circumstance arising after the initial plan agreement. (CCR § 10126(d).) For example, if your medical condition deteriorates to the point where you can no longer participate in the plan as drafted, your plan may be completely changed or modified to accommodate your new restrictions.

6. Receive Vocational Rehabilitation Benefits

While you're participating in the plan, make sure that you receive the correct amount of any temporary disability and maintenance allowance you may be entitled to, as discussed in Sections A2a and A2b, above.

In addition, your QRR should see to it that you're reimbursed for any costs you incur that are included in the plan. Make a written request to your QRR for reimbursement and include receipts to substantiate what you spent. You may use the same form that you use for requesting mileage and reimbursements for your medical treatment. (See Chapter 11, Sections A1 and A2.)

7. Problems With the Plan

Not every plan goes as smoothly as anticipated. It's possible that you or the insurance company may not live up to its terms. For instance, the insurance company may not pay vocational rehabilitation maintenance allowance at the correct rate, or you may develop transportation problems that prevent you from attending scheduled appointments.

In situations such as these, the Rehabilitation Unit may either order an extension of the plan or the development of a new plan, during which time you will continue to be paid vocational rehabilitation maintenance allowance.

If the insurance company gives you a written warning about your non-participation, you have ten days to comply. If you don't, the Rehabilitation Unit may, at the request of the insurance company, issue an order terminating your vocational rehabilitation benefits. Once a plan is terminated, it is difficult—but not impossible—to get another plan. You will have to convince the Rehabilitation Unit that this time you will actively participate.

Either of the following may also be grounds for termination of a plan:

- The insurance company fails to provide the necessary funds or services in sufficient time to enable you to participate in services specified in the plan.

    EXAMPLE: Connie's vocational rehabilitation plan specifies that the insurance company is to pay her $300 as soon as she is certified as a smog technician (the funds are necessary to obtain a license). The insurance company fails to do so despite numerous requests for payment. This may be deemed a breach by the insurance company that could entitle Connie to a new plan, because without a license she cannot obtain employment as a smog technician.

- You are unable to comply with the provisions of the approved plan, and fail to notify the QRR within five days of the reasons for your inability to comply.

    EXAMPLE: Thomas becomes so ill so that he cannot attend the classes specified in his plan. He has five days (assuming he is well enough to do so) to inform his QRR that illness precludes him from attending class.

If you receive a written warning from the insurance company alleging that you violated the vocational rehabilitation plan, and you disagree, you should immediately contact the insurance company. If you can't resolve the problem, you'll need to file for a dispute resolution right away. (Contact the Rehabilitation Unit for instructions on how to do this.)

G. Completing a Vocational Rehabilitation Plan

A vocational rehabilitation plan is complete when the insurance company and employee have fulfilled their respective obligations specified in the plan or when the maximum expenditures for vocational rehabilitation services have been reached, whichever occurs first.

It is not uncommon for an injured worker to complete a vocational rehabilitation plan and still not have found employment. Unfortunately, there is no guarantee that upon completing a vocational rehabilitation plan, you will have a job.

If the plan provided for modified or alternative work with the same employer, the insurance company must, upon completion of the plan, submit a request to conclude vocational rehabilitation services to the Rehabilitation Unit, along with a copy of the plan. (CCR §§ 10012(b), 10126(b).) The insurance company will generally want an order from the Rehabilitation Unit "closing rehabilitation services," meaning that the injured worker is not entitled to any additional benefits.

H. Where to Get Help With Vocational Rehabilitation

Various problems or disagreements may arise during the course of your vocational rehabilitation plan. Some of the more common problems include:

- the insurance company contests your right to rehabilitation benefits
- you and the insurance company are having trouble agreeing upon a QRR
- you and the QRR disagree about the details of your rehabilitation plan
- the insurance company fails to provide vocational rehabilitation services or benefits
- the insurance company files a request for termination of your rehabilitation services
- you are not happy with the way the plan is working, or
- the plan is over and you are not happy with the result.

1. Help From the Rehabilitation Unit

You can file certain documents with the Rehabilitation Unit to request resolution of your dispute. You may also request formal and informal conferences with Rehabilitation Unit representatives to help resolve issues. Prior to filing a formal request for dispute resolution, you must first contact the insurance carrier and request an informal conference. This is a meeting or discussion over the phone to try and resolve the issues in dispute.

Phone numbers for all Rehabilitation Units are listed in Appendix 5. The Rehabilitation Unit is usually located in the same building as the Workers' Compensation Appeals Board. However, because the office that is appropriate for you is determined by the zip code of your current home address (if you live outside of the state, this would be the zip code of your last California residence), it is possible that your workers' compensation case may be handled at one Appeals Board, and your vocational rehabilitation handled at a Rehabilitation Unit located at a different Appeals Board. Contact your local Appeals Board or Information and Assistance Officer for the address and telephone number of the Rehabilitation Unit that is appropriate for you.

You may also get the local address and phone number, along with instructions on filing documents with the Rehabilitation Unit by writing to:

Rehabilitation Unit Headquarters

P.O. Box 420603

San Francisco, CA 94141

You and the insurance company both have the right to appeal a decision of the Rehabilitation Unit. You must file your appeal with the Workers' Compensation Appeals Board within 20 days after you receive notice of a decision. This procedure is beyond the scope of the book, and you should see an attorney or request help from an Information and Assistance officer.

2. Help From an Information and Assistance Officer

If you have questions about vocational rehabilitation, you may request the assistance of the Information and Assistance Officer at your local Workers' Compensation Appeals Board. Information is provided in Chapter 26, Section A and in Appendix 5.

3. Hiring a Lawyer

If you hire a lawyer, she will keep track of the hours she worked on the vocational rehabilitation portion of your case and eventually be eligible for payment at an hourly rate. The insurance company may withhold 12% to 15% of your vocational rehabilitation costs for attorney fees.

Note that most lawyers will be more interested in representing you if your entire claim has not settled. If vocational rehabilitation is the only outstanding issue you need help with, it may be difficult to find a lawyer who is willing to accept your case. (If you want to hire a workers' compensation attorney, see Chapter 26, Section B.)

FORMS FILED WITH THE REHABILITATION UNIT

You may request assistance of the Rehabilitation Unit by filing the appropriate form. A copy of the form must be mailed to all the other parties at the same time you file it with the Rehabilitation Unit. (CCR § 10123(b).) Problems with vocational rehabilitation plans are usually resolved by filing one of these forms:

- RU-90: Treating Physician's Report of Disability Status
- RU-91: Description of the Employee's Job Duties
- RU-101: Case Initiation Document
- RU-102: Vocational Rehabilitation Plan
- RU-103: Request For Dispute Resolution
- RU-104: Employee's Request for Order of Vocational Rehabilitation Services
- RU-105: Employer's Request For Termination of Rehabilitation Services
- RU-107: Declination Of Vocational Rehabilitation Benefits

You can get these rehabilitation forms from your local Rehabilitation Unit or:

Rehabilitation Unit Headquarters

P.O. Box 3032

Sacramento, CA 95814-3032

They are also available on the Division of Workers' Compensation website, at http://www.dir.ca.gov/dwc/forms.html.

15

Death Benefits

When a work injury or illness causes or contributes to the death of an employee, the surviving dependents are entitled to recover death benefits. (LC § 4703.) These benefits consist of:

- a fixed sum of money; the amount depends on the number of surviving dependents and the date the injury occurred
- actual burial expenses up to $5,000, and
- retroactive temporary disability and accrued permanent disability payments (dependents get these only if they are also the worker's legal heirs).

It's also likely that surviving dependents may be eligible for benefits outside the workers' compensation system, such as Social Security; please refer to Chapter 17 for details.

⚠ MAKE SURE YOU RECEIVE ALL BENEFITS

Insurance companies sometimes try to pay less than a death claim is worth. Read this chapter carefully to make sure you (or any dependents) are not shortchanged.

💼 IF YOUR DEATH BENEFITS CLAIM IS DENIED

If the insurance carrier disputes your entitlement to death benefits as a surviving dependent of a deceased worker, you should immediately see an Information and Assistance officer or a competent workers' compensation attorney.

A. Who May Receive Death Benefits

You are entitled to death benefits if you are a surviving dependent of the deceased employee. This includes most surviving spouses and children under 18. While you do not have to be in these categories to be legally considered a surviving dependent, you must be able to prove that you were either totally or partially dependent upon the deceased employee for financial support. The date of the injury that resulted in death—not the date of death—is used to determine whether or not you qualify as a dependent.

Here's the difference between total and partial dependency:

- **Total dependent.** This person is presumed to have completely depended upon the deceased worker for support.
- **Partial dependent.** This person depended to some degree, but not totally, upon the deceased worker for support.

There are two situations where a surviving relative is conclusively presumed to be totally dependent for support upon the deceased employee. This means that the insurance carrier cannot deny total dependency, even if there is evidence to the contrary:

- **Spouse.** If a deceased employee was married at the time of death, and the surviving spouse earned $30,000 or less in the 12 months immediately preceding the death, the surviving spouse is conclusively presumed to be totally dependent for support upon the deceased employee. (LC § 3501.)
- **Children (by blood or adoption).** A minor child (under age 18), or an adult child who cannot earn a living due to physical or mental incapacity, is conclusively presumed to be totally dependent for support upon a deceased employee-parent if that child was living with the employee-parent at the time of injury. (LC § 3501.)

If neither of the situations listed above exists, the surviving relative must prove his financial dependence on the deceased employee.

> **EXAMPLE 1:** Tom and his mother were living with his father when he was killed in a freak accident at work. Tom was 12 years old at the time of his father's death, and his mother did not work. Both Tom and his mother are total dependents.

> **EXAMPLE 2:** Trevor is 22 years old and still lives with his parents. His father, John, is injured on the job and dies as a result of that injury. Because Trevor is over 18, and not physically or mentally incapacitated, to be entitled to any death benefit, he must prove that at the time of injury, he was totally or partially dependent upon his father for support. If Trevor was not working on the date of his father's injury, and had no source of income, he may be able to show total dependency upon his father, even if his mother was also working. If Trevor was working part-time, he may be able to show partial dependency upon his father for support.

B. Death Benefit Amount

The fixed-sum death benefit that surviving dependents are entitled to depends upon:

- the date of the injury that resulted in death, and
- the number of total and partial dependents the deceased wage earner had. (LC § 4702.)

The accompanying chart and following discussion cover how much total and partial dependents may be entitled to receive.

TOTAL AMOUNT OF DEATH BENEFITS		
Date of injury	One total dependent	More than one total dependent or one total dependent and one or more partial dependents
7/1/94-06/30/96	$115,000	$135,000 for 2 dependents $150,000 for 3 or more dependents
7/1/96 and later	$125,000	$145,000 for 2 dependents $160,000 for 3 or more dependents

1. One Total Dependent Only

If you are the sole surviving total dependent, and there are no partial dependents, you are entitled to the entire death benefit amount. Look at the accompanying chart and locate the date of injury. The amount you are entitled to is listed in the second column. For example, if the date of injury was 5/7/96, you would be entitled to $115,000. If the deceased employee was injured on 5/1/01, you would be entitled to $125,000.

2. Two or More Total Dependents

When there are at least two surviving total dependents, they will split the amount of money in the last column of the chart. In this situation, if there are any partial dependents, they are not entitled to anything.

EXAMPLE 1: Woody is injured on 12/5/00 and dies a month later, leaving a surviving wife and a small daughter. Woody's wife and daughter are entitled to split $145,000, or $72,500 each.

EXAMPLE 2: Assume the same facts, with the exception that Woody and his wife had two young daughters. In addition, Woody had a son from a previous marriage who partially depended on him for support. His surviving wife and two daughters are entitled to a third of $160,000, or $53,333 each. The son doesn't get anything.

3. One Total Dependent and One or More Partial Dependents

If there is only one total dependent, but one or more partial dependents, the total dependent is entitled to the entire sum of money in the second column entitled "One total dependent."

The partial dependents are also entitled to benefits. They receive four times the amount annually devoted to their support, as long as the total all partial dependents receive does not exceed the difference between the second and third columns in the chart. If the amount that partial dependents would be entitled to exceeds that difference, then each takes a proportionate share of the maximum amount available.

EXAMPLE: Charlie dies as a result of a 10/21/00 work injury, leaving one son from his current marriage and two sons from a previous marriage. Larry is found to be a total dependent, and is entitled to $125,000. Mo and Curly, who each received $6,000 per year in support, are determined to be partial dependents. They are entitled to a maximum of $24,000 each (four times $6,000), based upon four times the amount annually devoted to their support by their father. However, because only $35,000 is available between them ($160,000 – $125,000), Mo and Curly receive $17,500 each.

4. Partial Dependents Only

If there are no total dependents, the partial dependents are entitled to four times the amount annually devoted to their respective support by the deceased employee, not to exceed the amount in the second column, entitled "one total dependent." If the amount that partial dependents would be entitled to exceeds the amount in column 2, each takes a proportionate share of the maximum amount available.

EXAMPLE 1: Lori received a total of $10,500 per year from Ed for her support. Upon Ed's work-related death, Lori may be entitled to receive $42,000 (four times $10,500) if she qualifies as a partial dependent.

EXAMPLE 2: Sean partially supported her three college-aged children, Mike ($15,000 per year), Cathy ($7,000 per year) and Donna ($5,000 per year). Sean dies in an injury at work on 11/20/00, thus the maximum amount available to her dependents is $125,000. Mike may receive $60,000, Cathy may receive $28,000 and Donna may get $20,000. The total Sean's three children receive is $108,000.

C. Additional Payments for Dependent Minor Children

 See *Wright Schuchart-Harbor v. WCAB (Morrow, deceased)* and *Foodmaker v. WCAB (Prado-Lopez, deceased)* in Chapter 28.

In addition to any payments made according to the chart in Section B, above, payments of weekly death benefits will be made on behalf of any totally dependent minor children (by blood or adoption) until the youngest child reaches the age of 18. (LC § 4703.5.) Minor children who did not live with the deceased employee are eligible for death benefits if they were totally dependent upon the deceased employee for support. However, these children must prove their dependence.

This is a very valuable benefit that can be worth a lot of money. Weekly payments are paid in the same amount and manner as temporary disability payments would have been made to the deceased employee, except that no weekly payment will be less than $224. (See Chapter 12, Section B, for a discussion of temporary disability amounts.)

EXAMPLE: Juanita dies as a result of a work-related injury, leaving three children, ages 17, 11 and 2. In addition to any fixed-sum payments made according to the chart in Section B, above, the children will receive weekly payments of the greater of $224 or Juanita's temporary disability rate. This benefit will be divided three ways until the oldest child reaches age 18. It will then be divided equally between the remaining children until the middle one turns 18. After that point, the youngest child will continue to get weekly payments until age 18.

D. Burial Expense for Deceased Worker

In addition to any other benefits, actual burial expenses must be paid by the insurance carrier. The burial expense is payable up to $5,000. (LC § 4701.)

E. Unpaid Temporary or Permanent Disability Payments

 See *Manville Sales Corporation v. WCAB* in Chapter 28.

If the deceased employee was entitled to any unpaid temporary or permanent disability benefits at the time of death, that amount is due and payable to the surviving heirs. Surviving heirs are those entitled to the estate of the deceased either by will or, if there is no will, by succession of law. As a matter of course, the surviving heirs are often, but not necessarily, the same as the surviving dependents discussed in Section B, above.

Overdue disability amounts (and possibly penalties due, if payments were late) must be paid in addition to the other death benefits. See Chapter 12 for a discussion of temporary disability payments and Chapter 13 for information about permanent disability payments.

EXAMPLE: Martha was owed temporary disability payments in the amount of $12,500 at the time of her death. The insurance carrier had not been paying Martha her temporary disability checks, claiming she was not temporarily disabled for the period claimed. After Martha's death, the insurance carrier agreed to pay the past due amount. Martha's heirs are entitled to the $12,500, plus any penalties due.

F. How Death Benefits Are Distributed

All agreements between an insurance company and the dependent beneficiaries of a deceased worker regarding settlement of death benefit claims must be drafted in a settlement document. If the parties cannot agree on settlement of the death claim, a workers' compensation judge will hear the case in a trial and make a decision.

Although the Appeals Board generally distributes the death benefits according to the rules we have discussed, it may distribute death benefits in any manner that it deems is fair and equitable. The Appeals Board also determines whether the death benefit should be paid directly to the dependent or to a trustee appointed by the Appeals Board for the benefit of the dependent. (LC § 4704.)

IF DEPENDENT IS A MINOR

If a claim is being made for death benefits on behalf of a minor (person under age 18), an adult must be designated by the Appeals Board to represent the minor's interests in the claim. In legal jargon, this person is referred to as a guardian ad litem. Typically, but not always, the person appointed is the parent or legal guardian of the minor. A Petition for Appointment of Guardian ad Litem and Trustee is available from the Workers' Compensation Appeals Board. Check with an Information and Assistance officer if you need help filling it out.

16

Extraordinary Workers' Compensation Benefits and Remedies

The benefits and remedies discussed in this chapter are above and beyond a typical workers' compensation claim. It's unusual for the circumstances that give rise to these benefits to be present in a workers' compensation case, but it does happen. If you think that you may be entitled to one or more of these benefits, you should see a qualified workers' compensation attorney or consult an Information and Assistance officer.

Before we go on, let's define some jargon. When I mention "benefits" that are over and above what is normally allowed in the workers' compensation system, I'm referring to additional awards of money or the re-establishment of certain rights, such as getting your job back after being fired.

When I refer to "remedies," I mean legal action you may be able to take. This usually consists of filing additional claims within the workers' compensation system to recover damages you suffered as the result of someone else's improper actions.

The benefits and remedies discussed in this chapter will be of interest to you only if one of these fairly unusual situations applies:

- You had a prior injury or illness before your present workers' compensation injury; it does not matter if it happened at work. (Read Section A.)
- Your employer does not have workers' compensation insurance and is not self-insured. (Turn to Section B to learn about the Uninsured Employers' Fund.)
- You believe that your employer discriminated against you because you asserted your right to file a workers' compensation claim—for example, you were harassed or fired after you filed or threatened to file a workers' compensation claim. (Read Section C, on discrimination benefits.)
- You believe that your employer's seriously improper action or inaction, such as the failure to remedy an obvious safety violation, contributed to or caused your work injury. (Read Section D.)

IF YOUR SITUATION ISN'T UNUSUAL
If none of the situations described above applies to you, skip the rest of this chapter.

A. Subsequent Injuries Fund Benefits

The state-run Subsequent Injuries Fund is designed to provide a remedy for employees with pre-existing physical impairments who sustain a new injury at work. It allows these workers to recover benefits for their entire disability—the pre-existing disability and the new workers' compensation injury considered together. The prior impairment need not be work-related or it could be a previously compensated workers' compensation injury.

A little background is in order. In the event of an injury at work, an employer who hires a previously disabled worker is liable only for that percentage of the overall disability resulting from the new work injury—not for any portion of the injury that resulted from the prior disability. (LC § 4750.) This is fair, since most employers are not allowed to inquire as to the nature and extent of any prior disabilities while interviewing a prospective job applicant. (See a discussion of the Americans With Disabilities Act in Chapter 17, Section D.) This policy of holding employers liable only for the present injury also encourages employers to hire the physically disabled without fear of incurring workers' compensation liability for a pre-existing disability.

An injured worker with a permanent disability caused by the work injury will receive money from the insurance carrier. In addition, the worker may qualify for a money award that takes the entire disability into account, paid by the Subsequent Injuries Fund.

EXAMPLE: Jane injured her left leg in a horseback riding incident when she was a child. She injures her right leg on the job, which results in a permanent disability. Jane qualifies for workers' compensation, and her present employer's insurance company pays for the permanent disability to her right leg (none of this injury was the result of her prior condition). In addition, she should be entitled to money from the Subsequent Injuries Fund for the disability to her left leg, because the work injury has now increased her overall disability. In short, without the Subsequent Injuries Fund, Jane would have suffered a permanent disability greater than that for which the employer is liable, yet be unable to get compensated for her greater overall disability.

An injured worker with a prior disability may even be entitled to a life pension from the Subsequent Injuries Fund. The combined effect of the work injury and the earlier disability must, however, equal a permanent disability rating of 70% or more. (See Chapter 18 for more on rating disabilities.) In addition, at least one of the following must apply:

- The present work injury rates 35% or more when considered alone, without any adjustment for the employee's age or occupation, or
- The prior disability was to an eye, arm, hand, leg or foot, and the present work injury is to the opposite member

(the other eye, for example). The new disability must rate 5% or more when considered alone, without adjustment for the employee's age or occupation.

The time limitation for filing an application for Subsequent Injuries Fund benefits is the same as with workers' compensation benefits: one year from the date of injury. If, however, you did not know of your right to Subsequent Injury Fund benefits, you may have an extension to the filing deadline. This extension is typically for a "reasonable time" after learning about your right, even if more than one year has passed since the date of injury.

You generally will not know if you have a Subsequent Injuries Fund claim until after the doctors have determined your overall disability, as well as what portion of your disability is work related. Once this has been determined, file right away if you think you qualify.

 SEE A LAWYER TO MAKE A CLAIM AGAINST THE SUBSEQUENT INJURIES FUND

Because this is a complicated area, I highly recommend that you get help from an Information and Assistance officer or see an attorney.

B. The Uninsured Employers' Fund

The Uninsured Employers' Fund, which is set up and funded by the State of California, pays an injured employee's workers' compensation benefits if:

- the employer did not have workers' compensation insurance, or
- the employer is not permissibly self-insured. (LC §§ 3715, 3716.)

If you suffer an injury at work, and find out that your employer did not carry workers' compensation insurance, you may pursue your workers' compensation claim against the Uninsured Employers' Fund.

SEEK ASSISTANCE IF YOUR EMPLOYER IS UNINSURED

If you opt to file a claim against the state Uninsured Employers' Fund, it's likely you will need help, since you must meet very strict procedural requirements that are not covered in this book. Start by consulting with an Information and Assistance officer. You may also want to see a workers' compensation lawyer and possibly a civil litigation attorney, who should be able to provide you with information about whether you are likely to obtain a substantial recovery if you file a civil case.

You may also sue your employer. damages suffered as a result of your work injury. is serious, you may be able to recover more money through civil suit than you could through a workers' compensation claim. But there are downsides to lawsuits—they're time-consuming, emotionally draining and costly. In addition, before you proceed on this track, make sure your employer is financially sound. You won't be able to collect from a bankrupt or defunct employer.

C. Discrimination Benefits (Labor Code § 132(a))

If you believe your employer discriminated against you because you filed a workers' compensation claim, you may have certain legal remedies within the workers' compensation system. (You may also have rights outside of the workers' compensation system; see Chapter 17, Section D.)

If your employer discriminates against you, you may file a Petition Alleging Discrimination against your employer. (LC § 132(a).) This petition must be filed with the Workers' Compensation Appeals Board within one year from the date of the discriminatory action.

You may have a legitimate discrimination claim against your employer if you file or plan to file a workers' compensation claim and you are:

- **terminated from your job.** You are fired or laid off without good cause—that is, without a legitimate business reason.
- **harassed.** Your employer "writes you up" or embarrasses you in front of other employees or otherwise makes your work life more difficult without a legitimate business reason for doing so.
- **threatened.** Your employer threatens to terminate you or make your work life difficult if you proceed with your workers' compensation case.
- **subjected to an unreasonable change in working conditions.** For example, your shift is changed to a less desirable one or you're given extra work to do without a reasonable business necessity.
- **demoted or given a cut in pay.** Your seniority is taken away or your pay is decreased without a reasonable business necessity for doing so.
- **subjected to any other type of discriminatory action.** This may apply if other employees in like circumstances are not subjected to these actions or if your employer fails to offer reasonable accommodations for your disability.

If the Workers' Compensation Appeals Board determines that your employer discriminated against you, your employer will be guilty of a misdemeanor and you will be entitled to:

- a 50% increase in your workers' compensation award (all the benefits you receive), but in no event more than an additional $10,000
- costs and expenses not to exceed $250, and
- reinstatement in your job and reimbursement for lost wages and work benefits caused by your employer's actions.

All of this sounds great. But now for a reality check. An action for discrimination against an employer is difficult to prove under the best of circumstances. You must be able to show that the *only* reason your employer discriminated against you was because you filed, or threatened to file, a workers' compensation action. For example, you will probably not be successful in your discrimination petition if your employer can show that you were fired partially because you had a history of being late, your work was sub par or the company needed to cut back. This is true even if you are sure you were really terminated because you filed a workers' compensation claim.

WHICH DISCRIMINATION CLAIMS ARE LIKELY TO SUCCEED

A discrimination case with a reasonable chance of success contains most of the following factors:

- The employee has a clean work record, with few, if any, written warnings. If, however, the written warnings are made *after* a workers' compensation claim was filed, this may be evidence of an employer's plan to retaliate.
- The employee has written commendations in his employment file about a job well done.
- The employee has been employed for at least several years—the longer the better.
- The employer's reasons for terminating the employee do not make sense. For example, the employer claims the layoff was because of a lack of business, yet hires someone to replace the employee.
- The employer's discriminatory action occurs within a short time period of the employee's filing of a workers' compensation claim—for example, a week or two after the employee files a DWC-1 form.

D. Employer's Serious and Willful Misconduct

In unusual cases, a work injury or death may have been caused by an employer's serious and willful misconduct. (LC § 4553.) In legal jargon, serious and willful misconduct is behavior that goes well beyond the realm of negligence (carelessness). In short, the employer's actions must approach criminal conduct. Violations of certain health and safety codes, such as those promulgated by the California Occupational Safety and Health Administration (Cal-OSHA) may be considered serious and willful misconduct. Similarly, tampering with or removing safety devices on equipment would probably be viewed as serious and willful misconduct.

Many other actions would not, however, fall into this category. For instance, an employer who insists that employees work too many hours, or who speeds up the work process to a point where it causes injury to an employee, is certainly negligent. But those actions would probably not constitute serious and willful misconduct on the employer's part.

To have a valid claim against an employer, the employer must be responsible for the serious and willful misconduct. In other words, the misconduct generally must be committed by:

- the owner
- the store or business manager or supervisor
- where the employer is a partnership, one of the partners
- where the employer is a corporation, an executive, managing officer or general superintendent (supervisor).

A petition for serious and willful misconduct of an employer must be filed with the Workers' Compensation Appeals Board within 12 months from the date of the action in question. If it's successful, the employer may have to pay:

- a 50% increase in workers' compensation benefits (no limit on the amount), and
- costs and expenses not to exceed $250.

 SUCCESSFUL PETITIONS FOR SERIOUS AND WILLFUL MISCONDUCT ARE FAIRLY RARE

Petitions based on employer misconduct are complicated, with procedures and rules much like going to civil court. If you suspect that you have a serious and willful misconduct claim against your employer, I strongly recommend that you consult with a workers' compensation attorney. ■

Benefits and Remedies Outside the Workers' Compensation System

The workers' compensation system does not exist in a vacuum. It's quite possible that you may be entitled to benefits and remedies that fall beyond the scope of workers' compensation. Here we shift gears and talk about different state and federal agencies that may offer benefits to injured workers. We also discuss circumstances under which you may be entitled to legal recourse outside the workers' compensation arena.

If you're out of work or receiving a reduced income, it will be important for you to obtain all of the benefits to which you are entitled. Very few people can afford to be out of work without suffering some financial hardship. Your best approach will be to learn about your options and obtain *all* benefits you're entitled to. This chapter discusses:

- state disability insurance, or "SDI" (Section A)
- Social Security benefits (Section B)
- personal injury claims and lawsuits (Section C), and
- claims or lawsuits based on discrimination due to your disability (Section D).

OTHER SOURCES OF HELP

In addition to what's covered in this chapter, you may want to investigate the following important sources of income and benefits:

- Medicare
- Medi-Cal
- pensions
- disability policies
- vocational rehabilitation through the State Department of Rehabilitation, and
- public assistance (welfare).

A discussion of these benefits is beyond the scope of this book. You may find useful information in *Social Security, Medicare and Pensions,* by Joseph L. Matthews and Dorothy Matthews Berman (Nolo).

A. State Disability (SDI)

California employees who work for private employers have money automatically deducted from their paychecks to cover state disability insurance ("SDI"). A few groups of workers, such as state or federal employees, may not have this deduction taken, and are therefore not eligible for SDI benefits. If you aren't sure whether you are covered, look at one of your pay stubs or ask your employer. Look for a deduction entitled "SDI," which is usually only a few dollars per week.

The money you pay into the SDI system goes into your own personal "account." When you have paid in enough money over the required number of quarters (three-month increments), you normally are entitled to benefits if you're injured or ill. The amount of state disability benefits is roughly equivalent to workers' compensation temporary disability payments. You are paid out of your account until it is exhausted, at which time your payments stop.

Before we go on, let's emphasize the difference between SDI benefits and workers' compensation benefits. Only persons with a work-related injury are entitled to workers' compensation benefits. However, anyone who paid into the state disability system for the required period of time is entitled to state disability benefits if they cannot work due to any injury or illness, even if it's not work-related. A doctor must certify that you are unable to work because of your injury or illness.

If you sustained an injury at work, you should *immediately* apply for state disability, even if you are receiving temporary disability payments from the workers' compensation insurance company or have gone back to work. If you are receiving workers' compensation temporary disability, you will initially be denied SDI benefits, but that's okay. By filing for state disability as soon as possible, you "lock in" the date you applied. If you later need to re-apply because your workers' compensation benefits terminate, your qualification will be determined by the original date you applied. Although this sounds like a technical point, it is extremely important. Eligibility for state disability benefits is based upon previous quarters worked from the date of application. If, for example, you fail to apply soon after your injury and have to apply nine months later because you lost workers' compensation coverage, you may find that you do not qualify for benefits—simply because you did not work for the last nine months (three quarters).

REASONS TO APPLY FOR SDI

As mentioned, it's important to apply for SDI as soon as possible to "lock in" the benefit date and secure the maximum possible benefit, even if you believe you are covered by workers' compensation. This is because of the following possibilities:

- the insurance company may deny your workers' compensation claim
- the insurance company may interrupt your temporary disability benefits for some reason
- your doctor may claim that you are not temporarily disabled for workers' compensation purposes, or
- the insurance company may pay you at an incorrect rate and refuse to pay you at the correct rate; in that event, you may be able to receive the difference between the correct rate and the rate you're being paid for temporary disability.

---

1. How to Apply for State Disability

Contact your local office of the California Employment Development Department (EDD) to apply for state disability benefits. You can find the number in the front of the phone book under state agencies or call directory assistance.

2. If You Later Qualify for Workers' Compensation Benefits: The SDI Lien

It is not uncommon to receive state disability benefits for a few weeks or months and then discover that you should have been receiving temporary disability from the workers' compensation insurance company.

To recover its money, the state will file a lien (legal claim) in your workers' compensation case. At the time your case is resolved, the workers' compensation insurance company will have to negotiate with the state about how much money, if any, it must reimburse the state for state disability payments made to you. Money that is repaid to the state by the workers' compensation insurance company goes directly back into your SDI account and you are free to apply for those benefits again if needed. In fact, you may immediately qualify for state

disability indemnity if a doctor will certify that you are unable to work. This may be for a disability as a result of your present workers' compensation case (which you settled), a new workers' compensation case or a non-industrial injury.

SETTLEMENT DOCUMENTS MAY ADDRESS SDI LIEN
If you received SDI payments for any periods of time that you were entitled to receive permanent disability payments, the Employment Development Department (EDD) can have that amount deducted from your final permanent disability award. (LC § 4904.) This is usually a problem if your case goes to trial and the judge determines that you received SDI benefits after you were permanent and stationary. An Information and Assistance officer or workers' compensation attorney should be able to help. In addition, we discuss the settlement language that requires the insurance company to be responsible for the SDI lien (available if you settle by compromise and release) in Chapter 20, Section D2e.

B. Social Security Benefits

Social Security provides, among other things, benefits for seriously injured workers and their families. To qualify for Social Security benefits because of a disability:

- you must have a physical or mental impairment
- the impairment must prevent you from doing any "substantial gainful work," and
- the impairment must be expected to last, or have lasted, at least 12 months, or must be expected to result in death.

Of course, these terms are subject to different interpretations. Guidelines developed by Social Security and the courts provide details about the qualifications for disability.

Social Security disability will, over the long run, provide more benefits than will workers' compensation, so contact your local Social Security department if you may meet the above requirements.

If you receive Social Security benefits, such as Social Security disability or SSI (Supplemental Security Income), any money you later receive from your workers' compensation case may be credited against your Social Security benefits. In other words, if you settle your workers' compensation claim after you have received Social Security benefits, the Social Security department will want to offset the benefits it pays you against your workers' compensation benefits. Your Social Security benefit may be reduced by the amount of your workers' compensation settlement.

⚠ ADDRESS OFFSET IN SETTLEMENT DOCUMENTS

If it turns out that an offset may be taken against your workers' compensation claim, you should include some special language in your workers' compensation settlement documents. This language (which is only available with a compromise and release) is designed to minimize the amount of credit that Social Security will take against your workers' compensation award. You may want to consult with an Information and Assistance officer or see a workers' compensation attorney to make sure the appropriate language is included. (We discuss the required language in Chapter 20, Section D2e.)

C. Claims or Lawsuits for Personal Injuries

In fairly unusual circumstances, you may have the right to sue a third party (someone other than your employer or a co-worker), in addition to pursuing your workers' compensation remedies. This usually applies when a person or entity outside the employment arena caused or contributed to the cause of your injury.

The right to sue a third party may arise if you were injured because of circumstances such as these:

- **negligence** (for example, a careless driver with no relationship to your job hit you while you were on company business)
- **products liability** (for example, you were injured at work when a defective aerosol can blew up in your face)
- **intentional torts** (for example, a customer physically assaulted you), or
- **malpractice** (for example, you are further injured due to the malpractice of a doctor who treated you for your work injury).

It is usually advantageous to pursue a personal injury claim, because the amount you may recover is not restricted. Unlike workers' compensation, you may be entitled to compensation for your pain and suffering, property damage (such as damage to your car in an auto accident), loss of monetary support caused by the death or injury of a loved one, lost wages (past, present and future) and punitive damages where appropriate. However, unlike the workers' compensation system, which basically is a "no fault" system, you cannot recover damages unless you can show that the outside individual or entity caused or contributed to your injury.

To recover damages, you usually start by making a demand and trying to settle with the responsible party or that party's insurance company. If settlement negotiations fail, you must file a lawsuit within certain time frames (called the "statute of limitations"):

- You generally have one year from the date of your injury to sue third parties that may have caused or contributed to your injury. (Lawsuits against governmental agencies may require much quicker action on your part, often requiring an initial written claim within 180 days, and sometimes sooner.)
- You must bring a medical malpractice lawsuit within one year from the date the injury is discovered, or three years from the date the medical malpractice was committed, whichever date occurs first.
- For a negligence or products liability lawsuit, you must file within one year from the date of injury (except for government agencies, which may require you to file an initial written claim within about 180 days).

⚠ DON'T MISS THE FILING DEADLINE

If you don't file your lawsuit within the applicable statute of limitations, you could be forever barred from making any kind of recovery. See an attorney immediately if you think you have a personal injury claim.

IF YOU HAVE A THIRD PARTY CLAIM

Because laws are constantly changing, it is important that you get up-to-date information on the laws that apply to filing a lawsuit against third parties. Here are some resources from Nolo:

- *How to Win Your Personal Injury Claim,* by Joseph L. Matthews. If the third parties are covered by insurance, this book can help you through the insurance claims system. Use this book to protect your rights, understand what your claim is worth and negotiate a fair settlement.
- *Represent Yourself in Court,* by Paul Bergman and Sara J. Berman-Barrett. This book helps you analyze whether you have a good civil court case, present testimony and appear in court.

Understand that you cannot recover twice for the same injury. Each person you sue will be entitled to claim a credit against any settlement or recovery you receive from anyone else. This is called "subrogation."

EXAMPLE 1: Jenny is a driver for a courier service. While delivering a package, Jenny is seriously injured when another driver runs a red light and hits her van. She files a workers' compensation claim against her employer and a civil suit against the driver of the car that hit her. Jenny settles her civil suit first for $15,000. The workers' compensation insurance company is entitled to a credit of $15,000 (the net amount Jenny receive from her third party case) against any money Jenny may be entitled to in her workers' compensation case. If her workers' compensation case settles for less than $15,000, Jenny would not get any additional money.

EXAMPLE 2: Let's assume the same facts above, but this time Jenny settled her workers' compensation case first for $10,000. Now the insurance company in the third party case would be entitled to a credit of $10,000 (from Jenny's net recovery from her workers' compensation case) against any money it might have to pay her for her third party case.

If Jenny now settles her third party case for $15,000, she would only be entitled to an additional $5,000.

IF YOU'RE INVOLVED IN A CIVIL SUIT
Consider seeking representation by both a workers' compensation attorney and a civil attorney. Both attorneys will need to work together to maximize your recovery. If you go this route, you won't normally have to pay your lawyers upfront. The civil attorney will probably receive at least a third of any recovery in the form of the lawyer's "contingency fees," and the workers' compensation attorney will receive a percentage of your final workers' compensation settlement.

D. Claims or Lawsuits Based on Discrimination

Several laws may protect you if an employer, or a potential employer, discriminates against you because of your industrial injury and any resulting permanent disability. For example, if you are refused a new job, and you believe it is because you have a disability, you may have a claim under the Americans With Disabilities Act or the California Fair Employment Housing Act. Or if you are terminated from your present job because of your disability, you may have a discrimination claim.

SEE A LAWYER FOR A DISCRIMINATION CASE
If you believe you were discriminated against because of your disability, you should contact an attorney immediately. An in-depth discussion of your rights is beyond the scope of this book.

1. The Americans With Disabilities Act

The Americans With Disabilities Act (ADA) applies to private employers, state and local governments, employment agencies, labor unions and joint labor-management committees with 15 or more employees.

Here are the basics of the ADA. Employers cannot discriminate against people with disabilities in any aspect of the employment process. This includes application, testing, hiring, assignment, evaluation, disciplinary actions, training, promotion, medical examinations, layoff/recall, termination, compensation, leave and benefits.

Penalties for violation of the ADA include job reinstatement, back pay, payment for loss of future earnings and payment of legal fees, expert witness fees and court costs. Compensatory and punitive damages between $50,000 and $300,000 may also be awarded.

A charge of discrimination on the basis of disability must be filed with the Equal Employment Opportunity Commission (EEOC) within 180 days of the alleged discriminatory act. Call toll free 800-669-4000 to file a claim over the phone or to find out the location of the nearest EEOC office. After the EEOC issues a right-to-sue letter, you have one year to file a complaint in civil court.

Again, this is a very complex area of the law and generally requires legal representation. You may also want to consult *Your Rights in the Workplace*, by Barbara Kate Repa (Nolo), for more detailed information on the ADA.

2.   The California Fair Employment Housing Act

In addition to the ADA, you may have similar rights under a California law known as the California Fair Employment Housing Act (FEHA). The FEHA has very similar recovery provisions to the ADA discussed above. It requires that a claim be filed with the FEHA within one year from the alleged discriminatory act. After you receive a right-to-sue letter, you have one year to file a complaint in civil court. You can find the local address in your phone book under government agencies. ■

Rating Your Permanent Disability

IF YOU DON'T HAVE A PERMANENT PARTIAL DISABILITY
This chapter does not apply if you've recovered fully from your work injury with no disability whatsoever. This chapter also does not apply if you and the insurance company agree that you have a permanent disability rating of 100%, in which case you are entitled to receive payments at your temporary disability rate for the rest of your life. If you're not sure whether you have a permanent partial disability, turn to Chapter 13.

If you have a permanent disability, your disability will have to be "rated"—that is, assigned a numerical value. The rating in turn is plugged into a chart, which is the basis for determining the amount of money you'll receive. The process of rating disabilities is rather long and complicated. But it's also extremely important, because your rating determines how much money you'll be awarded for your permanent disability.

This chapter gives you an overview of the process involved in rating permanent disabilities. For most readers, the advantage to learning the basic principles involved in rating injuries lies in better understanding how the Administrative Director's result is arrived at (although some readers may wish to rate their own injury). Gaining a basic understanding of the process will:

- **help preserve your rights when seeking medical care.** All ratings are arrived at by analyzing medical reports. By understanding the process, you'll get a good idea of what a favorable medical report should contain. This may help you understand what the doctor is looking for and enable you to communicate better with the doctor. (See Chapter 9 for more on your medical case and Chapter 10 for information on the medical-legal evaluation process.)
- **help determine if the rating in your case is fair and equitable.** You'll have a good chance of spotting an unreasonably low rating, as well as the tools you'll need to challenge it.
- **provide the basis for negotiating a fair settlement.** Understanding the rating process will help you negotiate with the insurance adjuster. If the adjuster realizes that you understand your disability rating and how it was arrived at, he is much more likely to take your demands seriously.

A. Overview of the Rating Process

When and how an injury will be rated varies significantly from case to case. You may take an active role in getting your injury rated, or you may choose to sit back and wait until the system gets around to you. The following is an overview of how a rating is typically arrived at.

1. Reach Permanent and Stationary Status

Your permanent disability cannot be rated until you have been declared permanent and stationary by your treating doctor. (See Chapter 9, Section E, for a discussion of permanent and stationary status.) It is then time to determine the nature and extent of your permanent disability and your need for future medical treatment.

2. If You Want to Request an Advisory Rating

After you've been designated as permanent and stationary by the treating doctor, you may request that your disability be given an "advisory" rating, also referred to as a "summary" or "consultative" rating. The rating is called "advisory" because it is not legally binding. In other words, it is an opinion only. If your case goes to trial, the judge may use a different rating.

Advisory ratings are almost always obtained by unrepresented workers; if you have a lawyer, he'll do the rating.

Although you may request a rating of the treating doctor's permanent and stationary report at any time, it is in your best interest to do so as soon as possible to expedite settlement of your case.

To request your advisory rating, you'll need a copy of the treating doctor's permanent and stationary report. If for some reason you haven't received a copy, request one from the doctor or the insurance company. You'll need to send the report and a request for a calculation of your permanent disability rating to the Administrative Director—the person responsible for overseeing the worker's compensation system. (LC § 4061 (i).) Check with the clerk's office at your local Workers' Compensation Appeals Board to get the Administrative Director's correct address. The following is a sample letter.

4/14/year

Administrative Director

(address)

Re: Duane White

Case #: 1111

Claim #: 2222

Employer: Technology Unlimited

Date of injury: 12/24/year

Subject: Calculation of treating doctor's report dated 3/3/year

To Whom It May Concern:

Under the terms of Labor Code Section 4061(i), please calculate the rating of the enclosed permanent and stationary medical report of the treating doctor, Dr. Jennifer Smith, dated 3/3/year.

Sincerely,

Duane White

Duane White

(address and phone number)

Enclosure

cc: (name of insurance company)

3. Administrative Director Prepares Advisory Rating

Within 20 days of receipt of the treating doctor's medical evaluation, the Administrative Director is supposed to calculate the advisory rating based upon that report and mail a copy to you and your employer. As a practical matter, it usually takes months to get a rating back.

The advisory rating may be titled "Summary Rating" or something similar. At first, it will probably seem incomprehensible, with a phrase such as: "7.713-50%-11-H-56%-58:0%." Fortunately, this chapter will help you make sense out of that gobbledy-gook. Section C, below, takes you through the step-by-step process to rate relatively simple injuries yourself.

4. If You Agree With the Rating

If both you and the insurance company agree with the rating of the treating doctor's report, you can comfortably begin settlement negotiations. See Chapters 19 and 20 for more on settlement negotiations.

5. If You Disagree With the Rating

You may disagree with the rating of the treating doctor's report because:
- the rating was done incorrectly, or
- although the rating was accurate, you disagree with the basis for the rating—that is, the treating doctor's report itself.

COMMON REASONS TO DISPUTE A RATING

Ratings are often disputed for one or more of these reasons:
- wrong occupation or occupational group
- age not correctly taken into account
- work restrictions not taken into account or wrong work restrictions given by the doctor
- not all injuries taken into account
- standard disability rating doesn't use best choice of work restrictions or subjective findings—using other restrictions would result in a higher disability
- disputed physical findings contained in the treating doctor's report
- medical history relied upon by the treating doctor incomplete or inaccurate
- treating doctor did not review relevant tests or prior medical opinions in arriving at conclusions, or
- treating doctor did not correctly state subjective complaints.

If you arrived at a different rating altogether by rating your own disability, realize that unless you find a very basic error in the advisory rating, there is probably a good reason why it differs from yours. There are many advanced rating procedures, such as "overlap" and "pyramiding," that are simply beyond the scope of this book.

FURTHER INFORMATION

Check with the rating specialist at your local Workers' Compensation Appeals Board. He may be able to refer you to a seminar or educational course on rating disabilities. You may also find helpful information in *California Workers' Compensation Practice*, by Charles Laurence Swezey (California Continuing Education of the Bar), discussed in Chapter 27, Section B1. Or, consider trying to find a lawyer to take your case and rate your disability.

You can start by letting the insurance company know that you don't agree with the advisory rating. See if you and the adjuster can agree to a rating. If not, the judge will decide what the correct rating is at trial. The judge has a great deal of latitude. He may agree with your rating or the insurance company's rating, find that the rating is somewhere between the two, or find that the rating is higher or lower than either rating.

If you review the treating doctor's report and disagree with the medical findings, you can get a second opinion. You'll need to attend a qualified medical evaluation and get a medical-legal report. Contact the insurance company either by telephone or by letter and ask for a form you may use to request a QME panel. (To learn more about selecting a qualified medical evaluator, turn to Chapter 10, Section B.)

After you are examined, the QME (doctor) prepares a "formal medical evaluation." This report, along with a form summarizing its conclusions, is mailed by the doctor to the insurance company, you and the Disability Evaluation Unit for a new calculation of your permanent disability rating (independent and unrelated to the rating of the treating doctor's report).

The Administrative Director must calculate the permanent disability rating based upon the QME's medical evaluation and mail a copy to you and the insurance company.

6. If You Disagree With the New Rating of the QME

If you disagree with the new advisory rating of the QME's report, you have 30 days to request that the Administrative Director reconsider the recommended rating or obtain additional evaluations from a QME to address issues not dealt with or inadequately addressed in the QME report.

You must explain your reasons in a written request to the Disability Evaluation Unit, and send a copy to the defendants. The following is an example.

8/29/year

Administrative Director

(Address)

Re: Rating of Dr. Jones' Qualified Medical Examiner report dated 6/6/year

To whom it may concern:

I would appreciate a re-evaluation by the QME doctor, Dr. Jones, because he did not obtain an opinion from a neurologist regarding the nerve loss I sustained as evidenced by the EMG test performed by Dr. Smith on 3/3/year (copy enclosed.) I believe that an opinion from a neurologist regarding my disability is absolutely necessary to determine the nature and extent of my permanent disability.

Sincerely,

Jane Smith

Jane Smith

cc: Insurance company

B. What Is Involved in the Rating Process?

In the rest of this chapter, we explain the basic concepts of how to rate your permanent disability. Armed with this information, you should be able to rate some of the more common permanent partial disabilities.

RATING DISABILITIES IS A COMPLEX SUBJECT

This chapter cannot possibly make you an instant expert in rating permanent disabilities. If rating disabilities is important to you, you'll either need to do some additional studying on your own or get expert help from a lawyer to be sure your disability is rated correctly. You also might try checking with your local Information and Assistance officer.

1. The Rating Manual

There is simply no way around it: If you are going to rate your own permanent disability, you'll need to have access to a manual entitled *Schedule for Rating Permanent Disabilities Under the Labor Code of California,* informally referred to as "the rating manual." You may view the manual for free on the Internet at http://www.dir.ca.gov/DWC/PDR.pdf. You may also be able to locate one at a law library, or you can purchase your own. See Chapter 27, Section B1, for ordering information.

![warning icon] **USE OLD RATING MANUAL FOR INJURIES BEFORE 4/1/97**
If your injury occurred before 4/1/97, you must use the "old" rating manual to compute your permanent disability. The old rating manual (published in 1993), which is discussed beginning in Section E, below, is still used for all injuries prior to 4/1/97. It is not available on the Internet, but you may be able to locate one at a law library. To purchase your own, see Chapter 27, Section B1.

A quick review of the rating manual reveals that it contains seven main sections:
- Section 1 – Introduction and Instructions
- Section 2 – Disabilities and Standard Ratings
- Section 3 – Occupations and Group Numbers
- Section 4 – Occupational Variants
- Section 5 – Occupational Adjustment
- Section 6 – Age Adjustment
- Section 7 – Appendices

The rating manual contains various charts and graphs necessary to rate a permanent partial or permanent total disability. However, many disabilities and ratings are not contained in the rating manual, and are learned by many years of working in the workers' compensation field.

2. Eight-Step Rating Process

The rating process consists of eight basic steps. You'll need to use the rating manual in conjunction with the medical report being rated.

Step 1: Carefully read Section 1 of the rating manual for an overview of the rating process and a guide to rating your disability.

Step 2: Determine the disability number and standard rating for your disability.

Step 3: Determine your occupational group number.

Step 4: Determine the occupational variants for your disability and your occupation.

Step 5: Adjust the disability rating for your occupation.

Step 6: Adjust the disability rating for your age.

Step 7: Refer to the appendices to make final adjustments to the disability rating where necessary and to combine multiple disabilities, if applicable.

Step 8: Determine a dollar value for the disability rating.

Think of arriving at the disability formula and the value of your permanent disability as solving a puzzle. The puzzle has seven equally important pieces. Once you have all seven pieces (Steps 2 through 8) in place, you will know your "disability formula," which tells you your "disability rating." As you'll see from the example in Section C, below, it takes a fair amount of time and practice to accurately rate a disability.

C. Step-by-Step Example of How to Rate a Disability

We will now look at how to find and use each of the seven pieces of the puzzle. To help you through the process, we'll use a hypothetical case involving a woman named "Mary," who has suffered three common industrial injuries: a back injury, arm injuries and a leg injury.

Mary was injured while working as a meat wrapper for a major grocery chain. Her duties required her to regularly lift up to 25 pounds of meat at once. In addition, Mary constantly used machinery to measure and pre-wrap various meats, which required repetitive gripping and grasping motions.

Mary is claiming two dates for her injuries. The first was 10/23/99, when she slipped on some grease in the meat department and fell, injuring her back and right knee. The second injury is for continuous trauma (pain and disability) to both arms as a result of the repetitive meat wrapping motions. After the fall, Mary's doctor diagnosed carpal tunnel syndrome in both wrists and an ulnar nerve neuropathy in the left elbow. Mary has not worked since her fall on 10/23/99. For the second injury, she uses the dates of 10/23/98 to 10/23/99 as the period of injury. (See Chapter 5, Section C1b, for details on how to determine the injury date for a continuous trauma.)

Mary was 42 years old on the date of her fall. She was declared permanent and stationary by her treating doctor. Mary received copies of both the treating doctor's medical report and an advisory rating of her injury. (See sidebar, "Mary's Advisory Rating.")

Mary wants to determine her own disability rating for the injuries set forth in the treating doctor's report. She wants to understand how the advisory rating was arrived at, to be better prepared to deal with doctors and the insurance company's lawyers in the future.

Because Mary has injuries to three different parts of her body, she will have to figure out a disability formula for each body part. She'll then combine them using the multiple disability rating table (explained in Step 7, below).

UNDERSTANDING STANDARD DISABILITY PERCENTAGES

Leave it to workers' compensation to complicate even the way percentages are expressed. Percentages of disability are listed as a whole number followed by a colon (:), and then another number from 0 to 3. Here's what the numbers following the colon mean:

- the number 1 means .25%
- the number 2 means .50%, and
- the number 3 means .75%.

For example, 25:1% is equivalent to 25.25%, 25:2% is equivalent to 25.5% and 25:3% is equivalent to 25.75%.

MARY'S ADVISORY RATING

Mary receives an advisory disability rating in the mail. Here's what it reads, and what those numbers refer to. Each row refers to a different injury.

7.512 - 50% - 322G - 53% - 55%

12.1 - 15% - 322F - 15% - 16% > MDT 77%

14.511 - 25% - 322F - 25% - 27%

| disability numbers (Step 1) | "standard disability" ratings (Step 2) | occupational groups and variants (Step 3) | adjusted standard disabilities based on occupational variants (Step 4) | adjusted standard disability ratings for age (Step 5) | if more than one injury, adjustment for multiple disability rating (Step 6) |

💡 **DISABILITY RATING MEANS THE SAME THING AS DISABILITY PERCENTAGE**

In fact, the rating is always expressed as a percentage. We use these terms interchangeably in this chapter.

Step 1: Carefully Read Section 1 of the Rating Manual–Introduction and Instructions

Reading this section in the rating manual will give you a good overview of the rating process. It discusses the various factors used in rating a disability and the indexes you'll be using to calculate the components of your disability.

Step 2: Determine Disability Numbers for Parts of Body Injured and Their Respective Standard Ratings

This step consists of two parts: determining a disability number for the part of your body that's injured and assigning the standard rating to that disability.

a. Determine the Disability Number

The rating manual contains a section entitled "Section 2–Disabilities and Standard Ratings." Disabilities are listed by number ranging from 1 to 14. The smaller the number, the higher the injury is located on the body. Headaches, for example, are 1.7, while a toe injury is 14.7. Your objective is to find the number of the body part that most closely matches the injury location. This is not always easy because the rating manual does not precisely identify and cover each and every body part. You will have to extrapolate from time to time to get a number. For example, if you had an injury to your foot, you will note that the rating manual gives a disability number of 14.6 for ankle and 14.7 for toes, but there is no rating for foot. You would have to choose between the two given, depending upon which best describes your injury.

Here is an excerpt from Section 2 of the manual:

SECTION 2 – DISABILITIES AND STANDARD RATINGS

7.7 IMPAIRMENT OF FUNCTION, WRIST

Immobility of wrist joint in favorable position

7.711	Major	20%
7.712	Minor	17%
7.713	Both	50%

Note that the term major applies to the hand/wrist you are most proficient with (most people are right-handed) and minor applies to the less proficient hand/wrist.

Mary injured both arms, her back and her right knee. The disability number that most closely covers Mary's arm injuries is 7.713, which is "impairment of function" for both wrists. Section 2 also shows that the disability number for a back injury is 12.1, and the disability number for an injury to one knee is 14.511. Great, we have the first piece of our puzzle: Mary's disability numbers.

> **EXAMPLE:** The first part of Mary's disability rating:
>
> arms 7.713
> back 12.1
> knee 14.511

b.   Determine Standard Disability Rating

Be aware that the process of rating a permanent disability is an imprecise science. It is possible, even likely, that five knowledgeable raters might arrive at five different ratings for the same report. This is because some of the work restrictions and subjective findings contained in the doctor's medical report are subject to interpretation by the person doing the rating. In addition, doctors' reports typically differ in style and format, leading to different results when the doctor's findings are converted into numbers.

Knowing this, we'll go on to use the medical report to determine Mary's "standard disability" for each injured part of the body. Or to put it another way, we now need to find out how disabled the doctor thinks Mary is.

You should take several factors into consideration to arrive at any standard disability:

- **subjective complaints:** how much pain the doctor believes the patient is in
- **objective findings:** medical test results and examinations, and
- **work restrictions:** how the doctor feels the patient is limited in the open labor market as a result of the injury.

All three factors may be used to determine a standard disability, but often only one of the three is used. After you find separate standard ratings based upon subjective complaints, objective findings and work restrictions, you will compare the three and use the highest rating as your standard.

Mary's medical report covers objective and subjective factors of her disability and work restrictions, as do most medical reports that provide opinions on permanent disability. (If you're having trouble finding factors of disability, see "Where to Find Factors of Disability in a Medical Report," below.) Here's how her report reads:

FACTORS OF DISABILITY

A. Subjective
1. **Right & Left Arms:** Intermittent moderate pain.
2. **Low Back:** Intermittent slight to moderate pain.
3. **Right Knee:** Intermittent moderate pain.

B. Objective
1. **Left Elbow:** History of surgery with residual surgical scar.
2. **Right & Left Wrists:** (a) Decrease of grip bilaterally; (b) History of surgery bilaterally with residual scars.
3. **Low Back:** Positive MRI.
4. **Right Knee:** (a) Atrophy of the right calf; (b) History of surgery with residual surgical scars.

C. Work restrictions
1. **Right and left arms:** The patient should be prophylactically [preventively] restricted from heavy lifting, repetitive pushing and pulling with both arms, and repetitive and forceful gripping with both hands.
2. **Low back:** The patient should be prophylactically restricted from very heavy work.
3. **Right knee:** The patient should be prophylactically restricted from prolonged weight-bearing.

WHERE TO FIND FACTORS OF DISABILITY IN A MEDICAL REPORT

Most doctors who write reports for workers' compensation set out the factors of disability in a separate section. However, you may receive a report that is not well organized. If so, you'll have to locate language that deals with objective findings, subjective complaints and work restrictions. Here are some suggestions.

Objective Findings. In a typical report, objective factors are found throughout the report, and are summarized under the heading "Factors of Disability." Look for terms such as these:

- "objective findings of disability include…."
- "upon examination, the patient showed…."
- anything that supports the doctor's findings of "subjective factors of disability" or "work restrictions," including such terms as "loss of motion," "test results" or descriptions of "tenderness or pain" upon examination

Subjective Findings. Subjective factors of disability are found under a heading entitled "Subjective Factors of Disability." Look for terms such as these:

- "subjective complaints include…."
- "upon examination I would describe the patient's pain as…."
- language that deals with the doctor's opinion as to the type of pain you have in each part of body you injured. The pain may be described as the type of pain you have all the time, the type of pain you have upon doing certain activities or both. For example, "the patient has constant slight pain in the right upper extremity which increases to moderate upon heavy lifting."

Work Restrictions. Work restrictions are often listed under "Disability," "Permanent Disability" or "Work Restrictions." In some instances, however, you may have to read the report carefully to find where the doctor lists the work restrictions, such as:

- "work restrictions include…."
- "the patient should be precluded from doing the following types of activities…."
- language that describes limitations or things you can't do. These may be described as "actual" things the doctor says you physically can't do or "prophylactic" (preventive) things the doctor says you shouldn't do.

i.   Determine Subjective Standard Rating of Disability

The first basis for arriving at a standard disability rating is the doctor's opinion regarding subjective complaints. Some standard disability ratings for subjective complaints are set out in the rating manual—see the chart below. In addition, I have added a few extra ratings to help you rate your doctor's comments on your subjective complaints. I have compiled these extra ratings, which say "author's addition," on the basis of attending many courses and lectures on rating permanent disabilities and I believe them to be accurate.

Although the chart contains standard disability ratings for the most common subjective complaints, it does not list all possible variations. This means that sometimes you must extrapolate or modify the doctor's subjective factors to "fit" the chart.

Standard Disability Ratings for Subjective Complaints

occasional slight pain (author's addition)	3%
intermittent minimal to slight pain (author's addition)	3%
intermittent slight pain (author's addition)	5%
frequent slight pain (author's addition)	8%
constant slight pain	10%
constant slight to moderate pain	30%
constant moderate pain	50%

Mary uses the medical report to match her disabilities with the standard disability ratings of subjective factors. To do this, she must rate each of her disabilities separately, using the description from the medical report. Here's the process Mary undertakes.

- **Right & Left Arms:** "intermittent moderate pain." There is no listing for "intermittent moderate pain" on the chart. However, by looking at the chart we see that, in one instance at least, "intermittent" means one-half of "constant" pain. ("Constant slight pain" is a 10% disability, while intermittent slight pain is a 5% disability.) Therefore it's probably reasonable to extrapolate that if "constant moderate pain" is a 50% standard in the chart, "intermittent moderate pain," should be a 25% standard. So Mary lists her subjective arm standard at 25%.

- **Low Back:** "intermittent slight to moderate pain." Mary compares the subjective factors of disability given by the doctor to the standard disability ratings contained in the chart. By doing this, Mary finds she has a standard disability rating of 15% based on the same procedure that she used for her arms.
- **Right Knee:** "intermittent moderate pain." Comparing the subjective factors of disability given by the doctor for her right knee to the chart's ratings, Mary finds that she has a standard disability rating of 25%.

Here are Mary's subjective disability standards:

- 25% subjective standard (arms)
- 15% subjective standard (back), and
- 25% subjective standard (knee)

ii. Determine Standard Rating for Objective Findings

The rating manual lists standard disabilities and their ratings based on objective findings of the severity of a physical injury. As discussed in Section 2a, above, these are listed under "Section 2—Disabilities and Standard Ratings" in the rating manual. Because of the infinite number of possible objective findings, not all disabilities are in the rating manual.

Your specific disability may be listed in Section 2 of the rating manual. If, when you found your disability number (Step 2a, above), your exact disability was listed, you only need look at the corresponding standard rating to the right of the disability number. For instance, if you have severe mobility problems in both of your wrists, you could use a standard disability of 50% (see the chart in Step 2a, above, entitled Section 2–Disabilities and Standard Ratings).

For some injuries where you have only lost partial use of a body part, you'll have to take a fraction of that objective rating percentage given in Section 2 of the manual by using the charts in the appendix of the manual. This may apply to injuries involving vision; limitation of motion of finger, shoulder, hip or knee; reduction of grip strength; or thigh or calf atrophy (loss of muscle tissue).

Most of Mary's objective findings do not have a standard rating listed in the rating manual. This is not unusual. I would estimate that 80% of all injuries are rated based upon work restrictions, 15% on subjective findings and only 5% on objective findings. And in almost all cases, the rating based upon work restrictions, discussed in subsection c, below, will be greater. Mary will not use the objective findings for her elbow, low back or right knee to rate her disability.

Mary's loss of grip strength can be rated with the manual, by using the objective rating percentage in Section 2 of the manual and a chart in the appendix of the manual. Let's look at Mary's objective findings for grip loss.

Mary's doctor's report said she sustained grip loss bilaterally—for both hands (see "Factors of Disability" in subsection b, above). If you look in Section 2 of the rating manual, entitled Disabilities and Standard Ratings, you find that injuries to the grip are assigned the disability number 10.511, which is in turn assigned a disability percentage of 85%. (This percentage of disability applies to those who have lost *all* grip strength bilaterally.)

To find out how much grip strength she has lost, Mary should call or write the doctor for a supplemental report stating the percentage of grip loss the doctor estimates that she has sustained. When Mary receives the doctor's supplemental report on loss of grip strength, she'll refer to Table 4 in the Appendix of the rating manual (on page 7-6) to find her percentage of disability. If the doctor's supplemental report states that Mary has lost approximately 50% of her gripping capacity bilaterally, by reference to the table (reproduced below) we see that a 50% loss amounts to 1/3 of the disability percentage. Therefore a medical opinion that the applicant has lost 50% of her gripping capacity bilaterally results in 1/3 of 85%, or a 28.5% disability. We'll see in the section below that a disability rating based on Mary's work restrictions will actually give a higher rating for her arms (50%), so she won't use this 28.5% rating.

Percentage of Grip Strength Lost	Fraction
10%	0
15	1/20
20	1/12
25	1/8
30	1/6
35	1/5
40	1/4
45	3/10
50	1/3
55	2/5
60	4/9
65	1/2
70	3/5
75	2/3
80	3/4
85	4/5
90	5/6
95	1

TABLE 4—HAND-REDUCTION OF GRIP STRENGTH (DISABILITY NOS. 10.511, 10.512)

I know all this sounds confusing—believe me, it can be! The good news is it is much simpler to come up with a disability percentage using your work restrictions (see immediately below). And often a rating based upon work restrictions will be greater than one based on objective findings.

OBJECTIVE FINDINGS SHOULD SUPPORT WORK RESTRICTIONS

Objective findings are not only used to find the existence of a particular disability and to give a standard rating, but to support subjective complaints and work restrictions. For instance, an objective finding of an amputation of a finger on the right hand would support a work restriction of "no fine dexterous activities using the right hand."

In our example, Mary looks at the medical report to see if any of the objective findings can be rated for a standard disability. Mary has some very significant objective findings: a history of surgery to the left elbow, a decrease of grip strength in both hands, a history of surgery to both hands, a positive MRI for the back, a history of surgery for the right knee, as well as atrophy of the right calf. These findings strongly support the doctor's conclusions and opinions on subjective factors of disability, as well as recommended work restrictions.

But if you're satisfied with a medical report, don't worry if objective findings don't support subjective findings and work restrictions unless the insurance company raises this issue. Most insurance companies do not examine medical reports carefully enough to discover such inconsistencies. If the insurance company points out that the report does not contain objective findings to support the doctor's conclusions, you should write the doctor and request that she comment upon the objective findings in more detail. Hopefully, the doctor's report is only defective because of an oversight. But if the doctor simply can't find any objective findings, do your best to downplay this, since your subjective factors will, or should, support the doctor's work restrictions.

iii. Determine Standard Rating for Work Restrictions

 See *Capistrano Unified School District v. WCAB* in Chapter 28.

The doctor's medical report will explain that work restrictions are based on a combination of the subjective complaints of the patient as well as the objective findings.

Work restrictions can be of two types:

- actual, meaning you physically cannot do the restricted activity, and
- prophylactic, meaning that although you could do a certain activity, you should not do so prophylactically (preventively) because there is a high likelihood you will either reinjure or further injure yourself.

No matter how the doctor arrives at the restrictions (actual or prophylactic), the rating is the same.

Obviously, work restrictions are different for different parts of the body. For example, if you have an eye problem, what you can't, or shouldn't, do would differ from someone with a bad knee. Similarly, there are different percentages of disability and various levels of restrictions for each body part.

The rating manual lists disability percentages for two types of work restrictions. Listed in section 2, the rating manual has work restriction guidelines in "Spine and Torso Guidelines," page 2-14, and in "Lower Extremity Guidelines," page 2-19. The spine and torso guidelines can be used for injuries involving the abdomen or rib cage, problems with the neck, back or pelvis or pulmonary or heart disease. The lower extremity guidelines can be used for any injuries involving the legs, knees, feet, ankles or toes. Whether you have an injury to one or both legs, the disability percentages listed in the lower extremities chart are taken at full value. To put it another way, one leg gets the full value of the disability listed.

These charts are reprinted below. Note that these charts contain a few extra restrictions and corresponding percentages that are followed by the words "author's addition." I developed these ratings on the basis of workers' compensation lectures and seminars, on years of experience rating permanent disabilities and by extrapolating information from other disability percentages in the rating manual. They are believed, but not guaranteed, to be accurate.

SPINE AND TORSO GUIDELINES RATINGS FOR WORK RESTRICTIONS	
Disability precluding very heavy lifting	10%
Disability precluding very heavy work	15%
Disability precluding very heavy lifting and repeated bending and stooping (author's addition)	15%
Disability precluding repetitive motions of the neck or back	15%
Disability precluding heavy lifting	20%
Disability precluding heavy lifting and repeated bending and stooping	25%
Disability precluding heavy work	30%
Disability precluding substantial work	40%
Disability resulting in limitation to light work	50%
Disability resulting in limitation to semi-sedentary work	60%
Disability resulting in limitation to sedentary work	70%

LOWER EXTREMITY GUIDELINES RATINGS FOR WORK RESTRICTIONS	
Disability precluding repetitive squatting, kneeling or crawling (author's addition)	3%
Disability precluding squatting and/or kneeling	5%
Disability precluding work at unprotected heights (author's addition)	8%
Disability precluding climbing	10%
Disability precluding descending (author's addition)	10%
Disability precluding walking over uneven ground	10%
Disability precluding very heavy lifting	10%
Disability precluding prolonged sitting (author's addition)	10%
Disability precluding prolonged walking (author's addition)	10%
Disability precluding prolonged standing (author's addition)	20%
Disability precluding climbing, walking over uneven ground, squatting, kneeling, crouching, crawling and pivoting	20%
Disability precluding prolonged weight-bearing (can bear weight 75% of time)	10%
Disability precluding heavy lifting	20%
Disability precluding heavy lifting, squatting, kneeling, crawling, pushing, pulling or twisting (author's addition)	30%
Disability precluding heavy lifting, climbing, walking over uneven ground, squatting, kneeling, crouching, crawling and pivoting	30%
Disability precluding heavy lifting, prolonged weight-bearing, climbing, walking over uneven ground, squatting, kneeling, crouching, crawling and pivoting	40%
Disability resulting in limitation of weight-bearing to half time	40%
Use of cane required for work (author's addition)	40%
Disability resulting in limitation to semi-sedentary work	60%
Disability resulting in limitation to sedentary work	70%

for work restrictions involving the arms. Again, they are believed, but not guaranteed, to be accurate. Note that the term major applies to the arm/hand you are most proficient with (for example, most people are right-handed), and minor applies to the less proficient arm/hand.

UPPER EXTREMITY GUIDELINES RATINGS FOR WORK RESTRICTIONS	
Disability precluding pushing and pulling	
major	10%
minor	8%
both	18%
Disability precluding gripping and grasping	
major	15%
minor	13%
both arms	30%
Disability precluding very heavy lifting	
one arm	5%
both	10%
Disability precluding very heavy work	
one arm	8%
both	15%
Disability precluding heavy lifting	
one arm	10%
both	20%

One last rule: for disabilities above 24%, you round off to the nearest 5%. For instance, 58% rounds off to a 60% disability standard.

Now let's return to Mary and start by seeing how her doctor described her work restrictions, which were covered under a "Disability" category in her medical report:

If your injury is to your spine or torso or your legs or feet, you use the ratings, or disability percentages, in one of the charts printed above.

If your injury is to one or both arms, you may have a bit more difficulty rating your disability. The rating schedule does not set forth any standards for rating work restrictions for upper extremities, so they must be determined by analogy to other scheduled disabilities. However, on the basis of lectures and seminars, experience in rating permanent disabilities and extrapolation from other disability percentages in the rating manual, I have developed my own set of ratings

C. Work Restrictions

1. **Right and left arms:** The patient should be prophylactically restricted from heavy lifting, repetitive pushing and pulling with both arms, and repetitive and forceful gripping with both hands.
2. **Low back:** The patient should be prophylactically restricted from very heavy work.
3. **Right knee:** The patient should be prophylactically restricted from prolonged weight-bearing.

Now we'll see how all of these technicalities work out in arriving at a disability rating.

Arms: Using the work restrictions given by the doctor for Mary's right and left arms in the upper extremities chart, Mary finds that she has a standard work restriction for her arms of 50%. Whoa! How did Mary arrive at 50%? A step-by-step look at how she did this will not only make this clear, it will also introduce a very important rating principle known as "pyramiding." (see "Pyramiding: Multiple Work Restrictions for One Body Part," below.)

PYRAMIDING: MULTIPLE WORK RESTRICTIONS FOR ONE BODY PART

If you have more than one work restriction to the same body part, you are allowed to "pyramid" the restrictions—that is, apply more than one work restriction to the same part of the body. To do this, you take 100% of the greatest work restriction and add 50% of the combined total of all the other work restrictions.

For example, work restrictions of no heavy lifting (20%), no prolonged walking (10%) and no climbing (10%) would be 30%, a total of the entire amount of the greatest restriction (20%), plus half of the total of the other restrictions (10% + 10% x 1/2 = 10%).

According to the doctor's report, Mary should be "prophylactically restricted from heavy lifting, repetitive pushing and pulling with both arms, and repetitive and forceful gripping with both hands." Although this may seem like one large restriction, it is in fact three, as far as the workers' compensation rating system is concerned. This means Mary has to determine three different disability standards for her upper arms. Using the upper extremity chart, Mary finds:

- No heavy lifting with both arms is a 20% standard.
- No pushing and pulling with both arms is 18%.
- No gripping and grasping with both hands is 30%.

You might logically think that the standard disability would be the total of all three, or 68%. However, this is where the concept of pyramiding comes in. As discussed above, if you have more than one work restriction to the same part of the body, you first take the greatest restriction and then add to it one-half of the total of the remaining restrictions.

For Mary, the greatest of the three restrictions above is 30%. To this, she adds 19%, which is one-half of the total of the remaining restrictions (20% +18% = 38% x 1/2 is 19%). Adding 30% and 19% together gives Mary a 49% standard disability for her upper extremities. Finally, because disabilities above 24% are rounded off to the nearest 5%, Mary rounds off 49% to a 50% disability standard.

Low Back: Finding the work restriction given by the doctor for Mary's back (no very heavy work) in the spine and torso chart, Mary finds that she has a standard work restriction for her back of 15%.

Right Knee: Mary's doctor gives a work restriction of "no prolonged weight bearing," which is a 10% standard according to the lower extremity chart.

Mary comes up with the following work restrictions:
- arm restrictions: 50%
- back restrictions: 15%
- knee restrictions: 10%

If you aren't pleased with the medical report, study it carefully. If you can argue that the doctor's work restrictions are not correct, based upon the objective findings, you may be able to convince the insurance company that the injury is, in fact, more severe than the doctor finds.

iv. Determine Which Standard to Use

Usually you are not entitled to a work restriction rating based upon both subjective complaints and work restrictions. Instead, you are limited to the higher of the two for each body part. Of course, to know which is higher, you need to rate both, as covered above.

EXAMPLE: A comparison of Mary's subjective disabilities to her work restrictions shows:

Part of body	Subjective disabilities	Work restrictions
Arms	25%	50%
Back	15%	15%
Right knee	25%	10%

Taking the higher of the two ratings, Mary will use a standard of 50% for her upper arms, 15% for her back and 25% for her right knee.

Sometimes the same or similar work restrictions may be imposed on different body parts. This concept is called "overlap," as discussed below. If you have the same work restriction for two or more parts of the body, you are not entitled to total the two. Instead, you get one work restriction that covers both parts. In Mary's case, since she already has a work exclusion based on her arm problems of no heavy lifting, it does her no further good to claim a work restriction based on her back injury of no very heavy work (a restriction with a lesser disability percentage). In other words, Mary is already precluded from lifting for her arms, so an additional lesser lifting restriction would be irrelevant.

If asked by the insurance company how she arrived at her rating, Mary should explain that she used the 15% subjective findings for her back instead of the 15% work restriction. (She did this to avoid the overlapping work restrictions from her low back.)

OVERLAP

Overlap occurs when a work restriction for one part of the body also benefits another part of the body. If you are restricted from heavy lifting because of your back, your injured knees will also benefit from that restriction. Therefore a restriction of no very heavy lifting to the knees is absorbed in the no heavy lifting restriction for the back.

Overlap is not always easy to spot, and if your rating differs from that arrived at by an advisory rating, it is quite likely due to the application of this concept. The only way to spot overlaps is to check whether there are similar work restrictions to different parts of the body. If so, you must determine if you included both restrictions in your rating. Because this is impermissible, you must subtract out the duplicate rating. To avoid overlap, it is best to use subjective ratings for the body part that has no work restrictions or that has overlapping work restrictions.

Finally, Mary puts together the disability numbers (from Step 1, above) and the standard disability ratings she just came up with:

EXAMPLE: Mary's standard disability rating now consists of two parts:

arms ....7.713   -   50%

back ....12.1   -   15%

knee ....14.511   -   25%

Step 3: Determine Your Occupational Group Number

 See *Kochevar v. Fremont Unified School District* in Chapter 28.

The next factors in the formula are based upon your occupation. Different occupations will affect (increase or decrease) the standard rating for the same injury differently. For example, a cashier will be adversely affected by a hand injury to a greater degree than a restaurant hostess.

You need to search Section 3 of the rating manual called "Occupations and Group Numbers," to find your occupation (the list is not reprinted here due to size limitations). Occupations are listed in alphabetical order, and each has a corresponding group number. In Mary's case, looking up "meat clerk" in the rating manual tells us that the group number is 322. The occupation you use does not have to be the same one you listed in your Application for Adjudication of Claim.

Many occupations are not contained in the rating manual's list of occupations, with the result that you sometimes have to be creative and take a group number from a similar occupation. You should determine the basic activities of the occupation and relate it to a comparable occupation in the manual. If you find more than one group that your occupation could fit into, note all of them.

 ADVANTAGES TO CHANGING OCCUPATIONAL GROUP NUMBERS

You may be entitled to a larger permanent disability payment if you use a more advantageous occupational group number. This is covered below, in Step 4c.

Your occupational group number will be the third figure in your rating formula (see below).

Occupational Variant Table

		110	111	112	120	210	211	212	213	214	220	221	230	240	250	251	290	310	311	320	321	322	330
1.1	PARALYSIS	D	F	G	G	E	F	E	F	F	G	G	F	F	F	E	G	F	F	H	G	G	G
1.3	EPILEPSY	H	G	I		H	G	H	F	H	I		F	F	J	F	H		G	I		H	H
1.4	PSYCHIATRIC	J			H	I		H		H	J		F	G	H		H				H	G	F
1.5	PST-TRAUM HEAD	I	H	H	H	H	H	H			H		F	G	G	H	H	H	H	H	F	G	F
1.6	VERTIGO	D	D	D	D	E	D	C	H	H	H	D	E	F	G	G	E	E	F	F	F	F	F
1.7	HEADACHES	I	H	H	H	H	H		H	H	H	H	G	G	H	H	G	H	H	H	G	G	F
1.8	COGNITIVE DIS	I	H	H	H	H	H	H		H	H	G	F	H	G	G	G	H	H	H	F	G	F
2.1--	SIGHT-COSMETIC	I				J	I				J	H	G	G		J	J		J			H	G
2.2-2.6	VISION	H		J		I					J	H	G	G			I				H	H	G
2.7	LACRIMATION			J		J		C		J	J		F	G	H	H		J			H	H	G
3.1	HEARING LOSS	J	H	I	F	J	H		H		H	D	E	H	J	J		J	J	E	D	E	E
4.1	COSMETIC				H	J		C	H	J	J	G	F	J	F	J	J		J	E	E	E	E
4.3-4.4	SKULL	C	C	C	C	D	C	C	F	C	C	C	F	D	F	D	C	C	C	F	F	F	F
4.5	JAW	I		H	F	J	H			J	J	F	F	G	G		H	H	H	F	G	F	F
4.7	NOSE	H	H	H	F	H	H		H	H	G	F	E	H	H		H	F	F	F	H	E	H
5.2	SPEECH	J			F	J		J		J	J	G	D	J	J	J	J		J	D	C	C	D
5.31	SMELL	F	F	F	F	F	D	C	E	F	J	F	F	D	F	D	D	C	D	F	F	F	F
5.32	TASTE	F	F	F	F	F	D	C	F	F	J	F	F	G	E	H	H	H	H	F	G	H	E
5.33	SMELL, TASTE	F	F	F	F	F	F	C	F	F		F	E	H	J	J	H	F	F	F	F	F	F
6.1	SKIN-OUTSIDE	F	F	F	F	F	F	F	H	H	J	F	F	F	F	G		F	G	F	F	E	F
6.2	SKIN-WET WK	F	F	F	F	F	F	F	F	F	G	F	F	F	H	F	H	F	G	G	G	H	F
7.1	ARM AMP	E	G	H	H	E	G	E	F	G	H	F	G	G	F	G	G	F	G	F	H	G	G
7.3	SHOULDER	C	D	D	E	C	D	F	E	F	F	F	F	D	F	G	F	F	F	H	F	F	F
7.5	ELBOW	D	F	G	G	D	F	G	G	F	G	G	G	E	G	F	G	F	G	H	H	G	F
7.6	FOREARM	D	G	H	H	D	G	E	E	G	G	G	F	E	F	E	G	F	G		H	G	F
7.7	WRIST	D	G	H	H	D	G	F	G	G	H	H	G	E	F	F	H	G	G		G	H	F
8.11	THUMB AMP	F	G	H		E	E	F	H	G	H	H	G	E	F	F	H	F	G	F	G	G	G
8.12	INDEX AMP	F	H		H	E	H	F	F	H	H		G	E	F	F	H	G	H	F	H	F	G
8.13	MIDDLE AMP	F	H	I	H	E	H	F	F	G	H	H	G	E	F	F	H	G	H	G	H	H	G
8.14	RING AMP	F	G		G	E	G	F	F	G	G	G	G	E	F	F	F	F	G	H	G	G	F
8.15	LITTLE AMP	F	G	I	G	E	G	F	F	G	G	G	F	E	F	F	F	F	F	F	G	F	F

Step 4: Determine Your Occupational Variant

Next, we turn to Section 4 in the rating manual, entitled "Occupational Variants." This chart has the disability number (Step 2, above) down the left side of the page, and the occupational group numbers (Step 3, just above) across the top of the page. Where the two columns intersect, you will find a letter of the alphabet from "C" to "J." This letter is known as the "occupational variant," which is placed next to the occupation group number in the formula (see below).

With this occupational variant, you will be able to tell if one occupational group is better for you than another. The closer the letter is to "Z," the higher your disability rating will be. Here is the breakdown:

- Occupational variant of "F" is neutral—it will neither raise nor lower your standard disability rating.
- Occupational variant of "C," "D" or "E" will decrease your standard disability rating (C the most and E the least). This will result in a lower disability rating and thus less money.
- Occupational variant of "G" through "J" will increase your standard disability rating (G the least and J the most.) This means you'll end up with a higher disability rating, and thus more money.

Mary finds that the occupational variant for wrists (only the variant for the wrists can be found in the excerpt reprinted above) is G, the variant for her back is F, and the variant for her knee is F.

> **EXAMPLE:** Mary's standard disability formula now consists of three parts:
>
> arms .... 7.713 -   50%   -   322G
> back .... 12.1   -   15%   -   322F
> knee .... 14.5   -   25%   -   322F

 DECIDE WHETHER TO CHANGE OCCUPATIONAL GROUPS

As mentioned, oftentimes a change in your group number can make a significant difference in your disability rating, and thus the amount of disability that you are entitled to. That is because various work restrictions affect different occupations in different ways. For example, someone who has a work restriction of "no fine hand manipulations" will find that their standard rating goes up in value if their occupation requires fine hand manipulations, such as a typist or jeweler, and will go down for such occupations as a laborer, where fine hand manipulations are not required.

Just because your job title is listed in the section of the rating manual under occupational group numbers does not necessarily mean that you must use that group number. Look more to your job duties rather than your job title, to determine your group number(s). And don't be afraid to be creative. If your job title is "assembler" but your duties are really that of a "warehouseman," use the job classification that results in the most favorable occupational variant.

If it is possible that your job qualifies you for more than one group number, follow the instructions above and check all possible occupational groups to see which one results in an occupational variant that is best for you. Again, the point is that you want to locate and use the occupational group that gives you the greatest increase in your standard rating.

Step 5: Adjust the Standard Disability Rating Based on Your Occupational Variant

The next step is to determine the percentage of disability after "adjustment" for your occupation. As discussed in Step 4, just above, the adjustment is based upon how your disability affects your ability to work in your general occupation classification. Different occupations are affected differently by the same disability. (See "Decide Whether to Change Occupational Groups," just above, for information on how to decide which occupational group is best for you.)

Turning to Section 5 in the rating manual, entitled "Occupational Adjustment," Mary takes the standard ratings for each part of her body and finds the corresponding adjustment for her occupational variant.

The occupational adjustment table has the standard disability rating down the left side of the page, and the occupational variants from "C" through "J" across the top of the page. You need to find the intersection of the standard disability rating (from Step 3) and the occupational variant (from Step 4).

Looking up her disability rating for her arms, 50%, with an occupational variant of H, Mary finds that it adjusts to 56%. Looking up 15%, for her back, with an occupational variant of F, Mary finds that it remains at 15%. Looking up 25%, for her knee, with an occupational variant of F, Mary finds that it also remains at 25%.

> **EXAMPLE:** Mary's standard disability formula now consists of four parts:
>
> arms .... 7.713 -   50%   -   322G -   56%
> back .... 12.1   -   15%   -   322F -   15%
> knee .... 14.5   -   25%   -   322F -   25%

Occupational Adjustment Table

STANDARD RATING PERCENT	C	D	E	F	G	H	I	J
0	0	0	0	0	0	0	0	0
1	1	1	1	1	2	2	2	2
2	1	2	2	2	3	3	4	4
3	2	2	3	3	4	5	5	6
4	3	3	4	4	5	6	7	8
5	3	4	4	5	6	7	8	9
6	4	5	5	6	7	8	9	11
7	5	5	6	7	8	10	11	12
8	6	6	7	8	9	11	12	14
9	6	7	8	9	11	12	14	15
10	7	8	9	10	12	13	15	16
11	7	9	10	11	13	14	16	18
12	8	10	11	12	14	16	17	19
13	9	10	12	13	15	17	18	20
14	10	11	13	14	16	18	20	22
15	11	12	14	15	17	19	21	23
16	11	13	14	16	18	20	22	24
17	12	14	15	17	19	21	23	26
18	13	15	16	18	20	22	24	27
19	14	15	17	19	21	24	26	28
20	15	16	18	20	22	25	27	29
21	16	17	19	21	23	26	28	31
22	16	18	20	22	24	27	29	32
23	17	19	21	23	26	28	31	33
24	18	20	22	24	27	29	32	34
25	18	21	23	25	28	30	33	36

STANDARD RATING PERCENT	C	D	E	F	G	H	I	J
26	19	22	24	26	29	31	34	37
27	20	23	25	27	30	33	35	38
28	21	24	26	28	31	34	36	39
29	22	24	27	29	32	35	37	40
30	23	25	28	30	33	36	38	41
31	24	26	29	31	34	37	40	43
32	25	27	30	32	35	38	41	44
33	25	28	30	33	36	39	42	45
34	26	29	31	34	37	40	43	46
35	27	30	32	35	38	41	44	47
36	28	31	33	36	39	42	45	48
37	29	32	34	37	40	43	46	49
38	30	32	35	38	41	44	47	50
39	31	33	36	39	42	45	48	51
40	32	34	37	40	43	46	49	52
41	33	35	38	41	44	47	50	54
42	34	36	39	42	45	48	51	55
43	35	37	40	43	46	49	52	56
44	36	38	41	44	47	50	53	57
45	36	39	42	45	48	51	54	58
46	37	40	43	46	49	52	55	59
47	38	41	44	47	50	53	56	60
48	39	42	45	48	51	54	57	61
49	40	43	46	49	52	55	58	62
50	41	44	47	50	53	56	59	62

Step 6: Adjust the Standard Disability Rating for Your Age

The older a worker is at the time of injury, the greater will be the disability after adjustment for age. Age 39 is the median. For ages younger than 39, the disability will be adjusted downward, and above that age it will go up.

Here's the reasoning behind this. The younger someone is, the longer he has to figure out how to adjust to the disability and become a productive worker. The older a worker is, the less chance he will adapt to the disability in the work force.

In our example, Mary was 42 at time she was injured. In the rating manual, under Section 6, entitled "Age Adjustment," we find a table where the adjusted standard disability rating (from Step 5) is listed down the left side of the page, and

ages are listed across the top of the page. Where the two figures intersect on the page is the corresponding age-adjusted rating.

Looking up 56% (the adjusted rating for her arms), Mary finds that it adjusts to 58:0% for age 42. Looking up 15%, Mary finds that it adjusts to 16:0% for her age. Looking up 25%, Mary finds that it adjusts to 27:0% for her age. (Only adjusted ratings up to 25% are excerpted here from the manual.)

EXAMPLE: Mary's disability formula now consists of five parts:

arms .... 7.713 - 50% - 322G - 56% - 58.0%
back .... 12.1   - 15% - 322F - 15% - 16:0%
knee .... 14.5   - 25% - 322F - 25% - 27:0%

AGE ADJUSTMENT TABLE

AGE AT TIME OF INJURY

Rating	21 and under	22-26	27-31	32-36	37-41	42-46	47-51	52-56	57-61	62 and over
1	1	1	1	1	1	1	1	1	1	1
2	2	2	2	2	2	2	2	3	3	3
3	2	2	3	3	3	3	3	4	4	4
4	3	3	3	4	4	4	5	5	5	6
5	4	4	4	5	5	5	6	6	6	7
6	5	5	5	6	6	6	7	7	8	8
7	5	6	6	7	7	8	8	9	9	10
8	6	6	7	7	8	9	9	10	10	11
9	7	7	8	8	9	10	10	11	12	12
10	8	8	9	9	10	11	11	12	13	13
11	8	9	10	10	11	12	13	13	14	15
12	9	10	10	11	12	13	14	15	15	16
13	10	11	11	12	13	14	15	16	16	17
14	11	11	12	13	14	15	16	17	18	19
15	12	12	13	14	15	16	17	18	19	20
16	12	13	14	15	16	17	18	19	20	21
17	13	14	15	16	17	18	19	20	21	22
18	14	15	16	17	18	19	20	21	23	24
19	15	16	17	18	19	20	22	23	24	25
20	16	17	18	19	20	21	23	24	25	26
21	17	18	19	20	21	22	24	25	26	27
22	17	18	20	21	22	23	25	26	28	29
23	18	19	20	22	23	24	26	27	29	30
24	19	20	21	23	24	25	27	28	30	31
25	20	21	22	24	25	27	28	29	31	32

Step 7: Refer to the Appendices to Make Final Adjustments to the Rating Where Necessary and to Combine Multiple Disabilities If Applicable

If Mary had an injury to just one part of her body, say her back, she'd have figured out her permanent partial disability in Step 6, above. In our example, it would be 16% (her formula would be 12.1 - 15% - 322F - 15% - 16:0%), and she could skip this step.

However, where, as in Mary's case, there are disabilities to more than one part of the body, the individual disability totals must be combined into one grand total. This is done by referring to the "Multiple Disability Table" (also known as the MDT table) the last table in the appendices of the rating manual. This table has the disability rating across the top of the page in increments of 5%, as well as down the left side of the page in increments of 1%. (See table below.)

Here's how Mary proceeds. First she takes her largest disability, 58%, and finds the nearest number at the top of the page. The numbers are set forth in 5% increments, so Mary locates 60%.

Next, Mary will take her second largest disability and find it down the left side of the page. Although Mary's second largest disability was to her knee at 27%, we must subtract the 2% that we increased the largest disability to above (from 58% to 60%) when we rounded the number up. So Mary actually uses the 25% on the left side of the table. (If Mary needed to round her disability number down, she could have added it into one of her lower disability ratings.)

Now Mary is ready to compute the combined disability rating for the two disabilities. She does this by looking to see where the two numbers intersect. The number at the intersection is the percentage of disability for both injuries. In this instance, where 60% on top and 25% on the left intersect, the figure is 73%.

Now Mary must combine the 73% disability (gotten by combining her 58% and 27% disabilities) with her smallest disability of 16%. She follows the same procedure. Mary finds 75% (the closest 5% increment) across the top of the page for her biggest rating. Next, Mary will take her smallest disability and find it down the left side of the page. Although Mary's smallest disability was to her knee at 16%, we must subtract the 2% that we increased the largest disability to above (from

73% to 75%) when we rounded the number up to the closest increment. So Mary actually uses the 14% (16% minus 2%) on the left side of the table. She finds that these two percentages intersect at 80%.

After applying the multiple disability table to her three different disabilities, Mary finds that her permanent partial disability is 80%.

> **EXAMPLE:** Mary's completed disability formula:
> arms .... 7.713   -   50%   -   322G   -   56%   -   58.0%
> back .... 12.1   -   15%   -   322F   -   15%   -   16:0%
> knee .... 14.5   -   25%   -   322F   -   25%   -   27:0%
>
> Multiple Disability Rating (MDT) = 80%

Step 8: Determine a Dollar Value for the Disability

Now that your disability rating is complete, you're ready to determine the dollar value of your permanent disability. To do this, please refer to Chapter 13, Section E, for a detailed explanation on how to use the permanent disability table located in Appendix 3 of this book to determine the dollar value of your permanent disability.

 LIFE PENSION AVAILABLE FOR DISABILITIES OF 70% OR MORE

If you have a permanent disability rating of at least 70%, you are entitled to a life pension in addition to your permanent disability benefits. A life pension consists of a small amount of money that is payable every two weeks for as long as you live. See Chapter 13, Section F, on how to compute your life pension.

As you can see, the process of properly rating a permanent disability requires both time and effort. However, I believe that if you commit yourself to doing it, you will increase your chances of negotiating a fair settlement. By understanding your rating, you will be in a position to discuss your disability with the insurance claims adjuster intelligently and with the confidence that you know what you are talking about.

Multiple Disabilities Table

Rating for Major Disability–Percent

Rating for Secondary Disability-Percent

	5	10	15	20	25	30	35	40	45	50	55	60	65	70	75	80	85	90	95
5	10	15	20	25	29	34	39	44	48	53	58	63	67	72	77	82	86	91	96
6	11	16	21	25	30	35	40	44	49	54	58	63	68	72	77	82	87	91	96
7	12	17	22	26	31	36	40	45	50	54	59	64	68	73	77	82	87	91	96
8	13	18	23	27	32	36	41	46	50	55	59	64	69	73	78	82	87	92	96
9	14	19	24	28	33	37	42	46	51	55	60	65	69	74	78	83	87	92	96
10	15	20	25	29	33	38	43	47	52	56	61	65	70	74	79	83	88	92	97
11	16	21	25	30	34	39	43	48	52	57	61	66	70	74	79	83	88	92	97
12	17	22	26	31	35	40	44	48	53	57	62	66	70	75	79	84	88	92	97
13	18	23	27	32	36	40	45	49	53	58	62	67	71	75	80	84	88	93	97
14	19	24	28	33	37	41	46	50	54	58	63	67	71	76	80	84	89	93	97
15	20	25	29	34	38	42	46	51	55	59	63	68	72	76	80	85	89	93	97
16				34	39	43	47	51	55	60	64	68	72	76	81	85	89	93	97
17				35	39	44	48	52	56	60	64	69	73	77	81	85	89	93	98
18				36	40	44	49	53	57	61	65	69	73	77	81	85	90	94	98
19				37	41	45	49	53	57	61	65	70	74	78	82	86	90	94	98
20				38	42	46	50	54	58	62	66	70	74	78	82	86	90	94	98
21					43	47	51	55	59	63	67	71	74	78	82	86	90	94	98
22					44	48	52	55	59	63	67	71	75	79	83	87	91	94	98
23					45	48	52	56	60	64	68	72	75	79	83	87	91	95	98
24					45	49	53	57	61	64	68	72	76	80	83	87	91	95	99
25					46	50	54	58	61	65	69	73	76	80	84	88	91	95	99
26						51	55	58	62	66	69	73	77	80	84	88	92	95	99
27						52	55	59	63	66	70	74	77	81	84	88	92	95	99
28						52	56	60	63	67	70	74	78	81	85	88	92	96	99
29						53	57	60	64	67	71	75	78	82	85	89	92	96	99
30						54	58	61	65	68	72	75	79	82	86	89	93	96	100
31							58	62	65	69	72	76	79	82	86	89	93	96	100
32							59	62	66	69	73	76	79	83	86	90	93	96	100
33							60	63	66	70	73	77	80	83	87	90	93	97	100
34							61	64	67	70	74	77	80	84	87	90	94	97	100
35							61	65	68	71	74	78	81	84	87	91	94	97	100
36								65	68	72	75	78	81	84	88	91	94	97	100
37								66	69	72	75	79	82	85	88	91	94	97	100
38								67	70	73	76	79	82	85	88	91	95	98	100
39								67	70	73	76	80	83	86	89	92	95	98	100
40								68	71	74	77	80	83	86	89	92	95	98	100
41									72	75	78	81	83	86	89	92	95	98	100
42									72	75	78	81	84	87	90	93	96	98	100
43									73	76	79	82	84	87	90	93	96	99	100
44									74	76	79	82	85	88	90	93	96	99	100
45									74	77	80	83	85	88	91	94	96	99	100
46										78	80	83	86	88	91	94	97	99	100
47										78	81	84	86	89	91	94	97	99	100
48										79	81	84	87	89	92	94	97	100	100
49										79	82	85	87	90	92	95	97	100	100
50										80	83	85	88	90	93	95	98	100	100
51											83	86	88	90	93	95	98	100	100
52											84	86	88	91	93	96	98	100	100
53											84	87	89	91	94	96	98	100	100
54											85	87	89	92	94	96	99	100	100
55											85	88	90	92	94	97	99	100	100
56												88	90	92	95	97	99	100	100
57												89	91	93	95	97	99	100	100
58												89	91	93	95	97	100	100	100
59												90	92	94	96	98	100	100	100
60												90	92	94	96	98	100	100	100
61													92	94	96	98	100	100	100
62													93	95	97	99	100	100	100
63													93	95	97	99	100	100	100
64													94	96	97	99	100	100	100
65													94	96	98	100	100	100	100
66														96	98	100	100	100	100
67														97	98	100	100	100	100
68														97	99	100	100	100	100
69														98	99	100	100	100	100
70														98	100	100	100	100	100

CHECK FOR RATING PLATEAUS

If you take a look at the table of Permanent Partial Disability Rates in Chapter 13, Section E2, you will note that the weekly rate of permanent disability you are entitled to increases at various points. These are referred to in workers' compensation jargon as "plateaus." The following are the plateaus to watch for if you were injured on or after 7/1/94: 15%, 25% and 70%. If your advisory rating is close to the next "plateau," you should look for any means possible to increase your disability rate to reach that plateau. For example, if you can that argue for a different occupational group or a higher standard rating, do so.

D. Other Considerations in Rating a Permanent Disability

This section flags several more complicated issues that may come up when you're rating your disability. Although you will most likely need to see a lawyer or an Information and Assistance officer to deal with these, this overview will help you spot problem areas.

1. Apportionment of the Disability

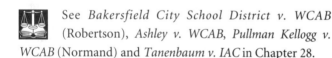 See *Bakersfield City School District v. WCAB* (Robertson), *Ashley v. WCAB, Pullman Kellogg v. WCAB* (Normand) and *Tanenbaum v. IAC* in Chapter 28.

Sometimes an insurance company will try to say that all or part of a permanent disability should be "apportioned" to outside factors. "Apportionment" is basically a concept that the insurance company uses to claim it is not responsible for paying permanent disability (or is responsible for a smaller payment) because it is not entirely attributable to the work injury.

EXAMPLE: Kathleen injured her left knee at work, and the treating doctor says she has a work restriction of no prolonged standing. The doctor also reports that prior medical records show that she injured the same knee while playing soccer in high school. The doctor concludes that 50% of Kathleen's present work restrictions are due to the prior sports injury. If she has a 30% disability rating for her knee, the insurance company would argue that it is really a 15% disability because only half is due to Kathleen's work injury.

DOCTOR'S OPINION ON APPORTIONMENT MUST NOT BE MERE SPECULATION

Just because a doctor says some part of your present work restrictions are due to a prior injury does not mean it is so. The doctor must support his conclusion with specific reasons. In the example above, a conclusion by Kathleen's doctor not substantiated by reasoning would not support a legal apportionment. So carefully read your doctor's opinion on apportionment to see if he explains why he came to his conclusion.

Apportionment can also be made on the basis of further injuries that take place after your work injury. For example, if a year after a work injury you are involved in an auto accident, it is possible that a doctor could apportion part of your disability to the subsequent auto accident, for which the insurance company would not be responsible.

Apportionment is determined by doctors and discussed in their medical reports. The doctor will note any prior or subsequent injuries and give an opinion as to whether any of your present problems would exist absent the work injury. The doctor considers such things as the amount of time between the work injury and the prior or subsequent injury, and whether you fully recovered from the prior or subsequent injury. (Chapter 3, Section B7, also discusses apportionment.)

If apportionment becomes an issue in your case, you should try to get the help of an experienced workers' compensation attorney or consult an Information and Assistance officer.

2. Employee Dies Before the Case Is Rated

If you are the surviving spouse or other dependent of a deceased worker who had an industrial injury, a determination will have to be made as to the nature and extent of the disability prior to death. This can be difficult if the injured worker passed away before undergoing medical examinations. In this situation, you should seek the help of a workers' compensation attorney.

E. How to Use the Old Rating Manual for Injuries That Occurred Before 4/1/97

IF YOUR INJURY WAS ON OR AFTER 4/1/97

This section affects you only if the date of your injury was BEFORE 4/1/97. If you were injured after that date, follow the instructions set forth in Sections B through D, above.

If you are going to rate your own disability you will need to refer to a copy of the old rating manual. It can be purchased from the California Applicants' Attorneys Association, 901-12th St., #201, Sacramento, CA 95814, (916) 444-5155, for $25.

To help you through the process, we'll use a hypothetical case involving a woman named "Mary," who has suffered the three most common industrial injuries: a back injury, arm injuries and a leg injury.

Mary was injured while working as a meat wrapper for a major grocery chain. Her duties required her to regularly lift up to 25 pounds of meat at once. Mary also constantly used machinery to measure and pre-wrap various meats, which required repetitive gripping and grasping motions.

Mary is claiming two dates for her injuries. The first was 1/23/94, when she slipped on some grease in the meat department and fell, injuring her back and right knee. The second injury is for continuous trauma (pain and disability) to both arms as a result of the repetitive meat wrapping motions. After the fall, Mary's doctor diagnosed carpal tunnel syndrome in both wrists and an ulnar nerve neuropathy in the left elbow. Mary has not worked since her fall on 1/23/94. For the second injury, she uses the dates of 1/23/93 to 1/23/94 as the period of injury. (See Chapter 5, Section C1b, for details on how to determine the injury date for a continuous trauma.)

Mary was 42 years old on the date of her fall. She was declared permanent and stationary by her treating doctor. Mary received copies of both the treating doctor's medical report and an advisory rating of her injury. (See "Mary's Advisory Rating," below.)

Mary wants to determine her own disability rating for the injuries set forth in the treating doctor's report. She wants to understand how the advisory rating was arrived at, to be better prepared to deal with doctors and the insurance company's lawyers in the future.

Because Mary has injuries to three different parts of her body, she will have to figure out a disability formula for each body part. She'll then combine them using the multiple disability rating table (explained in Step 6, below).

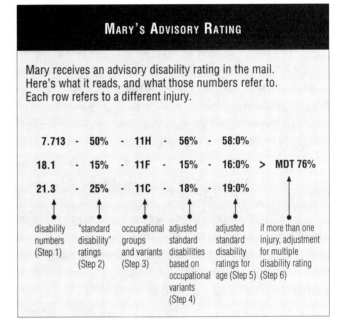

MARY'S ADVISORY RATING

Mary receives an advisory disability rating in the mail. Here's what it reads, and what those numbers refer to. Each row refers to a different injury.

7.713 -	50% -	11H -	56% -	58:0%	
18.1 -	15% -	11F -	15% -	16:0%	> MDT 76%
21.3 -	25% -	11C -	18% -	19:0%	

disability numbers (Step 1) / "standard disability" ratings (Step 2) / occupational groups and variants (Step 3) / adjusted standard disabilities based on occupational variants (Step 4) / adjusted standard disability ratings for age (Step 5) / if more than one injury, adjustment for multiple disability rating (Step 6)

UNDERSTANDING STANDARD DISABILITY PERCENTAGES

Leave it to workers' compensation to complicate even the way percentages are expressed. Percentages of disability are listed as a whole number followed by a colon (:), and then another number from 0 to 3. Here's what the numbers following the colon mean:

- the number 1 means .25%
- the number 2 means .50%, and
- the number 3 means .75%.

For example, 25:1% is equivalent to 25.25%, 25:2% is equivalent to 25.5% and 25:3% is equivalent to 25.75%.

Step 1: Determine Disability Numbers for Parts of Body Injured

The rating manual contains a section entitled "List of Disabilities and Standard Ratings." Disabilities are listed by number ranging from 1 to 21.8. The smaller the number, the higher the injury is located on the body. Headaches, for example, are 1.7, while a toe injury is 21.7. Your objective is to find the number of the body part that most closely matches the injury location. This is not always easy because the rating manual does not precisely identify and cover each and every body part. You will have to extrapolate from time to time to get a number. For example, if you had an injury to your foot, you will note that the rating manual gives a disability number of 21.6 for ankle and 21.7 for toes, but there is no rating for foot. You would have to choose between the two given, depending upon which best describes your injury.

Mary injured both arms, her back and her right knee. The disability number that most closely covers Mary's arm injuries is 7.713, which is "impairment of functions, both wrists." The chart also shows that the disability number for a back injury is 18.1, and the disability number for a knee injury is 21.3. Great; we have the first piece of our puzzle: Mary's disability numbers.

EXAMPLE: The first part of Mary's disability rating:

arms 7.713

back 18.1

knee 21.3

Step 2: Determine Standard Disability Rating

Be aware that the process of rating a permanent disability is an imprecise science. It is possible, even likely, that five knowledgeable raters might arrive at five different ratings for the same report. This is because some of the work restrictions and subjective findings contained in the doctor's medical report are subject to interpretation by the person doing the rating. In addition, doctors' reports typically differ in style and format, leading to different results when the doctor's findings are converted into numbers.

Knowing this, we'll go on to use the medical report to determine Mary's "standard disability" for each injured part of the body. Or to put it another way, we now need to find out how disabled the doctor thinks Mary is.

You should take several factors into consideration to arrive at any standard disability:

- **subjective complaints:** how much pain the doctor believes the patient is in
- **objective findings:** medical test results and examinations, and
- **work restrictions:** how the doctor feels the patient is limited in the open labor market as a result of the injury.

All three factors may be used to determine a standard disability, but often only one of the three is used. After you find separate standard ratings based upon subjective complaints, objective findings and work restrictions, you will compare the three and use the highest rating as your standard.

Mary's medical report covers objective and subjective factors of her disability and work restrictions, as do most medical reports that provide opinions on permanent disability. (If you're having trouble finding factors of disability, see "Where to Find Factors of Disability in a Medical Report," below.) Here's how her report reads:

FACTORS OF DISABILITY

A. Subjective

1. **Right & Left Arms:** Intermittent moderate pain.

2. **Low Back:** Intermittent slight to moderate pain.

3. **Right Knee:** Intermittent moderate pain.

B. Objective

1. **Left Elbow:** History of surgery with residual surgical scar.

2. **Right & Left Wrists:** (a) Decrease of grip bilaterally; (b) History of surgery bilaterally with residual scars.

3. **Low Back:** Positive MRI.

4. **Right Knee:** (a) Atrophy of the right calf; (b) History of surgery with residual surgical scars.

C. Work restrictions

1. **Right and left arms:** The patient should be prophylactically [preventively] restricted from heavy lifting, repetitive pushing and pulling with both arms, and repetitive and forceful gripping with both hands.

2. **Low back:** The patient should be prophylactically restricted from very heavy work.

3. **Right knee:** The patient should be prophylactically restricted from prolonged weight-bearing.

WHERE TO FIND FACTORS OF DISABILITY IN A MEDICAL REPORT

Most doctors who write reports for workers' compensation set out the factors of disability in a separate section. However, you may receive a report that is not well organized. If so, you'll have to locate language that deals with objective findings, subjective complaints and work restrictions. Here are some suggestions.

Objective Findings. In a typical report, objective factors are found throughout the report, and are summarized under the heading "Factors of Disability." Look for terms such as these:

• "objective findings of disability include…."
• "upon examination, the patient showed…."
• anything that supports the doctor's findings of "subjective factors of disability" or "work restrictions," including such terms as "loss of motion," "test results" or descriptions of "tenderness or pain" upon examination

Subjective Findings. Subjective factors of disability are found under a heading entitled "Subjective Factors of Disability." Look for terms such as these:

• "subjective complaints include…."
• "upon examination I would describe the patient's pain as…."
• language that deals with the doctor's opinion as to the type of pain you have in each part of body you injured. The pain may be described as the type of pain you have all the time, the type of pain you have upon doing certain activities or both. For example, "the patient has constant slight pain in the right upper extremity which increases to moderate upon heavy lifting."

Work Restrictions. Work restrictions are often listed under "Disability," "Permanent Disability" or "Work Restrictions." In some instances, however, you may have to read the report carefully to find where the doctor lists the work restrictions, such as:

• "work restrictions include…."
• "the patient should be precluded from doing the following types of activities…."
• language that describes limitations or things you can't do. These may be described as "actual" things the doctor says you physically can't do or "prophylactic" (preventive) things the doctor says you shouldn't do.

a.   Determine Subjective Standard of Disability

The first basis for arriving at a standard disability rating is the doctor's opinion regarding subjective complaints. Unfortunately, the standard disability ratings for subjective complaints are not set forth in the rating manual.

The standard disability ratings for subjective complaints listed below have been compiled by the author on the basis of attending many courses and lectures on rating permanent disabilities and are believed to be accurate. Although the chart contains standard disability ratings for the most common subjective complaints, it does not list all possible variations. This means that sometimes you must extrapolate or modify the doctor's subjective factors to "fit" the chart.

STANDARD DISABILITY RATINGS FOR SUBJECTIVE COMPLAINTS

occasional slight pain	3%
intermittent minimal to slight pain	3%
intermittent slight pain	5%
frequent slight pain	8%
constant slight pain	10%
constant slight to moderate pain	30%
constant moderate pain	50%

Mary uses the medical report to match her disabilities with the standard disability ratings of subjective factors. To do this, she must rate each of her disabilities separately, using the description from the medical report. Here's the process Mary undertakes.

• **Right & Left Arms: "intermittent moderate pain."** There is no listing for "intermittent moderate pain" on the chart. However, by looking at the chart we see that, in one instance at least, "intermittent" means one-half of "constant" pain. ("Constant slight pain" is a 10% disability, while intermittent slight pain is a 5% disability.) Therefore it's probably reasonable to extrapolate that if "constant moderate pain" is a 50% standard in the chart, "intermittent moderate pain," should be a 25% standard. So Mary lists her subjective arm standard at 25%.

• **Low Back: "intermittent slight to moderate pain."** Mary compares the subjective factors of disability given by the doctor to the standard disability ratings contained in the chart. By doing this, Mary finds she has a standard disability rating of 15% based on the same procedure that she used for her arms.

• **Right Knee: "intermittent moderate pain."** Comparing the subjective factors of disability given by the doctor for her right knee to the chart's ratings, Mary finds that she has a standard disability rating of 25%.

Here are Mary's subjective disability standards:

• 25% subjective standard (arms)
• 15% subjective standard (back), and
• 25% subjective standard (knee)

b.   Determine Objective Findings

The rating manual lists standard disabilities and their ratings based on objective findings of the severity of a physical injury. These are listed under "List of Disabilities and Standard Ratings" in the rating manual. Because of the infinite number of possible objective findings, not all disabilities are in the rating manual.

None of Mary's objective findings are listed in the rating manual for a standard rating. This is not unusual. I would estimate that 80% of all injuries are rated based upon work restrictions, 15% on subjective findings and only 5% on objective findings. This is because the only objective findings that can be rated are test results such as grip strength tests and range of motion tests, and in almost all cases, the rating based upon work restrictions, discussed below, will be greater. (There is a formula for determining a decrease in grip strength, but it is beyond the scope of this book. This formula, as well as other advanced rating formulas, may be obtained from the rating specialist at your local Appeals Board.)

OBJECTIVE FINDINGS SHOULD SUPPORT WORK RESTRICTIONS

Objective findings are not only used to find the existence of a particular disability and to give a standard rating, but to support subjective complaints and work restrictions. For instance, an objective finding of an amputation of a finger on the right hand would support a work restriction of "no fine dexterous activities using the right hand."

In our example, Mary looks at the medical report to see if any of the objective findings can be rated for a standard disability. Mary has some very significant objective findings: a history of surgery to the left elbow, a decrease of grip strength in both hands, a history of surgery to both hands, a positive MRI for the back, a history of surgery for the right knee, as well as atrophy of the right calf. These findings strongly support the doctor's conclusions and opinions on subjective factors of disability, as well as recommended work restrictions.

But if you're satisfied with a medical report, don't worry if objective findings don't support subjective findings and work restrictions unless the insurance company raises this issue. Most insurance companies do not examine medical reports carefully enough to discover such inconsistencies. If the insurance company points out that the report does not contain objective findings to support the doctor's conclusions, you should write the doctor and request that she comment upon the objective findings in more detail. Hopefully, the doctor's report is only defective because of an oversight. But if the doctor simply can't find any objective findings, do your best to downplay this, since your subjective factors will, or should, support the doctor's work restrictions.

c. Determine Disability Standard for Work Restrictions

 See *Capistrano Unified School District v. WCAB* in Chapter 28.

The doctor's medical report will explain that work restrictions are based on a combination of the subjective complaints of the patient as well as the objective findings.

Work restrictions can be of two types:

- **actual**, meaning you physically cannot do the restricted activity, and
- **prophylactic**, meaning that although you could do a certain activity, you should not do so prophylactically (preventively) because there is a high likelihood you will either reinjure or further injure yourself.

No matter how the doctor arrives at the restrictions (actual or prophylactic), the rating is the same.

Obviously, work restrictions are different for different parts of the body. For example, if you have an eye problem, what you can't, or shouldn't, do would differ from someone with a bad knee. Similarly, there are different percentages of disability and various levels of restrictions for each body part.

The most common work restrictions are shown in Chart A, below, as well as in the rating manual, titled "Guidelines for Work Capacity." These are also referred to as work capacity restrictions "A" through "H." There are no other work restrictions listed in the rating manual. The additional work restrictions listed below in Chart B, as well as all of the percentages listed in both charts, were compiled by the author on the basis of attending lectures and seminars on rating permanent disabilities. They are believed, but not guaranteed, to be accurate.

You may need to use one or more charts to find all your work restrictions. For example, a work restriction for the left leg of "no heavy lifting and no prolonged standing" would require you to use both Charts A and B. (But note that if you combine work restrictions, you'll have to take the concept of "pyramiding" into account, as discussed below.)

The work restrictions listed in Chart A apply to injuries involving pulmonary, heart disease, abdominal weakness and spinal (back) disabilities. Although not stated in the rating manual, these restrictions also apply to injuries involving the arms and legs (upper and lower extremities). If you have an injury to one or both legs, the work restrictions listed in the chart are taken at full value. To put it another way, one leg gets the full value of the disability listed.

 ### RATING FOR CHART A IS HALVED FOR INJURIES TO ONLY ONE ARM

If work restrictions apply to only one arm, the disability is one-half of the value listed in the chart. For example, a disability to both arms that precludes very heavy lifting is 10%. If only one arm is injured, the rating is one-half that amount, or a 5% disability standard.

One last rule: for disabilities above 24%, you round off to the nearest 5%. For instance, 58% rounds off to a 60% disability standard.

CHART A

RATINGS FOR WORK RESTRICTIONS: PULMONARY, HEART DISEASE, ABDOMINAL WEAKNESS, BOTH ARMS AND ONE OR BOTH LEGS

Following are the most common disability ratings for work restrictions due to any of the above disabilities.

a. disability precluding very heavy lifting	10%
b. disability precluding very heavy work	5%
By extrapolation—disability precluding very heavy lifting and repeated bending and stooping	15%
c. disability precluding heavy lifting	20%
d. disability precluding heavy lifting and repeated bending and stooping	25%
e. disability precluding heavy work	30%
f. disability resulting in limitation to light work	50%
g. disability resulting in limitation to semi-sedentary work	60%
h. disability resulting in limitation to sedentary work	70%

CHART B

RATINGS FOR WORK RESTRICTIONS TO KNEE, LEGS AND ARMS

Here are the most common work restrictions given for injuries to one or more knees, legs or arms.

Note: This chart is used for specific work restrictions. You can tell from the type of restriction as to whether it applies to the upper extremities or the lower extremities.

No repetitive kneeling, squatting or crawling	3%
No ascending, descending stairs and ladders	10%
No traversing uneven ground	10%
No working at unprotected heights	8%
No prolonged standing	20%
No prolonged weight bearing	20%
No prolonged walking	10%
No prolonged sitting	10%
No heavy lifting, crawling, kneeling, pushing, pulling, squatting or twisting	25%
No repeated pushing and pulling	
major	10%
minor	8%
No squatting	5%
No kneeling	5%
No climbing	10%
No descending	10%
No repeated gripping and grasping	
major	15%
minor	13%
bilateral	30%
Use of cane required	40%

Now let's return to Mary and start by seeing how her doctor described her work restrictions, which were covered under a "Disability" category in her medical report:

C. Work restrictions

1. **Right and left arms:** The patient should be prophylactically restricted from heavy lifting, repetitive pushing and pulling with both arms, and repetitive and forceful gripping with both hands.

2. **Low back:** The patient should be prophylactically restricted from very heavy work.

3. **Right knee:** The patient should be prophylactically restricted from prolonged weight-bearing.

Now we'll see how all of these technicalities work out in arriving at a disability rating.

Arms: Comparing the work restrictions given by the doctor for Mary's right and left arms in the medical report with the restrictions given in Charts A and B, Mary finds that she has a standard work restriction for her arms of 50%. Whoa! How did Mary arrive at 50%? A step-by-step look at how she did this will not only make this clear, it will also introduce a very important rating principle known as "pyramiding." (See "Pyramiding: Multiple Work Restrictions For One Body Part," below.)

PYRAMIDING: MULTIPLE WORK RESTRICTIONS FOR ONE BODY PART

If you have more than one work restriction to the same body part, you are allowed to "pyramid" the restrictions—that is, apply more than one work restriction to the same part of the body. To do this, you take 100% of the greatest work restriction and add 50% of the combined total of all the other work restrictions.

For example, work restrictions of no heavy lifting (20%), no prolonged walking (10%) and no climbing (10%) would be 30%, a total of the entire amount of the greatest restriction (20%) plus half of the total of the other restrictions (10% + 10% x 1/2 = 10%).

According to the doctor's report, Mary should be "pro-phylactically restricted from heavy lifting, repetitive pushing and pulling with both arms, and repetitive and forceful gripping with both hands." Although this may seem like one large restriction, it is in fact three, as far as the workers' compensation rating system is concerned. This means Mary has to determine three different disability standards for her upper arms. Using Charts A and B, Mary finds:

- No heavy lifting is a 20% standard.
- No repetitive pushing and pulling with both arms is the sum of 10% and 8% (the total of restrictions to the major and minor arms), or 18%.
- No repetitive gripping and grasping with both hands is 30%.

You might logically think that the standard disability would be the total of all three, or 68%. However, this is where the concept of pyramiding comes in. As discussed above, if you have more than one work restriction to the same part of the body, you first take the greatest restriction and then add to it one-half of the total of the remaining restrictions.

For Mary, the greatest of the three restrictions above is 30%. To this, she adds 19%, which is one-half of the total of the remaining restrictions (20% +18% = 38% x 1/2 is 19%). Adding 30% and 19% together gives Mary a 49% standard disability for her upper extremities. Finally, because disabilities above 24% are rounded off to the nearest 5%, Mary rounds off 49% to a 50% disability standard.

Low Back: Comparing the work restrictions given by the doctor for Mary's back (no very heavy work), to those in the charts, Mary finds that she has a standard work restriction for her back of 15%.

Right Knee: Mary's doctor gives a work restriction of "no prolonged weight bearing," which is a 20% standard according to Chart B.

Mary comes up with the following work restrictions:

- arm restrictions: 50%
- back restrictions: 15%, and
- knee restrictions: 20%

If you aren't pleased with the medical report, study it carefully. If you can argue that the doctor's work restrictions are not correct, based upon the objective findings, you may be able to convince the insurance company that the injury is, in fact, more severe than the doctor finds.

d.   Determine Which Standard to Use

Usually you are not entitled to a work restriction rating based upon both subjective complaints and work restrictions. Instead, you are limited to the higher of the two for each body part. Of course, to know which is higher, you need to rate both, as covered above.

EXAMPLE: A comparison of Mary's subjective disabilities to her work restrictions shows:

Part of body	Subjective disabilities	Work restrictions
Arms	25%	50%
Back	15%	15%
Right knee	25%	20%

Taking the higher of the two ratings, Mary will use a standard of 50% for her upper arms, 15% for her back and 25% for her right knee.

Sometimes the same work restrictions may be imposed on different body parts. This concept is called "overlap," as discussed below. If you have the same work restriction for two or more parts of the body, you are not entitled to total the two. Instead, you get one work restriction that covers both parts. In Mary's case, since she already has a work exclusion based on her arm problems of no heavy lifting, it does her no further good to claim a work restriction based on her back injury of no very heavy work (a restriction with a lesser disability percentage). In other words, Mary is already precluded from lifting for her arms, so an additional lesser lifting restriction would be irrelevant.

If asked by the insurance company how she arrived at her rating, Mary should explain that she used the 15% subjective findings for her back instead of the 15% work restriction. (She did this to avoid the overlapping work restrictions from her low back.)

OVERLAP

Overlap occurs when a work restriction for one part of the body also benefits another part of the body. If you are restricted from heavy lifting because of your back, your injured knees will also benefit from that restriction. Therefore a restriction of no very heavy lifting to the knees is absorbed in the no heavy lifting restriction for the back.

Overlap is not always easy to spot, and if your rating differs from that arrived at by an advisory rating, it is quite likely due to the application of this concept. The only real way to spot overlaps is to check whether there are similar work restrictions to different parts of the body. If so, you must determine if you included both restrictions in your rating. Because this is impermissible, you must subtract out the duplicate rating. To avoid overlap, it is best to use subjective ratings for the body part that has no work restrictions or that has no overlapping work restrictions.

Finally, Mary puts together the disability numbers (from Step 1, above) and the standard disability ratings she just came up with:

EXAMPLE: Mary's standard disability rating now consists of two parts:

arms	7.713	- 50%
back	18.1	- 15%
knee	21.3	- 25%

Step 3: Determine Occupational Group Number and Variant

 See *Kochevar v. Fremont Unified School District* in Chapter 28.

The next factors in the formula are based upon your occupation. Different occupations will affect (increase or decrease) the standard rating for the same injury differently. For example, a cashier will be adversely affected by a hand injury to a greater degree than a restaurant hostess.

a. Determine Occupational Group Number

The ratings manual contains a "list of occupations and occupational group numbers." Occupations are listed in alphabetical order, and each has a corresponding group number. In Mary's case, looking up meat "wrapper" in the rating manual tells us that the group number is 11. The occupation you use does not have to be the same one you listed in your Application for Adjudication of Claim.

Many occupations are not contained in the rating manual's list of occupations, with the result that you sometimes have to be creative and take a group number from a similar occupation. One method is to refer to the section of the rating manual near the back, titled "Outline of Occupational Groupings." You will find that the occupational groups listed begin with group 1 and go through group 56. Each group has a short description of the typical duties as well as examples of common occupations. Find the group that best describes your job duties. If you find more than one group that your occupation could fit into, note all of them.

 ADVANTAGES TO CHANGING OCCUPATIONAL GROUP NUMBERS

You may be entitled to a larger permanent disability payment if you use a more advantageous occupational group number. This is covered below, in Step 3c.

b. Determine Occupational Variant

Next, we turn to the section in the rating manual entitled "Column for disability-occupation combination" located toward the back part of the rating manual. This chart has the disability number (Step 1, above) down the left side of the page, and the occupational group numbers (Step 3a, just above) across the top of the page. Where the two columns intersect, you will find a letter of the alphabet from "A" to "L." This letter is known as the "occupational variant," which is placed next to the occupation group number in the formula.

With this occupational variant, you will be able to tell if one occupational group is better for you than another. The closer the letter is to "Z", the higher your disability rating. Here is the breakdown:

- **Occupational variant of "F"** is neutral—it will neither raise nor lower your standard disability rating.

SAMPLE FROM RATING MANUAL: COLUMN FOR DISABILITY-OCCUPATION COMBINATION

DISABILITY NUMBER	1	1A	2	3	4	5	6	7	8	9	10	11	12	13	14	15	16	17	18	19	20	21	22	23	24	25	26	27	28	29	30
18.__ NECK, SPINE, OR PELVIS																															
18.1_																															
18.12	H	*I*	F	F	F	F	F	F	F	C	H	F	H	E	G	G	C	F	F	F	G	F	F	F	G	F	H	H	H	K	K
18.14	H	*I*	F	F	F	F	F	F	F	C	H	F	H	E	G	G	C	F	F	F	G	F	F	F	G	F	H	C	H	K	K
18.16	100	*100*	100	100	100	100	100	100	100	100	100	100	100	100	100	100	100	100	100	100	100	100	100	100	100	100	100	100	100	100	100
18.3_																															
18.313	100	*100*	100	100	100	100	100	100	100	100	100	100	100	100	100	100	100	100	100	100	100	100	100	100	100	100	100	100	100	100	100
18.32	100	*100*	100	100	100	100	100	100	100	100	100	100	100	100	100	100	100	100	100	100	100	100	100	100	100	100	100	100	100	100	100
19.__ ABDOMEN																															
19.1_																															
19.111	G	*G*	F	D	F	F	F	F	F	C	F	F	G	F	G	G	C	F	F	F	G	F	F	F	F	F	G	D	F	J	J
19.113	G	*G*	F	D	F	F	F	F	F	C	F	F	G	F	G	G	C	F	F	F	G	F	F	F	F	F	G	D	F	J	J
19.121	G	*G*	F	D	F	F	F	F	F	C	F	F	G	F	G	G	C	F	F	F	G	F	F	F	F	F	G	D	F	J	J
19.131	G	*G*	F	D	F	F	F	F	F	C	F	F	G	F	G	G	C	F	F	F	G	F	F	F	F	F	G	D	F	J	J
19.2_																															
19.22	G	*G*	F	D	F	F	F	F	F	C	F	F	G	F	G	G	C	F	F	F	G	F	F	F	F	F	G	D	F	J	J
19.24	G	*G*	F	D	F	F	F	F	F	C	F	F	G	F	G	G	C	F	F	F	G	F	F	F	F	F	G	D	F	J	J
19.26	G	*G*	F	D	F	F	F	F	F	C	F	F	G	F	G	G	C	F	F	F	G	F	F	F	F	F	G	D	F	J	J
19.31	F	*F*	F	F	F	F	F	F	F	F	F	F	F	F	F	F	F	F	F	F	F	F	F	F	F	F	F	F	F	F	F
20.__ LOWER EXTREMITES—AMPUTATIONS AND SHORTENING																															
20.1_																															
20.111	G	*G*	F	C	C	C	C	D	F	B	F	C	F	F	G	F	B	F	C	D	F	F	D	F	F	D	G	G	G	L	K
20.113	100	*100*	100	100	100	100	100	100	100	100	100	100	100	100	100	100	100	100	100	100	100	100	100	100	100	100	100	100	100	100	100
20.121	G	*G*	F	C	C	C	C	D	F	B	F	C	F	F	G	F	B	F	C	D	F	F	D	F	F	D	G	G	G	L	K
20.123	G	*G*	F	C	C	C	C	D	F	B	F	C	F	F	G	F	B	F	C	D	F	F	D	F	F	D	G	G	G	L	K
20.131	G	*G*	F	C	C	C	C	D	F	B	F	C	F	F	G	F	B	F	C	D	F	F	D	F	F	D	G	G	G	L	K
20.133	100	*100*	100	100	100	100	100	100	100	100	100	100	100	100	100	100	100	100	100	100	100	100	100	100	100	100	100	100	100	100	100

GROUP NUMBER

Entries in italics apply to injuries occuring on and after January 1, 1961.

- **Occupational variant of "A" to "E"** will decrease your standard disability rating (A the most and E the least). This will result in a lower disability rating and thus less money.
- **Occupational variant of "G" through "L"** will increase your standard disability rating (G the least and L the most.) This means you'll end up with a higher disability rating, and thus more money.

Mary finds that the occupational variant for both upper extremities (arms) is H, the back is F, and the knee is C.

EXAMPLE: Mary's standard disability formula now consists of three parts:

arms 7.713	-	50%	- 11H
back 18.1	-	15%	- 11F
knee 21.3	-	25%	- 11C

c.   Decide Whether to Change Occupational Groups

As mentioned, oftentimes a change in your group number can make a significant difference in the amount of disability that you are entitled to. That is because various work restrictions affect different occupations in different ways. For example, someone who has a work restriction of "no fine hand manipulations" will find that their standard rating goes up in value if their occupation requires fine hand manipulations, such as a typist or jeweler, and will go down for such occupations as a laborer, where fine hand manipulations are not required.

Just because your job title is listed in the section of the rating manual under occupational group numbers does not necessarily mean that you must use that group number. Look more to your job *duties* rather than your job *title*, to determine your group number(s). And don't be afraid to be creative. If your job title is "assembler" but your duties are really that of a "warehouseman," use the job classification that results in the most favorable occupational variant.

If it is possible that your job qualifies you for more than one group number, follow the instructions above and check all possible occupational groups to see which one results in an occupational variant that is best for you. Again, the point is that you want to locate and use the occupational group that gives you the greatest increase in your standard rating.

Step 4: Adjust Standard Disability Rating Based on Occupational Variant

The next step is to determine the percentage of disability after "adjustment" for your occupation. As discussed in Step 3, above, the adjustment is based upon how your disability affects your ability to work in your general occupation classification. Different occupations are affected differently by the same disability. (See Step 3c, just above for information on how to decide which occupational group is best for you.)

Turning to the section in the rating manual entitled "Standard Range of Ratings," Mary takes the standard ratings for each part of her body and finds the corresponding adjustment for her occupational variant.

The chart has the standard rating down the left side of the page, and the occupational variants from "A" through "L" across the top of the page. You need to find the intersection of the standard rating (Step 2) and the occupational variant (Step 3).

SAMPLE FROM RATING MANUAL:
STANDARD RANGE OF RATINGS
PERCENT AT AGE 39

Standard Rating Percent	A	B	C	D	E	F	G	H	I	J	K	L
0	0	0	0	0	0	0	0	0	0	0	0	0
1	0	0	0	1	1	1	2	2	2	2	2	3
2	1	1	1	2	2	2	3	3	4	4	5	5
3	1	1	2	2	3	3	4	5	5	6	7	8
4	2	2	3	3	4	4	5	6	7	8	8	9
5	2	3	3	4	4	5	6	7	8	9	10	11
6	3	4	4	5	5	6	7	8	9	11	12	13
7	3	4	5	5	6	7	8	10	11	12	13	15
8	4	5	6	6	7	8	9	11	12	14	15	16
9	4	5	6	7	8	9	11	12	14	15	17	18
10	5	6	7	8	9	10	12	13	15	16	18	19
11	5	6	7	9	10	11	13	14	16	18	19	21
12	6	7	8	10	11	12	14	16	17	19	21	23
13	6	7	9	10	12	13	15	17	18	20	22	24
14	7	8	10	11	13	14	16	18	20	22	23	25
15	8	9	11	12	14	15	17	19	21	23	25	27
16	8	10	11	13	14	16	18	20	22	24	26	28
17	9	11	12	14	15	17	19	21	23	26	28	30
18	10	12	13	15	16	18	20	22	24	27	29	31
19	10	12	14	15	17	19	21	24	26	28	30	33
20	11	13	15	16	18	20	22	25	27	29	31	34
21	12	14	16	17	19	21	23	26	28	31	33	35
22	12	14	16	18	20	22	24	27	29	32	34	36
23	13	15	17	19	21	23	26	28	31	33	36	38
24	14	16	18	20	22	24	27	29	32	34	37	39
25	14	16	18	21	23	25	28	30	33	36	38	41

Looking up 50%, with an occupational variant of H, Mary finds that it adjusts to 56%. Looking up 15%, with an occupational variant of F, Mary finds that it remains at 15%. Looking up 25%, with an occupational variant of C, Mary finds that it adjusts down to 18%.

EXAMPLE: Mary's standard disability formula now consists of four parts:

arms .... 7.713 - 50% - 11H - 56%

back .... 18.1   - 15% - 11 F - 15%

knee .... 21.3   - 25% - 11C - 18%

Step 5: Adjust Standard Disability Rating for Age

The older a worker is at the time of injury, the greater will be the disability after adjustment for age. Age 39 is the median. For ages younger than 39, the disability will be adjusted downward, and above that age it will go up.

Here's the reasoning behind this. The younger someone is, the longer he has to figure out how to adjust to the disability and become a productive worker. The older a worker is, the less chance he will adapt to the disability in the work force.

In our example, Mary was 42 at time she was injured. In the rating manual, under the section entitled "Variation for Age in Ratings for Disability," we find a table where the adjusted standard disability rating (Step 4) is listed down the left side of the page, and ages are listed across the top of the page. Where the two figures intersect on the page is the corresponding rating, which has been adjusted for age.

Looking up 56%, Mary finds that it adjusts to 58:0% for age 42. Looking up 15%, Mary finds that it adjusts to 16:0% for her age. Looking up 18%, Mary finds that it adjusts to 19:0% for her age.

EXAMPLE: Mary's disability formula now consists of five parts:

arms .... 7.713 - 50% - 11H - 56% - 58.0%

back .... 18.1   - 15% - 11F - 15% - 16:0%

knee .... 21.3   - 25% - 11C - 18% - 19:0%

Step 6: Adjust for Multiple Disabilities, If Any

If Mary had an injury to just one part of her body, say her back, she'd have figured out her permanent partial disability in Step 5, above. In our example, it would be 16% and she could skip this step.

However, where, as in Mary's case, there are disabilities to more than one part of the body, the individual disability totals must be combined into one grand total. This is done by referring to the "Table for Determining Multiple Disability Ratings" (also known as the MDT table) in the rating manual. (See Section C, Step 7, above, for this chart.) This table has the disability rating across the top of the page in increments of 5%, as well as down the left side of the page in increments of 1%.

Here's how Mary proceeds. First she takes her largest disability, 58%, and finds the nearest number at the top of the page. The numbers are set forth in 5% increments, so Mary locates 60%. (If Mary needed to round her disability number down, she could save the percentage and add it into one of her lower disability ratings.)

Next, Mary takes her second largest disability, and finds it down the left side of the page. It is 19%. You do not need to round up or down the disability that is found on the left side of the page, as these are set forth in the table one percentage at a time.

Now Mary is ready to compute the combined disability rating for the two disabilities. She does this by looking to see where the two numbers intersect. The number at the intersection is the percentage of disability for both injuries. In this instance, where 60% on top and 19% on the left intersect, the figure is 70%.

Now Mary must combine the 70% disability (gotten by combining her 58% and 19% disabilities) with her smallest disability of 16%. She follows the same procedure. Mary finds 70% (the closest 5% increment) across the top of the page for her biggest rating. Mary finds 16% on the left side of the chart. Then she finds that these two percentages intersect at 76%.

After applying the multiple disability table to her three different disabilities, Mary finds that her permanent partial disability is 73%.

EXAMPLE: Mary's completed disability formula:

```
arms ........ 7.713  -  50%  -  11H  -  56%  -  58.0%
back ....... 18.1    -  15%  -  11F  -  15%  -  16:0%
knee ....... 21.3    -  25%  -  11C  -  18%  -  19:0%
```

Multiple Disability Rating (MDT) = 76%

Step 7: Determine a Dollar Value for the Disability

Now that your disability rating is complete, you're ready to determine the dollar value of your permanent disability. To do this, please refer to Chapter 13, Section E, for a detailed explanation on how to use the permanent disability table located in Appendix 3 of this book to determine the dollar value of your permanent disability.

LIFE PENSION AVAILABLE FOR DISABILITIES OF 70% OR MORE

If you have a permanent disability rating of at least 70%, you are entitled to a life pension in addition to your permanent disability benefits. A life pension consists of a small amount of money that is payable every two weeks for as long as you live. See Chapter 13, Section F, on how to compute your life pension.

As you can see, the process of properly rating a permanent disability requires both time and effort. However, I believe that if you commit yourself to doing it, you will increase your chances of negotiating a fair settlement. By understanding your rating, you will be in a position to discuss your disability with the adjuster intelligently and with the confidence that you know what you are talking about.

CHECK FOR RATING PLATEAUS

If you take a look at the table of Permanent Partial Disability Rates in Chapter 13, Section E2, you will note that the amount of permanent disability you are entitled to increases at various points in the chart. These are referred to in workers' compensation jargon as "plateaus." If your advisory rating is close to the next "plateau," you should look for any means possible to increase your disability rate to reach that plateau. For example, if you can argue a different occupational group, or higher standard rating, do so. The following are the plateaus to watch for: 15%, 25% and 70%. ■

Figure Out a Starting Settlement Amount

The vast majority of workers' compensation cases settle without the necessity of proceeding to a trial. Settling means you and the insurance company agree that you'll accept a certain amount of money (and perhaps future medical treatment) instead of having a workers' compensation judge decide these issues in a trial. This chapter will help you to arrive at the value of your workers' compensation case so that you can fairly assess any settlement offers made by the insurance company. Chapter 20 explains how to take this starting figure and negotiate a fair settlement.

A. What You May Receive in a Settlement

As you undoubtedly know by now, the sky is not the limit when it comes to how much you will receive to settle your workers' compensation case. You may, however, be entitled to some or all of the following:

- **permanent disability award.** This amount is based upon doctors' reports and a complicated rating system that puts a dollar value on your injuries.
- **life pension.** Your award may also include a small life pension, if you have a severe disability of over 70%.
- **retroactive (past due) temporary disability payments.** If you weren't paid all temporary disability payments you were entitled to receive while out of work and temporarily disabled, you are entitled to that amount.
- **retroactive (past due) maintenance allowance.** If you weren't paid all the vocational rehabilitation maintenance allowance that you were entitled to receive while participating in a vocational rehabilitation plan, you are entitled to that amount.
- **reimbursement for mileage.** You are entitled to reimbursement for mileage to and from your doctors' appointments.
- **medical expenses you paid.** You are entitled to be reimbursed for out-of-pocket expenses you incurred for medical treatment, hospital bills and doctors' fees, as well as costs of tests, prescriptions and medical supplies.
- **future medical expenses.** You may choose to be paid a sum of money in exchange for relieving the insurance company of the responsibility of paying for your future medical expenses. If, however, you want the insurance company to be responsible for those expenses, you will forego settlement money for future medical costs.
- **your right to petition to reopen your case.** If, within five years from the date of your injury, your medical condition deteriorates further as a result of your work injury (known

as "new and further disability" stemming from your original injury, in workers' compensation jargon), you may petition the Workers' Compensation Appeals Board for an additional permanent disability award. You may either reserve this right or possibly negotiate an additional sum of money in exchange for giving up this right.

- **penalties.** In some cases, the insurance company may be required to pay penalties for non-payment or late payment of your workers' compensation benefits.

In Section C of this chapter, we'll take a look at how to calculate the value of each of the above components of your settlement. But first, you'll need to understand your settlement options.

B. Two Kinds of Settlements

If you settle your case, you'll have two settlement alternatives:
- Stipulations with Request for Award (also referred to as "Stips"), or
- Compromise and Release (also known as C&R).

How much your case will settle for depends both on the severity of your injury and on which settlement option you use. In this section, we explain what this jargon means and how to decide which settlement option is best for you.

1. Stipulations With Request for Award (Stips)

As discussed in Section A, above, every case that settles is made up of several components. Here's what's unique to a settlement by Stipulations With Request for Award.

a. Permanent Disability Award Usually Paid Bi-Weekly

Permanent disability is paid to you based on a weekly amount and actually paid every two weeks—not in a lump sum—until the maximum amount is reached or until you die, whichever comes first. If you die, your surviving dependents (spouse or children, for example) are entitled to any unpaid permanent disability payments due on the date of your death, but not afterwards.

There are two exceptions to the bi-weekly payment schedule. First, remember that the insurance company is required to begin paying permanent disability starting the 14th day after the last payment of temporary disability. (LC § 4650.) Any permanent disability that wasn't paid and should have been is payable retroactively in one lump sum. Second, it's possible that an Appeals Board judge may grant a "commutation," where weekly payments are "commuted" to a lump sum payoff (but be aware that judges usually don't favor commutations).

If you received any permanent disability advances from the insurance company, you'll need to take that into account. The amount you received will be deducted from the end of your award. (See Chapter 13, Section D2, for more on permanent disability advances.)

EXAMPLE: Tom and the insurance company have agreed on the value of his permanent disability claim: 50 weeks of indemnity payable at $140 per week for a total of $7,000. Tom has already received 16 weeks of permanent disability advances paid at $140 per week, for a total of $2,240. Tom is entitled to receive the difference between the total amount due him and what he has already been advanced, or $4,760. The amount paid to Tom as permanent disability advances will be deducted from his total amount, and instead of 50 weeks of payments, Tom will receive 34 weeks of payments.

b.   Future Medical Expenses Are Paid by Company

With a settlement by Stips, the insurance company agrees to pay for any future medical treatments needed to cure or relieve your workplace injury, as indicated in your medical reports. You don't receive any settlement money for giving up this benefit. Future medical expenses may include prescriptions, examinations, tests, physical therapy and surgery, if the doctor has indicated that this may be necessary. If the doctor simply states that you may need future medical treatment and does not specify the type, you should be entitled to reasonably necessary treatment.

Note that the reasonableness or necessity of your future medical treatment is always subject to challenge by the insurance company, and it may be necessary to file for a hearing in the future to enforce your right to medical treatment.

c.   Right to Petition to Reopen Your Case

If you settle by Stips and your disability level increases (you have a new and further disability stemming from the original injury) within five years from the date of your injury, you may reopen your case. In other words, if your medical condition becomes worse and results in an increase in your permanent disability, you may be entitled to additional money.

2.   Compromise and Release (C&R)

Unlike Stips, discussed just above, with a Compromise and Release (C&R), the insurance company pays you your entire settlement in one lump sum. You agree to give up all rights to future medical treatment and the right to reopen your case. Here's how a C&R differs from Stips:

- **permanent disability award.** Your basic permanent disability value is computed in exactly the same way as in Stips, but it's paid in a lump sum.
- **future medical expenses.** With a C&R, the insurance company pays you a sum of money to buy out your right to future medical treatment. You add this amount to your settlement.
- **no right to reopen your case.** With a C&R, the insurance company may buy out your right to reopen your case.

3.   Which Is Right for You: Stips or Compromise and Release?

Whether it's best to settle by Stips or C&R depends upon your situation. There is no hard and fast answer that will fit everyone. However, there are several considerations that will tend to tilt your decision one way or the other. This chapter will help you figure out the settlement value of your case based upon both Stips and C&R to help you decide.

a.   Your Need for Future Medical Treatment

If your injury is likely to require expensive surgery or other treatment in the future, and you have no other insurance to pay for it, you will likely want to settle by Stips to reserve your right to future medical treatment. It makes no sense to take a lump sum now only to find out later that your medical treatment will cost many times what you received.

On the other hand, you might opt to cash out your future medical with a C&R in situations such as these:

- You have medical insurance that you're not in danger of losing anytime in the future.

- You are sure your injury will not require much in the way of future medical treatment.

The main reason for Stips instead of a C&R is to provide for future medical treatment. If you are fully recovered and unlikely to need future medical treatment, you would probably be better off with a C&R, which entitles you to a little more money, sooner.

b.   If You Need All the Money at Once

If your financial situation is such that you need to have your entire settlement paid to you in a lump sum, instead of weekly payments, you may want to settle by a C&R, as this is the only type of settlement that will give you a lump sum settlement. But don't jump to conclusions.

First of all, you don't want to make bad decisions by giving up your future rights because you're desperate for money now. Secondly, you may have a fair chunk of change coming to you in a lump sum with Stips if:

- you're owed a lot of retroactive temporary disability payments or reimbursement for medical expenses, or

- you stopped receiving temporary disability quite a while ago, and permanent disability payments did not commence 14 days after your last payment of temporary disability.

c.   If You Have Other Sources of Disability Income

Some disability programs, such as Social Security and certain private disability policy providers, will ordinarily take a credit or offset for money you receive in your workers' compensation settlement. In other words, if you're receiving benefits through these programs, your benefits may be reduced if you receive money in your workers' compensation case.

A C&R is the only type of settlement that allows you to insert language into the settlement document that may avoid or limit how much credit the disability provider may take. You do this by designating part of the settlement as future medical expenses, which won't ordinarily affect your disability benefits. If you're receiving Medicare or Medi-Cal, however, these programs may also take an offset against your settlement, even if the funds are earmarked for future medical expenses. (See Chapter 20, Section D2e, for a discussion.)

d. If You May Need to Reopen Your Case

If your disability worsens, settling by Stips preserves your right to reopen your workers' compensation case within five years from the date of injury. This is done by filing a petition to reopen (a procedure beyond the scope of this book). The right to reopen your case is extremely important if there's a good possibility that:

- you will undergo surgery or other serious medical procedures sometime in the future. (Your permanent disability may be greater following the procedure.) Or
- the medical reports on which your settlement was based aren't current (usually over 18 months old), and your condition has worsened since then.

EXAMPLE: Sid is injured on the job on 10/6/01. He settles his workers' compensation claim by Stips on 1/3/02. Sid has until 10/05/06 to file a petition to reopen his case for new and further disability. If Sid's condition gets worse during that period, he can have another chance at getting a bigger award. However, after five years from the date of injury, he can no longer reopen the case.

The closer you already are to the five-year anniversary of your injury, the less this becomes a major consideration. Also, if your injury (say a broken wrist) has healed with no problems for a year or more, there is little chance of needing to reopen your case. But obviously, if your injury is less certainly completely behind you (say a respiratory problem that keeps flaring up), it would not be wise to give up the right to reopen your case.

e. Stipulate Now, C&R Later

Another option is to enter into Stips now with the knowledge that you can always C&R your right to future medical treatment any time in the future. The insurance company should always be willing to C&R your case because it does not want to keep your file open indefinitely.

This option may be attractive if you don't have private health insurance or your coverage calls for high deductibles. Should you later acquire health insurance that will cover your industrial injury (a pre-existing condition), you can contact the insurance company and negotiate a settlement (C&R) of your future medical benefits.

The disadvantage to doing this is that you probably will not be able to get as much money to C&R your future medical treatment later. This is because the insurance company is anxious to C&R your case now. If you wait several years, during which time you need little or no medical treatment, the insurance company will not pay much to C&R because it will perceive its future liability to be very small.

COMPARISON OF WAYS TO SETTLE YOUR WORKERS' COMPENSATION CASE	Stipulations With Request for Award	Compromise and Release
Permanent Disability	Paid bi-weekly at permanent disability rate until settlement is paid off.	One lump sum payment made for the full value of permanent disability.
Medical Benefits	As long as reasonably necessary; you must make written demand on company for authorization for treatment. May later negotiate buyout of right to future medical treatment.	Money for future medical treatment is included in the lump sum settlement.
Right to Reopen Case	No later than five years from date of injury, you may petition to reopen your case for new and further permanent disability.	Money for waiving right to reopen case is included in the lump sum settlement.
Vocational Rehabilitation	No effect.	No effect.

C. Determine the Value of Your Claim Using the Settlement Worksheet

Before you try to settle your workers' compensation case, you need an accurate idea of what it's worth. Armed with this information, you can confidently negotiate a fair settlement without worrying about whether or not you're being bamboozled into settling for less then you should.

As you go through this section, use the form titled Settlement Worksheet: Value of Workers' Compensation Claim, provided in Appendix 4. The settlement worksheet will help you keep track of all components that make up the total value of your claim. You can also use the settlement worksheet to compare the two ways to settle your claim—by Stipulations with Request for Award or by Compromise and Release.

Here are line-by-line instructions for filling in the settlement worksheet.

IF YOU HAVE A LAWYER

Your attorney will enter into settlement negotiations with the insurance company. However, it's a good idea if you, too, go through the process in this chapter. You'll not only understand what your lawyer is doing, but will be in a more confident and informed position when it comes to discussing final decisions with your attorney.

Top of form. Fill in your name and the names of your employer and its insurance company. Provide the insurance company's claim number. If you have a disability rating, fill it in (see Chapter 18). Also, insert the Appeals Board case number if you have one.

1. Permanent Disability

The most important building block for any workers' compensation settlement is the permanent disability award. If you have a permanent work injury that affects your ability to participate in the open job market, you are entitled to a sum of money. How much you are entitled to is set by law.

Your permanent disability is expressed as a percentage of disability. Your permanent disability will be either partial (somewhere between .25% and 99.75%) or total (100% disability). The percentage of permanent disability is computed through a process called "rating" your permanent disability. This procedure, which is discussed in detail in Chapter 18, arrives at a percentage of permanent disability by converting the various restrictions on your ability to work into numerical values.

For a permanent partial disability, you are entitled to be paid the appropriate number of weeks (determined by the extent of your disability) at your permanent disability rate—which is usually less than your temporary disability rate. If you haven't already calculated the value of your permanent partial disability, turn to Chapter 13, Section E, for a detailed explanation.

However, if you have a 100% permanent total disability, you are entitled to receive payments at your temporary disability rate for the rest of your life. To determine the value of a lifetime permanent total disability, you need to determine the number of years you are expected to live; see the expectation of life chart below. Multiply the number of years by 52 (the number of weeks in the year) and then by your temporary disability rate (See Chapter 12, Section B).

	EXPECTATION OF LIFE*						
Age	Both	Male	Female	Age	Both	Male	Female
0	75.8	72.5	78.9	43	35.5	33.0	37.9
1	75.4	71.1	78.5	44	34.6	32.1	36.9
2	74.4	71.2	77.5	45	33.8	31.3	36.0
3	73.4	70.2	76.6	46	32.9	30.4	35.1
4	72.5	69.3	75.6	47	32.0	29.5	34.2
5	71.5	68.3	74.6	48	31.1	28.7	33.2
6	70.5	67.3	73.6	49	30.2	27.8	32.3
7	69.5	66.3	72.6	50	29.3	27.0	31.4
8	68.5	65.3	71.6	51	28.5	26.2	30.5
9	67.5	64.3	70.6	52	27.6	25.3	29.7
10	66.6	63.3	69.7	53	26.8	24.5	28.8
11	65.6	62.4	68.7	54	25.9	23.7	27.9
12	64.6	61.4	67.7	55	25.1	22.9	27.0
13	63.6	60.4	66.7	56	24.3	22.1	26.2
14	62.6	59.4	65.7	57	23.5	21.3	25.3
15	61.6	58.4	64.7	58	22.7	20.6	24.5
16	60.7	57.5	63.7	59	21.9	19.8	23.7
17	59.7	56.5	62.8	60	21.1	19.1	22.9
18	58.8	55.6	61.8	61	21.1	18.3	22.0
19	57.8	54.7	60.8	62	20.4	17.6	21.3
20	56.9	53.8	59.9	63	19.6	16.9	20.5
21	55.9	52.9	58.9	64	18.6	16.2	19.7
22	55.0	51.8	57.9	65	18.2	15.6	18.9
23	54.1	51.0	57.0	66	17.4	14.9	18.2
24	53.1	50.1	56.0	67	16.7	14.3	17.4
25	52.2	49.2	55.0	68	15.4	13.6	16.7
26	51.2	48.3	54.0	69	14.7	13.1	16.0
27	50.3	47.3	53.1	70	14.1	12.4	15.3
28	49.3	46.4	52.1	71	13.4	11.8	14.6
29	48.4	45.6	51.1	72	12.8	11.3	13.9
30	47.5	44.6	50.2	73	12.2	10.7	13.2
31	46.5	43.7	49.2	74	11.6	10.2	12.6
32	45.6	42.8	48.3	75	11.0	9.7	11.9
33	44.7	41.9	47.3	76	10.5	9.1	11.3
34	43.8	41.0	46.3	77	9.9	8.6	10.7
35	42.8	40.1	45.4	78	9.3	8.2	10.1
36	41.9	39.2	44.4	79	8.8	7.7	9.5
37	41.0	38.3	43.5	80	8.3	7.2	8.9
38	40.1	37.4	42.6	81	7.8	6.8	8.4
39	39.2	36.5	41.6	82	7.3	6.4	7.8
40	38.3	35.6	40.7	83	6.9	6.0	7.3
41	37.3	34.8	39.7	84	6.4	5.6	6.8
42	36.4	33.9	38.8	85	6.0	5.2	6.3

Source: *Vital Statistics of the U.S.*, Life Table Vol. II, Sec. 6, HHS Dept.
* Published 1995; more recent data may be available.

SETTLEMENT WORKSHEET:
Value of Workers' Compensation Claim

Name: _____   Employer: _____

Insurance Company: _____   Claim Number: _____

Rating: _____ ̄ _____ ̄ _____ ̄ _____ ̄ _____   Appeals Board Case Number: _____

	Stipulations With Request for Award (permanent disability and life pension paid bi-weekly)	Compromise and Release (lump sum payment)
1. Permanent disability (determined by rating) _____ weeks X $_____ per week	$ _____	$ _____
2. Life pension (available if rating is between 70 and 99.75)	$ _____	$ _____
3. Past due temporary disability	$ _____	$ _____
4. Past due vocational rehabilitation maintenance allowance	$ _____	$ _____
5. Reimbursement for mileage	$ _____	$ _____
6. Reimbursement for medical expenses	$ _____	$ _____
7. Future medical expenses, calculated at _____% of actual costs: $_____ medical examinations and hospital bills (including surgery, physical therapy, etc.) $_____ temporary disability (figured at _____ weeks X $_____ per week) $_____ medical costs (including prescriptions, tests, wheelchairs, hearing aids, braces, etc.)	No cash value	$ _____
8. Right to reopen case (five years from date of injury)	No cash value	$ _____
9. Penalties (specify):	$ _____	$ _____
10. Other (specify):	$ _____	$ _____
11. Total value of claim (sum of 1-10 above)	$ _____	$ _____
12. Attorney fees	$ (_____)	$ (_____)
13. Permanent disability advances	$ (_____)	$ (_____)
14. TOTAL YOU'LL RECEIVE (11 – sum of 12 + 13)	$ _____	$ _____

IF YOU ARE 100% DISABLED

When you are discussing settlement of a 100% disability case, you are going to be talking about significant amounts of money, and it would be prudent to solicit the help of a workers' compensation attorney as well as an accountant or investment counselor. They can help you calculate the dollar value and figure out the interrelationship with other benefits, such as Social Security.

Once you have determined the value of your permanent partial disability or permanent total disability, you will have a basic figure to work from. Insert this figure into the blank spaces on line 1 on your settlement worksheet.

2. Life Pension

Skip to Section 3, below, unless you have a permanent disability rating between 70% and 99.75%.

For any permanent disability of 70% to 99.75%, you are entitled to a small lifetime pension that is paid to you at a weekly rate (but actually paid every two weeks.) Please refer to Chapter 13, Section F, to learn how to figure out your weekly rate. Then take these steps:

Step 1: Determine your life expectancy using the expectation of life chart.

Step 2: Multiply your life expectancy figure in Step 1 by 52 to get the total number of weeks the actuaries say you will live.

Step 3: Multiply the figure in Step 2 by the weekly rate of your life pension to get a basic figure.

Step 4: To determine the present value of that money, you must then reduce (discount) it. You must figure out how much invested today would give you your weekly life pension amount per week for the rest of your life. The accepted interest rate in the workers' compensation community seems to be around 3% for purposes of this investment calculation. I will leave the actual computation of this figure to you, as it is beyond the scope of this book.

DISCOUNTED LIFE PENSION

If you don't have a workers' compensation lawyer to help you compute the discounted value of your life pension, check with an Information and Assistance officer. Or, see if your banker or life insurance agent can help with this computation.

Once you have determined the value of your life pension, insert that figure into line 2 of the settlement worksheet.

YOU CAN RECEIVE LIFE PENSION PAYMENTS ALL AT ONCE

A life pension is paid bi-weekly only if you settle your case by Stipulations With Request for Award or you are awarded a life pension after a trial. If, however, you settle your case by a Compromise and Release, you will receive all your pension payments in one lump sum.

3. Past Due Temporary Disability Payments

Next, you'll need to add in the value of any retroactive (past due) temporary disability payments. This consists of any past due temporary disability payments owed to you by the insurance company for any periods after your injury. We discuss how to arrive at this figure in Chapter 12, Section B. If you have been keeping accurate records, you can refer to your Record of Income and Benefits Received to verify the periods you received temporary disability. (See Chapter 6, Section C.) You may also ask the insurance company for a print-out of temporary disability benefits you've received.

Here's how to compute the amount you are due. First, determine the number of weeks you should have been paid but were not. Then multiply the number of weeks by your weekly temporary disability rate to arrive at the total owed. If you received state disability insurance, subtract that amount from the total.

EXAMPLE 1: Jed was temporarily disabled for approximately one year. Jed looks through his records and finds that during that time he was not paid temporary disability payments from the insurance company for a period of two weeks. During this period, Jed did not receive state disability. Jed's temporary disability rate was $336 per week. $336 per week multiplied by two weeks is $672. In figuring the settlement value of his case, Jed should insert $672 in line 3 of the settlement worksheet.

EXAMPLE 2: Let's take the same facts, but let's assume that during the two weeks, Jed was receiving state disability in the amount of $250 per week. The value of the retroactive temporary disability would be the difference between what Jed was entitled to from the insurance company ($336 per week) and what he actually received from the state ($250).

This amounts to $86 per week, for two weeks, or $172. Jed should insert $172 on line 3 of the settlement worksheet.

The insurance company may be required to pay you penalties as a result of its delay. We discuss that later, in Section C9.

4. Past Due Vocational Rehabilitation Maintenance Allowance (VRMA)

A vocational rehabilitation maintenance allowance consists of payments made to you once you qualify for and request a vocational rehabilitation program. Therefore, if you did not qualify for vocational rehabilitation benefits, you may skip this item. (See Chapter 14 for more on vocational rehabilitation and how to compute the maintenance allowance.)

You are entitled to be paid for any periods of time that you should have received vocational rehabilitation maintenance allowance (VRMA) payments, but did not. This includes all periods that the insurance company disputed your entitlement to vocational rehabilitation if it is ultimately determined that you were entitled. However, if you received temporary disability for any period you were in vocational rehabilitation, you are not entitled to VRMA for that period.

Here's how to calculate your retroactive VRMA. First, determine the number of weeks you should have been paid but were not. Ordinarily, you then multiply the number of weeks by your weekly vocational rehabilitation maintenance allowance to arrive at the total retroactive maintenance allowance you are owed. There is one important exception. If any VRMA payments were late, the insurance company must pay VRMA at the current temporary disability rate, set forth in Chapter 11, Section B. (LC § 4642.) This can mean a lot more money for you, so make sure all VRMA payments were made on time.

Vocational rehabilitation benefits are governed by the Labor Code, but are really a separate and distinct benefit. All issues regarding vocational rehabilitation, including payment of vocational rehabilitation maintenance allowance, must first be decided by the Rehabilitation Unit. (See Chapter 14, Section A1.) As a result, it is possible that at the time you're ready to start settlement negotiations on your workers' compensation case, your vocational rehabilitation program may still be going.

If you believe that you are owed any past due VRMA, contact the insurance company and see if it is willing to discuss settlement of this issue along with the rest of your case. It is in the insurance company's best interests to do so, because otherwise it will have to settle or litigate this issue with you at a later date. However, if the insurance company is denying that you are entitled to vocational rehabilitation benefits, it probably won't be willing to discuss settlement. That's okay. You can settle all other issues in your case except your retroactive VRMA. Because this is a separate benefit, you can resolve this issue later. Just make certain that if you do settle the rest of your case, you do not waive (give up the right) to any past due maintenance allowance prior to the date of the settlement documents.

If the insurance company is willing to negotiate settlement of retroactive maintenance allowance, insert the amount you believe you are owed on line 4 of the settlement worksheet.

5. Reimbursement for Mileage

You're entitled to reimbursement for your mileage expense for travel to and from doctor's appointments, physical therapy and pharmacies to pick up medication. If you are settling vocational rehabilitation issues, you should also include unreimbursed mileage to and from vocational rehabilitation appointments.

If you haven't been reimbursed for these costs, tally them up using the Record of Mileage and Transportation and Request for Reimbursement form and instructions in Chapter 11, Section A1. Fill in this amount on your settlement worksheet on line 5.

6. Reimbursement for Medical Expenses

The insurance company must reimburse you for any reasonable and necessary medical expenses you paid, including costs of prescription drugs and health aids.

If the insurance company refused to provide medical treatment, and you had to pay for it yourself, you're entitled to be repaid for out-of-pocket expenses you incurred as long as it was later determined that yours is an industrial injury. This would include, for example, an MRI exam requested by your treating doctor that you paid for because the insurance company refused to authorize it.

It's unlikely that you would have paid your own medical expenses, however. Many injured workers cannot afford to pay for treatment themselves, and most doctors and medical facilities want payment in advance before providing treatment. But if you've paid for any medical expenses, add them up using the Record of Medical Expenses and Request for Reimbursement form discussed in Chapter 11, Section A2. Be sure to include any medical expenses you are responsible for, even if you have not yet paid the bill. The insurance company will only be responsible for paying doctors and medical facilities that treated you without payment and instead filed a lien form with the Appeals Board.

 IF YOU OBTAINED TREATMENT THAT HAS NOT BEEN PAID FOR

Contact the doctors or medical facilities and request they file liens with the Workers' Compensation Appeals Board. (See Chapter 9, Section B2b.) If they do, you need not include their bill in this section, because the insurance company will have to pay or adjust their bill as part of the settlement documents you sign. However, if the doctor or the medical facility refuses or neglects to file a lien by the time you negotiate your settlement, those outstanding bills will be your responsibility. Because you will have to pay them out of your settlement proceeds, you should include them in your demand. Enter the total on line 6 of the settlement worksheet.

7. Value of Future Medical Treatment

 IF YOU PLAN TO SETTLE YOUR CASE BY STIPS

If you do not want to settle your case by Compromise and Release, you may skip this section. Remember, in Section B of this chapter, we discussed that reasonable future medical treatment will be paid for by the insurance company if you settle by Stips. That means you won't be paid anything for future medical treatment.

The only time you add in the value of your future medical treatment is if you are negotiating a settlement of your case by Compromise and Release, which is a full and complete settlement of your workers' compensation case. The value of your future medical treatment is the most difficult item to put a price tag on because you must estimate (or guess) as to what the cost of various medical treatments will be. If you hope to settle your case, it generally requires you to keep an open mind and to be flexible and open to compromise.

Future medical costs are almost certain to be a point of discussion between you and the insurance company. You can pretty much expect that the insurance company will not agree to pay you up front for the full value of future medical treatment you and your doctor believe may be necessary. That's because no one knows for sure whether or not you will ever have the treatment and what it will actually cost. For example, from the insurance company's point of view, just because your doctor says that you may need surgery in the future does not mean that you will ever decide to have it.

As a general rule, you can expect that an insurance company will try to pay no more than 25% to 35% of the value of your anticipated future medical treatment as part of a settlement. But there are no hard and fast rules. For example, you well may be able to negotiate to add as much as 75% of the value of your future medical treatment if your doctors present a very strong opinion that you will need treatment. (See Chapter 20, below, for more on negotiating a settlement).

How much you will end up with often depends on the words your doctor uses in his reports. Even seemingly similar reports can produce very different results. For example, when it comes to how much money you will receive, there is a big difference between a medical opinion that "the patient may need a laminectomy in the future if his symptoms significantly worsen," and one that states "the patient is presently a definite candidate for a laminectomy but has decided not to avail himself of this procedure at this time. However, this option must be kept open for him in the future." The first opinion will probably entitle you to no more than 30% (and probably much less) of the cost of a laminectomy and other related future medical expenses. The latter opinion is probably good for somewhere around 75% of the value.

Don't forget to add in the value of any other related expenses due to the various medical treatments you may require. If you have back surgery in the future and it is done within five years from the date of your injury, you would also

be entitled to an additional period of temporary disability payments. (See Chapter 12, Section B, to figure out the amount of your temporary disability benefits.)

In addition to temporary disability, other future medically related expenses to consider include:

- prescriptions
- non-prescription pain-killers and other over-the-counter medications
- physical therapy
- doctor's visits
- cost of tests, and
- the cost of apparatus, such as wheelchairs, hearing aids and braces.

You should also contact various hospitals and/or doctors' offices to get estimates regarding the cost of the type of medical treatment you may need in the future. This will give you a much more reliable dollar amount than would even an informed guess, and will impress the insurance adjuster if your figures are valid.

In deciding on a value to insert on your settlement worksheet for future medical treatment, I recommend starting in the 75%-80% range of the actual cost you estimate for future medical treatment. Indicate the percentage of actual costs you're using to come up with this figure. If you try demanding 100%, the insurance adjuster will not take you seriously and will categorize you along with all those other unrepresented workers who don't know what they're doing. By starting at 75%-80% and being willing to negotiate, the insurance adjuster should recognize that you understand how the system works and should take you seriously.

Once you determine the value of your future medical treatment, enter it on your settlement worksheet on line 7.

8. Value of Waiving Your Right to Reopen Your Case

 IF YOU DON'T WANT TO SETTLE BY COMPROMISE AND RELEASE

You may choose to skip this section if you are only interested in settling your case by Stips. Stips gives you the right to reopen your case and ask for more money if your condition gets worse within five years from the date of injury. (See Section B1c, above, for more on your right to reopen your case.)

If you want to settle your case using a Compromise and Release, realize that you will give up your right to reopen your case should your condition get worse. For example, if you

presently have a 10% permanent partial disability, and six months after you sign a Compromise and Release your disability worsens to a 50% disability, you would have given up your right to obtain any more money.

There's no set formula to follow in determining an amount for waiving your right to reopen your case. The amount you'll receive depends upon two factors:

- **whether your disability is likely to get worse in the future.** For example, if you have a progressive disability, such as a lung disease, you can probably expect to get more money for waiving your right to reopen than if you have an ankle fracture that has healed with a good result. That is because the ankle probably won't get any worse and require future care, while the lung disease probably will.
- **how much time is left to petition the Workers' Compensation Appeals Board to reopen your case.** If at the time of settlement, there are only five months left until the five-year anniversary date of your injury, you will not get nearly as much money as if there are three years until the five-year anniversary date of your injury.

In general, unless your condition is very likely to require lots more treatment (in which case you probably shouldn't waive your right to reopen your case in the first place), you should figure on getting anywhere from nothing to several thousand dollars to waive this right. As in all settlement figures, this amount is negotiable, and some insurance companies include it in future medical expenses. Insert the estimated value of this figure on line 8 of the settlement worksheet.

9. Penalties

 See *Pierce Enterprises, Argonaut Insurance Company, Petitioners v. WCAB and George Colchado, Respondents, Rhiner v. WCAB, Ready Home Health Care, Inc. v. WCAB (Sharp)* and *Christian v. WCAB* in Chapter 28.

If the insurance company failed to pay you benefits, or failed to pay them in a timely manner, you may be entitled to additional money in penalties unless the insurance company has a good reason for its action (or inaction).

Your employer may be subject to some of the following money penalties, which, after approval by the Appeals Board judge, may be tacked onto your workers' compensation award:

- **Failure to inform worker of rights.** If your benefits were delayed because you didn't have sufficient information about workers' compensation, your employer may be subject to a 10% penalty on the *entire amount* of all of your benefits. (LC § 5814.)

- **Delay or failure to provide benefits.** If the delay was unreasonable, the Appeals Board may assess a 10% penalty, calculated on the *entire amount* awarded for the particular delayed benefit, including temporary disability, permanent disability and medical treatment. (LC § 5814.)

- **Late payment of temporary disability or permanent disability.** This is an automatic 10% penalty on the delayed payment. (LC § 4650.) Make sure the insurance company hasn't already paid the penalty, discussed in Chapter 11, Section

C4. (Note that an additional 10% penalty on all temporary or permanent disability benefits may also apply under LC § 5814, as discussed just above.)

- **Employer's illegal hiring of a minor under age 16.** Unless the minor furnished falsified identification, the Appeals Board may award a 50% penalty on the workers' compensation award. (LC § 4557.)

- **Employer's serious or willful misconduct.** If your employer intentionally did something seriously wrong, such as endangering employees by violating Cal-OSHA regulations, the workers' compensation award is to be increased by 50%, excluding costs of medical treatment. (LC § 4553.) We cover this in Chapter 16, Section D. To qualify for this penalty, you

---

VOCATIONAL REHABILITATION CANNOT BE EXCHANGED FOR CASH—OR CAN IT?

Vocational rehabilitation is separate and apart from your workers' compensation case. Under the Labor Code, you cannot waive your right to vocational rehabilitation benefits in exchange for a sum of money. Theoretically, this is to prevent insurance companies from making a waiver of vocational rehabilitation benefits a condition of settlement. As a result, some judges will not allow you to waive your right to vocational rehabilitative benefits in exchange for money. However, there is nothing to stop you from trying.

The amount of money you ask for is up to you and should be negotiable. Remember that the cost to the insurance company for a vocational rehabilitation plan is limited to $16,000. If you can negotiate anywhere from $5,000 to $10,000 extra, you have done well. (Before waiving your rights, bear in mind that you may be able to get the entire $16,000 value of your plan by proposing a self-employment plan. See Chapter 14, Section B, Step 6.)

The insurance company will want to make sure that you won't take the money and later request vocational rehabilitation anyhow. Here are two methods to address this issue:

- **Sign a declination of vocational rehabilitation benefits.** This is known as an RU-107 form. It states that you do not want vocational rehabilitation benefits, even though you have been told that you're entitled to them. (There is some dispute over whether you can request benefits after having signed an RU-107; if

your employment status or medical condition changes, you probably will be able to request benefits. As a result, many insurance companies won't care if you sign an RU-107.)

- **Sign a Thomas waiver in the settlement documents.** This method is preferred by insurance companies. A Thomas waiver is a statement in your settlement document that if your case were to go to trial, there is the possibility that a judge might find that you did not have an industrial injury and that therefore you would not be entitled to any workers' compensation benefits, including vocational rehabilitation. There is really no risk in giving a Thomas waiver, as it is a hypothetical statement and you will still get all the compensation agreed to in your settlement. However, there must be some evidence to support the fact that you might be found not to have an industrial injury. Usually the insurance company will state in the Thomas waiver that certain witnesses would be called to testify that you didn't report the injury, or didn't have an injury, or something to that effect. If you received benefits, a Thomas waiver would not be appropriate. The Thomas waiver must be approved by a judge.

Regardless of how you proceed, make sure that any agreement to waive your rehabilitation rights for a sum of money is set out in writing in the settlement documents. (See Chapter 20, Section D2d.)

must file a separate application with the Appeals Board within one year of the date of injury. (CCR §§ 10440, 10445.) See a lawyer; the procedure is beyond the scope of this book.

- **Employer's discrimination against worker for filing claim.** As discussed in Chapter 16, Section C, an employer who fires, threatens to discharge or otherwise discriminates against an employee for filing a workers' compensation claim is subject to a 50% penalty on the award, up to $10,000. (LC § 132(a).) See a lawyer; you must file an application with the Appeals Board within one year from the date of the employer's discriminatory action.

Enter the value of any penalties on line 9 of the settlement worksheet.

10. Other

Specify any other expenses you may be entitled to and fill in the amounts. Here are some possibilities:

- costs of depositions, if you held any depositions (Chapter 21, Section C)
- costs of serving Subpoenas or Subpoenas Duces Tecum (Chapter 21, Section D)
- costs of having subpoenaed documents photocopied by an attorney service
- cash for vocational rehabilitation (see sidebar, "Vocational Rehabilitation Cannot Be Exchanged for Cash—or Can It?")

11. Total Value of Your Claim

Add the totals of lines 1 through 10 above. This is the figure you will use in starting your settlement negotiations. Enter the total on line 11 of the settlement worksheet. To determine how much you can expect to actually keep, complete lines 12 through 14, below.

12. Attorney Fees

If you do not have an attorney, enter 0 in this space. If you have or had an attorney, you'll need to enter the amount of the attorney fee on line 12. This is usually 12% to 15% of your settlement (the figure you ultimately agree to settle for). For starters, calculate 12% to 15% of the line 11 total.

13. Permanent Disability Advances

If you received permanent disability advances, explained in Chapter 13, Section D2, enter the total amount you received on this line. You are subtracting permanent disability advances to see how much "new money" you will get. Permanent disability advances are part of your settlement. Many injured workers forget this fact and pass up reasonable settlement offers because they will not net enough money.

EXAMPLE: Tom gets an offer of $3,000 to settle his case, which is reasonable. Tom has received $2,500 in permanent disability advances. Tom erroneously thinks that he is only going to get $500 for his case. While it is true that Tom will only get $500 in "new money" when his case settles, Tom has in fact received $3,000 to settle his case. He just got most of his settlement in advances.

14. Total You'll Receive

Subtract the total of lines 12 and 13 from line 11. This is what you can expect to receive in new money if you settle for the amount listed on line 11.

D. What to Do Next

Remember that the total represented on line 11 of your settlement worksheet is just the starting point for settlement negotiations. It is doubtful that you will get an offer from the insurance company at or even close to this figure. Armed with the information in the settlement worksheet, you may now begin the negotiating process to try to arrive at a final figure that you are willing to accept. Please proceed to Chapter 20 to learn how to use your newfound knowledge to negotiate a fair settlement of your case. ■

Negotiating a Settlement

This chapter covers what most people need to know about settling a workers' compensation claim. If you do not have an attorney, you will learn how to negotiate and settle your workers' compensation case. If you do have an attorney, this chapter will help you to understand what your attorney is going to do on your behalf, which should help you to better communicate your goals and desires.

If you've decided to negotiate the settlement of your case, you probably feel a little nervous. That's normal. Just remember that the insurance adjuster is as anxious as you are to settle your case, even if she doesn't act like it.

You also have the element of surprise on your side. Insurance adjusters often deal with injured workers who represent themselves. However, it's rare for an injured worker to know as much about how the system works as you probably do, having read this book. The claims adjuster may underestimate your ability to evaluate the value of your case and may be somewhat flustered when you're able to justify your demands with facts and figures.

Thousands of people have negotiated settlements of their cases even without the benefit of a self-help book. You should be able to do the same. If you feel overwhelmed, or feel you're not getting the results you want, you may seek the assistance of a workers' compensation attorney at any time. If you can't find a lawyer to represent you, or choose not to hire one, bear in mind that an Appeals Board judge will be reviewing your settlement documents. The judge will look particularly closely at a settlement negotiated by an unrepresented worker, and should approve it only if it's in your best interests.

A. Deciding Whether to Negotiate Your Own Settlement

There are many different negotiating styles. Some people can achieve more with a smile and a nod than others can by banging the table—but of course, the reverse is also true. In the last analysis, your negotiating style should be an extension of your personality, not something you put on for the day.

That said, it's also important to realize that good negotiating is a skill, and that the amount of your workers' compensation settlement will depend, to some degree, on your negotiating ability. If you are generally pretty good at bargaining for a good deal in other contexts (such as buying a car or getting a raise), you may want to negotiate your own workers' compensation settlement. But if you break out in a sweat, and can't open your mouth to speak at the thought of even calling the insurance adjuster, you will want to seriously consider getting a lawyer. See Chapter 26 for help finding a lawyer. As an alternative, you may have a knowledgeable non-lawyer friend negotiate on your behalf.

Some of the factors that come into play in determining your negotiating ability include:

- **personality.** Are you comfortable talking to people? Or do you avoid confronting difficult personal and business situations?
- **communication skills.** Are you able to effectively communicate in business transactions generally? Will you be able to make the adjuster understand your position?
- **confidence.** Do you feel confident in business dealings? When you speak, will the insurance adjuster be likely to take you seriously, or will you come across as being afraid or unsure?
- **objectivity.** Are you so angry or bitter about how your claim was handled that you can't talk about it without getting upset? If so, you'll probably have a hard time negotiating an equitable settlement.
- **knowledge.** When it comes to your workers' compensation claim, do you know what you're talking about? Have you read this book carefully and followed the suggestions to prepare your case?

Of all of the above factors, the most important is knowledge of the law and facts in your case. If you adequately study and prepare your case, the knowledge you acquire should help give you the confidence and the ability to persuade the insurance adjuster that you have correctly assessed your case.

This chapter will tell you what you need to know (knowledge!) in order to adequately prepare for settlement negotiations. It will discuss who to contact and when, and what to do if you can't settle your case. Finally, you will learn how to review settlement documents and get your settlement finalized.

BOOKS ON NEGOTIATING

Several books that can help you hone your negotiating skills include: *Getting to Yes: Negotiating Agreement Without Giving In,* by Roger Fisher, William Ury and Bruce Patton (Houghton Mifflin), *Getting Past No: Negotiating Your Way from Confrontation to Cooperation,* by William Ury (Bantam Books), and *You Can Negotiate Anything,* by Herb Cohen (Bantam Books).

IF YOU FIRED YOUR LAWYER

A workers' compensation lawyer will generally be entitled to a fee of 12% to 15% of your settlement. If you previously had an attorney, but you dropped him (substituted him out of your case, in legal jargon), the attorney must file a lien on your case for the reasonable value of his services. If so, you will have to negotiate a settlement of attorney's fees with your former lawyer at the time you settle your case. If your former attorney did not file a lien, you don't need to pay him to get your settlement approved. In that situation, he can't collect his fee from your settlement, but he could sue you in civil or small claims court (although that rarely happens) to collect his fees.

How much you end up paying your former attorney will depend on how long he represented you, what he accomplished and how much better you did after you dropped him. The worst you can do is to owe what the attorney would have been entitled to originally—12% to 15% of your settlement. If you had two or more attorneys who worked on your case, don't worry. The most you can owe is a total of 12% to 15% of your settlement. It is up to the attorneys to decide how that fee is to be split amongst them.

If you negotiate your own settlement, you will probably be able to negotiate an amount in the area of 6% or less of your settlement as attorney fees. If, however, the attorney did hardly any work on your case, he might even be willing to waive a fee. Once an agreement has been reached, request that your former attorney send you a letter confirming what he has agreed to accept to satisfy his lien, or send him a letter that states your agreement and request that he sign it and return it.

B. The Concept of Compromising

The basis for any out-of-court settlement is a principle known as compromising. Compromising is the process of giving up something you want, in return for the other side's giving up something it wants. In other words, each side gives a little to reach a settlement. If one, or both sides, is unwilling to compromise, there is little chance of settling the case without a trial. A willingness to compromise is the basis for any realistic and fruitful negotiation.

Sometimes—fortunately not very often—an insurance adjuster refuses to negotiate in good faith, or takes an outrageous position. In these rare situations, you will be left with no alternative but to proceed to trial. Don't worry or be discouraged; sometimes these things happen. We cover what to do in Section C4, below.

C. How to Negotiate a Settlement

Before you begin the actual negotiating process, you need to take two important steps:

Step 1: **Have a good grasp of how much your claim is worth.** Chapter 19 takes you step-by-step through the process. Once you have come to an educated estimate as to the value of your case, you will be in a position to begin settlement negotiations.

Step 2: **Learn about the different ways to settle your case.** If you haven't done so already, you need to decide what type of settlement you want: Stipulations with Request for Award or Compromise and Release. In Chapter 19, Section B, we discuss the advantages and disadvantages of each settlement approach. But it's important to understand that even after studying this material carefully, you may still be undecided. If so, you should make settlement demands, and solicit settlement offers, based upon both types of settlements. This is a fine, and probably smart, approach.

1. When to Settle

The best time to settle your workers' compensation claim is when there is nothing else left to do on your case except settle it or go to trial. In other words, the following should all apply:

- Your doctors have all said you are permanent and stationary—in other words, your medical condition has stabilized and future medical treatment at this time won't help you improve. (See Chapter 9, Section E.)
- You have obtained the medical reports you need to determine the nature and extent of your permanent disability and your need for future medical treatment, and have attended any medical appointments requested by the insurance company.
- You have determined a starting figure for the settlement value of your case and completed a settlement worksheet. (See Chapter 19, Section C.)

Sometimes financial circumstances may pressure you to try to settle your case in a hurry. Do your best to get financial assistance or seek permanent disability advances rather than rush into a settlement that's not to your advantage. (Chapter 13, Section D2, and Chapter 17 discuss these options.)

2. How to Initiate Settlement Negotiations

It is very possible that the insurance company will institute settlement negotiations. If so, you may receive a telephone call or a letter from the insurance adjuster setting forth an initial settlement offer. In fact, the insurance company may send you a filled out Stipulations With Request for Award with a cover letter saying that you must sign the agreement to ensure your rights to medical treatment, or even with a simple Post-It note saying, "Please sign and return." You do not have to sign and return it—this is just the insurance company's first settlement offer.

If you don't hear from the insurance company, when you're ready to begin settlement negotiations, you should take the initiative. Contact the person you have been dealing with all along—the insurance adjuster, the insurance company's attorney or the insurance company's hearing representative.

The quickest method of beginning settlement negotiations is by making a telephone call. Before you call, be prepared to discuss the basis for your demand in detail on the phone. You should have your settlement worksheet (Chapter 19, Section C) and all your figures and computations in front of you. Sometimes it is difficult to reach the person you need to discuss settlement with, in which case you should make your demand in writing.

Even if you do reach someone and discuss settlement, you should follow up the call with a letter to that person, setting forth your demand and any agreements you reached. I recommend sending all letters certified, return receipt requested, and keeping copies for your records. Make sure that your letter covers all the figures in your settlement worksheet. Also make sure your demand is reasonable, but not too low, as discussed in Section C3, below. You'll want some room to negotiate the settlement figure.

You should not expect any response to your correspondence in fewer than 30 days. It generally takes this long for the insurance adjuster or attorney to receive your letter, read it, obtain some authority to counter your settlement offer and respond. However, after about 30 days, you should follow up with another letter or a phone call. The follow-up letter should be short and have a deadline for the insurance company to respond. For example: "May I please have a response to my 7/3/01 letter. If I don't hear from you within 10 days, I will have no alternative but to set this matter for hearing." If you don't get a satisfactory response, you should probably set your matter for a hearing. Don't delay, as it may take months to get on the court's calendar. (See Chapter 22, Section D, for instructions.)

SAMPLE DEMAND LETTER

12/1/year

Mr. Mark Washington

Acme Insurance Co.

333 Tenth Ave.

Bartville, CA 99999

Applicant: Jean Mills

Employer: Ace Manufacturing

Date of injury: 3/12/year

Claim No: 12345

Appeals board Case No: 99999

Dear Mr. Washington:

Please be advised that I am in receipt of the advisory rating of the qualified medical evaluator's report, which indicates that I have a permanent partial disability of 33.5%. This is equivalent to $20,979, as I am a maximum earner for purposes of permanent disability.

In addition, I believe that I am owed retroactive temporary disability for the period 6/7/year through and including 2/2/year. As you know, Dr. Jones, the QME, states that I was temporarily totally disabled during this period of time, and you failed to pay me temporary disability benefits. This is equivalent to 241 days at $58 per day, or $13,978. I am also entitled to a 10% penalty of $1,398 under Labor Code Section 4560.

My records reflect that you did not pay me mileage reimbursement as I requested in my letter of 5/30/year. This amounts to $182.35.

Dr. Jones has indicated that I will require future medical treatment, including a possible laminectomy (surgery). I believe the value of my future medical treatment to be approximately $40,000. However, for settlement purposes, I am willing to accept $30,000 to waive my right to future medical treatment and my right to petition to reopen my case.

I am therefore willing to settle my workers' compensation claim by way of a Compromise and Release in the sum of $66,537.

If I have not heard from you within 30 days, I plan to file a Declaration of Readiness to Proceed to get this matter resolved before the Workers' Compensation Appeals Board. If I do, I will, of course, ask for the entire amount I believe I am owed. I look forward to your anticipated cooperation in resolving this matter.

Sincerely,

Jean Mills

Jean Mills

(Address)

(Telephone Number)

3. Settlement Negotiation Tips

Here are some tips you should keep in mind when negotiating your settlement.

Expect to negotiate the amount of permanent disability. The main area of dispute between you and the insurance adjuster will probably concern the value of your permanent disability. A dispute is likely to arise if you and the insurance adjuster are relying on the rating of different medical reports. The best way to negotiate the value of your permanent disability is to consider both reports (called "splitting the reports") and agree to a figure somewhere between the two. For example, if the treating doctor's report rates a 30% disability and the QME report rates a 20% disability, a reasonable compromise may be a 25% permanent partial disability. Especially if you are relying on the treating doctor's report, bear in mind that it is presumed correct under workers' compensation law. For example, if the treating doctor's report rates a 30% disability and a QME report rates a 10% disability, you would want to get much more than 20%.

Use the settlement worksheet to recalculate your award. Remember that your claim is made up of many different components. Once you've agreed to a particular part of the award, such as permanent disability, plug the agreed amount into your settlement worksheet (Chapter 19, Section C) and recompute your demand.

Your first demand should be more than you expect to receive. While your demand should be high, make sure it's reasonable or you'll damage your credibility. How much of a premium over your bottom line offer you should ask for initially depends on the situation, but 10-25% is usually about right. Thus if you figured out in the settlement worksheet (Chapter 19, Section C) that you are entitled to $20,000, you may want to ask for between $22,000 and $25,000 (again, depending on the circumstances).

Never negotiate with yourself. Never make two demands in a row without first having received a counteroffer from the insurance adjuster or attorney. Here's an example. You demand $15,000. The claims adjuster says, "I don't think I can get that much authority, what's the least you will take?" Don't reduce your demand! Explain that $15,000 is your demand and you would appreciate a response. The claims adjuster will either accept your demand (unlikely) or make a counterproposal.

If the insurance company raises its offer, use that figure as the new "floor" for negotiating. If you ask for $5,000 and the insurance adjuster offers $4,000, would you be willing to split the difference and accept $4,500 if the other side proposes it? If so, you have lots to learn about negotiating. Instead of accepting, you would be smarter to come back with $4,750 or $4,800. After all, the other side has already let you know they will pay $4,500, so you can probably get more.

You should not need to come down more than one or two times. In our example above, where your initial demand is $15,000, if the insurance adjuster makes a counter-proposal of $10,000, you might consider making a demand at $13,000. If your $13,000 demand is supported by facts and figures, this should be the end of the negotiations and the case should settle. If the insurance company makes yet another counter-proposal at, say, $11,000, you will have to reevaluate just how strong your case is and then decide whether to accept the $11,000 or, more likely, make a last counteroffer at $12,000.

Don't be intimidated. A good insurance adjuster will make it sound like you have the worst case in the world. That's her job—to try and punch as many holes in your case as possible and make you believe that you should accept the figure being offered. Most (if not all) of what the adjuster says is just "smoke" without substance. Stick to your guns unless you are presented with indisputable evidence to the contrary.

In addition, after you make a counter or a counteroffer, the insurance company may send you a letter saying that it is forwarding your file to an attorney to take over the case, or that if you do not agree to its offer, the insurance company will subpoena you and/or your doctor to come in for a deposition (a formal legal interview). These are normal procedures and shouldn't intimidate you. Don't be tempted to agree to their offer to avoid the legalities that may follow.

If you want any special provisions, ask for them. Some disability programs, such as Social Security and certain private disability policy providers, will ordinarily take a credit or offset for money you receive in your workers' compensation settlement. In other words, if you receive benefits from these disability providers, your benefits may be reduced after you receive your settlement. With a Compromise and Release, you may designate part of the settlement as future medical expenses, which won't ordinarily affect your disability benefits (although it may affect Medicare and Medi-Cal benefits). Section D2e, below, covers this issue in more detail.

4. If You Can't Settle

If you don't settle your case, it will go before a judge at the Workers' Compensation Appeals Board. Here are some issues to weigh if you're considering going to trial instead of settling.

a. Advantages of Going to Trial

There are several benefits of going to trial, including:
- Your case is decided on the true value of your situation; neither side gives up something to arrive at a settlement.
- If you are entitled to future medical treatment, you will get it.
- If your condition worsens within five years from the date of injury, you may petition the court to reopen your case for a determination of new and further disability.
- It is possible that you'll get more than has been previously offered by the insurance company.

b. Disadvantages of Going to Trial

Going to trial is time-consuming and complicated. In addition:
- You will not get your money as quickly by going to trial as you would by settling.

WORKERS' COMPENSATION APPEALS BOARD

STATE OF CALIFORNIA

Betty White   *Applicant*

vs.

Home Retail,
ABC Insurance

                               Defendants

Case No.

Stipulations
with Request
for Award

The parties hereto stipulate to the issuance of an Award and/or Order, based upon the following facts, and waive the requirements of Labor Code Section 5313:

1. _____Betty White_____ , born _____4/19/63_____ , while
   (Employee)

employed within the State of California as _____accountant_____ on ____8/28/XX_____ ,
                                               (Occupation)   (Date of Injury)

by___Home Retail_____ whose compensation insurance carrier was

___ABC Insurance___sustained injury arising out of and in the course of employment __both arms and back__ .
                                                                                      (Parts of body injured)

2. The injury caused temporary disability for the period ____8/28/XX_____

through___11/2/XX_____ for which indemnity is payable at $___406____ per

week, less credit for such payments previously made.

3. The injury caused permanent disability of____25____ %, for which indemnity is payble at $____140_____

per week beginning____3/2/XX_____ , in the sum of $_14,134.00_ , less credit for such

payments previously made.

An informal rating ~~has~~ has not been previously issued.
                    (Select one)

4. There is ~~XX XXX XX XXXXXXX~~ need for medical treatment to cure or relieve from the effects of said injury.
   (Select one)

DEPARTMENT OF INDUSTRIAL RELATIONS
DIVISION OF WORKERS' COMPENSATION

- You could end up getting less than was previously offered by the insurance company.
- If the insurance company has denied your claim, there is the possibility that you could lose and get nothing.
- Payments are made weekly at the maximum rate payable on the date of your injury, rather than in the lump sum available with a Compromise and Release. You will be entitled, however, to receive any past due payments that weren't paid beginning 14 days after your last payment of temporary disability, in a lump sum.
- You will not receive settlement money for your need for future medical treatment, so your cash award will usually be less than a settlement by a Compromise and Release. (Of course, this can be fine if you may need such treatment.)
- If you know that your case is going to trial, you may decide to get an attorney who will be entitled to a percentage (usually 12% to 15%) of your recovery. The attorney will be paid even if she negotiates a settlement without going to trial.

Chapters 21 through 24 cover the step-by-step process of preparing for and going to trial.

YOUR ATTORNEY IS NOT GOD

Workers' compensation lawyers don't get paid until your case settles or a Findings and Award is entered after trial. Although most workers' compensation lawyers are honest, you would be foolish if you did not pay attention to the fact that your lawyer will do a lot less work and get paid sooner if your case settles. In addition, your attorney will probably receive more money if you settle by a Compromise and Release. Don't feel bound to accept a settlement without question just because your lawyer recommends it. If you have done your numbers and are convinced you should get more, discuss your concerns with your attorney.

D. Review and Sign Settlement Documents

Whether you're settling by Stipulations with Request for Award or Compromise and Release, the insurance company will probably prepare the actual settlement document. There is no advantage to drafting the document yourself. It is, however, your responsibility—and to your advantage—to make sure the document correctly reflects what you've agreed to.

If you find a mistake in the settlement document, or discover a waiver or disclaimer you didn't agree to, contact the insurance company immediately and point out the error. Ask if you can handwrite the correction in the document, or whether the insurance company should make the necessary changes and send you a new set of papers for signing. If the insurance company insists on proceeding with the settlement as presented, you have two choices: You can agree to do it the insurance company's way, or you can refuse to sign the settlement papers and be ready to proceed to trial. If you want to make substantial changes, you will need to discuss them with the insurance representative to get approval. This may require some additional negotiations.

1.   Reviewing Stipulations with Request for Award (Stips)

The document your insurance company provides will already be filled in. Here are the important issues to look for in Stips; a sample follows.

Paragraph 1. Make sure your name is spelled correctly (it should be the same name you used when you filed your claim) and your date of birth is correct. Check to see that your occupation is accurately listed.

Carefully check the date(s) of injury listed. Sometimes the insurance company will try to include additional dates of injury to preclude any other potential claims you may have. For example, the insurance company may list all dates you were employed or list the entire year before your injury as a continuous trauma date of injury.

EXAMPLE: Assume the date of your injury was 9/9/01. The Stips lists 9/9/01, as well as a date of injury of 9/9/00 to 9/9/01. Unless your injury was caused in part by a cumulative trauma that occurred over this period of time, it's best not to accept this.

Check the accuracy of your employer's name and address and its insurance company's name and address.

Finally, make sure that all parts of your body that were injured are listed correctly. Because Stips include a provision for payment of your future medical treatment, the insurance company may try to omit a body part. Let's say that you injured your back, left leg, left shoulder and right arm. If the insurance company omits the right arm in the settlement documents, the insurance company may later refuse to provide medical treatment for that part of the body.

WORKERS' COMPENSATION APPEALS BOARD

STATE OF CALIFORNIA

5. Medical-legal expenses are payable by defendant as follows:

Dr. Clyde Smith is to be paid and adjusted for his lien
of 8/2/XX in the sum of $1,124.00

Dr. Helen Jones is to be paid the sum of $975.00

6. Applicant's attorney request a fee of $

None

7. Liens against compensation are payable as follows:

The lien of Acme Imaging to be paid by defendants in the sum
of $1,600.00

8. Other stipulations:

1. Applicant agees to waive all interest within 25 days after
the issuance of the Award.

_____
Dated

_____
Applicant

_____   _____
Social Security Number of Applicant   Address of Employer

_____   _____
Address of Applicant   Address of Insurance Company

_____   _____
Attorney for Applicant   Attorney or Authorized Representative for Defendant

_____   _____
Address of Attorney for Applicant   Address of Attorney or Authorized Representative

Paragraph 2. Make sure the dates are correct for the periods you were temporarily disabled. Check that the weekly indemnity amount you have been paid is accurate.

Paragraph 3. Make certain that the correct percentage of permanent disability is listed, as well as your correct indemnity rate and total sum due. Double-check this by comparing the figures in the document to those you agreed to.

In the blank after the words "per week beginning," you should see a date of 14 days after you last received temporary disability. Make sure this date is correct, and that it is *not* the date of the settlement agreement. This is important because you'll receive weekly payments (actually, every two weeks, but based on a weekly amount). If you last received temporary disability on 9/1/01 and you sign the settlement documents (Stips) on 3/15/02, you are already owed 24 weeks of permanent disability payments, which you will get in a lump sum check if you haven't already received it.

Paragraph 4. This paragraph is extremely important. Assuming there is a possibility you may need future medical treatment, it must be reflected here. Unless all of the medical reports relied upon to arrive at your settlement state that you are fully recovered, you will want to the paragraph to read "There *is* need for medical treatment…"

BEWARE OF OTHER STATEMENTS ON MEDICAL TREATMENT

If you sign an agreement stating that there is no need for any future medical treatment, you are out of luck if your injury flares up (although you may still reopen your case if your condition worsens and you have a "new and further disability"). You also want to object to a statement that says, "There *may be* need for medical treatment…" If this is included, you may have to prove you need future treatment before the company will authorize it. This can be a real hassle and could delay your ability to get needed medical treatment. If the carrier wants to include this statement, find out how you'd be entitled to medical treatment in the future.

Paragraph 5. Here you list all the liens for your medical-legal reports, if any. Medical-legal reports are those provided to prove your case (Chapter 10), not for medical treatment. See the discussion regarding Paragraph 7, below, and follow the precautions covered there, as they apply to medical-legal liens as well.

Paragraph 6. If you have a lawyer, she will list the attorney fee here. This must be in the percentage range listed on the Attorney Fee Disclosure Statement you signed—usually between 12% and 15%. The attorney may choose to list "reasonable fees" to be approved by the Appeals Board.

Paragraph 7. This paragraph is extremely important. It lists all of the outstanding liens (debts) the insurance company agrees to pay as part of the settlement, other than attorney fees. This includes bills owed to doctors, laboratories, pharmacies and interpreters.

Check the list and make sure no doctor, medical facility or anyone else who has provided you with medical treatment, tests, examinations and reports or other services to help prove your case has been overlooked. Only the listed bills will be paid by the insurance company. (Note that this should not address reimbursement for medical care you paid for yourself; those costs are listed in Paragraph 8.)

Even if the insurance company claims it paid a particular lien claimant, it is best to list it anyway, with the provision that "jurisdiction is reserved to the Appeals Board to resolve any disputes."

If there are outstanding medical bills for which no liens have been filed, you should do one of the following:

- Contact those doctors or companies and request that they file a lien before you sign the Stips. Then negotiate with the insurance company to agree to pay the bills by specifically listing them in the Stips.
- Get the insurance company to include language that it will pay or negotiate any outstanding bills that are a result of your injury. (Most insurance companies probably won't agree to this because there's no way to know what might be outstanding.)

OUTSTANDING BILLS MAY BE YOUR RESPONSIBILITY

If you do not make these specific arrangements for the insurance company to agree to be responsible for the bills, any bills that are outstanding after you sign the Stips will be your responsibility, and the creditor could sue you in civil court for the money.

Make sure that Employment Development Department (EDD) is listed here if it filed a lien in your case for reimbursement for money paid to you for disability periods that should have been the responsibility of the workers' compensation insurance company.

WORKERS' COMPENSATION APPEALS BOARD

STATE OF CALIFORNIA

AWARD

AWARD IS MADE in favor of __Betty White_____ against

__Home Retail, ABC Insurance_____ of:

(A) Temporary disability indemnity in accordance with paragraph 2 above,

(B) Permanent disability indemnity in accordance with paragraph 3 above,

    Less the sum of $__none____ payable to applicant's attorney as the reasonable value of services rendered.

    Less liens in accordance with Paragraph 7 above,

(C) Further medical treatment in accordance with Paragraph 4 above,

(D) Reimbursement for medical-legal expenses in accordance with Paragraph 5 above,

(E)

_____
Dated:

_____
Workers' Compensation Judge
WORKERS' COMPENSATION APPEALS BOARD

Copy served on all persons listed on
Official Address Record.

Date: _____

By: _____
            (Signature)

DWC WCAB FORM 3 (REV. 7-90)   (Page 3)   DEPARTMENT OF INDUSTRIAL RELATIONS
DIVISION OF WORKERS' COMPENSATION

⚠ THE SDI LIEN

If you received SDI (state disability insurance) payments from the EDD for any periods of time that you were entitled to receive permanent disability payments, the EDD can have that amount deducted from your final permanent disability award. (LC § 4904.) This is usually a problem only if your case goes to trial and the judge determines that you received SDI benefits after you were permanent and stationary. If your case settles, however, make sure the insurance company agrees to be responsible for the SDI lien.

You may also request that the following language be included in Paragraph 7: "The company agrees to hold the Applicant harmless therefrom." This means that if the insurance company can't successfully resolve the outstanding lien with the creditor, and the creditor attempts to sue you in civil court, the insurance company will agree to defend you. Many insurance adjusters won't agree to add this language, but it's worth asking. If yours refuses, press the issue but don't blow your settlement over the company's refusal to do so.

Paragraph 8. Any miscellaneous agreements between you and the company can, and usually should, be set out here. Here are some examples:

- Any agreement you have with the insurance company regarding waiving or declining vocational rehabilitation benefits should be explained in detail. Be sure to include any amount of money the insurance company has agreed to pay you, if appropriate.
- If you have agreed to accept cash to resolve a past due temporary disability issue, you and the insurance company might set forth your understanding that "retroactive temporary disability in the sum of (amount) is to be paid outside of this agreement within 25 days of approval."
- Include any agreement that the insurance company will reimburse you for your out-of-pocket mileage or medical expenses. This could include prescription as well as nonprescription drugs you paid for.

Signature: You must sign the Stipulations with Request for Award. There is no need to have it witnessed or notarized.

Once you sign the document, make a copy for your records and send the original to the insurance company. The Stips must be approved by a Workers' Compensation Appeals judge, and a document entitled "Award" must be signed by the judge. If the judge does not believe the agreement adequately compensates you, or finds other problems, the judge will point them out to you and ask you if you still want to proceed

with the settlement. (See Section E, below, for more on the hearing to approve your settlement.)

2. Reviewing a Compromise and Release (C&R)

It's extremely important to make sure all of the information in the Compromise and Release (C&R) document is correct. Understand that by signing this settlement document, you make a complete and final settlement of your workers' compensation claim. In other words, when you settle by C&R, you will no longer have any right to have your medical treatment paid by the insurance company, nor will you have the right to file a petition to reopen your case. What you agree to receive in the C&R will be the only money you'll get in your case.

Following is a sample C&R. The document the insurance company provides will already be filled in. Here are the important issues to look for.

Paragraph 1. Verify that your correct occupation is filled in. Next, make certain that the correct date of injury has been listed. Sometimes the insurance company will try to include additional dates of injury to preclude any other potential claims you may have. For example, the insurance company may list all dates you were employed or list the entire year before your injury as a continuous trauma date of injury.

COMPROMISE AND RELEASE
PLEASE SEE INSTRUCTIONS ON
REVERSE OF PAGE 2 BEFORE
COMPLETING FORM

STATE OF CALIFORNIA
DEPARTMENT OF INDUSTRIAL RELATIONS
DIVISION OF INDUSTRIAL ACCIDENTS
WORKERS' COMPENSATION APPEALS BOARD

CASE NO. __BV8888__

SOCIAL SECURITY NO. __999-99-9999__

Betty White
_____
APPLICANT (EMPLOYEE)

ADDRESS

Home Retail
_____
CORRECT NAME OF EMPLOYER

ADDRESS

ABC Insurance
_____
CORRECT NAME OF INSURANCE CARRIER

ADDRESS

1. The injured employee claims that while employed as a __accountant__
(OCCUPATION AT TIME OF INJURY)

on __8/28/XX__ at __Martinez__ , __CA__ , by the employer
(DATE OF INJURY)   (CITY)   (STATE)

(s)he sustained injury arising out of and in the course of employment to __both arms and back__ .
(STATE WHAT PARTS OF BODY WERE INJURED)

2. The parties hereby agree to settle any and all claims on account of said injury by the payment of the sum of $ __30,000__ in addition to any sums heretofore paid by the employer or the insurer to the employee, less amounts set forth in Paragraph No. 6.

3. Upon approval of this compromise agreement by the Workers' Compensation Appeals Board or a workers' compensation judge and payment in accordance with the provisions hereof, said employee releases and forever discharges said employer and insurance carrier from all claims and causes of action, whether now known or ascertained, or which may hereafter arise or develop as a result of said injury, including any and all liability of said employer and said insurance carrier and each of them to the dependents, heirs, executors, representatives, administrators or assigns of said employee.

4. Unless otherwise expressly provided herein, approval of this agreement RELEASES ANY AND ALL CLAIMS OF APPLICANT'S DEPENDENTS TO DEATH BENEFITS RELATING TO INJURY OR INJURIES COVERED BY THIS COMPROMISE AGREEMENT. The parties have considered the release of these benefits in arriving at the sum in Paragraph No. 2.

5. Unless otherwise expressly ordered by a workers' compensation judge, approval of this agreement DOES NOT RELEASE ANY CLAIM APPLICANT MAY NOW OR HEREAFTER HAVE FOR REHABILITATION OR BENEFITS IN CONNECTION WITH REHABILITATION.

6. The parties represent that the following facts are true: (If facts are disputed, state what each party contends under Paragraph No. 10.)

__4/19/63__   __$800/week__   __In dispute__
DATE OF BIRTH   ACTUAL EARNINGS AT TIME OF INJURY   LAST DAY OFF WORK DUE TO THIS INJURY

PAYMENTS MADE BY EMPLOYER OR INSURANCE CARRIER
TEMPORARY DISABILITY INDEMNITY   WEEKLY RATE   PERIODS COVERED

__Applicant has been adequately compensated to present__
PERMANENT DISABILITY INDEMNITY   TOTAL MEDICAL AND HOSPITAL BILLS
__$3,000__   __$7,990__

BENEFITS CLAIMED BY INJURED EMPLOYEE
BEGINNING AND ENDING DATES OF ALL PERIODS OFF DUE TO THIS INJURY   MEDICAL AND HOSPITAL BILLS PAID BY EMPLOYEE

__In dispute__   __Unknown__
TOTAL UNPAID MEDICAL AND HOSPITAL EXPENSE   ESTIMATED FUTURE MEDICAL EXPENSE

To Be Paid By: __Applicant except as set in Para 7__ To Be Paid By: __Applicant__

THE FOLLOWING AMOUNTS ARE TO BE DEDUCTED FROM THE SETTLEMENT AMOUNT:

$ __3,000__ PAYABLE TO __Applicant__ $ _____ PAYABLE TO _____

$ _____ PAYABLE TO _____ $ _____ PAYABLE TO _____

$ _____ PAYABLE TO _____ $ _____ PAYABLE TO _____

LEAVING A BALANCE OF $ __27,000__ , less approved attorney fee (See Paragraph No. 9), payable to applicant. (If payment is to be other than in a lump sum, or there is additional information, specify on separate page(s).)

151

DIA WCAB FORM 15 (REV. 1983) (PAGE 1)

88 84455

EXAMPLE: Assume the date of your injury was 9/9/01. The C&R lists 9/9/01, as well as a date of injury of 9/9/00 to 9/9/01. Unless your injury was caused in part by a cumulative trauma that occurred over this period of time, it's best not to accept this.

Check to see that the city and state where the injury occurred are correctly listed.

In the last blank, make sure the insurance company has listed only the parts of your body that you have injured. Some companies try to list other body parts that were not even claimed as injured. This may be important if you later need to file a new claim for a new body part, alleging injury to a body part the insurance company listed in the C&R. For example, if you only claimed you injured your right leg, don't allow the insurance company to add "back." If at a later date you want to file a claim for a back injury, you might have waived your right to do so.

Paragraph 2. Make certain the correct settlement amount is listed.

Paragraph 3. This is a standard clause that states you're settling all aspects of your case, including any and all injuries that resulted from or may arise in the future as a result of the date of injury. In other words, if you later learn of a new body part that was injured on the same date of injury, you can't file a new claim.

Paragraph 4. This is a standard clause that states that you are waiving any right that your dependents may have to recover death benefits in the event that you die as a result of this injury. In the vast majority of cases, this is fine, because the injury isn't that serious.

If, however, your injury is life-threatening (you may die within 240 weeks of the injury date), you should not agree to this paragraph unless the insurance company pays you for doing so. How much extra you can get will depend upon how likely or imminent your death is, and whether or not you have any dependents. Settling your death claim rights in a C&R will allow you, rather than your dependents, to get the money, if that's what you want. Or, if you don't waive death benefits and you should die as a result of your injury, your dependents may be entitled to recover death benefits. Chapter 15 explains what you or your dependents would be entitled to. Especially if you have dependents under the age of 18, this can entail a significant amount of money.

If there is any possibility that you could die as a result of your industrial injury, you may want to seriously consider seeing a workers' compensation attorney.

Paragraph 5. This standard paragraph states that unless otherwise stated in the C&R, you are not waiving any rights you may have to vocational rehabilitation benefits.

Paragraph 6. Carefully check this paragraph for accuracy. If you find any inaccuracies, you may contact the insurance company to make the correction or handwrite or type in the words "in dispute" in the appropriate place.

First, make certain your date of birth is correct. Next, check to see if you agree with the amount inserted as your average weekly wage. If you don't agree with the figure, contact the claims adjuster and request that the amount you believe is correct is inserted instead. If the insurance company won't agree, this should read "in dispute." The same goes for the last day off work due to the injury.

Under "payments made by employer or insurance company," review the amount of temporary disability indemnity paid to you, the weekly temporary disability rate and periods covered. If you do not agree with the amount, you can request that "in dispute" be inserted.

The insurance company will insert the amount it has paid you in permanent disability advances and the total value of the medical treatment it has paid on your behalf. Because all permanent disability advances will be deducted from the amount listed in Paragraph 2, make sure this figure is correct. However, any amounts listed for temporary disability or medical treatment paid will not be deducted from your settlement.

IF YOU DON'T KNOW HOW MUCH YOU'VE RECEIVED

You can ask the insurance company for a computer print-out of permanent disability advances (dates and amounts), or copies of canceled checks.

7. Liens not mentioned in Paragraph No. 6 are to be disposed of as follows: _____ Defendants to pay or adjust the liens of Dr. Smith, Dr. Jones, Acme Imaging with jurisdiction reserved with the WCAB, Applicant to be held harmless

8. For the purpose of determining the lien claim(s) filed for benefits paid pursuant to the Unemployment Insurance Code or for benefits furnished by lien claimants defined in Labor Code Sec. 4903.1, the parties propose reduction of the lien claim(s) in accordance with formulae attached.

9. Applicant's (employee's) attorney requests a fee of $ ___ N/A ___ . Amount of attorney fee previously paid, if any, $ ___ None ___ .

10. Reason for Compromise, special provisions regarding rehabilitation and death benefit claims, and additional information:

See Addenda "A," "B," "C" and "D."

11. It is agreed by all parties hereto that the filing of this document is the filing of an application on behalf of the employee, and that the WCAB may in its discretion set the matter for hearing as a regular application, reserving to the parties the right to put in issue any of the facts admitted herein, and that if hearing is held with this document used as an application the defendants shall have available to them all defenses that were available as of the date of filing of this document, and that the WCAB may thereafter either approve said Compromise Agreement and Release or disapprove the same and issue Findings and Award after hearing has been held and the matter regularly submitted for decision.

WITNESS *the signature hereof this* _____ *day of* _____ , 19 ___ , *at* _____

_____   _____
WITNESS   APPLICANT (EMPLOYEE)   (DATE)

_____   _____
WITNESS   (DATE)

THE APPLICANT'S (EMPLOYEE'S) SIGNATURE MUST BE ATTESTED BY TWO DISINTERESTED PERSONS   _____
OR ACKNOWLEDGED BEFORE A NOTARY PUBLIC.   (DATE)

                                                                              _____
                                                                              (DATE)

STATE OF CALIFORNIA   }
County of _____

On this _____ day of _____ A.D., 19 ___ , before me, _____ ,

a Notary Public in and for the said County and State, residing therein, duly commissioned and sworn, personally appeared _____

_____

known to me to be the person__ whose name__ _____
subscribed to the within Instrument, and acknowledged to me that __he__ executed the same.

IN WITNESS WHEREOF, I have hereunto set my hand and affixed my official seal the day and year in this Certificate first above written.

_____
Notary Public in and for said County and State of California

The next section of Paragraph 6 is "Benefits claimed by injured employee." Check that the correct date is listed for the beginning and ending dates of all periods off due to the injury. Make sure that the insurance company has inserted the amount you paid for hospital bills. If you disagree with any of these figures, you can have "in dispute" handwritten or typed in.

Under the section "Total unpaid medical and hospital expenses to be paid by," you will be lucky if the word "defendant" is inserted here. Defendant refers to the insurance company. This means that the insurance company agrees to pay for any outstanding medical bills as of the date of this agreement. Unfortunately, most insurance companies will not agree to this, and will include the phrase, "By applicant except as set forth in Paragraph 7." This means that the insurance company will agree to pay for all the medical bills where liens have been filed in the case, but you'll be responsible for payment of any outstanding bills where no liens have been filed. It is therefore important that you pay close attention to the discussion regarding Paragraph 7, below.

Under "Estimated future medical expenses to be paid by," the insurance company will have typed in "Applicant." This refers to you, since by agreeing to settle by a C&R, you are accepting responsibility for all your future medical treatment.

Under "The following amounts are to be deducted from the settlement amount," the insurance company will type in any amounts that it will take as a credit or deduction from the settlement amount set out in Paragraph 2. This would include any known amounts for money already advanced to you based on your permanent disability (also set forth in Paragraph 6 under "payments made by employer or insurance company").

Finally, under the section that begins "Leaving a balance of $_____ ," the insurance company will type in the amount you will receive after deducting credit for any permanent disability advances. Make sure this is the correct amount. You arrive at this figure by taking the gross settlement amount in Paragraph 2 and subtracting the amount you have already received by way of permanent disability advances, if any.

The insurance company will usually type in something like, "The insurance company will take credit for any permanent disability advances made to applicant subsequent to the date of this Compromise and Release." This is fine. The insurance company is just making sure that if it pays you any more advances after the date you sign this agreement, and before you receive your settlement check, it will get credit for the payments.

Paragraph 7. This paragraph is extremely important. It lists all of the outstanding liens (debts) the insurance company agrees to pay as part of the settlement, other than attorney fees and amounts for unpaid medical and hospital bills listed in Paragraph 6. (Note that this paragraph does not address reimbursement for medical care you paid for yourself; those costs are also listed in Paragraph 6.)

Make sure no doctor, medical facility or anyone else who has provided you with medical treatment, tests, examinations and reports or other services to help prove your case has been overlooked. Only the listed bills will be paid by the insurance company.

Even if the insurance company claims it paid a particular lien claimant, it is best to list it anyway, with the provision that "jurisdiction is reserved to the Appeals Board to resolve any disputes."

If there are outstanding medical bills for which no liens have been filed, you should do one of the following:

- Contact those doctors or companies and request that they file a lien before you sign the C&R. Then negotiate with the insurance company to agree to pay the bills by specifically listing them in the C&R.
- Get the insurance company to include language that it will pay or negotiate any outstanding bills that are a result of your injury. (Most insurance companies probably won't agree to this because there's no way to know what might be outstanding.)

⚠ OUTSTANDING BILLS MAY BE YOUR RESPONSIBILITY

If you do not make these specific arrangements for the insurance company to agree to be responsible for the bills, any bills that are outstanding after you sign the C&R will be your responsibility, and the creditor could sue you in civil court for the money.

Make sure that Employment Development Department (EDD) is listed here if it filed a lien in your case for reimbursement for money paid to you for disability periods that should have been the responsibility of the workers' compensation insurance company.

⚠ THE SDI LIEN

If you received SDI (state disability insurance) payments from the EDD for any periods of time that you were entitled to receive permanent disability payments, the EDD can have that amount deducted from your final permanent disability award. (LC § 4904.) This is usually a problem only if your case goes to trial and the judge determines that you received SDI benefits after you were permanent and stationary. If your case settles, however, make sure the insurance company agrees to be responsible for the SDI lien.

You may also request that the following language be included in Paragraph 7: "The company agrees to hold the Applicant harmless therefrom." This means that if the insurance company can't successfully resolve the outstanding lien with the creditor, and the creditor attempts to sue you in civil court, the insurance company will agree to defend you. Many insurance adjusters won't agree to add this language, but it's worth asking. If yours refuses, press the issue but don't blow your settlement over the company's refusal to do so.

Paragraph 8. This is standard language regarding payment of lien claimants.

Paragraph 9. This paragraph sets forth your attorney's fee, if you are represented. The amount of the attorney fee is generally between 12% and 15% of the amount set forth in Paragraph 2, and will be deducted from your settlement. This fee arrangement must be listed in a document you signed when your attorney took your case, called Attorney Fee Disclosure Statement. The attorney may choose to list "reasonable fees, to be approved by the Appeals Board."

Paragraph 10. Here you'll find the reasons for the Compromise and Release. Due to lack of room on the form, the insurance company will usually refer to addenda (usually labeled "A," "B," "C" and so on). The following are samples of the most common addenda you'll likely run into. Although each C&R may be arranged a little differently, most will cover the issues presented below, although not necessarily in the same order.

⚠ ADDENDA USUALLY CONTAIN BOILERPLATE LANGUAGE
The insurance company will probably use standard, boilerplate language in the addenda. If you've agreed to anything out of the ordinary, it may not be correctly stated, so check each addendum carefully.

a. Addendum A (Waivers and Agreements)

This addendum sets forth the various waivers and miscellaneous agreements between the parties.

Paragraph 1 explains the reasons you and the defendants have decided to settle your case.

Paragraph 2 is called a "Sumner Waiver" in workers' compensation jargon. It is standard in almost all workers' compensation settlements and is always referred to by its name. The Sumner Waiver waives your dependents' right to any workers' compensation death benefits in the event you should die as a result of your industrial injury. This is really just a restatement of Paragraph 4 of the main body of the C&R. If there is any possibility that your injury may result in your death (within 240 weeks from the date of injury), you should not allow a Sumner Waiver. You should also seek the advice of an attorney.

Paragraph 3 of addendum A is what is referred to in workers' compensation jargon as a "Rogers Waiver," or a "Carter Waiver." We'll refer to it as a Rogers Waiver. A Rogers Waiver is only significant if you are going to participate in vocational rehabilitation training. This waiver states that if you are injured or need treatment while participating in your vocational rehabilitation plan, you will not be able to file a workers' compensation claim for a new injury.

If you are participating in vocational rehabilitation, consider the likelihood of getting injured and decide whether or not you want to agree to a Rogers Waiver. If you don't sign the waiver and you suffer a new injury while participating in vocational rehabilitation, that injury is covered by workers' compensation; if you sign a Rogers Waiver, it isn't. The insurance company will probably want a Rogers Waiver to settle your case if you are still participating in vocational rehabilitation. But this is a matter for negotiation. Workers' compensation lawyers consider that a Rogers Waiver may be worth some money (up to a couple of thousand dollars), depending upon how badly the insurance company wants to settle. On the other hand, the insurance company may refuse to settle until you complete vocational rehabilitation or sign a Rogers waiver. This is where negotiating skills will prove valuable.

Paragraph 4 is an agreement that the defendants are only responsible for those liens (debts) that are listed in the C&R. We already discussed this issue for Paragraph 7 of the main text of the document. If the insurance company includes this clause, make doubly sure that all doctors and others who provided you services have been paid or are listed, and that no outstanding bills remain unaccounted for.

Paragraph 5 is a catchall clause waiving claims to any and all injuries and claims (such as discrimination or wrongful termination) you may have sustained while working for your employer. This is a sneaky way an insurance company may try to get you to unknowingly waive all other potential claims against your employer for which you have not yet filed, including cumulative trauma injuries. Ordinarily, you should not allow a catchall waiver in the agreement unless the defendants pay additional money for it. Remember, the C&R is a settlement of *this* claim; it should not be used to settle potential future claims you may have. If, however, you are certain that you will not be filing any more claims against your employer, you should try to negotiate some additional money for the waiver. The amount is entirely negotiable, but a figure of up to $1,000 or so is probably reasonable for a waiver where you really don't have any potential claims outstanding. If you may have a legitimate claim, the amount should be much higher, if you agree to it at all. Of course, the statute of limitations may determine if you have the right to file any other claim. In short, in many cases you'll be waiving little, if anything by agreeing to waive all future claims.

Paragraph 6 is a standard clause that most insurance companies put in Compromise and Release agreements. This clause says you agree to waive your rights under §1542 of the Civil Code of California. By agreeing to this waiver you are confirming that the Compromise and Release settles any and all claims you may have against this employer for this date of injury, and that you are giving up your right to file for any additional injuries that you might discover later. For example, if you have a back injury and you sign a C&R for the date of injury in which you injured your back, then you later find out that you injured your liver as a result of the same injury, you can't file a new claim.

This is standard procedure for settlement by a Compromise and Release, and it really shouldn't present any problem since, by the time of settlement, any and all parts of body that you injured on that particular date of injury should have been determined and treated. However, because this clause may also bar any other claims for damages you may have outside the workers' compensation claim (see *Jefferson v. California Department of Youth Authority* in Chapter 28), you should always add the following language to the end of that clause: "This clause applies only to this claim."

ADDENDUM "A"

1. A bona fide dispute exists between the parties as to injury, nature, extent and duration of permanent disability, occupation, employment, need for future medical treatment, liability for self-procured medical treatment, medical/legal costs, earnings, temporary disability, rehabilitation, apportionment, transportation expenses, penalties and all other issues. All parties desire to avoid the hazards and delays of litigation. Applicant wishes to receive a lump sum settlement and to control all future medical care; defendants by this settlement are buying their peace.

2. The parties have taken into consideration the release of any and all claims of applicant's dependents to death benefits relating to the injury covered by this Compromise and Release. The parties have considered the release of these benefits in arriving at the amount of this Compromise and Release and the attention of the judge is directed to this fact.

3. In the event applicant elects to participate in vocational rehabilitation at some future date and is found to be a qualified injured worker, applicant expressly waives any potential claims for ordinary compensation benefits and medical treatment for any injury that may be sustained while participating in vocational rehabilitation in compliance with *Rogers vs. WCAB* 168 Cal.App.3rd (1985), *Carter vs. County of L.A.*, 51 CCC 255 (1985), *Weatherspoon vs. St. Ferdinand's School*, 51 CCC 255 (1985) and *Constancio vs. L.A. County* 51 CCC 255 (1986).

4. The only lien claims in existence are stated in this agreement. The applicant guarantees and warrants there are no other or further lien claims and thereby agrees to hold defendants harmless from any claims or cause of action commenced or presented by any lien claimants other than those accounted for herein.

5. This agreement represents full and final settlement of any liability on account of (employer) and the carrier (insurance company) with respect to any and all employment at (employer) during any period when (insurance company) was the workers' compensation insurance carrier, and further is based upon any cumulative trauma or specific injuries that may have occurred during such employment at (employer).

6. Applicant agrees that this release will apply to all unknown and unanticipated injuries and damages resulting from such accident, and all rights under §1542 of the Civil Code of California are hereby expressly waived. Applicant agrees that this release extends and covers employees of the defendants. This clause applies only to this claim.

BY: _____

    Applicant

b. Addendum B (Standard Agreements and Waivers)

Addendum B contains standard language that further clarifies the understanding of the parties. Again, the paragraphs may not appear in the same order or be in the same wording as discussed here.

Paragraph 1 explains that the C&R you are signing is a contract and is the only agreement between you and the defendants on this subject. This is additional legal jargon that is really not needed, but if the insurance company wants to put it in, it's no problem.

Paragraph 2 gives the defendants 25-30 days to mail your settlement check before they are responsible for paying you any interest on the money you settled for. This standard paragraph is okay.

Paragraph 3 tells the Workers' Compensation Appeals Board that you have read the entire C&R, that you understand it and are aware of its legal effect. It further states that you understand that it is a complete and final settlement of your workers' compensation case for all injuries arising out of the dates of injury that are specified in the agreement. In other words, if you later develop problems as a result of your injury, you cannot file a workers' compensation claim.

⚠️ IF YOU ANTICIPATE FUTURE PROBLEMS

As I have repeatedly emphasized, if you don't want to sign away your right to future claims because you believe you later may have problems arising out of your injury, you should not agree to a Compromise and Release. Instead you should settle by way of Stipulations with Request for Award. (See Section D1, above.)

Paragraph 4 states in legal lingo that you are settling your claim on behalf of not only yourself, but anyone else who may have any future claim to these benefits. This is okay.

Paragraph 5 simply states that you have read and understood the agreement and agree to be bound by its terms and provisions.

ADDENDUM "B"

1. This Compromise and Release and attachments contain the entire agreement between the parties hereto and the terms of this release are contractual in nature and not merely a recital.

2. THE CONSIDERATION FOR THIS COMPROMISE AND RELEASE SET FORTH IN PARAGRAPH 2 INCLUDES ANY INTEREST WHICH MAY OTHERWISE BE DUE PRIOR TO THE 25th DAY AFTER APPROVAL THEREOF.

3. The undersigned hereby affirms and acknowledges that he has read the foregoing Compromise and Release Agreement, or had it fully explained to him, and fully understands and appreciates the foregoing words, terms and their legal effect and that this is a full, final compromise, release and settlement of all claims, demands, actions or causes of action, known or unknown, suspected or unsuspected, arising out of his employment with the employer set forth within this Compromise and Release. Further, it is agreed this Compromise and Release shall extend to and pertain to any and all injuries known or unknown, to any and all parts of the body, whether by way of specific injury or continuous trauma, arising out of the employment with the employer set forth herein.

4. In further consideration of the payment of the aforesaid sum, applicant agrees that this release extends to and covers the executors, administrators, representatives, heirs and successors, assigns, officers, directors, agents, servants and employees of the defendants, and each of them, and the physicians, surgeons and nurses retained by the defendants, and each of them, whether acting individually or on behalf of them, or either of them.

5. THE PERSON WHOSE SIGNATURE APPEARS BELOW HAS READ AND UNDERSTOOD EACH ATTACHMENT AND FURTHER TERMS OF COMPROMISE AND RELEASE AND HEREBY AGREES TO ALL PROVISIONS.

BY: _____

    Applicant

c. Addendum C (Non-Interest in Vocational Rehabilitation)

  See *Cisneros v. WCAB* in Chapter 28.

Addendum C addresses vocational rehabilitation. If you have completed a vocational rehabilitation program or are currently participating in one, this addendum will probably not be attached to your C&R. If you have not participated in vocational rehabilitation, it likely will be included and you should read it carefully.

The provisions in the addendum normally state that you have indicated that, for the present time, you are not interested in participating in vocational rehabilitation, and are not entitled to retroactive vocational rehabilitation benefits. It will state that should you want to participate in the future, you will notify the insurance company. It also sets forth the time period you have in which to request vocational rehabilitation benefits.

Here are the things to watch out for in this type of addendum. If these issues affect you, negotiate with the insurance company to have them crossed out or modified.

- Language that says you are not a qualified injured worker (QIW). You must be a QIW to be entitled to vocational rehabilitation benefits.
- If it has already been determined that you are a qualified injured worker, language stating that the insurance company does not admit that you are entitled to benefits, or that your entitlement to vocational rehabilitation benefits will be determined in the future.
- Language that waives your right to collect retroactive maintenance allowance (VRMA), unless the amount you are settling for includes settlement of that issue.

ADDENDUM "C"

DECLARATION OF NON-INTEREST/REHABILITATION WAIVER

Applicant realizes that vocational rehabilitation is voluntary on his part and the applicant does not wish to undergo any such rehabilitation at this time. Furthermore, the applicant understands his right to rehabilitation benefits, but does not now nor has he in the past had any interest in pursuing rehabilitation benefits.

Applicant hereby waives all rights to rehabilitation benefits until such time that he notifies the defendants that he wishes a determination of Qualified Injured Worker status and a decision as to whether or not he is entitled to vocational rehabilitation benefits.

Any claim for present or past rehabilitation is waived, with the understanding that such waiver will be effective until such time as applicant manifests his desire for a determination regarding his rehabilitation status and makes a written, timely and proper demand for rehabilitation benefits upon the defendants.

No admission is made by the defendants that the applicant is a Qualified Injured Worker entitled to vocational rehabilitation benefits, and any determination regarding the applicant's entitlement to vocational rehabilitation benefits will be made in the future, in the event the employee wishes to pursue his possible right to vocational rehabilitation benefits.

The period within which applicant may request vocational rehabilitation benefits is one year from the date of the last finding of permanent disability by the Appeals Board, one year from the date the Appeals Board approves a Compromise and Release, or five years from the date of injury, where the original injury causes a need for vocational rehabilitation services, whichever is later (Labor Code Section 5405.5).

BY: _____

   Applicant

d. Addendum D (Waiver of Rights to Vocational Rehabilitation)

Addendum D, also called the "Thomas Waiver" in workers' compensation jargon, should not be present in your agreement unless AOE/COE is an issue—whether your injury was caused by your employment. This addendum constitutes a complete waiver of any rights you have to vocational rehabilitation based upon the theory that if your case were to go to trial, the Appeals Board would probably find that you did not have a work injury. If you have little or no chance of winning if you go to trial, as a last resort you may choose to sign this waiver to induce the defendants to pay a small amount to settle the case. You and the insurance company must provide the facts on which the waiver is based. (See Chapter 3, Section C8, for more on AOE/COE.)

ADDENDUM "D"

STIPULATION RE LABOR CODE SECTION 139.5 REHAB

Applicant hereby agrees that he has been fully compensated for any claim for vocational rehabilitation benefits which may have accrued through the date of his signing this Compromise and Release, and he further states that he is not presently interested in vocational rehabilitation benefits.

The parties further request a finding by the Board that there exists a reasonable and serious dispute as to whether the claimed disabilities arose from the employment and that therefore the defendants are relieved from any liability for benefits under Labor Code Section 139.5.

The factual basis for such a finding is as follows. If this matter were to go to trial, defendants would produce witnesses that would testify that the applicant was not injured as a result of his fall, but injured himself as a result of an accident while driving his all-terrain vehicle the following day.

A serious AOE/COE question exists as to applicant's injuries. Therefore, this stipulation is made and a finding requested pursuant to *Thomas vs. Sports Chalet*, 42 CCC 625 (1977).

BY: _____

    Applicant

e. Addendum E (Characterization of Settlement Proceeds)

If you are receiving Social Security disability, Supplemental Security Income or payments from a private disability policy, it may be extremely important that your C&R addresses how your settlement proceeds are to be characterized. Let's back up just a bit.

Some disability programs will take a credit or offset for moneys you receive in your workers' compensation settlement, and reduce or limit the disability benefits you're entitled to. Many disability policy providers will not, however, take credit for money that is earmarked to help pay your future medical expenses (although Medicare and Medi-Cal may take a credit for those payments).

For these reasons, it may be prudent to designate in the C&R that a certain sum of the settlement is for future medical expenses and is being paid to you at a designated monthly rate. Addendum E explains how the money you will receive is to be classified. That means you may designate part of the settlement as future medical expenses. Accompanying Addendum E is a supplemental order to be signed by a judge. This order reiterates the characterization of settlement proceeds set forth in Addendum E.

RESEARCH CREDIT OR OFFSET RULES
To find out if your workers' compensation settlement will affect benefits you're currently receiving, contact the appropriate disability providers or agencies. You may also wish to consult with an Information and Assistance officer or a workers' compensation attorney to make sure you're making the best possible arrangements in your settlement.

ADDENDUM "E"

CHARACTERIZATION OF SETTLEMENT

(A) After negotiation between the parties, the following items have been reached in regard to the settlement proceeds being received:

(1) Total amount of Compromise and Release: $25,000

(2) Temporary disability should have been paid to the Applicant between 3/1/year and 9/7/year.

(3) Temporary disability should have been paid at the rate of $336/week.

(4) Total temporary disability benefits that should have been paid to the Applicant: $10,000.

(5) Applicant was actually paid temporary disability benefits in the amount of $7,000.

(6) Of the above referenced Compromise and Release amount, $3,000 is being paid to Applicant for temporary disability.

(7) Included in the Compromise and Release, is the sum of $10,000 to be used for future medical care, in accordance with the recommendation of Dr. Shirley Smith.

(8) After deduction for attorney fees, medical care and temporary disability, the sum of $12,000 remains. This sum is being paid to Applicant Jane Dowry due to lifelong permanent disability which will interfere with Applicant's ability to engage in gainful employment for the remainder of her life. This sum is being paid to Applicant in a lump sum based upon a life expectancy of 25 years and payments at the rate of $40/week beginning on 11/1/year at the rate of $173 per month. This is based upon *Sciarotta vs. Bowen*, 837 F.2d 135, using the "Hartman" formula.

(B) The specific characterization of the settlement proceeds in this matter, as set forth above, are an essential element of the Compromise and Release in this matter and it is specifically requested that the judge reviewing this Compromise and Release make a specific finding in the order of approval as to the characterization of the benefits set forth in this Compromise and Release.

(C) A finding is requested as to the life expectancy of the employee based upon the life expectancy tables found in the *Vital Statistics of the United States,* 1988, Life Tables Volume 2, Section 6, DHHS Pub. No. (OHS) 89-1147, to wit; Employees' life expectancy as a female, as of 11/1/year is 25 years.

(D) It is agreed between the parties that this settlement shall be paid in a lump sum, but it shall be prorated over the life expectancy of the employee since this is a lifetime settlement. The rate per week would be found by dividing the net lump sum amount to the employee by the number of weeks of her life expectancy. Proration shall start the month of receipt of the lump sum and will continue into the future.

(E) Paragraph D referring to the proration has been noted and is approved. As of this date, the employee's life expectancy is 25 years. Paragraph A is noted and approved.

SUPPLEMENTAL ORDER APPROVING
COMPROMISE AND RELEASE AND
FINDINGS OF FACTS

Compromise and Release having been submitted in the above referenced matter, and order approving having been issued this date, the following additional findings are made:

(1) That the terms of the Compromise and Release agreement set forth herein are incorporated in whole in this order approving.

(2) That Applicant Jane Dowry will receive, after attorney's fees are deducted, the sum of $25,000. That amount is to be construed as follows:

　(a) $3,000 is to be construed as temporary disability benefits that should have been provided during the period of 3/1/year to 9/7/year.

　(b) $10,000 is to be construed as payments for future medical care as deemed necessary by the treating doctors.

　(c) The lump sum remainder of the Compromise and Release amount is to be construed as periodic payments of permanent disability at the rate of $40 per week for the remainder of Applicant's lifetime.

_____   _____
Date   WORKERS' COMPENSATION JUDGE

---

f. Signing the C&R

Make sure you review the entire C&R agreement carefully, including all the addenda. If you've received permission from the insurance company to cross out any language or write anything in, initial each instance.

Your signature must either be witnessed by two people who are not related to you, or it must be notarized. Legally, it doesn't matter which route you follow—do whichever is easier. If you're having two witnesses sign, they must be over age 18 and not be related to you or entitled to receive money from your workers' compensation case. If you want your signature notarized, you can look in the phone book under "notary public" to find a notary. Notaries may charge up to $10 to notarize a document. Or check with your bank or a real estate office, which may do the notarization for free.

Once you sign the C&R, make a photocopy for your records and send the original back to the insurance company.

E. Attend an Adequacy Hearing

You will need to attend an adequacy hearing at the Workers' Compensation Appeals Board. This is a short meeting in which a judge reviews the proposed settlement documents and decides if they are adequate. (See Chapter 24, Section B2, for more on adequacy hearings.) ■

Preparing Your Case

I f your workers' compensation case goes to trial, you and the insurance company will appear before a Workers' Compensation Appeals Board judge. If you don't have a lawyer, the judge will walk you through the trial process. The proceeding is designed to get at the truth without scaring you half to death.

Appeals Board hearings are relatively informal and the judge will give you the benefit of the doubt. You won't need to follow the rules of evidence lawyers love to spout in court trials (for example, "I object, your honor, on the basis that no foundation has been laid for the introduction of that document").

During the trial, you will probably need to present evidence—information you want the judge to consider as the basis for making decisions in your favor. Evidence may take many forms, including your oral (spoken) testimony, testimony of witnesses, medical reports and documents such as wage statements and injury reports.

Now, here is a crucial point. *You should begin preparing your case as if it were going to result in a contested trial from the moment you file your claim.* This is true even though most cases settle and never actually go to trial. It's only common sense to ask, "Why prepare for a trial that may never occur?" If you wait until you realize that settlement won't be possible, it will be too late to gather and organize the necessary evidence.

If you've followed the suggestions in Chapter 6, you probably have the evidence you need. In this chapter, you'll learn how to put your evidence in the context of the possible issues (disputes) that are likely to be decided at your trial. You'll also learn about legal procedures for obtaining any evidence you may be missing. Finally, you'll find out how to prepare for your upcoming hearing.

WHAT ARE TRIALS AND HEARINGS?

The terms "trials" and "hearings" are often used interchangeably in this book. But in case you are thinking that, for once, workers' compensation terms have been made easy to understand, think again. It turns out that while a trial is always a hearing, a hearing is not necessarily a trial. Here's how to differentiate between the two:

- **Hearing.** This refers to any time your claim is set before the Workers' Compensation Appeals Board for any reason. A hearing would include a pre-trial conference or Mandatory Settlement Conference to try to settle your case, a "lien conference" to deal with the payment of medical bills, a hearing in which a judge orders a party to do something prior to trial (such as to attend a medical appointment or pay benefits), as well as an actual trial.
- **Trial (which by definition is also a hearing).** This refers to a proceeding heard before a workers' compensation judge, where both sides offer evidence and put on witnesses trying to prove or disprove issues regarding a workers' compensation claim.

A. Identify Possible Issues in Dispute

To properly prepare for your trial, it will help to identify and understand all issues that may be in dispute (not agreed upon). Disputed issues may be raised by the insurance company at the outset of your case. However, it's quite likely that some issues will be added and others eliminated as your case proceeds. For this reason, it's wise to assume that the insurance company may contest all aspects of your claim, until you know for certain otherwise. This will allow you to be prepared for all possible contingencies.

The following two-page "Issues That May Be In Dispute" chart lists key disputed issues that may be resolved at workers' compensation hearings. Scan the first column and check all issues that are in dispute. Then look over the second column to see if you have the evidence to back up your claim. If you don't, you'll need to do your best to find documentation or testimony that will help prove your case.

ISSUES THAT MAY BE IN DISPUTE

Issues in dispute (and where to get more information)	Evidence that may support your point of view

COVERAGE OF CLAIM

☐ **AOE/COE:** whether injury arose out of and occurred in the course of employment (Chapter 3, Section C8)

injury reports, emergency room records, medical reports, your testimony, testimony of witnesses who saw the injury occur

☐ **insurance company at time of injury:** which company is responsible for paying benefits (Chapter 1, Section C1; also see Chapter 8, Section C1, if employer was not insured)

search by Workers' Compensation Insurance Rating Bureau (WCIRB), letters from insurance companies

☐ **employment:** whether you were an employee or an independent contractor (Chapter 3, Section A2)

witnesses who can attest to your job duties, employment contracts, your testimony, W-2 tax forms

JOB AND WAGES

☐ **wages at time of injury:** how much you earned determines your disability rates

pay stubs (last 12 months of employment), W-2 tax forms from previous year, your personnel records, employer's testimony, your testimony, testimony of co-workers

☐ **occupation:** determines your employment group number, which affects your permanent disability rating

testimony of co-workers, your testimony, documents that describe your job duties (if you agree with the description)

INJURY AND TREATMENT

☐ **date of injury:** determines your disability rate

completed DWC-1 form, work accident report, medical records, employee's personnel records, your testimony, testimony of witnesses who saw the injury occur

☐ **part(s) of body injured:** whether denied injury will be covered

medical reports, your testimony, testimony of witnesses who saw the injury occur, completed DWC-1 form

☐ **nature and extent of injury:** whether you injured yourself as badly as you claim

medical reports, your testimony (note that the insurance company may have photos or videotapes of you doing activities you claim you can't)

☐ **date of permanent and stationary status:** determines when temporary disability ends (Chapter 9, Section E)

medical reports, your testimony

☐ **type of current medical treatment needed:** determines reasonableness and necessity of treatment when disputed

medical reports, your testimony

BENEFITS

☐ **past due temporary disability**

medical reports, your testimony, EDD certifications of disability

☐ **temporary disability rate**

wage statements for last year of employment, W-2 tax forms from previous year, employer's testimony, personnel records, your testimony, testimony of co-workers

(continued)

ISSUES THAT MAY BE IN DISPUTE (CONTINUED)

Issues in dispute (and where to get more information)	Evidence that may support your point of view
☐ **permanent disability amount**	wage statements for the last year of employment, W-2 tax forms from previous year, employer's testimony, personnel records, your testimony, testimony of co-workers, collective bargaining agreement showing scheduled wage and salary increases
☐ **medical costs and mileage paid for and not reimbursed**	your testimony, receipts, canceled checks, requests for reimbursement, mileage logs
☐ **need for particular medical treatment**	medical records, medical reports, your testimony, letters from insurance carrier
☐ **need for future medical**	medical reports, test results, your testimony
☐ **penalties for late payment of benefits** (See Chapter 19, Section C9)	your testimony, postmarked envelope showing when checks were sent, copies of bills from medical providers showing unpaid balances

LIENS AND ATTORNEY FEES

☐ **medical liens**	copies of green liens, your testimony, bills
☐ **other liens,** including Employment Development Department (EDD) liens and liens by attorneys	copies of liens, copies of EDD goldenrod liens, your testimony
☐ **attorney fees,** if you previously had a lawyer and there is dispute over how much he is entitled to	copies of liens, your testimony, prior signed Attorney Fee Disclosure Statements

OTHER MATTERS

☐ **treating doctor,** if you have seen more than one doctor	your testimony, medical records
☐ **apportionment:** where insurance company claims your medical condition is partially or all due to a pre-existing or subsequent condition or event	medical reports, medical records, your testimony *(See an Information and Assistance officer or a lawyer; this is beyond scope of the book)*
☐ **statute of limitations:** where insurance company alleges you did not file your workers' compensation claim on time	your testimony, DWC-1 form, medical reports *(See an Information and Assistance officer or a lawyer; this is beyond scope of the book)*
☐ **death case:** who are total and partial surviving dependents	copies of tax returns, birth certificates, marriage certificates
☐ **death case:** amount of burial expenses or death benefits	copies of bills for burial expenses, canceled checks
☐ **rehabilitation appeal**	*(See an Information and Assistance officer or a lawyer; this is beyond scope of the book)*
☐ **unlawful discrimination**	*(See an Information and Assistance officer or a lawyer; this is beyond scope of the book)*
☐ **other:**	

PERIODICALLY REVIEW ISSUES IN DISPUTE

As your case progresses, the issues in dispute may change. Do your best to keep track of the issues in dispute. This will allow you to always know what you may have to deal with at trial, and therefore help you be prepared.

B. How to Prove (or Disprove) Disputed Issues

If there are any issues in dispute, the parties (you and the workers' compensation insurance company) will have to provide evidence to prove or disprove a particular point of view.

If your case goes to trial, you, as the injured worker, will testify first. This should allow you to establish your basic case. Only after you testify (and call any witnesses to support your position), may the insurance company offer evidence that your claim is not true. If you're not represented by a lawyer, make sure you have your evidence organized and readily accessible. A judge will help you through the process.

> **EXAMPLE:** Raphael claims that he injured himself at work and therefore is entitled to workers' compensation benefits. The workers' compensation insurance company disputes this, claiming he hurt himself playing football. It's up to Raphael to introduce at least some evidence that what he claims is true. Once he establishes his basic case, the insurance company will have a chance to offer evidence that he did not suffer an injury at work.

1. Ways to Prove Your Case

"Proving your case" simply refers to establishing by 51% of the evidence that the issues you are trying to prove at your hearing are true. Proving your case can be accomplished in a variety of ways. These are the most common methods:

- presumptions—this sounds complicated but it's simply a fact or legal issue that is considered to be true until proven otherwise (Section B3, below, covers this)
- your testimony in court
- testimony of other witnesses in court
- documents, such as payroll slips, W-2 forms, employment records and injury reports
- medical evidence, such as doctor's reports or other medical records and test results, and

- deposition testimony—prior testimony of witnesses taken under oath in front of a court reporter and then transcribed and signed by the witness under penalty of perjury.

2. Insurance Company May Raise Affirmative Defenses

The insurance company may try to raise issues that are known as "affirmative defenses"—issues that, if proven, will either defeat or limit your entitlement to some workers' compensation benefits.

The insurance company may try to raise (and if it does, has the burden of proof on) some of these affirmative issues:

- **Independent contractor status.** The insurance company may try to show that you were an independent contractor, not an employee, and therefore excluded from receiving workers' compensation benefits. (To help prepare your response, see Chapter 3, Section A2.)
- **Intoxication.** The insurance company may try to prove that your injury was caused by intoxication from alcohol or misuse of drugs, thereby making you ineligible for workers' compensation benefits. (See Chapter 3, Section C1.)
- **Willful misconduct.** The insurance company may try to show that you are ineligible for workers' compensation benefits because your injury was caused by intentional misconduct, such as horseplay or disobeying a company policy. (To help prepare your defense if this issue is raised, see Chapter 3, Section C4.)
- **Aggravation of disability by unreasonable conduct.** The insurance company may try to show that your actions unreasonably contributed to or aggravated your injury. If it is determined that your conduct was unreasonable, the insurance company is entitled to subtract whatever percentage of permanent disability your misconduct contributed to the overall disability. For example, this might be a situation where you unreasonably refused medical treatment, which resulted in further injury.
- **Failure to report the injury.** The insurance company may try to prove that you failed to notify your employer of the injury as required by law, thereby precluding entitlement to workers' compensation benefits. (LC §§ 5400, 5401, 5705.) Chapter 5, Section B, explains how and when to report an injury.
- **Apportionment of permanent disability.** The insurance company may try to prove that part or all of your permanent disability is due to non-industrial causes. (See Chapter 3, Section B7, for more information.)

• **Statute of limitations.** The insurance company may try to show that your claim for workers' compensation benefits is barred by the statute of limitations.

3. Identify Presumptions in Your Favor

Simply put, a "presumption" is a belief established by law that something is considered to be true, unless evidence is presented that proves otherwise. If you have a presumption in your favor, it's like having a head start in a race—and if the other side has no convincing evidence to present to overcome, it can amount to winning the race by default.

Although the judge could raise a presumption or give you the benefit of it without being asked, it's unwise to leave something this important to chance. The appropriate time and place to make the judge aware of any presumptions is before your case goes to trial, at a pre-trial conference (discussed in Chapter 22, Section A1, and Chapter 24, Section B).

 DON'T CONCERN YOURSELF WITH PRESUMPTIONS AGAINST YOU

There are very few presumptions that the insurance company could try to assert in its favor. Don't waste your time looking for presumptions that may hurt you. It's up to the insurance company to raise them.

a. Identify Conclusive (Irrebuttable) Presumptions

A conclusive presumption (also called an irrebuttable presumption) cannot be disproved. In other words, if you can show that the presumption applies to you, no evidence—no matter how strong—can overturn this presumption. Unfortunately, there are very few of these and it's unlikely that one will apply to your case. But look over this list to be sure:

• These are conclusively presumed to be total (100%) permanent disabilities: (a) loss of both eyes or sight in both eyes, (b) loss of both hands or the use of both hands, (c) an injury resulting in practically total paralysis, or (d) an injury to the brain resulting in incurable imbecility or insanity—the inability to manage one's own affairs due to being mentally incompetent. (LC § 4662.)

• A spouse who earned less than $30,000 in the year preceding a worker's death is conclusively presumed to have been a dependent of a deceased spouse. (LC § 3501.)

• A minor (person under age 18), or an adult who is physically or mentally incapable of performing work for wages is conclusively presumed to be wholly dependent for support upon a deceased employee-parent if he was living with the employee-parent at the time of an injury that resulted in the parent's death. (LC § 3501.)

b. Identify Rebuttable (Disputable) Presumptions

 See *SCIF v. WCAB (Welcher)* and *Rodriguez v. WCAB* in Chapter 28.

A rebuttable presumption (also known as a disputable presumption) is drawn from the facts in a case. It holds good unless it is invalidated by evidence to the contrary or by a stronger presumption.

Here are the main rebuttable presumptions that may apply to a workers' compensation case:

• If you filed a workers' compensation claim, and more than 90 days passed with no rejection of the claim by your employer or its insurance company, there is a rebuttable presumption that the claim is compensable. The 90 days starts to run from the date that you filed a DWC-1 claim form or first requested the DWC-1 form, if your employer did not provide it to you within 24 hours of making the request. The presumption is rebuttable only by evidence discovered after the 90-day period. (LC § 5402.) In other words, any evidence that the employer should have been able to obtain prior to the expiration of 90 days cannot be used to deny the claim.

• If you are temporarily totally disabled and you are off work due to the industrial injury for more than 365 days, there is a rebuttable presumption that you are a qualified injured worker (QIW)—that is, you're medically eligible for vocational rehabilitation services if you haven't already been identified as such. (LC § 4636(c).)

• Peace officers, fire fighters and safety officers who suffer from heart disease, tuberculosis, hernia, pneumonia, and cancer that manifests itself during their employment (and for a limited time after retirement) are presumed to have a condition that arose out of the employment. (LC §§ 3212-3214.)

• Any person rendering service for another is presumed to be an employee unless the person is an independent contractor or expressly excluded as an employee by the Labor Code. (LC § 3357.)

C. Depositions

A deposition is a proceeding in which a party or witness is asked to answer questions orally under oath so the other side can determine what she knows and may say about the case if called to testify at a trial. Depositions take place at a location away from the court, often at a lawyer's or doctor's office. Questions are usually asked by the lawyer for each side; if you represent yourself, you may ask questions as a party to the workers' compensation action. A court reporter (someone who makes a permanent record of the deposition by means of an electronic device) records the testimony and later prepares a written transcript of the entire proceeding.

Depositions are expensive. The court reporter is paid several hundred dollars. In addition, the person conducting the deposition may be required to pay witness fees, which can range from under $100 for non-experts to much more for experts, such as doctors. The person setting up the deposition is usually required to pay these amounts up front. If you conduct a deposition, however, you may be entitled to recover deposition costs when your case settles or goes to trial.

1. Reasons for You to Conduct a Deposition

Injured workers rarely conduct depositions. However, it may make sense to take the deposition of a witness to your case, in instances such as these:

- You feel that information gained at the deposition might persuade the insurance company to settle your case or change its position on a particular issue. For example, suppose the insurance company disputes that your injury really occurred. If you take the deposition of a witness who testifies that she saw you injure yourself as you claimed, it may persuade the insurance company to accept your claim.
- A witness is out-of-state or likely to be unavailable at trial due to poor health or death. If you take the deposition of a witness who is later unavailable for trial, the deposition transcript can be entered into evidence.

IF YOU NEED TO TAKE A DEPOSITION

A deposition of a doctor will not be necessary unless the doctor's report is very bad for your case. If you decide to conduct a deposition, please refer to *Nolo's Deposition Hand-*

book, by Paul Bergman and Albert Moore (Nolo). This book will give you guidance on depositions, whether you're being deposed or need to depose someone else. Or you may choose to see an attorney and discuss the alternative of having her take over your case.

2. Attending Your Own Deposition

In workers' compensation cases, the insurance company usually takes the injured worker's deposition. That way, the insurance company can determine the facts of the case and the extent of its liability. In most workers' compensation cases, the injured worker is the only person who is deposed. Attending your own deposition shouldn't be a problem as long as you always tell the truth. If things get out of hand, you can always stop the deposition and get a lawyer.

If you receive a notice that your deposition will be taken, read it carefully. Make sure you can appear at the date, time and place it's scheduled. If you can't attend, call the other side well in advance and make arrangements for a new date. If you don't show up, your benefits may be cut off immediately, and you may need to arrange for a hearing at the Appeals Board to get benefits. This may cause a delay of up to several months.

On the day of the deposition, show up a little early. Do not bring any documents with you unless you have been instructed to do so. Such a request may be made in advance in a self-explanatory document: either a Notice to Produce or a Deposition Subpoena for Personal Appearance and Production of Documents and Things.

To begin the deposition, the court reporter will ask you to raise your right hand and take the same oath to tell the truth that you would in a court of law. This oath carries with it criminal penalties if you knowingly tell a falsehood.

The attorney will then advise you of some ground rules that will be followed in the deposition. These instructions will mainly be about how to best answer the questions so that the court reporter can understand you.

The questions the attorney will ask probably will cover the following areas:

- your personal history, including your name, current home address, social security number, driver's license number, where you have lived for the past ten years, your educational background, family members and whether you have ever been convicted of a felony.

HOW TO HANDLE THE FELONY QUESTION

The other side is allowed to ask you if you have ever been convicted of a felony (a crime punishable by a jail sentence of more than one year—lesser crimes are misdemeanors). The purpose of this question is to lessen your credibility if you have had a felony conviction, with the idea that someone convicted of a felony presumably might not tell the truth. If you've been convicted of a felony, limit your answer to yes or no and the type of felony conviction. You should refuse to answer all other questions regarding this issue.

- your employment history from the time you got out of school to the present, including questions about your various job duties, why you left and whether or not you had any injuries at those jobs
- your claim of industrial injury, including how it happened, whether you reported it and whether there were witnesses
- your past and current medical history, including the names and addresses of doctors you have seen, who sent you to which doctors, what they did for you, and whether or not you are still being treated by a doctor, and
- your present complaints regarding your industrial injury. You will probably be asked to state the various parts of your body that still bother you, what kinds of activities and movements you can no longer do and what types of pain you have.

WHEN NOT TO ANSWER PSYCHIATRIC OR STRESS-RELATED QUESTIONS

Unless you have some kind of a stress-related injury, do not answer any questions regarding psychiatric problems, personal problems (alcoholism, divorce and the like) or treatment. This includes questions about whether you have ever seen a psychiatrist, and any questions of a very personal nature that would have to do only with your emotional welfare. Simply state that you object to the question as being irrelevant and don't answer.

a. Rules to Follow at Your Deposition

At a deposition, it's always a good idea to abide by these general rules:

- **Tell the truth.** Always tell the truth, even if you feel it might be detrimental to your case. But it's fine to frame the truth in its most favorable light to you. For example, you are asked, "Can you lift heavy objects without experiencing

SAMPLE NOTICE OF DEPOSITION

Name
Mailing address
City, State, Zip
Phone number
In Pro Per

BEFORE THE WORKERS' COMPENSATION APPEALS BOARD
OF THE STATE OF CALIFORNIA

[Name of employee] Applicant, vs. [Name of employer and its insurance company] Defendants	Case No. [Case Number] **NOTICE OF DEPOSITION**

YOU ARE HEREBY NOTIFIED that the deposition of [Name of person being deposed] has been scheduled for [Date] at [Time, a.m. or p.m.] at [Address] before a Notary Public for the State of California.

This Notice is being served by mail on all persons shown on the attached Proof of Service.

Date: _____   Signature: _____

Printed Name: _____

pain?" If the truth is that yes, at the time you don't feel pain, but the next day you'll have severe stiffness and pain, make both points in your answer.

• **Be polite and courteous**. Don't argue with the person asking the question or treat him rudely, no matter what you privately think about that person.

• **Make sure you understand the question**. If you don't hear or aren't certain that you understand the question, ask that it be repeated or explained. Always make sure you fully understand the question before you start answering.

• **Answer only the question asked.** If you can comfortably answer a question with a "yes," "no," "I don't know," or "I don't remember," give that answer. This will make for a clear record, as well as prevent you from providing information that your opponent may have never thought to ask. If the person asking the question wants an explanation, he will ask for it.

• **Don't guess.** You may give your best estimate if you really have one, but don't guess. If your answer is a guess, just say "I don't know."

• **Take a break when you need one.** You may take as many breaks as you need. This may be especially important if your injury is acute. For example, you may want time to use the rest room, or simply to regain your composure if you find yourself getting tired or angry. Try to limit a break to five or ten minutes.

b.   Potential Problems at Your Deposition

In 90% of workers' compensation cases, the attorney asking the questions will be polite and will not try to trick you. You should be on guard, however, for the other 10%. Here are the kinds of questions to watch out for:

• **Questions about irrelevant information.** If you're asked for information not relevant to your case, first say, "For the record, I object to this question as being irrelevant." By objecting for the record, you can later object to your answer being admitted into evidence at the time of trial. Wait and see if the attorney asks you to answer the question anyway. If she does, you may choose to answer it if the question is harmless. If you refuse to answer, the attorney's only recourse is to seek a hearing before a judge and get an order for you to answer at a later date.

• **Repetition of the same question.** If the attorney badgers you by repeatedly asking the same question, you have the right

to object. Simply say, "The question has been asked and answered," and refuse to answer it again.

• **Trick questions.** Watch out for questions that tend to box in your testimony, such as "please tell me *everything* that bothers you, that you attribute to your injury." If you testify at trial to something you failed to list, the defendants may try to discredit your testimony by pointing out that you testified differently at your deposition. You should answer these types of questions by first qualifying your answer, such as "As best as I can recall at this time" or, "At this moment, the following things bother me…." Or, if the question is phrased in such a way as to elicit a certain response, such as when you are asked if you can walk 50 feet—the answer is yes, but you know you can't walk 100 feet—answer in such a way as to make your limitations known.

c.   Terminating the Deposition

It's quite common to end a deposition because of health reasons. If at any time during the deposition you do not feel capable of continuing because you feel lousy, inform the attorney of this, and say that you are willing to finish it at a later date.

You may also end a deposition if the attorney is harassing you (say, by asking offensive personal questions). Be aware, however, that the insurance company could use this as an excuse to cut off benefits. So before taking such a drastic move, follow the suggestions in Section D2b, above, for handling problem questions. If the attorney continues to harass you, you may choose to end the deposition. Inform the attorney that you will no longer tolerate her actions and that you are leaving.

STATE OF CALIFORNIA
DEPARTMENT OF INDUSTRIAL RELATIONS
DIVISION OF WORKERS' COMPENSATION

WORKERS' COMPENSATION APPEALS BOARD

Jeffrey O'Conner

Claimant/Applicant,

vs.

XYZ Corporation, SCIF

Employer/Insurance Carrier/Defendant.

Case No. XX 1112

(IF APPLICATION HAS BEEN FILED, CASE NUMBER
MUST BE INDICATED REGARDLESS OF DATE OF INJURY.)

SUBPOENA DUCES TECUM

(When records are mailed, identify them by using above
case number or attaching a copy of subpoena)

Where no application has been filed for injuries on or after
January 1, 1990 and before January 1, 1994, subpoena will
be valid without a case number, but subpoena must be served
on claimant and employer and/or insurance carrier.

See instructions below.*

The People of the State of California Send Greetings to:

WE COMMAND YOU to appear before __Worker's Compensation Appeals Board__

at __50 "D" Street, Santa Rosa, CA 95404__

on the ____18th____ day of ____August____ , 19 _9X_ , at _1:00_ o'clock __P__.M., to testify in the above-
entitled matter and to bring with you and produce the following described documents, papers, books and records:
Employment records of Jeffrey O'Conner, SS #555-55-5555

(Do not produce X-rays unless specifically mentioned above.)

For failure to attend as required, you may be deemed guilty of a contempt and liable to pay to the parties aggrieved all
losses and damages sustained thereby and forfeit one hundred dollars in addition thereto.

This subpoena is issued at the request of the person making the declaration on the reverse hereof, or on the copy which is
served herewith.

Date ____July 20____ , 19_9X_

WORKERS' COMPENSATION APPEALS BOARD
OF THE STATE OF CALIFORNIA

_____
Secretary, Assistant Secretary, Workers' Compensation Judge

***FOR INJURIES OCCURRING ON OR AFTER JANUARY 1, 1990
AND BEFORE JANUARY 1, 1994:**
If no Application for Adjudication of Claim has been filed, a declaration under
penalty of perjury that the Employee's Claim for Workers' Compensation Benefits
(Form DWC-1) has been filed pursuant to Labor Code Section 5401 must be executed
properly.

**SEE REVERSE SIDE
[SUBPOENA INVALID WITHOUT DECLARATION]**

You may fully comply with this subpoena by mailing the records described (or authenticated copies, Evid. Code 1561) to the person and place
stated above within ten (10) days of the date of service of this subpoena.

This subpoena does not apply to any member of the Highway Patrol, Sheriff's Office or city Police Department unless accompanied by notice
from this Board that deposit of the witness fee has been made in accordance with Government Code 68097.2, et seq.

DIA WCAB 32 (Side 1) (REV. 06/94)

The attorney may threaten to obtain a judge's order to force you to complete the deposition. Tell the attorney that is fine. If the attorney gets such an order, you will be notified of the time and place. You will have an opportunity to tell the judge what happened at the deposition and to request that the judge order the attorney to stop harassing you.

If you terminate a deposition, you should only agree to a subsequent deposition if you get a lawyer or first obtain an order from a workers' compensation judge restraining the defense attorney from harassing you.

D. Subpoenaing Witnesses and Documents

In this section, we show you how to use legal procedures to require someone to show up at a hearing or provide you with copies of documents that will help you win your case:

- **Subpoena.** A Subpoena requires someone to appear at a deposition or hearing to answer questions.
- **Subpoena Duces Tecum.** A Subpoena Duces Tecum requires the production of documents.

To require someone's personal appearance *and* the production of documents, you'll need both a Subpoena and a Subpoena Duces Tecum.

When one party wants another *party* to produce documents, a Notice to Produce Documents is generally used instead of a Subpoena Duces Tecum. To require another *party* to attend a deposition or hearing, a Notice of Deposition is usually used instead of a Subpoena. You may, however, use a Subpoena Duces Tecum or Subpoena with a party such as the insurance company and your employer.

1. Subpoena Duces Tecum

IF YOU WANT DOCUMENTS FROM A PARTY
Send your employer or the insurance company a copy of the letter provided in Chapter 6, Section D. You don't need to use a Subpoena Duces Tecum.

A Subpoena Duces Tecum is a powerful tool. You may use it to require any person or business to produce books, accounts, papers and other documents relevant to your workers' compensation case. In addition, you may require not only the production of documents that you know about, but also any relevant documents that you don't even know exist!

This self-explanatory document must be signed by a judge or stamped with a judge's signature. You can get a Subpoena by making a written request to the Workers' Compensation Appeals Board, or by going to the Appeals Board office and asking a clerk for one. If you need help filling it in, see an Information and Assistance officer.

The person being served will have a minimum of 15 days to comply with the Subpoena Duces Tecum. As a practical matter, you will want to issue your Subpoena Duces Tecum long before your case is set for trial. This allows you to use it to discover any possibly relevant information that may help you to settle your case, or that may point to other documents that you may want to obtain.

2. Subpoena

To be sure witnesses will actually show up at your workers' compensation hearing, you need a court order requiring their presence, called a Subpoena. This document must be signed by a judge or stamped with a judge's signature. You can get a Subpoena by making a written request to the Workers' Compensation Appeals Board, or by going to the Appeals Board office and asking a clerk for one.

Most subpoenaed witnesses may request $35 for a day's appearance, plus 31 cents per mile from their home to the place of the hearing. In the unlikely event that you subpoena an expert witness (not an eyewitness), such as your treating doctor, you must pay that person an expert witness fees. (Government Code § 68092.5.) Expert witness fees can easily total hundreds of dollars, and must be agreed upon in advance. That is why doctors' medical reports are routinely admitted into evidence in workers' compensation cases without the necessity of having the doctor appear at the hearing. In fact, I have never had to subpoena an expert witness to a trial.

If the witness is "friendly" to your case—that is, someone who will voluntarily appear in court when needed and give testimony in your favor, you may think you won't need to serve a Subpoena. This is risky, however, because your witness may change his mind. Here are some reasons to subpoena even friendly witnesses:

- If something "better to do" comes up on the date of your hearing, a witness will think twice before deciding not to attend your hearing.
- If the witness gets cold feet or is pressured by the employer or others not to testify, she must still appear.

STATE OF CALIFORNIA
DEPARTMENT OF INDUSTRIAL RELATIONS
DIVISION OF WORKERS' COMPENSATION

WORKERS' COMPENSATION APPEALS BOARD
San Francisco, CA

Case No. AA 1234

(IF APPLICATION HAS BEEN FILED, CASE NUMBER
MUST BE INDICATED REGARDLESS OF DATE OF INJURY)

Mary Smith   S&S Company, SCIF

vs.

Claimant/Applicant   Employer/Insurance Carrier/Defendant

SUBPOENA

The People of the State of California Send Greetings to:

Alan Baker

YOU ARE HEREBY COMMANDED to appear before a Workers' Compensation Judge of the WORKERS' COMPENSATION APPEALS BOARD OF THE STATE OF CALIFORNIA at Worker's Compensation Appeals Board, 525 Golden Gate Avenue, San Francisco, CA 94102

on the   13th   day of   June   , 19 9X   , at   9:00   o'clock   A. M., to testify in the above-entitled action.

For failure to attend as required, you may be deemed guilty of contempt and liable to pay to the parties aggrieved all losses and damages sustained thereby and forfeit one hundred dollars in addition thereto. This subpoena is issued at request of Mary Smith   , Telephone No.   415-555-1234

WORKERS' COMPENSATION APPEALS BOARD
OF THE STATE OF CALIFORNIA

_____
Secretary, Assistant Secretary, Workers' Compensation Judge

Date_____ , 19_____

This subpoena does not apply to any member of the Highway Patrol, Sheriff's Office or city Police Department unless accompanied by notice from the Board that deposit of the witness fee has been made in accordance with Government Code 68097.2, et seq.

FOR INJURIES OCCURRING ON OR AFTER JANUARY 1, 1990 AND BEFORE JANUARY 1, 1994:

If no Application for Adjudication of Claim has been filed, a declaration under penalty of perjury that the Employee's Claim for Workers' Compensation Benefits (Form DWC-1) has been filed pursuant to Labor Code Section 5401 must be executed properly.

[SUBPOENA INVALID WITHOUT DECLARATION]

DIA WCAB 30 (Side 1) (Rev. 06/94)

- If the witness fails to show up, the judge is more likely to postpone ("continue") the hearing rather than proceed without the person's testimony.
- The Subpoena can provide a witness with the necessary reason or excuse to get time off from work to testify.

a. Which Witnesses to Subpoena

The issues that are contested by the insurance company in your case will usually determine what witnesses you will need to subpoena to help prove your case. They may include:

- your supervisor
- co-workers who witnessed the accident
- anyone who can substantiate your physical or mental limitations, and
- co-workers or others who know what your job duties were.

There are some restrictions as to who may be subpoenaed. A witness is not required to attend a Workers' Compensation Appeals Board hearing if it's located out of the county in which she resides, unless the distance is less than 75 miles from her place of residence to the place of the hearing. (Evidence Code § 1989.) If you can't subpoena someone because the distance is too great, you could take her deposition. (See Section C1, above.)

b. How to Fill in a Subpoena

If you want someone to appear at a hearing, you should serve a Subpoena only after you've received a Notice of Hearing in the mail. You'll use information from the Notice of Hearing to complete the Subpoena. If you can't find the Notice of Hearing, you can get another by contacting the Workers' Compensation Appeals Board where your case was filed. (A sample Notice of Hearing is provided in Chapter 22, Section F.)

You may type in the information or neatly handwrite the Subpoena. Here's how to fill it out.

County. In the blank line after the words "Workers' Compensation Appeals Board," fill in the name of the county in which your matter has been filed. For example, "San Bernardino County, California."

Case Number. Fill in your case number, which is the number assigned to your claim when you file an Application for Adjudication of Claim.

Applicant. That's you; fill in your name.

Defendant. Fill in the name of both your employer and its insurance company.

The People of the State of California Send Greetings to. Fill in the name and address of the witness you wish to have present at your hearing. You must use one Subpoena for each witness. If you've unsuccessfully attempted to determine the person's full legal name, identify her sufficiently so that the person serving the Subpoena can find the right person. For example, "Mary, Dispatcher for Anderson Trucking."

In the next blank, after the sentence "YOU ARE HEREBY COMMANDED to appear before a Workers' Compensation Judge of the WORKERS' COMPENSATION APPEALS BOARD OF THE STATE OF CALIFORNIA at," fill in the name of the Appeals Board that appears on the Notice of Hearing. For example, "Workers' Compensation Appeals Board, Long Beach," and give the address.

Next, insert the date and time the witness is to appear. For example, "on the 3rd day of September, 2003, at 10:00 A.M."

Finally, fill in your name and telephone number as the requesting party.

Leave the rest of the form blank.

3. Serving a Subpoena or Subpoena Duces Tecum

How to serve (provide copies) of documents is covered in Chapter 23. You'll follow different rules depending on whether you're serving a Subpoena or a Subpoena Duces Tecum:

- **Subpoena Duces Tecum:** The easiest way to serve a Subpoena Duces Tecum is by mail, although it may be served personally. You must give the recipient at least 20 days to comply. For example, if you mail the Subpoena Duces Tecum on October 1, the person served has until October 21 to produce the documents. (If the Subpoena Duces Tecum is served personally, you need only give 15 days.)
- **Subpoena:** A Subpoena must be personally served no less than 10 days before the hearing. If, at the time of service, the witness demands a witness fee, the person serving must immediately pay $35 for one day's appearance plus 20 cents per mile for the total number of miles the witness must drive to the Workers' Compensation Appeals Board. (Government Code § 68093.) In the rare event that you are using an expert witness, that person must be contacted in advance and a fee must be agreed upon.

After you serve documents, you'll need to complete a Proof of Service form, which states when and how service occurred. For more on completing Proofs of Service, see Chapter 23, Sections B and C.

E. Preparing for a Pre-Trial Hearing (Mandatory Settlement Conference)

If settlement efforts prove fruitless, you will have to move into high gear when it comes to getting ready for your day in court. You may request a pre-trial conference (sometimes called a pre-trial hearing, Mandatory Settlement Conference or MSC, for short); instructions are in Chapter 22, Section D. It's more likely, however, that you will receive a Notice of Hearing of your pre-trial conference in the mail. Look it over carefully to find the conference date and time. (A sample Notice of Hearing is provided in Chapter 22, Section F.)

1. Review Issues in Dispute

About 30 days before the pre-trial conference date, you should figure out what issues are still in dispute. You may find that some of the issues you originally listed as disputed have been accepted by the insurance company, while others you thought were accepted are now in dispute. Turn to Section A, above, for an Issues That May Be In Dispute form you can use.

Review the letters from the insurance company, notes about your conversations with the insurance adjuster, and any Answer filed by the insurance company to your Application. (As explained in Chapter 5, Section D, the insurance company can file a document called an Answer that sets forth the issues it is agreeing to or disputing.)

If any issues are in dispute at this stage, you'll need to organize the evidence that you are going to offer at the trial. You will be required to list all of your evidence at the pre-trial conference.

⚠ ANY EVIDENCE YOU DON'T LIST WILL NOT BE ALLOWED
If you need evidence—including doctor's reports—you should get it before you go to the pre-trial conference. If you don't have a medical report you need, make an appointment with your doctor before the hearing so you can list the report as evidence.

ISSUES LIKELY TO ARISE AFTER YOU BECOME PERMANENT AND STATIONARY

After you have been declared permanent and stationary, you should be looking for one or more of the following new issues:

- **Retroactive temporary disability indemnity.** Determine if the insurance company owes you temporary disability indemnity for periods off work due to your work injury. If so, organize all medical reports and records that would show that you were temporarily disabled during the periods you have claimed.
- **Permanent disability indemnity.** You or the insurance company may dispute the doctor's opinion regarding the nature and extent of your permanent disability. Review the treating doctor's opinion to determine if you will be relying on her report (it's presumed to be accurate), rather than a QME's evaluation.
- **Need for future medical treatment.** How much, and what kind of medical treatment you will need in the future is almost always disputed. As with permanent disability indemnity, you will need to rely on the treating doctor's report or a medical-legal opinion to substantiate your need for future medical treatment. (See Chapter 10, Section D.)
- **Self-procured medical treatment.** If you had to pay for any medical expenses yourself, you should acquire copies of all receipts and canceled checks, and add up the total amount you spent. (See Chapter 11, Section A.)
- **Liens.** Make a list of all the medical facilities, doctors, the Employment Development Department, attorneys, or any others who have filed liens (formal requests for payment) against your case. You should have received copies of all liens filed in your case. If you know that any particular medical facilities failed to file a lien, contact them and see that they do so. You will want to make sure that the insurance company pays these off.
- **Apportionment.** If any medical reports (usually by doctor's you were sent to by the insurance company), indicate that part of your present disability is due to pre-existing conditions or other outside factors, you should have obtained medical-legal reports to substantiate that all of your present disability is due to your industrial injury.

2. Review Your File and Serve Documents

Take a thorough look through your file, from beginning to end. Make sure you have all the documents you're using as evidence to prove your case. Also check to see that you have not overlooked anything, such as a demand for mileage that was never paid.

File and serve upon the Appeals Board and the insurance company any documents you intend to use at the trial that have not been previously filed. All written documents must be filed and served within 20 days of the conference or the judge may not allow them into evidence. (How to do this is covered in Chapter 23.)

 IF YOU DIDN'T RECEIVE DOCUMENTS FROM THE INSURANCE COMPANY

If you made a request to the insurance company to send you medical reports or other documents and you didn't receive them, write a letter to the judge before the pre-trial conference and send a copy to the insurance company. Request that the judge issue an order asking for the document. It's unlikely that the judge will comply with your request, but it will be a big help for the judge to know that you requested, but weren't sent, certain evidence.

SPECIAL RULES FOR MEDICAL REPORTS

Medical reports are important because they are used as evidence to prove (or disprove) medical issues in your case. A party files medical reports with the Workers' Compensation Appeals Board along with a Declaration of Readiness to Proceed to Trial. The opposing party has six days from service of a Declaration of Readiness (11 days if service is by mail) to file medical reports with the Appeals Board. (CCR § 10879.)

In most cases, you will have already served most, if not all, of your medical reports on opposing parties and lien claimants. Once a request for medical reports has been made, it is considered an ongoing request, and the party to whom the request was directed must serve and file any new doctors' reports within five days of receipt.

Remember, there is a difference between medical reports and medical records. You are required to file and serve medical reports, not medical records. Do not send X-rays or other records, such as the results of tests, to the Appeals Board unless the Board requests it.

---

3. Review Your Witness List

Check over your list of witnesses, if any. You will be required to list all your witnesses at the pre-trial conference. There's no harm in listing witnesses you may not end up calling to testify; you can always decide not to call them. But if you neglect to list someone, you will not be permitted to call that person to testify.

F. Preparing for a Trial

Once you've received your Notice of Hearing for your trial (a preliminary hearing, expedited hearing or trial on the case-in-chief), you should be in a "countdown mode." For the first time, you know the exact date and time of your trial. (See Chapter 22, Section F, for more on the Notice of Hearing.)

At least 30 days before the trial, you should prepare your case for presentation to the judge. All of the preliminary work has now been done. As we discuss in Chapter 24, Section B, you may have attended a pre-trial conference (where you were unable to settle your case) and completed the Joint Pre-Trial Statement, listing all the evidence and witnesses you intend to present at trial. Now it is just a matter of organizing your medical reports, witnesses and documentary evidence for the actual trial.

GET A HEAD START BY WATCHING A TRIAL

You'll want to be sure you know what you're up against. If possible, go to the Workers' Compensation Appeals Board to observe a trial, preferably by the judge who will be hearing your case. Ask the clerk to direct you to courtrooms where trials are going to begin. Before the trial gets started, walk up to the judge when she has a free moment and ask if it would be okay for you to sit in and watch. As long as you check with the judge first, you should have no problem sitting in on a workers' compensation trial to get a feel of what is going to happen in your case.

When you observe a trial, take some notes as to how things proceed. Note the order in which people testify, what kinds of questions are asked and what types of testimony are most effective.

1. Prepare Your Evidence

Organize all of the medical reports that you listed at the pre-trial conference and wish to admit into evidence. They should be organized in chronological order, with all the proofs of service attached to each report indicating when it was served. All of your original medical reports should have already been filed and served upon the Workers' Compensation Appeals Board.

Have an extra copy of every piece of evidence you intend to offer at your trial, so that in the event that anything was misplaced, you can provide the judge with another copy.

Write out all the issues you need to offer evidence on at the trial, using the Issues That May Be in Dispute Chart in Section A. Decide what issues you and any other witnesses will offer testimony on. You will generally testify first. Decide in what order you will call your remaining witnesses, and write out a list.

MAKE CERTAIN THAT YOU HAVE SUBPOENAED ALL YOUR WITNESSES

If you haven't, do so now. Your witnesses must be served at least ten days before the trial. (See Section D for instructions.)

2. Consider Trying to Exclude Medical Reports

In some cases, the insurance company will have obtained medical evidence in violation of the rules or regulations of the Labor Code. If it did, the medical evidence may be inadmissible at a workers' compensation hearing. In other words, you may be able to persuade the judge to not allow those reports into evidence at trial.

For example, unless there has been a qualified medical evaluation by a doctor you chose from a panel of three doctors, generally no medical reports, other than those of the treating physician, may be admitted into evidence in a proceeding before the Workers' Compensation Appeals Board. (See Chapter 10, Sections D and E.) The practical application of this comes into play when the insurance company attempts to offer into evidence medical reports from doctors they have sent you to without having complied with the requirements of the Labor Code.

REVIEW LC §§ 4060, 4061 AND 4062

These three Labor Code sections are critical when it comes to admissibility of medical evidence. If at all possible, you should carefully review those code sections. (See Chapter 27 on legal research.) ■

Arranging for a Hearing or Trial

At a hearing or trial, you'll have an opportunity to present your case to a workers' compensation judge and to have a decision rendered on any issues in dispute. This chapter discusses the how, what, when and why of getting a hearing or trial date set with the Workers' Compensation Appeals Board.

Let's back up a bit and explain some legal jargon. Cases heard before the Workers' Compensation Appeals Board are sometimes referred to as "conferences," sometimes "trials" and sometimes "hearings." And unlike a civil court case, you may have more than one trial during the course of your workers' compensation case. Don't let the legal lingo throw you; it's not that difficult to sort it out, and once you do, you'll realize that even lawyers are prone to jumble it up.

A. Kinds of Hearings

"Hearing" is a generic term that refers to any matter set before the Workers' Compensation Appeals Board. A workers' compensation hearing usually takes one of two forms: a conference or a trial.

1. Pre-Trial Conferences (Mandatory Settlement Conferences)

A pre-trial conference is sometimes called a pre-trial hearing, a Mandatory Settlement Conference, or MSC. This hearing is almost always set by the Workers' Compensation Appeals Board when you or the insurance company request that the case be set for a trial. Only if settlement isn't possible will the matter be set (assigned a date) for trial.

No evidence or testimony is allowed at a pre-trial hearing. If you aren't represented, a judge may facilitate a discussion about settling the case. Otherwise, you and the insurance company will meet in the courtroom, discuss settlement and tell the judge the outcome. If you reach an impasse and the judge can't help, the matter will be set for trial.

2. Pre-Trial Discovery Motions

A pre-trial discovery motion requests that the workers' compensation judge issue an order requiring the other side to take, or stop taking, a particular action.

Insurance companies might file a pre-trial discovery motion to compel you to:

- attend a deposition if you failed to appear for your deposition at least once before
- attend a medical examination scheduled by the insurance company where you have failed to appear at a scheduled appointment at least once before, or
- produce certain documents, if you have refused to do so.

You could file a pre-trial discovery order to compel the insurance company to stop harassing you at your deposition, comply with your request to produce documents or get permission to not comply with Subpoenas or not go to a deposition.

If a hearing is set, you will receive notice of the date and time to appear. This will be a short hearing where each side will tell the judge why the order should be granted or denied.

3. Trials on Preliminary Issues and Trial on the "Case-in-Chief"

A "trial" refers to any hearing before a workers' compensation judge in which you have an opportunity to present your case and to have a decision rendered on issues in dispute. As noted earlier, a trial may also be referred to as a hearing. Trials come in two broad varieties:

- mini-trials, to resolve a particular issue that develops as you go along, such as eligibility for medical treatment, and
- your main trial, to deal with the final value of your case. Lawyers often call this the trial on your case-in-chief.

B. Trial on Preliminary Issues (Case Not Ready to Settle)

As your case progresses, you may find it necessary to have one or more mini-trials to resolve important preliminary issues, but not to settle the entire case. For example, if the insurance company refuses to pay for surgery recommended by the treating doctor, you may need a trial to have a judge decide whether surgery is reasonable and necessary. At a trial on preliminary issues, evidence is presented and testimony given before a workers' compensation judge, who then makes a decision on the issues.

1. Kinds of Preliminary Issues

A mini-trial on preliminary issues may be necessary if you believe you are entitled to certain benefits, such as medical treatment or temporary disability payments, and the insurance company refuses to provide them. A hearing may also be needed if the insurance company is denying your claim altogether.

a. Preliminary Issue of Whether Injury Is Compensable

"Compensability" is a broad term that means your claim is valid and therefore you are entitled to benefits. If the insurance company asserts that you don't have a compensable injury, it is denying your claim altogether. (LC § 4060(a).) We cover compensability issues in Chapter 3, Section B.

You are entitled to set a matter for trial at any time to resolve the issue of compensability. If the insurance company claims your injury is noncompensable (denies your claim), you will always have other issues as well, such as the insurance company's failure to pay you temporary disability or provide medical treatment. So, as a practical matter, there is no point in requesting a trial solely on the issue of compensability; you'll want to resolve the other issues as well.

IF YOUR CLAIM IS DISPUTED
If the insurance company disputes the basic issue of whether you have a compensable injury (whether or not you are entitled to any workers' compensation benefits), obtain the help of a competent workers' compensation attorney, if possible. If this issue is decided against you, you will be precluded from obtaining any workers' compensation benefits whatsoever.

b. Other Preliminary Issues (Accepted Case)

It's possible that your claim was accepted by the insurance company, but you and the insurance company disagree over one or more preliminary issues, such as these:

- Is your medical condition permanent and stationary? (See Chapter 9, Section E.)
- What should be the extent and scope of your present medical treatment?
- Do you have a new and further disability?

- Are you entitled to receive temporary disability indemnity, which the insurance company refuses to pay?
- How much temporary disability should the insurance company be paying?
- Are you entitled to medical treatment, which the insurance company refuses to authorize?
- Who is your treating physician? (See Chapter 9, Sections A, B and C.)
- Are you entitled to vocational rehabilitation benefits?

NOW ABOUT YOUR CLAIM...

2. When to File for a Hearing on Preliminary Issues

Before you file for a hearing before the Workers' Compensation Appeals Board to deal with any preliminary issues, consider whether it may make more sense to wait and resolve these issues when your entire case is ready for trial. Consider the following criteria in deciding whether to get a separate hearing (trial) date on a preliminary issue:

- **How serious is the issue?** Don't get a trial date for a relatively insignificant issue. For example, if the issue is your entitlement to temporary disability payments and you have no other source of income, you probably need a hearing to resolve that issue. However, if the issue is your right to $22.95 for mileage reimbursement, you should wait to resolve this issue when your case is ready to settle.

- **Do you have any alternatives?** There's no point in going through the hassles of an extra trial if there are easy options that will solve your problem. Let's say the issue is your entitlement to a particular medical treatment. If your doctor is willing to file a "green lien," you might decide to wait to resolve the issue when your case is ready to settle.

- **How strong is your position?** If you proceed to trial on an issue, what are your chances of winning? The best way to make an educated guess is to carefully read the appropriate sections of this book on the particular issue to first determine what you must convince the judge of at a trial. Then carefully consider whether you will be able to do so.

3. Medical Examination Requirements for Hearing on Preliminary Issues

Before you may request a trial on any preliminary issues, you must satisfy certain medical requirements. No disputed medical issue (preliminary issue) may come before a workers' compensation judge unless there has first been an evaluation of the injured worker by:

- the treating doctor
- a qualified medical evaluator (QME), if the employee does not have a lawyer, or
- an agreed medical examiner (AME), if the employee is represented by an attorney. (LC § 4062(e).)

If the insurance company has denied compensability, you may need to use your group medical insurance doctor as the treating doctor or find a doctor willing to treat you on a lien.

(See Chapter 9, Section B2b.) You are still entitled to a QME evaluation, however. (See Chapter 10, Section C.)

4. Regular and Expedited Preliminary Hearings

A regular preliminary hearing (trial) usually does not occur for 45-180 days after you request it. Because trials on preliminary issues are generally urgent in nature, that just won't do. For example, preliminary issues may cover authorization for medical treatment or granting of temporary disability payments to help pay bills. As a result, preliminary issues may sometimes be decided earlier, using what is known as an expedited hearing procedure.

a. Regular Preliminary Hearing

Any hearing (trial) set on the regular trial calendar will first be set for a pre-trial conference date, typically 30 to 60 days after the hearing is requested.

If the issue can't be resolved at the pre-trial conference, a trial will then be set, usually 60 to 120 days after the pre-trial conference date.

WHEN WILL YOUR TRIAL BE SET?
Check with your local Workers' Compensation Appeals Board to find out how quickly it is setting hearings. How long it will take will vary greatly depending upon how heavy the particular Appeals Board calendar is, and how many judges hear workers' compensation cases. If regular hearings are being set fairly quickly, you may not need to request an expedited hearing.

b. Expedited Hearings

The hearing (trial) is given priority over regular trial dates, and is usually set for trial within 30-90 days of request. No pre-trial conference is scheduled. Although we are really referring to an expedited trial, the common workers' compensation jargon refers to them as expedited hearings.

There are certain limits on your right to an expedited hearing. You're only entitled to an expedited hearing if the insurance company has accepted your workers' compensation claim—in other words, the issue of whether you're covered (compensability) cannot be determined in an expedited hearing. In general, only the following issues may be resolved in an expedited hearing:

- entitlement to medical treatment
- entitlement to temporary disability payments or the amount of those payments
- enforcement or termination of vocational rehabilitation or
- dispute between employers or insurance companies as to liability for payment of benefits.

How to file the documents to obtain an expedited hearing is covered in Section D2, below.

c. Hardship Hearings

When you can't qualify for an Expedited Hearing, the Appeals Board may grant a hearing on a priority basis if waiting for the regular hearing date would cause you undue hardship. The hearing will probably be set sooner than a regular hearing, but not as quickly as an expedited hearing. There are no hard and fast rules on what constitutes a hardship; requests will be considered on a case-by-case basis. (We discuss how to request a hardship hearing in Section D3, below.)

C. Trial on Entire Case (the Case-in-Chief)

When your entire case is ready to be heard, it's referred to as the "case-in-chief" in workers' compensation slang. Generally speaking, the main issue that must be resolved at a hearing is the settlement value of your case. The hearing generally centers around the nature and extent of the permanent disability and need for future medical treatment. It also addresses any other unresolved issues, such as your right to retroactive temporary disability.

1. When to Set a Trial on the Case-in-Chief

If either of the following two issues exist, your matter is considered a trial on your case-in-chief:

- the nature and extent of permanent disability, or
- your need for future medical treatment. (LC § 4061.)

At a trial on the case-in-chief, evidence is presented and testimony given before a workers' compensation judge, who then makes a decision on the issues.

A hearing on the case-in-chief generally occurs when all of the following apply:

- you have been declared permanent and stationary
- you are no longer receiving temporary disability payments, and
- you have been unable to reach a settlement with the insurance company on the remaining issues in your case. (Issues that may remain unresolved are set forth in Chapter 21, Section A.)

2. Medical Examination Requirements for Setting a Trial on the Case-in-Chief

Any disputed medical issue regarding the existence or extent of permanent disability and limitations or the need for continuing medical care may be decided in a trial on the case-in-chief only if there has been an evaluation of the injured worker by:

- the treating doctor
- a qualified medical evaluator (QME), if the employee is not represented, or
- an agreed medical examiner (AME), if the employee is represented by an attorney. (LC § 4061(m).)

D. Complete Documents to Set Your Case for Hearing

To set your case for hearing (whether on preliminary issues or the case-in-chief, and whether expedited or regular) you or the insurance company will need to file and serve a Declaration of Readiness to Proceed.

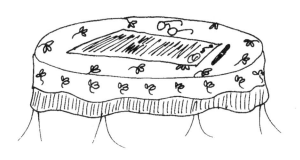

DECIDING WHO TO PROCEED AGAINST

In most workers' compensation cases, you will have only one employer and its one insurance company as defendants in your case. If, however, you have filed claims against more than one employer or more than one insurance company, you have a choice of who to proceed against. For example, if you have claimed a continuous trauma injury, and you worked for two different employers during the continuous trauma period, you will have two different employers and probably at least two different insurance companies who are responsible for paying you benefits.

If you are eligible to proceed against more than one party, you may:

- proceed against all employers and their insurance companies, or
- pursue your claim against one of the employers and its insurance company. That employer would be responsible for paying for the entire claim, but would be free to look to the others for contribution.

It is generally best to proceed against all employers if you are dealing with three or fewer employers. However, electing against an employer or insurance company can be helpful in complicated cases involving multiple defendants, where you do not want to go to court against three or four attorneys. For example, you may choose the employer who has not prepared its case for trial or has not obtained any medical evidence. Be aware, however, that if you lose your case against the employer you elected against, all other employers are "off the hook" also. I recommend that you discuss your situation with a workers' compensation attorney before deciding what to do.

are step-by-step instructions as well as a completed sample. You may either type or neatly print the information.

Case Number. When you filed an Application for Adjudication of Claim, a number was assigned to your case. Insert the number here.

Applicant. Fill in your name. This should be the same name you listed on the Application for Adjudication of Claim.

Defendants. Enter the names of the employer(s) as well as its insurance company. This information is contained on the DWC-1 form you filed.

The Employee or Applicant. Check the box before the words "Employee or applicant." This indicates that you—the employee/applicant—are filing the Declaration of Readiness to Proceed.

Place. Enter the city where you want your case to be heard. This is usually the same place where you filed your Application.

Issues. On this line, briefly explain what efforts you have made to settle your case with the insurance company. If possible, list the dates of letters and phone calls made to the insurance company, as well as the result of those efforts. Then state, "Assistance of the Appeals Board is necessary to resolve the issues in dispute." For example: "Defendant has failed to respond to Applicant's settlement offers of 3/11/XX and 4/20/XX. Assistance of the Appeals Board is necessary to resolve the issues in dispute."

Declarant requests. You will check one of the boxes on this line:

Regular Hearing. If you have previously attended a pre-trial conference (Mandatory Settlement Conference), check this box to get the matter set for a trial date.

Conference Pre-Trial. If you have not been to a pre-trial conference, check this box. In this situation, you may be assigned a pre-trial conference date even if you check the box entitled "Regular Hearing."

Rating Pre-Trial. If you want the assistance of the rater at the Appeals Board to help resolve a dispute over the rating of a medical report, check this box.

1. Complete the Declaration of Readiness to Proceed

In a Declaration of Readiness to Proceed (also called a "DOR"), the person completing the document states under penalty of perjury that she is ready to proceed to a hearing on the issues specified. The document also indicates what efforts were made to resolve the issues. (CCR § 10414.)

It's easy to complete a Declaration of Readiness to Proceed. Start by locating the form in Appendix 4. Following

WORKERS' COMPENSATION APPEALS BOARD
STATE OF CALIFORNIA

Kenneth Gomez

Applicant

vs.

A-1 Technologies, Best
Insurance Company, Inc.
Defendants

Case No.

DECLARATION OF READINESS
TO PROCEED

NOTICE: "Any objection to the proceedings requested by a Declaration of Readiness to proceed shall be filed and served within ten (10) days after service of the Declaration.   (Rule 10416)

The | [X] Employee or applicant
[ ] Defendant
[ ] Lien Claimant

requests that this case be set for hearing at

San Jose, California
(Place)

and declarant states under penalty of perjury that he or she is presently ready to proceed to hearing on the issues below and has made the following efforts to resolve these issues. letters proposing settlement dated 4/5/XX, 6/21/XX and 7/8/XX have gone unanswered by defenants. Assistance of the Appeals Board is required.

Declarant requests:

    [ ] Regular Hearing   [X] Conference Pre-trial   [ ] Rating Pre-trial

(SEE REVERSE SIDE FOR INSTRUCTIONS)

At the present time the principal issues are—

[X] Compensation Rate   [ ] Rehabilitation
[X] Temporary Disability   [X] Self-procured Treatment
[X] Permanent Disability   [ ] Future Medical Treatment
[X] Other penalties and unreimbursed mileage .

Employee [ ] is (or) [ ] is not presently receiving compensation payments.
Employee's condition following injury is permanent and stationary as shown by the report(s) of
Doctor(s) Dr. Sheila Holmes   Dated 3/2/XX ,
filed and served on 4/5/XX .
I expect to present 1 witnesses, including 0 medical witnesses, and estimate the time required for the hearing will be 2 hours.
I have completed discovery and all medical reports in my possession or control have been filed and served as required by WCAB Rules of Practices and Procedure.
Adverse parties [X] have (or) [ ] have not served me with medical reports.
Copies of this Declaration have been served this date as shown below.

Name (Print or Type) Kenneth Gomez

Declarant's signature *Kenneth Gomez*

Address 191 North First St., San Jose, CA 95113   Phone 408-555-2000

Date 2/7/XX

SERVICE

Type or print names and addresses of parties, including attorneys and representatives served with a copy of this Declaration:

A-1 Technologies   200 W. Hedding St., San Jose, CA 95110

Best Insurance Company, Inc.   270 Grant Ave., Palo Alto, CA 94306

(SEE REVERSE SIDE FOR INSTRUCTIONS)

DIA WCAB 9 (REV. 2/89)   89 52346

At the present time the principal issues are. Check *all* issues that apply, as follows:

Compensation Rate. Put an "X "in this box only if there is an issue over how much per week you made at your employment. Your average weekly wage affects your temporary disability and permanent disability rates.

Temporary Disability. Put an "X "in this box if you believe that there were periods of time that you were off work as a result of your injury and the insurance company failed to pay you temporary disability benefits. Also check this box if you are currently temporarily disabled and not getting paid.

Future Medical Treatment. Check this box if you are in need of medical treatment for your injury and the insurance company refuses to authorize it, or there is a dispute as to the nature of the present or future treatment you require.

Permanent Disability. Check this box if you have been declared permanent and stationary, your case is ready to settle, and you need a determination by the Appeals Board as to the nature and extent of your permanent disability.

Self-procured Treatment. Check this box if the insurance company has not repaid you for all out-of-pocket expenses you incurred for medical treatment or medication. This includes prescription medications as well as over-the-counter medication. For example, check this box if you paid $500 for an MRI test and $32 for over-the-counter painkillers and were not reimbursed.

Rehabilitation. Check this box if you are appealing a decision of the Rehabilitation Unit or you are trying to enforce an order from the Rehabilitation Unit. (Note that a rehabilitation appeal is beyond the scope of this book. You should seek the assistance of an Information and Assistance officer or a qualified workers' compensation attorney.)

Other. On these lines, describe any other issues you want resolved, such as:

- penalties and interest (Chapter 19, Section C9)
- mileage reimbursement (Chapter 11, Section A1), or
- AOE/COE (arising out of employment/in the course of employment). This involves the issue of whether the injury resulted from work. (See Chapter 3, Section C8.)

Employee is or is not presently receiving compensation payments. Check the appropriate box, depending on whether or not you are receiving any temporary disability, vocational rehabilitation maintenance allowance or permanent disability payments.

Doctor(s). Fill in the name of the doctor who wrote the medical report upon which you are relying, usually the one who determined permanent disability most favorably for you.

Dated. Enter the date of the medical report upon which you are relying to establish your permanent and stationary date.

Filed and served on. Enter the date you filed and served (sent to the insurance company) the medical report you are relying on.

Witnesses. In the first blank, list the total number of witnesses you intend to call at the trial. For most cases, this is going to be one witness—you.

In the next blank, indicate how many of your witnesses will be medical witnesses (such as doctors or chiropractors). If, as is common, you won't call a medical witness in person—but instead will rely on written reports—put "none."

Time required for hearing. Enter the number of hours you believe your matter will take to hear. If you are the only witness, estimate two hours. Add half an hour for each additional witness.

Adverse parties. Check the appropriate box to indicate whether or not adverse parties—generally the insurance company—have served you (provided you) with copies of their medical reports. If you don't know, leave this blank.

Name (Print or Type). Enter your name.

Declarant's Signature. Sign your name with your usual signature.

Address. Enter your current mailing address.

Phone. Fill in your current home telephone number.

Date. Enter today's date.

Service. Fill in the names and addresses of the opposing parties and their attorneys. As we'll explain later, you will need to send them copies of the Declaration of Readiness to Proceed.

2. Request for Expedited Hearing (Optional)

If you do not wish to request, or do not qualify for, an expedited hearing, you can skip this section. (See Section B4, above, for guidelines on when to request an expedited hearing.)

If you qualify for an expedited hearing, you'll need to complete a Request for Expedited Hearing and Decision. A blank copy of this very simple form is contained in Appendix 4. Either type or neatly print the information. Have your completed Declaration of Readiness to Proceed handy, as you'll need the information you provided there.

Case Number. Fill in the number assigned to your case.

Applicant. Enter your name.

Defendants. Enter the name of the defendants in your case as is listed on your Declaration of Readiness to Proceed.

WORKERS' COMPENSATION APPEALS BOARD
STATE OF CALIFORNIA

CASE NO.____DD1234_____

Karen Yamamoto_____
Applicant

REQUEST FOR EXPEDITED
HEARING AND DECISION
[LABOR CODE SECTION 5502 (B)]

VS.

Dave's Garden Center, Acme Insurance
_____
Defendants

The applicant herein, having filed an application for benefits this date, requests that this case be set

for expedited hearing and decision at____Oakland, CA_____
Workers' Compensation Appeals Board

on the following issues:

__X__ Entitlement to Medical Treatment per L.C. 4600
__X__ Entitlement to Temporary Disability, or disagreement on amount of Temporary Disability
____ Appeal From Decision and Order of Rehabilitaiton Bureau
____ Entitlement to Compensation in Dispute Because of Disagreement between Employers and/or Carriers

Explanation: _____Despite demands for authorization for surgery and payment of_____

temporary disability benefits, defendants have failed to authorize sur-

gery and pay disability indemnity.

APPLICANT STATES UNDER PENALTY OF PERJURY THAT THERE IS A BONA FIDE DISPUTE; THAT HE/SHE IS PRESENTLY READY TO PROCEED TO HEARING; THAT HIS/HER DISCOVERY IS COMPLETE ON SAID ISSUES; THAT THE TIME REQUIRED FOR HEARING WILL BE _2_.

Name (Print or Type)_Karen Yamamoto_____

Signature of Applicant___*Karen Yamamoto*_____

Signature of Attorney (if represented)_By:_____

Date:__2/7/XX___

INSTRUCTION FOR FILING
This request must be filed with an application for Benefits at the office of Benefit Assistance and Enforcement (OBAE). For location of the OBAE office nearest you, call 1-800-736-7401.

SERVICE
Type or print names and addresses of parties, including attorneys and representatives served with a copy of this request:
Dave's Garden Center, 1225 Fallon St., Oakland, CA 94612
Acme Insurance, P.O. Box 123, Berkeley, CA 94704

DWC Form 4 (1/1/90)

You will want to list your employer and its workers' compensation insurance company.

Workers' Compensation Appeals Board. Enter the city and state of the Workers' Compensation Appeals Board that your case is filed in.

Next you will check off the issues that are the subject of the expedited hearing:

Entitlement to Medical Treatment per L. C. 4600. Check this line if you want a judge to resolve your need for medical treatment and the insurance company's refusal to provide it.

Entitlement to Temporary Disability, or disagreement on the amount of Temporary Disability. Check this line if this is an issue to be resolved at the expedited hearing.

Appeal From Decision and Order of Rehabilitation Bureau. Check this line if you are appealing or requesting enforcement of a decision and order of the Rehabilitation Bureau. (This issue is beyond the scope of this book.)

Entitlement to Compensation in Dispute Because of Disagreement between Employers and/or Carriers. Check this line if you're involved in a situation where there is more than one employer and/or insurance company possibly liable for your industrial injury, and each is claiming the other is responsible, with neither providing you any benefits.

Explanation. State the reason why you need the assistance of the Workers' Compensation Appeals Board. If you can, you should refer to specific dates where you contacted the defendants either by phone or letter and attempted to resolve the dispute. For example, "Defendants failed to respond to my letter proposing settlement of 4/5/XX and the assistance of the Appeals Board is necessary to resolve the issues in dispute." This should be the same explanation as listed on the Declaration of Readiness to Proceed.

Name. Print or type your name.

Signature of Applicant. Sign your name.

Signature of Attorney. Leave this blank if you don't have a lawyer.

Date. Enter the date on which you are signing the document.

Service. At the bottom of this page, type or print the names and addresses of the insurance company or its attorney (if it has one). If your employer is self-insured, list your employer or its attorney (if it has one).

 REQUEST FOR EXPEDITED HEARING FORM CAN'T BE FILED BY ITSELF

The Request for Expedited Hearing form must be attached to a Declaration of Readiness to Proceed. The Request for Expedited Hearing requests that the Appeals Board act on the attached documents in an expedited manner, so without the Declaration, there is nothing for the Appeals Board to act on.

3. Attachment Letters (Optional)

You will need to attach a letter to your Declaration of Readiness to Proceed in situations such as these:

- **You are requesting that your matter be set on a priority basis.** If, because of hardship or other good cause (discussed in Section B4c, above), you want an earlier hearing, write a letter specifying in detail the nature of the hardship and the reason why an early hearing is required. This would be important, for example, if the insurance company has denied your case (therefore you are not entitled to file for an expedited hearing) and you are experiencing financial hardship due to the insurance company's failure to provide benefits.

- **You may want to bypass the pre-trial settlement conference procedure because you have previously been to one.** The Appeals Board may schedule you for another pre-trial conference unless you attach a letter explaining that you have previously attended a pre-trial conference and you would prefer to have your matter set directly for trial.

E. Copy, Serve and File Documents

Once you've prepared the documents necessary to request a hearing, you'll need to make copies, serve the defendants and file the papers with the court. Chapter 23 explains how to file and serve documents. Note that you may serve the defendant by mail.

If you or the insurance company requested an expedited hearing, the Appeals Board must review the request within two business days. If approved, the request will be referred to the presiding workers' compensation judge for placement on a separate and faster trial schedule. (CCR § 10136.)

DIVISION OF WORKERS' COMPENSATION

WORKERS' COMPENSATION APPEALS BOARD

NOTICE OF HEARING

DATE OF SERVICE: *12/16/XX*

WCAB CASE NBR(s): XX 0000

EMPLOYEE: Allen Mar

EMPLOYER: Sandy's Restaurant

INSURER: *AAA Insurance Company*

TYPE OF HEARING: *MANDATORY SETTLEMENT*

DATE OF HEARING: *02/22/XX TUESDAY*

TIME OF HEARING: *9:00 A.M.*

LENGTH OF HEARING:

LOCATION: *303 W. Third Street #640*
SAN BERNARDINO CA 92401

JUDGE: John Justice
(909) 555-2222

You are hereby notified that the above-entitled case is set for hearing before the Division of Workers' Compensation of the State of California. Continuances are not favored and will be granted only upon clear showing of good cause. Please arrive before scheduled appearance time.

NOTICE TO INSURER: The employer will not receive Notice of Hearing.

SPECIAL COMMENTS/INSTRUCTIONS:

WC01

F. Receiving Notice of a Hearing

After you (or the insurance company) file a Declaration of Readiness to Proceed with the Workers' Compensation Appeals Board, you will receive a notice in the mail, called a Notice of Hearing. This document contains important information about your case, which will assist you at the time of your hearing. Carefully look over the Notice of Hearing and find:

- the type of hearing you are set for, such as a pre-trial settlement conference
- the date and time of your hearing (often several weeks or months away)
- the address of the Workers' Compensation Appeals Board where your matter will be heard, and
- the department or judge who will hear your matter.

Depending on the calendar (schedule) at your local Workers' Compensation Appeals Board, your matter will be set either for a pre-trial conference (Mandatory Settlement Conference), or a trial. Typically you will only go directly to trial if you have requested an expedited hearing or sometimes where there has already been a pre-trial conference.

1. If the Insurance Company Requested the Hearing

Within six days of being served with a Declaration of Readiness to Proceed (11 days if it was mailed to you), you must file with the Workers' Compensation Appeals Board, and serve upon opposing parties, any medical reports that you have in your possession or under your control, unless they've been previously filed in the proceeding. (CCR § 10979.) See the instructions in the sidebar in Chapter 21, Section E2.

2. How to Object to a Hearing

If the insurance company filed a Declaration of Readiness to Proceed on any issues (preliminary or on the case-in-chief), you will be served with a copy of the document. It's possible that you won't be ready to go to trial for reasons such as these:

- You are still receiving medical treatment and are not yet permanent and stationary.
- You have not yet seen a QME to determine the nature and extent of your permanent disability.
- You are still participating in a vocational rehabilitation program and do not want to settle your case until it is completed.

If you are served with a Declaration of Readiness to Proceed, you must either attend the hearing once it's set, or object to the hearing being set. Here's how to object to having the hearing set for trial. You write and file an "objection letter," which must be signed under penalty of perjury. In the letter you explain the specific reasons why you feel your matter is not yet ready to be heard.

Any objection to your matter being set for a hearing must be sent to the Workers' Compensation Appeals Board (and a copy served upon opposing parties) within ten days (15 days if you were mailed a copy) of the date of service of the Declaration

of Readiness to Proceed by the insurance company. If you don't object within the time allotted, your case will be set for a hearing on the issues listed in the Declaration of Readiness to Proceed. You will have to appear and request that the case be taken off calendar at that time or proceed with the hearing.

File your letter with the Appeals Board and serve copies on all opposing parties in your case within the required time limits. (See Chapter 23, Section D, for instructions). You should receive a response from the Appeals Board within 30 days.

3. Prepare for the Hearing

Turn to Chapter 21 for information on how to prepare for the hearing. Then read Chapter 24 to learn about what to expect when you attend a hearing. ∎

SAMPLE OBJECTION LETTER

June 12, year

Presiding Judge

Workers' Compensation Appeals Board

(address)

Re: Donna Goldstein v. SQ Industries, A & A Insurance Company

Case # BV 0000

Objection to Defendants' Declaration of Readiness to Proceed

Your Honor,

I have been served with a copy of a Declaration of Readiness to Proceed filed by A & A Insurance Company, a copy of which is attached to this letter.

I object to the Declaration of Readiness and request that this case not be set for a hearing at this time because I am still treating with Dr. Smith for my back injury, and have not yet been declared permanent and stationary *(or whatever reasons you have)*.

I respectfully request that the Declaration of Readiness filed by A & A Insurance Company be set aside.

I declare under penalty of perjury under the laws of State of California that the facts contained in this letter are true and correct to the best of my knowledge.

Sincerely,

Donna Goldstein

Donna Goldstein

(address)

cc: A & A Insurance Company

(address)

How to File and Serve Documents

I f you're handling your own workers' compensation case, you'll need to comply with the legal requirement that opposing parties must be served (provided) with copies of all important documents. You'll also need to file certain documents with the Workers' Compensation Appeals Board.

Various rules govern who must be served with which documents and whether or not copies must be filed with the Appeals Board. Why are all these procedures so important? Because most of the key issues of your case will be determined on the basis of written documents, such as medical reports, your DWC-1 form, your Application for Adjudication of Claim forms and work injury reports.

This chapter gives step-by-step instructions on how to:

- serve (provide) the other side with copies of documents pertaining to your case, and
- file documents with the Workers' Compensation Appeals Board to insure that all relevant evidence in your case is part of your Appeals Board file.

A. What Is Service of Documents?

"Serving papers" refers to the process of providing copies of documents to people. In a workers' compensation case, documents are usually served by sending them via regular U.S. mail. Documents may also be served if they are personally handed to someone.

1. Who Must Be Served?

Your employer and the workers' compensation insurance company may be referred to as defendants or opposing parties, because their interest in the process is directly opposed to yours.

Every document that you file with the Appeals Board (and some that you don't) must be served on opposing parties. If your employer is represented by an insurance company, you only need to serve the insurance company, unless you're advised differently.

If a party (such as the insurance company) hires an attorney, service should be made on the attorney rather than the party. (CCR § 10510.)

You must also serve any persons or entities who have an interest in the outcome of your claim. This would include any doctors, hospitals or others yet to be paid (called lien claimants).

2. When and What Documents Must Be Served?

All documents that are filed with the Workers' Compensation Appeals Board must also be served on opposing parties. This includes all of the documents in the accompanying chart.

You must also serve opposing parties with certain documents that are not filed with the Appeals Board if:

- the documents require action on the part of the other party, or
- you intend to submit the documents into evidence at your trial.

Examples of documents that are not initially filed with the Appeals Board, but that must be served on opposing parties, include medical reports, Subpoenas and Subpoenas Duces Tecum. See the chart below for details.

3. Who Is Responsible for Serving Documents?

As a general rule, each party has the responsibility of serving documents on the other parties. In some instances, the Workers' Compensation Appeals Board may serve parties with documents filed there. You should not, however, rely on this. Get into the practice of always serving the parties with copies of any documents that are listed in the accompanying chart. Serving documents consists of putting copies in the mail and filling out a simple proof of service form, so there is really no reason not to do it as a matter of course.

B. How to Serve Documents by Mail

Documents other than Subpoenas may all be served by mail. (See Section C, below, for instructions on how to serve documents personally.) Subpoenas Duces Tecum may be served either personally or by mail.

1. Complete Proof of Service Form

A proof of service is simply a form in which you state that you mailed a certain document to a particular person or entity on a certain date. Any time you serve the opposing parties with a document, you must prepare a proof of service and staple one copy to the document you are serving. (CCR § 10324.)

DOCUMENTS TO BE SERVED AND FILED

Document	When to Serve Defendants	When to File with Workers' Compensation Appeals Board
Application for Adjudication of Claim	Appeals Board will serve if you don't have a lawyer	Within one year of the date of injury
DWC-1 form	Within one year of the date of injury	At the time you file a Declaration of Readiness
Declaration of Readiness to Proceed	At the time you file a Declaration of Readiness with the Appeals Board	When you're ready to set your matter for a hearing
Subpoena	At the time you serve Subpoena on individual being subpoenaed	Only if (and when) you need to get an order enforcing the Subpoena
Subpoena Duces Tecum	At the time you serve Subpoena Duces Tecum on the individual or entity you want to produce records	Only if (and when) you need to get an order enforcing the Subpoena Duces Tecum
Medical reports	Within five days of receipt	At the time you file a Declaration of Readiness or Application
Medical records	Not required if you don't intend to submit as evidence	If you intend to submit as evidence, serve records at the time you file a Declaration of Readiness or Application
Written evidence to be presented at trial, such as W-2 forms, pay stubs, letters, pain diaries	Not less than 20 days before hearing	At the time you file a Declaration of Readiness
X-rays	Not required	Not required; judges generally don't want to see X-rays
Letters you write to the Appeals Board judge regarding your matter	At the time you send letter to Appeals Board	Not applicable

The proof of service must give the names and addresses of all persons served, specify how service was made, provide the date of service and either the place of personal service or the address to which mailing was made. Refer to the sample proof of service, below, as a guide. A tear-out form is provided in Appendix 4.

After you've completed the proof of service form, proceed to Section B2, below, for instructions on how to copy and serve the legal documents.

FIVE DAYS ADDED FOR SERVICE BY MAIL

The time limitations for serving documents is extended by an additional five days if the documents being served are in response to documents received by mail. (CCR § 10507; California Code of Civil Procedure § 1013.)

EXAMPLE: Craig is mailed a Declaration of Readiness to Proceed. He has a total of 15 days from the date he received the Declaration to object if he wants to—that is, the normal 10 days plus five additional days because the document was served by mail.

---

2. Copy and Mail Documents

Here's what you do to serve papers through the mail:

Step 1. Gather together the papers you want to serve.

Step 2. Make photocopies of the papers, including the signed proof of service. You'll need one copy of each set of papers for every opposing party, plus two copies for filing.

Step 3. Staple the signed proof of service form to the top of the documents you are mailing.

Step 4. Put a copy of the papers, including a copy of the proof of service, in an envelope addressed to each party being served. If there is an attorney of record, remember to serve the attorney instead of the party.

Step 5. Put sufficient postage on each envelope for first-class delivery.

Step 6. Deposit the envelope in the mail box. Or, if you are mailing the papers from work, you may deposit them in the business's mail if it will be taken for collection that day.

Step 7. Keep the original signed documents and proof of service. You may need to file these with the court; turn to Section D for instructions.

C. How to Serve Documents Personally

Subpoenas must be served personally—that is, personally handed or delivered to the person being served. Subpoenas Duces Tecum and other documents may be served either personally or by mail. (How to serve documents by mail is covered in Section B, just above.)

In a workers' compensation case, you (the injured worker) or any adult may perform service. If it's convenient, have someone other than you serve the documents. Here's how to serve papers personally:

Step 1. Gather together the papers you want served.

Step 2. Fill in a proof of service form provided in Appendix 4. Follow the sample shown, and check the appropriate box to indicate personal service rather than service by mail. If more than one person is being personally served, fill out a separate proof of service for each. Don't sign the proof of service yet.

Step 3. Make copies of the papers, including the proof of service. You'll need one set for the person being served, one set for every opposing party, two copies for filing, plus the original.

Step 4. Staple the proof of service to the top of the documents you are serving.

Step 5. Shortly before serving the person (perhaps outside the person's home or office), fill in the date and time of service and sign and date the proof of service. Simply hand a completed proof of service and documents to the person being served. The person need not accept the documents. It's fine to put them as near as possible to the person being served and say "This is for you" or "These are legal documents."

Step 6. If you served someone other than the opposing parties (a witness, for example), you'll need to serve the opposing parties with copies of those documents you served, including the completed proof of service. Follow the directions in Section B for serving documents by mail.

Step 7. Keep the original signed documents and proof of service. You may need to file these with the court; turn to Section D for instructions.

IF YOU ANTICIPATE PROBLEMS SERVING SOMEONE
For people who are difficult to serve—for example, it's hard to find them or they don't want to be served—your best bet may be to hire a professional process server. Check in the Yellow Pages of the telephone directory under "process servers" or "attorney services." Process servers generally charge around $25 for personal service and sometimes more, especially if service is difficult. I highly recommend using professionals for personal service.

D. How to File Documents With the Workers' Compensation Appeals Board

To file a document with the Workers' Compensation Appeals Board, you take or mail it to the Appeals Board, where it is recorded (date stamped as received) and placed in your official case file. Before any document can be reviewed and considered by a judge, it must first be filed with the Appeals Board. Documents may be filed either in person or by mail.

You'll file all papers and documents at the Appeals Board office where your case is being heard. This office is usually located in the county where you live. If you're not sure which office to file in, see Chapter 5, Section C4c, for an explanation of how to figure this out.

1. When and What Documents Must Be Filed

Before you file any documents with the Workers' Compensation Appeals Board, turn to the chart above, "Documents to Be Served and Filed." Make sure that:

- you have served the opposing parties
- you are filing the document at the appropriate time, and
- you are permitted (or required) to file the document with the Appeals Board.

If you aren't certain whether or not to file particular documents, check with an Information and Assistance officer.

SAMPLE PROOF OF SERVICE FOR SERVICE BY MAIL OR PERSONAL SERVICE

STATE OF CALIFORNIA
DEPARTMENT OF INDUSTRIAL RELATIONS

WORKERS' COMPENSATION APPEALS BOARD

_____

Applicant

Case No. _____

vs.

PROOF OF SERVICE

_____

Defendants

I declare that:

1. At the time of service I was at least 18 years of age.

2. My business or residence address is: _____
_____

3. If service is by mail, I am a resident of or employed in the county where the mailing occurred.

4. I served copies of the following papers _(list exact titles of papers served):_
_____
_____
_____

5. Manner of service _(check one box):_

☐ a. By placing true copies in a sealed envelope with postage fully prepaid and depositing the envelope in the United States Mail on
_____, 20_____ at _(city and state):_ _____

☐ b. _(If deposited at a business):_ By placing true copies for collection and mailing following ordinary business practices. I am readily familiar with the business' practice for collection and processing of correspondence for mailing with the United States Post Office. The correspondence is/was scheduled to be deposited with the United States Post office in the ordinary course of business on _____, 20_____ at _(business address, city and state):_ _____

☐ c. By personally delivering true copies on _____, 20_____, at _____ _(time)._

6. Name and address of each party/person served:
_____
_____
_____
_____

7. I declare under penalty of perjury under the laws of the State of California that the foregoing is true and correct.

Date: _____   Signature: _____

Printed Name: _____

SOME DOCUMENTS CANNOT BE FILED WITH THE APPEALS BOARD

Certain documents cannot be filed with, or sent to, the Workers' Compensation Appeals Board. If you try to file these documents, the Appeals Board may send them back to you. Worse yet, the Appeals Board could simply discard them and not tell you. Do not try to file:

- letters to opposing parties or lawyers
- Subpoenas and Subpoenas Duces Tecum
- notices of taking deposition, and
- medical appointment letters.

---

2. Requirements for Filing Documents

All legal documents (such as completed forms, letters, petitions, briefs and notices) filed with the Workers' Compensation Appeals Board must meet certain requirements:

- Documents must be on 8¹/2 X 11 inch, white paper, with two holes punched at the top and centered (the holes should be 2³/4 inches apart.)
- All documents must have a heading that includes the name of the injured employee and the Workers' Compensation Appeals Board case number, if one has been assigned.
- Copies must be served on opposing parties, either by mail or in person. To show that service was made, you must include a proof of service. (See Sections B and C, above.)

3. How to File Documents in Person

Make at least one extra copy of the documents (and proofs of service) you're planning to serve. There are two ways that a document may be filed in person:

- You or someone else may take the document to the clerk's office at the Workers' Compensation Appeals Board. Simply ask the clerk to file the documents. Some Appeals Boards have baskets where you drop documents off for filing the next day. Before placing the document in the basket, you need to "file-stamp" it. There will be a ma-

chine similar to a time clock. Insert your document for stamping. Remember to file-stamp an extra copy for your records.

- If you're going to a settlement conference, hearing or trial, file-stamp your documents as discussed just above. You'll then need to take the original file-stamped document to the courtroom for filing in your Board file. Do not leave your documents with the clerk, as they won't make it into your file in time for the hearing.

Make sure you get back an extra copy of every document you file, file-stamped for your records. Also get an extra file-stamped copy for the opposing parties if they have not yet been served.

4. How to File Documents by Mail

Make at least two extra copies of each document (and proof of service or service letter) you're filing by mail. If you mail two or more documents in the same case at one time, you must staple them to a cover letter, which includes your name, Appeals Board case number and lists each document by name and date. (CCR § 10392.)

You will find a form cover letter to the Appeals Board in Appendix 4. Complete this self-explanatory service letter using the following sample as a guide.

Mail the documents to the Workers' Compensation Appeals Board. Include a self-addressed stamped envelope, because you're asking the Appeals Board to send you a file-stamped copy. Documents filed by mail are deemed filed on the date they are received by the Workers' Compensation Appeals Board, not on the date the stamp on the envelope is canceled. (CCR § 10390.) It is best to send important mail like this by certified mail, return receipt requested.

APPEALS BOARDS AREN'T RIGID ON FILING AND SERVICE OF EVIDENCE

Most Appeals Board judges are lenient about the rules for filing and serving medical reports and other evidence. Unless the other side objects, any evidence you file—even on the day of a hearing—will generally be allowed. Even if the other side objects, there is a very good chance the judge will allow you to file and serve your evidence anyway, reasoning you don't have an attorney and "don't know any better."

COVER LETTER TO APPEALS BOARD

Date: _August 29, XXXX_

State of California
Workers' Compensation Appeals Board

Oakland Office

1111 Jackson Street

Oakland, CA 94602

Re: Workers' Compensation Claim

Injured Worker: _Juan Martinez_

Employer: _Creekside Development_

Insurance Company: _SCIF_

Appeals Board Case Number: _BD 121_

To whom it may concern:

Enclosed please find the original and _____1_____ copy/copies of the following documents *(list exact title and date of each document):*

Medical report and bill of Dr. Smith dated June 1, year.

_____

_____

_____

_____

_____

_____

Please file the original documents and return date-stamped copies to me. I have enclosed a self-addressed, stamped envelope. Thank you.

Signature: _Juan Martinez_

Printed Name: _Juan Martinez_

Mailing Address: _P.O. Box 101010_

City, State, Zip: _Oakland, CA 94606_

Telephone Number: (_510_) _555-8181_

CHAPTER

24

Going to a Hearing or Trial

T his chapter assumes the necessary papers have been filed with the Workers' Compensation Appeals Board and your case is scheduled for a hearing or trial. (How to complete the required paperwork is covered in Chapter 22.)

If you do not have an attorney, this chapter will take you through the basics of handling your own hearing. If you have a lawyer, she will handle the procedural details for you, but this chapter will still be very useful.

Prior to reading this chapter, you should review Chapter 21 and make sure that you've adequately prepared for your hearing. If you've followed our advice, you will have already observed a workers' compensation hearing to get a feel for what goes on.

It is a good idea to read this chapter at least twice. Read it a minimum of several weeks before your hearing date so you have plenty of time to prepare. Then reread this chapter shortly before your hearing, to keep the information fresh in your mind.

Here's what this chapter covers:

- Section A discusses practical aspects of appearing at the Workers' Compensation Appeals Board. This information applies for all types of hearings and trials. You'll learn, among other things, how to check in, find your hearing room, locate your file and find the insurance company representative.
- Section B covers pre-trial conferences (often called Mandatory Settlement Conferences or pre-trial hearings). You will find out how to go about settling your case and what to do if you can't settle.
- Section C discusses trials. You'll find material on final negotiations, as well as advice on when to proceed to trial and when to continue (postpone) your case. You'll learn how to submit medical evidence and other exhibits, stipulate (agree with your opponent) to issues, and generally set the stage for the trial. Finally, you'll learn about the trial itself: questions you will be asked and how best to cross-examine witnesses.
- In Section D, we cover the judge's decision, which will be set out in a document called the Findings and Award.

JUDGE OR REFEREE: IT MAKES LITTLE DIFFERENCE
Whenever I use the term "judge," I refer to people who may technically be classified as either a judge or a referee in the workers' compensation bureaucracy. But as far as you are concerned, workers' compensation referees and judges have the same basic responsibilities and therefore it makes no difference who hears your case. Out of respect, I refer to both referees and judges as judges, and suggest you do the same.

A. Finding Your Way Around the Appeals Board

By now, you have prepared your case for the hearing, filed and served appropriate documents, notified any witnesses and organized your papers so that you can easily lay your hands on any documents you may need.

1. Several Days Before Your Hearing

Double check that your paperwork and evidence are in order. If anything's missing, leave yourself enough time to get it and make copies. You won't want to be in a rush before your hearing.

2. The Day Before Your Hearing

The night before your big day, lay out the clothes you plan to wear. If possible, men should wear a dress shirt and tie. Women should wear appropriate clothing, as if attending a business meeting. Finally, get to bed early, and get a good night's sleep.

3. Getting to the Appeals Board

If you have never been to the Appeals Board before, be sure to call well in advance and get directions. You will have enough on your mind on the day of your hearing; you don't need to worry about directions.

Plan on arriving at the Appeals Board at least 30 minutes before your designated hearing time. This will allow you time to get oriented and find out where you're supposed to be. (Information about the hearing date, time and location are contained in the Notice of Hearing. See Chapter 22, Section F.)

Expect to spend the better part of the day at the Appeals Board (although you will probably end up staying for a shorter time, such as a morning or an afternoon). For example, park your car where you won't have to move it, and don't make appointments you'll need to rush to.

Your promptness at hearings is a reflection on you, so be on time unless an emergency arises. If you can't avoid being late (flat tire or some other unavoidable reason), call the Appeals Board and leave a message telling when you can be expected. The Appeals Board operates rather informally, so if you have a good reason for being late, it shouldn't be a problem as long as you notify the Board.

4. Checking In at the Appeals Board

When you arrive at the Appeals Board, job one is to check in. Almost all Appeals Boards have a main assembly area, with posted lists of matters to be heard that day.

Look at the list of cases under the name of the judge who has been assigned to your case (the judge's name is on your Notice of Hearing). The list should have your name, the name of your employer, as well as the name of attorneys representing any of the parties. Place your signature or initials next to your name. This will notify anyone checking the list that you are present. Also look to see if a representative from the insurance company has signed in and make a note of the name.

If there is no list, check with a clerk at the main desk (clerk's office) and inquire if you need to sign in anywhere. If your name is not on the list of matters to be heard that day, find out from the clerk's office why you're not scheduled to appear.

5. Find the Courtroom

After checking in, you'll need to find the courtroom where your matter will be heard. Many Appeals Boards take security precautions to prevent entry by anyone carrying weapons or who is otherwise unauthorized to enter. As a party to a proceeding, you are permitted to enter the security area, but of course, you must comply with all required measures.

Individual courtrooms are often identified by the name of the judge or referee, rather than a room number. The sign-in sheet will have the judge's room number listed if room numbers are used.

If you have any difficulty finding the courtroom, don't hesitate to ask a clerk at the main desk. Or you might ask someone in a suit with a briefcase. Chances are that person is an attorney who is familiar with the Appeals Board.

Once you find the courtroom, enter and take a moment to get acquainted with the room. The hearing room is generally small. At some Appeals Boards, there will be an office room adjoining the hearing room, which is known as the judge's chambers. Judges sometimes hear matters that can be resolved quickly in their chambers. At other Appeals Boards, the judge's chambers and the hearing room are one and the same. If there is a judge's chambers, don't enter it.

The time for your hearing will be listed on your Notice of Hearing. Most morning calendars (schedules) begin at 9:00 a.m. and finish by noon, while the afternoon calendar generally begins at 1:30 p.m. and finishes by 4:30 p.m. You will probably not see much activity in the courtroom until it's time to begin. If no hearing or trial is in progress, you can sit anywhere.

TYPICAL COURTROOM

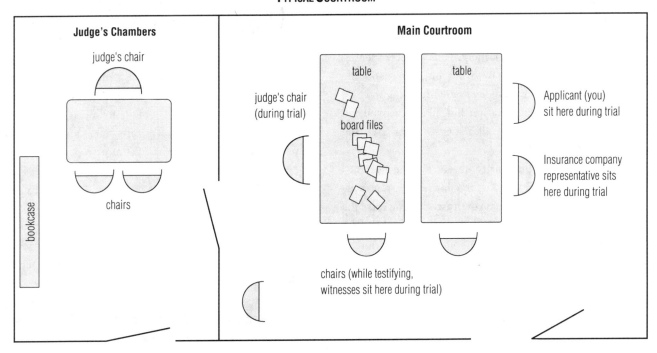

6. Find the Board File

The board file is the master file that contains all of the legal documents and medical reports that have been filed in your case. In some Appeals Boards, board files are in a box on one of the tables, or may be lying on a table.

If you can't find your board file, check with the judge's secretary, who can usually be found at a desk within close proximity to the judge's office, or ask the court clerk. Find out if your board file is available; some judges will keep the board file until it's time for your hearing.

If you have time, carefully look through your board file and make sure that it contains copies of all medical reports and other documents you have filed in your case. If anything is missing, make a note so that you can give the judge a copy of the missing document before you begin your hearing. (Chapter 21, Section E2, explains how to prepare documents for filing with the Appeals Board.)

7. Find the Opposing Parties

If the insurance company representative or attorney has checked in, you'll want to locate that person. Unless your employer is permissibly self-insured, or has been asked to appear as a witness in your case, it is rare for the employer to appear at Appeals Board hearings. Announce to those persons in the courtroom, "Is anyone here on the (your name) matter?" Do this every so often until you find the representative.

You will probably want to make one last effort to settle your case before going before the judge. You might try opening up the lines of communication by saying something about the issues to be resolved. For example, if you are trying to settle your overall case, you might say something like, "Have you had an opportunity to review my file?" or "Do you have any settlement authority today?"

If there is room in the courtroom, you and the insurance company's representative (we'll refer to him as "the representative") can sit down and discuss your case. You can leave the courtroom if you'd like. You should not need to take the board file with you if you leave the room, but if you wish to, get permission from the judge first.

Don't be afraid to tell the representative what you want and why you feel you are entitled to it. Listen very carefully to the representative's opinion regarding the issues you are trying to resolve. If anything said casts a new light on your case, you will need to make a quick analysis to see if you wish to change your position. The key to doing this is to understand your case very well in the first place.

If you are dealing with an attorney, don't let him intimidate you. If you ever had any suppressed desires to be an actor, use them now. Even if you're nervous, act with authority and confidence. Demonstrate your knowledge of the case and your determination to see it through. If the representative realizes you know what you are talking about, he is less likely to try to put something over on you.

Above all, don't cave in to what you know to be an unreasonable proposal by the representative. Be aware that representatives often use the tactic of waiting to the last moment before trial begins to settle—hoping that you will be too nervous to go to trial and will settle on their terms. So make up your mind in advance that you are fully prepared to try your case if necessary. Remember, the judge will help you through the hearing or trial.

B. Pre-Trial Conference (Mandatory Settlement Conference)

The pre-trial conference you'll be assigned is known by several terms, including "Mandatory Settlement Conference," "MSC," "pre-trial settlement conference" and "pre-trial hearing."

The purpose of a pre-trial conference is to help the parties settle the issues in dispute, rather than having a judge resolve them. A pre-trial conference is really just a meeting at the Appeals Board between you and the insurance company.

By the time your pre-trial conference rolls around, you should have already considered the key issues in your case. (See Chapter 21, Sections A and E1, for a more detailed discussion.) You should be able to answer all of the following questions:

- Do you have all the medical reports you require or do you need to see other doctors and get more reports?
- Have you prepared all your documentary evidence, such as pay stubs and W-2 forms?
- Do you know who your witnesses will be, if any?
- Has your permanent disability been rated?
- Do you have a settlement amount (often called a demand) in mind? See Chapter 19 for a step-by-step approach to figuring out this amount.

Expect to spend the entire morning or afternoon at your pre-trial conference, as the case may be. With a little luck, you might wrap things up in under two hours, but plan on spending at least three. As you'll learn, it's to your advantage to set aside plenty of time for your pre-trial conference.

At the pre-trial conference, you cannot offer evidence or testimony, and the judge will not decide the issues in your case. (That will come later, at a trial if you're unable to settle.) Although a judge will always be present at the pre-trial conference, her function is to informally assist you and the insurance company in arriving at a settlement.

SETTLEMENT CONFERENCE PROCEDURES CAN VARY

The material that follows reviews the rules and procedures applicable to pre-trial conferences. However, please understand that the procedures may be a little different at your pre-trial conference.

1. Try to Settle Your Case

You will usually be discussing settlement with an attorney or a hearing representative—a non-attorney who acts as an attorney for the insurance company. Sometimes an insurance company will send a claims adjuster (whose job is to settle workers' compensation claims), possibly the same adjuster you have been dealing with all along. No matter who you are dealing with, don't be intimidated. As discussed earlier, put on your best acting face and pretend that you also are an expert.

The best way to describe the atmosphere is to say the hearing room often looks like a crowded bus. It is not uncommon for there to be 20 or more people in a 10' by 10' room, all trying to find a place to sit and discuss their case. Typically, there will be at least half a dozen conversations taking place at once.

The judge will probably not participate in the actual settlement discussions, so you and the insurance company's representative may discuss the matter there in the courtroom or go anywhere else in the building. Because you may need help from the judge, however, you probably won't want to stray too far from the courtroom. If you need to take the board file with you for any reason, remember to first get the judge's permission.

a. If the Representative Is Pressed for Time

Often lawyers and insurance adjusters are in a hurry. This is because once an argument—or impasse—is reached, it must be presented to the judge, which is done on a first come, first served basis. Lawyers, anxious to get back to their offices, want to be at the front of the line.

If you sense that the insurance company's representative is eager to get going, use it to your advantage. For starters, make a demand that is slightly higher than what your opening demand was going to be and see what the response is. You may very well end up with extra cash simply because the insurance company representative wants to get back to the office.

You also might let the representative know you've set aside the whole day to settle your case. The rule here is, don't be rushed. By taking your time, you have everything to gain and nothing to lose.

b. Settlement Tips

Before you attend a pre-trial conference, spend a little time reviewing Chapter 20 on the art of negotiating a settlement. Remember that once the insurance company raises the offer to a new high, that figure becomes the new "floor" for your case. Any further negotiations between your demands and their offer should begin with the new floor, not with the insurance company's original offer.

Be clear about your goal at the pre-trial conference. It's the same as at any other settlement meeting: to arrive at a fair and equitable resolution of your case. Please understand that there is no urgency to settle the case now. There will be plenty of time between the pre-trial conference and the trial date to try to settle your case. In addition, you will have one final opportunity to settle before your hearing begins on the trial date. And if you just can't settle, there should be no harm in going to trial.

You might expect the insurance company to sweeten its previous offer to try and arrive at a fair compromise at a pre-trial conference. While this sometimes happens, it's also very possible that the insurance company will play hardball and, hoping that you will want to avoid a trial, make an inferior offer. Often times, the insurance company will wait to the day of trial to offer a reasonable settlement, and will do so only after realizing that you're perfectly willing to go to trial.

DON'T BE SWAYED BY HARDBALL TACTICS!

It is the insurance representative's job to convince you that your case is weak in order to scare you into settling for less than you want. *Don't allow yourself to be intimidated!* If you are adequately prepared, you will know when the representative is "blowing smoke." If you're not sure, set the matter for trial and then research the points brought by the representative.

Some attorneys may initially refuse to negotiate with you, claiming that your demand is unreasonable or that they don't have any settlement authority from their client (the insurance company). Don't believe it! If the attorney refuses to talk to you about settlement, take your time. Tell her you have all day if necessary, and you want her to seriously consider your demand or make a reasonable counteroffer.

At any time during the pre-trial conference, you may ask the judge to help you. Judges have an interest in seeing that matters are settled at the pre-trial conference if at all possible, and they are often helpful in assisting parties to reach settlement. For example, if the attorney is uncooperative, walk up to the judge and explain that the attorney is unwilling to negotiate a settlement in good faith and ask for the judge's help. Tell the judge you want to settle your case today if at all possible.

 BOTH PARTIES MUST BE PRESENT WHEN SPEAKING WITH THE JUDGE

Anytime you speak to the judge, you must do so in the presence of the insurance company representative and vice versa. Talking to a judge outside the presence of the other side is called "ex parte communication" and is not allowed.

> ### RESOLVING A DISAGREEMENT OVER AN ADVISORY RATING
>
> At some Appeals Boards, the Rating Bureau will allow parties on certain days to come in and have their medical reports rated on an informal basis. If there has not previously been an advisory rating in your case or a disagreement over your permanent disability rating is hindering settlement, try to see if the rater is available to give you and the insurance representative an advisory rating.
>
> If you are at a hearing, you can inquire of the judge or ask the Appeals Board clerk about its policy for getting advisory ratings done at the Appeals Board.

2. If You Settle Your Case

If you and the insurance company reach an agreement, you must sign the appropriate settlement documents: a Compromise and Release or Stipulations with Request for Award. A line-by-line look at these settlement documents is discussed in Chapter 20, Sections D1 and D2.

You may want to have the signed settlement documents submitted to the judge at a pre-trial conference, because doing this will expedite the receipt of your check by at least 30 days. Assuming the settlement documents are prepared to your satisfaction, you and the insurance representative will get in line to see the judge. The judge must review the settlement documents to determine if they are fair and adequate.

 SETTLEMENTS MUST ALWAYS BE APPROVED BY A JUDGE

A great advantage you have when you are not represented by an attorney is that the judge will look very carefully at any settlement proposal you and the insurance company present for approval. If she does not feel that it is fair, it will not be approved. This is kind of like having a security blanket. Don't be afraid to ask the judge for an opinion regarding the adequacy of the settlement. This will insure that she reviews the medical reports upon which the settlement is based, as well as the settlement amount and terms.

If you feel uncomfortable because things are just going too fast and you want to review the documents at home, don't sign. It's perfectly reasonable to get your check later in exchange for being able to carefully review the settlement documents at your leisure.

It's also possible that the representative will state that the documents cannot be completed at the Board (sometimes this happens and there is really nothing you can do about it). If you've reached a settlement, you and the insurance representative should inform the judge. Explain that the matter has been settled and request that the pre-trial conference be taken off calendar pending receipt of the settlement documents, usually within 30 days. In workers' compensation jargon, this is referred to as "30 days for C&R" or "30 days for Stips." Ask the judge for a hearing date, at which she will review the settlement documents, also known as an "adequacy hearing." You will need to come back to the Appeals Board for the adequacy hearing, discussed below.

ADEQUACY HEARINGS

If you have already agreed to settle your case by Stipulations with Request for Award or Compromise and Release, the insurance company will file a Declaration of Readiness to Proceed and request that your matter be set on calendar for a hearing to approve your settlement. The notice may be titled "Pre-Trial Conference," followed by wording in the document such as "Hearing is set over issue of adequacy of C&R" or something similar.

The adequacy hearing is a short meeting with a judge at the Workers' Compensation Appeals Board. At the hearing, the judge reviews the proposed settlement documents and decides if they are adequate. If the judge feels that the settlement agreement is adequate, she will approve it. If the judge does not feel it's appropriate, she will instruct the insurance company to first make certain changes to the agreement, which could even include more money for you.

You should always attend this hearing, even if some Boards may allow you to waive this procedure. This is a good way to find out if you have negotiated a fair settlement. At the hearing, bring up any questions or concerns you have and ask the judge for an opinion.

---

3. If You Cannot Settle Your Case

If you and the insurance representative cannot come to a settlement agreement, you may request the judge's assistance. As mentioned earlier, the judge wants you and the representative to settle, and will do her best to help you do so. If you feel the insurance representative is being unreasonable, or won't agree to your demand because of a belief that your demand is not supported by the facts or the law, tell the representative that you want to ask the judge's opinion. You have this right—and should use it—even if the insurance representative doesn't want you to. Stand in line and wait to see the judge.

When your turn comes to see the judge, you'll be directed to a seat. The insurance representative will also be present. If you have the board file, hand it to the judge. Always remember to address the judge as "Your Honor." Answer the judge's questions clearly, giving all the necessary information, but no more. Don't ramble or get off track into irrelevant issues. Above all, be calm, courteous and patient.

Tell the judge the one or two main points in your case that are preventing you and the insurance company from reaching a settlement. For example, let's say the insurance representative contends that based on the medical reports, your case is only worth $3,000 in permanent disability while you contend that it is worth $10,000. The judge will review the reports and probably give an opinion on the value of your permanent disability. Depending on what the judge says, the insurance company or you may decide to reconsider settlement.

By law, the judge must protect your best interests. The judge's point of view will give you very valuable information about the true value of your case as well as the likely outcome of crucial issues if your case proceeds to trial. The judge may make suggestions to you or the insurance representative about settlement. Listen carefully and, if possible, take notes on comments the judge may make.

If you cannot settle your case, even with the assistance of the judge, you must do one of the following:

- **Ask the judge to take the matter off calendar (postpone the trial).** This means that you want your case be taken off the court's system for setting trials at this time.
- **Ask the judge to continue the pre-trial conference to another date.** This means that you can't resolve your matter at the present time, but may be able to do so in the future.
- **Set your case for trial.** This means you and the representative will get a date for the issues to be decided by a judge. This requires that you and the insurance representative fill

out a Joint Pre-Trial Statement, perhaps with a judge's assistance. (See Section B4, below for instructions.)

Now let's look at these options in more detail.

a.   Take the Matter Off Calendar

On the basis of what you learn prior to or at the pre-trial conference, you may want to delay your trial date. This may be necessary because you realize that your situation has changed since your case was set for hearing and other things need to be done before the case is ready for trial. For example, your medical condition may have deteriorated since you last saw a QME, and you may need to be reexamined to substantiate your medical condition.

The workers' compensation jargon for taking your matter off the trial calendar is "order taken off calendar," or OTOC (pronounced Oh-tock). This amounts to a request that the judge take your case out of the loop and not set it for a new pre-trial conference or trial date. (If you OTOC your case, you do not need to fill out the Joint Pre-Trial Statement form covered in Section B4, below.)

To OTOC your case, you must get the judge's permission. How to proceed depends on who set the matter for trial—that is, who filed the Declaration of Readiness to Proceed.

• **If you set the matter for trial**. Ask the judge in the presence of the insurance company representative that the matter be OTOCed, and state your reasons.

• **If the insurance company set the matter for trial**. In this case, it is more difficult to get the matter taken off calendar. Because the insurance company has requested that the matter be set for trial, it probably will object to your OTOC request. If you previously objected to the insurance company's filing of the Declaration of Readiness to Proceed, you should point that out to the judge. (See Chapter 22, Section F2.) If you did not object, your position is much weaker. However, if your reasons are good, the judge nevertheless may OTOC the matter.

b.   Request a Continuance of the Pre-Trial Conference

A continuance consists of rescheduling your pre-trial conference at a later date. The reasons and factors discussed above regarding OTOCing also apply to continuing (postponing) the pre-trial conference. This makes sense. They both accomplish the same objective: to acquire additional time to do something before the matter is set for a trial. (If you continue the pre-trial conference, you do not need to fill out a Joint Pre-trial Statement, covered in Section B4, below.)

Continuing the pre-trial conference has the advantage of keeping your case in the pre-trial conference/trial loop. This means you'll save time because you won't need to file another Declaration of Readiness to Proceed. Note, however, that not all judges will allow you to continue the pre-trial conference, so you may be required to either OTOC it or set your case for trial.

 CONTINUANCE TO A "RATING CALENDAR"
If one of the stumbling blocks in settling your case is a dispute about the rating of any medical report, request that the judge continue your pre-trial conference to a "Rating Calendar." At the next pre-trial conference, you will be able to get the report in question rated by the Appeals Board rater.

c.   Set Your Case for Trial

If you can't settle your case at the pre-trial conference, you may choose to set your case for trial. At this time, you and the insurance company's representative must fill out a Joint Pre-Trial Statement form, perhaps with the judge's assistance (as discussed in Section B4, below).

Some judges may assign a trial date themselves. Sometimes the trial will be set "on notice," which means that you won't find out the date and time of the trial until you receive a Notice of Hearing in the mail. At other times, the judge will give you the board file and send you and the insurance company representative down the hall to the calendar clerk, who will assign a trial date and note it on the board file.

4.   How to Complete the Joint Pre-Trial Statement

 See *Early California Foods v. WCAB* and *Henley v. I.I.* in Chapter 28.

A JOINT PRE-TRIAL STATEMENT IS REQUIRED ONLY WHEN A MATTER IS SET FOR TRIAL
You need not complete the Joint Pre-Trial Statement if you have settled your case, OTOCed your case or requested a continuance of the pre-trial conference. This form is required only if you are setting your matter for a trial date.

The Joint Pre-Trial Statement gives basic information about your injury and employment. In addition, you and the insurance company's representative must list each and every piece of evidence you want to offer at your trial, as well as the names of any and all witnesses you will be calling. The Joint Pre-Trial Statement also sets out all issues that you and the insurance company agree upon, as well as all issues that the judge will be required to decide. As the name implies, this is a joint statement, meaning that you and the insurance company representative will fill it out together.

It is important to take as much time as you need to complete the Joint Pre-Trial Statement, even if it means that the insurance company has to wait for you. Above all, don't sign anything that you haven't had the time to review carefully. If you don't have a lawyer, the judge may help you fill out the Joint Pre-Trial Statement. If this happens, feel free to ask the judge to explain anything you don't understand.

FILLING OUT JOINT PRE-TRIAL STATEMENT HAS IMPORTANT LEGAL CONSEQUENCES

When you fill out your Joint Pre-Trial Statement, you must make certain that you list all the issues you want resolved and all evidence and witnesses you plan to present at trial. *Anything that you fail to list on this statement may be excluded from consideration at the trial.*

If the judge does not help you fill out the Joint Pre-Trial Statement, ask the insurance company representative to complete it first, since this is routine. Then carefully review the form and fill in any blanks or make changes.

If you attempt to complete the Joint Pre-Trial Statement first, realize that the form asks for some information that only the insurance company may know, such as the total amount of benefits paid. Leave these questions blank if you don't know the answer, and the insurance company representative will fill them in.

Remember to pay particular attention to information on your witnesses and evidence; anything you fail to list may not be admissible at trial. Slow down and use the information you have prepared in earlier chapters.

As of the date of this printing, most Workers' Compensation Appeals Boards are using a form entitled "Stipulations and Issues" rather than Joint Pre-Trial Statement, but the forms are very similar. Each Appeals Board, and in fact, each judge, may have a slight variation of this form, but basically it should resemble the sample that follows.

Case Number. Insert your Appeals Board case number(s) here and any other time the form asks for your case number(s). You will find this on your Notice of Hearing. Remember, you will have a separate case number for each date of injury.

Date of Pre-Trial Conference. Insert the date of the pre-trial conference (Mandatory Settlement Conference) proceeding.

Judge. Enter the name of the judge.

Employer. Insert the name of your employer.

Applicant. Insert your name.

Insurance company. Insert the name of the workers' compensation insurance company.

Counsel/Applicant: If you have an attorney, her name goes here. Otherwise, insert "None."

Counsel/Defense: This will be filled in by the representative for the insurance company.

Other: If you know someone other than you or the insurance company representative will appear at the hearing, list the name. For example, this might be a lien representative—someone representing the interests of a doctor or medical group that has filed a lien for payment. If none, fill in "None."

The following facts are admitted. This section lists all the facts that you and the insurance company agree on. If any fact is in dispute, insert "in dispute" on the line provided. *Do not admit to facts you disagree with or aren't sure about.*

1. Insert your name here.

Born. Insert your date of birth here.

While employed. Here you list your injury date or period of injury. Check one or two boxes, depending on your situation:

- Check the first box if your injury—or one of your injuries—was a specific injury. (See Chapter 3, Section B1, if you're not sure about the type of injury.) Insert the date of your injury.

- Check the second box if your injury—or one of your injuries—was a cumulative trauma injury. (See Chapter 3, Section B2, if you're not sure about the type of injury.) After the words "during the period," insert the date of injury—for example, 12/2/00 to 12/2/01.

As a (occupation). Put in your job title as of the date you were injured. After the word "at," list the city in which you were working when injured. This may not necessarily be the same city as your employment address. For example, if you were a truck driver and reported to Los Angeles each morning to get your truck, and were involved in an accident in Banning, California, the city of your injury would be Banning, not Los Angeles.

By (employer). Insert the name of the employer you were working for at the time of your injury. If you had other jobs, you need not list them unless you are claiming that they caused your injury.

Sustained or claims to have sustained. If the insurance company has admitted that your injury arose out of and was sustained in the course of your employment, check the first box. (See Chapter 3, Section C8, for more on AOE/COE.)

If the insurance company is denying that you were injured on the job (AOE/COE is an issue), check the second box. Sometimes the insurance company may admit injury to some parts of your body and deny injury to other parts you have claimed. It may be appropriate in some cases to check both boxes.

Injury arising out of and in the course of employment (AOE/COE) to. In the blank, list all of the parts of your body you claim to have injured.

2. If your employer was insured, insert the name of the workers' compensation insurance company in the blank.

Or, if your employer did not have a workers' compensation insurance company, check the appropriate box to indi-cate that the employer was either permissibly self-insured or was uninsured.

3. In the first blank, if you and the insurance company agree on how much you were earning at the time of your injury, fill in the amount. If you and the insurance company dispute this figure, instead enter "in dispute."

In the second blank, insert how much per week you would be entitled to for temporary disability payments, based upon your average weekly wage. If you and the insurance company agree upon a figure, insert it here. If not, insert "in dispute." (See Chapter 12, Section B, for information on how to compute your temporary disability rate.)

In the last blank, insert how much per week you would be entitled to for permanent disability indemnity based upon your average weekly wage. If you can agree upon a figure, insert it here. If not, insert "in dispute." (See Chapter 13, Section E, for information on how to compute your perma-nent disability indemnity.)

4. Here you list the various types of compensation you have been paid by the insurance company. It's generally best to let the insurance company fill this part out, since they usually have a computer print-out of all benefits paid to date.

Case Number(s): _DC1000_____

JOINT PRE-TRIAL STATEMENT

DATE OF PRE-TRIAL CONFERENCE: _11/5/XX_____   JUDGE: _Debra Cook_____

EMPLOYER: _____Davidson Builders_____

APPLICANT: _____Mark Nakayama_____

INSURANCE COMPANY: _Insurance Company of America_____

COUNSEL/APPLICANT: _None_____

COUNSEL/DEFENSE: _None_____

OTHER: _____

The following facts are admitted:

1. ___Mark Nakayama_____

    born _____May 17_____, _1965_, while employed

    ☒ on _____March 24_____, 20_XX__

    ☐ during the period _____

    as a (occupation) _carpenter_____

    at _____Eureka_____ , California

    by (employer) __Davidson Builders_____

    ☒ sustained   ☒ claims to have sustained

    injury arising out of and in the course of employment (AOE/COE) to: _both legs, right shoulder_____

2. At the time of injury:

    ☒ The employer's workers' compensation carrier was: _Insurance of America_____

    ☐ The employer was permissibly self-insured.   ☐ The employer was uninsured.

3. At the time of injury, the worker's earnings were $_in dispute_ per week, warranting indemnity rates of $_in dispute_ for temporary disability and $_in dispute_ for permanent disability.

4. The carrier/employer has paid compensation as follows:

Type	Weekly Rate	Period		Type	Weekly Rate	Period
___	___	___		___	___	___
___	___	___		___	___	___

    ☐ The worker has been adequately compensated for all periods of temporary disability claimed.

    The employer has furnished   ☐ all   ☒ some   ☐ no medical treatment.

Check the box before the words, "The worker has been adequately compensated for all periods of temporary disability claimed," only if you agree that you have been paid for all periods of temporary disability that you claimed. *Do not check this box if you believe the insurance company owes you some retroactive temporary disability payments.*

Check the appropriate box before the word "all," "some" or "no" to indicate whether the insurance company has paid for all, some or none of your medical treatment.

5. Check this box if no attorney fees have been paid and you do not have an attorney fee agreement. If you had a prior attorney, you should check this box.

6. This item deals with vocational rehabilitation. Check the appropriate box to indicate whether vocational rehabilitation benefits have been requested, and whether it has been completed. If neither applies, do not check them.

Benefits have been or are being provided as follows. Check this box if the insurance company has provided any vocational rehabilitation benefits, including vocational rehabilitation maintenance allowance, or VRMA. (See Chapter 14, Section A2b.) On the line, insert the dates of any benefits paid by the insurance company and the type of benefits provided.

Action pending before the Rehabilitation Unit. Check this box if there is any action pending before the Rehabilitation Unit. Fill in a short description of the action pending in your vocational rehabilitation program.

7. Other stipulations. Check this box and write in other stipulations (agreements) you and the insurance company want to make, if any. For example, you might list an agreement that the issue of retroactive temporary disability owed is resolved for the sum of $1,100.

Issues. In this section of the form, you indicate which issues are to be resolved at the trial. Check each relevant box if there is a dispute on a given issue. Do not check the box if you and the insurance company agree on the facts involving that issue. Following are possible issues in dispute.

8. Employment. Check this box if the insurance company is denying that you were an employee.

9. Insurance coverage. Check this box only if the insurance company is denying that it insured your employer for the date of injury you have claimed. (This issue is both unusual and beyond the scope of this book; seek the help of a workers' compensation lawyer. See Chapter 26.)

10. Injury arising out of and in the course of employment (AOE/COE). Check this box if AOE/COE is an issue. AOE/COE is a critical issue, so if this relates to your case, you should consider seeking the help of an Information and Assistance officer or a workers' compensation lawyer.

11. Parts of body injured. Check this box only if the insurance company is disputing your claim that you injured certain parts of the body. If you do check this box, list all parts of body that the insurance company either admits or denies. For example, "defendant admits back but denies knees."

12. Earnings. Check this box if you and the insurance company cannot agree on a figure for your average weekly earnings. After the words "Worker claims," insert the amount you believe you earned on a weekly basis at the time of your injury. Then fill in the basis for your claim, such as pay stubs, W-2s received from employer or a recent raise. Let the insurance company fill in what it claims to be the amount you earned.

13. Temporary disability. Check this box if you claim that the insurance company owes you any retroactive temporary disability. Then fill in the dates for which you should have received temporary disability. (See Chapter 12 for more on temporary disability benefits.)

14. Permanent and stationary date. Check this box if there is a dispute as to the date that your medical condition became permanent and stationary (discussed in Chapter 9, Section E). This is important for determining when the insurance company's obligation for payment of temporary disability payments ended (unless you returned to work on an earlier date). After the words "Worker claims," insert the date you claim you became permanent and stationary. Let the insurance company insert the date it claims you became permanent and stationary.

15. Occupation. Check this box if you and the insurance company cannot agree on your occupational group number. Fill in the group number you claim, and let the insurance company fill in the group number that it claims. The occupational group number is the number assigned according to your occupational duties.

16. Apportionment. Check this box if apportionment is an issue to be resolved. (How to present the issue of apportionment at a contested hearing is beyond the scope of this book. Seek the help of an Information and Assistance officer or a workers' compensation lawyer; see Chapter 26.)

17. Permanent disability. Check this box if permanent disability is an issue to be resolved.

18. Need of further medical treatment. Check this box if the insurance company is denying that you should be entitled to future medical treatment.

☐ 5. No attorney fees have been paid and no attorney fee agreements have been made.

☐ 6. Vocational rehabilitation benefits have been requested   ☐ Rehabilitation completed   ☐ Benefits have been or are being provided as follows:

_____

☐ Action pending before the Rehabilitation Unit: _____

☐ 7. Other stipulations: _____

The following issues are in dispute:

☐ 8. Employment _____

☐ 9. Insurance coverage _____

☐ 10. Injury arising out of and in the course of employment (AOE/COE)

☒ 11. Parts of body injured   _Defendant admits legs but denies shoulder_____

☒ 12. Earnings: Worker claims $_800/wk____ based on _pay stubs_____

      Employer/carrier claims $_500/wk____ based on _____

☐ 13. Temporary disability, the worker claiming _____

☒ 14. Permanent and stationary date:

      Worker claims _4/22/XX_____   Employer/carrier claims _9/19/XX_____

☐ 15. Occupation: Group claimed by worker _____   Group claimed by employer/carrier _____

☐ 16. Apportionment

☒ 17. Permanent disability

☒ 18. Need of further medical treatment

☒ 19. Liability for self-procured medical treatment

☒ 20. Liability for medical-legal expense

☒ 21. Liens:

Lien Claimant	Type	Amount
Kaiser	medical	$580

☐ 22. Attorney fees

☐ 23. Other issues: _____

The above stipulations and issues are correct.

_____   _____
Date   Worker's attorney

_____   _____
Date   Employer's/carrier's attorney

DEFENDANT'S MEMORANDUM FOR TRIAL

EXHIBITS   [X] To be offered at regular hearing   ☐ Admitted

Party	Exhibit No.	Description	Date

WITNESSES:

APPLICANT'S MEMORANDUM FOR TRIAL

EXHIBITS   [X] To be offered at regular hearing   ☐ Admitted

Party	Exhibit No.	Description	Date
Mark Nakayama	1	Wage statements	1/1/XX—12/31/XX
Mark Nakayama	2	Dr. Jones' medical report	3/24/XX
Mark Nakayama	3	Dr. Jones' medical report	8/1/XX
Mark Nakayama	4	Dr. Rich's medical report	4/22/XX

WITNESSES:

Mark Nakayama

Brian Davidson

19. Liability for self-procured medical treatment. Check this box if the insurance company disputes that it should be required to pay you for any expenses you incurred getting medical treatment. Note that this refers to money actually spent for medical treatment, not mileage.

20. Liability for medical-legal expense. Check this box if the insurance company is disputing its liability for paying any medical-legal expenses you incurred. Medical-legal expenses refer to the costs of medical examinations and reports obtained to prove your case, as discussed in Chapter 10.

21. Liens. Check this box if there are any outstanding liens to be paid in your case, such as liens filed for payment of medical treatment, medical tests performed, interpreter fees, and pharmaceutical liens. List each of the liens on the lines provided. Also, check the board file and make sure that copies of all of the liens are in the file.

22. Attorney fees. Check this box if you have or previously had an attorney who claims attorney fees on your case. If you do not know, leave this blank.

23. Other issues. Check this box to list any other issues in your case not covered above. This might include reimbursement for mileage, or penalties for non-payment or late payment of benefits. (See sidebar, "You May Be Required to Submit Your Rating Formula," for information on why you may want to list additional issues.)

Worker's attorney. If you aren't represented by a lawyer, cross this off and write "in pro per." Then sign your name and enter the date. The insurance company representative will sign in the appropriate place.

Defendant's Memorandum for Trial. In this section, the representative for the insurance company will list all of its exhibits to be offered at the trial as well as its witnesses, if any.

Applicant's Memorandum for Trial. In this section, you'll list all of your exhibits to be offered at the trial as well as any witnesses.

Check the box indicating that the exhibits are "to be offered at regular hearing."

Under the section entitled "Exhibits," list all of the medical reports and other documents you want the judge to consider in your case. Make sure you list everything you want to present at your trial. If you leave anything out, the judge may not allow you to present it at trial if the defendants object, unless you can give a good reason why you failed to list it here.

Next, list all witnesses. Make certain you list yourself as a witness, as well as anyone else you will call to testify at your trial. If you fail to list a witness here, the judge may not allow that witness to testify at your trial if the defendants object, unless you can give a good reason why you failed to list them here.

C. Trial

If you have already been to a pre-trial conference, covered in Section B, above, your matter may be set for trial. You'll either be notified of the hearing date by mail or at the pre-trial conference.

When you arrive at the Appeals Board, look for any witnesses you have subpoenaed and do your best to keep them advised of when your case will be ready to be heard. You might suggest that they wait in the designated assembly room, or in the coffee shop, if there is one.

SEND SUBPOENAS BEFORE TRIAL DATE
Immediately upon learning of your hearing date, send out any subpoenas you need to assure the attendance of any witnesses. (See Chapter 21, Section D, for instructions.)

1.   Try (Again) to Settle Your Case

Before your case is heard by a judge, you should try to try to settle it one last time. For the most part, you'll follow the same settlement procedures discussed in Section B2, above.

Your case will probably be one of several set for trial that day. Therefore, the sooner you can determine whether you can settle your case or will need to go to trial, the better. That is because the judge will generally only have time to put on one or two trials.

Keep one eye on the judge, as it is possible that if you take too long in settlement negotiations, the judge may start another trial. If you see the judge is preparing to start a trial, you and the insurance company's representative should ask the judge if you can interrupt when you know what you want to do. However, don't allow yourself to be rushed if you feel additional discussion may settle the case. Be prepared to stay for a few hours, if necessary.

The pressure to settle at this stage is more intense than at the pre-trial conference, as both sides realize that trial is imminent. If you have done your homework, you will know the strength of your case. The stronger your case, the firmer your position should be to settle at, or close to, your terms. Bear in mind that the insurance company does not really want to go to trial. It's quite common for insurance companies to settle at the last moment.

Let me say something about negotiating a settlement at this stage of the game. By now, you should know whether you want to settle your case by Compromise and Release or by Stipulations with Request for Award. (These forms of settlement are discussed in detail in Chapter 19, Section B.) If a lump sum settlement is important to you, this is your last chance to negotiate one. You can only get a lump sum settlement by a Compromise and Release. If you proceed to trial, you will be paid in the same manner as if you negotiated a settlement by Stips.

How much you are willing to come down from your original demand will depend upon many factors, including what you expect if you proceed to trial. When I have gotten as far as the day of trial without being able to settle the case, it is usually because the insurance company has not been willing to negotiate in good faith. My attitude is that they have forced me to do all the work and preparation necessary to prepare for a trial. As long as I am at the Appeals Board and ready for trial, I'll go ahead—unless I can get an offer pretty close to my demand or my case is really weak. I recommend that you take the same approach. Remember, if you don't have a lawyer, the Appeals Board judge will help you through the trial.

Be aware that the insurance company representative may not be well prepared. It is not unusual for the insurance company to turn over a file to their attorney the day before the case goes to trial. Rarely is everything in order, which gives you a big advantage. If you are fully prepared and determined to try the case if necessary—and more important, your opponent realizes that you are willing to do so—you will have a strong advantage in final settlement negotiations.

WHEN TO CONTINUE (POSTPONE) YOUR TRIAL

You or the insurance company may ask the judge for a continuance, which means postponing your trial to a later date, in situations such as these:

- Your physical condition has significantly changed since the pre-trial conference, and you need an additional medical exam and report. For example, if your medical condition has become much worse, you might want to be reevaluated to see if the medical examiner thinks your permanent disability has increased.
- One or more witnesses for either side did not appear although they were subpoenaed.
- One of the parties is ill and unable to proceed.

But be forewarned: simply not being prepared is *not* an acceptable reason for a continuance.

---

2.   Appearing Before the Judge

By the time you and the insurance representative make the decision to proceed to trial, there will probably be a line of people waiting to see the judge. Take your place in line and wait.

When your turn comes, explain to the judge that you and the insurance company cannot settle your case, so you will need to go to trial. The judge may ask questions of both of you and make recommendations about settlement. Most judges will try to get you to settle first.

Neither of you is under any obligation to follow the judge's recommendations, but as the injured worker, realize that the judge is supposed to have your best interests in mind. In fact, it is his legal duty to assist you, and only to approve fair settlement agreements you reach with the insurance company. If the judge tells you that you should settle because the insurance company's offer is higher than what you are likely to get at trial, you're probably wise to settle. Unless you have very strong evidence the judge has not yet considered, you run the risk that the judge will render a decision that awards you less than what was offered in the settlement proposal.

If it is clear that you're not going to be able to settle the case (the parties are too far apart on the amount, or one or the other side is being stubborn and won't negotiate in good faith), the judge will advise you of the status of the trial calendar. It is not uncommon for there to be three or more trials set for a particular day, as well as many pre-trial conferences. It's likely that you'll have to wait a few hours while the judge takes care of the pre-trial conferences first.

If other cases set for trial in addition to yours do not settle, the judge will have to decide which cases to hear that day and which to delay until a future date. If you are asked to return on a different day for your trial, and you have subpoe-

naed any witnesses, ask the judge to order that those witnesses appear at the continued trial.

If the judge says that he will hear your case that day, he will also tell you when to report back to his chambers or courtroom for your hearing. Be sure to arrive at least 15 minutes prior to the designated time. Bring your file, documents and witnesses.

3. Setting the Groundwork for the Trial

At the designated time, the judge will take you and the insurance company through several pre-trial procedures.

a. Submit Medical Evidence

The judge may go through the board file and read off the reports that are in the file for consideration. The judge may then ask you if he has omitted any reports that you previously listed. It's also possible that the judge will ask you and the representative to review the board file and sort out any medical evidence you want considered when the judge makes a decision.

PREPARATION PAYS OFF

Anticipating the judge's request, you should have reviewed all medical reports before your hearing. Be prepared to tell the judge what you believe to be the key medical evidence.

Also, bring extra copies of every medical report you want to submit to the judge. If, for any reason, a particular report is not in the file, let the judge know and provide a copy of the missing report. This is all done rather informally.

b.   Submit Additional Exhibits

Tell the judge what non-medical exhibits (documents) you would like her to examine before making a decision. (For a list of what evidence to use, see the Issues That May Be in Dispute chart in Chapter 21, Section A.)

c.   When to Object to the Insurance Company's Evidence

If the representative for the insurance company offers something into evidence that was not listed on the Joint Pre-Trial Statement, you should object. You do this by speaking up and saying "Objection, Your Honor. This evidence was not previously listed on the Joint Pre-Trial Statement."

d.   Identify Stipulated Issues

The judge will ask each of you what issues can be stipulated to (agreed upon). The judge will go through the potential issues and ask each of you if there is any agreement. If not, the judge will designate that issue as something to be decided at trial. The issues are the same ones you have been working with throughout your case, and are set forth in the Joint Pre-Trial Statement you filled out.

Once all the issues to be decided at trial have been identified, the judge will enter the various medical reports and exhibits into evidence. This simply means that after the hearing, the judge will read and consider each of those pieces of information before rendering a decision in your case.

e.   Final Preparations Before the Trial

The judge will then call for a court reporter. The court reporter uses a machine to make a written record of every word that is said in the courtroom as part of the proceeding. When the court reporter arrives, most people will leave the room. Unless there is an objection by the other side, you may have your witnesses (if any), sit in the back of the room so you may call them as needed. If the other side objects, the judge may instruct them to wait in the hallway, where they'll be called as needed.

IF THE INSURANCE COMPANY HAS WITNESSES
Ask the judge to exclude the insurance company's witnesses from the courtroom until they testify. This will prevent any possibility of one witness's testimony being influenced by another's.

4.   The Trial Begins

The judge will start things off by asking you to call your first witness. Tell the judge that you will testify first. It's important for you to do so, even if you have other witnesses. That way, you can state the facts that may be substantiated by other witnesses.

The judge will instruct the court reporter to swear you in. An advantage to representing yourself is that the judge will almost always act as your attorney and ask you all the necessary questions to establish and prove your case.

IF YOU DON'T HAVE A LAWYER
Take advantage of your right to get help from the judge. Ask her to explain anything you don't understand. For example, you may want an explanation of issues, stipulations and what evidence may be admitted.

a.   Questions a Judge Usually Asks

The following questions are typical of the questions you can expect. Some questions may not be asked if the issue concerning those questions has been stipulated to.

BRING THESE QUESTIONS WITH YOU
Have a copy of these questions handy at your trial. In the event the judge does not ask you specific questions (not likely), you can simply go down this list and answer the relevant questions. Skip over any questions that deal with issues that have been stipulated to (that are not disputed).

1. By whom were you employed on the date of injury?
2. When were your first employed by your employer?

3. How did your injury occur?

    Hint: *Take your time and carefully explain how the injury occurred. You want to make sure the judge knows why your injury is work-related.*

4. What symptoms did you notice?

    Hint: *Describe what you felt immediately after the accident. You want the judge to understand that your problems were a result of the work injury.*

5. Did you request—and did your employer provide—medical treatment?

6. Did you seek medical treatment on your own? If so, when?

7. Who treated you?

8. What was the reason for any delay in obtaining medical treatment?

9. Who paid for your medical treatment?

10. Were you reimbursed for any medical expenses you personally incurred?

11. Did you report the injury? If so, when and to whom?

12. Did you lose time off from work due to the injury?

13. What dates were you off work, and for how long were you off work as a result of your injury?

14. Did you receive any compensation while you were off work?

15. Who paid you compensation while you were off work?

16. How much per week did you receive while you were off work?

17. Are there any periods that you were off work as a result of your injury for which you did not receive payment from the insurance company?

18. Had you ever injured your [part of body injured] before? If so, when and how?

    Hint: *Be truthful. Explain to the judge why you feel that the prior injury or subsequent injury has nothing to do with your present problems.*

19. As a result of your prior injury, did you have to limit your work activities in any way before your current date of injury?

20. Did you see a qualified medical examiner on [date of the exam]?

21. Did you give that doctor an accurate and complete history of your injuries and problems?

22. Did you read the report of [name of doctor] dated [date of the report]?

23. Do you consider the report to be accurate? If not, in what way is the report inaccurate?

    Hint: *Hopefully your report is accurate and you agree with it. If you disagree with any part of the report, say so and explain why.*

24. Did you have to pay [name of doctor] anything?

    Note: The judge will probably ask the same questions (#20 to #24) for each doctor you saw who rendered a medical opinion about your injury.

25. What are your current complaints that you attribute to your injury?

    Hint: *Slow down and carefully tell the judge all of your present complaints. Start with the top of your head and go down to your toes, discussing each body part that still bothers you.*

26. What can't you do now that you used to be able to do?

    Hint: *Explain your physical limitations. If you used to play sports and now you can't, say so. If the QME report says you shouldn't lift more than 30 pounds, tell what happens if you do. Or tell the judge you really can't lift more than 20 pounds if that's true.*

27. On a scale of 1 to 10, with 1 being minimal pain, and 10 being terrible pain, how would you describe your pain to your [part of body injured] on a typical day?

    Hint: *Don't be a whiner, but don't underrate your condition either. Be truthful.*

28. Depending upon the part of body injured, the judge may ask particular questions about your ability to do such things as lift heavy objects, bend, stoop, walk for extended periods, stand for extended periods, grip and grasp items.

    Hint: *Again, don't be a "crybaby," but make sure you let the judge know your new limitations.*

29. What was the date you last worked?

30. When were last able to work?

31. Are you currently employed? If so, by whom, and what are your duties? If not working, why not?

32. Could you return to your former job duties? If not, why not?

33. Have any doctors told you that you will need additional medical care? If so, which doctors?

34. What kind of treatment do the doctors say you need?

b. Cross-Examination

When the judge has finished asking you questions, the attorney or other representative for the insurance company will ask you questions about your testimony. This is called "cross-examination." When answering the questions proposed by the insurance representative, be calm, courteous and truthful. Do not become upset or hostile.

What questions the representative will ask depends entirely upon the contested issues. For example, if the main issue involves the nature and extent of your permanent disability, you may be asked very specific questions about whether or not you can do certain things. The insurance representative can only ask you questions on cross-examination that deal with your original testimony. You should object to any questions that deal with new subject matter.

Sometimes the insurance company will plan to show a videotape of you doing certain things you claim you cannot do. If you're asked very specific questions like, "Can you change a flat tire?" you should suspect that they have film on you. If the representative did not list the video tape on the Joint Pre-Trial Statement, object to it being shown. The insurance company is required to provide you with a copy for review upon request before the trial. If the insurance company representative plans on showing a film to the judge, the person who took the film must testify as to its authenticity. If this witness was not listed on the Joint Pre-Trial Statement, object to his testimony.

After the attorney has finished questioning you, you may comment or explain anything you want to clear up regarding what the representative asked you. This is called "re-direct." The representative may then ask you additional questions if he wishes within the scope of what you just testified to. This is called "re-cross."

ASK THE JUDGE FOR HELP IF YOU NEED IT

If you feel you or any of your witnesses are being badgered by the representative for the insurance company, don't be afraid to ask the judge for help. Simply tell the judge you (or any of your witnesses) feel you are being unreasonably badgered and request that he tell the representative to be civil.

c. Witnesses Testify

When you are done with your testimony, you may call any other witnesses you have. The order in which they are called to testify is not really important. Ask each witness the questions you have prepared and practiced in advance.

For example, if you have called a co-employee as your witness because she saw your injury occur, your questions might go like this:

1. Please state your name.
2. Where do you work?
3. Were you working on [date of injury]?
4. Did you witness anything unusual? [Your witness will describe what she saw.]
5. Ask any other relevant questions regarding what she saw, such as what happened immediately after the accident and how you reacted.

After you are done questioning the witness, the attorney for the insurance company may ask additional questions. After she has finished, you may do the same. This process continues until each of you indicates that you have no more questions for that witness.

After all your witnesses have testified, the insurance company may call its witnesses. You have the right to question each one after the defense attorney finishes asking questions. You will have to make an immediate decision as to whether or not you want to ask a defense witness questions. It is not necessary unless, in your opinion, her testimony has hurt your case. Even then, do so only if you feel you have questions that will show the witness to be mistaken or to be biased. Otherwise, you may just reinforce the witness's testimony.

The following are reasons you may want to cross-examine a defense witness:

- **You want to discredit the witness.** You might inquire whether anyone told him he had to testify today, or whether he is being paid to testify.
- **The witness has made a statement that directly contradicts another credible witness.** You might ask him to explain the discrepancy.
- **The witness has contradicted himself.** You should point this out.

You can also recall any of your witnesses to rebut (refute) any damaging testimony. Put your witness back on the stand and ask her questions that will clear up any testimony that the insurance company's witness gave.

d. Judge Takes Matter Under Submission

When the defendants are done presenting their witnesses, the trial is over and the matter will stand submitted. That means the judge will review her notes on all testimony given. The judge will also consider the exhibits and medical evidence, and then make a decision within about 30-90 days. The judge will rarely make a decision the same day.

The judge should tell you that prior to receiving the Findings and Award, you will be mailed a copy of the judge's Summary of Evidence, which consists of notes the judge took on the trial. The judge will also tell you how many days the parties will have to review the Summary of Evidence before she issues a Findings and Award. Make careful note of this deadline.

When you receive the Summary of Evidence, read it very carefully. If you think the judge failed to note important testimony or evidence, or that she noted something incorrectly, immediately write the judge a letter and explain your understanding of the discrepancy. Be sure to serve (mail) a copy of your letter on the insurance company.

D. Findings and Award

The judge's decision, called the Findings and Award, will be mailed to you. It will generally include a summary of evidence and an explanation of the rationale that the judge relied upon to make a decision on each disputed issue. The Findings and Award also sets forth the benefits to which you are entitled. Short of an appeal, it's the final decision in your case.

PETITION FOR COMMUTATION

As you know by now, the only sure way to get all your settlement in one lump sum check is by settling your case with a Compromise and Release. If you settle your case by Stips, or you get a Findings and Award following a trial, you will receive your permanent disability award in weekly payments (paid every two weeks) until paid in full. If you want a judge to commute payments, you'll need to file a Petition for Commutation. The process is beyond the scope of this book; check with an Information and Assistance officer or see a lawyer.

SAMPLE FINDINGS AND AWARD

STATE OF CALIFORNIA
DIVISION OF WORKERS' COMPENSATION

[name of injured worker],

                Applicant,   CASE No. [number]

    vs.   JOINT FINDINGS, AWARD & ORDER

[name of employer and insurance company],

                Defendants

[name of attorney], Attorney for Applicant

[name of attorney], Attorney for Defendants.

The above-entitled matter having been heard and regularly submitted, the Honorable [judge's name], Workers' Compensation Judge, makes his/her decision as follows:

Re: Case No. [number]

FINDINGS OF FACT

1. [Name of injured worker], born April 29, 1944, while employed during the period of May 30, 20XX, through March 30, 20XX, as an irrigation specialist, occupational group number of 5, at Crockett, California, by [employer], insured by [insurance company], sustained injury arising out of and in the course of said employment to his low back and neck.

2. Average weekly earnings at injury were $336 per week for temporary disability and $148 per week for permanent disability.

3. There is need for medical treatment to cure or relieve the effects of said injury.

4. Said injury caused temporary total disability as follows: Beginning May 30, 20XX, to and including August 24, 20XX, payable at weekly rate of $336 per week.

5. Said injury caused permanent disability of 61 percent.

6. Applicant is entitled to unapportioned award.

7. All self-procured medical treatment costs shall be paid.

8. All medical-legal costs shall be paid pursuant to the current provisions of the Labor Code.

9. The reasonable value of services and disbursements of applicant's attorneys is $7,000, payable to [name of present attorneys] and $200 to [name of prior attorney].

10. The following liens are found to be reasonable and necessary and ordered paid: Bayside Medical Group. $5,237.32; Signal Radiology Medical Group, $1,327; Parker Pharmacy, $560.30; and Barry Bradstreet, D.C., $945.30.

11. The lien of Dalton Drug Company in the sum of $1,982 is excessive and unreasonable.

AWARD

AWARD IS MADE in favor of [injured worker] against [insurance company], of temporary disability indemnity of $336 per week for the periods, specified in Finding of Fact 4; of permanent disability indemnity of $___41,366.00___, payable at the rate of $148 per week, beginning ___March 4, 20XX___, for 279.50 weeks, less attorneys fees in the sum of $___7,000.00___ to [name of present attorneys] and $200 to [name of prior attorney]; together with further medical treatment as set forth in Finding of Fact 3; together with reimbursement for self-procured medical treatment as set forth in Finding of Fact 7; together with reimbursement for medical-legal costs as set forth in Finding of Fact 8; and payment of liens as set forth in Finding of Fact 10.

ORDER

IT IS HEREBY ORDERED that Defendants adjust or litigate the lien of Dalton Drug Company.

FINDINGS OF FACT

1. Applicant did not sustain an injury to his left shoulder and psyche while employed as an irrigation specialist at [employer], during the period of May 30, 20XX, through March 30, 20XX.

2. All other issues are moot.

ORDER

IT IS HEREBY ORDERED that Applicant takes nothing further herein.

Filed and Served by mail on: MARCH 4, 20XX

On all parties on the Official address Record

_____
WORKERS' COMPENSATION JUDGE

By:_____

Appealing a Workers' Compensation Decision

This chapter gives an overview of your right to appeal, the grounds (basis) for an appeal and the appeals process. The step-by-step procedure involved in appealing a workers' compensation case is, however, beyond the scope of this book.

SEEK OUTSIDE HELP IF YOU PLAN TO APPEAL

If you think you have grounds for appealing an adverse decision in your workers' compensation case, check with an Information and Assistance officer or try to find a workers' compensation attorney who is interested in taking your case. Bear in mind that most attorneys will not be interested. If you do find a lawyer, at least 15% of any judgment you win on appeal will go to the attorney.

WORKERS' COMPENSATION APPEALS BOARD

Many people are confused about the different uses of the term "Workers' Compensation Appeals Board" or "Appeals Board." The confusion is for good reason. These terms may refer to the place where you file your papers and your case is heard by a judge or referee (not an appeal at all—just your first chance to go to court). But these terms also refer to the actual seven-member Appeals Board located in San Francisco that hears the first step in an appeal if you are unhappy with how your case was initially decided and file a Petition for Reconsideration.

A. The Three-Step Appeal Process

There are three separate and distinct levels of appeal in a workers' compensation case. You must start with the first level; if you lose, you may appeal to the next level, and so on. The three levels are:
- the Petition for Reconsideration
- the Writ of Review in the Appellate Court, and
- the Writ of Review in the California Supreme Court.

THE APPEAL PROCESS

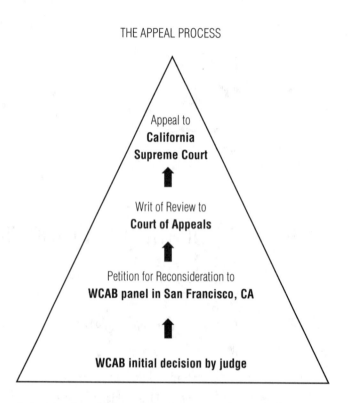

A decision by a higher authority supersedes and takes precedence over that of a lower court or authority. For example, a decision by the Court of Appeals would take precedence (would be followed by later courts) over that of an opposite decision by the WCAB.

B. Petition for Reconsideration

Any person who is affected by a final decision, award or order made by a workers' compensation judge, referee or arbitrator may petition the Workers' Compensation Appeals Board for reconsideration on any matter covered by the order. (CCR § 10988, LC § 5900.) This would be you, the employer, the insurance company, a lien claimant (such as a doctor who filed a green lien) or anyone else who is legally bound by the order.

To appeal your case, you file a document called a Petition for Reconsideration with the Workers' Compensation Board where your case was heard. The petition is directed to the seven-member Appeals Board panel in San Francisco. Usually only three members of the panel will handle a given appeal.

It is not hard to file a Petition for Reconsideration. An Information and Assistance officer should be able to provide you with a form and help you complete it. Be aware that you must act fast, as you'll only have 20-25 days from the date you received your decision, award or order.

VOCATIONAL REHABILITATION APPEALS

A vocational rehabilitation appeal differs from an appeal from an order of the Appeals Board. This is because the initial order in a vocational rehabilitation matter is made by the Rehabilitation Unit, not the Appeals Board.

If you decide to appeal, you must request that the issue be heard by a judge or referee at the local Board (not the Appeals Board panel in San Francisco). To do this, you file a petition in which you give your reasons for the appeal. Next, you file a Declaration of Readiness to Proceed. (CCR § 10992.) Copies of all pleadings, notices and orders must be served on the Office of Benefit Determination, Vocational Rehabilitation Unit.

1. Rules for Filing a Petition

A Petition for Reconsideration must be filed within 20 to 25 days of the date that the judge signs the order, decision or award. (LC § 5903.) When you receive your copy of the signed order in the mail, check for the date the judge signed it. If you received your notice in the mail (rather than receiving a copy of the order in person), you may add five days, giving you a total of 25 days to file your Petition.

Don't miss this deadline. If you fail to file your Petition within the 20 to 25 days, the Appeals Board will probably not hear your appeal, especially if the insurance company files an opposition to your appeal pointing out that you failed to file on time.

To win your appeal, you must have a sound reason why the Appeals board decision is unjust or unlawful. Your Petition must identify every issue you want the Appeals Board to consider. Specifically, your Petition may be made upon one or more of the following grounds—and no others:

- The Appeals Board acted without or in excess of its powers when it made the order, decision, or award.
- The order, decision, or award was procured by fraud.
- You discovered new important evidence, which you could not, with reasonable diligence, have discovered and produced at the hearing.
- The evidence presented before the Appeals Board does not justify the Appeals board's Findings of Fact. This means that the judge's opinion on the facts of your case are mistaken given the evidence presented at your trial. For example, if the judge listed in her Findings of Fact that you purposefully jumped off a roof at work, there would have to be some evidence to support that finding. If there was testimony or any other evidence to indicate that in fact you fell off the roof, the evidence would not justify that finding of fact. (A sample Findings of Fact is provided in Chapter 24, Section D.)
- The Findings of Fact by the Appeals Board judge do not support the order, decision or award. (LC § 5903.) In short, given the facts of the case as found by the judge, her order is plainly incorrect. For example, if the judge found that you sustained an injury at work, and then issued a decision that your injury is not industrial, the Findings of Fact would not support the decision.

Don't get bogged down by these categories. Just list each reason why the judge made a mistake on a given issue. Then point to the evidence that supports your viewpoint and explain why it does.

The Petition must contain a general statement of any evidence or other matters upon which you rely to support your petition. (LC § 5902.) Finally, the petition must be verified under oath, meaning that you are stating under penalty of perjury that the facts contained in your Petition are true and correct to the best of your knowledge.

2. Service of the Petition and Answer

If you decide to appeal, you must immediately serve a copy of the Petition for Reconsideration upon all opposing parties. This may be done by mail. (Instructions are in Chapter 23, Section B.)

Any opposing party may file an Answer to your Petition within 10 days of the date of service and serve a copy on you. An Answer is the opposing party's position regarding the merits of your Petition. The Answer must also be verified.

3. Action by the Appeals Board on the Petition

Once you file a Petition for Reconsideration, the Appeals Board usually must decide to accept it or deny it within 60 days from the date of the filing, otherwise the Petition is automatically considered denied.

The Appeals Board has the power to affirm, rescind or change the original decision, order or award upon which your Petition for Reconsideration is based. The Appeals Board may proceed by either:

- going ahead and deciding the appeal without further notice to you or without any further proceedings, or
- scheduling a hearing to take additional evidence. In this rare situation, you'll be mailed a notice of the time and place of any hearing. Information on the hearing will also be sent to opposing parties.

If the Appeals Board grants or denies a Petition for Reconsideration or otherwise upholds, cancels or changes the original order, a majority of the Appeals Board members assigned to hear it (usually two out of three) must sign the decision. The Board must state the evidence it relied upon for the new decision and specify in detail the reasons for making it. (LC § 5908.5.) All parties are mailed a copy of the decision.

4. Effect on the Original Order

If you file a Petition for Reconsideration, the order, decision or award that you're appealing is automatically suspended for ten days, unless otherwise ordered by the Appeals Board. (LC § 5910.) A suspension means that no action need be taken on the order. Let's say an order required the insurance company to immediately pay you retroactive temporary disability bene-

fits. If the insurance company appeals, the automatic suspension means that it does not have to comply with the order yet. The Appeals Board may delay the order, decision or award for as long as it takes to act on the Petition.

Any order the Appeals Board makes after reconsideration will not affect the original order or its enforceability unless the Appeals Board says so. (LC § 5908.) In other words, the Appeals Board must specifically state that the original order or decision is changed or no longer enforceable. Normally, the original order is suspended until after the appeal, and the insurance company does not have to pay during that time.

C. Writ of Review With the Appellate Court

If you or the insurance company are unhappy with the Appeals Board's decision on the Petition, a second appeal is possible, this time to the Appellate Court (also called the Court of Appeal) for a Writ of Review. The Appellate Court is the same court that you would appeal a regular court case to; it is not part of the workers' compensation court system.

The purpose of the Writ of Review is to inquire into, and determine the lawfulness of the original order, decision or award if the Petition was denied, or of the order, decision or award following reconsideration if the Petition was granted and a subsequent order issued. (LC § 5950.)

The Appellate Court can't make its own determination of what the facts are in the case—for example, it cannot hold a new trial, take evidence or exercise its independent judgment on the evidence. (LC § 5952.) It must assume that the facts found by the Appeals Board are correct. (The entire record of the Appeals Board will be certified as true and correct by the Appeals Board.) However, the court can look into whether, given the facts, the Appeals Board could have reasonably arrived at its decision.

1. Rules for Filing a Writ of Review

The application for Writ of Review must be filed:

- within 45 days after a Petition for Reconsideration is denied, or
- within 45 days after the filing an order, decision or award after a Petition for Reconsideration was granted. (LC § 5950.)

The only issues that can be determined on appeal are whether:

- The Appeals Board acted without or in excess of its powers.
- The order, decision or award was procured by fraud.
- The order, decision or award was unreasonable.
- The order, decision or award was not supported by substantial evidence.
- If Findings of Fact were made, they do not support the order, decision or award under review.

2. Service of Pleadings

A copy of every pleading that was filed with the Appellate Court by any party must be served on:

- the Appeals Board, and
- every opposing party who appeared in the action.

Instructions for serving papers are in Chapter 23.

3. Suspension of Previous Appeals Board Decision

By filing a Writ of Review with the Appellate Court, previous Appeals Board orders, decisions or awards are not automatically suspended. The court before which the petition is filed may, however, choose to suspend part or all of a previous decision. (LC § 5956.)

4. Right to Appear and Judgment

The Appeals Board, and each party to the action or proceeding before the Appeals Board, has the right to have their positions heard in the review by the Appellate Court. The overwhelming majority of cases appealed are affirmed by the Appellate Court, so you really need to give a lot of thought before you file an appeal.

There are no deadlines set forth in the Labor Code regarding when you must be notified or when a hearing by the Appellate Court must be scheduled. It typically takes six to 12 months.

At the hearing, the court will enter judgment either affirming or canceling the order, decision or award, or the court may return the case for further proceedings to the original Appeals Board where the case was considered in the first place. If the case is returned to the original Appeals Board, further proceedings will be held according to the instructions given by the Appellate Court. In other words, you may need to have a new trial on one or more issues in your case.

D. Writ of Appeal to the California Supreme Court

The final step in the appeal process is to appeal your case to the California Supreme Court if you are not satisfied with the decision of the Appellate Court. Appeals to the Supreme Court are rarely granted. Carefully consider whether the remote chance of success makes an appeal worthwhile.

All of the rules and procedures set forth under Section C, above, apply to Writs of Appeal to the Supreme Court of California. The only difference is that the Supreme Court will decide the issue instead of the Appellate Court. ■

Lawyers and Other Sources of Assistance

Although this book covers the basic information you need to handle your own workers' compensation case, a unique situation or issue in your particular case may require that you seek assistance from:

- a workers' compensation Information and Assistance officer, and/or
- a lawyer.

This chapter discusses how you may best use these resources.

A. Information and Assistance Officers

Each Workers' Compensation Appeals Board has a minimum of one Information and Assistance officer available to help you pursue your workers' compensation claim. Information and Assistance officers not only help workers, but provide information and help to employers, lien claimants and other interested parties. They are an excellent source of free assistance in such areas as:

- providing legal information
- contacting the insurance company to determine why benefits were not provided
- filling out forms
- resolving disputes, and
- reviewing settlement documents.

Because Information and Assistance officers are very busy, you may have to be extremely patient and persistent. If possible, you may want to meet with your local Information and Assistance officer, explain your case and establish a good working relationship. This may prove helpful later if you require assistance at a critical stage in your case.

To reach a local Information and Assistance officer, see Appendix 5 for the number to your local workers' compensation office. You may also reach the Workers' Compensation Information and Assistance Unit at 800-736-7401. This unit at this 800 number can answer your questions and refer you to the Information and Assistance officer closest to you.

B. Hiring a Lawyer

If you meet with a workers' compensation lawyer to discuss your case, your initial consultation must be free. Fees must be awarded on a contingency basis and are paid out of your

settlement after approval by a workers' compensation judge. (LC § 4906.) Typically, fees will amount to 12% to 15% of your permanent disability recovery.

1. Where to Find a Good Workers' Compensation Lawyer

Any attorney who is licensed to practice law in California may represent you in your workers' compensation matter. However, you should limit your search to attorneys who practice exclusively in this area. Workers' compensation has become a very complicated area of the law and requires an attorney who is very knowledgeable regarding the many new laws and procedures. Here are some suggestions.

Personal referrals. Seek out information from friends or acquaintances who hired attorneys to handle their workers' compensation case. Give serious consideration to an attorney who gets rave reviews. Watch out for the "I have a friend whose second cousin is a workers' compensation attorney" type recommendation. Also, pay attention to who is making the recommendation. Is this person really savvy, or is it someone whose judgment you often question?

Professional workers' compensation organizations. Several organizations provide a regular forum for the exchange of ideas and for learning new developments in the workers' compensation field. Because participation by lawyers is voluntary, membership can be a good indication that the attorney is willing to put forth the extra effort required to be at the forefront of the field. Ask any prospective attorney if she is a member of either of these professional organizations:

- **The California Applicants' Attorneys Association (CAAA).** The CAAA is an organization of lawyers affiliated for the purpose of protecting the legal rights of California's injured workers. These lawyers usually work exclusively for injured workers (applicants). You can reach the CAAA at 801 - 12th Street, Suite 201, Sacramento, CA 95814, 916-444-5155, and request a list of workers' compensation applicant attorneys in your area.
- **The Workers' Compensation Division of the California State Bar.** Contact your local bar association. You can find the number in the telephone book or through directory assistance. If you request a list of attorneys in your area, make sure you contact applicant attorneys only (defense attorneys represent insurance companies and employers).

Information and Assistance Office. This office may have a list of applicant attorneys who practice workers' compensation in your area.

Yellow Pages. While not highly recommended, a careful reading of the various ads can alert you to attorneys who specialize in workers' compensation and have been in practice for many years. But be wary here; the fact that a lawyer bought a splashy ad promising big recoveries is no guarantee of competence. Be sure you carefully check up on and interview any lawyer you find this way.

2. What to Look for in a Lawyer

As emphasized, you should do your best to find a lawyer with substantial experience in the workers' compensation field. When you interview an attorney about your case, do not be afraid to ask about her experience. Find out how long the lawyer has been practicing in the workers' compensation field, as well as what organizations the attorney belongs to, such as the California Applicants' Attorneys Association (CAAA) and the Workers' Compensation Division of the California State Bar.

In my opinion, you should limit your choices to attorneys who practice workers' compensation law *full-time* as an applicant (injured worker) attorney. If an attorney you speak to also practices family law, real estate or anything else, move on. Assuming the lawyer practices only in the workers' compensation area, ask if she exclusively represents injured workers. If the answer is "No, I also represent insurance companies," it's my opinion that you should look elsewhere.

3. Interview Prospective Lawyers

Once you have an attorney in mind, call her office and explain that you have a workers' compensation case. The secretary, paralegal or other staff person will ask you some preliminary questions, designed to determine whether or not the attorney

would be interested in talking to you. This will often depend on whether or not you have suffered a permanent disability. As mentioned, workers' compensation attorneys generally work on a 12% to 15% contingency fee, so they will rarely accept workers' compensation cases where there is little or no permanent disability. If they do, the final settlement will be too low to reasonably compensate them for their time.

EXAMPLE 1: James severed the tip of his little finger at work. Since this will generally result in a permanent disability of 5% or less, most attorneys will not be interested in representing James.

EXAMPLE 2: Marna fractured her hip in a fall at work. She had a total hip replacement. This injury will result in a substantial permanent disability, so any attorney should be interested in representing Marna.

EXAMPLE 3: Antonio hurt his elbow from repetitive use of a hammer at work. The doctor suspects ulnar nerve entrapment. Because Antonio's permanent disability is an unknown quantity, some attorneys will and some won't want to represent Antonio.

As pointed out earlier, you cannot be charged a fee for an initial consultation with a workers' compensation attorney. If a lawyer attempts to charge you a fee for a consultation, do not make an appointment. The lawyer is either unethical or does not know the law regarding workers' compensation fees. Either way, you don't want to be represented by that person.

In addition to asking the lawyer the questions discussed just above, ask yourself whether you like the attorney you are considering hiring. You are going to have to work together, perhaps for several years. Make certain that you are at ease and feel comfortable with your choice. Are you able to communicate with the lawyer? Does he take the time to answer your questions to your satisfaction?

Ask the attorney his policy regarding returning your phone calls and answering your letters. Any workers' compensation attorney who is being up-front and honest with you should say that because of a large caseload, it is very difficult to return all phone calls immediately, but that he will either return your call or have someone from the office capable of answering your questions call you as soon as possible, usually within five days.

THE ATTORNEY'S INTERVIEW OF YOU

The better workers' compensation lawyers can afford to turn down three or four cases for every case they accept. At the same time you are interviewing a lawyer, you are also being interviewed! Or put bluntly, the lawyer wants to determine if you are someone she would feel comfortable representing, and whether your case will produce a large enough settlement to be worth her time.

With this in mind, let me give you some ground rules about how to approach your initial interview if you want an attorney to take your case:

- Show up on time for your appointment. Be sure you are neat and presentable. (If you can't keep an appointment, call ahead of time to cancel.)
- If possible, have a copy of your DWC-1 form and all correspondence and paperwork from the insurance company and your employer.
- Answer questions honestly and specifically. Be prepared to tell the lawyer exactly how you injured yourself and what you did afterward. Have a concise history of your medical treatment to date. Because of the relatively low fees, workers' compensation lawyers have many clients, and they don't have time for people who ramble on and on.
- Completely and accurately fill out any questionnaires given to you by the attorney.
- Don't sound like a know-it-all. While it is true that if you've read this book, you will know a great deal about workers' compensation law, don't use the interview as a way to impress the lawyer.
- It is usually a mistake to say that you have spoken to another attorney, unless you can't avoid it. Even if you decided not to hire another attorney, you may be perceived as having been turned down. This can be a red flag to a lawyer who may wonder why the other lawyer rejected your case.
- Be reasonable with regard to your case. Avoid making belligerent statements such as, "I won't settle for anything less than…" or "I don't care if I ever get a dime, I just want to get back at them…" The attorney is looking for someone who is realistic and willing to listen to good advice. It's fine to be knowledgeable and want to be involved in your case, but if an attorney sees you as uncontrollable, chances are she will decide not to represent you.

4. How Workers' Compensation Attorneys Are Paid

The only way an applicant's workers' compensation attorney can earn money is by a contingency agreement or contract. That means that the attorney earns a fee based upon a percentage of your recovery. If you do not get a recovery, you do not owe the attorney a penny. If the attorney asks you for a retainer, or any money up front, get up and leave! This is a violation of the law. You may also want to consider reporting the attorney to the State Bar. You can find the number of the local state bar by calling information or referring to the telephone directory.

The lawyer's fee percentage of your recovery varies slightly from county to county, and depends in part on the complexity of your case. For example, in some counties, a judge may award 10% for a very easy case, 12% for an average case, and 15% where the attorney has done a bang up job in a highly complex situation.

Considering the amount of work involved in a typical workers' compensation case, a 12% to 15% fee based upon the amount the attorney recovers for you is a bargain. If you had another kind of case, you wouldn't be as lucky. For instance, contingency fees in auto accident and other types of personal injury cases usually run from 25% to 40% of the recovery.

The amount of the attorney fee is calculated on:
- the amount of your permanent disability award
- the amount of any *retroactive* temporary disability payments
- any money received to settle your future medical treatment
- any money you receive by way of *retroactive* vocational rehabilitation maintenance allowance, and
- any penalties you recover.

EXAMPLE: Nina's case settles for $10,000 for permanent disability plus $3,000 for past due temporary disability payments. Her attorney's fee is based upon a percentage (10%, 12% or 15%) of the $13,000. Fees are not calculated on any amounts she receives for voluntary current temporary disability payments or payment of her outstanding medical bills and related costs. If, prior to retaining an attorney, the insurance company had offered Nina $13,000 to settle her case, and she settles for $13,000 after hiring an attorney, the attorney still would be entitled to a fee based on the $13,000 settlement.

In addition to charging a fee based on your permanent disability award and retroactive benefits recovered, most lawyers will also insist that they represent you if you are entitled to and want vocational rehabilitation benefits. If you don't want representation and want to handle your own vocational rehabilitation case, you will have to find an attorney willing to take only the workers' compensation portion of your case. Vocational rehabilitation is an additional service for which the attorney is entitled to another fee (usually about 12%) based upon the temporary maintenance allowance you receive while you are being retrained. For example, if you are receiving $246 per week maintenance allowance while participating in retraining, 12% (or $29.52) would be deducted each week and set aside for attorney fees.

OUT-OF-POCKET LEGAL EXPENSES ARE PAID BY THE ATTORNEY

Any legal expenses, such as costs of depositions or Subpoena costs are advanced by your attorney and will be reimbursed by the insurance company when your case settles.

5. Pro Per Advice Only

Unlike other areas of the law, workers' compensation attorneys are not allowed to charge an hourly rate for representing you in a workers' compensation matter. (LC § 4906.) This apparently includes giving advice to pro pers (people representing themselves), as all workers' compensation fees received must first be approved by a workers' compensation judge.

If you want to hire a lawyer by the hour to help or advise you on a difficult issue in your case, it's possible that a judge would allow you to do so. If a judge were to approve an hourly fee, you should be free to find an attorney willing to help. You might try asking a judge if he would be willing to issue an order allowing an attorney you choose to bill for services for a few hours. You'd make this request by filing documents with the Appeals Board and arranging for a hearing before a judge, as described in Chapter 22.

6. How to Work With a Lawyer

Because workers' compensation lawyers have very high caseloads, their time is at a very high premium. Against this background, let's look at how to keep in touch with your lawyer so that you stay informed, provide help as needed, but respect the fact that your lawyer likely has hundreds of other cases to attend to.

Start by understanding that most offices specializing in workers' compensation cases have sophisticated systems to successfully process a case from beginning to end. Very often, the attorney relies on trained paralegals and other support personnel to handle the routine aspects of each case. The lawyers devote most of their time to appearing in court, attending depositions, negotiating with defendants and interviewing clients.

In most offices, legal assistants are trained to answer routine questions. They are likely to be more up-to-date on the status of your case than your lawyer. So as long as you get reasonably prompt and solid answers to your questions, do not feel neglected or slighted if you have a difficult time reaching your lawyer directly.

If you simply must communicate with your lawyer, and your request is ignored, realize that it is much easier to get in touch by writing than by telephone. Write your attorney a letter and address it "personal and confidential." This will assure that your letter goes directly to your lawyer. Keep your letter polite, short and to the point, such as the following example.

You naturally want to know the status of your case at all times. However, don't let this fact cause you to be overly anxious or concerned if you haven't heard from your attorney for several months. As you know from reading this book, the workers' compensation system is very slow, and it is not unusual for months to go by without hearing anything—because nothing significant has happened.

Make use of the knowledge you've gleaned from this book and ask specific questions of your lawyer. If you ask, "How is my case going?" you're liable to get a response such as "Fine." However, if you ask "Now that Dr. Smith has declared me to be permanent and stationary, are you planning to set up an agreed medical examination, and if so when?" you should get an answer to your question or at least a call back within a day or two with a solid answer.

Make sure you advise your lawyer of any changes in your address or phone number. Always advise her of any letters you receive from the insurance company, such as notices of medical appointments or changes in benefits.

SET AN APPOINTMENT WHEN NECESSARY

Asking to have an appointment with your attorney should be a last resort. However, it may be necessary if you have a new injury, get fired by your employer or some other major event occurs in your case. When all else fails, set an appointment to review your concerns.

SAMPLE

March 10, 20XX

Dear Ms. Watson:

I have been trying to reach you for several weeks regarding an issue that is very important to me. [State problem.]

Your legal assistant, Darlene Gray, while very competent, is unable to answer my questions to my satisfaction.

I realize you are very busy. However, I would appreciate speaking with you at your earliest convenience. If I haven't heard from you by March 29, I will call your office for an appointment. I would very much appreciate if you would leave word with your assistant to set an appointment date for me when I call.

Sincerely,
Susan Sheridan
Susan Sheridan
[address and phone number]

HOW TO WORK WITH A LAW FIRM

If you retain a law firm with more than one attorney, realize that you are hiring the *firm* and not that particular attorney. It is common practice for attorneys within the same firm to appear on each other's cases. For example, if "your" attorney is on vacation or has a calendar conflict, another attorney from the firm may show up to cover a deposition, settlement conference or trial. Also, the attorney who handles your case may leave the firm and another attorney may be assigned to your case.

Don't let the fact that you may have several different attorneys throughout your case upset you. They should all become completely familiar with your case and capable of representing your interests. You won't be responsible for additional attorney fees.

7.   How to Fire Your Attorney

Getting rid of your lawyer is fairly simple. Simply advise the lawyer in writing that you no longer want him to represent you. This is your right; the lawyer can't continue to represent you if you don't want him to.

Once a lawyer is notified that you wish to end the relationship, he should mail you a self-explanatory substitution of attorney form to fill out and return. You may also get a substitution of attorney form from the Appeals Board. Your old attorney and your new attorney (or you, if you will be representing yourself) must sign. Your old attorney must file the substitution of attorney form with the Workers' Compensation Board and send you your file.

In those rare cases where the attorney will not cooperate with you, you'll need to fill out a "withdrawal of attorney fee disclosure form" and "dismissal of attorney" form. You can get these forms from the Workers' Compensation Appeals Board. Go to the law office and present them with a copy and request your file, or mail your lawyer copies by certified mail, return receipt requested. If your lawyer won't cooperate, call the State Bar of California and lodge a complaint. This will generally get you quick results. You can find the number in the phone book or by calling information.

If you fire an attorney, he will be entitled to a reasonable fee based upon the amount of work done prior to termination. To guarantee that he receives it, he will likely file a lien with the Workers' Compensation Appeals Board asking for a "reasonable fee." When your case is ready to settle, you—or your new lawyer—will have to negotiate your prior attorney's lien. Obviously, you will want to convince the attorney to accept as little as possible, as the fee will come out of your settlement.

DON'T FIRE YOUR LAWYER WITHOUT GOOD REASON
If your case was sufficiently complex that your attorney agreed to take it on, you likely will benefit from formal legal representation. Once you fire an attorney, finding a new one may be very difficult, particularly if the original attorney is well-regarded in the community. Workers' compensation attorneys often have far more injured workers seeking their services than they can accept as clients. They can be, and are, very selective about the cases they take. If you are seen as a difficult, demanding client, you will likely be turned down, even if you have a good case. Some attorneys have a rigid "two attorney" rule—if you have fired two prior attorneys, they will not accept your case under any circumstances. ■

27

Legal Research

A number of books aimed at lawyers have been written about workers' compensation. Most of these are dry and technical, but nevertheless can be a gold mine of useful information. Although these books often cost upwards of $100, most are available for use at a good law library. Going that extra mile to look up the law on a troublesome issue in your case can sometimes mean the difference between receiving or losing important workers' compensation benefits.

A. Find a Law Library

All California counties have at least one law library open to the public, usually located in the main county courthouse where the Superior Court is headquartered. Publicly funded law schools at UCLA, UC Berkeley, UC Davis and Hastings College of the Law (San Francisco) also have excellent law libraries open to the public.

While you will be able to find laws and regulations online (see Section B2, below), to find cases and background sources on workers' compensation law, you'll need to go to the law library.

B. The Basics of Legal Research

The law library contains four very important sources of information on workers' compensation law. They are:

- California Labor Code (this is also available at many larger public libraries and online)
- California Code of Regulations, which defines and interprets the Labor Code (also available online)
- case law (court decisions), and
- background resources (textbooks), which cover California workers' compensation law.

 STEP-BY-STEP METHOD FOR ANSWERING LEGAL QUESTIONS

Please refer to *Legal Research: How to Find and Understand the Law*, by Stephen Elias and Susan Levinkind (Nolo). This excellent work covers in detail how to find statutes, regulations and cases.

The first step in doing legal research is to figure out what you are looking for. Formulate one or more questions that deal with your subject. For example, if the insurance company raised the statute of limitations (the time period in which you have to take a particular action) as a defense to your workers' compensation case, you may want to know:

- What is the statute of limitations?
- Does it apply to my case?
- Are there any exceptions to the statute of limitations that may apply?

Next, you will want to break down your subject into key words or phrases that will allow you to easily find your topic in various indexes to statutes, cases or background resources. For example, statute of limitations might be categorized in an index under such headings as: statute of limitations, statute/limitation of, limitation of actions or time limitations. Use the indexes in the various background resources listed below, to find the information you are looking for.

1. Find a Good Background Resource

When starting a legal research task, it's often best to get an overview of how the legal issues connected with your question fit into the larger legal fabric. Assuming you need a more detailed treatment of the subject than presented here, you'll want to refer to other books written by experts on the subject.

In order of importance or usefulness, here is a list of good resources for researching workers' compensation topics or issues:

- ***Workers' Compensation Laws of California*** (Matthew Bender). This soft-bound book contains the various laws governing workers' compensation, such as the Labor Code, Insurance Code and the Rules and Regulations. It does not, however, give any comments or discussions on the laws. Most workers' compensation attorneys (including myself) use this book on a daily basis. It contains an excellent index that allows you to easily find the law that applies to your situation. If you can afford it (the cost is about $41 plus tax), consider purchasing a copy. (Call the publisher at 800-223-1940 for ordering information.)
- ***California Workers' Compensation Practice***, by Charles Laurence Swezey (California Continuing Education of the Bar). This 900+ page book contains a good treatment of California workers' compensation laws set out by subject matter. This book is written to assist the practicing workers' compensation attorney. It is comprehensive and includes sample forms. Good treatment of the appeals and rating processes.

- *California Workers' Compensation Law and Practice*, Fourth Edition, by Sheldon C. St. Clair (California Compensation Seminars). This two-volume set gives a very thorough discussion by subject matter. St. Clair is considered to be an authority on the subject and is often cited as law.
- *The California Workers' Compensation Handbook: A Practical Guide to Workers' Compensation Laws of California*, by Stanford D. Herlick (Parker and Son). A thorough and readable treatment of California workers' compensation laws. This book gives a detailed discussion on all subject matter, including references to applicable case law.
- *Schedule for Rating Permanent Disability Under the Labor Code of California*, by the Division of Industrial Accidents, State of California. A "must have" manual on rating permanent disabilities, discussed in Chapter 18. Without it, it is impossible to rate permanent disability yourself. If you don't want to spend hours at a law library, you may order a copy from the California Applicants' Attorneys Association, 801 - 12th Street, Suite 201, Sacramento, CA 95814, 916-444-5155. The manual sold by the association now includes both the "old" and the "new" manual and is $65. Even better, view it on the Internet for free at http://www.dir.ca.gov/dwc/pdr.pdf.
- *California Law of Employee Injuries and Workers' Compensation*, by Warren L. Hanna (Matthew Bender). A three-volume set containing the Rules and Regulations, sample forms, tables, an index as well as a thorough discussion of the law by subject matter. (This is similar to the Matthew Bender book mentioned above in scope and depth; try the other book first.)
- *California Workers' Compensation Claims and Benefits*, by David O'Brien (Parker and Son). A large three-binder manual containing over 1,100 pages of information, featuring a thorough discussion of each workers' compensation law. Includes references and citations to applicable case law. A great way to find out if courts have ruled on any of the key legal issues in your case.
- *California Civil Practice—Workers' Compensation*, by Judge Alan Eskenazi, Raymond E. Frost and Lynn Pearce Peterson (Bancroft Whitney). A two-volume set containing a very good discussion of workers' compensation laws. This book is set out by subject matter, starting with an overview and proceeding through various topics. It is similar in scope to the O'Brien book, listed above.
- *Workers' Compensation Rehabilitation Manual* (Work-Comp Communications). A must for injured workers handling their own vocational rehabilitation programs. This book contains forms, Administrative Rules and Administrative Guidelines. It also lists citations to cases and various Labor Code sections, as well as giving interpretations of what the various codes and rules say. It does not, however, provide step-by-step instructions on how to handle a vocational rehabilitation case. You may order copies for $48.50 from Work-Comp Communications, P.O. Box 325, Verdugo City, CA 91046, 818-249-2120.
- *Rules, Decisions and Forms,* by David W. O'Brien (Parker and Son). Contains a good discussion of California workers' compensation, as well as sample forms and case law decisions. Good book for assisting you in filing documents and forms.

2. Read California Workers' Compensation Laws and Rules

After you review background resources, you will want to proceed to the law itself. In most instances, you'll start by consulting statutes and rules organized into groups of laws known as codes.

I estimate that 95% of all laws you will be concerned with in your workers' compensation case are either in the Labor Code or in the California Code of Regulations (also referred to as CCR or Rules and Regulations).

a. Statutes (Codes)

California laws regarding the subject of labor are contained in the Labor Code. You can find the Labor Code, which is published by a number of different publishers, in most larger public libraries as well as all law libraries. You will find various divisions, which cover different aspects of the general subject of labor. Division 4 specifically deals with workers' compensation laws. It is subdivided into chapters, which are set out in a very logical fashion. When it comes to workers' compensation, you will almost always work with the Labor Code.

To find California statutes online, go to http://www.leginfo.ca.gov/calaw.html. Check the box for Labor Code. Go to the bottom of the page to the "search for keywords" box. If you know the number of the code section (for example, LC §5412), you can put this into the box. Otherwise, enter a word or two describing your topic (for example, for the date of injury, enter "date" and "injury"). Click on search. A page will come up with a list of the laws that contain the keywords you entered. The laws at the top of the list have more instances of those keywords than the ones at the bottom of the list. Click on the law at the top of the list and browse through it to see if it answers your question (your keywords will be in bold). If it doesn't answer your question, go to the next law. If you get too many laws, you may want to refine your search. Go back to the previous search screen and either add another word or change one of the words to be more specific. If you get too few laws, or none, go back to the previous search screen and either remove a keyword or change a keyword to be more general. Click on search again.

Occasionally you may need to refer to another code, normally the Code of Civil Procedure or the Insurance Code. All of these codes are available at most of the larger public libraries and at all law libraries, or you can search the codes online at the same URL above, by checking the box for the appropriate code, rather than for Labor Code.

Whenever you refer to a code section in the library, make sure you always check the "pocket part" inside the back cover of the code book to see if there is a current supplement. The supplement, which is also organized numerically by code section, will contain the latest version of the law.

If possible, refer to the annotated version of the Labor Code (and any other relevant codes), which is available in law libraries. In addition to the actual words of the statute, annotated codes contain extremely valuable references to related court cases, other relevant code sections, key law journal articles, commentaries on the statute, and a discussion of how the code section has been interpreted.

b. California Code of Regulations (CCR)

You will often hear the California Code of Regulations (CCR) referred to as the "Rules and Regulations" or the "Rules and Regs." The Rules and Regulations that apply to workers' compensation are an extension of the Labor Code. They mostly expand upon and clarify the procedural aspects of processing a workers' compensation claim.

You can find all the regulations that apply to workers' compensation online at http://www.dir.ca.gov/samples/search/querydwc.htm.

The best way to understand the purpose of the Rules and Regulations is to review the synopsis in the front. The section that is applicable is Title 8. Like the Labor Code, it is set forth in a very logical manner.

Always check the "pocket part" of the Rules and Regulations to see if there is a current supplement that contains the latest version of the law.

3. Find Relevant Cases

Most of the laws you will deal with in workers' compensation can be found in the Labor Code, the Rules and Regulations and a few other codes, discussed just above. Additional laws have come about as a result of decisions made by the California Appellate or California Supreme courts. You may need to research case law to see how various issues have been decided by the courts. The process of referring to a case as precedent for a legal point is known as "citing a case" or "case citation."

Workers' compensation cases generally fall into one of three categories:

- Workers' Compensation Appeals Board decisions that have been denied judicial review
- California Appellate Court opinions. Certain decisions are certified for publication in the official reports and may be cited as law to the court. Those cases that have not been certified for publication in the official reports may *not* be cited as law to the court, and
- California Supreme Court decisions.

Before you do the legal research necessary to find court decisions that may help you win your case, you'll need to know how cases are referred to, or "cited." Citations start with the name of the case, usually in italics or underlined. For example: *Massey v. WCAB.* (In this case Massey is the injured worker and, of course, WCAB stands for Workers' Compensation Appeals Board.) Immediately following the name are the locations (books) where the case can be found. For example: 58 CCC 367, 21 CWCR 189. CCC refers to a set of books called *California Compensation Cases*, which is available in many law libraries; 58 refers to the volume number and 367 the page number where the Massey case starts. CWCR refers to *California Workers' Compensation Reporter*, another set of books where the same court decision can also be found; 21 refers to the correct volume and 189 to the page where the Massey decision begins.

Finally, in parentheses, some cites will tell you the court that made the decision. Sometimes this information will be very easy to understand, as would be true for (California Supreme Court) or (Court of Appeal, Appellate District). But you will also encounter the more confusing term (Writ denied). This means that the Court of Appeal decided not to consider a case, which has the effect of leaving the decision of the Workers' Compensation Appeals Board intact. (See Chapter 25, Appealing a Workers' Compensation Decision, for an explanation of the workers' compensation appeals process.)

Case law can also be very helpful at the time of trial if your right to certain benefits turns upon an interpretation of a particular section of the labor code. If you know how to do case research, you have the opportunity to find and call the judge's attention to helpful decisions. And if the judge asks each side to submit "points and authorities" (jargon that means citations to relevant cases), you'll know how to respond.

Fortunately, because workers' compensation is a relatively narrow field, it's not difficult to locate significant court decisions. In fact, most of the collection work has already been done for you by the authors of the books listed in Section B1, above. In addition, the following books, which are available in law libraries, contain virtually every case relevant to workers' compensation:

- **California Compensation Cases (CCC)** (Matthew Bender). This is probably the best source of case law for workers' compensation. All cases are grouped by year from 1936 to the present. New cases are set forth in monthly advance sheets (loose leaf publications usually found in a three-ring binder near the bound volumes). Best of all, the cases are grouped in the index by subject matter, which allows you to easily find cases relevant to your situation. Each case is discussed, including what the case held or stands for under workers' compensation law.
- **California Workers' Compensation Reporter** (Melvin S. Witt, P.O. Box 975, Berkeley, CA 94701). A monthly bulletin of key developments in workers' compensation law. (Some information is available online at http://www.cwcrwitt.com.)
- **West's California Reporter** (West Publishing Co.). This multi-volume set contains cases of Supreme Court, Courts of Appeal, Superior Court and Appellate Courts of California.
- **Shepard's Citations for Statutes** contains cross-references to all relevant case law that supports or gives an opposing opinion to a particular case.
- **California Appellate Reports** (Bernard and Whitney Company). 1st through 4th series. A multi-volume set containing all Appellate Court decisions.

a.   How to Find a Case

Here are several methods or sources for finding relevant case law:
- **Annotated codes.** As mentioned, if you look up a particular law in an annotated version of the Labor Code (available in law libraries), you'll find short summaries of all court cases that interpret the statute directly following the notes on the statute's history. Annotated codes also provide information on the statute's history (when it was adopted and modified) and case law interpretation. (See Section B2a for more on using annotated codes.)
- **Background resources.** Most of the workers' compensation texts discussed in Section B1 are copiously footnoted with citations to cases that discuss specific points of law covered in the main discussion. Thus, if you read the commentary about legal issues that affect your case, you'll almost surely find that key court cases are mentioned.

- **Shepard's Citations for Statutes.** This resource provides a complete listing of each time a particular statute, regulation or constitutional provision has been referred to and perhaps interpreted by a published decision of a federal or state court. We are, of course, interested only in California state court citations. To Shepardize state statutes, note the year the statute you wish to Shepardize was passed. Find the Shepard's volume of your state's statutes, and select all volumes covering the years since the statute was passed. Next, find the Labor Code in the upper margin in boldface. Locate the section number of the statute. Finally, note the citations under the section number. These citations are to the book and pages where the statute is referred to. Follow this process for all volumes and pamphlets up to the most recent case.

USING SHEPARD'S

It is not always easy for a novice to use Shepard's. Fortunately, the details of how to do it are covered in detail in *Legal Research: How to Find and Understand the Law,* by Stephen Elias and Susan Levinkind (Nolo).

- **Case digest subject index.** Digests are collections of brief summaries (called headnotes) from cases, which are organized according to subject and indexed. It's easy to use the subject index or table of contents in a case digest to find the court cases that deal with your legal questions. For example, look up "statute of limitations" (or other appropriate words or phrases) to find a long list of cases on that subject. The two main digests are *Shepard's California Citations* and *West's California Citations.*
- **Digest table of cases.** It is common to hear well-known cases referred to by name only. For example, a letter advising that an employee may have a workers' compensation claim is known as a "Reynolds" letter because of the case of *Reynolds vs. Appeals Board*, 12 Cal.3d 726, 39 CCC

768 (1974). If you know the name of a case only, you'll need to find its citation to find the book and page where it's located. To do this, the West Digest system is extremely helpful. Each digest (collection of summaries of cases) is accompanied by a Table of Cases that lists all the cases referred to in that digest.

- **California Reporter.** The *California Reporter* is a multi-volume set of books listing all the California cases in detail. Each *California Reporter* has a subject index, usually at the back, as well as a table of cases, usually at the front. This table contains a listing of all cases in that volume of the report and their page references.

CHAPTER 28 - CASE LAW REVIEW

In addition to the sources for finding relevant workers' compensation case law listed here, please refer to Chapter 28, Case Law Review. This chapter digests many court decisions in key legal areas. You may find case law on your "legal issue" in this chapter. For easy reference the cases have been arranged by topic and refer to the chapter and page in the book where the material is discussed.

---

b.   How to Find Related Cases

Once you've found a relevant case, you may find similar cases, or cases that affect the validity of the case you've found. The tools used to find these cases are *Shepard's Citations for Cases* and the *West* digest system. Explaining exactly how to use these systems is beyond the scope of this book. You may want to ask the law librarian for assistance. ■

CHAPTER

28

Case Law Review

Most of the laws you will deal with in workers' compensation can be found in the California Labor Code, the California Code of Regulations and a few other codes. All important ones are discussed in this book as part of our detailed review of the process of applying for workers' compensation benefits. But in many substantive legal areas we have not had the space to discuss how courts have applied the law to particular fact situations. This is where case law comes in.

If you have a particular problem in your case, it is likely that others have faced a similar situation. This means by finding a prior reported case that deals with your problem or issue—or even a similar one—you can often learn if the court that will consider your case is likely to agree or disagree with your position. In addition, you will be in a position to tell the court about the existence of the earlier case, something they may or may not discover on their own. The process of referring to a court case as precedent for a legal point is known as "citing a case" or a "case citation." (See Sidebar: "Precedent: Why One Court Follows the Decisions of Another.")

Case law is not magic. It doesn't just "appear" one day for everybody to read and benefit from. It is "created" by people, just like you, who are not willing to accept a "mistaken" decision by a workers' compensation judge. When faced with what they believe to be a wrong interpretation of a particular labor code or regulation, these people appeal their cases to a higher court (see Chapter 25, Appealing a Workers' Compensation Decision). The resulting court opinions then act as precedent to be applied by workers' compensation judges in the future.

PRECEDENT: WHY ONE COURT FOLLOWS THE DECISIONS OF ANOTHER

In any hearing before a workers' compensation judge (as well as any other court of law), the judge will base her decision on the written laws and regulations. Sometimes, however, the meaning of the law is not absolutely clear, but instead subject to different interpretations given the facts of a particular case.

To avoid different decisions on the same or similar fact situations, the judge will look to how other judges have "interpreted" the meaning of the law by looking at other case decisions. The procedure of deciding a case based upon an interpretation of the law as made by another judge is known as "case law precedent." The previous case sets a "precedent" to be followed by other judges. In order for precedent to be applicable, however, the facts in the two cases must be the same or very similar. In addition, to understand whether a second court *must* follow a previous court's decision (precedent is binding) or *may* consider it, but nevertheless arrive at a different decision (precedent is advisory), it is necessary to understand the hierarchy or pecking order of the courts. As the state's highest court, decisions by the California Supreme Court must be followed by lower state courts and the Workers' Compensation Appeals Board. As California's second highest court, the Court of Appeals must follow cases (precedent) decided by the California Supreme Court, but can treat opinions at the WCAB level as being advisory. The judges at the Workers' Compensation Appeals Board must follow the decisions of both the Court of Appeals and the California Supreme Court.

For instance, when Labor Code §4600 was written to provide the level of medical treatment an injured worker is entitled to, it was only a matter of time before judges were faced with deciding whether particular injured workers qualified for benefits under its terms; they "interpreted" and "defined" its meaning. And each time a higher court did this, it created new case law, or precedent, for lower courts to follow when faced with the same fact situation. Another way of saying this is that, when courts make law, they are fitting statutes to real life situations. And because this is true you will often want to check to see if any of this judge-made law affects you.

EXAMPLE: Your doctor states in writing that you can hire someone to do your housekeeping for you since you are physically unable to do it yourself. But the insurance adjuster claims that under the law you are not entitled to this benefit. You disagree and the dispute ends up in court. You do some legal research and locate a previous court case where a court said that the injured worker was entitled to payment of housekeeping services (see *Gardner v. WCAB*, 20 CWCR 295). You call this precedent to the attention of the judge hearing your case.

The rest of this chapter identifies and briefly discusses what I believe to be the most important recent workers' compensation cases, following the same subject organization as used in the book itself. By important, I mean a case which casts important light beyond what can be found in a statute or regulation on a fact situation which many injured workers face. But please understand that there are thousands of other cases I do not discuss. So please treat the cases discussed in this chapter as only a starting place for your case law research (see Chapter 27 for more on legal research).

⚠️ **READ THE CASE, NOT JUST OUR COMMENTS**
In a very short space below we summarize what we believe each noteworthy case means. By definition this sort of legal shorthand is an imperfect science—if you think a case may have a bearing on your situation, look it up and read it in its entirety.

CHAPTER 3—IS YOUR INJURY COVERED BY WORKERS' COMPENSATION?

The cases discussed here deal with issues involving whether or not your injury is covered by workers' compensation in the first place. Please refer to Chapter 3 for a detailed review of this subject.

1. AREA OF LAW:

The issue is whether an injured worker can file a worker's compensation claim after the worker has been terminated or laid off. If a claim for workers' compensation benefits is not filed until after the injured worker has been laid off or fired, the claim will not be allowed unless the worker can prove one or both of the following:
- the worker received medical treatment for the work-related injury prior to receiving the notice of layoff or termination, or
- the employer had knowledge of the injury prior to the notice of layoff or termination.

NAME OF CASE: *Jeffrey Mabe v. Mike's Trucking and California Indemnity Insurance Company*, 26 CWCR 381

This case says: An injured worker can file a claim for workers' compensation benefits after he quits, provided that the worker did not have prior notice of a potential for layoff or termination.

2. AREA OF LAW:

Psychiatric injury—is it covered by workers' compensation? **Jargon Note:** For workers' compensation purposes, a psychiatric and a psychological injury are the same thing. In different cases, you will see one or the other term used—there is no real difference.

NAME OF CASE: *Rodriguez v. WCAB*, 59 CCC 14, 22 CWCR 12
This case says: Rodriguez claimed that he suffered a psychiatric injury as a consequence of dealing with a physical injury. (This case does not involve a claim of a psychiatric injury due to the stress and strain of the job.) The case holds (rules) that psychological stress and strain from dealing with the workers' compensation process (dealing with court hearings, coping with results of medical reports, etc.) is *not* compensable (recoverable) under workers' compensation. However, it also says that workers' compensation does cover a situation where a psychiatric injury results from another related work injury. For example, under the reasoning of this case you can qualify for workers' compensation if you establish that as a result of the stress and strain of dealing with the consequences of your severe back injury you have sustained a psychological injury. It follows that you should advise your doctor that, if possible, her report should contain language to the effect that your psychiatric problems are due to the frustrations of dealing with the pain and limitations of the *injury*, not as a result of the many frustrations inherent in the workers' compensation litigation process.

NAME OF CASE: *California Youth Authority v. WCAB (Walker)*, 60 CCC 1099
This case says: This case plows some of the same ground as the Rodriguez case discussed just above, but deals with psychiatric stress injuries. It holds that when an original injury is psychiatric in nature, the need for additional temporary disability and medical treatment is compensable as a combined effect of the industrial injury and the workers' compensation litigation process. In this case the

applicant had an admitted psychiatric injury covered by workers' compensation and had been receiving disability payments (see Chapter 12, Section A). Applicant then requested a permanent disability advance in order to pay for his sons' college education. The carrier delayed payment (whether or not the delay was reasonable or not is of no consequence) of the lump sum advance pending an Agreed Medical Examiner's (AME) evaluation (see Chapter 10, Section A). As a result of the delay applicant suffered a significant depressive episode and required a new period of temporary disability (see Chapter 12, Section A). The insurance carrier argued that since the aggravation of the condition was a result of the worker's compensation litigation process, they should not be responsible for the additional temporary disability. The court stated that this case involved "an original injury to the psyche and need for medical treatment should major recurrent depressive episodes and/or psychological reversal occur" and that "since the original industrial injury triggered the employee's psychiatric condition, the employee's later need for treatment and temporary disability is on an industrial basis." In other words, if the original injury is psychiatric in nature (not purely physical as in *Rodriguez*, above) the aggravation due to the workers' compensation litigation process is compensable.

3. AREA OF LAW:

A normal personnel action by the employer, such as writing the employee up for alleged misconduct, cannot give rise to psychiatric injury covered by workers' compensation. And this is true even if the action was unfair. To recover, an employee who suffers a psychological injury must show that the employer acted in bad faith—that is, had some ulterior motive or reason, outside of the immediate needs of the job, to act the way he did. For example, a bad faith action by an employer might consist of writing up an innocent employee for stealing because the supervisor did not like the employee.

NAME OF CASE: *Cristobal v. WCAB*, 61 CCC 65
This case says: In this case the injured worker claimed a psychiatric injury as a result of a verbal altercation with his supervisor related to a change in the applicant's work shift. Since the court decided that the source of the stress that caused the psychiatric injury was a good faith person-

nel action by the employer, the applicant's injury was determined to be non-industrial and, therefore, not covered by workers' compensation. In other words, a *personnel action by the employer* undertaken in good faith (the employer was motivated by needs of the job) does not give rise to an injury arising out of or occurring in the course of his employment based on Labor Code §3208.3.

CHAPTER 5—WHAT TO DO IF YOU'RE INJURED

The cases that follow deal with when you are injured at work. Please refer to Chapter 5 for a more complete discussion of this subject.

1. AREA OF LAW:

Failure to report the injury on time. As discussed in Chapter 5, Section C1, if you fail to promptly report your injury and file a timely workers' compensation claim, your right to receive benefits may be barred by the "statute of limitations."

NAME OF CASE: *Reynolds v. Workmen's Comp. Appeals Bd.* (1974), 12 Cal. 3d 726, 39 CCC 768 (California Supreme Court case)
This case says: If your employer fails to follow the law and advise an injured worker in writing of his right to file a workers' compensation claim, the employer is not allowed to assert that your claim has been filed too late (is barred by the statute of limitations). But once you receive actual knowledge that you may be entitled to benefits under the workers' compensation system, the statute of limitations period (usually one year from the date of your injury) can begin to be counted.

2. AREA OF LAW:

Date of injury for continuous trauma injuries. The date of injury you use can affect the disability rate at which you are paid, for both temporary disability (see Temporary Disability Rates table in Chapter 12, Section B) and permanent disability (see Permanent Disability Rates table in Chapter 13, Section E2). The later your date of injury, the higher your disability rate will be. But for a continuous trauma injury, your insurance carrier will probably want to make the date of injury the day you first started having symptoms, saw a doctor or filed a claim. As discussed in Chapter 5, Section C1b, the date of injury should be the first day you took off work. The following cases clarify Labor Code §5412, which says that the date of injury is when you first suffered a disability *and* knew or (should have) that the disability was caused by your employment.

NAME OF CASE: *Globe Indemnity Co. v. IAC*, 125 Cal. App. 2d 763
This case says: For purposes of compensation in a progressive disease case, the injury dates from the time when the condition culminated in incapacity to work. Therefore, if you worked for several months or years after the beginning of symptoms, your rate will be that in effect on your first day off work, not on the first day you experienced symptoms.

NAME OF CASE: *Thorp v. WCAB*, 153 Cal. App. 3d 327
This case says: The date of injury is when bodily impairment results in impairment of earnings capacity. This can be the day you are eligible to receive temporary total or partial disability or permanent disability.

NAME OF CASE: *Dickow v. WCAB*, 34 Cal. 3d 762, 33 CCC 664
This case says: To calculate your disability rate, you use the rate that is in effect on the date of your disability.

CHAPTER 9—TAKING CHARGE OF YOUR MEDICAL CASE

The cases that follow deal with issues involving the treating doctor. Since this doctor determines many of the issues in your case, it is very important that you control who this person is. Please read Chapter 9 for a review of this subject matter.

1. AREA OF LAW:

The treating doctor's permanent and stationary report is presumed to be correct under Labor Code §4062.9. (See Sidebar in Chapter 9, "Treating Doctor's Report Is Presumed Correct," for more on how this presumption works.)

NAME OF CASE: *Minniear v. Mt. San Antonio Community College*, 61 CCC 1055
This case says: This very important case says that the treating doctor's report is presumed to be correct and must be followed by the trial judge unless there is clear and convincing evidence to show that it is wrong. In short, if you (or the insurance company) have the treating doctor's report in your favor, you have a very big advantage over the other side.

NAME OF CASE: *Davis v. WCAB*, 65 CCC 1038
This case says: A party who wishes to rely upon Labor Code §4062.9, which says that the findings of the treating physician are presumed to be correct, must raise that issue no later than at the time of trial. Although it is prudent to raise the issue before or during the mandatory settlement conference, failure to do so does not waive the presumption of the correctness of the treating doctor.

2. AREA OF LAW:

You are entitled to change treating doctors after the first 30 days (a longer wait is required in certain circumstances). Please refer to Chapter 9, Section C5, for a review of this subject matter.

NAME OF CASE: *Ralph's Grocery Store v. WCAB (Lara)*, 45 Cal. Rptr. 2d 197, 38 Cal. App. 4th 820, 60 CCC 840, 23 CWCR 249
This case says: This case dispels the myth that you are only allowed to change your treating doctors once. In fact, you can have more than one change of treating doctors if reasonably necessary.

NAME OF CASE: *Tenet/Centinela Hospital Medical Center v. Carolyn Rushing and WCAB* (May 2000)
This case says: This case involves a situation that occurs quite often, if you are initially sent to the company doctor for treatment (because your employer generally has the right to control your medical treatment for the first 30

days; see Chapter 9, Section C). Before you have a chance to change treating doctors, the company doctor may write a report saying that you are permanent and stationary (see Chapter 9, Section E) and that you do not need ongoing or continuing medical treatment, but you may need future medical treatment. This case says that you cannot change treating doctors because the first doctor says you don't need treatment. If you dispute the treating doctor's opinion that you are permanent and stationary and that you don't need current treatment, you must advise the insurance company, pursuant to Labor Code §§4061 and 4062, that you want to see a QME (see Chapter 10). You should dispute the original treating doctor's report within 30 days of receiving it. Only if the QME says you need more treatment can you change doctors and get more treatment.

If the insurance company tries to tell you can't change treating doctors, you should cite the next case (*Krueger*), which appears to give workers the right to change treating doctors at any time, in support of your right to do so.

Another way to overcome this problem would be to demand in writing to the insurance company that you be seen again by the original treating doctor because you feel you need treatment pursuant to the future medical provisions of his report. If the doctor refuses to see you, or the insurance company refuses to authorize treatment, you can advise the insurance company that you can change treating doctors. If the doctor agrees to see you and puts you back on a treatment program, you can then change treating doctors because you are currently being treated. If the doctor examines you and again says you are not in need of treatment than you will have to dispute his findings pursuant to Labor Code §§4061 and 4062 (see above).

NAME OF CASE: *Krueger v. Republic Indemnity Company of America*, 28 CWCR 44
This case says: You have the right to change treating doctors at any time pursuant to Labor Code §4060 and that the AD Rule 9785 is invalid. AD Rule 9785 provides:

"There shall be no more than one primary treating physician at a time. Where the primary treating physician discharges the employee from further medical treatment and there is a dispute concerning the need for continuing treatment, no other primary treating physician shall be identified unless and until the dispute is resolved. If it is determined that there is no further need for continuing treatment, then the physician who discharged the employee shall remain the primary treating physician. If it is determined that there is further need for continuing treatment, a new primary treating physician may be selected."

This AD Rule 9785 was the basis for the *Tenet*, decision above. This case says AD Rule 9785 is invalid because it is inconsistent with the right of an injured worker to the "free choice of physician" guaranteed by Labor Code §4600. Therefore under this case you do not need to request a QME evaluation, and you can change treating doctors.

CHAPTER 10—MEDICAL-LEGAL EVALUATIONS

The cases that follow deal with the area of law concerning your right to have a doctor of your choice determine whether or not you are entitled to workers' compensation benefits (a process that is called the medical-legal evaluation). Remember, as discussed in Chapter 10, different rules apply when you are represented by an attorney or represent yourself.

1. AREA OF LAW:

Whether an insurance company can require an injured worker to attend a rebuttal medical evaluation in a situation in which the self-represented applicant obtained and relied on a Board panel Qualified Medical Examiner. (Please refer to Chapter 10, Section B, for a detailed discussion regarding the QME process.)

NAME OF CASE: *Regents of University of California, Lawrence Berkeley Laboratories v. WCAB (Ford)*, 60 CCC 1246
This case says: The court concludes that the defendant insurance company was not entitled to obtain a rebuttal report to the Board panel QME under Labor Code §4050. The important point here is that if you have already gone to a panel QME and are relying on that report, you do not have to attend another exam set by the defendants. Instead, you should set your case for hearing by filing a Declaration of Readiness or an Application for Adjudication of Claim (see Chapter 22, Section D).

2. AREA OF LAW:

Whether you are entitled to obtain multiple medical-legal evaluations at the insurance company's expense, when the insurance company has obtained multiple medical-legal evaluations to address allegations arising from a single injury to multiple body parts.

> **NAME OF CASE:** *Donald W. Gubbins v. Metropolitan Insurance Company, Travelers Indemnity Company* (Board panel decision), 62 CCC 946
>
> This case says: The WCAB concluded that when the insurance company has set up three separate medical-legal evaluations because there are three separate and distinct body parts involved, the injured worker can obtain three similar evaluations at the insurance company's expense. It its decision, the WCAB acknowledged that it would not be possible to obtain an opinion from any one of the physicians to cover all the aspects of the claim. (Labor Code §§4060, 4064 and 4621.)

3. AREA OF LAW:

A party who disagrees with a report issued by the treating physician has to object within a reasonable time or it may lose the right to obtain a qualified medical evaluation (QME) report.

> **NAME OF CASE:** *Strawn v. Golden Eagle Insurance Company*, 28 CWCR 105
>
> This case says: In this case the insurance company objected to a treating doctor's report and obtained a qualified medical evaluation four months after the report was issued. The court stated that despite the absence of a specific time limit set forth in Labor Code §4061, an objection to the treating doctor's report is required within a reasonable period of time. In this case, the judge found a four-month delay in objecting to the report to be unreasonable.

CHAPTER 11—PAYMENT OF MEDICAL BENEFITS

The cases that follow deal with the subject of payment of medical benefits. Please see Chapter 11 for a detailed discussion of this important subject.

1. AREA OF LAW:

Future medical care. If the doctor(s) say you will need future medical care for your injuries, you are entitled to it.

> **NAME OF CASE:** *Gardner v. WCAB*, 20 CWCR 295
>
> This case says: An unrestricted award for future medical treatment covers any psychiatric problems that develop later as a result of the original injury. It also appears that this case requires that where there is a non-specific award (or a general medical award) virtually any medical need that is a direct result of the industrial injury is to be covered. Therefore, based on this reasoning, when you are negotiating a settlement by stipulation (see Chapter 20, Section D), it makes sense to try to include very general language covering the need for future medical treatment, such as "Applicant will need future medical treatment." Unfortunately, it also means that the insurance company will likely be bargaining for language that is very limiting, such as "Applicant's medical treatment is limited to medications and physical therapy as needed."

> **NAME OF CASE:** *Stott v. WCAB*, 57 CCC 22, 26 CWCR 3
>
> This case says: If an industrial injury aggravates a pre-existing condition then further medical treatment should be awarded. In this case the injured worker's industrial injury aggravated pre-existing multiple sclerosis. The court held that the defendants are responsible for treating the pre-existing multiple sclerosis for life since there is no way to apportion treatment between the applicant's current injury and the multiple sclerosis in a situation where the multiple sclerosis is made worse by the industrial injury. Of course the defendants are also responsible for treating the industrial injury.

2. AREA OF LAW:

Can future medical treatment also include paying for house-keeping services?

> **NAME OF CASE:** *Jensen v. WCAB*, 57 CCC 19, 20 CWCR 10
> This case says: If the doctor says housekeeping services are a medical necessity the insurance carrier must pay for them.

CHAPTER 12—TEMPORARY DISABILITY BENEFITS

The cases that follow deal with temporary disability benefits payable to the injured worker while she cannot work as a result of a work-related injury. (Please refer to Chapter 12 for a detailed review of this subject.)

1. AREA OF LAW:

Establishing the amount of temporary disability benefit. Generally, as discussed in Chapter 12, this benefit is payable at two-thirds of the worker's average weekly wage with certain minimum and maximum amounts based upon the date of injury. (See Chart in Chapter 12, Section B, "Temporary Disability and Minimum/Maximum Rates for the First Two Years From Your Date of Injury.")

> **NAME OF CASE:** *Hofmeister v. WCAB* (1984), 49 CCC 438; 12 CWCR 155
> This case says: Temporary disability benefits, whether paid on time (or past due), which are paid more than two years after the date of injury, must be paid at the current temporary disability rate. For example, assume the date of injury is 5/2/94 and the injured worker is entitled to the maximum temporary disability rate of $336 (see Chapter 11, Section B). But because of procedural delays, benefits are not paid. Over two years later the applicant finally receives temporary disability payments. They would be paid the maximum rate of $448 as of 1996 (or at two-thirds of actual wages for workers who don't qualify for the maximum).

> **NAME OF CASE:** *Placer County Office of Education v. WCAB (Halkyard)*, 60 CCC 641
> This case says: This older case, which is still good law, concerns how the amount of temporary disability is determined for people who ordinarily work less than a full year. It is important to teachers and seasonal workers. Here the applicant was a teacher who was off during the summer and therefore only worked ten months out of the year. She earned a total salary of $12,400 for the year. The insurance company tried to argue that during the summer months, when the teacher ordinarily received no income, it should not have to pay her anything. The court disagreed, ruling that the teacher is entitled to temporary disability for the entire year because it is her earning *capacity* that is being replaced, not her actual lost wages. The court then went on to compute the teacher's benefits based on two different rates. The first rate, payable during the ten months when she would ordinarily be working, was based on the $12,400 divided by the 40.71 weeks of the school year. It worked out to a weekly wage of $304.59. (The teacher got two-thirds of this figure, or $203.06 per week, for temporary disability.) The court then ruled that during the remaining 11.29 weeks when she did not teach, she would be entitled to a temporary disability rate of $158.97. This was computed by taking the $12,400 and dividing it by 52 weeks for an average weekly wage of $238.40. Two-thirds of this figure produced the temporary disability rate of $158.97 payable during the summer months. Despite this case, an insurance carrier will probably try to pay disability based on the 52-week average wage (in this case, $158.97). Don't let them get away with it.

2. AREA OF LAW:

Defendant's right to deduct any money earned by the injured worker from temporary disability amounts owed to the worker. Please see Chapter 12, Section A2, for a detailed discussion of temporary partial disability.

> **NAME OF CASE:** *Hupp v. WCAB*, 60 CCC 928, 45 Cal. Rptr. 2d 859; 23 CWCR 275
> This case says: When the injured worker is engaged in a self-employment activity, the defendant insurance carrier is only entitled to offset (take credit for) the *net* income earned from the injured worker's self-employment after

all necessary business expenses are deducted. The defendant argued that they should be entitled to deduct applicant's gross receipts (money received from self-employment before the cost of doing business was subtracted) from the amount of temporary disability owed. The court obviously did not agree.

3. AREA OF LAW:

Applicant's right to receive temporary disability while receiving treatment for a non-industrial condition that must be treated before applicant's industrial injury can be properly treated. (Please refer to Chapter 11 for a detailed discussion of medical treatment.)

> **NAME OF CASE:** *Fremont Medical Center v. WCAB (Easley)*, 61 CCC 110
> This case says: Applicant was scheduled for shoulder surgery for an industrial injury. During the surgery work-up it was discovered that applicant had anemia which needed to be controlled before surgery could proceed. Applicant was entitled to receive temporary disability payments during the period it took to cure the anemia so that surgery could take place.

4. AREA OF LAW:

Entitlement to temporary disability after retirement age.

> **NAME OF CASE:** *Gonzales v. WCAB*, 63 CCC 147
> This case says that an injured worker is not entitled to temporary disability benefits after retirement unless she has made known her intention to return to the labor market. In this case, the injured worker turned 65 while on temporary total disability and had previously made known her intention to retire at age 65. The court said that since the injured worker had removed herself from the labor market, she was not entitled to temporary disability benefits. If you are close to age 65 and still temporarily totally disabled (see Chapter 12), make sure your employer and the insurance company know you intend to keep working after age 65 or retirement.

CHAPTER 13—PERMANENT DISABILITY

The cases that follow deal with the permanent disability benefit payable to an injured worker. Specifically, they concern the issue of how the permanent disability affects the worker's future ability to participate in the labor market. (Please refer to Chapter 13 for a review of the permanent disability benefit.)

1. AREA OF LAW:

You are entitled to up to two-thirds of your average weekly wage as a permanent disability benefit, according to your date of injury, within the minimum and maximum amounts allowed by law. (Please refer to Chapter 13, Section E, for a review of this benefit.)

> **NAME OF CASE:** *Wilkinson v. WCAB*, 42 CCC 402, 5 CWCR 87, 19 Cal. 3d 491
> This case says: Where there are two separate injuries with the same employer and the condition resulting from the first injury became permanent and stationary after the date of the second injury, the Appeals Board (rather than calculating the amount of benefits payable on the percentage of disability assigned to each injury separately) must calculate the amount on the combined total disability resulting from both injuries (but also see the Parker case just below, which limits the Wilkinson rule to two or more injuries involving the *same body part*).

 ALWAYS CITE THIS CASE WHEN YOU HAVE TWO OR MORE INJURIES TO THE SAME BODY PART

You should definitely refer to this famous and often cited case if you have two or more injuries to the same body part that become permanent and stationary at the same time. Under its reasoning, you will get more money for your permanent disability because of the progressive escalation in your benefit amount as your percentage of disability goes up. Example: Two separate injuries to the same body part, each by themselves having a 10% disability, result in a larger disability payment if computed as an overall 20% disability—as required by the Wilkinson case (rather than 10% plus 10%). Also, the fact that the date of the last injury is used for computational purposes is another reason why you may end up with a higher permanent disability rate.

NAME OF CASE: *Parker v. WCAB*, 57 CCC 608, 12 Cal. Rptr. 2d 370

This case says: The use of the Wilkinson case doctrine discussed just above only applies to situations where the same part of the body is involved in a successive injury. So if you have an ankle injury and a back injury that both become permanent and stationary at the same time, Wilkinson does not apply and you have two separate permanent disability awards (they can't be combined). However, if you have two successive back injuries that become permanent and stationary at the same time, they can be combined for a higher permanent disability rating. (Although not definitively determined, this is probably true if the injuries are to a part of the body covered by the same workers' compensation number—a back injury and a neck injury, for example, are both classified under the number 18.1 for workers' compensation purposes (see Chapter 18, Rating Your Permanent Disability), and therefore should be able to be combined under Wilkinson.

NAME OF CASE: *Rumbaugh v. WCAB*, 87 Cal. Ap. 3d 907, 43 CCC 1399

This case says: In this case an injured worker had two successive injuries to the same part of body that became permanent and stationary at the same time. However, the injuries did not occur at the same employer. The court said that the worker can combine those injuries for rating purposes even if the injuries do not occur with the same employer, abandoning the same employer rule from the *Wilkinson* case, above.

NAME OF CASE: *Nuelle v. WCAB*, 92 Cal. Ap. 3d. 239, 44 CCC 1399

This case says: When a worker is injured on two separate dates, the worker is entitled to all permanent disability benefits at the rate in effect as of the last date of injury.

NAME OF CASE: *Harold v. WCAB*, 100 Cal. 3d. 772, 45 CCC 77

This case says: Where a worker is injured on two separate dates and both of the injuries become permanent and stationary at the same time, the injuries may be combined for permanent disability rating purposes even if the inju-

ries were to different parts of body. The court said that what matters is not the parts of the body injured, but what parts are causing the permanent disability.

NAME OF CASE: *LeBoeuf v. WCAB* (1983), 48 CCC 587

This case says: The amount of your permanent disability may be determined by factors in addition to the medical reports. Specifically, evidence can be considered at trial to the point that the injured worker is precluded from receiving rehabilitation benefits because the worker's injury is so serious he is found to be non-feasible (non-eligible) for vocational rehabilitation (see Chapter 14, Section C2). Similarly, evidence that the applicant can't function in the open labor market and is in fact 100% disabled can also be considered.

NAME OF CASE: *Sandlin v. WCAB*, 55 CCC 277

This case says: Permanent disability encompasses not only impairment of the normal use of a portion of the body, but also impairment of earning capacity and the diminished ability of the injured worker to compete in an open labor market. In this case the injured worker was unable to perform work for over two hours at a stretch due to back pain and was not a feasible candidate for vocational rehabilitation and was therefore found to be permanently and totally disabled.

2. AREA OF LAW:

Credit for payment of prior disability award. When you file a petition to reopen your case based on a new and further disability (see Chapter 19, Section B), the defendant is entitled to a credit (deduction) for prior payments. Start by understanding you are entitled to additional permanent disability payments for any increase in your disability as a result of the natural progression of your prior injury. For example, if your prior permanent disability award was 20% and you now (within five years of the date of your injury) have a permanent disability of 40%, you are entitled to additional benefits. But in computing them, the insurance carrier is entitled to deduct the money already paid based on your 20% disability from the 40% you are now entitled to with the result that you get an additional permanent disability award of 20%. This is also true when you have a new injury. For example, let's say you injured your back in 1991 and settled that case in 1993 for a permanent disability of 30%. You now have a new injury to your back (not a natural progression from your prior injury) that results in a permanent disability of 50%. The defendant is entitled to deduct the money already paid for the disability from what is now due for the 50% disability, *unless you can show that you rehabilitated yourself from the prior injury*. In other words if, since 1993, you exercised and strengthened your back to the point where your back was no longer disabled (or, for example, improved it to be only 10% disabled), the insurance carrier would not be entitled to deduct the prior 30%. In the case of your strengthening it so you only had a 10% disability from the first injury, that's the amount they could deduct from the subsequent amount.

NAME OF CASE: *The Home Depot v. WCAB (Smith)*, 60 CCC 449

This case says: If the original award is for a partial disability (let's say 20%) and after petitioning to reopen the case you are found to have a larger overall disability (say, 36%), the defendant will argue that your disability should be figured by simply subtracting the original percentage from the higher percentage of your overall disability (36% minus 20% = 16%). This case says the correct way to do this is to take the dollar value of 36% and subtract the dollar value of the prior award. Although this sounds like a highly technical distinction, it's important, since doing it this way will always result in more money in your pocket.

EXAMPLE: Using the figures above for a 7/2/97 date of injury, 16% disability is equivalent to $8,680. So if the subtraction method were used above (36% minus 20% = 16%), the injured worker would get $8,680. However, the dollar value of 36% disability is $28,560. Subtracting his prior award of 20% ($11,280) leaves $17,280. As you can see this results in substantially more money ($17,280 as compared to $8,680).

3. AREA OF LAW:

Where you have more than one injury and suffer a separate permanent disability to each injured body part, the important principle known as "overlap" may apply. Simply stated, over-

lap occurs when a work restriction for one part of the body also benefits another part of the body. For example, if you are restricted from heavy lifting because of your back, your injured knees will also benefit from that restriction. Unfortunately, because the restriction of no heavy lifting as regards your knees is "absorbed" in the no heavy lifting restriction for your back, the insurance carrier will use this principle to reduce the amount of disability you get. In response, you should claim that the doctrine of absorption doesn't apply and you are entitled to a permanent disability award for each part of your body that you injured. Please see Chapter 18, Section C, Step 2d, for a detailed review of this subject matter.

NAME OF CASE: *County of Los Angeles v. WCAB (McLaughlin)*, 56 CCC 510

This case says: If a non-industrial medical condition develops concurrently with an industrial condition (injury), the doctrine of overlap will not apply. In this case the applicant developed non-industrial obstructive lung disease due to smoking. At the same time, due to exposure to asbestos at work the applicant developed a restrictive lung condition that was not as severe as the non-industrial condition. The insurance carrier argued that the less severe work-related condition was completely absorbed (complete overlap occurred) by the non-industrial condition. Their point was that absent the industrial injury the applicant would have still had at least this amount of disability and that therefore the industrial injury didn't really cause any additional disability. The court did not agree, holding that there can be no apportionment (overlap) between a medical condition covered by workers' compensation and one that developed off the job (a non-industrial condition) at the same time. The effect of the court's ruling is that when you have a non-industrial disability that develops at the same time as your industrial disability, the insurance carrier can't use that against you to deny you benefits for your industrial injury.

4. AREA OF LAW:

Using the treating doctor's report to establish permanent disability. (See Chapter 13, Section A, for a discussion about permanent disability.)

NAME OF CASE: *Peterson v. Wausau*, 20 CWCR 250

This case says: For dates of injury between 1/1/91 and 12/31/93, the treating doctor's report cannot be relied upon for determining the amount of your permanent disability. The law requires that you obtain a QME evaluation. But for injuries on or after 1/1/94 you can rely on the treating doctor's report to determine the amount of permanent disability if you want to.

 STARTING IN 1994, YOUR TREATING DOCTOR'S REPORT CARRIES LOTS OF WEIGHT

For injuries on or after 1/1/94, the treating doctor's report is given a presumption of being correct. This means you will normally want to rely on this report if it is favorable to you. To try to counter this report your insurance carrier will likely request a panel QME report (see Chapter 10, Section B). You, in turn, should continue to emphasize that you want to rely on the treating doctor's report.

CHAPTER 14—VOCATIONAL REHABILITATION BENEFITS

The cases that follow deal with vocational rehabilitation. This is a workers' compensation benefit available to those injured workers who have been determined to be "qualified injured workers" and therefore unable to return to their previous type of work due to their injuries. Please refer to Chapter 14 to review this subject matter.

1. AREA OF LAW:

To start vocational rehabilitation, you must request it. But fortunately, there are many ways you can do this. (This is discussed in Chapter 14, Section D.)

NAME OF CASE: *Visalia School District, Petitioner v. WCAB and Lube Hernandez, Respondents*, 60 CCC 1158, 40 Cal. App. 4th 1211

This case says: A telephone call to the insurance company requesting vocational rehabilitation benefits is sufficient to get the ball rolling. To be entitled to vocational rehabilitation, you do not need to make a written request (although it is always a good idea for later proof purposes).

2. AREA OF LAW:

Vocational Rehabilitation Maintenance Allowance (VRMA). VRMA is paid every two weeks while you are participating in vocational rehabilitation. It is based upon two-thirds of your average weekly wage up to a maximum of $246 per week. (Please refer to Chapter 14, Section A2, for a detailed explanation of this benefit.)

NAME OF CASE: *Double D Transport Company v. WCAB (Copeland)*, 60 CCC 757

This case says: Applicant, who was ultimately found not to be a qualified injured worker (and therefore not entitled to vocational rehabilitation benefits) *was entitled* to retroactive vocational rehabilitation maintenance allowance (VRMA) when defendant was aware that applicant was temporarily disabled for 90 consecutive days but failed to notify applicant of his vocational rehabilitation rights under Labor Code §4636(a). Applicant was awarded VRMA from the date that medical temporary disability payments were canceled by the insurance carrier through the date of the award finding that applicant was not entitled to vocational rehabilitation benefits. The point of the case is the insurance carrier has a duty to contact a qualified injured worker after 90 days and advise him of his possible right to rehabilitation benefits. If the carrier fails to do so, it is responsible for making vocational rehabilitation payments to the worker until his rights to such benefits are determined one way or the other.

NAME OF CASE: *Industrial Indemnity v. WCAB (Elizondo)*, 50 CCC 171, 165 Cal. App. 3d 633, 211 Cal. Rptr. 683

This case says: This important case says that an injured worker who was ultimately determined *not* to be a qualified injured worker (and therefore *not* entitled to vocational rehabilitation benefits) is nevertheless entitled to rehabilitation benefits during his evaluation period because at the time vocational rehabilitation was requested there existed good faith issues that might have been resolved in the applicant's favor. This is an important case because it is very common to have a dispute as to whether a person is eligible for vocational rehabilitation benefits. For example, assume your doctor says you are entitled to vocational rehabilitation benefits, while the insurance company's doctor says you are not. The issue can't be resolved for six months, when you go to a Qualified

Medical Examiner (QME) (see Chapter 10, Section A) who agrees with one party or the other. Again, the point of this case is that the insurance company owes you vocational rehabilitation maintenance allowance from the date of your first request for benefits (you should have requested benefits right after your doctor says you are entitled to benefits—see Chapter 14, Section D4) to the date the QME says you are not entitled to benefits. If this takes six months, you are entitled to six months of VRMA plus penalties if payment is made late, even if it is eventually decided that you are not eligible.

3.   AREA OF LAW:

Signing a form declining rehabilitation services simultaneous to signing the compromise and release. Please review Chapter 19, Sections D2c and D2d, for a complete review of the declination of vocational rehabilitation benefits in the settlement document.

> **NAME OF CASE:** *Cisneros v. WCAB*, 60 CCC 1144, 48 Cal. Rptr. 2d 265
> This case says: If you sign a document declining your rights to vocational rehabilitation services as part of an agreement to settle your workers' compensation claim, you may be forever barred from requesting vocational rehabilitation services again unless you can show a change of circumstances that did not exist at the time of the signing. A mere change of mind will not be sufficient to allow you to obtain additional benefits. So think twice before you do this.

CHAPTER 15—DEATH BENEFITS

The cases that follow deal with benefits payable to the surviving dependents of a deceased worker whose death was the result of his employment. Please refer to Chapter 15 for a review of the benefits for which surviving dependents are eligible.

1.   AREA OF LAW:

Death benefit amount payable to minor children. The amount of the death benefit is determined by the date of injury that resulted in death and is payable at the temporary disability rate in effect for that date. (This issue is discussed in Chapter 15, Section C.)

> **NAME OF CASE:** *Wright Schuchart-Harbor v. WCAB (Morrow, deceased)*, 60 CCC 1066 (Writ denied), also *Foodmaker v. WCAB (Prado-Lopez, deceased)*, 60 CCC 124 (Writ denied)
> This case says: If there is a demonstrated need, the judge has the discretion to award death benefits at a rate higher than was in force at the date the worker was injured, up to the amount payable on the date of the request. In the example given in Chapter 15, Section C, Juanita's children could ask the judge to award their payments at the current temporary disability rate of $490 per week instead of $224 per week in force when her husband was injured if they can show financial necessity for the increase. The judges' discretion is limited to the maximum temporary disability rate in effect at the time of the request.

DO A BUDGET TO SHOW FINANCIAL NECESSITY
Financial necessity justifying higher death benefits might be shown if the deceased workers' dependents can show that the lower amount in force at the date of the injury is not sufficient to pay the essential living expenses of the family, such as for shelter, clothing, food and medical care.

2.   AREA OF LAW:

Unpaid temporary disability payments. If a deceased employee was entitled to any unpaid temporary or permanent disability benefits at the time of death, that amount is due and payable to his surviving heirs. (This issue is discussed in Chapter 15, Section E.)

> **NAME OF CASE:** *Manville Sales Corporation v. WCAB*, 59 CCC 1093 (Writ denied)
> This case says: A surviving heir is entitled to payment for any unpaid temporary disability from the time the deceased worker became physically unable to work (in this

case from 1985) to his death (on October 10, 1990). This case confirms that the surviving heirs of a deceased employee are entitled to receive the temporary disability benefits that the decedent would have been entitled to.

3. AREA OF LAW:

The rate of death benefits is usually determined by the date of injury.

> **NAME OF CASE:** *Sacramento Municipal Utilities District v. WCAB (Phillips, deceased)*, 63 CCC 1091
> This case says: The WCAB affirmed that since the payment of death benefits is to be paid in the same manner as temporary disability benefits, an increase in rate is called for after two years under Labor Code §4661.5. The WCAB has jurisdiction to order payment of death benefits at a rate higher than was in existence at the time of death of the injured worker (after two or more years from the date of injury). This decision applies to injury dates on or after 7/30/98.

CHAPTER 16—EXTRAORDINARY WORKERS' COMPENSATION BENEFITS AND REMEDIES

The case that follows deals with employers who discriminate against employees who file workers' compensation claims. (See Chapter 16, Section C for a review of this subject.)

1. AREA OF LAW:

Employers who discriminate against an employee who has filed or is about to file a workers' compensation claim are in violation of Labor Code §132a.

> **NAME OF CASE:** *Abratte v. WCAB*, 65 CCC 790
> This case says: Where an employer terminates an employee's health benefits after a worker is injured on the job, the employer is in violation of Labor Code §132a, unless the employer can show there was a business necessity for terminating the benefits.

CHAPTER 18—RATING YOUR PERMANENT DISABILITY

The cases that follow deal with how to determine the dollar amount of permanent disability you are entitled to as a result of your injury.

1. AREA OF LAW:

Rating of upper extremities (hands, arms, shoulders) based upon work restrictions such as "no repetitive pushing and pulling with both upper extremities" or "no repetitive forceful gripping with both hands." (See Chapter 18, Section C, Step 2c, for details concerning this situation.)

> **NAME OF CASE:** *Capistrano Unified School District v. WCAB*, 61 CCC 844
> This case says: A permanent disability rating for upper extremity disability based upon a description of lost ability to use the upper extremities is proper. This is a very important concept. Some disability raters had been taking the position that if a work restriction given by a doctor for an upper extremity was not specifically listed in the rating manual, they would not assign any amount of permanent disability to it. This case says that they are wrong! It is now clear that even if there is no scheduled rating for a given work restriction in the manual, the court or rater may arrive at a permanent disability by interpolation and analogy. In this case, the doctor used the term "loss of use" of an arm—a term not listed in the manual. But instead of saying there was no disability because of use of incorrect terminology, the court looked at the fact that the doctor found that the applicant had lost 75% of his pre-injury capacity to use his right arm and equated this to an amputation (which is a scheduled rating). The result was the court used 75% of the disability rating for an amputated right arm.

2. AREA OF LAW:

Apportionment of a disability. Apportionment is a concept that an insurance company uses to claim it is not responsible for paying permanent disability because it is not fully attributable to the work injury. (See Chapter 18, Section D, for a review of this subject.)

NAME OF CASE: *Bakersfield City School District v. WCAB (Robertson)*, 61 CCC 260 (Writ denied)

This case says: Apportionment of a disability to outside factors (factors other than the work injury) is not proper where no evidence is presented to establish that the disability would have existed absent applicant's industrial injury. In the example in Chapter 18, Section D1, this means the unsupported conclusion by the doctor that Kathleen's disability is 50% due to the prior sports injury is not valid apportionment. The doctor would have had to find that Kathleen had an actual disability immediately prior to the industrial injury as a result of the prior sports injury. For example, an apportionment would be proper if the doctor said that, based upon his review of medical records, it is clear that Kathleen had treatment for her prior high school injury all the way up to a few weeks before her industrial injury, indicating she still had a disability from the prior injury.

NAME OF CASE: *Monterey County v. WCAB (Moses)*, 61 CCC 273 (Writ denied)

This case says: Apportionment to the natural progression of a pre-existing condition is not valid where the doctor does not specifically state that the natural progression would have occurred absent the industrial injury or exposure. In the example in Section D1, the doctor would have to find that as a result of the natural progression of Kathleen's sports injury, she would have 50% of her current disability absent her industrial injury (for valid apportionment to the natural progression of a pre-existing injury).

NAME OF CASE: *Ashley v. WCAB*, 43 Cal. Rptr. 2d 589, 60 CCC 683

This case says: Labor Code §4750.5 says: "An employee who has sustained a compensable injury covered by workers' compensation and who subsequently sustains an unrelated condition, shall not receive permanent disability indemnity for any permanent disability caused solely by the subsequent condition." The key issue here is that Labor Code §4750.5 requires apportionment only when an injury covered by workers' compensation (a compensable injury) is followed by one not covered by workers' compensation (a non-compensable injury) and does not apply when an applicant becomes pregnant or unemployed, since neither condition constitutes a "non-compensable injury" within the meaning of the statute. In other words, for apportionment of benefits to apply, there must be a real "non-compensable injury." Pregnancy and/or periods of unemployment are simply not considered "injuries" within the meaning of Labor Code §4750.5.

NAME OF CASE: *Pullman Kellogg v. WCAB (Normand)*, 26 Cal. 3d 450, 45 CCC 170 (California Supreme Court case)

This case says: The defendant insurance company always has the burden of proving that there should be apportionment between injuries covered and not covered by workers' compensation, based on their claim that part of your overall disability is due to non-work-related factors. In short, you do not have to prove anything unless the insurance company presents convincing evidence that an apportionment should be made.

NAME OF CASE: *Tanenbaum v. IAC* (1935), 4 Cal. 2d 615

This case says: For workers' compensation purposes, an employer takes the employee as he finds him at the time of employment. This means, when an industrial injury aggravates a previously existing condition with the result that the worker becomes disabled, there should be no apportionment of part of the disability to the previous condition unless the present disability would still have existed in absence of the new industrial injury. The fact that if the employee had been stronger or healthier at the time of the injury (that is, had no previous injury or health problem) there would have been no disability (or a less severe disability) is not a reason to apportion disability benefits unless the prior condition was so serious that it alone would have led to the current disability. For example: Mary had a history of pre-existing asthma. However, when she went to work for Racafrax Chemical Co., it had been dormant and under control for five years. But as a result of exposure to toxic chemicals at Racafrax, Mary's asthma is aggravated and becomes disabling. There should be no apportionment of Mary's benefits to the pre-existing asthma condition just because it probably made her more susceptible to the toxic chemicals, causing her to again suffer asthma.

3. AREA OF LAW:

Occupational variant. As discussed in Chapter 18, one of the steps in rating your permanent disability is to determine your "occupational variant." This variant is determined by the type of job duties you did in the occupation in which you were injured, and is based on the concept that a particular injury may be more or less limiting depending on the type of work you do. (Please see Chapter 18, Section C, Step 3b, for a complete discussion of this concept.)

NAME OF CASE: *Kochevar v. Fremont Unified School District*, 19 CWCR 290

This case says: Lots of jobs have a mix of duties at different rating levels. Where this is true, the question becomes *how should the activities be rated?* The answer is, if some degree of higher-rated activities are an integral part of your job, even though most of the duties of that job have a lower rating, then the higher rating occupational variant should be used. In this case the applicant spent about a hundred minutes of a 40-hour work week engaged in strenuous physical education activities that included demonstrating basketball dribbling and shooting, foot dribbling in soccer, use of a balance beam and jumping rope. The issue the court considered was whether she should be given a group 59 rate for athlete (which would give her a very high permanent disability rating) or a group 41 rating reflecting her job title of school teacher (which would result in a lower permanent disability rating). The court found that since the athlete's duties were an integral part of this applicant's duties use of the higher rating variant was proper.

CHAPTER 19—FIGURE OUT A STARTING SETTLEMENT AMOUNT

Once you have completed your medical treatment and have obtained medical opinions on how much permanent disability you have, you must figure out how much your case is worth and make a settlement demand upon the insurance company. The cases that follow deal with the elements that you must consider when you figure out your starting settlement proposal. You should consider a number of things, including the dollar value of your permanent disability, the amount of any past due temporary disability and/or vocational rehabilitation

maintenance allowance, past due mileage, reimbursement for self-procured medical benefits, penalties and interest. Please refer to Chapter 19 for a review of this subject matter.

1. AREA OF LAW:

Penalties. If the insurance carrier failed to pay you the benefits you were entitled to on time, you should consider the dollar value of any penalties you might be entitled to as a result of their unreasonable delay. (Please see Chapter 19, Section C9, for a review of the types of monetary penalties you can petition the court for if the insurance carrier pays your benefits late.)

NAME OF CASE: *Pierce Enterprises, Argonaut Insurance Company, Petitioners v. WCAB and George Colchado, Respondents*, 60 CCC 1052

This case says: Because the insurance carrier committed separate and distinct acts of delay or non-payment of a disability award, the WCAB properly awarded five separate 10% penalties as part of setting a temporary disability. The point here is that the insurance company is liable for a separate 10% penalty (figured as a percentage of the total value of the temporary disability benefit) for each act of late or non-payment, not just one 10% penalty covering all the late payments. Also, see *Christian v. WCAB*, discussed below, which discusses what constitutes a separate and distinct act of delay.

 IF YOUR INSURANCE COMPANY IS REFUSING TO PAY YOU, READ THIS ENTIRE CASE
Pierce Enterprises, Argonaut Insurance Company, Petitioners v. WCAB and George Colchado, Respondents presents a good review of the different types of misconduct by an insurance carrier that can constitute grounds for establishing a penalty.

NAME OF CASE: *Christian v. WCAB*, 15 Cal. 4th 505, 24 CWCR 193, 62 CCC 576 (California Supreme Court case)
This case says: The Supreme Court of California held that for multiple and successive penalties to apply to an insurance carrier's improper failure to pay temporary disability benefits, there must be distinct and separate acts of delay. The failure of the insurance carrier to pay temporary disability is one act. The fact that this occurred every two

weeks does not make it a separate and distinct act each time the insurance company failed to pay. However, if some intervening event were to occur—for example, after refusing to pay benefits the insurance company paid them for awhile before once again improperly refusing to pay—this would constitute a separate and distinct act and lead to a second penalty. For example, XYZ Insurance improperly fails to pay temporary disability for six consecutive weeks (since this is one act, one penalty would be allowed—not a penalty for each two-week period). Then XYZ pays temporary disability for four weeks before again delaying payment. A new and separate penalty would arise for this second separate and distinct act of delay.

NAME OF CASE: *Rhiner v. WCAB* (1993), 4 Cal. 4th 1213, 18 Cal. Rptr. 2d 129, 58 CCC 172 (California Supreme Court case)

This case says: This very important case establishes that when an insurance company is guilty of unreasonable delays in paying benefits, the applicant is entitled to a 10% penalty based on the dollar amount of the entire benefit (in workers' compensation jargon, the "entire species of benefit") and not just on the improperly delayed portion of the benefit. For example, if the carrier unreasonably delays paying you one temporary disability check of, say, $772 the penalty is not just 10% of that amount, or $77.20. It is 10% of your entire temporary disability benefit (past, present and future). So if your entire benefit totals $25,000, you are entitled to a penalty of $2,500 for the delayed payment of $772!

NAME OF CASE: *Ready Home Health Care, Inc. v. WCAB (Sharp)*, 61 CCC 891 (Writ denied)

This case says: An unreasonable failure to timely pay reimbursement for mileage to and from medical appointments is a basis for an award of a 10% penalty against the entire medical treatment portion (species) of benefits. For example, if an injured worker who needs to drive a considerable distance to the doctor submits a request for mileage reimbursement of $50 and the insurance carrier does not pay within a reasonable time period the applicant may be able to get a 10% penalty on the value of her medical treatment (past, present and future). This means if the

value of this treatment is $75,000, applicant could obtain a $7,500 penalty for failure to timely pay $50!

 PAYMENTS AFTER 30 DAYS OF REQUEST FOR REIMBURSEMENT MAY BE UNREASONABLE

It is up to the court to decide what constitutes a reasonable—or unreasonable—time in which to reimburse an applicant for covered expenses. But I would argue that 30 days is ample time to process such a claim and anything over that is unreasonable.

NAME OF CASE: *Avalon Bay Foods v. WCAB (Moore)*, 63 CCC 902 (California Supreme Court)

This case says: When an insurance company is 60 days late or more in paying medically related transportation expenses (mileage reimbursement), there is a Labor Code §5814 penalty owed on all medical treatment benefits (of which mileage is a part).

NAME OF CASE: *Moulton v. WCAB*, 28 CWCR 293

This case says: A worker may be entitled to multiple penalties under Labor Code §5814 if the insurance company has failed to pay permanent disability in a timely fashion. If you received a portion of your permanent disability payments late, the insurance company must include an automatic 10% penalty on the portion that was late. (Labor Code §4650(d); see Chapter 19, Section C9.) If it does not automatically pay you this penalty, you are entitled to a 10% penalty on the entire amount awarded for permanent disability (Labor Code §5814).

CHAPTER 20—NEGOTIATING A SETTLEMENT

1. AREA OF LAW:

Signing a form declining rehabilitation services simultaneous to signing the compromise and release. (Please review Chapter 20, Sections D2c and D2d for a complete review of the issue of declining vocational rehabilitation benefits in a settlement document.)

NAME OF CASE: *Cisneros v. WCAB*, 60 CCC 1144, 48 Cal. Rptr. 2d 655

This case says: If you sign a document declining your rights to vocational rehabilitation services as part of an agreement to settle your workers' compensation claim, you may be forever barred from requesting vocational rehabilitation services again unless you can show a change of circumstances. A mere change of mind will not be sufficient to allow you to obtain additional benefits. So think twice before you say no to vocational rehabilitation benefits.

2. AREA OF LAW:

When you have agreed on a settlement of your claim by Compromise and Release (see Chapter 20), the insurance company will prepare the settlement document and send it to you for signature. You will then have to review it and make sure it is correct and does not contain objectionable language.

NAME OF CASE: *Jefferson v. California Department of Youth Authority*, 66 CCC 343

This case says: In this case, the insurance company included an attachment to the Compromise and Release that contained a general release under Civil Code §1542. This attachment barred a claim under the California Fair Employment and Housing Act (FEHA) and any other third-party claims the worker may have had, such as a wrongful termination lawsuit or a civil complaint against any party involving the same date of injury.

Note: All Compromise and Release documents contain this general release under Civil Code §1542. You should add the following additional language to the end of the clause: "This clause applies to this claim only."

CHAPTER 21—PREPARING YOUR CASE

The cases that follow deal with issues you should consider when preparing your case for trial. These include identifying possible issues in dispute, how to prove or disprove disputed issues, taking depositions of witnesses, subpoenaing witnesses and documents, preparing for a mandatory settlement conference and preparing for trial. Please refer to Chapter 21 for a detailed review of this subject matter.

1. AREA OF LAW:

Presumption of compensable injury. If you filed a workers' compensation claim and more than 90 days pass with no rejection of the claim by your employer or its insurance carrier, there is a rebuttable presumption that the claim is valid and benefits should be paid. (Please refer to Chapter 21, Section B3b.)

NAME OF CASE: *SCIF v. WCAB (Welcher)*, 60 CCC 717, 32 CWCR 213, 43 Cal. Rptr. 2d 660

This case says: Defendant's failure to reject applicant's claim for workers' compensation within 90 days created a presumption that benefits should be paid ("compensability" exists) under Labor Code §5402. It further held that evidence contained in defendant's later submitted medical reports was inadmissible to rebut the presumption of compensability since such evidence could have reasonably been obtained and submitted by the carrier within the 90-day period.

 ARGUE THAT AN INSURANCE CARRIER MUST SHOW THAT NEW EVIDENCE CAME TO LIGHT, TO REJECT APPLICANT'S CLAIM AFTER 90 DAYS FROM SUBMISSION

After 90 days from the submission of a worker's claim, the insurance carrier should only be able to rebut the presumption that benefits should be paid (compensability exists) with new evidence that could not have been reasonably obtained within the first 90 days after the injury was reported. (But see the Rodriguez case below, which casts doubt on this argument in some circumstances.)

NAME OF CASE: *Rodriguez v. WCAB*, 35 Cal. Rptr. 2d 713; 59 CCC 857

This case says: This is a bad case for injured workers! Nevertheless, you need to be aware of it and hope your opposition isn't. In this case the insurance carrier failed to deny the claim until 96 days following completion of the DWC-1. The worker asserted that after 90 days from his application for benefits, the rebuttable presumption under Labor Code §5402 (discussed in the previous case) meant that his claim could only be rejected if the insurance company based the rejection on evidence not already available. In my view this argument should have been strong enough to result in the worker being deemed eligible for benefits. But the court held that all that is required of the defendants is that it made a *determination* to deny the claim within the 90 days even though the applicant was not told that the claim was denied until after the 90 days. In this case the insurance carrier was allowed to use oral testimony from a claims examiner who said that she had decided to deny the claim within the 90 days. Probably one factor contributing to the carrier's victory here was the fact that benefits were denied just six days after the end of the 90-day period. A longer delay by the insurance company might have produced a different result.

2. AREA OF LAW:

The insurance company may take your statement or set a deposition (a formal legal interview) for you. At the deposition it will ask you many questions (see Chapter 21, Section C). The following case addresses the issue of what medical questions are relevant and which are not.

NAME OF CASE: *Carol Allison v. WCAB*, 64 CCC 624
This case says: The court stated that, at a deposition, the worker is not required to answer questions about her medical history that are not relevant to the workers' compensation matter. The court said that questions about medical history should be limited to the past 10 years and should deal only with the parts of body injured. Questions that are overly broad are not proper and are a violation of worker's doctor/patient privilege and right to privacy.

CHAPTER 22—ARRANGING FOR A HEARING OR TRIAL

The following cases involve the various types of hearings that you can request before the Workers' Compensation Appeals Board, including a mandatory settlement conference.

1. AREA OF LAW:

When you file a declaration of readiness to proceed, requesting that your matter be set for a mandatory settlement conference, you should be prepared to go forward to trial if you can't settle your case. (See Chapter 22.)

NAME OF CASE: *County of Sacramento v. WCAB (Estrada)*, 64 CCC 26
This case says: You must never file a declaration of readiness to proceed requesting a mandatory settlement conference unless you are certain you have all the evidence you will need at trial. If you don't have the proper evidence, the judge at a mandatory settlement conference does not have the authority to order a continuance or leave the record open for further discovery unless you can show good cause as to why the evidence was not obtainable prior to the conference. If the insurance company files a declaration of readiness to proceed and you are not ready to go to trial, be sure you immediately object to the conference (see Chapter 22).

2. AREA OF LAW:

At the mandatory settlement conference, both sides should be prepared to discuss settlement of the case and should have the authority to enter into a settlement.

NAME OF CASE: *Rochin v. State of California, Department of Corrections*, 26 CWCR 290
This case says: The workers' compensation insurance company must have someone available, either in person at the mandatory settlement conference or by telephone (so that the representative at the hearing can call him), who has the authority to approve a settlement of the claim. If the attorney or representative for the insurance company tells you that he can't reach anyone who can give him settlement authority, then the insurance company is subject to sanctions for failure to have proper settlement authority as required by WCAB Rule 10563.

CHAPTER 24—GOING TO A HEARING OR TRIAL

The cases that follow deal with issues that may arise at a hearing or trial before a judge at the Workers' Compensation Appeals Board. Please refer to Chapter 24 for a detailed review of this subject matter.

1. AREA OF LAW:

The amount the injured worker earns—her average weekly wage—determines how much she is entitled to for temporary or permanent disability payments. (Please see Chapter 12, Section B, for a discussion of how to compute your average weekly wage.) The case discussed below concerns when a defendant can raise a dispute over the amount of the applicant's earnings. This issue can be important because an insurance carrier will often try to argue you earned less than you really did in an effort to reduce the amount it has to pay you.

> **NAME OF CASE:** *Early California Foods v. WCAB (Ellis)*, 56 CCC 137
>
> This case says: A two-year delay in raising the issue of earnings will justify the workers' compensation judge's denial of the defendant's request to dispute the applicants' average weekly wage. In this case the defendant waited until the time of trial to dispute how much the applicant earned for purposes of determining the applicant's temporary disability and permanent disability rate, even though the company had been paying the applicant's temporary disability benefits at the maximum allowable rate for over a year, and had made three appearances at the WCAB without raising the issue. The judge held that waiting for two years from the date of injury to try to raise the issue meant that the defendant forever waived their right to do so. (The judge relied on Administrative Rule 10484, which gives him the discretion to allow or disallow evidence upon matters not previously pleaded.)

 CITE THIS CASE WHENEVER A DEFENDANT WAITS UNTIL TRIAL TO RAISE A NEW ISSUE

New issues should rarely be raised for the first time at trial. If the defendant tries to do so, refer to the *Early California Foods* case as part of your argument that the issue in question has been waived, by not having been raised earlier.

2. AREA OF LAW:

Admissibility of a medical report where the exam was set up before the Mandatory Settlement Conference (MSC—see Chapter 24, Section B) but was not actually held until after the MSC.

> **NAME OF CASE:** *Henley v. I.I.*, 20 CWCR 188
>
> This case says: This case is important if the defendants have filed a Declaration of Readiness to Proceed (see Chapter 22, Section D) and have gotten a date for an MSC in a situation where the applicant has requested a medical examination by a qualified medical examiner. The case says if you have requested your Qualified Medical Examination (QME—see Chapter 10, Section A) prior to the date of the MSC, the report should be allowed into evidence even if the actual date of the appointment is not until sometime after the date of the MSC. So even if you are caught "off guard" by the carrier's request to proceed to trial, you can still request your QME appointment and have the results considered. ■

Appendix
Table of Contents

Appendix 1

Summary of Important Workers' Compensation Laws for Injuries Between 1/1/90 and 12/31/93

The text of this book applies to workers' compensation injuries that occurred on or after 1/1/94. This Appendix highlights how most of the important laws and rules for injuries between 1/1/90 and 12/31/93 apply to this book. If you were injured prior to 1/1/94, important laws that affect your particular case may have a significant impact. Please don't rely solely on this Appendix; also check with an Information and Assistance officer or see a lawyer. (See Chapter 26.)

Chapter 1. Introduction to Workers' Compensation

■ To file a workers' compensation claim, injured workers must fill out and file a DWC-1 form with their employers within one year of injury, preferably as soon as possible after the injury.

Chapter 2. Overview of a Workers' Compensation Claim

■ To file a workers' compensation claim, injured workers must fill out and file a DWC-1 form with their employers within one year of injury, preferably as soon as possible after the injury.

■ Qualified medical examiners (QMEs), or agreed medical examiners (AMEs), rather than the treating doctor, prepare a medical report for rating. The injured worker is entitled to one medical evaluator in each medical specialty. A treating doctor's report may, however, be ratable and may be considered by a judge.

Chapter 3. Is Your Injury Covered by Workers' Compensation?

■ To file a workers' compensation claim, injured workers must fill out and file a DWC-1 form with their employers within one year of injury, preferably as soon as possible after the injury.

■ For stress claims between 1/1/90 and 7/15/93, an injured worker was only required to show that the stress at work contributed at least 10% to the overall psychiatric injury. An employer's claim that the stress was caused by a good faith personnel action is not a defense.

■ Injuries before 7/16/93 are not subject to special rules if the employee was terminated or laid off.

■ Claims are prohibited within the first six months of employment due to stress caused by regular and routine employment event, including lawful, good faith non-discriminatory personnel action.

Chapter 5. What to Do If You're Injured

■ To file a workers' compensation claim, injured workers must fill out and file a DWC-1 form with their employers within one year of injury, preferably as soon as possible after the injury. Eventually an Application must be filed to obtain a hearing before the Appeals Board.

Chapter 6.   Keep Good Records to Protect Your Claim

■ *No significant changes.*

Chapter 7.   The Insurance Company's Role

■ *No significant changes.*

Chapter 8.   Dealing With Your Employer

■ Employers do not have the right to object to how the insurance company chooses to settle a workers' compensation case (although many insurance contracts provide that the carrier needs the employer's permission).

■ Employers must post notices informing employees of their right to designate their doctors in advance. However, no categories of employers need to advise employees of their right to pre-designate their treating doctors at the time of hiring and at least once a year thereafter.

■ Offers of modified or alternate work with the same employer will not necessarily affect an injured workers' rights to vocational rehabilitation benefits. The modified or alternate work may, however, be incorporated into the rehabilitation plan.

■ To file a workers' compensation claim, injured workers must fill out and file a DWC-1 form with their employers within one year of injury, preferably as soon as possible after the injury.

Chapter 9.   Taking Charge of Your Medical Case

■ There is no "primary" treating doctor, although a single doctor will probably manage a worker's treatment and make referrals to other doctors. Specialists write their own medical reports.

■ The treating doctor's report is not automatically rated.

■ There is no 20- or 30-day time limit for objecting to a treating doctor's report.

■ Employers must post notices informing employees of their right to designate their doctors in advance. However, no categories of employers need to advise employees of their right to pre-designate their treating doctors at the time of hiring and at least once a year thereafter.

■ Rules pertaining to employers that offer a choice of at least two health care organizations do not apply.

■ An employer must notify an employee of the right to obtain an evaluation to determine a permanent disability rating.

Chapter 10. Medical-Legal Evaluations

■ Qualified medical examiners (QMEs), or agreed medical examiners (AMEs), rather than the treating doctor, write medical-legal reports that address whether an injured worker has a permanent disability, needs future medical care and qualifies for vocational rehabilitation. For unrepresented workers, the evaluation is done by a QME. When an injured employee has an attorney, an AME is used if the parties agree. Otherwise, a QME can be used by each side. A QME for each medical specialty can be used.

■ If a QME report requires the insurance carrier to either pay compensation or commence proceedings before the Appeals Board, and the insurance carrier opts to commence proceedings rather than pay compensation, the injured worker's attorney fees must be paid by the insurance carrier.

■ If an injured employee gets a medical-legal evaluation before a claim is denied or presumed compensable, the employee may be personally liable for paying for the report.

■ For injuries that occurred between 1/1/90 to 12/31/90, there is no provision for a QME panel to be provided to a nonrepresented injured worker. An injured worker may get a medical-legal evaluation from any doctor and may get one for each specialty required.

■ For injuries that occurred between 1/1/91 to 12/31/93, a QME panel is provided to the employee. If not satisfied with the QME evaluation, the employee may get a lawyer and is entitled to another QME exam at the employer's expense.

Chapter 11. Payment of Medical Benefits

■ *No significant changes.* (Also see above summaries for Chapters 9 and 10.)

Chapter 12. Temporary Disability Benefits

■ Depending on the date of injury, different rates may apply for temporary disability.

Chapter 13. Permanent Disability (and Life Pension)

▧ A medical evaluator generally writes a medical-legal report that addresses whether the injured worker has a permanent disability, although the treating doctor can also write such an evaluation for consideration by a judge.

▧ Depending on the date of injury, different rates may apply for permanent partial disability, permanent total disability and life pension.

▧ There is no limitation on a judge's determination of permanent disability rating.

Chapter 14. Vocational Rehabilitation Benefits

▧ Offers of modified or alternate work with the same employer will not necessarily affect an injured workers' rights to vocational rehabilitation benefits. The modified or alternate work may, however, be incorporated into the rehabilitation plan.

▧ There is no limit on the cost of a vocational rehabilitation plan, but the rehabilitation counselor's fee is limited to $5,700.

▧ The plan may be in-state or out of California.

▧ There is no restriction on the length of time needed to complete the plan. Maintenance allowance payments are unlimited, and must be paid for the entire period for which the injured worker is participating or is entitled to participate in vocational rehabilitation.

▧ There are no limits on the number of plans, but the Rehabilitation Unit must approve additional plans.

▧ An employee must use the services of a vocational rehabilitation counselor.

▧ For injuries between 1/1/91 and 12/31/93, an injured worker is eligible for vocational rehabilitation if the treating doctor's final report finds an inability to return to the worker's usual occupation or the occupation in which the worker was employed at the time of injury. Workers need a lawyer if they disagree with the treating doctor's opinion on their entitlement to vocational rehabilitation benefits and want to get another medical opinion. Labor Code Section 4062, which determines how and when the parties may obtain additional medical opinions on this issue, applies only to represented workers.

▧ After injured workers have been temporarily totally disabled for a period of 90 days, the insurance company must appoint a qualified rehabilitation representative (QRR).

(LC § 4636(a), 1993 edition.) The QRR may not be an in-house insurance company employee.

▧ For dates of injury between 1/1/91 and 12/31/93, the qualified rehabilitation representative (QRR) is responsible for preparing a job analysis and monitoring the injured worker's progress.

Chapter 15. Death Benefits

▧ Depending on the date of injury, different amounts of death benefits may be available.

▧ Burial expenses are limited to $2,000 for injuries occurring between 1/1/90 and 12/31/90. Burial expenses increase to up to $5,000 for dates of injury on or after 1/1/91.

Chapter 16. Extraordinary Workers' Compensation Benefits and Remedies

▧ *No significant changes.*

Chapter 17. Benefits and Remedies Outside the Workers' Compensation System

▧ The Americans With Disabilities Act (ADA) went into effect on July 25, 1992, for employers with at least 25 employees. As of July 25, 1994, the ADA applies to employers with at least 15 employees.

Chapter 18. Rating Your Permanent Disability

▧ For injuries before 7/1/94, the rating plateaus are 25% and 70%.

▧ A medical evaluator generally writes a medical-legal report that addresses whether the injured worker has a permanent disability, although the treating doctor can also write such an evaluation for consideration by a judge.

Chapter 19. Figuring Out a Starting Settlement Amount

▧ *No significant changes.*

Chapter 20. Negotiating a Settlement

■ *No significant changes.*

Chapter 21. Preparing Your Case

■ An Application for Adjudication of Claim, rather than a Declaration of Readiness to Proceed, must be filed to set a case for a hearing or trial. Rules pertaining to the Declaration apply to an Application. (Note that this Application form is different from the one used to file a workers' compensation claim for injuries after 1/1/94.)

Chapter 22. Arranging for a Hearing or Trial

■ Evidence and other documents are usually filed with the Workers' Compensation Appeals Board after an Application for Adjudication of Claim has been filed setting the matter for trial. If, however, there are pre-hearing disputes, any party may file a pre-hearing petition, such as a Petition for Pre-Trial Discovery Order, and a case number will be established by the Appeals Board.

■ Before filing for a hearing, an injured worker must have a medical-legal evaluation by a medical evaluator (QME or AME) if the hearing addresses the existence or extent of permanent disability or the need for future medical care. (LC § 4060.)

■ In addition to other documents, a one-page Data Entry Sheet form may be required to set a case before the Appeals Board.

■ Any objection to a case being set for trial must be filed and served within ten days of service if the Application was filed on or before 12/31/90, or within six days if the Application was filed on or after 1/1/91. (Five extra days are allowed if service was made by mail.)

■ The injured worker must obtain a medical-legal report from a medical evaluator (QME or AME), although a judge may also consider the treating doctor's report. (See Chapter 9.)

Chapter 23. How to File and Serve Documents

■ Evidence and other documents are usually filed with the Workers' Compensation Appeals Board after an Application for Adjudication of Claim has been filed setting the matter for trial. If, however, there are pre-hearing disputes, any party may file a pre-hearing petition, such as a Petition for Pre-Trial Discovery Order, and a case number will be established by the Appeals Board.

Chapter 24. Going to a Hearing or Trial

■ For injury dates before 1/1/94, a rating formula is not required on a joint pre-trial statement.

Chapter 25. Appealing a Workers' Compensation Decision

■ *No significant changes.*

Chapter 26. Lawyers and Other Sources of Assistance

■ *No significant changes.*

Chapter 27. Legal Research

■ *No significant changes.* ■

Appendix 2

Temporary Disability Benefits Compensation Chart

Actual Weekly Wage	Weekly Comp. Rate	Actual Weekly Wage	Weekly Comp. Rate	Actual Weekly Wage	Weekly Comp. Rate	Actual Weekly Wage	Weekly Comp. Rate	Actual Weekly Wage	Weekly Comp. Rate	Actual Weekly Wage	Weekly Comp. Rate	Actual Weekly Wage	Weekly Comp. Rate	Actual Weekly Wage	Weekly Comp. Rate
168.00	112.00	197.00	131.33	226.00	150.67	255.00	170.00	284.00	189.33	313.00	208.67	342.00	228.00	371.00	247.33
169.00	112.67	198.00	132.00	227.00	151.33	256.00	170.67	285.00	190.00	314.00	209.33	343.00	228.67	372.00	248.00
170.00	113.33	199.00	132.67	228.00	152.00	257.00	171.33	286.00	190.67	315.00	210.00	344.00	229.33	373.00	248.67
171.00	114.00	200.00	133.33	229.00	152.67	258.00	172.00	287.00	191.33	316.00	210.67	345.00	230.00	374.00	249.33
172.00	114.67	201.00	134.00	230.00	153.33	259.00	172.67	288.00	192.00	317.00	211.33	346.00	230.67	375.00	250.00
173.00	115.33	202.00	134.67	231.00	154.00	260.00	173.33	289.00	192.67	318.00	212.00	347.00	231.33	376.00	250.67
174.00	116.00	203.00	135.33	232.00	154.67	261.00	174.00	290.00	193.33	319.00	212.67	348.00	232.00	377.00	251.33
175.00	116.67	204.00	136.00	233.00	155.33	262.00	174.67	291.00	194.00	320.00	213.33	349.00	232.67	378.00	252.00
176.00	117.33	205.00	136.67	234.00	156.00	263.00	175.33	292.00	194.67	321.00	214.00	350.00	233.33	379.00	252.67
177.00	118.00	206.00	137.33	235.00	156.67	264.00	176.00	293.00	195.33	322.00	214.67	351.00	234.00	380.00	253.33
178.00	118.67	207.00	138.00	236.00	157.33	265.00	176.67	294.00	196.00	323.00	215.33	352.00	234.67	381.00	254.00
179.00	119.33	208.00	138.67	237.00	158.00	266.00	177.33	295.00	196.67	324.00	216.00	353.00	235.33	382.00	254.67
180.00	120.00	209.00	139.33	238.00	158.67	267.00	178.00	296.00	197.33	325.00	216.67	354.00	236.00	383.00	255.33
181.00	120.67	210.00	140.00	239.00	159.33	268.00	178.67	297.00	198.00	326.00	217.33	355.00	236.67	384.00	256.00
182.00	121.33	211.00	140.67	240.00	160.00	269.00	179.33	298.00	198.67	327.00	218.00	356.00	237.33	385.00	256.67
183.00	122.00	212.00	141.33	241.00	160.67	270.00	180.00	299.00	199.33	328.00	218.67	357.00	238.00	386.00	257.33
184.00	122.67	213.00	142.00	242.00	161.33	271.00	180.67	300.00	200.00	329.00	219.33	358.00	238.67	387.00	258.00
185.00	123.33	214.00	142.67	243.00	162.00	272.00	181.33	301.00	200.67	330.00	220.00	359.00	239.33	388.00	258.67
186.00	124.00	215.00	143.33	244.00	162.67	273.00	182.00	302.00	201.33	331.00	220.67	360.00	240.00	389.00	259.33
187.00	124.67	216.00	144.00	245.00	163.33	274.00	182.67	303.00	202.00	332.00	221.33	361.00	240.67	390.00	260.00
188.00	125.33	217.00	144.67	246.00	164.00	275.00	183.33	304.00	202.67	333.00	222.00	362.00	241.33	391.00	260.67
189.00	126.00	218.00	145.33	247.00	164.67	276.00	184.00	305.00	203.33	334.00	222.67	363.00	242.00	392.00	261.33
190.00	126.67	219.00	146.00	248.00	165.33	277.00	184.67	306.00	204.00	335.00	223.33	364.00	242.67	393.00	262.00
191.00	127.33	220.00	146.67	249.00	166.00	278.00	185.33	307.00	204.67	336.00	224.00	365.00	243.33	394.00	262.67
192.00	128.00	221.00	147.33	250.00	166.67	279.00	186.00	308.00	205.33	337.00	224.67	366.00	244.00	395.00	263.33
193.00	128.67	222.00	148.00	251.00	167.33	280.00	186.67	309.00	206.00	338.00	225.33	367.00	244.67	396.00	264.00
194.00	129.33	223.00	148.67	252.00	168.00	281.00	187.33	310.00	206.67	339.00	226.00	368.00	245.33	397.00	264.67
195.00	130.00	224.00	149.33	253.00	168.67	282.00	188.00	311.00	207.33	340.00	226.67	369.00	246.00	398.00	265.33
196.00	130.67	225.00	150.00	254.00	169.33	283.00	188.67	312.00	208.00	341.00	227.33	370.00	246.67	399.00	266.00

Actual Weekly Wage	Weekly Comp. Rate	Actual Weekly Wage	Weekly Comp. Rate	Actual Weekly Wage	Weekly Comp. Rate	Actual Weekly Wage	Weekly Comp. Rate	Actual Weekly Wage	Weekly Comp. Rate	Actual Weekly Wage	Weekly Comp. Rate	Actual Weekly Wage	Weekly Comp. Rate	Actual Weekly Wage	Weekly Comp. Rate
400.00	266.67	442.00	294.67	484.00	322.67	526.00	350.67	568.00	378.67	610.00	406.67	652.00	434.67	694.00	462.67
401.00	267.33	443.00	295.33	485.00	323.33	527.00	351.33	569.00	379.33	611.00	407.33	653.00	435.33	695.00	463.33
402.00	268.00	444.00	296.00	486.00	324.00	528.00	352.00	570.00	380.00	612.00	408.00	654.00	436.00	696.00	464.00
403.00	268.67	445.00	296.67	487.00	324.67	529.00	352.67	571.00	380.67	613.00	408.67	655.00	436.67	697.00	464.67
404.00	269.33	446.00	297.33	488.00	325.33	530.00	353.33	572.00	381.33	614.00	409.33	656.00	437.33	698.00	465.33
405.00	270.00	447.00	298.00	489.00	326.00	531.00	354.00	573.00	382.00	615.00	410.00	657.00	438.00	699.00	466.00
406.00	270.67	448.00	298.67	490.00	326.67	532.00	354.67	574.00	382.67	616.00	410.67	658.00	438.67	700.00	466.67
407.00	271.33	449.00	299.33	491.00	327.33	533.00	355.33	575.00	383.33	617.00	411.33	659.00	439.33	701.00	467.33
408.00	272.00	450.00	300.00	492.00	328.00	534.00	356.00	576.00	384.00	618.00	412.00	660.00	440.00	702.00	468.00
409.00	272.67	451.00	300.67	493.00	328.67	535.00	356.67	577.00	384.67	619.00	412.67	661.00	440.67	703.00	468.67
410.00	273.33	452.00	301.33	494.00	329.33	536.00	357.33	578.00	385.33	620.00	413.33	662.00	441.33	704.00	469.33
411.00	274.00	453.00	302.00	495.00	330.00	537.00	358.00	579.00	386.00	621.00	414.00	663.00	442.00	705.00	470.00
412.00	274.67	454.00	302.67	496.00	330.67	538.00	358.67	580.00	386.67	622.00	414.67	664.00	442.67	706.00	470.67
413.00	275.33	455.00	303.33	497.00	331.33	539.00	359.33	581.00	387.33	623.00	415.33	665.00	443.33	707.00	471.33
414.00	276.00	456.00	304.00	498.00	332.00	540.00	360.00	582.00	388.00	624.00	416.00	666.00	444.00	708.00	472.00
415.00	276.67	457.00	304.67	499.00	332.67	541.00	360.67	583.00	388.67	625.00	416.67	667.00	444.67	709.00	472.67
416.00	277.33	458.00	305.33	500.00	333.33	542.00	361.33	584.00	389.33	626.00	417.33	668.00	445.33	710.00	473.33
417.00	278.00	459.00	306.00	501.00	334.00	543.00	362.00	585.00	390.00	627.00	418.00	669.00	446.00	711.00	474.00
418.00	278.67	460.00	306.67	502.00	334.67	544.00	362.67	586.00	390.67	628.00	418.67	670.00	446.67	712.00	474.67
419.00	279.33	461.00	307.33	503.00	335.33	545.00	363.33	587.00	391.33	629.00	419.33	671.00	447.33	713.00	475.33
420.00	280.00	462.00	308.00	504.00	336.00	546.00	364.00	588.00	392.00	630.00	420.00	672.00	448.00	714.00	476.00
421.00	280.67	463.00	308.67	505.00	336.67	547.00	364.67	589.00	392.67	631.00	420.67	673.00	448.67	715.00	476.67
422.00	281.33	464.00	309.33	506.00	337.33	548.00	365.33	590.00	393.33	632.00	421.33	674.00	449.33	716.00	477.33
423.00	282.00	465.00	310.00	507.00	338.00	549.00	366.00	591.00	394.00	633.00	422.00	675.00	450.00	717.00	478.00
424.00	282.67	466.00	310.67	508.00	338.67	550.00	366.67	592.00	394.67	634.00	422.67	676.00	450.67	718.00	478.67
425.00	283.33	467.00	311.33	509.00	339.33	551.00	367.33	593.00	395.33	635.00	423.33	677.00	451.33	719.00	479.33
426.00	284.00	468.00	312.00	510.00	340.00	552.00	368.00	594.00	396.00	636.00	424.00	678.00	452.00	720.00	480.00
427.00	284.67	469.00	312.67	511.00	340.67	553.00	368.67	595.00	396.67	637.00	424.67	679.00	452.67	721.00	480.67
428.00	285.33	470.00	313.33	512.00	341.33	554.00	369.33	596.00	397.33	638.00	425.33	680.00	453.33	722.00	481.33
429.00	286.00	471.00	314.00	513.00	342.00	555.00	370.00	597.00	398.00	639.00	426.00	681.00	454.00	723.00	482.00
430.00	286.67	472.00	314.67	514.00	342.67	556.00	370.67	598.00	398.67	640.00	426.67	682.00	454.67	724.00	482.67
431.00	287.33	473.00	315.33	515.00	343.33	557.00	371.33	599.00	399.33	641.00	427.33	683.00	455.33	725.00	483.33
432.00	288.00	474.00	316.00	516.00	344.00	558.00	372.00	600.00	400.00	642.00	428.00	684.00	456.00	726.00	484.00
433.00	288.67	475.00	316.67	517.00	344.67	559.00	372.67	601.00	400.67	643.00	428.67	685.00	456.67	727.00	484.67
434.00	289.33	476.00	317.33	518.00	345.33	560.00	373.33	602.00	401.33	644.00	429.33	686.00	457.33	728.00	485.33
435.00	290.00	477.00	318.00	519.00	346.00	561.00	374.00	603.00	402.00	645.00	430.00	687.00	458.00	729.00	486.00
436.00	290.67	478.00	318.67	520.00	346.67	562.00	374.67	604.00	402.67	646.00	430.67	688.00	458.67	730.00	486.67
437.00	291.33	479.00	319.33	521.00	347.33	563.00	375.33	605.00	403.33	647.00	431.33	689.00	459.33	731.00	487.33
438.00	292.00	480.00	320.00	522.00	348.00	564.00	376.00	606.00	404.00	648.00	432.00	690.00	460.00	732.00	488.00
439.00	292.67	481.00	320.67	523.00	348.67	565.00	376.67	607.00	404.67	649.00	432.67	691.00	460.67	733.00	488.67
440.00	293.33	482.00	321.33	524.00	349.33	566.00	377.33	608.00	405.33	650.00	433.33	692.00	461.33	734.00	489.33
441.00	294.00	483.00	322.00	525.00	350.00	567.00	378.00	609.00	406.00	651.00	434.00	693.00	462.00	735.00	490.00

Appendix 3

Permanent Disability Indemnity Chart

PD%	7/1/94–6/30/95	7/1/95–6/30/96	7/1/96>	PD%	7/1/94–6/30/95	7/1/95–6/30/96	7/1/96>
1.00	420.00	420.00	420.00	9.00	3,780.00	3,780.00	3,780.00
1.25	525.00	525.00	525.00	9.25	3,885.00	3,885.00	3,885.00
1.50	630.00	630.00	630.00	9.50	3,990.00	3,990.00	3,990.00
1.75	735.00	735.00	735.00	9.75	4,095.00	4,095.00	4,095.00
2.00	840.00	840.00	840.00	10.00	4,235.00	4,235.00	4,235.00
2.25	945.00	945.00	945.00	10.25	4,375.00	4,375.00	4,375.00
2.50	1,050.00	1,050.00	1,050.00	10.50	4,515.00	4,515.00	4,515.00
2.75	1,155.00	1,155.00	1,155.00	10.75	4,655.00	4,655.00	4,655.00
3.00	1,260.00	1,260.00	1,260.00	11.00	4,795.00	4,795.00	4,795.00
3.25	1,365.00	1,365.00	1,365.00	11.25	4,935.00	4,935.00	4,935.00
3.50	1,470.00	1,470.00	1,470.00	11.50	5,075.00	5,075.00	5,075.00
3.75	1,575.00	1,575.00	1,575.00	11.75	5,215.00	5,215.00	5,215.00
4.00	1,680.00	1,680.00	1,680.00	12.00	5,355.00	5,355.00	5,355.00
4.25	1,785.00	1,785.00	1,785.00	12.25	5,495.00	5,495.00	5,495.00
4.50	1,890.00	1,890.00	1,890.00	12.50	5,635.00	5,635.00	5,635.00
4.75	1,995.00	1,995.00	1,995.00	12.75	5,775.00	5,775.00	5,775.00
5.00	2,100.00	2,100.00	2,100.00	13.00	5,915.00	5,915.00	5,915.00
5.25	2,205.00	2,205.00	2,205.00	13.25	6,055.00	6,055.00	6,055.00
5.50	2,310.00	2,310.00	2,310.00	13.50	6,195.00	6,195.00	6,195.00
5.75	2,415.00	2,415.00	2,415.00	13.75	6,335.00	6,335.00	6,335.00
6.00	2,520.00	2,520.00	2,520.00	14.00	6,475.00	6,475.00	6,475.00
6.25	2,625.00	2,625.00	2,625.00	14.25	6,615.00	6,615.00	6,615.00
6.50	2,730.00	2,730.00	2,730.00	14.50	6,755.00	6,755.00	6,755.00
6.75	2,835.00	2,835.00	2,835.00	14.75	6,895.00	6,895.00	6,895.00
7.00	2,940.00	2,940.00	2,940.00	15.00	7,437.00	7,738.50	8,040.00
7.25	3,045.00	3,045.00	3,045.00	15.25	7,585.00	7,892.50	8,200.00
7.50	3,150.00	3,150.00	3,150.00	15.50	7,733.00	8,046.50	8,360.00
7.75	3,255.00	3,255.00	3,255.00	15.75	7,881.00	8,200.50	8,520.00
8.00	3,360.00	3,360.00	3,360.00	16.00	8,029.00	8,354.50	8,680.00
8.25	3,465.00	3,465.00	3,465.00	16.25	8,177.00	8,508.50	8,840.00
8.50	3,570.00	3,570.00	3,570.00	16.50	8,325.00	8,662.50	9,000.00
8.75	3,675.00	3,675.00	3,675.00	16.75	8,473.00	8,816.50	9,160.00

PD%	7/1/94–6/30/95	7/1/95–6/30/96	7/1/96>	PD%	7/1/94–6/30/95	7/1/95–6/30/96	7/1/96>
17.00	8,621.00	8,970.50	9,320.00	**30.00**	19,908.00	20,664.00	21,420.00
17.25	8,769.00	9,124.50	9,480.00	**30.25**	20,184.50	20,951.00	21,717.50
17.50	8,917.00	9,278.50	9,640.00	**30.50**	20,461.00	21,238.00	22,015.00
17.75	9,065.00	9,432.50	9,800.00	**30.75**	20,737.50	21,525.00	22,312.50
18.00	9,213.00	9,586.50	9,960.00	**31.00**	21,014.00	21,812.00	22,610.00
18.25	9,361.00	9,740.50	10,120.00	**31.25**	21,290.50	22,099.00	22,907.50
18.50	9,509.00	9,894.50	10,280.00	**31.50**	21,567.00	22,386.00	23,205.00
18.75	9,657.00	10,048.50	10,440.00	**31.75**	21,843.50	22,673.00	23,502.50
19.00	9,805.00	10,202.50	10,600.00	**32.00**	22,120.00	22,960.00	23,800.00
19.25	9,953.00	10,356.50	10,760.00	**32.25**	22,396.50	23,247.00	24,097.50
19.50	10,101.00	10,510.50	10,920.00	**32.50**	22,673.00	23,534.00	24,395.00
19.75	10,249.00	10,664.50	11,080.00	**32.75**	22,949.50	23,821.00	24,692.50
20.00	10,434.00	10,857.00	11,280.00	**33.00**	23,226.00	24,108.00	24,990.00
20.25	10,619.00	11,049.50	11,480.00	**33.25**	23,502.50	24,395.00	25,287.50
20.50	10,804.00	11,242.00	11,680.00	**33.50**	23,779.00	24,682.00	25,585.00
20.75	10,989.00	11,434.50	11,880.00	**33.75**	24,055.50	24,969.00	25,882.50
21.00	11,174.00	11,627.00	12,080.00	**34.00**	24,332.00	25,256.00	26,180.00
21.25	11,359.00	11,819.50	12,280.00	**34.25**	24,608.50	25,543.00	26,477.50
21.50	11,544.00	12,012.00	12,480.00	**34.50**	24,885.00	25,830.00	26,775.00
21.75	11,729.00	12,204.50	12,680.00	**34.75**	25,161.50	26,117.00	27,072.50
22.00	11,914.00	12,397.00	12,880.00	**35.00**	25,438.00	26,404.00	27,370.00
22.25	12,099.00	12,589.50	13,080.00	**35.25**	25,714.50	26,691.00	27,667.50
22.50	12,284.00	12,782.00	13,280.00	**35.50**	25,991.00	26,978.00	27,965.00
22.75	12,469.00	12,974.50	13,480.00	**35.75**	26,267.50	27,265.00	28,262.50
23.00	12,654.00	13,167.00	13,680.00	**36.00**	26,544.00	27,552.00	28,560.00
23.25	12,839.00	13,359.50	13,880.00	**36.25**	26,820.50	27,839.00	28,857.50
23.50	13,024.00	13,552.00	14,080.00	**36.50**	27,097.00	28,126.00	29,155.00
23.75	13,209.00	13,744.50	14,280.00	**36.75**	27,373.50	28,413.00	29,452.50
24.00	13,394.00	13,937.00	14,480.00	**37.00**	27,650.00	28,700.00	29,750.00
24.25	13,579.00	14,129.50	14,680.00	**37.25**	27,926.50	28,987.00	30,047.50
24.50	13,764.00	14,322.00	14,880.00	**37.50**	28,203.00	29,274.00	30,345.00
24.75	13,949.00	14,514.50	15,080.00	**37.75**	28,479.50	29,561.00	30,642.50
25.00	15,128.50	15,703.00	16,277.50	**38.00**	28,756.00	29,848.00	30,940.00
25.25	15,365.50	15,949.00	16,532.50	**38.25**	29,032.50	30,135.00	31,237.50
25.50	15,602.50	16,195.00	16,787.50	**38.50**	29,309.00	30,422.00	31,535.00
25.75	15,839.50	16,441.00	17,042.50	**38.75**	29,585.50	30,709.00	31,832.50
26.00	16,076.50	16,687.00	17,297.50	**39.00**	29,862.00	30,996.00	32,130.00
26.25	16,313.50	16,933.00	17,552.50	**39.25**	30,138.50	31,283.00	32,427.50
26.50	16,550.50	17,179.00	17,807.50	**39.50**	30,415.00	31,570.00	32,725.00
26.75	16,787.50	17,425.00	18,062.50	**39.75**	30,691.50	31,857.00	33,022.50
27.00	17,024.50	17,671.00	18,317.50	**40.00**	30,968.00	32,144.00	33,320.00
27.25	17,261.50	17,917.00	18,572.50	**40.25**	31,244.50	32,431.00	33,617.50
27.50	17,498.50	18,163.00	18,827.50	**40.50**	31,521.00	32,718.00	33,915.00
27.75	17,735.50	18,409.00	19,082.50	**40.75**	31,797.50	33,005.00	34,212.50
28.00	17,972.50	18,655.00	19,337.50	**41.00**	32,074.00	33,292.00	34,510.00
28.25	18,209.50	18,901.00	19,592.50	**41.25**	32,350.50	33,579.00	34,807.50
28.50	18,446.50	19,147.00	19,847.50	**41.50**	32,627.00	33,866.00	35,105.00
28.75	18,683.50	19,393.00	20,102.50	**41.75**	32,903.50	34,153.00	35,402.50
29.00	18,920.50	19,639.00	20,357.50	**42.00**	33,180.00	34,440.00	35,700.00
29.25	19,157.50	19,885.00	20,612.50	**42.25**	33,456.50	34,727.00	35,997.50
29.50	19,394.50	20,131.00	20,867.50	**42.50**	33,733.00	35,014.00	36,295.00
29.75	19,631.50	20,377.00	21,122.50	**42.75**	34,009.50	35,301.00	36,592.50

PD%	7/1/94–6/30/95	7/1/95–6/30/96	7/1/96>	PD%	7/1/94–6/30/95	7/1/95–6/30/96	7/1/96>
43.00	34,286.00	35,588.00	36,890.00	**56.00**	49,651.50	51,537.00	53,422.50
43.25	34,562.50	35,875.00	37,187.50	**56.25**	49,967.50	51,865.00	53,762.50
43.50	34,839.00	36,162.00	37,485.00	**56.50**	50,283.50	52,193.00	54,102.50
43.75	35,115.50	36,449.00	37,782.50	**56.75**	50,599.50	52,521.00	54,442.50
44.00	35,392.00	36,736.00	38,080.00	**57.00**	50,915.50	52,849.00	54,782.50
44.25	35,668.50	37,023.00	38,377.50	**57.25**	51,231.50	53,177.00	55,122.50
44.50	35,945.00	37,310.00	38,675.00	**57.50**	51,547.50	53,505.00	55,462.50
44.75	36,221.50	37,597.00	38,972.50	**57.75**	51,863.50	53,833.00	55,802.50
45.00	36,498.00	37,884.00	39,270.00	**58.00**	52,179.50	54,161.00	56,142.50
45.25	36,774.50	38,171.00	39,567.50	**58.25**	52,495.50	54,489.00	56,482.50
45.50	37,051.00	38,458.00	39,865.00	**58.50**	52,811.50	54,817.00	56,822.50
45.75	37,327.50	38,745.00	40,162.50	**58.75**	53,127.50	55,145.00	57,162.50
46.00	37,604.00	39,032.00	40,460.00	**59.00**	53,443.50	55,473.00	57,502.50
46.25	37,880.50	39,319.00	40,757.50	**59.25**	53,759.50	55,801.00	57,842.50
46.50	38,157.00	39,606.00	41,055.00	**59.50**	54,075.50	56,129.00	58,182.50
46.75	38,433.50	39,893.00	41,352.50	**59.75**	54,391.50	56,457.00	58,522.50
47.00	38,710.00	40,180.00	41,650.00	**60.00**	54,707.50	56,785.00	58,862.50
47.25	38,986.50	40,467.00	41,947.50	**60.25**	55,023.50	57,113.00	59,202.50
47.50	39,263.00	40,754.00	42,245.00	**60.50**	55,339.50	57,441.00	59,542.50
47.75	39,539.50	41,041.00	42,542.50	**60.75**	55,655.50	57,769.00	59,882.50
48.00	39,816.00	41,328.00	42,840.00	**61.00**	55,971.50	58,097.00	60,222.50
48.25	40,092.50	41,615.00	43,137.50	**61.25**	56,287.50	58,425.00	60,562.50
48.50	40,369.00	41,902.00	43,435.00	**61.50**	56,603.50	58,753.00	60,902.50
48.75	40,645.50	42,189.00	43,732.50	**61.75**	56,919.50	59,081.00	61,242.50
49.00	40,922.00	42,476.00	44,030.00	**62.00**	57,235.50	59,409.00	61,582.50
49.25	41,198.50	42,763.00	44,327.50	**62.25**	57,551.50	59,737.00	61,922.50
49.50	41,475.00	43,050.00	44,625.00	**62.50**	57,867.50	60,065.00	62,262.50
49.75	41,751.50	43,337.00	44,922.50	**62.75**	58,183.50	60,393.00	62,602.50
50.00	42,067.50	43,665.00	45,262.50	**63.00**	58,499.50	60,721.00	62,942.50
50.25	42,383.50	43,993.00	45,602.50	**63.25**	58,815.50	61,049.00	63,282.50
50.50	42,699.50	44,321.00	45,942.50	**63.50**	59,131.50	61,377.00	63,622.50
50.75	43,015.50	44,649.00	46,282.50	**63.75**	59,447.50	61,705.00	63,962.50
51.00	43,331.50	44,977.00	46,622.50	**64.00**	59,763.50	62,033.00	64,302.50
51.25	43,647.50	45,305.00	46,962.50	**64.25**	60,079.50	62,361.00	64,642.50
51.50	43,963.50	45,633.00	47,302.50	**64.50**	60,395.50	62,689.00	64,982.50
51.75	44,279.50	45,961.00	47,642.50	**64.75**	60,711.50	63,017.00	65,322.50
52.00	44,595.50	46,289.00	47,982.50	**65.00**	61,027.50	63,345.00	65,662.50
52.25	44,911.50	46,617.00	48,322.50	**65.25**	61,343.50	63,673.00	66,002.50
52.50	45,227.50	46,945.00	48,662.50	**65.50**	61,659.50	64,001.00	66,342.50
52.75	45,543.50	47,273.00	49,002.50	**65.75**	61,975.50	64,329.00	66,682.50
53.00	45,859.50	47,601.00	49,342.50	**66.00**	62,291.50	64,657.00	67,022.50
53.25	46,175.50	47,929.00	49,682.50	**66.25**	62,607.50	64,985.00	67,362.50
53.50	46,491.50	48,257.00	50,022.50	**66.50**	62,923.50	65,313.00	67,702.50
53.75	46,807.50	48,585.00	50,362.50	**66.75**	63,239.50	65,641.00	68,042.50
54.00	47,123.50	48,913.00	50,702.50	**67.00**	63,555.50	65,969.00	68,382.50
54.25	47,439.50	49,241.00	51,042.50	**67.25**	63,871.50	66,297.00	68,722.50
54.50	47,755.50	49,569.00	51,382.50	**67.50**	64,187.50	66,625.00	69,062.50
54.75	48,071.50	49,897.00	51,722.50	**67.75**	64,503.50	66,953.00	69,402.50
55.00	48,387.50	50,225.00	52,062.50	**68.00**	64,819.50	67,281.00	69,742.50
55.25	48,703.50	50,553.00	52,402.50	**68.25**	65,135.50	67,609.00	70,082.50
55.50	49,019.50	50,881.00	52,742.50	**68.50**	65,451.50	67,937.00	70,422.50
55.75	49,335.50	51,209.00	53,082.50	**68.75**	65,767.50	68,265.00	70,762.50

PD%	7/1/94–6/30/95	7/1/95–6/30/96	7/1/96>	PD%	7/1/94–6/30/95	7/1/95–6/30/96	7/1/96>
69.00	66,083.50	68,593.00	71,102.50	82.00	89,796.00	105,831.00	122,935.00
69.25	66,399.50	68,921.00	71,442.50	82.25	90,174.00	106,276.00	123,452.50
69.50	66,715.50	69,249.00	71,782.50	82.50	90,552.00	106,722.00	123,970.00
69.75	67,031.50	69,577.00	72,122.50	82.75	90,930.00	107,167.00	124,487.50
70.00	71,652.00	84,447.00	98,095.00	83.00	91,308.00	107,613.00	125,005.00
70.25	72,030.00	84,892.50	98,612.50	83.25	91,686.00	108,058.50	125,522.50
70.50	72,408.00	85,338.00	99,130.00	83.50	92,064.00	108,504.00	126,040.00
70.75	72,786.00	85,783.50	99,647.50	83.75	92,442.00	108,949.50	126,557.50
71.00	73,164.00	86,229.00	100,165.00	84.00	92,820.00	109,395.00	127,075.00
71.25	73,542.00	86,674.50	100,682.50	84.25	93,198.00	109,840.50	127,592.50
71.50	73,920.00	87,120.00	101,200.00	84.50	93,576.00	110,286.00	128,110.00
71.75	74,298.00	87,565.50	101,717.50	84.75	93,954.00	110,731.50	128,627.50
72.00	74,676.00	88,011.00	102,235.00	85.00	94,332.00	111,177.00	129,145.00
72.25	75,054.00	88,456.50	102,752.50	85.25	94,710.00	111,622.50	129,662.50
72.50	75,432.00	88,902.00	103,270.00	85.50	95,088.00	112,068.00	130,180.00
72.75	75,810.00	89,347.50	103,787.50	85.75	95,466.00	112,513.50	130,697.50
73.00	76,188.00	89,793.00	104,305.00	86.00	95,844.00	112,959.00	131,215.00
73.25	76,566.00	90,238.50	104,822.50	86.25	96,222.00	113,404.50	131,732.50
73.50	76,944.00	90,684.00	105,340.00	86.50	96,600.00	113,850.00	132,250.00
73.75	77,322.00	91,129.50	105,857.50	86.75	96,978.00	114,295.50	132,767.50
74.00	77,700.00	91,575.00	106,375.00	87.00	97,356.00	114,741.00	133,285.00
74.25	78,078.00	92,020.50	106,892.50	87.25	97,734.00	115,186.50	133,802.50
74.50	78,456.00	92,466.00	107,410.00	87.50	98,112.00	115,632.00	134,320.00
74.75	78,834.00	92,911.50	107,927.50	87.75	98,490.00	116,077.50	134,837.50
75.00	79,212.00	93,357.00	108,445.00	88.00	98,868.00	116,523.00	135,355.00
75.25	79,590.00	93,802.50	108,962.50	88.25	99,246.00	116,968.50	135,872.50
75.50	79,968.00	94,248.00	109,480.00	88.50	99,624.00	117,414.00	136,390.00
75.75	80,346.00	94,693.50	109,997.50	88.75	100,002.00	117,859.50	136,907.50
76.00	80,724.00	95,139.00	110,515.00	89.00	100,380.00	118,305.00	137,425.00
76.25	81,102.00	95,584.50	111,032.50	89.25	100,758.00	118,750.50	137,942.50
76.50	81,480.00	96,030.00	111,550.00	89.50	101,136.00	119,196.00	138,460.00
76.75	81,858.00	96,475.50	112,067.50	89.75	101,514.00	119,641.50	138,977.50
77.00	82,236.00	96,921.00	112,585.00	90.00	101,892.00	120,087.00	139,495.00
77.25	82,614.00	97,366.50	113,102.50	90.25	102,270.00	120,532.50	140,012.50
77.50	82,992.00	97,812.00	113,620.00	90.50	102,648.00	120,978.00	140,530.00
77.75	83,370.00	98,257.50	114,137.50	90.75	103,026.00	121,423.50	141,047.50
78.00	83,748.00	98,703.00	114,655.00	91.00	103,404.00	121,869.00	141,565.00
78.25	84,126.00	99,148.50	115,172.50	91.25	103,782.00	122,314.50	142,082.50
78.50	84,504.00	99,594.00	115,690.00	91.50	104,160.00	122,760.00	142,600.00
78.75	84,882.00	100,039.50	116,207.50	91.75	104,538.00	123,205.50	143,117.50
79.00	85,260.00	100,485.00	116,725.00	92.00	104,916.00	123,651.00	143,635.00
79.25	85,638.00	100,930.50	117,242.50	92.25	105,294.00	124,096.50	144,152.50
79.50	86,016.00	101,376.00	117,760.00	92.50	105,672.00	124,542.00	144,670.00
79.75	86,394.00	101,821.50	118,277.50	92.75	106,050.00	124,987.50	145,187.50
80.00	86,772.00	102,267.00	118,795.00	93.00	106,428.00	125,433.00	145,705.00
80.25	87,150.00	102,712.50	119,312.50	93.25	106,806.00	125,878.50	146,222.50
80.50	87,528.00	103,158.00	119,830.00	93.50	107,184.00	126,324.00	146,740.00
80.75	87,906.00	103,603.50	120,347.50	93.75	107,562.00	126,769.50	147,257.50
81.00	88,284.00	104,049.00	120,865.00	94.00	107,940.00	127,215.00	147,775.00
81.25	88,662.00	104,494.50	121,382.50	94.25	108,318.00	127,660.50	148,292.50
81.50	89,040.00	104,940.00	121,900.00	94.50	108,696.00	128,106.00	148,810.00
81.75	89,418.00	105,385.00	122,417.50	94.75	109,074.00	128,551.50	149,327.50

PD%	7/1/94–6/30/95	7/1/95–6/30/96	7/1/96>
95.00	109,452.00	128,997.00	149,845.00
95.25	109,830.00	129,442.50	150,362.50
95.50	110,208.00	129,888.00	150,880.00
95.75	110,586.00	130,333.50	151,397.50
96.00	110,964.00	130,779.00	151,915.00
96.25	111,342.00	131,224.50	152,432.50
96.50	111,720.00	131,670.00	152,950.00
96.75	112,098.00	132,115.50	153,467.50
97.00	112,476.00	132,561.00	153,985.00
97.25	112,854.00	133,006.50	154,502.50
97.50	113,232.00	133,452.00	155,020.00
97.75	113,610.00	133,897.50	155,537.50
98.00	113,988.00	134,343.00	156,055.00
98.25	114,366.00	134,788.50	156,572.50
98.50	114,744.00	135,234.00	157,090.00
98.75	115,122.00	135,679.50	157,607.50
99.00	115,500.00	136,125.00	158,125.00
99.25	115,878.00	136,570.50	158,642.50
99.50	116,256.00	137,016.00	159,160.00
99.75	116,634.00	137,461.50	159,677.50

Appendix 4

Workers' Compensation Forms

Instructions for the forms in this appendix can be found in the following chapters:

State of California
Department of Industrial Relations
DIVISION OF WORKERS' COMPENSATION

EMPLOYEE'S CLAIM FOR WORKERS' COMPENSATION BENEFITS

If you are injured or become ill because of your job, you may be entitled to workers' compensation benefits.

Complete the **"Employee"** section and give the form to your employer. Keep the copy marked **"Employee's Temporary Receipt"** until you receive the dated copy from your employer. You may call the Division of Workers' Compensation at **1-800-736-7401** if you need help in filling out this form or in obtaining your benefits. An explanation of workers' compensation benefits is included on the back of this form.

You should also have received a pamphlet from your employer describing workers' compensation benefits and the procedures to obtain them.

Any person who makes or causes to be made any knowingly false or fraudulent material statement or material representation for the purpose of obtaining or denying workers' compensation benefits or payments is guilty of a felony.

Estado de California
Departamento de Relaciones Industriales
DIVISION DE COMPENSACIÓN AL TRABAJADOR

PETICION DEL EMPLEADO PARA BENEFICIOS DE COMPENSACIÓN DEL TRABAJADOR

Si Ud. se ha lesionado o se ha enfermado a causa de su trabajo, Ud. tiene derecho a recibir beneficios de compensación al trabajador.
Complete la sección "Empleado" y entregue la forma a su empleador. Quédese con la copia designada "Recibo Temporal del Empleado" hasta que Ud. reciba la copia fechada de su empleador. Si Ud. necesita ayuda para completar esta forma o para obtener sus beneficios, Ud. puede hablar con la Division de Compensación al Trabajador llamando al 1-800-736-7401. En la parte de atrás de esta forma se encuentra una explicación de los beneficios de compensación al trabajador.

Ud. también debería haber recibido de su empleador un folleto describiendo los beneficios de compensación al trabajador lesionado y los procedimientos para obtenerlos.

Toda aquella persona que a propósito haga o cause que se produzca cualquier declaración o representación material falsa o fraudulenta con el fin de obtener o negar beneficios o pagos de compensación a trabajadores lesionados es culpable de un crimen mayor "felonía".

Employee: *Empleado:*

1. Name. *Nombre.* _____ Today's Date. *Fecha de Hoy.* _____

2. Home Address. *Dirección Residencial.* _____

3. City. *Ciudad.* _____ State. *Estado.* _____ Zip. *Código Postal.* _____

4. Date of Injury. *Fecha de la lesión(accidente).* _____ Time of Injury. *Hora en que ocurrió.* _____ a.m._____ p.m.

5. Address and description of where injury happened. *Dirección/lugar dónde occurió el accidente.* _____

6. Describe injury and part of body affected. *Describa la lesión y parte del cuerpo afectada.* _____

7. Social Security Number. *Número de Seguro Social del Empleado.* _____

8. Signature of employee. *Firma del empleado.* _____

Employer—complete this section and give the employee a copy immediately as a receipt.
Empleador—complete esta sección y déle inmediatamente una copia al empleado como recibo.

9. Name of employer. *Nombre del empleador.* _____

10. Address. *Dirección.* _____

11. Date employer first knew of injury. *Fecha en que el empleador supo por primera vez de la lesión o accidente.* _____

12. Date claim form was provided to employee. *Fecha en que se le entregó al empleado la petición.* _____

13. Date employer received claim form. *Fecha en que el empleado devolvió la petición al empleador.* _____

14. Name and address of insurance carrier or adjusting agency. *Nombre y dirección de la compañía de seguros o agencia administradora de seguros.* _____

15. Insurance Policy Number. *El número de la póliza del Seguro.* _____

16. Signature of employer representative. *Firma del representante del empleador.* _____

17. Title. *Título.* _____ 18. Telephone. *Teléfono.* _____

Employer: You are required to date this form and provide copies to your insurer or claims administrator and to the employee, dependent or representative who filed the claim within **one working day** of receipt of the form from the employee.

SIGNING THIS FORM IS NOT AN ADMISSION OF LIABILITY

*Empleador: Se requiere que Ud. feche esta forma y que provéa copias a su compañía de seguros, administrador de reclamos, o dependiente/representante de reclamos y al empleado que hayan presentado esta petición dentro del plazo de **un día hábil** desde el momento de haber sido recibida la forma del empleado.*

EL FIRMAR ESTA FORMA NO SIGNIFICA ADMISION DE RESPONSABILIDAD

WORKERS' COMPENSATION BENEFITS

Medical Care. All medical care for your work injury or illness will be paid for by your employer or employer's insurance company. Medical benefits may include treatment by a doctor, hospital services, physical therapy, lab tests, x-rays, and medicines. Your employer or employer's insurance company will pay the cost directly so you should never see a bill.

Payment for Lost Wages. If you can't work because of a job injury or illness, you will receive "temporary disability" benefit payments. The payments will stop when your doctor says you are able to return to work. These benefits are tax-free. Temporary disability payments are two-thirds of your average weekly pay, up to a maximum set by state law. Payments are not made for the first three days you are off the job unless you are hospitalized or cannot work for more than 14 days.

Payment for Permanent Disability. If the injury or illness results in a permanent handicap, permanent disability benefit payments will be paid after recovery. The amount of benefits will depend on the type of injury, and your age and occupation.

Rehabilitation. If the injury or illness prevents you from returning to the same type of job, you may qualify for "vocational rehabilitation benefits". These benefits include services to help you get back to work. If you qualify for vocational rehabilitation, the costs will be paid by your employer or employer's insurance company, up to a maximum set by state law.

Death Benefits. If the injury or illness causes death, payments may be made to relatives or household members who were financially dependent on the worker.

Disclosure of Medical Records. After you make a claim for workers' compensation benefits, your medical records will not have the same privacy that people usually expect for medical records. Records of all medical treatment you have received, even for injuries or illnesses that are not caused by your work, may be read by a variety of people. If you do not agree to voluntarily release medical records, they can be "subpoenaed" and ordered to be released. A workers' compensation judge may "seal" (keep private) certain medical records if the worker requests privacy.

For More Information. If you need help filling out this form, or if you have questions about workers' compensation benefits, please call an Information and Assistance Officer in the local office of the Division of Workers' Compensation. You may hear recorded information and a list of local offices by calling this toll free number: 1-800-736-7401. This is a free service of the State of California. You may also consult an attorney.

BENEFICIOS DE COMPENSACIÓN AL TRABAJADOR

Cuidado Médico. Todo el cuidado médico por su lesión o enfermedad causada en el trabajo será pagado por su empleador/patrón o su compañía de seguros. Los beneficios médicos pueden incluír tratamiento por un doctor, servicios de hospital, fisioterapia, análisis de laboratorio, rayos-x, y medicamentos. Su empleador o la compañía de seguros de su empleador pagará directamente el costo, así Ud. nunca tendrá que ver una cuenta.

Pago por Pérdida de Sueldos. Si Ud. no puede trabajar debido a una enfermedad o lesión causada en el trabajo, Ud. recibirá pagos de beneficio de "incapacidad temporal". Los pagos se detendrán cuando su médico indique que Ud. puede volver a su trabajo. Estos beneficios son libres de impuestos. Los pagos por incapacidad temporal son dos-tercios del promedio de su pago semanal, hasta un máximo asignado por la ley del estado. No se efectúa pago por los tres primeros días que Ud. esta incapacitado a menos que Ud. este hospitalizado o no pueda trabajar por mas de 14 días.

Pagos por Incapacidad Permanente. Si los resultados de la lesión o enfermedad producen un impedimento o incapacidad permanente, se efectuarán pagos de incapacidad permanente después de la recuperación.

Rehabilitación. Si la lesión o enfermedad le impide a Ud. volver al mismo trabajo, puede ser que Ud. califique para los "beneficios de rehabilitación vocacional". Estos beneficios incluyen servicios para ayudarlo a que Ud. vuelva a trabajar. Si Ud califica para rehabilitación vocacional, los costos serán pagados por su empleador o su compañía de seguros, hasta un maximo asignado por la ley del estado.

Beneficios de Muerte. Si la lesión o emfermedad resulta en muerte, los pagos pueden ser efectuados a parientes o a miembros de la familia quienes dependen financieramente del trabajador.

Revelación de Expedientes Médicos. Después de que Ud. efectúa un reclamo para beneficios de compensación del trabajador sus expedientes médicos no tendrán la misma privacidad que la gente por lo general espera de los expedientes médicos. Un expediente de todos los tratamientos médicos que Ud. haya recibido, inclusive de lesiones o enfermedades que no hayan sido causadas por su trabajo, pueden ser leídos por distintas personas. Si Ud. no esta de acuerdo a entregar voluntariamente los archivos médicos, pueden ser ordenados en un "comparendo" (orden judicial) y que ordenan su entrega. Un juez de compensaciones al trabajador, puede "cerrar" (mantenidos en privado) ciertos expedientes médicos si el trabajador solicita privacidad.

Información y Asistencia. Si Ud. necesita ayuda para completar esta forma, o si Ud. tiene preguntas relacionadas con sus beneficios, por favor póngase en contacto con un Oficial de Información y Asistencia en la oficina local de la División de Compensación al Trabajador. Ud. puede escuchar información grabada y una lista de las oficinas locales llamando gratis al número: 1-800-736-7401. Este es un servicio gratis del Estado de California. Ud. también puede consultar a un abogado.

WORKERS' COMPENSATION APPEALS BOARD

SEE REVERSE SIDE
FOR INSTRUCTIONS

APPLICATION FOR ADJUDICATION OF CLAIM

CASE No. _____

(PRINT OR TYPE NAMES AND ADDRESSES)

M _____

_____
(INJURED EMPLOYEE'S ADDRESS AND ZIP CODE)

Social Security No.: _____

_____

_____
(APPLICANT, IF OTHER THAN INJURED EMPLOYEE)
VS.

_____
(APPLICANT'S ADDRESS AND ZIP CODE)

_____
(EMPLOYER — STATE IF SELF-INSURED)

_____
(EMPLOYER'S ADDRESS AND ZIP CODE)

_____
(EMPLOYER'S INSURANCE CARRIER OR, IF SELF-INSURED, ADJUSTING AGENCY)

_____
(INSURANCE CARRIER OR ADJUSTING AGENCY'S ADDRESS)

IT IS CLAIMED THAT:

1. The injured employee, born _____, while employed as a _____
   (DATE OF BIRTH)   (OCCUPATION AT TIME OF INJURY)
   on _____ at _____
      (DATE OF INJURY)   (ADDRESS)   (CITY)   (STATE)   (ZIP CODE)
   By the employer sustained injury arising out of and in the course of employment to

   _____
   (STATE WHAT PARTS OF BODY WERE INJURED)

2. The injury occurred as follows: _____
   (EXPLAIN WHAT EMPLOYEE WAS DOING AT TIME OF INJURY AND HOW INJURY WAS RECEIVED)

3. Actual earnings at time of injury were: _____
   (GIVE WEEKLY OR MONTHLY SALARY OF HOURLY RATE AND NUMBER OF HOURS WORKED PER WEEK)

   _____
   (SEPARATELY STATE VALUE PER WEEK OR MONTH OF TIPS, MEALS, LODGING OR OTHER ADVANTAGES REGULARLY RECEIVED)

4. The injury caused disability as follows: _____
   (SPECIFY LAST DAY OFF WORK DUE TO THIS INJURY AND BEGINNING AND ENDING DATES OF ALL PERIODS OFF DUE TO THIS INJURY)

5. Compensation was paid _____ _____ $_____ $_____ _____
                          (YES) (NO) (TOTAL PAID) (WEEKLY RATE)   (DATE OF LAST PAYMENT)

6. Unemployment insurance or unemployment compensation disability benefits have been received since the date of injury
   _____ _____
   (YES) (NO)

7. Medical treatment was received _____ _____ _____ All treatment was furnished by
                                   (YES) (NO)   (DATE OF LAST TREATMENT)
   the Employer or Insurance Company _____ _____ Other treatment was provided or paid for by _____
                                      (YES) (NO)
   _____ Did Medi-Cal pay for any health care
   (NAME OF PERSON OR AGENCY PROVIDING OR PAYING FOR MEDICAL CARE)
   related to this claim _____ _____ doctors not provided or paid for by employer or insurance company who treated or examined
                          (YES) (NO)
   for this injury are _____
                       (STATE NAMES AND ADDRESSES OF SUCH DOCTORS AND NAMES OF HOSPITALS TO WHICH SUCH DOCTORS ADMITTED INJURED)

8. Other cases have been filed for industrial injuries by this employee as follows: _____

   _____
   (SPECIFY CASE NUMBER AND CITY WHERE FILED)

9. This application is filed because of a disagreement regarding liability for: Temporary disability indemnity _____

   Permanent disability indemnity _____   Reimbursement for medical expense _____   Medical treatment _____

   Compensation at proper rate _____   Rehabilitation _____   Other (Specify) _____
                                                                                    AND APPLICANT REQUESTS A HEARING AND AWARD OF

   _____
   THE SAME, AND FOR ALL OTHER APPROPRIATE BENEFITS PROVIDED BY LAW.
Dated at _____ California, _____
              (CITY)   (DATE)

_____
(APPLICANT'S ATTORNEY)

_____
(APPLICANT'S SIGNATURE)

_____
(ADDRESS AND TELEPHONE NUMBER OF ATTORNEY)

INSTRUCTIONS

FILING AND SERVICE OF A DECLARATION OF READINESS (DIA/WCAB Form 9) IS PREREQUISITE TO THE SETTING OF A CASE FOR HEARING.

Effect of Filing Application

Filing of this application begins formal proceedings against the defendants named in your application.

Assistance in Filling Out Application

You may request the assistance of an information and assistance officer of the Division of Industrial Accidents.

Right to Attorney

You may be represented by an attorney or agent, or you may represent yourself. The attorney fee will be set by the Board at the time the case is decided and is ordinarily payable out of your award.

Filling Out Application

All blanks in the application shall be completed. Where the information is unknown, place "unknown" in the blank. If medical treatment is paid for by *Medi-Cal, Medicare, group health insurance or private carrier, please specify.*

Service of Documents

Your attorney or agent will serve all documents in accord with Labor Code Section 5501 and Section 10500 of the Workers' Compensation Appeals Board's Rules of Practice and Procedure.

If you have no attorney or agent, copies of this application will be served by the Workers' Compensation Appeals Board on all parties. If you file any other document, you must mail or deliver a copy of the document to all parties in the case.

IMPORTANT!

If any applicant is under 18 years of age, it will be necessary to file Petition for Appointment of Guardian ad Litem. Forms for this purpose may be obtained at the office of the Workers' Compensation Appeals Board.

DECLARATION IN COMPLIANCE WITH LABOR CODE SECTION 4906(G)

The undersigned swear under penalty of perjury that they have to the best of their information and belief not violated California Labor Code Section 139.3 and they have not offered, delivered, received or accepted any rebate, refund, commission, preference, patronage, dividend, discount or other consideration, whether in the form of money or otherwise, as compensation or inducement for any referred examination or evaluation.

_____   _____
Date   Employee

_____   _____
Date   Employee's Attorney

_____   _____
Date   Employer

_____   _____
Date   Insurer

_____   _____
Date   Employer's/Insurer's Attorney

The document filed is an Application, Answer, Case Opening Compromise and Release or Case Opening Stipulations with Request for Award.
(Circle the document(s) filed.)

RECORD OF INCOME AND BENEFITS RECEIVED

Name: _____   Employer: _____

Insurance Carrier: _____   Claim Number: _____

Date check received	Check number	Period (starting date through ending date)	Amount of check	Reason for check (temporary disability, permanent disability advance, vocational rehabilitation, unemployment, Social Security, etc.)

RECORD OF INCOME AND BENEFITS RECEIVED

Name: _____   Employer: _____

Insurance Carrier: _____   Claim Number: _____

Date check received	Check number	Period (starting date through ending date)	Amount of check	Reason for check (temporary disability, permanent disability advance, vocational rehabilitation, unemployment, Social Security, etc.)

RECORD OF TIME OFF WORK

Name: _____   Employer: _____

Insurance Carrier: _____   Claim Number: _____

Starting Date	Ending date	Doctor's report or off work order?	Reason for time off work

RECORD OF TIME OFF WORK

Name: _____   Employer: _____

Insurance Carrier: _____   Claim Number: _____

Starting Date	Ending date	Doctor's report or off work order?	Reason for time off work

Date: _____

_____

_____

_____

_____

Re: Workers' Compensation Claim

Injured Worker: _____

Injury Date: _____

Claim No: _____

Dear: _____

I request that you, your insurance carrier or administrator send me copies of the following:

1. All of my medical reports.

2. My wage statement.

3. Any statements taken from me pertaining to my injury.

4. Investigation reports regarding my injury.

5. Copies of any videotapes, film and/or photographs that have been taken of me.

6. Any statements made by me with reference to my right or desire to participate in vocational rehabilitation.

7. A history of all benefits paid, the dates and amounts.

8. Any statements prepared by a Qualified Rehabilitation Representative in my case.

9. Any reports or statements prepared by a case management worker in my case.

10. Other: _____

Please consider this a *continuing demand*, and serve me with the above if you should receive them in the future.

Thank you for your anticipated cooperation.

Sincerely,

_____

Mailing Address: _____

City, State, Zip: _____

Telephone Number: (_____) _____

cc: Insurance Company: _____

WORKERS' COMPENSATION APPEALS BOARD

_____

Applicant

VS.

_____

Defendants

Case No. _____

NOTICE OF CHANGE OF ADDRESS

To all parties and their attorneys of record:

PLEASE TAKE NOTICE THAT Applicant in this case has moved to:

New mailing address: _____

_____

_____

New street address: _____

_____

_____

New telephone number: (_____) _____

All communications to Applicant in this case should be directed to such address.

Date: _____   Signature: _____

Printed Name: _____

EMPLOYEE'S DESIGNATION OF PERSONAL PHYSICIAN
(California Labor Code Section 4600)

To _____ :
   Name of Employer

In the event I am injured at work and require medical treatment, I designate the following as my personal physician:

_____
Name of Physician, Chiropractor or Medical Facility

_____
Address of Physician, Chiropractor or Medical Facility

_____
Telephone Number

_____   _____
Date   Signature of Employee

Given to: _____
               Name of Employer Representative

- -

EMPLOYEE'S DESIGNATION OF PERSONAL PHYSICIAN
(California Labor Code Section 4600)

To _____ :
   Name of Employer

In the event I am injured at work and require medical treatment, I designate the following as my personal physician:

_____
Name of Physician, Chiropractor or Medical Facility

_____
Address of Physician, Chiropractor or Medical Facility

_____
Telephone Number

_____   _____
Date   Signature of Employee

Given to: _____
               Name of Employer Representative

RECORD OF MILEAGE & TRANSPORTATION AND REQUEST FOR REIMBURSEMENT

Name: _____

Address: _____

Employer: _____

Claim Number: _____ Today's Date: _____

To (Insurance Carrier): _____

I have incurred the expenses listed below in connection with trips for medical examinations, treatment and/or vocational rehabilitation. Receipts, if available, are attached. Pursuant to the California Labor Code, I request immediate reimbursement. Please send the payment to me at the address listed above.

Date	Medical or vocational rehabilitation appointment with (specify)	Parking fees/actual transportation fees	Mileage (round trip)
_____	_____	_____	_____
_____	_____	_____	_____
_____	_____	_____	_____
_____	_____	_____	_____
_____	_____	_____	_____
_____	_____	_____	_____
_____	_____	_____	_____
_____	_____	_____	_____
_____	_____	_____	_____
_____	_____	_____	_____
_____	_____	_____	_____
_____	_____	_____	_____
_____	_____	_____	_____

Total parking fees/actual transportation costs _____

Total mileage _____

Total cost of mileage (Total mileage X .31) _____

Total fees to be reimbursed
(Total cost of mileage + Total parking fees/actual transportation costs) ===========================

RECORD OF MEDICAL EXPENSES AND REQUEST FOR REIMBURSEMENT

Name: _____

Address: _____

Employer: _____

Claim Number: _____   Today's Date: _____

To (Insurance Carrier): _____

I have incurred the medical expenses listed below for prescriptions, medical treatment and other medical costs. Receipts for these expenses are attached. Pursuant to the California Labor Code, I request immediate reimbursement. Please send the payment to me at the address listed above.

Date expense incurred	Specify expense	Reason for expense	Amount spent

Total expenses to be reimbursed _____

SETTLEMENT WORKSHEET:
Value of Workers' Compensation Claim

Name: _____   Employer: _____

Insurance Company: _____   Claim Number: _____

Rating: _____ ‾ _____ ‾ _____ ‾ _____ ‾ _____   Appeals Board Case Number: _____

	Stipulations With Request for Award (permanent disability and life pension paid bi-weekly)	**Compromise and Release** (lump sum payment)
1. Permanent disability (determined by rating) _____ weeks X $_____ per week	$ _____	$ _____
2. Life pension (available if rating is between 70 and 99.75)	$ _____	$ _____
3. Past due temporary disability	$ _____	$ _____
4. Past due vocational rehabilitation maintenance allowance	$ _____	$ _____
5. Reimbursement for mileage	$ _____	$ _____
6. Reimbursement for medical expenses	$ _____	$ _____
7. Future medical expenses, calculated at _____% of actual costs: $_____ medical examinations and hospital bills (including surgery, physical therapy, etc.) $_____ temporary disability (figured at _____ weeks X $_____ per week) $_____ medical costs (including prescriptions, tests, wheelchairs, hearing aids, braces, etc.)	No cash value	$ _____
8. Right to reopen case (five years from date of injury)	No cash value	$ _____
9. Penalties (specify):	$ _____	$ _____
10. Other (specify):	$ _____	$ _____
11. Total value of claim (sum of 1-10 above)	$ _____	$ _____
12. Attorney fees	$ (_____)	$ (_____)
13. Permanent disability advances	$ (_____)	$ (_____)
14. TOTAL YOU'LL RECEIVE (11 – sum of 12 + 13)	$ _____	$ _____

WORKERS' COMPENSATION APPEALS BOARD

STATE OF CALIFORNIA

_____

Applicant

vs.

Defendants

Case No. _____

Stipulations
with Request
for Award

The parties hereto stipulate to the issuance of an Award and/or Order, based upon the following facts, and waive the requirements of Labor Code Section 5313:

1. _____ , born _____ , while
   (Employee)

employed within the State of California as _____ on _____ ,
                                            (Occupation)   (Date of Injury)

by_____ whose compensation insurance carrier was
   (Employer)

_____ sustained injury arising out of and in the course of employment _____ .
                                                                                            (Parts of body injured)

2. The injury caused temporary disability for the period _____

through_____ for which indemnity is payable at $_____ per

week, less credit for such payments previously made.

3. The injury caused permanent disability of_____ %, for which indemnity is payble at $_____

per week beginning _____ , in the sum of $_____ , less credit for such

payments previously made.

An informal rating has   has not   been previously issued.
                  (Select one)

4. There is   is not   may be need for medical treatment to cure or relieve from the effects of said injury.
       (Select one)

DEPARTMENT OF INDUSTRIAL RELATIONS
DIVISION OF WORKERS' COMPENSATION

WORKERS' COMPENSATION APPEALS BOARD
STATE OF CALIFORNIA

5. Medical-legal expenses are payable by defendant as follows:

6. Applicant's attorney request a fee of $

7. Liens against compensation are payable as follows:

8. Other stipulations:

_____
Dated

_____
Applicant

_____   _____
Social Security Number of Applicant   Address of Employer

_____   _____
Address of Applicant   Address of Insurance Company

_____   _____
Attorney for Applicant   Attorney or Authorized Representative for Defendant

_____   _____
Address of Attorney for Applicant   Address of Attorney or Authorized Representative

WORKERS' COMPENSATION APPEALS BOARD

STATE OF CALIFORNIA

AWARD

AWARD IS MADE in favor of _____ against

_____ of:

(A) Temporary disability indemnity in accordance with paragraph 2 above,

(B) Permanent disability indemnity in accordance with paragraph 3 above,

    Less the sum of $_____ payable to applicant's attorney as the reasonable value of services rendered.

    Less liens in accordance with Paragraph 7 above,

(C) Further medical treatment in accordance with Paragraph 4 above,

(D) Reimbursement for medical-legal expenses in accordance with Paragraph 5 above,

(E)

_____
Dated:

_____
Workers' Compensation Judge
WORKERS' COMPENSATION APPEALS BOARD

Copy served on all persons listed on
Official Address Record.

Date: _____

By: _____
          (Signature)

DEPARTMENT OF INDUSTRIAL RELATIONS
DIVISION OF WORKERS' COMPENSATION

COMPROMISE AND RELEASE

PLEASE SEE INSTRUCTIONS ON
REVERSE OF PAGE 2 BEFORE
COMPLETING FORM

STATE OF CALIFORNIA
DEPARTMENT OF INDUSTRIAL RELATIONS
DIVISION OF INDUSTRIAL ACCIDENTS
WORKERS' COMPENSATION APPEALS BOARD

CASE NO. _____

SOCIAL SECURITY NO. _____

_____
APPLICANT (EMPLOYEE)

_____
ADDRESS

_____
CORRECT NAME OF EMPLOYER

_____
ADDRESS

_____
CORRECT NAME OF INSURANCE CARRIER

_____
ADDRESS

1. The injured employee claims that while employed as a _____
(OCCUPATION AT TIME OF INJURY)

on _____ at _____ , _____ , by the employer
(DATE OF INJURY)   (CITY)   (STATE)

(s)he sustained injury arising out of and in the course of employment to _____ .
(STATE WHAT PARTS OF BODY WERE INJURED)

2. The parties hereby agree to settle any and all claims on account of said injury by the payment of the sum of $ _____ in addition to any sums heretofore paid by the employer or the insurer to the employee, less amounts set forth in Paragraph No. 6.

3. Upon approval of this compromise agreement by the Workers' Compensation Appeals Board or a workers' compensation judge and payment in accordance with the provisions hereof, said employee releases and forever discharges said employer and insurance carrier from all claims and causes of action, whether now known or ascertained, or which may hereafter arise or develop as a result of said injury, including any and all liability of said employer and said insurance carrier and each of them to the dependents, heirs, executors, representatives, administrators or assigns of said employee.

4. Unless otherwise expressly provided herein, approval of this agreement RELEASES ANY AND ALL CLAIMS OF APPLICANT'S DEPENDENTS TO DEATH BENEFITS RELATING TO INJURY OR INJURIES COVERED BY THIS COMPROMISE AGREEMENT. The parties have considered the release of these benefits in arriving at the sum in Paragraph No. 2.

5. Unless otherwise expressly ordered by a workers' compensation judge, approval of this agreement DOES NOT RELEASE ANY CLAIM APPLICANT MAY NOW OR HEREAFTER HAVE FOR REHABILITATION OR BENEFITS IN CONNECTION WITH REHABILITATION.

6. The parties represent that the following facts are true: (If facts are disputed, state what each party contends under Paragraph No. 10.)

_____
DATE OF BIRTH

_____
ACTUAL EARNINGS AT TIME OF INJURY

_____
LAST DAY OFF WORK DUE TO THIS INJURY

PAYMENTS MADE BY EMPLOYER OR INSURANCE CARRIER

TEMPORARY DISABILITY INDEMNITY	WEEKLY RATE	PERIODS COVERED	

PERMANENT DISABILITY INDEMNITY		TOTAL MEDICAL AND HOSPITAL BILLS	

BENEFITS CLAIMED BY INJURED EMPLOYEE

BEGINNING AND ENDING DATES OF ALL PERIODS OFF DUE TO THIS INJURY

MEDICAL AND HOSPITAL BILLS PAID BY EMPLOYEE

TOTAL UNPAID MEDICAL AND HOSPITAL EXPENSE
To Be Paid By:

ESTIMATED FUTURE MEDICAL EXPENSE
To Be Paid By:

THE FOLLOWING AMOUNTS ARE TO BE DEDUCTED FROM THE SETTLEMENT AMOUNT:

$ _____ PAYABLE TO _____ $ _____ PAYABLE TO _____

$ _____ PAYABLE TO _____ $ _____ PAYABLE TO _____

$ _____ PAYABLE TO _____ $ _____ PAYABLE TO _____

LEAVING A BALANCE OF $ _____ , less approved attorney fee (See Paragraph No. 9), payable to applicant. (If payment is to be other than in a lump sum, or there is additional information, specify on separate page(s).)

INSTRUCTIONS

1. Do not use this form in death cases. Use Form 16. Do not use in third-party cases. Use Form 17.

2. If the injured employee be under 18 years of age and a guardian ad litem has not been previously appointed, a petition for appointment of guardian ad litem and trustee must accompany this agreement.

3. The guardian must sign this agreement on behalf of an injured employee who is under 18 years of age. If the minor is above the age of 14, such minor should also sign this agreement.

4. Attach all medical reports not heretofore submitted to the Workers' Compensation Appeals Board and advise when other reports were filed.

5. Proposals for reduction of liens must be fair and reasonable and must be based on the real facts of the case. There should be no attempt made to deprive lien claimants of a reasonable recovery consistent with all the amounts involved.

6. If the parties intend that the right to rehabilitation will be foreclosed, Paragraph No. 10 must contain (1) a statement that there are genuine issues which would defeat applicant's entire claim if resolved against applicant, (2) a description of these issues and (3) a fair summary of the evidence which would be presented on the issues. The right to rehabilitation will not be foreclosed unless the workers' compensation judge or appeals board makes a finding supported by the record that there are such genuine issues.

7. If the parties intend to release the applicant's dependents' claim to death benefits (See Paragraph No. 4 of Compromise and Release), they must indicate in clear language in Paragraph No. 10 of the Compromise and Release that they have considered the release of death benefits in arriving at their agreement and direct the attention of the workers' compensation judge to that fact.

7. Liens not mentioned in Paragraph No. 6 are to be disposed of as follows: _____
_____

8. For the purpose of determining the lien claim(s) filed for benefits paid pursuant to the Unemployment Insurance Code or for benefits furnished by lien claimants defined in Labor Code Sec. 4903.1, the parties propose reduction of the lien claim(s) in accordance with formulae attached.

9. Applicant's (employee's) attorney requests a fee of $ _____ . Amount of attorney fee previously paid, if any, $ _____ .

10. Reason for Compromise, special provisions regarding rehabilitation and death benefit claims, and additional information:

11. It is agreed by all parties hereto that the filing of this document is the filing of an application on behalf of the employee, and that the WCAB may in its discretion set the matter for hearing as a regular application, reserving to the parties the right to put in issue any of the facts admitted herein, and that if hearing is held with this document used as an application the defendants shall have available to them all defenses that were available as of the date of filing of this document, and that the WCAB may thereafter either approve said Compromise Agreement and Release or disapprove the same and issue Findings and Award after hearing has been held and the matter regularly submitted for decision.

WITNESS *the signature hereof this* _____ *day of* _____ , 19 _____ , *at* _____

_____	_____
WITNESS	APPLICANT (EMPLOYEE) (DATE)
_____	_____
WITNESS	(DATE)
THE APPLICANT'S (EMPLOYEE'S) SIGNATURE MUST BE ATTESTED BY TWO DISINTERESTED PERSONS **OR** ACKNOWLEDGED BEFORE A NOTARY PUBLIC.	_____ (DATE)
	_____ (DATE)

STATE OF CALIFORNIA
County of _____ }

On this _____ day of _____ A.D., 19 _____, before me, _____ ,

a Notary Public in and for the said County and State, residing therein, duly commissioned and sworn, personally appeared _____
_____

known to me to be the person___ whose name_____
subscribed to the within Instrument, and acknowledged to me that ___he___ executed the same.

IN WITNESS WHEREOF, I have hereunto set my hand and affixed my official seal the day and year in this Certificate first above written.

_____
Notary Public in and for said County and State of California

WORKERS' COMPENSATION APPEALS BOARD
STATE OF CALIFORNIA

Case No. _____

Applicant	
VS.	
Defendants	

DECLARATION OF READINESS TO PROCEED

> NOTICE: "Any objection to the proceedings requested by a Declaration of Readiness to proceed shall be filed and served within ten (10) days after service of the Declaration.
> (Rule 10416)

The
[ ] Employee or applicant
[ ] Defendant
[ ] Lien Claimant

requests that this case be set for hearing at

_____
(Place)

and declarant states under penalty of perjury that he or she is presently ready to proceed to hearing on the issues below and has made the following efforts to resolve these issues. _____

_____

Declarant requests:

[ ] Regular Hearing   [ ] Conference Pre-trial   [ ] Rating Pre-trial

(SEE REVERSE SIDE FOR INSTRUCTIONS)

At the present time the principal issues are—
[ ] Compensation Rate   [ ] Rehabilitation
[ ] Temporary Disability   [ ] Self-procured Treatment
[ ] Permanent Disability   [ ] Future Medical Treatment
[ ] Other _____.

Employee [ ] is (or) [ ] is not presently receiving compensation payments.
Employee's condition following injury is permanent and stationary as shown by the report(s) of Doctor(s) _____ Dated _____,
filed and served on _____
I expect to present _____ witnesses, including _____ medical witnesses, and estimate the time required for the hearing will be _____ hours.
I have completed discovery and all medical reports in my possession or control have been filed and served as required by WCAB Rules of Practices and Procedure.
Adverse parties [ ] have (or) [ ] have not served me with medical reports.
Copies of this Declaration have been served this date as shown below.

Name (Print or Type) _____

Declarant's signature _____

Address _____ Phone _____

Date _____

SERVICE
Type or print names and addresses of parties, including attorneys and representatives served with a copy of this Declaration:

_____   _____

_____   _____

_____   _____

_____   _____

(SEE REVERSE SIDE FOR INSTRUCTIONS)

DIA WCAB 9 (REV. 2/89)   89 52346

INSTRUCTIONS

1. This declaration must be completed and filed before any case will be set for hearing at the request of any party.

A hearing includes either a conference hearing or regular hearing. A conference hearing includes conference pre-trial to frame issues, record stipulations and join necessary parties and any other setting (such as rating pre-trial and/or standby calendar) for the purpose of assisting the parties in resolving disputes.

A regular hearing is set for the purpose of receiving evidence.

2. Unless notified otherwise, no witness other than the applicant need attend conference pre-trial hearings.

3. The party producing a non-English-speaking witness must arrange for the presence of a certified interpreter.

4. Continuances are not favored and none will be granted after filing of this Declaration without a clear and timely showing of good cause.

5. The Workers' Compensation Appeals Board favors the presentation of medical evidence in the form of written reports.

6. If setting on a priority basis because of hardship or other good cause, a letter should be attached specifying in detail the nature of the hardship and the reason why early setting is requested.

If setting is requested on any calendar other than the conference pre-trial or regular hearing, a letter should be attached to the Declaration of Readiness specifying in detail just why such setting is requested.

If a regular hearing is requested, a letter should be attached to the Declaration of Readiness specifying in detail why the matter is not suitable for a conference pre-trial or other setting.

The Board, upon the receipt of the Declaration of Readiness, may set the case for a type of proceeding other than the one requested (Rule 10417).

WORKERS' COMPENSATION APPEALS BOARD
455 Golden Gate Avenue, San Francisco 94102-3678

DISTRICT OFFICES

BAKERSFIELD	5555 California Ave. (93309-1615)	(805) 395-2723	
EUREKA	619 Second St. (95501-0423)	(707) 445-6518	
FRESNO	2550 Mariposa St. (93721-2280)	(209) 445-5051	
LONG BEACH	245 W Broadway (90802-4490)	(213) 590-5001	
LOS ANGELES	107 S Broadway (90012-4578)	(213) 620-2880	
NORWALK	12440 Firestone Blvd. (90650-4328)	(213) 864-7452	
OAKLAND	1111 Jackson St. (94607-4967)	(415) 464-0500	
POMONA	300 S Park Ave. (91766-1501)	(714) 623-4301	
REDDING	2115 Akard Ave. (96001-2796)	(916) 225-2845	
SACRAMENTO	1006 Fourth St. (95814-3373)	(916) 445-5812	
SALINAS	21 W Laurel Dr. (93906-3486)	(408) 443-3060	
SAN BERNARDINO	303 W Third St. (92401-1888)	(714) 383-4341	
SAN DIEGO	1350 Front St. (92101-3690)	(619) 237-7321	
SAN FRANCISCO	525 Golden Gate Ave. (94102-3284)	(415) 557-0680	
SAN JOSE	100 Paseo de San Antonio (95113-1482)	(408) 277-1246	
SANTA ANA	28 Civic Center Pl. (92701-4070)	(714) 558-4121	
SANTA BARBARA	411 E Canon Perdido (93101-1598)	(805) 966-1527	
SANTA MONICA	2701 Ocean Park Blvd., Ste. 220, (90405)	(213) 452-9114	
SANTA ROSA	50 "D" St. (95404-4760)	(707) 576-2391	
STOCKTON	31 E Channel St. (95202-2314)	(209) 948-7759	
VAN NUYS	6150 Van Nuys Bl. (91401-3373)	(818) 901-5367	
VENTURA	5810 Ralston St. (93003-6085)	(805) 654-4674	

WORKERS' COMPENSATION APPEALS BOARD
STATE OF CALIFORNIA

CASE NO._____

_____
Applicant

VS.

_____
Defendants

REQUEST FOR EXPEDITED
HEARING AND DECISION
[LABOR CODE SECTION 5502 (B)]

The applicant herein, having filed an application for benefits this date, requests that this case be set

for expedited hearing and decision at_____
Workers' Compensation Appeals Board

on the following issues:

____ Entitlement to Medical Treatment per L.C. 4600
____ Entitlement to Temporary Disability, or disagreement on amount of Temporary Disability
____ Appeal From Decision and Order of Rehabilitaiton Bureau
____ Entitlement to Compensation in Dispute Because of Disagreement between Employers and/or Carriers

Explanation: _____

_____

_____

_____

APPLICANT STATES UNDER PENALTY OF PERJURY THAT THERE IS A BONA FIDE DISPUTE; THAT HE/SHE IS PRESENTLY READY TO PROCEED TO HEARING; THAT HIS/HER DISCOVERY IS COMPLETE ON SAID ISSUES; THAT THE TIME REQUIRED FOR HEARING WILL BE____.

Name (Print or Type)_____

Signature of Applicant_____

Signature of Attorney (if represented)_By:_____

Date:_____

INSTRUCTION FOR FILING
This request must be filed with an application for Benefits at the office of Benefit Assistance and Enforcement (OBAE). For location of the OBAE office nearest you, call 1-800-736-7401.

SERVICE
Type or print names and addresses of parties, including attorneys and representatives served with a copy of this request:

_____   _____

WORKERS' COMPENSATION APPEALS BOARD

_____

Applicant

vs.

Defendants

Case No. _____

PROOF OF SERVICE

I declare that:

1. At the time of service I was at least 18 years of age.

2. My business or residence address is: _____

_____

3. If service is by mail, I am a resident of or employed in the county where the mailing occurred.

4. I served copies of the following papers _(list exact titles of papers served):_

_____

_____

_____

5. Manner of service _(check one box):_

☐ a. By placing true copies in a sealed envelope with postage fully prepaid and depositing the envelope in the United States Mail on _____, 19_____ at _(city and state):_ _____

☐ b. _(If deposited at a business):_ By placing true copies for collection and mailing following ordinary business practices. I am readily familiar with the business' practice for collection and processing of correspondence for mailing with the United States Post Office. The correspondence is/was scheduled to be deposited with the United States Post office in the ordinary course of business on _____, 20_____ at _(business address, city and state):_ _____

☐ c. By personally delivering true copies on _____, 20_____, at _____ _(time)._

6. Name and address of each party/person served:

_____

_____

_____

_____

7. I declare under penalty of perjury under the laws of the State of California that the foregoing is true and correct.

Date: _____   Signature: _____

Printed Name: _____

Date: _____

State of California
Workers' Compensation Appeals Board

_____

_____

_____

Re: Workers' Compensation Claim

Injured Worker: _____

Employer: _____

Insurance Company: _____

Appeals Board Case Number: _____

To whom it may concern:

Enclosed please find the original and _____ copy/copies of the following documents *(list exact title and date of each document):*

_____

_____

_____

_____

_____

_____

_____

_____

Please file the original documents and return date-stamped copies to me. I have enclosed a self-addressed, stamped envelope. Thank you.

Signature: _____

Printed Name: _____

Mailing Address: _____

City, State, Zip: _____

Telephone Number: (_____) _____

Appendix 5

Workers' Compensation—District Offices

City	Information and Assistance	Vocational Rehabilitation
Anaheim	714-738-4038	714-558-4581
Bakersfield	661-395-2514	209-445-5066
Eureka	707-441-5723	707-576-2427
Fresno	559-445-5355	559-445-5066
Goleta	805-966-9872	805-968-7678
Grover Beach	805-481-3380	805-568-0266
Long Beach	562-590-5240	562-590-5033
Los Angeles	213-576-7389	213-576-7397
Oakland	510-622-2861	510-622-2860
Oxnard	805-485-3528	805-485-3144
Pomona	909-623-8568	909-623-8767
Redding	530-225-2047	530-225-2659
Riverside	909-782-4347	909-782-4347
Sacramento	916-263-2718	916-263-2930
Salinas	831-443-3058	408-277-1102
San Bernardino	909-383-4522	909-383-4073
San Diego	619-767-2082	619-767-2085
San Francisco	415-703-5020	415-703-5031
San Jose	408-277-1292	408-277-1102
Santa Ana	714-558-4597	714-558-4581
Santa Monica	310-452-1188	310-452-4166
Santa Rosa	707-756-2452	707-756-2427
Stockton	209-948-7980	209-948-3608
Van Nuys	818-901-5374	818-901-5443
Walnut Creek	925-977-8343	925-977-8318

Index

CATALOG

...more from Nolo

	PRICE	CODE

BUSINESS

	PRICE	CODE
Avoid Employee Lawsuits	$24.95	AVEL
The CA Nonprofit Corporation Kit (Binder w/CD-ROM)	$59.95	CNP
Consultant & Independent Contractor Agreements (Book w/CD-ROM)	$29.95	CICA
The Corporate Minutes Book (Book w/CD-ROM)	$69.99	CORMI
The Employer's Legal Handbook	$39.99	EMPL
Everyday Employment Law	$29.99	ELBA
Drive a Modest Car & 16 Other Keys to Small Business Success	$24.99	DRIV
Firing Without Fear	$29.95	FEAR
Form Your Own Limited Liability Company (Book w/CD-ROM)	$44.99	LIAB
Hiring Independent Contractors: The Employer's Legal Guide (Book w/CD-ROM)	$34.95	HICI
How to Create a Buy-Sell Agreement & Control the Destiny of your Small Business (Book w/Disk-PC)	$49.95	BSAG
How to Create a Noncompete Agreement	$44.95	NOCMP
How to Form a California Professional Corporation (Book w/CD-ROM)	$59.95	PROF
How to Form a Nonprofit Corporation (Book w/CD-ROM)—National Edition	$44.99	NNP
How to Form a Nonprofit Corporation in California (Book w/CD-ROM)	$44.99	NON
How to Form Your Own California Corporation (Binder w/CD-ROM)	$39.95	CACI
How to Form Your Own California Corporation (Book w/CD-ROM)	$34.95	CCOR
How to Form Your Own New York Corporation (Book w/Disk—PC)	$39.95	NYCO
How to Form Your Own Texas Corporation (Book w/CD-ROM)	$39.95	TCOR
How to Get Your Business on the Web	$29.99	WEBS
How to Write a Business Plan	$29.99	SBS
The Independent Paralegal's Handbook	$29.95	PARA
Leasing Space for Your Small Business	$34.95	LESP
Legal Guide for Starting & Running a Small Business	$34.99	RUNS
Legal Forms for Starting & Running a Small Business (Book w/CD-ROM)	$29.95	RUNS2
Marketing Without Advertising	$22.00	MWAD
Music Law (Book w/CD-ROM)	$34.99	ML
Nolo's California Quick Corp	$19.95	QINC
Nolo's Guide to Social Security Disability	$29.99	QSS
Nolo's Quick LLC	$24.95	LLCQ
Nondisclosure Agreements	$39.95	NAG
The Small Business Start-up Kit (Book w/CD-ROM)	$29.99	SMBU
The Small Business Start-up Kit for California (Book w/CD-ROM)	$34.99	OPEN
The Partnership Book: How to Write a Partnership Agreement (Book w/CD-ROM)	$39.95	PART
Sexual Harassment on the Job	$24.95	HARS
Starting & Running a Successful Newsletter or Magazine	$29.95	MAG
Tax Savvy for Small Business	$34.95	SAVVY
Working for Yourself: Law & Taxes for the Self-Employed	$39.95	WAGE
Your Limited Liability Company: An Operating Manual (Book w/CD-ROM)	$49.99	LOP
Your Rights in the Workplace	$29.95	YRW

CONSUMER

	PRICE	CODE
Fed Up with the Legal System: What's Wrong & How to Fix It	$9.95	LEG
How to Win Your Personal Injury Claim	$29.95	PICL
Nolo's Encyclopedia of Everyday Law	$29.99	EVL
Nolo's Pocket Guide to California Law	$24.95	CLAW
Trouble-Free Travel...And What to Do When Things Go Wrong	$14.95	TRAV

Prices subject to change.

	PRICE	CODE
Student & Tourist Visas	$29.99	ISTU
U.S. Immigration Made Easy	$44.99	IMEZ

MONEY MATTERS

101 Law Forms for Personal Use (Book w/CD-ROM)	$29.95	SPOT
Bankruptcy: Is It the Right Solution to Your Debt Problems?	$19.99	BRS
Chapter 13 Bankruptcy: Repay Your Debts	$34.99	CH13
Creating Your Own Retirement Plan	$29.99	YROP
Credit Repair (Quick & Legal Series, Book w/CD-ROM)	$19.99	CREP
How to File for Chapter 7 Bankruptcy	$34.99	HFB
IRAs, 401(k)s & Other Retirement Plans: Taking Your Money Out	$29.99	RET
Money Troubles: Legal Strategies to Cope With Your Debts	$29.95	MT
Nolo's Law Form Kit: Personal Bankruptcy	$24.95	KBNK
Stand Up to the IRS	$24.95	SIRS
Surviving an IRS Tax Audit	$24.95	SAUD
Take Control of Your Student Loan Debt	$26.95	SLOAN

PATENTS AND COPYRIGHTS

The Copyright Handbook: How to Protect and Use Written Works (Book w/CD-ROM)	$34.95	COHA
Copyright Your Software	$34.95	CYS
Domain Names	$26.95	DOM
Getting Permission: How to License and Clear Copyrighted Materials Online and Off (Book w/CD-ROM)	$34.99	RIPER
How to Make Patent Drawings Yourself	$29.99	DRAW
The Inventor's Notebook	$24.99	INOT
Nolo's Patents for Beginners	$29.99	QPAT
License Your Invention (Book w/Disk—PC)	$39.95	LICE
Patent, Copyright & Trademark	$34.95	PCTM
Patent It Yourself	$49.99	PAT
Patent Searching Made Easy	$29.95	PATSE
The Public Domain	$34.95	PUBL
Web and Software Development: A Legal Guide (Book w/ CD-ROM)	$44.95	SFT
Trademark: Legal Care for Your Business and Product Name	$39.95	TRD

RESEARCH & REFERENCE

Legal Research: How to Find & Understand the Law	$34.95	LRES

SENIORS

Beat the Nursing Home Trap: A Consumer's Guide to Assisted Living and Long-Term Care	$21.95	ELD
The Conservatorship Book for California	$44.95	CNSV
Social Security, Medicare & Goverment Pensions	$29.99	SOA

SOFTWARE
Call or check our website at www.nolo.com
for special discounts on Software!

LeaseWriter CD—Windows	$129.95	LWD1
LLC Maker—Windows	$89.95	LLP1
PatentPro Plus—Windows	$399.99	PAPL
Personal RecordKeeper 5.0 CD—Windows	$59.95	RKD5
Quicken Lawyer 2002 Business Deluxe—Windows	$79.95	SBQB2
Quicken Lawyer 2002 Personal Deluxe—Windows	$69.95	WQP2

Special Upgrade Offer
Save 35% on the latest edition of your Nolo book

Because laws and legal procedures change often, we update our books regularly. To help keep you up-to-date, we are extending this special upgrade offer. Cut out and mail the title portion of the cover of your old Nolo book and we'll give you **35% off** the retail price of the NEW EDITION of that book when you purchase directly from Nolo. This offer is to individuals only.

Prices and offer subject to change without notice.

Order Form

Name

Address

City

State, Zip

Daytime Phone

E-mail

Item Code	Quantity	Item	Unit Price	Total Price

Method of payment

☐ Check   ☐ VISA   ☐ MasterCard
☐ Discover Card   ☐ American Express

Subtotal	
Add your local sales tax (California only)	
Shipping: RUSH $9, Basic $5 (See below)	
"I bought 3, ship it to me FREE!"(Ground shipping only)	
TOTAL	

Account Number

Expiration Date

Signature

Shipping and Handling

Rush Delivery—Only $9

We'll ship any order to any street address in the U.S. by UPS 2nd Day Air* for only $9!

* Order by noon Pacific Time and get your order in 2 business days. Orders placed after noon Pacific Time will arrive in 3 business days. P.O. boxes and S.F. Bay Area use basic shipping. Alaska and Hawaii use 2nd Day Air or Priority Mail.

Basic Shipping—$5

Use for P.O. Boxes, Northern California and Ground Service.

Allow 1-2 weeks for delivery. U.S. addresses only.

For faster service, use your credit card and our toll-free numbers

**Call our customer service group
Monday thru Friday 7am to 7pm PST**

Phone   1-800-728-3555
Fax   1-800-645-0895
Mail   Nolo
         950 Parker St.
         Berkeley, CA 94710

**Order 24 hours a day @
www.nolo.com**

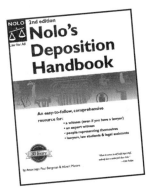

Remember:

Little publishers have big ears.
We really listen to you.

Take 2 Minutes & Give Us Your 2 cents

Your comments make a big difference in the development and revision of Nolo books and software. Please take a few minutes and register your Nolo product—and your comments—with us. Not only will your input make a difference, you'll receive special offers available only to registered owners of Nolo products on our newest books and software. Register now by:

PHONE
1-800-728-3555

FAX
1-800-645-0895

EMAIL
cs@nolo.com

or **MAIL** us
this registration card

fold here

Registration Card

NAME _____ DATE _____

ADDRESS _____

_____

CITY _____ STATE _____ ZIP _____

PHONE _____ E-MAIL _____

WHERE DID YOU HEAR ABOUT THIS PRODUCT? _____

WHERE DID YOU PURCHASE THIS PRODUCT? _____

DID YOU CONSULT A LAWYER? (PLEASE CIRCLE ONE)   YES   NO   NOT APPLICABLE

DID YOU FIND THIS BOOK HELPFUL?   (VERY)   5   4   3   2   1   (NOT AT ALL)

COMMENTS _____

_____

_____

WAS IT EASY TO USE?   (VERY EASY)   5   4   3   2   1   (VERY DIFFICULT)

We occasionally make our mailing list available to carefully selected companies whose products may be of interest to you.

❑   If you do not wish to receive mailings from these companies, please check this box.

❑   You can quote me in future Nolo promotional materials.
Daytime phone number _____ .

WORK 3.0

Nolo *in the* **NEWS**

"Nolo helps lay people perform legal tasks without the aid—or fees—of lawyers."

—USA TODAY

Nolo books are ..."written in plain language, free of legal mumbo jumbo, and spiced with witty personal observations."

—ASSOCIATED PRESS

"...Nolo publications...guide people simply through the how, when, where and why of law."

—WASHINGTON POST

"Increasingly, people who are not lawyers are performing tasks usually regarded as legal work... And consumers, using books like Nolo's, do routine legal work themselves."

—NEW YORK TIMES

"...All of [Nolo's] books are easy-to-understand, are updated regularly, provide pull-out forms...and are often quite moving in their sense of compassion for the struggles of the lay reader."

—SAN FRANCISCO CHRONICLE

fold here

- -

Place
stamp here

Nolo
950 Parker Street
Berkeley, CA 94710-9867

Attn: WORK 3.0